The Complete NetWare® Construction Kit

A Professional Blueprint for Designing, Installing, and Managing LANs

DAVID JAMES CLARKE IV

John Wiley & Sons, Inc.

New York • Chichester • Brisbane • Toronto • Singapore

Associate Publisher: Katherine Schowalter
Senior Acquisitions Editor: Diane Cerra
Associate Editor: Terri Hudson
Managing Editor: Jacqueline A. Martin
Editorial Supervision: Lynn Brown, Brown Editorial Service
Composition: Impressions, A Division of Edwards Brothers, Inc.

This text is printed on acid-free paper.

NetWare is a registered trademark of Novell Corporation. Designations used by companies to distinguish their products are often claimed as trademarks. In all instances where John Wiley & Sons, Inc., is aware of a claim, the product names appear in initial capital or all capital letters. Readers, however, should contact the appropriate companies for more complete information regarding trademarks and registration.

This publication is designed to provide accurate and authoritative information in regard to the subject matter covered. It is sold with the understanding that the publisher is not engaged in rendering legal, accounting, or other professional service. If legal advice or other expert assistance is required, the services of a competent professional person should be sought. FROM A DECLARATION OF PRINCIPLES JOINTLY ADOPTED BY A COMMITTEE OF THE AMERICAN BAR ASSOCIATION AND A COMMITTEE OF PUBLISHERS.

Library of Congress Cataloging–in–Publication Data

Clarke, David James
    The complete NetWare construction kit: a professional blueprint
for designing, installing, and managing LANs / David James Clarke
IV.
      p. cm.
   Includes index.
   ISBN 0-471-58259-X (alk. paper)
   1. NetWare (Computer file) 2. Local area networks (Computer
networks) I. Title.
TK5105.7.C6   1993
004.6'8—dc20   92-38970
                                    CIP

Printed in the United States of America
10 9 8 7 6 5 4 3

*I dedicate this book to the human race
for never ceasing to amaze me.*

CONTENTS

v

ACKNOWLEDGMENTS

I guess it's corny to say "I couldn't have done it without the following people." Well, it's true. I am a mosaic of experiences from family, friends, and everybody else in between. My wife, Mary, deserves the most credit for supporting my work and bringing a great deal of happiness to my life. Thanks.

What no wife of a writer can ever understand is that a writer is working when he's staring out of a window.

—Burton Rascoe

It all started with my family—literally. I owe a great deal to my parents for their financial, emotional, and physical support, and I plan to pay them back someday. I would like to thank my little sister, Athena, for putting up with me through childhood, and her husband, Ralph, for giving me the brother I never had. Speaking of brothers, thanks to Keith and Bob for providing me with perspective and, of course, my newly adopted parents-in-law for giving me a home away from home.

My writing style is a combination of lessons I learned from Dr. James Buxbaum and Rene Mendoza, to whom I owe a great deal. I would like to thank Ken Applegate and the Walt Disney Company for providing me with the opportunity to experience the world of networking firsthand on their dime, and to the gang at Diablo Valley College for giving me the opportunity to talk about it. I would like to thank Joyce Arntson and my classmates at Irvine Valley College for the C.N.I.—on my dime—and Marty Carter at U.C. Berkeley for providing me with a platform for new ideas.

In publishing this book, there are many wonderful people to acknowledge. First, thanks to Diane Cerra and Terri Hudson at John Wiley & Sons, who worked night and day in making *The Complete NetWare Construction Kit* a success. Speaking of working night and day, I owe a great deal of gratitude to the following three people for their excellence in editing and production: Lynn Brown of Brown Editorial Service, Joyce Jackson at Impressions, and Jackie Martin of John Wiley & Sons. They are the glue that holds this book together.

Thanks to Rose Kearsley of Novell Press for being so cooperative and nice, and thanks to Adnan Kandah of Novell Education for his professionalism and candor. Thanks to the following experts for their insight and contribution: Debbie Fields for graphics, Matt Anderson for illustrations, Steve Schleiger for cabling, Larry Gunn for troubleshooting, Lori Jorgeson for documentation, Paul Wildrick for printing, and Dan Peterson for Windows NT. A special thanks goes out to Michael L. Kim for his exceptional work on the chapter cover cartoons. His sense of humor is inspiring.

Finally, I would like to save the best for last. Thanks to *you* for caring enough about networking to buy this book. You deserve a great deal of credit for your enthusiasm and discerning eye. I think Ronald Reagan expressed it best when he said, "You can tell a lot about a fellow's character by the way he eats jelly beans." Good luck with your LAN and enjoy the book.

PREFACE

You are probably asking yourself, "What is a NetWare Construction Kit?" and "Why is it complete?" What a dilemma! Questions like these have inspired great progress, wisdom, and fortune cookies. Have no fear, the answers are here. In this Preface, I answer these and other pressing questions: "What's with all the TLAs?" "Who can help me?" and "Why am I here?"

What Is a NetWare Construction Kit?

I don't pretend to understand the universe; it is a great deal bigger than I am.

—Thomas Carlyle

The Complete NetWare Construction Kit provides all the information you need to build a NetWare local area network (LAN)—the plans, the tools, the questions, and the answers—in essence, a construction kit (LAN components not included). The book started with an idea: "Building a LAN is like building anything." You begin with a plan, buy the materials, and build it. Sounds simple, right? It is. If you break down the process into tiny manageable pieces, the prospect of building a NetWare LAN isn't so overwhelming.

There are three primary phases in constructing your NetWare home: design, installation, and management.

The *design* phase is the most important and time-consuming of the three phases. It involves many different professionals with many skills: The developer finds the land, the buyer establishes requirements, the architect designs the structure, and the seller sets a price. Often the design phase is overlooked in exchange for the more glamorous installation process, but that's a mistake. Decisions made early in the construction process will have a profound effect on the success of your LAN. Imagine choosing a carpet color on a whim. A week later, purple and green doesn't seem so cool.

Installation refers to the adventure of materializing the plan. The installation team purchases the materials, lays the foundation, pounds the nails, and molds vaporware into a living, breathing LAN.

The final phase, *management,* refers to the challenge of adding purpose to the structure. A house, a castle, a car, and a LAN all share one common construction thread: They were built for a reason. During the management phase, you must determine the purpose of your LAN and strive to accomplish it. NetWare management also includes maintenance and troubleshooting, which are facets that often remain overlooked until it is too late.

The Complete NetWare Construction Kit follows these three simple construction phases. After laying the foundation in Part I, "Fundamentals," Part II, entitled "Building NetWare LANs: Analysis and Design" starts at the beginning by asking "Why do you need a LAN?" We perform systems analysis, build a requirements report, and ultimately develop the hardware/software design. In Part III, "Building NetWare LANs: Installation," we use the design to purchase the LAN materials and launch hardware installation. At this point, we construct the foundation of the LAN: NetWare. NetWare installation guides you through the peaks and valleys of NetWare v2.2, v3.11, and v4.0 procedures. The final part,

"Building NetWare LANs: Network Management," is dominated by chapters covering directory structures, system configurations, users and groups, and printing. Here is where we add value and function to the LAN—its network applications, menu systems, printing, and shared directory structures. The final chapter's exploration of NetWare construction concerns keeping the LAN alive—maintenance and troubleshooting. Be prepared for a wild ride. Building NetWare LANs is exciting, rewarding, and painful. You will find this book to be helpful, informative, interesting, and fun; don't leave home without it!

Why Is This Book Complete?

Some books are to be tasted, others swallowed, and some few to be chewed and digested.

—Francis Bacon

In order to accomplish the monumental task of building a NetWare LAN, you must arm yourself with as many tools and skills as you can. This book is dedicated to providing you with a complete set of NetWare concepts, skills, tools, secrets, resources, guidelines, and answers. To accommodate the huge wealth of NetWare knowledge, I have incorporated a variety of different learning tools: text, laboratories, case studies, examples, and icons. The majority of the information is in the text. This format is flexible, and I have made every effort to provide you with an enjoyable level of readability. I believe learning doesn't have to be torture.

The *laboratories* provide you with hands-on experience. Concepts are important, but the real mettle is in the doing. I provide five laboratory exercises designed for NetWare users. These user labs will walk first-time users through introductory NetWare concepts. The supervisor labs encompass all facets of network management.

Four *case studies* are included to afford you an opportunity to practice systems analysis and design. These cases have been very successful in my NetWare classes—take them seriously.

Examples are scattered throughout the text to inject reality, perspective, and conceptual highlights.

Finally, the *icons* are my pride and joy. These quips provide instant information in the form of Quotes, Knowledge, and Construction Tips. Here is how the major icons are organized:

      These add flavor and insight from people more dazzling than myself.

      These point out critical concepts and delectable facts.

      The tips highlight time-proven construction techniques.

In addition, mini-icons highlight items that are of interest for software, hardware, and communications purposes:

These lightning symbols denote telecommunications topics.

These symbols mark discussions that are network hardware-oriented.

Symbols like these flag discussions that describe network software concerns.

What's with All the TLAs?

A good catchword can obscure analysis for fifty years.

—Wendell L. Willkie

TLAs make the network world go 'round! TLAs are three-lettered acronyms—even the definition is a TLA. The NetWare environment is full of complex theories and fancy machinery; TLAs provide a level of simplicity and sophistication. The problem is remembering them all. Throughout the book, I will introduce you to the most important network, hardware, software, and communications acronyms. I will define them and point out when and where they should be used. With considerable restraint, I will ignore meaningless and frivolous acronyms. However, in case you become overwhelmed with the plethora of apparently meaningless series of capital letters and the cutesy words other abbreviations form, refer to Appendix A, which presents a cheat sheet of common and uncommon abbreviations and their expanded names.

In addition to TLAs, the LAN industry has adopted some ETLAs—extended three-lettered acronyms. These four-lettered acronyms are used to outline concepts and LAN fundamentals. TLAs are bad enough, so try not to get drowned in the ETLA backwash. Some TLAs to look out for:

LAN	WAN	MAN	OSI	ISO
NIC	CPU	FEP	MAU	RAM
ROM	SNA	UNA	SAA	XNS
UTP	UPS	STP	DOS	NFS
SFT	WOS	IPX	NOS	BNC

This is an *abbreviated* list, of course. I counted well more than 200 different TLAs throughout the book. Extra points if you can find them all.

Who Can Help Me?

An ounce of action is worth a ton of theory.

—Friedrich Engels

Inevitably at some point, you are going to want to apply this great NetWare knowledge to some physical structure—a LAN, perhaps. I'm assuming that you will act on this book's concepts, theories, methods, and procedures. It would be horribly negligent and irresponsible of me to abandon you at the very point you need the most help: construction. So in an attempt to provide you with the most complete assistance possible, I have created an organization called LANimation. LANimation is an organization of CNEs, students, authors, and professionals who have banded together to offer NetWare assistance to readers of this book, *free*! We will answer all of your LAN questions with accuracy and within a reasonable period of time. LANimation can be reached by any of the following means:

Electronic Mail	COMPUSERVE at David James Clarke, IV–71700,403
	INTERNET at DCIV@Garnet.Berkeley.EDU
Phone	LANimation at (510) NET-FONE (Voice) or (510) 432–4405 (Fax)
Physical Mail	LANimation at 500 Ygnacio Valley Road, Suite 250, Walnut Creek, California 94596
PC Anywhere	L.I.N.C. at (510) 432–4404

In addition to LAN tips and answers, LANimation provides a remote on-line NetWare LAN for readers who don't have a network of their own. You can use the system to complete the User Labs, explore on your own, or just practice what I preach. The system is called L.I.N.C. (LAN Innovators for Networking Communities), and it requires a PC, modem (up to 9600 baud rates are supported), and PC Anywhere remote communications software.

Why Am I Here?

All the animals except man know that the principal business of life is to enjoy it.

—Samuel Butler

Network Supervisors commonly ponder the major question of why they are here during those frustrating moments of network installation—and on bad days thereafter.

So why are we here? This is a difficult question. Some existentialists believe we are here merely to exist, which sounds boring. Some philosophers believe we are figments of our own minds, which sounds crazy. And most pop culturalists would have us believe that the purpose of life is to consume, which sounds destructive. No, I'm with Samuel Butler: I believe we are here to live, love, prosper, and build NetWare LANs—not necessarily in that order.

Good luck with your LAN, and I hope you have as much fun using this book as I have had building it. I will leave you with one parting thought.

Politics is applesauce.

—Will Rogers

ABOUT THE AUTHOR

David James Clarke, IV, is a certified NetWare instructor (CNI) and certified NetWare engineer (C.N.E.). As a professor of networking at Diablo Valley and Las Positas colleges in Northern California, David has an opportunity to share his NetWare secrets with classrooms full of future CNEs. In addition, he is currently developing a series of new NetWare v4.0 courses for a very successful Novell Authorized Education Center in the San Francisco Bay area.

After studying data communications in graduate school, David began his career in networking at the Walt Disney Studios as a member of the systems integration group. After years of constructing local and wide area networks in Los Angeles, Mr. Clarke moved to the Bay Area and founded a network management consulting firm. He is currently creating a technical consortium of NetWare professionals called LANimation.

The Complete NetWare Construction Kit is a product of David's lecture notes and theories as a CNI professor and his diverse experiences as a network management consultant. With his unique blend of technical expertise and instructional savvy, David has created a remarkable book that is informative, humorous, and easy to understand.

Part I

Fundamentals

Information storage and retrieval problems have been around since humans started writing. Transmitting pyramid records from field offices down the Nile to an irate boss at the main office probably consisted of etching or painting icons of wheat onto clay tablets. Data was lost by any number of mishaps along the way, including sinking boats and crocodiles.

As the years passed, paper and pencils, and then typewriters, filing cabinets, and postal services made data transfer more practical and safe. During the late 1940s and early 1950s, people made a significant advance by inventing the electronic computer. Office environments could now send batches of information to a central location and have the computer do their information processing. The problem was that the information, punched into boxes full of cards, still had to be hand carried to the central processing location. An event that was not to be taken lightly, such as an accidental slip in chocolate milk, could render the thousands of sorted punch cards useless.

The 1960s spawned advancements that moved the input terminal from the central processing room onto the office worker's desk. This enabled the user to avoid long, messy corridors and input the information directly into the central processing computer. But the telephone lines and primitive protocols meant that users would have to wait hours to receive results. In the mid-1970s, silicon chip technology had made it possible for manufacturers to build more intelligence into the desktop terminal. Suddenly, office workers could replace their dumb terminals with miniature versions of the big central processing computer. A lot more of the work was done locally, leaving all of the big processing for the big machines. By the early 1980s, microcomputers had completely revolutionized the concept of electronic computing. Managers of large, centralized information systems were losing their domains as computing became more decentralized. Computer prices were so affordable that most of America's businesses quickly joined the new technobandwagon.

The personal computer revolution spawned many improvements that directly benefited users: more numerous and varied applications; lower costs; and a gentler, kinder user interface. One disadvantage of personal computers was decentralization. The distributed personal computers had a very hard time exchanging data and information. The answer came along in the floppy disk. Floppy disks could store entire file cabinets worth of information. Once again the world was a happy place. But as time moved on, the substantial increase in productivity spawned an even larger volume of data and information. Suddenly users were carrying stacks of floppy disks back and forth instead of stacks of punch cards. The computer revolution took two large steps back toward the dark ages.

The Winchester (hard) disk came to the rescue. It allowed shared storage capacities starting at 5 megabytes and growing to 100. Unfortunately, early hard disks were too expensive. Another dilemma was created in how to share storage at a reasonable cost. Manufacturers began experimenting with different storage technologies, and the traditional mainframe scientists began exploring data communications at the PC level; local area networking was born.

Early networks were disk-serving networks. They gave multiple users shared access to all parts of one central hard disk. This caused obvious problems: organization, security, and data integrity. Novell Inc. introduced the first file server network in 1983. The file server system was based on software, not hardware. Novell NetWare quickly evolved into the networking standard because it was flexible, cost-effective, secure, and most importantly, hardware independent.

Today, local area networking is a multibillion-dollar business. Many new competitors have joined Novell at the top of the networking heap: Banyan, IBM, Apple, and Microsoft. Novell's NetWare still leads in sophistication, security, and cost-effectiveness. The latest NetWare release, version 4.0, represents Novell's ninth-generation network operating system. Computing has come a long way since the early days of punch cards and clay tablets.

The longer the island of knowledge, the longer the shoreline of wonder.

—Ralph W. Sockman

Chapter 1

Data Communications Fundamentals

In the beginning, Man had no computer, no data, and used clubs in a futile attempt to communicate with rocks.

C omputers were first linked across distances in 1940, when a simple collection of electronic syllables were sent over telegraph lines from a computer at Dartmouth College in New Hampshire to a calculating machine at Bell Laboratories in New York City. The distance traveled in 1940 makes international communications from San Francisco to Tokyo look like a pilgrimage, but that event did mark the birth of *data communications*: computer systems that use telecommunications for the exchange of data or information.

Since 1940, advances in computer science and communications technology have resulted in mind-boggling networks and a worldwide explosion of data communications. Data sent over telephone lines is bounced off satellites and carried through the air by microwaves. Just make sure not to get in the way of those microwaves, or your goose will literally be cooked! The relationship of data communications to networking technology is that of a parent to a child, with the child greatly exceeding the expectations of the parent. To fully explore the networking child, we must first examine the basic elements of the data communications parent.

Data communications fundamentals are a critical aspect of building NetWare local area networks (LANs). The information you gain here will provide you with a strong LAN foundation on which to expand. Without a fundamental understanding of data communications, you could make some serious mistakes in building your NetWare LAN. Sure it's boring, but I guarantee that you will thank me when it's over. I'll be with you every step of the way. To enhance your understanding of data communications fundamentals, I will use numerous analogies, examples, and icons. The analogy I like best is the building of a castle. Throughout this book, I will relate the process of building NetWare LANs to building large, medieval castles. So keep your eyes open for castle analogies and medieval icons.

When Dr. George Stibbitz sent his experimental data from Dartmouth to Bell Labs in 1940, he could never have imagined The Home Shopping Channel. Today Prodigy and CompuServe bring data communications into the home in the guise of everything from trading stock to baseball cards, buying shoes, and exchanging electronic golf courses. NASA uses data communications to control the space shuttle and realign geosynchronous satellites. Surgeons perform computerized operations from miles away. Because of data communications, today's workforce is better able to balance home and work by working from home (telecommuting).

Housework can kill you . . . if done right!

—Erma Bombeck

Data communications is having a profound effect on all our lives and shows every sign of becoming even more pervasive. The grasp of networking is reaching out from cubicles to buildings to countries. The next two chapters introduce the basic elements and fundamentals of today's data communications. Then we will focus our communications microscope on the most exciting subset of data communications: local area networking. Further exploration into the practical details of networking will create a strong foundation for building your NetWare LAN.

Overview of Data Communications

Four basic elements compose a functional data communications system: a sender, the message, a medium, and the receiver. Figure 1.1 illustrates these four elements and shows how they work in concert to create a viable, productive data communications system.

The *sender* is the device that transmits the data or information. This is also where data is originally conceived and prepared for transmission. The sender can be anything from a computer to a terminal or an ATM machine.

The *message* is the digital data that is actually transmitted from the sender to the receiver. It can consist of a spreadsheet, a database file, or even a marriage proposal. The functionality of the message is governed by the wisdom of the data communications software.

The *medium* is the communication path between the sender and receiver. It carries the message from one location to the other using a set of rules called "protocols." The medium may consist of telephone wire, fiber optic cable, or satellite transmissions.

The *receiver* is the destination device for data communications data. It can be the same type of device as the sender, as is the case with most local area networks, or it can be a totally unrelated type of device, in which case it becomes necessary to use interconnectivity devices such as bridges or gateways.

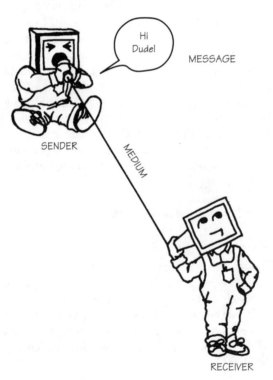

FIGURE 1.1   The Basic Data Communications System

Each of these data communications elements has a specific purpose. They rely on each other in the same way your thumb counts on your index finger. Imagine how hard it would be to grasp these concepts without a pinkie. Although functionally distinct, these four data communications elements can be classified into three important computer science categories:

Element	Category
Sender and Receiver	Data Communications Hardware
Message	Data Communications Software
Medium	Communications Channels

To simplify matters, this book follows a consistent pattern of icon uses:

Data Communications Hardware

Data Communications Software

Communication Channels

Data Communications Hardware Components

Data communications hardware is the first of the three computer science categories. it embodies the classical view of data communications as a collection of connected computer systems.

> ⇨ **DATA COMMUNICATIONS:** *A computer system that uses telecommunications for the exchange of data or information.*

The computer system is at the heart of data communications. It is the equipment that creates, sends, receives, and processes the data or information. The computer system is data communications hardware—terminals, modems, interface units, and computers—that is integrated into the elements known as sender and receiver.

The data communications hardware is organized into two primary processing systems: centralized and distributed. The *centralized* data communications system relies almost exclusively on the processing capabilities of one central computer (the *host*). The connected terminals *(clients)* have varying degrees of intelligence but in most cases act rather "dumb" in comparison to the central host. Typically, 95 to 100 percent of all the processing within the system is handled by the central computer. The host has central control of files, *shared resources* (files, hard disks, or computers that multiple people use), security, and all data communications. Each additional user diminishes the power available to any one other user, and if the central computer blows its top, the whole network goes down.

The *distributed* processing scheme works just the opposite from the centralized one: The host computer performs mostly organizational tasks—the housekeeping—and the true grunt work is handled by intelligent clients. All computers on the network are equipped with internal processing chips and contribute to the system's overall data processing performance. Every added user in this system increases the processing power of the network, and if any one computer goes down, no adverse effect is felt on most of the other computers. Today's most advanced NetWare LANs are prime examples of productive, successful distributed data communications systems.

Data Communications Software Components

Data communications software is a set of network protocols that translate the message from something the hardware understands to something the communications channel can use. Data communications software is also a collection of operating systems that guide and control network resources. These key software components are the stop lights and road signs of your network thoroughfare. Imagine New York City as a LAN.

Traffic signals in New York are just rough guidelines.

—David Letterman

There are two different types of data communications software: shells and operating systems. Data communications *shells* are small networking programs that grab the message from the sender and package it in a specific way. The communications channel then takes the package and sends it along to the receiver according to a specific set of rules *(protocol)*. Once the receiver has it, the message is unwrapped by a similar data communications shell and processed. The shells are written for specific types of networking protocols, which in turn are controlled by the system's *topology* (physical arrangement of components). This is a good example of the inseparable link between data communications hardware and data communications software.

Operating systems control the processing and functionality of the data communications system. In a centralized system, the operating system resides only on the central host and is responsible for all the facets of processing, security, file transfer, resource utilization, and communications. In a distributed system, the operating systems reside on both the central host and the distributed clients. The host operating system (network operating system or NOS—in our case, NetWare) handles central file storage, security, and resource usage. The client operating system (workstation operating system or WOS) is responsible for processing, communications, and local file storage. These two operating systems must work very closely together to ensure software compatibility and network integrity.

Communication Channels

One of the first data communications systems was conceived in a sunny backyard on a lazy August afternoon somewhere in Indiana. Two young boys were fooling around with tin cans and string (see Figure 1.1). They noticed that vibrations along the string could carry their voices from one end of the yard to the other. They probably didn't realize that the string served as a communications channel, linking the two computer systems (boys) through network topology components (tin cans) in a distributed data communications system.

Today's advanced networks have come a long way since those early days of tin cans and string. A network's tin cans are much more expensive and the string can handle many more voices. But the simple concept holds true: Communications channels unite data communications hardware devices and provide a physical pathway for the exchange of data. The functional scope of data communications channels embraces more than just the physical medium. It also includes important support mechanisms such as transmission characteristics, protocols, and topology. When configured correctly, these components provide the network with a fast, reliable pathway from sender to receiver.

The physical medium of the communications channel describes the specific structure of the pathway that houses the data communications message. The message is "carried" along the physical medium by a series of repeating electronic signals. These signals are either bound (in cabling) or unbound (sent across airwaves). The transmission characteristics of the medium strongly affect the performance of the electronic signals as they carry the message from sender to receiver. There are three primary characteristics that clearly influence the transmission of the message over data communications channels: speed, direction, and mode. Later in this chapter these characteristics are described in greater depth.

Data communications *protocol* describes the set of rules and procedures that govern the transmission of the message over data communications channels. Protocols spell out in detail how to initiate and maintain viable telecommunications and are intended to encourage peaceful coexistence between the system's many different topology components. Today's advanced data communications systems use one of three protocols: CSMA, polling, and token-passing.

Data communications topology describes the physical layout of the communications medium. It dictates the orientation of the hardware components and has great influence over the productivity, efficiency, and reliability of the data communications system. In most cases, the topology and protocol are combined into one communications standard. These standards are governed by the Institute of Electrical and Electronic Engineers (IEEE) organization and determine many of the characteristics of today's advanced data communications hardware. There are currently three generally accepted topology arrangements: bus, star, and ring.

The protocol and topology standards play an important role in the development of local area networks. A typical network designer agonizes over this decision more than any other. The chosen standard impacts many other decisions: physical medium; workstations; topology components; and, most importantly, cost. The complexities of these decisions and the relationship of topology/protocol standards to network design will be discussed later in this book.

If you are thirsting for more detailed data communications knowledge, stick around. The rest of this chapter explores all of these general concepts in more depth.

I took a course in speed reading and was able to read *War and Peace* in twenty minutes. It's about Russia.

—Woody Allen

So you want to be a *communications cowboy*. An exciting life to be sure, but there are many, many things to learn. Today's successful diskette jockey is well versed in OSI, IEEE, VM, and IPX. The arena is a multilayered LAN with routing bridges and multiplexing gateways. The NICs connect to hubs, and network chippers toss three-lettered acronyms across crowded motherboards. There's HOS, NOS, and WOS. LAN, WAN, and MAN. And don't forget UTP, STP, MAC, LLC, and DIX.

Today's world of data communications is crazy enough to make your head spin. That's O.K. Let's stop, take a deep breath, and then proceed by using normal words. Now, start at the beginning and walk through the maze one step at a time, and amazing things will happen—networking's many acronyms and data communications strategies will start to make sense. Components will fall into place. Believe me, it is all done with smoke and mirrors. Once you get past all of the nonsense, the real data communications fundamentals will present themselves.

The book will cover both centralized and distributed systems, stressing the components of the distributed LAN. To help you make the transition into Chapter 2 of the book, "Local Area Networking Fundamentals," this chapter introduces LAN protocols, topologies, and standards. So much to learn, and so few pages. Let's begin with data communications hardware.

Data Communications Hardware

The overview earlier defined data communications hardware as the computer equipment that creates, sends, receives, and processes data. This equipment is organized into one of two different processing systems: centralized or distributed. Centralized hardware includes host mainframe computers, front-end processors, terminals, and telecommunications devices. Distributed hardware includes file servers, personal computer workstations, topology components, and interconnectivity devices.

Before we begin our in-depth exploration of these data communications hardware components, let's spend a moment looking at architecture standards. Architecture standards are the framework on which networks are built. Without these strong foundations, today's communications systems would be isolated, useless islands of information.

Architecture Standards

Architecture standards establish models for the interconnectivity of like and unlike systems. These models are developed by the International Standards Organization (ISO) for data communications throughout the world. The ISO's most famous model, OSI (Open Systems Interconnection), consists of seven layers that incrementally describe the levels of interconnectivity within and between centralized and distributed communications systems. Figure 1.2 is a graphical illustration of the seven-layer OSI model and how it relates to NetWare LANs. The network message travels through the OSI layers one at a time. The message receives modifications as it goes "down" the sender's end and subsequently loses those modifications as it travels "up" the receiver's architecture. The message is more English toward the top of the model and more digital toward the bottom.

With the OSI model, any two data communications systems can communicate over great geographic boundaries. Every hardware manufacturer must adhere to the OSI model in order to ensure industry-wide compatibility. Some influential computer manufacturers have created their own interpretations of this model: IBM uses the SNA (Systems Network Architecture) and SAA (Systems Application Architecture) interpretations, Digital Equipment Corporation has developed its own DNA (Digital Network Architecture) model, Xerox uses XNS (Xerox Network System), and Novell has developed UNA (Universal NetWare Architecture) for standardization among Novell protocols.

OSI Model	DOS-based LANS	NetWare			Protocols	
APPLICATION Layer 7	DOS	NetWare Applications				
PRESENTATION Layer 6	Windows	NetWare Core Protocols (NCP)	NetWare			
SESSION Layer 5	Network Basic Input/Output	NetWare Communication Systems				
TRANSPORT Layer 4	System (NetBIOS)	NetWare Sequenced Packet Exchange - SPX		SNA	OSI	
NETWORK Layer 3	Network driver	NetWare Internet Packet Exchange IPX				
DATA LINK Layer 2	Ethernet	Open Data-link Interface (ODI) Token-Ring FDDI				Ethernet Token- Ring ARCNet
PHYSICAL Layer 1	10BaseT, Thick, Thin coaxial	Unshielded Twisted Pair, Shielded Twisted-pair				

FIGURE 1.2   The OSI Model and Correspondence of Its Layers to DOS and NetWare

A committee is a cul-de-sac down which ideas are lured and then quietly strangled.

—Sir Barnett Cocks

The OSI model consists of the following seven layers, listed here from the topmost layer (the application level with which all users are familiar) down to the most concrete layer (hardware level):

7. *Application:* The top layer is where the message originates. The user and his or her software applications work together to create a useful, important data file. Let's say Mary writes a letter to her mom. The application layer takes the data file and converts it to a digital format—a series of 0s and 1s. This layer adds a header to designate the sender/receiver and forwards the message to the presentation layer. In our example, Mary would look into her Rolodex, find mom's address, and label the envelope accordingly.

6. *Presentation:* The presentation layer establishes an appropriate data code set— ASCII for microcomputers or EBCDIC for mainframes—and converts the message into the established code. Mary writes the letter in English.

5. *Session:* The session layer grabs the message from the presentation layer and opens a communications path between the sender and receiver. This layer also brackets the message to distinguish the beginning and the end. Mary adds a stamp to the envelope and completes the greetings/salutations.

4. *Transport:* Once the message has been completed, the transport layer breaks it into smaller, more manageable segments. Error checking is added to each segment and a backup copy is made. In our example, Mary photocopies the letter for her files and takes it down to the local post office.

3. *Network:* The network layer takes the message segments and breaks them down into even smaller units called *packets.* The packets are organized and classified with communications headers, then sent on to the data link layer. The post office indexes Mary's letter and stores it in the appropriate mail slot.

2. *Data Link:* The data link layer receives the collection of classified packets and adds final preparations before transmission: checksum trailers and address headers. The postal carrier picks up Mary's letter and prepares it for tomorrow's delivery route.

1. *Physical:* The lowermost layer of the OSI model, the physical layer represents the physical communications link between the sender and the receiver. The communications channels are opened and the packets are sent as a stream of electronic bits. Finally, Mary's letter is delivered to her mom.

The OSI model serves as a guideline for standardization within the data communications industry. As I mentioned earlier, many of the leading manufacturers have opted for their own interpretations of this seven-layer model. IBM's SNA architecture is the most widely used of the independent architectures, simply because there is such a huge number of IBM machines in use. SAA is an offshoot from the SNA standard that focuses on users, programming, and application interfaces. The DNA model has eight layers and works only within DEC systems. XNS is a four-layered model that still maintains all of the functionality of the seven-layered OSI model. The most interesting of the independent models is Novell's UNA architecture.

NetWare exists at the top three layers of the OSI model—session, presentation, and application. IPX exists at the middle two layers of the OSI model—network and transport. Ethernet exists at the bottom two layers of the OSI model—physical and data link.

UNA follows the OSI model very closely. It also supports APPC (Advanced Program-to-Program Communication) and LU type 6.2. None of this modeling is as important as the protocols UNA supports. UNA was originally conceived to give users the flexibility to stay within the NetWare environment as they used many different technologies. UNA accomplishes this flexible autonomy through the use of two unique packet-exchange protocols (IPX and SPX) and one network communications standard (NetBIOS). IPX, Internetwork Packet Exchange, provides interconnectivity support for all NetWare LANs on the network layer of the OSI model. SPX, Sequenced Packet Exchange, provides error checking, windowing, and flow control for IPX on the transport layer. Finally, IBM developed NetBIOS (Network Basic Input/Output System) to provide standard peer-to-peer interfaces on the session and transport layers of the OSI model.

All of this nonsense can become quite overwhelming very quickly. Fortunately, you don't need to work with these standards on a daily basis. Most of this stuff is transparently built into "off-the-shelf" data communications systems. What I would like you to walk away from this discussion with is a strong appreciation for the necessity of standards in today's quickly changing communications environment. Be aware of these architecture models, but don't lose sleep over them.

Centralized Data Communications Hardware

Centralized data communications systems share data through one central location: the host. Each of the terminal clients communicates with the host through the use of advanced telecommunications devices. Following is a detailed description of the host mainframe computers, front-end processors, terminals, and telecommunication devices that make up the centralized data communications hardware. Figure 1.3 demonstrates these components in their native environments.

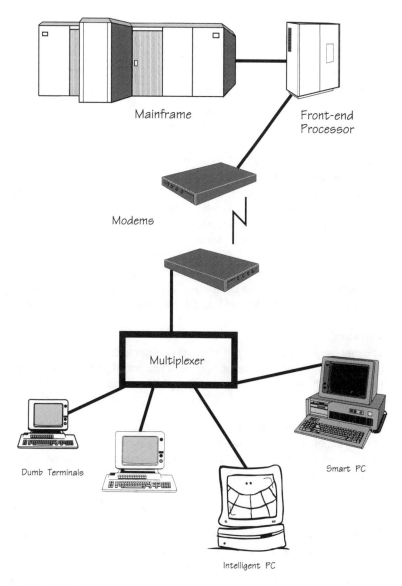

FIGURE 1.3 Centralized Data Communications Network Design

Host Mainframe Computers

Centralized data communications systems rely almost exclusively on the processing capabilities of one central computer: the host. The power of the host computer depends entirely on the "number-crunching" needs of the data communications clients. Most systems use a mainframe class computer that is capable of processing 50 to 200 million instructions per second (MIPS). These host computers are ideal for large corporations, government, and university installations. Smaller systems use minicomputer hosts with 10 to 50 MIPS capacities, whereas large technology networks rely on amazing supercomputers for their centralized processing: 4 billion instructions per second.

PCs have varying degrees of speed:

Pentium	100 MIPS	80486	41 MIPS
80386	11 MIPS	80286	3 MIPS
8088	0.33 MIPS		

Front-End Processors

A good portion of the host's processing tasks are administrative. The central processor can quickly become bogged down with requests for access control, security, protocol translation, and data transmission procedures. In large data communications systems these tasks are off-loaded to an auxiliary mainframe computer, the front-end processor. The *front-end processor* is the point of entry for all the mainframe's clients. It checks passwords, converts data transmission codes, switches communications lines, allocates host resources, and tracks system usage. In some cases, the addition of a front-end processor triples the processing capabilities of a centralized data communications network by off-loading the trivial administrative tasks and leaving the number crunching to the central mainframe.

Terminals

The most important resource of any data communications system is the user. Users use terminals—dumb terminals, smart terminals, and intelligent terminals. The difference among them lies in how much local processing the terminal can handle independently from the central host.

Dumb Terminals. Most centralized data communications terminals are dumb, capable of no local processing. Dumb terminals are only simple input/output devices. They send keystrokes from an internal keyboard (input) and display text on a 12-inch monochrome monitor (output). Dumb terminals are also known as *CRTs (cathode ray tubes)* and *VDTs (video display terminals)*. Some of the older models send the text to an external printer instead of the built-in monitor. These devices are known as hard-copy terminals.

Smart Terminals. Some of today's advanced data communications systems require a slightly more intelligent terminal. Smart terminals are simple input/output devices with an added twist: 5 percent local processing. They are capable of storing and processing a small amount of the system's data without having to send it to the central host computer. Smart terminals give the user the added functionality of customized display screens, programmable keyboards, and limited internal memory. Some examples of smart terminals are data collection terminals, automated teller machines (ATMs), point-of-sale (POS) terminals, and credit authorization terminals.

Intelligent Terminals. With the incredible invasion of microcomputing over the last 10 years, users are beginning to integrate personal computers into centralized data communications systems. These intelligent terminals are capable of just as much local processing as the host mainframe. Unfortunately, most centralized systems are not adequately equipped to handle more than one processor. In these cases, the microcomputer client is made to act as a dumb or smart terminal through a process known as *terminal emulation.* Through the use of complex communications software, microcomputers can emulate any type of manufacturer-specific dumb terminal. Some examples of intelligent terminals are the IBM 3270, TeleVideo 925, ADDS Viewpoint A2, Wyse 50, ANSI, VT-100, and VT-220.

Telecommunications Devices

The world has always been fascinated with the process of moving from point A to point B. Telecommunications devices facilitate the movement of digital data from computer system A to computer system B. Ninety-five percent of the time these devices must rely on existing analog telecommunications networks: phone lines! Modems, multiplexers, and data concentrators tame these lines so that centralized host computers can communicate with their geographically separated clients.

Modem. An acronym for MOdulator/DEModulator, which is a device that modifies the data signal as it travels from computer system A through the telecommunications network to computer system B. *Modulation* is the process of translating digital signals to their analog equivalents. The reverse is known as *demodulation.* Computers understand the world of 0s and 1s (digital). Phone lines understand the world of in-between (analog). A modem enables these two worlds to communicate. The modem is connected to the client terminal through an internal serial port and to the phone line through a standard RJ-11 telephone jack. The client software calls the central host modem and establishes a handshake. The sending modem then transmits the data at the highest possible speed, from 300 to 64,000 bits per second (bps). *Electromagnetic interference (EMI)* or "noise" from the telecommunications network can impede the signal and slow down transmission rates. Large data communications systems lease dedicated phone lines and condition them for reliable data transmission at very high speeds. T-1 lines, for example, use expensive modems to send digital messages over great distances at a rate of 1,540,000 bps.

Multiplexer (mux). A device that enables multiple clients to communicate on one phone line. Thirty-two clients, for example, are connected to one multiplexer in Los Angeles. The multiplexer is in turn connected to a modem that transmits data to a modem in Chicago over one dedicated phone line. The receiving modem in Chicago is connected to another multiplexer that serves a front-end processor and eventually the central host mainframe. *Frequency division multiplexing (FDM)* provides each of the 32 clients with simultaneous access to the single telecommunications line by varying their transmission frequencies. In *time division multiplexing (TDM),* each client is allocated a small fraction of the total time on the line. Multiplexers are expensive, but they pay for themselves very quickly by substantially lowering telecommunications costs.

Data Concentrator. A specialized multiplexer that enhances transmission speeds by buffering infrequent client requests, concentrating them, then sending the data in large packets at high speeds. Concentrators are more practical than time division multiplexers because they do not require clients to send their requests at exact designated intervals; users are generally not this precise. A concentrator enables users to be less precise with their timing and still conduct multiple sessions on the same telecommunications line. The Los Angeles office would be best served with a frequency division multiplexer or a data concentrator.

Centralized data communications systems have evolved over the past 40 years into enormous networks with mammoth processing capabilities. At the same time, the world of business has diversified. Recent advancements in computer technology have brought the power to the people. The new cry is "a computer in every office." Today's monstrous centralized systems are shrinking. The movement is toward a more flexible, distributed network with multiple processors and more intelligent clients. The time is right for local area networking.

Distributed Data Communications Hardware

Distributed data communications systems are the wave of the future. This book is your surfboard. As with surfing, balance is the key. File servers and personal computer workstations must balance local processing with centralized applications. The topology components balance speed and reliability. Interconnectivity devices balance local, wide, and metropolitan area networks (LANs, WANs, and MANs). You get the point. Figure 1.4 illustrates a typical LAN layout.

File Servers

The distributed data communications system relies less on a central host computer and more on its distributed clients. Ninety-five percent of all network processing occurs at the user's workstation, leaving the 5 percent administrative load for the central file server to handle. The file server is primarily responsible for allocating shared network resources, processing user requests, and storing/retrieving central data files.

The most important file server function is in housing the heart of the LAN—the network operating system (NetWare). NetWare directly controls all network communications, establishes user restrictions and security, provides system fault tolerance, and allows interconnectivity within and among distributed networks. Additional computer resources such as printers, modems, and CD-ROMs can be shared by the entire LAN when they are addressed by the central server.

Personal Computer Workstations

The true workhorses of a distributed LAN are the personal computer workstations. Each workstation is equipped with a *network interface card (NIC)* that allows it to communicate with the central file server. The workstation reaches out to the server for a copy of any centrally stored application and downloads the program into local RAM (random-access memory). Once loaded, the application is run and data is processed using the workstation's own built-in microprocessor. Files can be stored locally on the workstation's hard disk or at the central file server for shared network access. This level of connected autonomy is

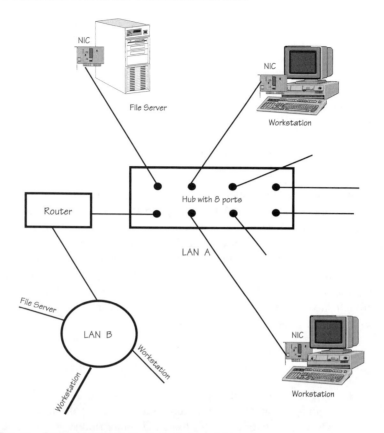

FIGURE 1.4 Distributed Data Communications Network

very productive in business environments that use multiple applications and rely on commonly shared data files. Any type of personal computer can be integrated into a distributed system. Color monitors, ergonomic keyboards, and fuzzy mice are enhancements to the cold dumb terminal. Personal computer manufacturers are making the interfaces more friendly and the network users more productive.

One machine can do the work of fifty ordinary men. No machine can do the work of one extraordinary man.

—Elbert Hubbard

Topology Components

The network show is ready to begin; the servers and workstations are in place. But who controls the strings? *Topology,* you may recall, was defined as the physical arrangement of the network nodes (servers and workstations), whereas a *protocol* is the set of rules that control the topology. Topology components are distributed devices that establish the network protocol and facilitate the movement of messages throughout the topology. NICs and hubs control the strings.

NICs. NICs contain the electronic components that establish and control network communications. They are advanced modems that transmit digital packets of data over short distances (1,000 feet) at very high speeds (10 million bps). The NIC is the principal network hardware device that differentiates a network node from a stand-alone microcomputer. There are thousands of different types and manufacturers of NICs, but most of them conform to one of five distinct topology standards: Ethernet Bus, Ethernet 10Base-T, ARCNet, Token Ring, or LocalTalk. Most NICs are 8-bit or 16-bit cards, but some more advanced file server NICs are now taking advantage of the 80486 32-bit EISA architecture. These high-end boards can increase network throughput as much as 400 percent by eliminating key bottlenecks on the file server bus.

Hubs. Some topology standards use a star configuration. The physical star cabling scheme relies on a central hub for communications integrity. The Ethernet 10Base-T standard uses a punchdown block for cabling connectivity and then fastens the block to an electronic 10Base-T hub for network trafficking. ARCNet systems employ a combination of passive, active, and intelligent hubs for their distributed star arrangement. The Token Ring LAN is more intriguing. It's structured as a physical star/logical ring and relies exclusively on a central *multistation access unit (MSAU)*. All MSAUs are then linked together through auxiliary ring-in and ring-out ports to complete the logical ring. Chapter 2 describes these standards in more depth.

Interconnectivity Devices

Let's review the scale of the network types we've been discussing:

1. A LAN links a small group of functionally similar workstations within a local geographic area: a series of adjacent cubicles or offices on the same floor.
2. Once the network expands to include other floors, or even other LANs, it ceases to be local and becomes a wide area network (WAN)—a LAN of LANs.
3. To take it one step farther, a WAN of functionally similar WANs within a municipal region is called a metropolitan area network (MAN).

LANs, WANs, and MANs each speak their own language. In a few cases, the data is written in the same networking language. In most cases, the LANs use completely different topology standards; the WANs use many different dialects; and the MANs don't (yet) have a standard. In all cases, the process of connecting multiple dissimilar systems requires very flexible, advanced interconnectivity devices: repeaters, bridges, routers, and gateways.

Repeaters. *Repeaters* are simple interconnectivity devices that connect two identical cabling segments of a LAN. A repeater accepts weak signals, electrically regenerates them, and then sends the messages back on their way. You must include a repeater when a cabling segment exceeds the topology's inherent distance limitation. The trunk of an Ethernet bus, for example, is limited to 607 feet. To extend beyond this technical restriction would require a repeater. The repeater effectively doubles the network's size by connecting two 607-foot segments. Distance limitations are a product of the media's transmission characteristics and the electronic demands made on it by the LAN protocol. The signal strength of distributed messages degrades as they travel down the communications channel. Repeaters operate at the electronic level, and contain no real intelligence. In order to expand beyond a few cabling segments, let's say to another LAN, we would need to use a bridge.

Bridges. *Bridges* are more intelligent than repeaters; they go beyond simply regenerating weak signals. Bridges process network signals and ensure smooth passage from LAN to LAN and from LAN to WAN. A message traveling from Token Ring LAN A to Ethernet LAN B has a destination address programmed into it. The file server on LAN A doesn't recognize the address, so it sends the message off to the bridge. The bridge processes the address, compares it to an internal routing table, and forwards the message to LAN B. It is imperative, though, for LAN A and LAN B to share the same Media Access Control or MAC-layer communications protocol (TCP/IP, NetBIOS, or IPX). All NetWare LANs use the IPX communications standard. In cases where the communications protocols differ among LANS, a router is more appropriate.

Routers. *Routers* are more intelligent than bridges; the routers process and understand all communications languages. Routers contain advanced algorithms that allow them to make intelligent decisions about where a message should go and what path to use for greatest efficiency. A message traveling from Token Ring LAN A to TCP/IP Internet WAN B contains destination addressing in different languages. The file server in LAN A is so clueless it doesn't see the message. The packet is sent directly from the workstation in LAN A to the router. The router strips off the IPX information, reads the TCP/IP subnet address, and packages the packet for the destination protocol. The message is then forwarded to a router in the WAN B system.

Sometimes the functions of bridging and routing are combined in a single interconnectivity device. These communications oddities are called *brouters*—no really, I'm serious!

Gateways. *Gateways* approach interconnectivity from a completely different angle. These devices use more software translation than hardware routing. Gateways are required when network messages travel between two entirely different systems. The most classic example is the exchange of data between centralized and distributed data communications systems. Say that you're connecting two systems. System A is a distributed Token Ring LAN. System B is a centralized IBM mainframe. System A speaks IPX token-ring. System B speaks SNA. In order for these two systems to communicate, the gateway will need to read the network addresses; reconfigure the packet protocols; translate the operating software; and in most cases, completely rewrite the data alphabet. Gateways are the most expensive and complex interconnectivity devices. Here is a brief list of some additional gateways: asynchronous communications gateways, satellite gateways, DNA gateways, XNS gateways, and X.25 gateways.

Data Communications Standards Organizations

That completes our discussion of data communications hardware. Next we will explore data communications software and its administrative role in oversight of mindless communications hardware. But before we go on, I would like to take this opportunity to mention a few more of the standards organizations that work so hard to ensure compatibility among networks.

- The *CCITT (International Consultative Committee for Telegraph and Telephone)* makes recommendations for international data communications standards. This group lists "V" standards for telephone circuits and "X" standards for public data networks. Some of their more famous standards are V.32/V.42 modem protocols and the X.25 packet switching network.
- The *EIA (Electronic Industries Association)* sets standard specifications for communications interfaces. This group created the RS-232C serial interface standard.
- The *IEEE (Institute of Electrical and Electronic Engineers)* is responsible for most of the standards in the electronics industry. This organization sets the stage for the development and maintenance of network interface cards and topology hubs. The IEEE 802.3 topology is Ethernet, and the 802.5 standard describes Token Ring. IEEE is also responsible for guaranteeing that every NIC created in the world is manufactured with a unique internal address.

Data Communications Software

Previously, data communications software was defined as both a set of protocols that translate network messages and a collection of operating systems that guide and control network resources. Communications software is very different from the application programs you are used to. These advanced subroutines are a good example of substance over style: They provide very little user interface and a lot of network functionality. Another key point for data communications software is *transparent connectivity,* the concept that successful networks perform complex connectivity operations without the user's knowledge or worry. The NetWare network operating system is a good example of transparent connectivity.

Data communications software comprises shells and operating systems. *Shells* are small networking programs that establish dialogs between system hardware and communications protocols. *Operating systems* are complete software packages that control the processing and functionality of centralized host mainframes, distributed network file servers, and personal computer workstations.

Shells

Network shells integrate the communications technologies of LAN software and LAN hardware. These shells are complex command programs that link operating systems and topology components. IPX, for example, is so hardware-specific it requires a software driver from the NIC manufacturer.

Centralized systems have very little use for network shells, because 100 percent of the processing occurs at the central host. Dumb and smart terminals rely on host software for routine communications operations. Some simple subroutines are programmed into these terminals, but for the most part, they act in concert with the host and not independently of it. Intelligent terminals, on the other hand, require terminal emulation programs. These programs are network shells that facilitate data exchanges between distributed microcomputers and centralized mainframes. In some cases, additional hardware is installed in the personal computer—an IBM 3270 emulation board. These centralized NICs are connected directly to IBM control units that forward communications to the IBM host.

Through the use of shells, NetWare can support a variety of different platforms:

Clients—DOS, OS/2, UNIX, Macintosh

Hosts—SNA, VAX, UNIX, OSI

Distributed communications systems rely a great deal on network shells, because roughly 100 percent of the processing occurs at the personal computer workstation. Shells reside on distributed clients and perform a variety of functions. They forward network requests from the WOS to the NOS, they process incoming network messages, they specifically configure network interface cards, and they establish communications between the distributed workstation and central file server. There are currently seven different shells used in the NetWare environment: IPX, NETx, NetBIOS, ODI, LSL, NetWare Requester for OS/2, and Chooser. We will explore these shells in much more detail later in the book.

Network shells are critical components of data communications software, but they are not complete software packages. Operating systems are complete software packages that control and manage network resources.

Operating Systems

Operating systems exist in all types of computer systems: microcomputers, mainframes, networks, supercomputers, and so on. An operating system is a collection of programs and utilities that control, support, and manage computer hardware/software resources. Operating systems control hardware resources such as central processing units, random access memory, disk storage, and auxiliary input/output devices. Operating systems control software resources such as communications protocols, shells, software applications, and telecommunications programs. Operating systems are the interface between these resources and the user—*you*. You can imagine how much users have to say in the success or failure of an operating system. Thus, the most popular operating systems are user friendly: Windows, Macintosh System 7, NetWare, and DOS. The less popular operating systems are sometimes more powerful, but not friendly enough to be productive: UNIX, OS/400, and IBM's VM systems.

Only three types of operating systems have an impact on today's data communications systems: the host operating system (HOS), network operating system (NOS), and workstation operating system (WOS).

Host Operating Systems

Host operating systems are large, complex, cumbersome processor cows. But they work. They are multiuser, multitasking systems that contain extremely sophisticated multiprocessing subroutines. Their job is not an enviable one: They control hundreds of users with thousands of requests for millions of bytes of data, all simultaneously! Specialized front-end processors help off-load some of the communications burden, but 100 percent of the system's processing is still handled by the central host mainframe and its internal operating system. Probably the most advanced host operating system is IBM's VM system. VM (virtual machine) can make a single IBM mainframe appear to be a variety of different machines to different users. VM simulates many different machines by creating virtual processors, virtual storage, and virtual I/O (input/output). To each user it appears as though he or she has an isolated mainframe, which of course is not the case. VM is actually four different operating systems in one: multitasking, multiprocessing, time-sharing, and virtual storage. Some people have said that IBM = VM^2.

Network Operating System

The *network operating system* is the "brains" of distributed data communications systems. The NOS resides on the central file server and handles critical network tasks such as local and global communications, security, resource allocation, and central data storage. The key to a successful network operating system is balance: balance between networking functionality and user interface. Networking functionality describes the complex set of instructions that is required for the type of multiuser, multirouting tasks most LANs demand. On the other hand, the NOS must have a consistent, familiar user interface in order to avoid the dreaded "B" word—*baffling*. There is nothing less successful than a functionally superior NOS that nobody knows how to use. Of all the NOSs currently available, Novell NetWare seems to have struck the right balance, providing the functionality of VM and the user friendliness of DOS. The next chapter takes a closer look at the four most popular network operating systems: NetWare, Banyan VINES, LAN Manager, and Windows NT.

Workstation Operating Systems

Workstation operating systems reside on the personal computer client and handle the processing requirements of local applications. The WOS defines the user's interface before and after network applications have been loaded. It is critical for the WOS and the NOS to like each other and get along. The interface between these two is the responsibility of network shells. Among the most popular WOSs are DOS, UNIX, OS/2, Windows NT, and System 7. We will learn more about these popular operating systems in the next chapter, "Local Area Networking Fundamentals."

I admit that twice two makes four is an excellent thing, but if we are to give everything its due, twice two makes five is sometimes a very charming thing too.

—Fëdor Dostoevski

Communications Channels

The previous section described the communications channels as the string between two cans. Communications channels unite data communications hardware and provide a physical pathway for the exchange of data. This physical medium is the most critical link in the data communications system. If the link is broken, the message dies. Channel reliability and performance are paramount to the construction of a solid, successful NetWare LAN.

Communications channels are built on four basic principles: physical medium, transmission characteristics, protocol, and topology. The physical medium describes the specific structure of the channel: bound or unbound. The transmission characteristics of the channel dictate speed, reliability, throughput, and cost. Protocols control the messages as they traverse the channel, and topologies determine the geographic arrangement of the data communications hardware. Together, these four principles create a solid pathway on which important messages can travel. This section explores these channels in greater depth.

Physical Medium

The physical medium of the communications channel describes the actual structure of the path traveled by the data communications message. The message is carried along the physical medium by communications signals. These signals are either bound or unbound.

Bound

Bound media generally consist of wire and glass cables. Wire types include unshielded twisted-pair (UTP), shielded twisted-pair (STP), and coaxial cable. These wires consist of solid or twisted copper cores surrounded with metal shielding and a polyvinyl jacket. Fiber optic cabling is the newest technology and uses light signals through a pure glass core, as Figure 1.5 shows.

Unbound

Unbound signals are carried by electromagnetic waves. Unless restricted, these signals radiate freely through space and continue for very long distances. A variety of different radio frequencies are used to carry data communications signals from transmitters at one

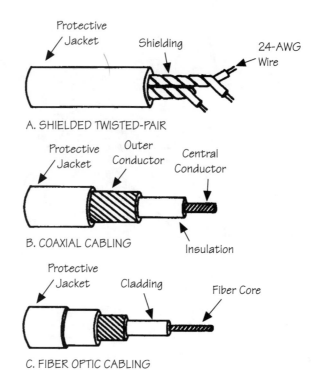

FIGURE 1.5 Cable Types

end to receivers at the other. The most common data communications frequencies are microwave and satellite. Private use of microwave or satellite technology is expensive and generally limited to large organizations. Infrared frequencies provide a less expensive solution. These communications channels use a similar technology to the one in your TV's remote control unit. Figure 1.6 illustrates microwave and satellite communications.

Transmission Characteristics

The *transmission characteristics* of the communications channel determine the system's performance. These components can be divided into three functional groups: transmission speed, transmission direction, and transmission mode.

Speed

The *transmission speed* of a communications channel determines how much data can be transmitted over the physical medium in a given period of time. This rate is usually mea-

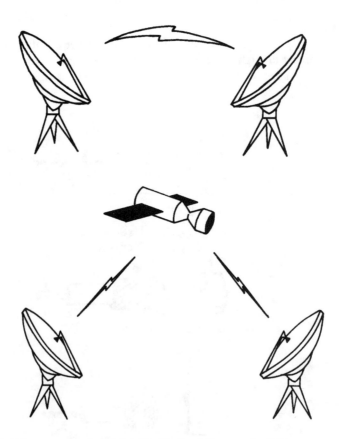

FIGURE 1.6 Microwave (Top) and Satellite (Bottom) Communications

sured in bps. Many communications systems measure speed in changes of state per second, or *baud*:

System	Bits-per-Second for Every Baud
Monobit	1 (1200 baud = 1200 bps)
Dibit	2 (1200 baud = 2400 bps)
Quadbit	4 (2400 baud = 9600 bps)

Typical 2400-baud modems are actually 1200 baud at dibit, whereas 9600-baud modems are usually transmitting 2400 baud at quadbit. The most critical transmission characteristic that affects speed is bandwidth. *Bandwidth* describes the range of frequencies a given medium can handle: The larger the range, the greater the data throughput. Think of bandwidth as the number of lanes on a freeway. More lanes equal less traffic and higher speeds. Communications channels are classified by bandwidth into narrowband, voiceband, and broadband.

Narrowband Channels. Narrowband channels have a bandwidth of less than 2,000 hertz (Hz) and a transmission rate between 7 and 30 characters per second. Telegraph lines are examples of narrowband channels.

Voiceband Channels. Voiceband channels provide a bandwidth of about 3,000 Hz and transmission rates up to about 960 characters per second (cps). Telephones use voiceband channels.

Broadband Channels. Broadband channels have a bandwidth up to several hundred million hertz and transmission rates up to 125 million cps. Coaxial cables, microwave systems, and fiber optic cables use broadband channels. Broadband communications channels are the transmission media of choice for distributed data communications systems.

Direction

The *transmission direction* of a communications channel refers to the ability of the media to handle simultaneous transmissions. *Simplex channels* can only handle "one-way" transmissions. Devices connected to simplex channels can either send or receive, but not both, as in a one-way broadcast radio. *Half-duplex channels* allow for both sending and receiving, but only one at a time, as in the classic walkie-talkie scenario. *Full-duplex channels* also allow for both sending and receiving, but these devices can operate simultaneously. The telephone is an example of a full-duplex device. Full-duplex communications channels can handle large volumes of data at very high speeds. They are ideal for local area networking. Most of today's data communications devices use full-duplex channels.

Mode

The *transmission mode* of a communications channel refers to the bit-level organization of the data and the way it is transmitted over the physical medium. Inside computers and terminals, data is handled in a parallel fashion—multiple bytes together over 8, 16, or 32 parallel channels. The computer chip and internal bus (or motherboard) each use parallel data communications in unique ways. Herein lies the difference among the 80286, 80386/486, and 80386SX architectures:

Chip and Bus	CPU	Channel
80286DX	16-bit	16-bit
80386DX/80486DX	32-bit	32-bit
80386SX	32-bit	16-bit

External data communications, on the other hand, use serial transmissions, with one bit after another. Two common modes of serializing data are asynchronous and synchronous transmission.

Asynchronous. An *asynchronous transmission* involves the sending of one character (or byte) at a time. To separate the characters, a "start bit" and one or more "stop bits" are added to each end of the individual 8-bit character code. This mode of communications is slow and wasteful because the system must support 11 bits per byte, instead of the standard 8. That equates to approximately 27 percent overhead. Inexpensive modems use asynchronous transmissions.

Synchronous. A *synchronous transmission* involves the sending of organized blocks of characters, sometimes called *frames* or *packets.* These packets of data are carefully "synchronized" so that the sending and receiving devices can distinguish the boundaries of each character. Because fewer bits are actually sent with this transmission mode, it tends to be faster and more efficient. Synchronous transmissions are ideal for high-speed modems and NICs.

The transmission characteristics of the centralized or distributed system can have a profound impact on the network's performance and durability. In general:

- Centralized data communications systems use synchronous modems for the exchange of full-duplex signals over voiceband channels.
- Distributed networks use network interface cards for the exchange of full-duplex signals over broadband channels. Local area network packets travel throughout distributed channels with the help of network protocols, topologies, and standards.

Protocols, Topologies, and Standards

The *protocol* of a communications channel describes the set of rules and procedures that govern the transmission of messages over the physical medium. The *topology* of the system describes its geographic orientation and the arrangement of the networking components. Protocol and topology combine to create *networking standards.* These standards are developed and controlled by the IEEE. Standards are important because they lay down guidelines for the manufacture and installation of distributed and centralized data communications systems.

Three LAN protocols (CSMA, polling, token-passing) combine with three respective LAN topologies (bus, star, ring) to create three major networking standards (Ethernet, ARCNet, Token Ring).

Protocols

The sole purpose of the protocol is to provide guidance to the communications channel and to promote harmonious connectivity between the many network components. Protocols work at the electronic level. They are initiated and controlled by advanced subroutines built into each NIC. LANs commonly use one of three communications protocols: CSMA, polling, and token-passing.

CSMA

Carrier Sense Multiple Access (CSMA) relies on a shared "trunk" of cabling. The trunk is a single run of cabling that extends throughout the topology of the LAN. Each workstation connects to the trunk directly and communicates with the LAN through an internal NIC. Figure 1.7 shows the CSMA trunk. Here is how the protocol does its thing:

1. Workstation A has a message for workstation B. Workstation A listens to the trunk and waits until all is clear (carrier sensing).
2. When A detects that the trunk is clear, the workstation marks the message with a destination address and sends it over the trunk. All of the other workstations continually monitor the trunk for a message with their address (multiple access).
3. Workstation B finds a match, accepts the message, and returns an acknowledgment of receipt. Problems occur when multiple nodes send messages simultaneously—collision!

To deal with imminent collisions, the CSMA protocol has adopted a subprotocol called *collision detection*. In the event of a collision, workstation A will stop transmitting, wait a random period of time, and resend (collision detection). If collisions persist, workstation A will systematically double the random delay up to 10 collisions. Random delays are calculated according to the following formula: $0 < r < 2^n$. This approach, known as *binary exponential backoff,* is used to optimize the randomness of the delay without having the workstation wait too long. It is possible for a workstation to wait an indefinite period of time, but typically CSMA nodes crash after 16 collisions.

Polling

Polling relies on a central controlling node (workstation or file server). The central node polls each workstation to determine whether there is a message to be sent. When a sending workstation is ready, the central node reserves the network channel and the message is sent. Polling is typically used in a centralized system because this type of protocol relies exclusively on the intelligence and dexterity of the central controlling node. If the central machine becomes flustered or confused, the network dies. Also, the polling process can slow down tremendously in distributed systems because of the demand placed on the central node by each intelligent workstation. For these reasons, polling is no longer used as a LAN protocol. Figure 1.8 gives a graphic illustration of polling.

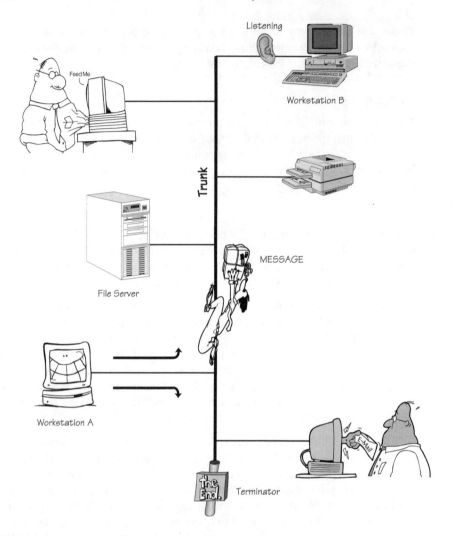

FIGURE 1.7   The CSMA Protocol on a Bus Topology

Token Passing

The token-passing protocol relies on a control signal: the token. A *token* is a 24-bit packet that circulates throughout the network from NIC to NIC in an orderly fashion. If a workstation wants to transmit a message, it must seize the token and thus control the communications channel. The existence of only one token eliminates the possibility of signal collisions. The token is originally created by the first initialized workstation. This special node, called the *active monitor,* is responsible for ensuring the integrity of the token as it travels along the channel. If the token is damaged by line noise or a workstation crash, the active monitor waits seven seconds and then generates a new token. This level of fault tolerance, along with the civilized manner in which the token travels, makes token passing an excellent choice for large networks with medium to heavy load requirements.

FIGURE 1.8 The Polling Protocol on a Star Topology

Topologies

Topologies define the geographic arrangement of the data communications hardware. There are strict guidelines that network installers follow when they install NICs and configure network nodes. File servers and workstations are arranged according to a variety of factors: speed, cost, reliability, distance, and load requirements. Each topology is ideally suited for a different combination of these factors:

- The bus is fast, cheap, and unreliable.
- The star is slow, large, and reliable.
- The ring is fast, expensive, and reliable.

Bus

The *bus topology* is the simplest and most widely used of the network topologies. It consists of one continuous length of LAN cabling *(trunk)* and a terminating resistor *(terminator)* at each end. The data communications message travels along the bus in both directions until it is picked up by a workstation NIC. Figure 1.7 illustrates a typical bus topology. If the message is missed or not recognized, it reaches the end of the cabling and dissipates at the terminating resistor. If the message did not dissipate at the end of the trunk, it would reflect back toward the trunk and cause harmful collisions. All nodes on the bus topology have equal access to the trunk; no discrimination here. Also, the number of nodes and length of the trunk can be easily expanded. On the down side, the bus topology requires a high level of techno-babysitting. If a break occurs in the cabling or too many nodes try to access the trunk simultaneously, the whole topology crashes. In general, the bus topology is flexible and inexpensive—ideal for small to medium-sized word-processing LANs. Its only drawback is its unreliability.

Star

The *star topology* is ideal in two other ways. Each node sits at the end of a dedicated leg just like points of a star, as Figure 1.8 shows. The central controlling node, which is usually the file server, handles all network requests and routes messages from the sender across the star to the receiver. The workstations enjoy a dedicated line to the server, which prevents collisions and therefore keeps the network free from becoming bogged down by fancy communications monitoring devices. If a leg fails, the topology continues to operate normally. A network star can be constructed with any of the four LAN media: unshielded twisted-pair (UTP), shielded twisted-pair (STP), coaxial, and fiber optic cabling. The most common star media are UTP and coaxial. In general, the star topology is inexpensive and reliable—ideal for medium to large word processing and spreadsheeting LANs. Its only disadvantage is its slow speed.

Ring

The ring topology arranges network nodes in a circular channel. Messages travel around the ring from node to node in a very organized manner. Figure 1.9 illustrates a typical ring topology.

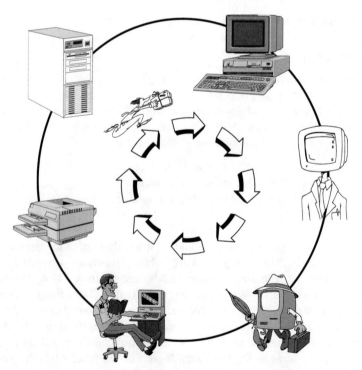

FIGURE 1.9 The Token-Passing Protocol on a Ring Topology

As network messages flow, each workstation checks the message for a matching destination address. If the address doesn't match, the node simply regenerates the message and sends it back on its way. If the address matches, the node accepts the message and sends a reply to the sending workstation. The ring topology is extremely durable. The civilized ring design and node-to-node pathway eliminate many of the problems associated with the earlier topologies: no collisions and no need for a central controlling node. On the down side, there is a speed limit on the ring channel. The messages travel at a fixed rate regardless of the number of nodes or network load requirements. In general, the ring topology is expensive and durable—ideal for large database LANs with high load requirements. The ring's disadvantage is its high cost.

The 802 Series Standards for Protocols and Topologies

Although conceptually independent, protocols and topologies are optimized when they are intelligently combined. CSMA works best in a bus, polling with a star, and token passing as a ring. The IEEE developed a series of standards in the spring of 1980 to outline exactly which combinations work best. In an effort to create the most bizarre and obscure name possible, the IEEE named these standards "802"—that is, 80 for the year and 2 for the month of February. Here is what the IEEE group came up with:

- *802.1.* The data link layer of the OSI model is broken into two sublayers: Media Access Control (MAC) and Logical Link Control (LLC). This standard describes the high-level interfaces at the MAC layer. These interfaces deal with procedures for sharing physical networking media—the internetworking standard.
- *802.2.* This standard describes the LLC layer and procedures for sharing common protocol schemes.
- *802.3.* The Ethernet standard. 802.3 describes the Carrier Sense Multiple Access/Collision Detection (CSMA/CD) protocol over a bus topology. A recent variation on this standard has been adopted by the IEEE, which supports 10-Mb/s CSMA over a twisted-pair star. This new standard is called *Ethernet 10Base-T*.
- *802.4.* The ARCNet standard (almost). 802.4 describes the token passing protocol over a star/bus topology. ARCNet is not explicitly supported by the IEEE 802.4 standard, because it uses a slight variation of the token bus design.
- *802.5.* The Token Ring standard. 802.5 describes the token-passing protocol over a star/ring topology. IBM has worked very closely with the IEEE to ensure that IBM's products adhere to the strict 802.5 guidelines. Currently, IBM and Synoptics Communications are proposing a variation on the 802.5 standard that will support 16-Mb/s token passing over unshielded twisted-pair (UTP) media.
- *802.6.* The next four standards focus on higher-level networks and media specifications. 802.6 describes procedures for developing and maintaining metropolitan area networks (MANs). Currently there are MAN pilot programs going on in Canada and the eastern United States.
- *802.7.* This standard is not yet a standard. 802.7 consists of a technical advisory group that is focusing on standards for broadband (bound) communications.

- *802.8*. This standard is also not yet a standard. 802.8 consists of a technical advisory group that is focusing on standards for fiber optic cabling. There is much speculation about and interest in the results of the 802.8 standard.
- *802.9*. The final 802 standard deals with procedures for integrating data and voice networks. 802.9 is a critical element in the development of successful wide and metropolitan area networks.

Diplomacy is the art of saying "Nice Doggie" until you can find a rock.

—Will Rogers

All of the 802 standards are important for the development of successful data communications systems. The middle three—802.3, 802.4, and 802.5—are especially important in the construction of distributed NetWare LANs. Digital, Intel, and Xerox (DIX) proposed the adoption of 802.3 Ethernet as the global LAN standard, and IBM pushed 802.5 Token Ring. DIX and IBM continue to feud over these two standards, prompting the industry to take sides with either Ethernet or Token Ring.

In ending this discussion of data communications fundamentals and beginning our exploration of local area networking, I would like to spend a moment outlining the three major LAN standards, Ethernet, ARCNet, and Token Ring.

Ethernet

The name Ethernet was conceived by Robert Metcalfe and David Boggs at the Xerox PARC facility in Palo Alto, California, to honor the bizarre substance *ether*. (Ether was once thought to carry electromagnetic radiation through unseen channels of space.) Whatever the reasoning, Ethernet has really taken off since its inception in 1973. Digital, Intel, and Xerox have fueled the Ethernet bandwagon to a new standard called DIX 2.0 or Ethernet II. Both Ethernet 802.3 and Ethernet II frame types are supported by NetWare LANs. The Ethernet standard uses CSMA/CD protocol over a bus topology. Ethernet data packets carry 1024-byte messages over coaxial or UTP cabling at a maximum rate of 10 million bits per second (10 Mb/s). That means a packet enters the trunk every 820 microseconds. In real life, Ethernet packets can slow to 1 Mb/s over crowded trunks with many multiple collisions. The Ethernet standard is ideal for small to medium-sized LANs within a tight geographic area. Word processing and spreadsheet applications should work fine, but I would stay away from using it for large databases or mission-critical environments.

ARCNet

ARCNet was developed at the Datapoint Corporation in 1977 by a scientist named John Murphy. ARCNet, an acronym for *Attached Resource Computer Network*, was somewhat of an underground favorite until it reached international attention in 1982. It was then that SMC (Standard Microsystems Corporation) released an ARCNet chip set to many other NIC manufacturers. ARCNet follows the IEEE 802.4 ruling, but it is not officially IEEE rated.

The ARCNet standard uses the token-passing protocol over a star/bus topology. The star/bus topology combines the flexibility of a star with the simplicity and throughput of a bus. Chapter 2 discusses this unique design in more detail. The ARCNet token carries 512-byte messages over coaxial cabling at a fixed rate of 2.5 Mb/s. Because the token passing throughput is fixed, the ARCNet design cannot slow down in high-load environments. The ARCNet standard is ideal for medium- to large-sized LANs that span multiple star topologies. ARCNet's slow speed does not support quick response times, as are often needed for large database queries, but it does work well with disk-intensive applications and mission critical environments.

Token Ring

IBM pretty much owns the Token Ring standard. Ring-oriented networks have been around since Ethernet, but IBM substantially enhanced the old design in 1984 with the introduction of IBM Token Ring. Since its inception, IBM Token Ring has been completely proprietary and only operated on IBM equipment over IBM-type cabling. Recently, IBM has relaxed its ownership of this IEEE standard and has allowed other manufacturers to introduce Token Ring components. The leading competitor in this arena is Proteon, Inc., with the ProNet series. The Token Ring standard uses token passing protocol over a physical star, logical ring topology. The star/ring topology is physically wired as a star, but the token must circle the LAN in a logical ring.

The original Token Ring standard passed 245 tokens each second over STP cabling (a 2048-byte token at 4 Mb/s). At the outset, many of the token passing advocates were excited about this new IBM standard, but they couldn't justify the switch from ARCNet because of the high costs and the marginally faster 4 Mb/s throughput. At the turn of the decade, IBM answered these critics with the introduction of a much faster standard: the IBM 16-Mb/s Token Ring. The 16-Mb/s standard also operates on STP IBM-type cabling, although some industry professionals are pushing for 16-Mb/s Token Ring on UTP. IBM currently supports 4 Mb/s over UTP cabling.

The Token Ring standard is far and away the ideal LAN standard. It is fast, reliable, and supported by an industry leader. But unfortunately we don't live in an ideal world. On the down side, Token Ring is just too darned expensive. Only large corporations, rich industries, or IBM-supported schools can afford the Token Ring design. For them it is ideal; for the rest of us ARCNet and Ethernet will probably have to do.

What sculpture is to a block of marble, education is to the soul.

—Joseph Addison

Most local area networks, including NetWare LANs, use a combination of the many data communications fundamentals we explored in this chapter. The real trick in designing a successful LAN is finding the right combination: synergy, or the quest for a perfect balance among data communications hardware, software, communications channels, and topology. Let me ease your mind: Nothing is perfect! The remaining chapters of this book do everything possible to achieve NetWare nirvana. We might fall short, but it doesn't matter. The learning is in the journey, not the destination.

Chapter 2

Local Area Networking Fundamentals

"Okay, Mr. Zablinski, for the money, the car, and the trip around the world—what is *transparent connectivity*?"

Chapter 1 defined data communications as a computer system that uses telecommunications for the exchange of data. Furthermore, you learned that distributed data communications involves a computer system that combines intelligent workstations for local processing, a central host for administrative tasks, topology standards for communications control, and operating systems for productivity and user interface. The local area network (LAN) epitomizes distributed data communications:

- LANs operate within local geographic areas.
- LANs use high-speed protocols over a diverse collection of cabling.
- LANs balance advanced hardware components with sophisticated software applications.

Chapter 1 also explored the basic elements that compose the distributed data communications system: file servers, workstations, topology components, cabling, operating systems, and shells. This chapter continues our study of these components by showing how they work in concert to create a LAN structure. This chapter refines your understanding of these specific distributed data communications fundamentals. This understanding will evolve into a set of networking skills that will serve you well in building your NetWare LAN, just as architects and construction teams need tools to build a skyscraper, a house, or a castle. They rely on steel and brawn, whereas you rely on silicon and brains. We begin with the essence of networking—the concept of transparent connectivity.

Transparent Connectivity

I asked a classroom full of students to define transparent connectivity. Their responses included these:

- a technique used by psychics
- a technique used by marriage counselors
- a new type of paint
- quick-drying glue
- the latest Stephen King novel

Not even close! *Transparent connectivity* is a network buzzword that describes the productive marriage of a user and his or her LAN. Connectivity is the goal of every good LAN. The higher the level of connectivity, the more powerful the LAN. Transparency is the goal of every good user. The more transparent the LAN, the easier it is to use. Transparent connectivity makes for productive LANs and happy users.

So, how does one achieve transparent connectivity? *Balance* is the key to successful networking. Transparent connectivity is achieved through the balance of hardware and software resources. The LAN hardware provides network connectivity. The LAN software provides user transparency, that is, productivity without knowing it. The combination is a powerful force in office automation, telecommuting, electronic mail, videoconferencing, funds transfer, and information brokering.

This chapter uses the concept of transparent connectivity to examine the fundamentals of LAN hardware and LAN software. This discussion will arm you with the tools you need to build successful NetWare LANs: A clear blueprint, the hammer of knowledge, and the cement of understanding.

Today's LANs are similar to the pioneering systems in concept and design, but there the similarities end. Huge breakthroughs in hardware and software technology have increased the horsepower of local area networking tremendously. In today's LANs, the hardware and software components together create LAN synergy: The network as a whole is more useful than each of the components alone.

LAN components can be organized into two functional groups: hardware and software. Later you'll learn how to successfully balance these components through network design, installation, and management. But for now, we need to start by exploring the basic principles that govern local area networking fundamentals. Here they are:

LAN Hardware

Topology Components	Workstations
Cabling	System Fault Tolerance (SFT) Components
File Server	

LAN Software

Network Operating System	Network Applications
Workstation Operating Systems	Office Systems Design
Menu Systems	

LAN Hardware

LAN hardware describes the components you can "touch." It provides the system with processing; communications; fault tolerance; and most importantly, connectivity.

The *topology components* provide the network messages with a highway to travel on. They also create, maintain, and support the rules of the road. The *cabling* is the actual road. It provides the physical pathway for the message's journey and most of the time determines the speed of travel. The *file server* is the network boss. It establishes the communications procedures for network workstations and allocates shared LAN resources. The file server also houses the all-important network operating system. The *workstations* are the true workhorses of the LAN. They handle 95 percent of the network's processing load. Also, each workstation represents its user's link to the LAN. Workstations must be as user friendly as they are smart. Finally, the often-overlooked *system fault tolerance components* represent the LAN's only protection against data corruption, power outages, data loss, and network crashes. Let's take a closer look at these critical LAN hardware components.

Topology Components

Chapter 1 touched on the three major topology standards: Ethernet, ARCNet, and Token Ring. This chapter explores these three LAN standards in more depth, concentrating on the components themselves and how they fit together. Chapter 5 will examine each of these standards in greater depth with the goal of developing a complete NetWare LAN design.

Ethernet

The Ethernet standard uses Carrier Sense Multiple Access (CSMA) protocol over a bus topology. In the event of a collision, Ethernet employs the collision detection (CSMA/CD) subprotocol solution. Ethernet is available in three different designs: thin Ethernet bus, thick Ethernet bus, and the Ethernet 10Base-T star. The Ethernet bus design is the oldest and most established topology standard. It is also the simplest, with all nodes connected to a single linear trunk. The Ethernet 10Base-T star is the youngest of the topology standards, only recently earning its Institute of Electrical and Electronic Engineers (IEEE) rating.

The key hardware components of the Ethernet bus standard are the network interface card (NIC), BNC T-connector, and BNC 50-ohm terminator. The NIC plugs into an intelligent workstation and sends a signal through the BNC T-connector to the linear trunk. Transmissions flow in both directions toward the terminating ends of the coaxial cable. Transmissions over thin Ethernet cabling travel at 0.65 times the speed of light, whereas thick Ethernet transmissions can accelerate to 0.77 times the speed of light.

All Ethernet NICs have unique internal addresses. These addresses are 12 characters (hexadecimal) and are programmed onto the cards at the factory. Each manufacturer is given a large bank of addresses by the Ethernet governing body, the IEEE. As the messages travel along the linear trunk, all NICs on the LAN monitor the cable and grab packets with matching destination addresses. Unclaimed packets are absorbed at each end of the trunk by the BNC 50-ohm terminators.

Ethernet 10Base-T is popular because it operates over existing telephone wire—UTP. This convenience is overshadowed by the fact that the telephone wire was not originally designed to handle high-speed LAN communications. The 10Base-T design is unstable in high load environments and instances of electromagnetic interference (EMI). Possible sources of EMI include fluorescent lighting, elevator motors, coffee machines, and power cables.

The key components of the Ethernet 10Base-T standard are the NIC and 10Base-T hub (sometimes called a *concentrator*). The Ethernet 10Base-T standard is so named for the 10-Mb/s transmission speed and twisted-pair cabling. It uses the same CSMA/CD protocol as the traditional Ethernet, except that the normal linear trunk is organized into a linear star. At the center of the Ethernet star is the 10Base-T hub. Each hub can connect up to 12 cabling trunks directly to 12 workstation NICs, each with its own dedicated leg. The topology design is rather confusing though, because the 12 independent legs are actually treated as one single trunk. The same collisions occur as with the traditional bus design, but the star configuration provides an additional level of cabling fault tolerance.

All three designs share one common thread: the Ethernet NIC. The Ethernet network interface card uses essentially the same components regardless of the topology or media. The NIC contains an internal transceiver, network address read-only memory (ROM), and CSMA protocol firmware. The only difference between the thin, thick, and 10Base-T NICs is the cabling port. Thin Ethernet uses a BNC connector that plugs directly into the coaxial trunk through a BNC T-connector. Thick Ethernet uses a DIX (Digital/Intel/Xerox) 15-pin connector that attaches to an external transceiver. Ethernet 10Base-T NICs have an internal RJ-45 port for direct connection to UTP and a DIX port for connection to a thick or thin external transceiver. In addition, a thin or thick Ethernet NIC can be used in a 10Base-T design by connecting its DIX port to an external 10Base-T transceiver. Here are the advantages and disadvantages of Ethernet:

Advantages	Disadvantages
Fast at 10 Mb/s	Slows down in high traffic
Simple, inexpensive components	Vulnerable bus topology
High level of connectivity	

ARCNet

The ARCNet standard uses token-passing protocol over a star/bus topology. ARCNet was conceived at the Datapoint Corporation in 1977 as a means for sharing data among the many different Datapoint machines of that era. It uses a relatively small packet size (512KB) for flexibility, travels at a fixed rate (2.5 Mb/s) for reliability, and operates over IBM's 3270 terminal cabling (RG/62 93-ohm coaxial) for connectivity. Back in 1977, these features made sense. Today they are obsolete. The ARCNet Trader's Association (ATA) is working on a new ARCNet standard (ARCNet Plus) that will operate at 20 Mb/s over various types of media. Many industry professionals believe that the only reason ARCNet has not achieved IEEE approval is because it didn't have an IBM or Digital pushing the issue. The ATA will pursue an IEEE rating for ARCNet Plus.

The ARCNet design is truly unique. Its token-passing protocol over a star/bus topology requires specialized programming. Only a couple of manufacturers produce the ARCNet chip sets for all 150 NIC suppliers. The key to ARCNet's design is the node address of each workstation NIC. The node address is an eight-digit binary equivalent of the numbers 1 through 255. The address is represented by a block of eight on/off switches on the ARCNet NIC and is programmed manually by the network designer. In an ARCNet LAN, messages are broadcast over the coaxial star in the same manner as the Ethernet bus, with one important distinction: The ARCNet NIC cannot broadcast on the star trunk unless the token says it can. This approach differs from Token Ring in that the token doesn't carry the message, it just signals the release of one. The ARCNet token (called an *ITT—invitation to transmit*) travels along the star topology in address order. It passes from 1 to 2 to 3 and up to 255 and back to 1 in a logical ring. When a workstation NIC has the token, that NIC broadcasts its message throughout the entire star topology.

The star bus design terminates each leg at the workstation NIC; no external terminator is needed. Once the destination NIC receives the message, it sends an acknowledgment back to the sender and the token is released to the next higher address. This deterministic protocol makes for strange token paths if successive workstations are located at opposite ends of the topology. It is important to note that the ARCNet token travels at a fixed rate. This feature slows down the LAN, but it also provides a high level of reliability, because there are no collisions.

The key components of the ARCNet standard are the NIC, active hub, and passive hub. The ARCNet NIC contains an internal 93-ohm terminator, node address bank, and token-passing firmware. The ARCNet NIC port uses the same BNC connector as Ethernet. Each workstation leg connects directly to the central point of the star (active hub). The active hub contains 4, 8, or 20 BNC connections and accepts legs from network workstations, servers, or gateways. The active hub amplifies and reconditions ARCNet broadcasts as they travel throughout the star topology. Passive hubs simply redirect the signal; they don't condition it. The ARCNet standard enables you to connect multiple active hubs in a distributed star configuration. This feature gives you the flexibility to span great distances by using the repeater characteristics of the active hub. In addition, manufacturers are providing active hub cards that plug into workstations and feed off the computer's internal power supply.

The ARCNet Plus design will *octuple* the speed of original ARCNet. Today's ARCNet relies on sine wave intervals of 400 nanoseconds to send 1 bit of data. The ARCNet Plus protocol uses amplitude modulation to send 4 bits of data every 200 nanoseconds. (Hence, 2.5 Mb/s becomes 20 Mb/s.) Another useful feature of ARCNet Plus is automatic stepdown: ARCNet Plus NICs will communicate with other ARCNet Plus NICs at 20 Mb/s, or they can step down automatically to communicate with original ARCNet NICs at 2.5 Mb/s. All that the manufacturer asks is that you use ARCNet Plus active hubs and not the original ones. ARCNet's comparison:

Advantages	Disadvantages
Fixed speed in high traffic	Slow speed at 2.5 Mb/s
Inexpensive components	Not officially IEEE rated
Reliable star topology	
Supports a large, distributed layout	

Token Ring

The Token Ring standard uses the token-passing protocol over a star/ring topology. The physical star, logical ring topology is unique to Token Ring and provides many levels of system fault tolerance. The central point of the physical star configuration is a Token Ring hub called the *MultiStation Access Unit, MSAU* (pronounced "msaooow"). The term MSAU is used to avoid confusion with the 802.3 MAU, or Media Attached Unit. The MSAUs form a logical ring through special end connectors called ring-in (RI) and ring-out (RO) receptacles. The RO from the first MSAU plugs into the RI of its neighbor. The neighbor's RO plugs into the next MSAU's RI, and so on. The entire topology follows this convention until the last RO finds the first RI, creating a closed ring. IBM's MSAU is a passive (no electricity), nonintelligent hub that can handle up to eight simultaneous connections, called an IBM 8228 MSAU.

The IBM 8228 brings workstations in and out of the ring through the use of an old-fashioned internal relay; if the port's relay is open, the workstation is in the ring. In many cases, the relays trip open during transport, so IBM has included an 8228 Setup Aid (for $50) that reinitializes the internal relays and ensures that the workstation ports are open and the empty ports are closed. IBM also offers an intelligent MSAU that includes internal network management features and software-controlled access to internal relays. These specialized devices are called *Controller Access Units,* or *CAUs* (pronounced "cows"). Who says IBM doesn't have a sense of humor?

As discussed earlier, the token-passing protocol relies on a 24-bit control signal, the token. The token circulates the ring 245 times a second and stops to visit each workstation along the way. The NIC that controls the token has exclusive access to the channel and may send a 2,048-byte message without any interference. Token ring NICs exist in one of four different states: transmit, bypass, listen, and receive. The token passing works like this:

1. Workstation A has a message for workstation D. Workstation A enters into transmit mode and captures the free-flowing token.
2. Workstation A attaches its message to the token, marks it with a destination address, and sends the token along the network channel.
3. Workstation B is off, remaining in bypass mode. So the token continues straight through B's NIC and on to the next node.
4. Workstation C, in listen mode, notices the passing token and checks the destination address. No match. C sends the token back on its way.
5. Workstation D, also in listen mode, notices the token and checks the destination address. Now there's a match.
6. D switches into receive mode and copies the message into workstation memory. It is important to note at this point that workstation A still has control of the token. Thus, D must attach an acknowledgment packet to the token and send it back to A.
7. Once A receives the acknowledgment message from workstation D, A releases the token and enters into listen mode.

A special node, called the *active monitor,* is responsible for ensuring the integrity of the token as it circles the ring. Token passing was initially defined by the IEEE under grouping 802.5. The protocol was originally designed to operate at 4 Mb/s, but recently IBM has introduced enhancements to this design that increase the speed 300 percent, to 16 Mb/s. The 16-Mb/s design uses the *early release token mechanism.* This feature allows multiple workstations simultaneous access to the ring by eliminating the need for acknowledgment packets. The sending workstation releases the token without confirmation that the receiving node ever actually accepted the message. This design has obvious flaws, but in "real life," 16-Mb/s Token Ring is just as reliable as the original design.

The Token Ring standard is inherently proprietary; it has IBM written all over it. The IBM specification requires IBM NICs, IBM-type patch cables, and IBM-type adapter cables. The real oddity in Token Ring is the proprietary IBM data connector: It is *hermaphroditic.* Usually, cables are classified as male (pin) or female (port). The IBM data connector is both—or neither, depending on your point of view. Token Ring NICs are too small to support these monstrous connectors, so they use 15-pin AUI (auxiliary unit interface) connectors.

The Token Ring NIC comes in four flavors: 4 and 16 Mb/s for standard IBM PCs (ISA), or 4 and 16 Mb/s for IBM PS/2 Microchannel machines. The 16-Mb/s NICs can run at either 4 or 16 Mb/s but not at both. The entire Token Ring LAN will operate at the speed of the slowest workstation NIC.

Node addressing for Token Ring is handled in the same manner as Ethernet—the 12-digit, hexadecimal codes are programmed onto the cards at the factory and controlled by the IEEE organization. The only difference is that Token Ring NICs come with software that enables you to change the node address. This is a double-edged sword. On the one hand, it offers great flexibility in case you need to swap NICs, and other network devices are looking for a given address. On the other hand, it presents the network manager with a bureaucratic nightmare. Take your pick. I recommend you leave the node addresses alone. Here is a brief look at Token Ring's advantages and disadvantages:

Advantages	Disadvantages
Fixed speed in high traffic	Very expensive components
IBM connectivity	Highly proprietary cabling
Fast at 16 Mb/s	Complex topology installation
Reliable star topology	

Token Ring is the ideal LAN standard. It offers flexibility, speed, reliability, and IBM connectivity. Unfortunately, all good things have a price, and Token Ring's price is very high. Workstation NICs, IBM-type cabling, and network management tools cost 300 to 400 percent more than similar devices for Ethernet and ARCNet.

Cabling

The topology components must connect somehow; this is the role of cabling. LANs rely on cabling for connectivity, reliability, and speed. In the past, cabling choices were driven by topology standards: Ethernet and coaxial, ARCNet and coaxial, Token Ring and STP. Times have changed. Today, the industry is flexible enough that any topology design can run on almost any kind of cabling. This discussion explores the many types of LAN cabling and the variety of workable combinations of media and topology. Also, I would like to spend a moment discussing the prospects of wide area networking and connecting LANs through unbound media.

The light at the end of the tunnel has a train attached.

—Anonymous

LAN Media

The term *local area network* implies a communications scheme within a tight geographic zone. LAN cabling is produced with this idea in mind. Each of these four media is a true cable—that is, the communications channel is housed within a physical wire or fiber. This property has advantages in security, reliability, and speed. There are many factors to consider beyond price and performance when you choose a LAN cable: durability, reliability, ease of installation, fire codes, standardization, maintenance, and troubleshooting.

Currently, four different types of media are specifically suited for local area networking:

LAN Media

UTP (Unshielded Twisted Pair)	Coaxial
STP (Shielded Twisted Pair)	Fiber Optics

UTP (Unshielded Twisted-Pair). UTP comprises two solid or stranded copper wires braided together to decrease susceptibility to EMI. The quality of the copper wire is measured according to a rating scheme called the American Wire Gauge (AWG). The AWG number of the wire describes characteristics such as diameter and composition. Most UTP wires are 22-AWG or 24-AWG. Three additional characteristics of the wire that directly affect its reliability as a LAN medium are attenuation, capacitance, and crosstalk. UTP can handle a maximum speed of around 10 Mb/s. UTP is not a great LAN medium, but unfortunately many network managers choose UTP for convenience.

STP (Shielded Twisted-Pair). STP consists of the same copper wire core as UTP, but STP has the added protection of a foil or mesh shield—usually, aluminum/polyester. The added shield of STP allows for less crosstalk and thus accommodates higher transmission rates, up to a maximum speed of 65 Mb/s. STP cabling is used almost exclusively in the Token Ring design. Almost all of the proprietary IBM-type cabling is made of shielded twisted pair. STP is also a great fit for Ethernet 10Base-T; nobody says you have to use UTP.

Coaxial. Coaxial cable, commonly known as *coax,* consists of a central conducting copper core that is enclosed in Teflon insulation. The insulation is then further encased in a second layer of conducting material, usually a wire mesh or solid copper jacket. All of this is covered by a tinted jacket of Teflon. Coaxial cabling is measured by the same cable properties as UTP and STP, and performs better with respect to capacitance and attenuation. In addition, coax connectivity is rated according to impedance. *Impedance* concerns the relationship of current to voltage in a coax cable. NICs and coax media must be tuned into the same level of impedance: 50 ohms for Ethernet and 93 ohms for ARCNet. LANs cabled with the wrong impedance will not work. This is a common source of frustration and hair loss. Coaxial cabling supports a much higher transmission rate than UTP or STP, with a maximum of 100 Mb/s. Coax is ideal for both Ethernet and ARCNet designs. I prefer it to UTP or STP in many situations.

Fiber Optic. Fiber optic technology is the future of network cabling. For some the future is here today. The Ethernet, ARCNet, and Token Ring standards currently support fiber optic cabling. An industry standard has been developed to help manufacturers deal with the complexities of fiber optics in a LAN environment. This standard, called *Fiber Distributed Data Interface (FDDI),* establishes transmission protocols at 100 Mb/s. Fiber optic cabling consists of a very fine optical fiber made from two types of glass—one for the inner core and one for the outer core (cladding). The inner and outer cores have different indexes of refraction, and that causes the light signal to bounce back and forth as it travels along the fiber cabling. Fiber optic cabling is measured by the diameter of the core fiber. Most LAN components require 62.5 micron fiber. Fiber optic technology relies on the properties and characteristics of light instead of electricity. These properties are completely immune to electrical or electromagnetic interference. In addition, light transmission allows for an almost infinite bandwidth, which in turn equates to incredible speeds—up to 200 gigabits per second.

WAN Media

The term *wide area network* implies a communications scheme beyond geographic boundaries. WAN communications media must be able to extend beyond buildings, cities, and even countries. Only one of the four WAN media is composed of physical cabling: T-1. T-1 is described more accurately as a communications protocol, not an actual medium. The rest of the WAN channels use the characteristics of unbound communications, including lack of physical restrictions, larger bandwidths, and unique frequencies. These properties make it possible for geographically distributed LANs to communicate with one another on a real-time basis.

Currently, four types of media are specifically suited for wide area networking:

WAN Media

Infrared	Satellite
Microwave	T-1

Infrared. Infrared communications are best suited for attaching LANs that are less than a mile apart. Infrared transmission is similar to the signals used by your TV's remote control. Infrared does not require an FCC license to use, and it promises WAN transmission speeds of approximately 10 Mb/s. The hardware components are relatively inexpensive compared to the other WAN alternatives. On the down side, infrared is susceptible to environmental interference from fog, rain, snow, or birds.

Microwave. Microwave communications extend the geographic boundaries of your WAN approximately 30 miles. Microwave relay towers (MRT) can extend communications beyond the 30-mile limit. Microwave signals are sent as frequency-specific radio waves from a parabolic sending antenna to a similar parabolic receiving antenna. Microwave communications are also *line-of-sight,* subject to interference from large obstructions. The U.S. Federal Communications Commission (FCC) requires organizations to license their microwave frequencies, and this process can prove to be quite expensive and time-consuming. Microwaves have large bandwidths, of 10 to 30 Mb/s.

Satellite. The most spectacular advancement in data communications has been made in the area of satellite transmission. This WAN medium virtually opens the entire globe to any network. Satellite transmissions are sent as high-frequency—4- to 30-gigahertz (GHz)—radio waves from an earth uplink station to a geosynchronous satellite orbiting 22,300 miles above the earth. The satellite relays the message to a second earth station (downlink station) that transmits the message to the LAN through conventional bound media. There are currently over 20 communications satellites in orbit. Unfortunately, these satellites are highly saturated and it is quite expensive to buy bandwidth. Satellite communications are sophisticated and extremely expensive, but for global wide area networking they provide the only choice.

T-1. The T-1 standard connects geographically separated LANs in a cost-effective manner. T-1 operates as a digital signal level 1 (DS-1) over phone-company networks at a transmission rate of approximately 1.544 Mb/s. The T-1 protocol breaks a DS-1 signal into 24 DS-0 64-Kb/s channels. These 24 channels can be shared by many devices (fractional T-1) or monopolized by one large piece of equipment. The T-1 WAN standard is cost-effective for large corporations whose users require real-time network access.

File Server

The file server has a substantial impact on network performance. It houses the network operating system, processes disk requests, stores LAN applications and data, controls network security, and provides central system fault tolerance. If there is one critical hardware component, it is the network file server. Keep in mind, though, that a LAN is a distributed data communications system. This means that 95 percent of the network processing occurs at the workstation, not at the file server. The file server's processing capability is not as important as these other features:

Feature	Types
Bus type	ISA, EISA, or Microchannel
Disk type	MFM, RLL, ESDI, SCSI, or IDE
NIC architecture	8-bit, 16-bit, or 32-bit bus mastering

At a minimum, the NetWare file server must have the following:

- an Intel-based 80286 processor
- 12-MHz clock speed
- memory addressing of up to 16MB

Before we can explore what makes a file server good, you must first understand what the file server is designed to do. Its primary function is to process requests from the LAN by accepting incoming data packets and shuffling them off to internal random-access memory (RAM). RAM acts as a holding cell until the file server central processing unit (CPU) is ready to work on the request. Typically, the network packet consists of a request for specific data located at a specific address somewhere inside the file server disk. The CPU locates the data and sends the packet back to RAM where it waits until the requested data arrives. Once the data arrives, it is attached to a reply packet and sent off to the original workstation through the file server NIC. In this scenario, many file server components affect network performance:

Component	Performance Effect
Topology	The time it takes for the request to reach the file server and the reply packet to return
File server NIC architecture	The time it takes for the file server NIC to shuffle the request to internal RAM
CPU clock speed	The length of time the request waits in RAM
RAM-to-CPU channel	The throughput from memory to the CPU
Disk type	The speed of the disk and the time it takes for the drive to retrieve the data
Disk-to-RAM channel	The throughput from server disk to RAM
File server NIC architecture	The time it takes for the file server NIC to shuffle the request from RAM to the topology

The topology performance is fairly fixed. Once the network manager chooses a given topology, the file server has no control over the time it takes for LAN requests to travel from workstation to server. The following factors *do* affect performance:

- The file server NIC architecture is very important and affects network performance dramatically. A shallow NIC can create bottlenecks of network traffic and slow file server performance up to 300 percent.
- CPU clock speed is important in ISA machines. It becomes almost obsolete, though, in EISA and Microchannel architectures.
- The RAM-to-CPU channel and disk-to-RAM channel are controlled by the file server bus type. The ISA, EISA, and Microchannel architectures provide various degrees of channel dedication to the CPU, hard disk, and memory.
- The speed of the disk drive itself has a great deal to do with how quickly data can move from point A to point B.

Disk channel bottlenecks are more severe than NIC clogs. Let's spend a moment to explore the three file server components that have the greatest impact on network performance: bus type, disk type, and NIC architecture.

Bus Type

The microcomputer motherboard is designed around two data transfer components: the data bus and the expansion bus. The term bus was originally conceived to illustrate the process of transporting (busing) critical data bits to and from the computer's electronic hardware: CPU, RAM, and expansion cards—printers, mice, modems, sound, disk, NIC, and video. The data bus furnishes the system with connections between CPU and RAM, while the expansion bus offers communications pathways to the expansion cards. The file server's bus type is important because it defines the path network requests travel. A slow, narrow bus will bog down in heavy loads and negatively affect network performance. A fast, intelligent bus can make a noticeable difference in the time it takes for workstation requests to be returned. Currently, there are three common bus types: ISA, EISA, and Microchannel.

ISA. The Industry Standard Architecture (ISA) bus describes the original IBM AT design. ISA is universally accepted as the microcomputer standard. It uses 8-, 16-, or 32-bit channels to transfer data from expansion card to RAM to CPU. The throughput of the ISA bus is dictated by the Intel-based CPU, as discussed in Chapter 1. Most of these machines only support 8-bit or 16-bit expansion cards.

EISA. In September 1988 a consortium of nine computer manufacturers announced a new ISA standard called the *Extended Industry Standard Architecture (EISA)*. The Gang of Nine consisted of Compaq, AST, Epson, Hewlett-Packard, NEC, Olivetti, Tandy, Wyse, and Zenith. The EISA standard did not replace ISA but merely enhanced it. The EISA bus offers 32-bit channels from expansion cards to RAM to CPU. The 32-bit EISA expansion slots support both 32-bit EISA expansion cards or the traditional 16-bit ISA cards. The most exciting enhancement, though, is bus mastering. *Bus mastering* provides a means whereby an expansion device does not necessarily have to wait for the CPU to transfer data to and from memory. Instead of the original design, in which the CPU must handle all requests from expansion cards to RAM—a disk request (wait), a NIC request (wait), a video request (wait)—bus mastering expansion cards contain internal processors that take control of the EISA bus and bypass the busy CPU. Bus mastering NICs send data requests directly to bus mastering disk controllers. This EISA feature can increase network performance up to 400 percent.

Microchannel. In 1987 IBM's leaders decided to take matters into their own hands, and they developed a proprietary improvement to the ISA standard: Microchannel Architecture. Originally, IBM used the acronym MCA to designate this architecture, but that acronym was dropped after multiple lawsuits from the Music Corporation of America (MCA). Microchannel is the basis for the IBM PS/2 line of computers and has many advantages and disadvantages compared with ISA. The biggest disappointment is that Microchannel bus slots do not support ISA expansion cards. Microchannel is also a 32-bit bus and offers its own version of bus mastering.

Disk Type

The file server's disk houses most of the LAN's primary resources: the network operating system, shared data, and network applications. The file server disk comprises two components: the disk drive itself and a matching disk controller. The *controller* plugs into the microcomputer bus and translates address requests from the CPU into specific sectors on the disk. Speed, size, and reliability are key factors in choosing a file server disk. There are currently five different file server disk types: MFM, RLL, ESDI, SCSI, and IDE.

MFM. The early AT-class computers used a disk data encoding scheme called modified frequency modulation (MFM). MFM drives use clock heartbeats from the controller to distinguish the presence of a 0 bit or 1 bit. The bits are organized on the disk in 512-byte sectors, with 17 sectors per track. MFM controllers transfer data to and from the disk at 5 Mb/s.

RLL. IBM quickly developed an improvement to MFM called run length limited (RLL). RLL disks have 50 percent greater capacity than MFM drives because the RLL format uses 25 sectors per track. RLL disks are also faster, at a data transfer rate of 7.5 Mb/s. RLL quickly became the industry standard in the early 1980s with almost 90 percent of the industry manufacturers following its design.

ESDI. In the mid-1980s, a consortium of disk manufacturers banded together and developed the enhanced small device interface (ESDI) standard. ESDI drives move the pulse-driven intelligence from the controller to the disk itself. Another key advancement is the use of digital communications rather than analog. ESDI drives use 53 sectors per track for a data transfer rate of 10 to 24 Mb/s. ESDI is common among older NetWare file servers.

SCSI. SCSI, or small computer systems interface (pronounced "scuzzy"), drives differ from ESDI in a few critical ways. First, ESDI drives transfer data in a serial fashion—one bit at a time. SCSI drives use parallel communications to transfer 8 bits simultaneously. Second, SCSI handles data in blocks, not sectors. This leads to greater flexibility in the SCSI device. SCSI is not a disk controller protocol; it is more of a systems interface protocol. SCSI controllers can handle a variety of devices: hard disks, CD-ROMs, tape drives, and external subsystems. Up to eight SCSI devices can be daisy-chained from one controller. SCSI controllers can transfer data to and from the disk at 32 Mb/s. SCSI is the best choice for NetWare server disks.

IDE. IDE disk technology was recently developed by the Western Digital Corporation. IDE stands for intelligent drive interface, integrated drive electronics, or intelligent David entertainment—take your pick. IDE technology is similar to SCSI in that the controller electronics are on the drive itself. IDE disks borrow the best features from all the previous designs: they have the speed of ESDI, the intelligence of SCSI, and compression encoding schemes of RLL. IDE has become the new industry standard for microcomputers, replacing ESDI. IDE is a solid standard, but I still prefer the flexibility and stability of SCSI for network file server disks.

NIC Architecture

The throughput of the file server NIC is the most critical topology point on the LAN. Workstation NICs handle singular requests, whereas the file server NIC handles multiple simultaneous requests. File server throughput is determined by one factor: the size of the channel from NIC to RAM. Standard AT NICs offer an 8-bit channel to memory; only 8 bits of information can travel from the NIC to memory simultaneously. The typical Token Ring data packet is 2,048 bits, and it circles the ring up to 980 times a second. Simple math shows that the typical AT NIC must handle 250,880 trips to RAM each second, creating a major bottleneck. To improve the throughput from the file server NIC to memory, manufacturers have produced network interface cards that take advantage of the 16- and 32-bit bus architectures. Also, recent advancements in NIC design have produced cards that can take advantage of bus mastering in the EISA and Microchannel environments.

Workstations

Although the file server is the focus of network performance, the workstation is the LAN workhorse. In a distributed data communications system, the workstation handles 95 percent of the network processing. Bus type, disk type, and NIC architecture are not the critical issues here. Instead, workstations are designed for processing, memory, and ergonomics. You saw earlier in the chapter that a NetWare file server is restricted to only IBM PC-compatible machines. Fortunately the choice of workstation is not nearly as prohibitive. NetWare currently supports workstations based on the following three architectures:

- IBM-compatible
- Macintosh
- UNIX workstations

Each of these architectures is best suited for specific workstation tasks. The IBM-compatible workstations are flexible, cheap, and easily expanded. The Macintosh computers are powerful, have exceptional graphics capabilities, and are easy to use. The UNIX workstations have superior processing power and work well for scientific and engineering applications. One of the strengths of NetWare is that it simultaneously supports such a wide variety of platforms, giving it the reputation for transparent connectivity.

IBM-Compatible

The IBM PC family of computers stretches well beyond the original IBM PC. Today, the IBM-compatible family opens its arms to Compaq, NEC, AST, Toshiba, Zenith, Dell, and thousands of no-name clone manufacturers. Fortunately, all of these different machines have a few things in common: processor, bus, memory, disk, video, ports, and configuration. The typical IBM-compatible workstation uses an Intel-based microprocessor with 16- or 32-bit bus channels. The workstation has 4 to 8MB of RAM, high-density floppy drives, and an EGA or VGA monitor. Look for one serial and one parallel port, each set to the correct interrupt and I/O address. Let's spend a few minutes exploring the IBM-compatible workstation in more detail.

Processor. The IBM-compatible workstation includes the Intel-based microprocessor. There are currently five generations of this chip: 8086/8088, 80286, 80386, 80486, and Pentium (80586). Rumor has it that the Intel Corporation has already finished the next two generations, and Intel's engineers are currently working on the 80886 family.

Here are the milestones in the Intel processor family tree:

1. The 8086 is the original Intel chip. It was introduced in 1978 with a 16-bit data bus.
2. Existing hardware could only support 8 bits, so Intel shelved the 8086 and introduced the 8088—an 8-bit version of the 8086. The first microprocessors could only address 1MB of RAM and operated at 4.77 MHz.
3. In 1984, Intel introduced the 80286, with a 16-bit data bus. The 80286 can address 16MB of RAM and operates at 6 to 20 MHz. The significance of the 80286 is capability of real versus protected addressing. In real mode, the 80286 emulates the 8086/8088 and can access only 1MB of memory. In protected mode, the 80286 can access the remaining 15MB of memory and protect the system from application faults. This feature was the driving force behind the development of Microsoft Windows.
4. The next significant workstation advancement was from 16- to 32-bit processing. The Intel 80386 was introduced as a true 32-bit processor together with a 32-bit data bus.
5. Soon afterwards, the 80386SX was introduced—mostly as a marketing ploy. The 80386SX is also a true 32-bit processor, but it only operates with a 16-bit bus. The 80386 is capable of addressing 4GB (gigabytes) of memory and operates at 16 to 40 MHz.
6. The next two generations have seen less significant improvements. The Intel 80486 is simply an 80386 with a built-in math coprocessor and 8KB of processor cache.
7. Intel's newest wonder, the Pentium, is an 80586 with a new name, apparently to distinguish between Intel's chip and the numerous clone copies. The Pentium is a much improved 80486 with high memory capacities and a faster clock speed. The major improvement in the Pentium is processing capabilities—over 100 million instructions per second—faster than most minicomputers.

The engineers at Intel are reaching the limits of the current technology. There is talk that they are working on a completely different approach to microprocessing: photonics. *Photonics* is processing based on light instead of electricity.

Bus. The discussion under Bus Type discussed the microcomputer bus in detail. The bus type is much less critical for network workstations. Most IBM-compatible workstations are based on the ISA architecture. It doesn't make sense to spend the money on EISA or Microchannel for independent workstations.

Memory. The memory requirements of IBM-compatible workstations are driven by network applications. RAM is so named because of its ability to address any location at any time without regard for the last location that was addressed. RAM is vital to the performance of any type of network workstation. RAM stores requests before and after processing, it stores application instructions, and it houses critical NetWare communications parameters. It comes in many different shapes and sizes. The most common implementation is SIMMs (Single In-line Memory Modules). SIMM describes a small circuit board that plugs into a special SIMM socket on 80286, 80386, 80486, and Pentium motherboards. The SIMM boards contain a number of RAM chips in increments of 1MB, 4MB, 8MB, or 16MB. The most important issue with SIMMs is that board sizes must match; you can't mix 1MB with 4MB chips on a single board.

Workstation RAM is organized into three functional groups: conventional, expanded, and extended. *Conventional RAM* is the first 640KB of memory that is addressable by DOS. DOS has a serious problem with this 640KB barrier: RAM cram. *RAM cram* is the situation most network workstations endure as they try to cope with communications shells, network applications, and system configurations all in the first 640KB. Software manufacturers have been quite clever in their quest to break the 640KB barrier, but for DOS it will always be there. Expanded and extended RAM are addressed above the 640KB barrier in different ways. *Expanded memory* uses the LIM (Lotus/Intel/Microsoft) EMS 4.0 (Expanded Memory Specification) standard to address up to 32MB of workstation RAM. *Extended memory* requires the LIM XMS (Extended Memory Specification) driver for access to additional RAM. Chapters 5 and 6 discuss memory management in more detail.

Disk. Local disk storage is not critical for network workstations. The purpose of a central file server is the storage of centrally shared applications and data. Workstation hard disks defeat this purpose. Unfortunately, users have become accustomed to accessing their own local drives and do not take kindly to network managers with screwdrivers. NetWare provides the capability of remote booting for diskless workstations. An image of the boot files is stored on the file server, and an internal workstation boot chip—*programmable read-only memory (PROM)*—redirects system startup procedures to the correct central location. Diskless workstations provide additional levels of workstation security and virus protection.

Video. There are two basic modes of workstation video: text and graphics. Text monitors can display only simple ASCII characters. Graphics monitors can display thousands of colors in a variety of different resolutions. *Resolution* is the measure of fineness in picture quality. Workstation screens display images as a collection of dots called *pixels* (picture elements). The greater the number of dots, the sharper the picture. Video is a combination of the workstation monitor and an internal video adapter. CGA (Color Graphics Adapter) systems have the poorest resolution, and one step up is EGA (Enhanced Graphics Adapter), succeeded by the VGA (Video Graphics Array) and Super VGA. VGA monitors can display 640 by 480 pixels in 16 colors, whereas Super VGA monitors can display 800 by 600 pixels in 256 colors. Quality video resolution can have a positive impact on user productivity and workstation effectiveness. Currently, the most exciting improvements in workstation video are 32-bit on-bus VGA and acceleration cards for advanced graphics and Microsoft Windows.

Ports. Two workstation ports affect the network: parallel and serial. The workstation parallel port is used for local and remote network printing. The serial port is used for communications. NetWare provides utilities for shared access to both parallel and serial workstation ports.

Configuration. The IBM-compatible workstation bus is a complex freeway of system requests and application instructions. The various workstation hardware components compete for local resources: CPU, RAM, and disk. To organize these communications, the IBM-compatible world has adopted three configuration methods: interrupts, memory addresses, and I/O (input/output). Interrupt requests (IRQ) are hardware signals sent from NICs, keyboards, disk controllers, video, and other devices, that tell the CPU it's time to listen. The interrupting hardware device sends this signal over a dedicated IRQ line. Each hardware device in the workstation must have a unique IRQ. The memory address is a range of workstation RAM dedicated to a specific hardware device.

The I/O address is similar to IRQ. It represents a dedicated door to the workstation CPU. Each hardware device must have a unique I/O address. Other critical workstation configurations are stored in a battery-powered ROM chip called the *CMOS (complementary metal-oxide semiconductor)*. The CMOS permanently stores disk parameters, clock-calendar functions, and system start-up configurations.

Macintosh

Apple Macintosh computers are becoming more powerful. At the same time, they are becoming more popular. Today's sophisticated user is more educated and curious. He or she is exposed to a variety of different platforms and switches easily among the traditional PC, an Apple Macintosh, and a Sun UNIX machine. As workstation platforms diversify, users are demanding transparent connectivity between unlike machines. NetWare is the leader in multiple platform integration. Macintosh connectivity is achieved through two NetWare products: NetWare for Macintosh VAP (Version 2.2) and NetWare for Macintosh NLM (Versions 3.11 and 4.0). There are four primary Macintosh-specific components that exaggerate the difference between Apple and IBM-compatible workstations: communications, filing, printing, and user interface.

The Macintosh communicates with other systems through an internal network interface card. The Macintosh NIC uses a proprietary Apple topology design called LocalTalk. LocalTalk uses the CSMA protocol with Collision Avoidance (CA) at 0.254 Mb/s, which is 40 times slower than Ethernet. Macintosh workstations communicate with NetWare servers through a proprietary protocol called AppleTalk. Macintosh filing systems are unique as well. They rely on another proprietary protocol called AppleTalk Filing Protocol (AFP). AFP structures data files into two components: the data fork and resource fork. The *data fork* contains the data, and the *resource fork* keeps track of the application used to create the data.

Macintosh filenames are case-sensitive, allow spaces, and can be up to 32 characters long. UNIX filenames are even more flexible, consisting of up to 128 characters. DOS filenames are extremely limited, consisting of just 11 characters and no spaces.

Macintosh printing services use LocalTalk ports to communicate with Apple ImageWriters and LaserWriters. NetWare print queues give Macintosh and IBM users shared access to Apple Postscript printers. The Macintosh user interface remains intact when connected to NetWare servers. The dazzling graphical user interface (GUI) that has become the Macintosh trademark is not sacrificed at all. Macintosh users connect to a NetWare file server through the Chooser utility. In addition to Chooser, NetWare provides two Macintosh-specific utilities: NetWare DA (Desk Accessory) and the NetWare Control Center. The NetWare DA gives Macintosh users the ability to send messages to other PC users, view and manage NetWare print queues, and manage rights within a file folder. The NetWare Control Center is the Macintosh equivalent to SYSCON and FILER. These administrative utilities give Macintosh supervisors the ability to create users, change security, delete files, delete folders, change servers, and manage volume rights.

UNIX Workstations

The UNIX environment was initially designed to serve large corporate systems. It is traditionally text-based and is designed for cryptic tasks like protocol translation, interoperability, and multitasking. None of these features endears UNIX to the network user. As a matter of fact, the early UNIX systems were coined *user hostile.*

Recent advances, though, have changed the face of UNIX, and now it is a powerful, user-friendly alternative for advanced network users. UNIX entered the GUI world with the release of *X Windows*, a wonderful multitasking windows interface. The UNIX system runs on high-end, proprietary engineering machines. These computers are capable of 50 to 100 million instructions per second. Sun Microsystems, Inc., and Digital Equipment Corporation (DEC) are the leading manufacturers of high-end UNIX workstations. These microcomputers have always been thought to occupy a transient classification somewhere between minicomputer and microcomputer.

UNIX workstations communicate with each other through TCP/IP (Transmission Control Protocol/Internet Protocol). TCP/IP is actually a group of network protocols that define data communications among a broad range of computers. UNIX machines speaking TCP/IP can communicate with NetWare computers speaking IPX/SPX through a variety of different NetWare products: NetWare TCP/IP, NetWare NFS, and LAN WorkPlace for DOS. Other UNIX network standards include File Transfer Protocol (FTP), Network File System (NFS), TELNET, and Simple Mail Transfer Protocol (SMTP).

SFT Components

System fault tolerance (SFT) is a measure of how tolerant a system is to destructive faults. Makes sense, right? A high level of SFT means that a LAN can withstand disk crashes, power outages, file corruption, and total data loss. The only thing SFT cannot protect you from is coffee spills on the keyboard. A low level of SFT opens your LAN to a variety of minor disasters, any of which can cause early retirement.

There are two major types of system faults: energy failures and data loss. *Energy failures* occur when the power from the wall either spikes (there's too much juice) or dies (there's not enough). Energy failures can cause workstation crashes, file server crashes, disk crashes, and data loss. Also, energy spikes have proven to destroy sensitive microcomputer motherboards.

Data loss is most frequently attributed to file server disk failures. Data loss can also occur when users delete files, corrupt files, or introduce destructive network viruses. NetWare and third-party manufacturers provide a variety of SFT components to help prevent and recover from destructive system faults.

Energy Loss + Data Loss = Hair Loss

Energy SFT. *Energy SFT* components protect file servers, workstations, and active topology components from power surges, brownouts, and blackouts. Energy SFT is provided by three components: the surge protector, standby power supply (SPS), and uninterruptible power supply (UPS).

Surge protectors are the first line of defense. These inexpensive devices sit in-line between the computer and the wall. They monitor incoming voltage levels and send spikes beyond 250 volts to the ground. Energy spikes can cause a wide range of damage to motherboards, NICs, power supplies, and workstation peripherals.

The *SPS* works similarly to the surge protector in location and function, but the SPS provides an additional level of network defense: It will switch over to battery power in the event of an energy blackout. The problem with this scenario is the time it takes the SPS to switch from commercial power to its internal battery. In some cases, this delay is substantial enough to crash the file server anyway.

In comes the *UPS,* which feeds conditioned power to the computer at all times, so there is no switching after power outages. Conditioned power is energy from the UPS's internal battery. If commercial power fails, the UPS continues to feed the network device and sends a message to the file server that it's time to close down. UPS components offer the highest level of energy SFT.

Storage SFT. *Storage SFT* components protect network users from data loss, disk crashes, and file corruption. Storage SFT is provided by two components: tape backups and on-line redundancy. *Tape backup systems* are the most effective protection against data loss and file corruption. It is a strange fact that most people fully realize the value of their data once it is gone. Many factors contribute to the reliability of a tape backup system: flexibility, data encoding scheme, security, speed, storage capacity, encryption, and media. The tape backup hardware is useless without a good implementation plan. The backup implementation schedule should optimize data recovery by rotating tapes in combination with off-site storage.

On-line redundancy protects network data in "real time." This level of storage SFT relies on internal NetWare commands and additional disk hardware. Sometimes referred to as *SFT Level II,* on-line redundancy employs four recovery strategies: hot fix, transactional tracking (TTS), disk mirroring, and disk duplexing. Hot fix and TTS do not require additional hardware. Disk mirroring and duplexing require various levels of hardware redundancy. The ultimate level of on-line redundancy can be found in SFT Level III: full server duplexing. SFT Level III links two redundant servers with a speedy fiber optic cable. Full server duplexing offers SFT protection at all hardware levels—NIC, disk, and CPU.

The question of common sense is always "What is it good for?"—a question which would abolish the rose and be answered triumphantly by the cabbage.

—James Russell Lowell

LAN Software

LAN software describes the components you cannot "touch." It provides the system with productivity; user interface; system management; and most importantly, user transparency. LAN software consists of five components: network operating system (NOS), workstation operating systems (WOSs), menu systems, network applications, and office systems design.

The NOS is the heart of the LAN. It resides on the central file server and controls critical network operations such as file requests, packet routing, network security, interconnectivity, and system management.

WOSs reside on distributed workstations and handle local processing, network applications, and resource allocation.

Menu systems provide the LAN with a productive, friendly user interface. Such systems integrate network applications, direct LAN functions, and continually monitor resource usage.

Network applications are productivity tools that add value to the LAN. These tools create and interpret the messages that bounce from computer to computer. Without network applications, the LAN would be nothing more than an electronic merry-go-round.

Finally, the office systems design components offer task integration for network users. Sometimes called *groupware,* these components handle electronic mail, automated group scheduling, calendars, and network management.

Let's take a closer look at these critical LAN software components.

Network Operating Systems

The true brains of the LAN are stuffed into the NOS. It manages file server memory, users and groups, network applications, data, security, CPU usage, and shared resources. In most cases, the NOS resides on a central controlling node—the file server. Workstations use network shells to communicate with the NOS. This setup is called the *client/server model.* In a few cases, the NOS is distributed equally among the workstations through a peer-to-peer design. In *peer-to-peer networks,* the distributed nodes share the load of LAN administration and resource allocation. Local hard disks become network drives, and distributed printers join one common pool.

NOS systems span the top five layers of the OSI model. The data link and physical layers handle LAN topology components. The main function of the NOS is to interface between the communications segment (topology) and application resources (disk drives, security, and applications such as WordPerfect). To perform this task, the NOS uses three components: network drivers, subnet protocols, and application layer protocols.

Network drivers interface between the NOS software and the topology hardware. The NOS uses network drivers to communicate with the file server NIC and receive incoming data packets.

Subnet protocols span layers 3, 4, and 5 of the OSI model. These protocols converse with network drivers and application layer protocols. Some examples of subnet protocols include IPX/SPX and TCP/IP.

The *application layer protocols* are sometimes called *Application Programming Interfaces (APIs)*. These protocols receive data requests from subnet protocols and direct them to appropriate application resources. Novell programmers use APIs to expand the functionality of NetWare systems—NLMs and VAPs. Later, this book discusses these important NetWare APIs.

Client/Server OSs

There are currently seven viable network operating systems:

Client/Server	Peer-to-Peer
NetWare	NetWare Lite
Banyan VINES	LANtastic
LAN Manager/LAN Server	Windows NT
Appleshare	

We will focus on the four most popular client/server network operating systems: NetWare, VINES, LAN Manager, and Appleshare. Then the discussion shifts to peer-to-peer systems, NetWare Lite, LANtastic, and Windows NT.

NetWare. Novell has released nine generations of NetWare: NetWare/286 v2.0a, v2.15 Adv, v2.15 SFT, v2.2, NetWare ELS I, ELS II, NetWare/386 v3.0, v3.11, and NetWare v4.0. Only three of these generations are currently supported: NetWare v2.2, v3.11, and v4.0. NetWare commands 70 percent of the NOS market, although Novell won't admit it, because competitors are screaming "Monopoly!" Novell has done a wonderful job in distributing its organizational structure. The company uses a complex affiliate program to extend key management functions beyond corporate boundaries: education (NAEC, CNE, CNI, and NTI), support (VAR and NTS), marketing (NUI), and development (VAR, NTI, and TSA).

The key to NetWare's success is familiarity; simply stated, it looks like DOS. It isn't based on DOS, it doesn't use DOS, it just *looks* like DOS. DOS users feel comfortable using the system and quickly pick up the subtle NetWare differences. Using familiarity as a springboard, Novell has pushed NetWare in many exciting directions. Currently, NetWare's functionality is based on seven LAN principles:

- configuration
- security
- SFT
- speed
- connectivity

- user interface
- network management

Chapter 6 provides a detailed discussion of these important NetWare principles.

Banyan VINES. Banyan VINES is the second-rated NOS and is expecting a significant release during the second quarter of 1993. VINES (Virtual Network System) is based on the interface and functionality of UNIX System V. Banyan has created a powerful, interconnected NOS that is difficult to use and understand. Although baffling, VINES has a variety of terrific features: the StreetTalk global naming scheme, fine-tuning maintenance, broad auditing capabilities, and excellent internal bridging. VINES uses TCP/IP for communications, FTP for file transfers, and NFS for filing. Users who are familiar with the UNIX arena have no problem adjusting to VINES. Incidentally, Novell uses a variation of StreetTalk as the basis of NetWare V4.0's NetWare Directory services.

LAN Manager/LAN Server. LAN Manager is Microsoft's product and LAN Server is IBM's. Both of these network operating systems are based on the OS/2 WOS. OS/2 has many inherent features that make it an ideal network operating system: multitasking, programming flexibility, 32-bit architecture, and High Performance File System (HPFS). The concept of using OS/2 as a NOS was originally conceived in a joint effort by IBM and Microsoft, but they didn't see eye to eye and divorced in late 1991. IBM is firmly committed to OS/2 as a platform for LAN Server, whereas Microsoft redesigned LAN Manager and released it with Windows NT (New Technology). LAN Manager and LAN Server differ in only subtle ways. The heart of the NOS is in the features and benefits of OS/2.

Appleshare. Appleshare is Apple's hat in the ring. It is a slow, low-powered NOS with nothing to offer except terrific user interface and a low price tag. Appleshare uses Macintosh's internal LocalTalk topology and AppleTalk protocol. This NOS only runs on Macintosh file servers. Appleshare's NOS functionality falls well short of the previous three systems, but it supports a wide variety of groupware applications that can enhance the productivity of a small to medium-sized Macintosh office. Most Appleshare LANs quickly upgrade to NetWare for Macintosh.

Peer-to-Peer

In additon to the four client/server NOSs, we can choose among less powerful, peer-to-peer systems: NetWare Lite, LANtastic, and NT.

NetWare Lite. Novell introduced NetWare Lite in the fall of 1991. It was designed to offer a low-cost, simple NOS alternative for small, first-time network installations. It has exceeded Novell's expectations. NetWare Lite loads into each workstation's conventional RAM as a peer-to-peer NOS. It monitors other stations on the LAN and establishes drive mappings and printer redirections to local resources. NetWare Lite emulates client/server NetWare in a few key categories: auditing, security, drive mapping, resource sharing, messages, network backup, and user administration. It is a miniversion of the real thing. The obvious limitations of NetWare Lite are linked to its peer-to-peer nature: it handles a limited number of nodes, it features no centralized resources, it provides limited interconnectivity, and it includes no wide area networking capability. NetWare Lite also is limited to

25 users. NetWare Lite provides first-time LAN users with an easy-to-use, partial version of NetWare. NetWare Lite costs $99 retail per workstation, although it's advertised for under $50. NetWare Lite is a good stepping stone to NetWare v3.11.

LANtastic. Artisoft's LANtastic has been the leader in peer-to-peer technology since 1987. LANtastic was the first noncentralized NOS and offers several convenient and useful features: excellent printer sharing, small memory overhead, CD-ROM sharing, proprietary topology components, and electronic mail. In addition, LANtastic 4.0 recently added Windows administration, hardware independence, and support for up to 300 workstations. LANtastic compares to NetWare Lite in functionality and ease of use but falls well short in performance and reliability.

Cost is a tricky issue with LANtastic. Artisoft will sell you a 300-user pack for $699—that's $2.33 per workstation, a steal! Not so fast. You must add the LANtastic Ethernet cards at $299 apiece. Suddenly, the tab totals $301.33 per workstation. Artisoft will sell you special hardware-independent LANtastic at $99 per workstation, and you can add Intel's superior Ethernet card for $150—that's $249 per workstation.

Windows NT. Windows NT is Microsoft's latest addition to the networking market. NT has replaced OS/2 as the networking foundation of LAN Manager. In its basic form (without LAN Manager), Windows NT provides distributed users with peer-to-peer functionality through a sophisticated set of networking hooks and multitasking programs. NT is a true 32-bit operating system like NetWare and OS/2 but offers a little bit more: security, file browsing, print browsing, and multiprotocol support. The other peer-to-peer network operating systems sit on top of DOS. Windows NT is different; NT is its own fully functional 32-bit operating system. It comes with a feature called Flexboot, which gives users the choice between booting NT or booting DOS. When a user boots NT, he or she receives a login message to press Ctrl+Alt+Del simultaneously. This flushes out any non-NT intruders.

After entering a correct username and password, the user is brought into a Windows 3.1 environment. NT looks like Windows 3.1, but it is much more: NT includes the NT File System (NTFS), remote NT printer administration, server functions, network utilities, UPS services, file recovery system, CD player, and many various administrative tools.

Once NT has loaded, it looks to a network configuration file to determine whether it is running on a peer-to-peer client or a centralized LAN Manager server. If you're running NT in peer-to-peer mode, the system sends out a message to other clients on the LAN and attaches to their local file and printing resources. Windows NT uses two protocols for peer-to-peer communications: TCP/IP and NetBEUI (for LAN Manager support). Chapter 6 discusses Windows NT in more detail.

Workstation Operating Systems

If the workhorse of the LAN is the workstation, the reins are controlled by the workstation operating system (WOS). The WOS manages local processing and workstation resources while maintaining a stable link to the distributed LAN. In most cases, a specific WOS gets along best with a specific NOS: DOS with NetWare, OS/2 with LAN Server, NT with LAN Manager, UNIX with VINES, and System 7 with Appleshare.

The WOS resides on the workstation and handles processing requirements for NIC communications, local computer functions, and distributed network applications. The WOS defines the user's interface before and after the network applications have been loaded. The most important functions of the WOS are compatibility, user interface, and interoperability. The most popular workstation operating systems are DOS, OS/2, Windows NT, UNIX, and System 7.

DOS

The leading WOS is the longstanding disk operating system (DOS). DOS currently comes in three flavors: MS-DOS from Microsoft, PC DOS from IBM, and DR (Digital Research) DOS from Novell. In addition, there are a few proprietary variations available from Compaq, Toshiba, and DEC. MS-DOS and PC DOS are virtually identical. DR DOS has a few special quirks.

Here's a synopsis of Novell's relationship to DOS as it was coproduced by Microsoft and IBM:

1. The early versions of DOS (V1.x and V2.x) were marginally supported by Novell, because they lacked the many subtle hooks needed to communicate in a network environment.
2. DOS became networkable in November 1984 with the release of version 3.1.
3. DOS V4.x was a flop.
4. DOS V5.0, on the other hand, was a savior; it offered many new networking advantages, especially in the areas of disk handling, memory management, and communications. At this point, IBM ceased to coproduce the system with Microsoft, turning its attention instead to refining OS/2.
5. DOS 6.0 is here. It offers all of the features of DOS 5.0, plus more networkability, memory management, and disk optimization. DOS 6.0 also includes the Microsoft antivirus, flexible configuration files, peer-to-peer networking, and much better on-line help.

All of the features and benefits of MS-DOS are duplicated in DR DOS. As a matter of fact, there are many who believe that DR DOS is superior to Microsoft's product in its memory management, task integration, and disk handling features. But the real key to DR DOS is its networkability. Digital Research was purchased by Novell in 1991. This move was interpreted by many as a commitment by Novell to superior connectivity between NOS (NetWare) and WOS (DR DOS). DR DOS 6.0 has enhanced many of the MS-DOS 5.0 features, with MemoryMAX for memory management, DiskMAX for disk caching, and DOSBOOK for on-line help.

DR DOS 6.0 has also exceeded many of MS-DOS 6.0's features—ViewMAX for GUI interface, TaskMAX for instant multitasking, and built-in NetWare shells.

OS/2

OS/2 was developed as a joint effort by Microsoft and IBM. OS/2 was intended to replace DOS as the premier workstation operating system—hence the name Operating System 2 (OS/2). The following capsule history of this system covers its ups and downs:

1. The original version of OS/2 (version 1.0) was doomed from the start. It was completely proprietary, was left unsupported by leading applications, and required googols of memory in a time when RAM was very expensive.

2. The next release (version 1.1) offered a few technical compromises, but the operating system still didn't have the support it needed from software manufacturers like Lotus, Ashton-Tate, and Borland. Microsoft also lagged in its OS/2 application offerings.

3. During development of the next release (version 2.0), IBM and Microsoft reached an insurmountable impasse. They wanted to move OS/2 in different directions: IBM wanted to concentrate on hardware; Microsoft saw the future in diversified software support. They split. IBM continued its efforts and released OS/2 version 2.0. Microsoft, on the other hand, funneled its OS/2 efforts into a completely different product called Windows NT.

OS/2 has its clear advantages: it can run multiple applications simultaneously and supports application RAM in excess of 640KB. OS/2 is a true 32-bit operating system, which means it can take advantage of the superior speed and throughput of the 80386, 80486, and Pentium machines. Also, OS/2 comes with an internal Windows-like GUI, Presentation Manager. The problem with OS/2 is its heavy hardware overhead. It requires fast, expensive machines with tons of internal RAM. Also, OS/2 hasn't yet caught on as a stable 32-bit application platform. Keep in mind that it does support 16-bit DOS applications in DOS-emulation mode.

Windows NT

Windows NT is Microsoft's 32-bit, multitasking WOS. Its processing core is founded on the principles of OS/2, whereas its interface emulates Windows 3.1. Windows NT also has built-in LAN Manager workstation and server capabilities. The most substantial networking features of Windows NT are security, registry, filing, and network management. Windows NT supports administrators, power users, users, and guests. The NT configuration information is stored in a database called the *registry*. The registry is organized in a tree format, much like the DOS file system, and provides users with the ability to change critical configuration files from a central location. Local and network filing is handled by the Windows NT File System (NTFS). NTFS provides three main features: no file size limits, excellent recoverability, and security.

Windows NT provides excellent GUI-based network management facilities. In addition to the standard Windows 3.1 control panel, file manager, and print manager is a set of enhanced administrative tools. The Windows NT administrative tools include performance monitor, event viewer, backup, disk manager, and user manager. Windows NT is an intense 32-bit GUI operating system. Like OS/2, it requires heavy hardware overhead. Windows NT will only run on a 32-bit workstation (80386, 80486, or Pentium) with 8MB of RAM and a minimum of 55MB of local hard disk storage.

UNIX

UNIX is inherently networkable. It was originally designed at Bell Laboratories as a communications platform for the development of the C programming language. C is a versatile language that changed the face of computing. Variations of C have been used to develop applications and operating systems like NetWare, Microsoft Windows, Windows NT, WordPerfect, Quattro Pro, System 7, and Microsoft Word.

UNIX comprises local and networking features. Local features include the UNIX File System (UFS) and X Windows. Network features include TCP/IP, FTP, NFS, and various network commands/utilities. TCP/IP's communications protocols establish connectivity between UNIX workstations and UNIX servers. FTP supports a variety of file formats and includes an internal file conversion utility. NFS is a proprietary NOS that was developed by Sun Microsystems. NFS sits on top of TCP/IP and provides UNIX users with the ability to access remote files as if they were local. The many UNIX network commands and utilities include Simple Mail Transfer Protocol (SMTP), TELNET, rlogin, rcp, and ping.

System 7

System 7 is the latest WOS in a long line of Macintosh operating systems. System 7 is considerably more networkable than the earlier versions. It contains peer-to-peer file sharing, interapplication communications (IAC), Apple Events Messaging (AEM), and multiprotocol driver support.

The heart of the Macintosh environment is user friendliness. Apple was the first to popularize GUI, and its desktop interface has come to represent user productivity and effectiveness. The introduction of System 7 had very little effect on the actual look and feel of the Macintosh computer. Instead, the new WOS increased the workstation's power and connectivity.

System 7's peer-to-peer file sharing is achieved through direct LocalTalk connections. Workstations can share files, folders, hard disks, or CD-ROMs. The Macintosh Control Panel utilities (termed *CDEVs*) manage file sharing, object security, and user access. IAC is a new System 7 feature that enables users to exchange critical application updates across the LAN. Any network-aware application can publish updates to all workstations that subscribe to it.

Apple Events Messaging is another file-sharing mechanism that works on the basis of the client/server model. Any workstation application can request the services of another LAN application through messages called *Apple Events*. Events can be internal or external and include files, hard disks, indexing, formatting, applications, printing, and security. The communications core of System 7 is the AppleTalk protocol and LocalTalk topology. Together they are known as the Macintosh Communications Standard (MCS).

Menu Systems

The WOS controls the workstation environment. It manages input, processing, storage, and output. Many of today's WOSs integrate a graphical user interface. This interface is the user's link to network applications and productivity; its importance cannot be overestimated. Later in the book, we will talk about ergonomics. *Ergonomics* (pronounced "air-go-NOM-iks") is the study of how people interface with their surroundings. An ergonomic chair, for example, is comfortable and pleasing to the eye. To build an ergonomic chair, one must concentrate on how people sit and what they like.

The same holds true for menu systems. To design an ergonomic menu system is to create an interface that people enjoy and understand. A few network menu systems are both ergonomic and network-aware. Microsoft Windows is the first that comes to mind. In addition, there are many worthy GUI menu systems, such as Windows Manager II, GeoWorks Ensemble, and SuperGUI. For those who don't like GUI, there are some nice network-aware text-based menu systems, including Novell's own internal menu utility (MENU).

Microsoft Windows

Contrary to popular opinion, Microsoft Windows is *not* a workstation operating system. Windows runs on top of DOS and relies on it for internal commands, procedure calls, and resource allocation. Microsoft Windows is a very popular menu system that provides network users with a GUI look-and-feel, multitasking, and additional application utilities. Microsoft Windows 3.1 adds multimedia support, enhanced graphics, and workstation disk optimization.

Probably the most important feature of Microsoft Windows is application consistency. All applications that are written to the Windows standard must follow consistent menu structures and a specific GUI look and feel. Microsoft strongly enforces these standards. You cannot argue with the results. Microsoft has gained momentum with the immense success of Windows and recently launched three network-related applications: Windows NT, Windows for Workgroups, and LAN Manager for Windows NT. The ultimate acceptance of Windows is illustrated by Novell's commitment to GUI in the new NetWare Graphical Administrator, a NetWare version 4.0 management utility based on the Windows interface. Soon Microsoft will release a flood of 32-bit applications and a new version of Windows—version 4.0.

Microsoft Windows 3.1 requires a minimum of 1MB of workstation RAM and an 80286, 80386, 80486, or Pentium processor. At least 2MB of RAM and a pointing device (mouse, pen, or trackball) are recommended.

Windows currently operates in either of two modes: standard and enhanced. *Standard mode* is intended for 80286 workstations with limited internal RAM. In standard mode, non-Windows applications cannot multitask. *Enhanced mode* takes full advantage of the advanced workstation processors and additional internal RAM. The Windows environment consists of four components: shells, tools, applications, and programming. The Windows shells are Program Manager, File Manager, and Print Manager. The Windows tools include desktop accessories, the Clipboard, DDE (Dynamic Data Exchange), OLE (Object Linking and Embedding), Control Panel, TrueType Fonts, and Multimedia. The Windows applications are Write, Terminal, Paintbrush, and Solitaire. The Windows programming features include .INI (initialization) files, drivers, virtual memory, and network shells.

Microsoft Windows interfaces with NetWare through the IPX and NETx workstation shells. These shells initialize the internal NIC and control the interface between DOS, Windows, and NetWare. Windows' performance is optimized when you run it on a local workstation disk, but it can also operate from the central file server. In the case of the latter, 16MB of program files are placed in a shared directory called WINSHARE, and specialized workstation configuration files are stored in individual user subdirectories.

Other GUI Menu Systems

Beyond Microsoft Windows is a world of secondary GUI products. None of these menu systems has Microsoft's golden touch, but they do have some great networking features—security, encryption, resource tracking, and application integration. Some of the most interesting GUI menu systems are these:

- GeoWorks Ensemble
- NCDware
- PM Assistant

- SuperGUI
- WISh2

Text-Based Menu Systems

If Microsoft Windows is just too overwhelming and you're sick of workstation RAM cram, there are some text-based menu systems that work well in a NetWare environment. The critical function of a text-based menu system is memory consumption: How much RAM overhead does it take? Also, users are concerned with the menu-building language: Does it take a PhD to understand? Some of the most unobtrusive and easy to understand menu systems include these:

- +Menu
- LANMenu
- Direct Access Network
- Automenu
- NetWare's Menu

- EASY-DOS-IT
- Turbo Menu
- Lazy Susan
- Q*Menu
- WordPerfect Library

Network Applications

Network applications are productivity tools that add value to the NetWare LAN. These tools create and interpret network messages as they bounce from computer to computer. Network applications can be likened to the swords that users wield to carve out company profits. The proper mix of network applications can save thousands of dollars in increased productivity and overall office efficiency.

As we saw earlier, NetWare was designed with DOS in mind. NetWare adheres to many of the DOS programming standards that enable thousands of different applications to exist in the IBM-compatible environment. This means that most applications that run under DOS will also run under NetWare.

There are two types of network applications: stand-alone and network-aware. *Stand-alone software* includes applications that were never intended to run on a LAN. These network applications can nevertheless operate on a NetWare server, but their file sharing functionality is severely limited. *Network-aware software* is more complex and designed to take full advantage of NetWare's multiuser environment.

Most of the major software manufacturers are developing network-aware versions of popular stand-alone applications. Additional functionality includes application security, file sharing, record locking, convenience, easy upgrades, cost savings, and storage efficiency.

Network-aware applications are organized into five categories: word processing, spreadsheets, database, integrated software, and miscellaneous network applications.

Word Processing

Word processing is the most common network application. It is used by more network users than all of the other applications combined. Using a word processor in a network environment provides several advantages: file sharing, security, printer sharing, performance, and enhanced disk storage. The network operating system handles data security and organization, and the word processing software provides formatting features and user functionality. Some of the most network-aware word processing applications are these:

- Microsoft Word
- WordPerfect
- Borland Multimate
- Borland Fullwrite Professional for Mac
- Lotus Manuscript

Spreadsheets

Network-aware spreadsheet applications provide users with the ability to consolidate financial models across multiple platforms. In addition, these advanced spreadsheets provide file locking, cell-level locking, file sharing, and common templates. Workgroup spreadsheeting has become so popular that Lotus Development Corporation has invented a workgroup manager for 1-2-3 called Chronicle. Chronicle is a sister product for 1-2-3 that applies tracking technology to multiuser spreadsheets.

Some other network spreadsheets include these:

- Microsoft Excel
- Borland Quattro Pro
- Lotus 1-2-3
- PlanPerfect
- Borland Full Impact for Mac

Databases

A *database* is a collection of related information that you enter as "records" and that you can output in the forms of reports, indexes, lists, notes, and tables. Some advanced database systems also support graphics, sound, and video—in other words, multimedia. A LAN is a very natural place to find databases. Databases are designed to allow multiuser access and simultaneous report generation. Today's database management systems (DBMSs) go one step farther and combine a friendly user interface with fuzzy-logic searches (that is, searches that imitate how the human mind makes connections). These are very powerful systems.

Following are the most common database products for networks:

- Borland Paradox
- dBASE IV
- Fox Pro
- R:Base
- DataPerfect

Integrated Software

Integrated software combines word processing, spreadsheets, database management, graphics, and communications in one package. The problem with integrated software is consistency. These five components are so dissimilar in function that it's almost impossible to combine them with any sense of unity. As of yet, no manufacturer has been able to put together a successful combination. Here is a list of the best integrated software products:

- Microsoft Works
- WordPerfect Works

- Lotus Symphony
- Borland Framework IV

Office Systems Design

Office systems design software is an integral part of today's new electronic office. Sometimes called *groupware,* these applications provide network users with electronic task integration. The need for groupware in today's electronic office is becoming more apparent as managers grapple with cyberphobia, increased paperwork, decreased efficiency, and an incongruous workforce.

Of all the groupware functions, electronic mail (E-mail) has had the most noticeable impact. Mail is the most voluminous and popular form of communications within and among businesses. If we could transfer 1 percent of the annual paper mail in the United States to electronic mail, we could make a huge dent in the destruction of the rainforest. NetWare has an internal mail routing protocol called the Message Handling Service (MHS).

Here is a list of some of the best groupware available:

- Microsoft Windows for Workgroups
- WordPerfect Office
- Higgins for Windows

I like work; it fascinates me. I can sit and look at it for hours. I love to keep it by me; the idea of getting rid of it nearly breaks my heart.

—Jerome K. Jerome

Well, that's it for LANs. This chapter talked about transparent connectivity, LAN topology, file servers, SFT, NOSs, WOSs, and network applications. These first two chapters were designed to create a strong foundation of data communications and local area networking fundamentals. Now that we have poured the concrete, it is time to don our hard-hats and begin the real fun: building my castle—no, building NetWare LANs. First, we take time out to survey the full range of Novell products so you can determine which one best suits your needs. Then, Part II's chapters explore network design, Part III's chapters concern installation, and Part IV deals with building the LAN itself.

The information you gather in the next chapter will prepare you for the process of designing, installing, and managing NetWare LANs.

Chapter 3

Novell and NetWare

I n order to achieve NetWare Nirvana, you must create a perfect balance between purpose and application. The purpose of your LAN is established in the systems analysis and design phase, which is covered in the next chapter. You must consider all aspects of network hardware and software, then develop a sound design that encompasses your purpose. The second step is application. The application of your purpose is defined by available LAN resources. The more resources you have available, the more successful the application. This chapter is about NetWare resources.

Novell, Inc.

Novell, Inc., of Provo, Utah, designs and manufactures microcomputer-based software products that substantially improve local area network performance. Novell's software-intensive approach to LANs provides

- compatibility among dissimilar hardware and software platforms
- simultaneous data access and manipulation
- enhanced minicomputer-like capabilities
- compatibility with off-the-shelf applications
- versatile interconnectivity
- portability
- ease of use

Novell's mission statement is simply "to accelerate the growth of network computing" (as stated in the *NetWare Buyer's Guide*). Novell was the first LAN product manufacturer to offer software-based distributed processing and continues to dominate the world market in connectivity and multiplatform development. Novell has grown from 14 employees in 1983 to over 3,200 employees currently working worldwide. In 1992, Novell's sales topped the $1 billion mark. Industry analysts have estimated that over 70 percent of the world's 4 million LANs are either using or connected to Novell products. Not bad.

In the Beginning

It all started for Novell in 1983 with the introduction of the first software-based LAN. The product, called NetWare (combining "network software"), revolutionized people's thinking about multitasking, security, and shared resources. Prior to 1983, LANs consisted of shared disk servers. These disk servers simply provided shared hard disks with no security, no multitasking, and very limited file structures.

Novell introduced NetWare v1.0 in 1983 along with Btrieve, the first multiuser database application for LANs. The first NetWare operating system contained multilayered security, DOS connectivity, menu-driven utilities, and early Ethernet topology support. Novell expanded the NetWare concept in 1985 to include database support for client/server architectures.

In 1986, Novell introduced a new generation of NetWare that supported the 80286 16-bit AT architecture: NetWare v2.0a. The new 80286-based NetWare provided considerable enhancements—system fault tolerance level I, internal bridging, Token Ring support, and LAN-to-IBM host connectivity. The next year, Novell announced the release of

NetWare v2.15 SFT, which included system fault tolerance level II. In 1988, Novell added three important platforms to its list of supported workstations: OS/2, Apple Macintosh, and VMS (for DEC VAX minicomputers). The current application of Novell's 80286-based NOS is NetWare v2.2.

In 1989, Novell began an incredible run of five straight years in each of which management announced at least one substantial revolution in the connectivity and functionality of NetWare. In 1989, the company introduced NetWare v3.0, the first 32-bit network operating system for Intel 80386-based servers. NetWare v3.0 represented a considerable improvement in the functionality of NetWare: modularity. All aspects of the operating system could be loaded and unloaded independently. NetWare v3.0 also included a high-capacity file system, remote printing, versatile workstation connectivity, and remote management facilities. The current application of Novell's 80386-based NOS is NetWare v3.11.

Also in 1989, Novell began licensing NetWare to UNIX vendors for portability to the UNIX server platform. In 1990, NetWare expanded to SNA hosts with LU 6.2 support. Novell also introduced NetWare SQL, a relational client/server database management system.

In 1991, Novell announced a considerable marketing merger with IBM. The new agreement called for NetWare distribution through IBM channels—a monumental achievement for the formerly small Novell. Also in 1991, Novell added three more connectivity platforms to the NetWare family: NetWare NFS for UNIX systems, NetWare SAA for IBM hosts and AS/400 connectivity, and NetWare FTAM to support OSI standards and the U.S. government's GOSIP (Government OSI Protocols) solution. One of the most interesting offerings in 1991 was the introduction of NetWare Lite, the small, peer-to-peer NOS designed for LANs that can't justify the costs of the original client/server model. NetWare Lite has met with mixed support.

The world is moving so fast these days that the man who says it can't be done is generally interrupted by someone doing it.

—Elbert Hubbard

In 1992, Novell announced another startling merger. This time it was a technology agreement between Novell corporate and UNIX System Laboratories. The new company, Univel, is charged with providing open system software solutions for distributed enterprise-wide LANs. The first Univel product, called UnixWare, was released in late 1992. Novell began to restructure its support foundation in 1992, providing two additional Certified NetWare Engineer (CNE) certifications (ECNE and CNA) and introducing a new on-line technology service, NetWare Express.

Also in 1992, NetWare began working very hard on the new desktop WOS offerings, with improvements to DR DOS 6.0 (1991) and DR Multi-user DOS. Novell released an upgrade patch to NetWare v3.11, a NetWare v2.2-to-v3.11 migration utility, and various drivers to support the enhanced Windows 3.1 platform.

And 1993 was a banner year for Novell. Their most notable success was the introduction of NetWare v4.0. NetWare v4.0 represents the most advanced generation of NetWare available. It includes an object-oriented NetWare Directory Service, data compression,

GUI administration, and an enhanced file management system. There was a great deal of enthusiasm surrounding the release of NetWare v4.0, and nobody has been disappointed. Also in 1993, Novell announced a restructured education program with all-new NetWare v4.0 courses and computer-based training. Today, Novell ushers the networking industry into brave new frontiers: hardware-independent NOS modularity, 64-bit multiprocessing, SFT Level III, and transparent global connectivity.

Here is a brief summary of where Novell has been:

1983	NetWare released as the first software-based LAN.
	Btrieve issued as the multiuser database system for LANs.
1986	NetWare v2.0a marketed as the first 16-bit NOS for Intel 80286-based servers.
	LAN-to-IBM host connectivity established.
	SFT level I created.
1987	NetWare v2.15 SFT released with SFT level II.
1988	NetWare connectivity for OS/2 developed.
	NetWare connectivity for Macintosh developed.
	NetWare connectivity for UNIX developed.
1989	NetWare v3.0 released as the first 32-bit NOS for Intel 80386-based servers.
	NetWare for UNIX developed as the first NetWare NOS to run on UNIX servers.
1990	NetWare SNA Gateway marketed.
	NetWare SQL released as the first relational database engine for NetWare servers.
1991	NetWare/IBM distribution merger finalized.
	NetWare for NFS released for UNIX connectivity.
	NetWare SAA produced for enhanced AS/400 connectivity.
	NetWare FTAM created for OSI and GOSIP connectivity.
	NetWare Lite developed as peer-to-peer NOS with NetWare functionality.
1992	Univel created from Novell merger with UNIX System Laboratories.
	ECNE and CNA certifications supported.
	Upgrade patch to NetWare v3.11 released.
1993	NetWare v4.0 released as the most advanced NetWare generation to date.
	UnixWare developed with NetWare functionality and UNIX connectivity.
	Education enhanced with new courses and new CBT programs.

The Novell Organization

Novell is organized around three business groups that are responsible for product development and marketing: NetWare Systems Group, Interoperability Systems Group, and Desktop Systems Group. In addition, these three product groups are provided centralized sales and support services from the Corporate Services Group. The executive vice presidents of Novell's four corporate groups are Jan Newman, Kanwal Rekhi, John Edwards, and Mary Burnside, respectively. These corporate officers report directly to Raymond J. Noorda, president and CEO. Mr. Noorda reports to the Novell board of directors, and specifically Adolf A. Paier, chairman of the board. The Corporate Sales Group provides the following services: sales, marketing, engineering, and administration.

NetWare

The cornerstone of Novell's product matrix and business philosophy is the NetWare network operating system. NetWare has evolved over nine generations to become a comprehensive, high-performance LAN solution. The next section discusses the ten most substantial features of NetWare:

- speed
- user interface
- resource sharing
- print spooling
- security
- system fault tolerance
- network management
- interconnectivity
- multiuser functionality
- interoperability

Novell's Other Products and Services

In order to satisfy its mission statement, Novell spends a large amount of time and resources on software development and product integration. The company has expanded its product line beyond simply NetWare and its accessories. Currently, there are many Novell products that stand alone: DR DOS 6.0, LANalyzer, NE3200, and LAN WorkPlace. In addition, Novell offers numerous service programs to support and educate the users of its product lines. Later, this chapter examines the Novell product matrix.

(handwritten margin note: "to accelerate the growth of network computing" (as stated in the Netware Buyer's guide))

Features and Benefits of NetWare

Now let's focus on the features and benefits of the NetWare network operating system. NetWare has some of the following features in common with other NOSs, but most are unique to NetWare. The goal here is to provide you with a general understanding of the concepts and techniques associated with building a NetWare LAN. Subsequent chapters explore these concepts in much greater depth.

In this section I will outline the 10 NetWare features and then offer a brief description of associated benefits. The benefits will be bold for emphasis.

Speed

NetWare was designed to provide high-performance file and print services to distributed workstation clients. NetWare currently incorporates five performance features that contribute to high network speeds: distributed processing, directory caching, directory hashing, file caching, and elevator seeking.

Distributed Processing

Distributed processing acknowledges each workstation as a computer capable of executing its own applications. NetWare exploits this fact, so that each station functions as if it were the only network workstation. Overall processing power increases as additional workstations are added to the NetWare LAN.

> **Benefits: With computing power equally available to each individual workstation, speed and efficiency are significantly increased.**

Directory Caching

Directory caching is the process of storing the NetWare Directory Entry Table (DET) and File Allocation Table (FAT) in server RAM. When a user requests a network file, NetWare uses the RAM-stored FAT to find the file's address. This stops the file server from making those extra trips to the hard disk for the DET and FAT.

> **Benefits: The addressing of disk-stored DET and FAT tables is kept in RAM instead of on the disk. Workstations can read and write network data from memory 100 times faster than from network disks. Directory caching also eliminates potential disk-access bottlenecks.**

Directory Hashing

Directory hashing is the process of indexing network DET and FAT tables. It enables the system to find correct addresses by examining only a few directories or file entries.

> **Benefits: A hashed FAT reduces the response time of disk input/output (I/O) requests by 30 percent.**

File Caching

NetWare *file caching* procedures store the most heavily used network files and applications in file server RAM. The first request for a file moves it from the disk to RAM, where the file is stored for subsequent requests. The system monitors the file caching area of RAM and determines which files are most frequently used. Once RAM is full, the least used files are overwritten by new requests. NetWare will use all available server RAM for caching.

> **Benefits: Subsequent requests for cached network files are answered 100 times faster. RAM caching improves performance and decreases disk thrashing.**

Elevator Seeking

Elevator seeking is a disk management process designed to prioritize buffers of I/O requests according to their disk addresses. Prioritization depends on the address's positional relationship to the current position of the disk head and the other current buffered I/O addresses. Figure 3.1 demonstrates a simple process, with four I/O requests in a current buffer.

> **Benefits: Elevator seeking techniques speed disk access by 40 percent. In addition, they significantly decrease disk thrashing, minimize disk wear, and increase the disk throughput by up to 50 percent.**

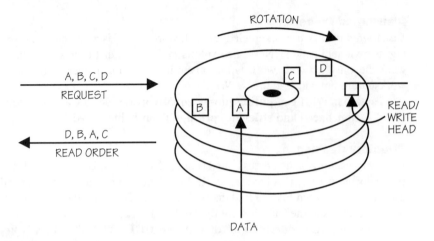

FIGURE 3.1   Prioritizing I/O Through Elevator Seeking

User Interface

NetWare's command-line utilities and administrative menu utilities resemble those of DOS and Windows. Their functionality, on the other hand, emulates networking hooks in OS/2 and UNIX. In addition, NetWare provides extensive context-sensitive on-line help facilities. Users can take advantage of over 200 menu-driven help screens. NetWare v4.0 provides workstation files that customize the user interface for DOS, Windows, or OS/2 environments.

> **Benefits: Users accustomed to DOS, Windows, OS/2, Macintosh, or UNIX find the NetWare command structure comfortable and easy to understand. This factor, along with extensive on-line help facilities, provides a shallow network learning curve.**

Shared Resources

NetWare supports hard disk systems ranging in size from 10 megabytes to more than 32 terabytes. NetWare's high-capacity file system can take advantage of new technology with nearly unlimited volume and directory sizes. NetWare also supports shared printers, modems, CD-ROMs, and gateways to larger systems.

> **Benefits: NetWare provides multiuser access to shared resources on the LAN. This is a cost-effective solution for small networks sharing documents or large enterprise WANs sharing distributed database applications.**

Print Spooling

NetWare is equipped with a fully functional print spooler that supports up to 16 printers per server and 100 files per queue. Each printer on the system can have its own queue, or multiple printers can share one queue. The spooler supports any batch printing device and supports multiple forms. With NetWare's inherent print management utilities, users can cancel their own print jobs, monitor queue loads, and operate up to three serial and/or parallel printing devices simultaneously.

> **Benefits: Individual users control print requests from their own workstations as needed. Users can view or modify their jobs' print number, status, form type, job sequence, filename, banner specification, number of copies, format, and job time at any point. Print spooling also frees valuable workstation processors as lengthy jobs are queued to the server.**

Security

NetWare provides the system Supervisor with extensive facilities to create a security system as simple or as sophisticated as desired. NetWare security is a multilayered system consisting of login names, passwords, user restrictions, group assignments, directory rights, file flags, and console commands. Partial lockout is available at the user and group levels. Total lockout is available through login names and passwords.

In addition, NetWare v4.0 offers advanced security at the global directory level (NDS) and independent auditing services. A user independent from the Supervisor can audit network usage and track user actions.

> **Benefits: The NetWare security system protects against accidental or intentional disclosure of confidential information. Data is easily protected, and the security is flexible. The password, user, group, and directory rights, along with file/directory flags, combine in a logical, sequential manner, making security management easy and comprehensive. Auditing services allows for independent tracking of network usage and user activities.**

System Fault Tolerance

System fault tolerance (SFT) is an essential part of the NetWare operating system. SFT verifies writes, protects data, provides dynamic bad block remapping, and guards against hardware failure. Some of the most important SFT features are built into NetWare and require no additional hardware. Others are dependent on expensive disk subsystems and redundant LAN hardware. NetWare categorizes these features as SFT levels I, II, and III.

SFT Level I

This original level of NetWare SFT is available in all the product's versions. It includes fundamental reliability features: read-after-write verification, duplicate directory entry tables (DETs), and duplicate File Allocation Tables (FATs). Read-after-write verification ensures that the data stored on disk matches the original information in RAM. Duplicate disk tables provide additional insurance against network data loss.

SFT Level II

This level of NetWare SFT became available in 1987 with the introduction of NetWare/286 SFT. SFT level II incorporates hot fixing, disk mirroring/duplexing, UPS monitoring, and the NetWare transactional tracking system.

Hot fix detects disk media defects and corrects them on the fly. When a bad block is detected during a write operation, the data is moved to a safe area of the disk and the bad block is marked unusable. This process is also known as *dynamic bad-block remapping* and is shown in Figure 3.2.

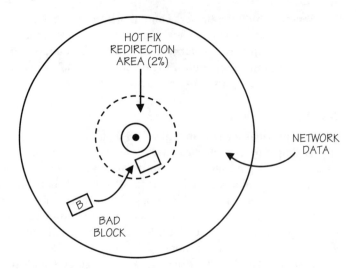

FIGURE 3.2   Detecting Media Problems with Hot Fix

Disk mirroring duplicates the contents of an entire hard disk on a second hard disk. If the original disk fails, the duplicate (mirrored) disk automatically takes over without sacrificing any important data. *Disk duplexing* duplicates the disk coprocessor board, cable unit, and drive controllers as well as the hard disk. Data loss is prevented along the entire channel from the server to the disk. Figure 3.3 illustrates disk mirroring and disk duplexing.

UPS monitoring provides a warm link between the server and the Energy SFT device. In the case of a power loss, the server is notified and NetWare closes down gracefully. The *Transactional Tracking System (TTS)* is a database protection option that preserves database integrity when applications, workstations, or file servers crash. When a failure occurs, TTS automatically rolls back or aborts database changes to the previous point of consistency.

SFT Level III

The highest level of NetWare SFT incorporates server redundancy. The concept is similar to disk duplexing but on a grander scale. In this case, the entire server and network operating system are duplexed to a backup system. A high-speed fiber optic connection keeps both systems in synch. This level of SFT protection is available as an enhancement to NetWare v3.11 or NetWare v4.0.

> **Benefits: NetWare SFT provides the maximum level of protection for valuable network data. SFT protects everything on the LAN from storage media to critical application files. In an environment where information is everything, most business LANs cannot live without the highest level of reliability.**

Network Management

NetWare provides the system Supervisor with a sophisticated, multifaceted system of network management. Printer control, users and groups, system security, and maintenance are all performed with the use of GUI menu-driven utilities. NetWare provides three types of

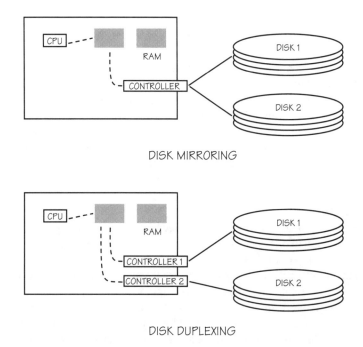

DISK MIRRORING

DISK DUPLEXING

FIGURE 3.3   System Fault Tolerance Through Disk Mirroring and Duplexing

network utilities: text, menu, and GUI. Text utilities can be entered at the workstation command line or file server console. Extensive help screens are available to explain the various parameters and options. Menu utilities incorporate many of the text-based commands and some additional commands not available at the command line. System configurations, printing, and network directory structures are managed from intuitive, easy-to-use menus. GUI utilities are new with NetWare v4.0. The friendlier interface provides additional functionality and more efficient command structures. Network management facilities are available in varying degrees to users, workgroup managers, operators, and the system Supervisor.

> **Benefits: The NetWare operating system has been designed to put maximum control and maintenance capabilities in the hands of the network Supervisor. Network management is completely centralized and creates a constructive environment from which the Supervisor can perform his or her magic. In addition, the three interface types provide flexibility to perform network operations from a variety of different angles.**

Interconnectivity

NetWare includes built-in interconnectivity features. LAN-to-LAN communications is achieved through internal bridging, external routers, and asynchronous server products. In addition, NetWare supports the OSI seven-layer communications model. This standardization enables NetWare to interface with a wide variety of like and unlike systems: IBM mainframes, TCP/IP, VMS systems, and UNIX WANs. NetWare uses three methods for interconnectivity: multiple servers, routing, and gateways.

Multiple Servers

NetWare supports multiple file servers on the same LAN. Users can log in to all servers simultaneously with one login using NetWare's Name Service. Some complex LANs run 5 to 10 different file servers simultaneously, and users switch from one to another as applications change.

> **Benefits: A company could purchase a network now and as it grows continue to install more file servers and workstations. Marketing, sales, accounting, and manufacturing departments could each have its own file server and continue to communicate as if the entire company were on one small network. Security features apply to multiple file server networks in exactly the same way they apply to a single server network.**

Routing

NetWare provides the facility to bridge between different types of networks, each running the same network operating system. This internetworking function greatly increases the expandability of the LAN and allows networks of different topologies or protocols to communicate effortlessly. NetWare's internal and external routing functions intelligently guide packets over similar or dissimilar configurations.

> **Benefits: A small network architecture can expand as the need for high-performance hardware arises. The key is that the software remains the same as the hardware evolves. The NetWare operating system automatically handles multi-LAN routing.**

Gateways

NetWare also provides the facility to bridge between a NetWare LAN and any other type of data communications system. This type of bridge between a LAN and an unrelated DC device is called a *gateway*. Gateways exist between any of a variety of different systems, including IBM mainframes, TCP/IP, VMS minicomputers, and UNIX WANs.

> **Benefits: An established NetWare LAN can easily expand into other data communications environments without sacrificing the processing capabilities of the local high-performance system.**

Multiuser Functionality

NetWare is a true multiuser network operating system that provides users with the ability to share software resources. These resources can include program files as well as data files. It also provides functions to allow transparent communications between stations on the network and functions to send information from any network station to networks beyond the local arena.

> **Benefits: One multiuser licensed program can be placed on the system and serve all of the user's needs instantaneously. This makes the system Supervisor's job a lot easier. It also eliminates the need for users to keep a floppy disk copy of each program they use. Shared data files can be kept in a public directory, whereas private files are protected under specific directory securities. This resource centralization allows for more efficient and effective disaster recovery as well as for system fault tolerance.**

Interoperability

NetWare is platform independent, topology independent, and client independent. One of its most amazing features is its ability to transparently support such a wide variety of different environments. *Platform independence* relates to the ability to interface with a variety of processors and operating systems: all Intel-based chips, UNIX systems, and VMS minicomputers. *Topology independence* describes the ability to handle requests from a variety of different topology designs: Ethernet, ARCNet, Token Ring, LocalTalk, and TCP/IP. *Client independence* defines NetWare's support of many client machines and operating systems: DOS, OS/2, Macintosh, UNIX, OSI, IBM's SNA, and Microsoft Windows NT.

> **Benefits: NetWare network managers have the flexibility to design any type of LAN system around NetWare's interoperability. The NOS can share resources and data files among countless combinations of platform, topology, and client architectures.**

Novell's Products and Services

Novell's product matrix is comprehensive and diverse. It includes a wide variety of network products and services designed to support NetWare and provide a complete LAN solution. Novell's products and services are organized into four categories:

- NetWare operating system products

- network services products

- distributed application development tools

- support and training

This section explores each product category in depth. A comprehensive understanding of Novell's product matrix is valuable to you as you analyze and design a network. Study this section carefully, because many NetWare accessories are designed to support the LAN construction process. Think of these products as the tools you need to build your NetWare LAN. Without a hammer, ladder, nails, and concrete, I wouldn't get very far building my castle. Likewise, the following product matrix will round out your Novell tool chest. In addition, if you are having a network crisis, the answers are probably here.

NetWare Operating System Products

The NetWare operating system products are at the pinnacle of Novell's product line. These products are organized into three groups: Network operating system products, workstation operating system products, and network adapters and hardware drivers.

Network Operating System Products

Network operating systems form the foundation of Novell's product line. They provide solutions for a variety of needs, including support for client/server and peer-to-peer systems.

NetWare Lite is a simple, inexpensive peer-to-peer NOS for networks with 2 to 25 users. NetWare Lite offers basic LAN functionality at a very low price. Features include security, resource sharing, network printing, network file structure, and audit trails.

NetWare version 2.2 is Novell's basic-level client/server NOS. It is ideally suited for small to medium-sized businesses or departmental workgroups within large corporations. NetWare v2.2 can operate dedicated or nondedicated within an 80286 computer or above. Features include comprehensive network management, internetworking, system fault tolerance, and multilayered security.

NetWare version 3.11 is Novell's 80386-based operating system. It provides a migration path from workgroup LANs (NetWare v2.2) to enterprise WANs (NetWare v4.0). NetWare v3.11 is currently the most popular NOS, largely because of its modular design, versatility, and high performance. Features include multivendor integration, mainframe connectivity, development support, and 80486 awareness.

NetWare version 4.0 is Novell's crowning achievement. It supports all previous levels of NetWare plus some hooks to future functionality. NetWare v4.0 was designed to connect existing NetWare v2.2 and NetWare v3.11 LANs into global NetWare enterprise WANs. Features include NetWare Directory Services, data compression, GUI utilities, international languages, and multiprotocol support.

NetWare for UNIX is a version of NetWare designed to run under general-purpose operating systems like UNIX. NetWare for UNIX acts as a set of nonnative application programs and provides a stable interface between NetWare environments and non-NetWare operating systems. Features include host/PC integration, transparent print services, combined security, and multiprotocol compatibility.

NetWare for UNIX has taken on new importance for Novell in light of Novell's purchase of AT&T's UNIX. Look for native UNIX connectivity in the next release of NetWare.

NetWare for UNIX has taken on new importance for Novell in light of Novell's purchase of AT&T's UNIX. Look for native UNIX connectivity in the next release of NetWare.

Workstation Operating System Products
On the heels of purchasing Digital Research in October 1991, Novell developed an advanced set of desktop WOSs to complement NetWare. DR DOS 6.0 leads the way with pseudomultitasking functionality. DR DOS 6.0 is a substantial improvement on conventional DOS with improved memory management, superior disk performance, built-in security features, and dynamic on-the-fly compression. DR Multi-user DOS is an almost-NOS multiuser operating system for small businesses and departmental workgroups. This WOS supports 16 terminals for file sharing, printing, and general resource allocation.

Network Adapters and Hardware Drivers
Novell licenses Ethernet adapters from various manufacturers, including Eagle, Shiva, and Federal Technology Corporation. In addition, Novell licenses the NE3200 32-bit bus mastering Ethernet adapter for optimizing the NetWare v3.11 and NetWare v4.0 server platforms. Beyond Novell-licensed products are the myriad Novell-certified hardware

products. Novell encourages the development of third-party network products and works closely with these manufacturers to ensure NetWare compatibility. Novell-certified hardware products include adapters, hubs, disk drives, workstations, file servers, tape backup systems, and SFT. This alliance materializes in the form of NetWare-supported hardware drivers.

ᗊ Network Services Products

Network services products support the NetWare LAN. These products provide connectivity, interconnectivity, network management, and general network services.

Connectivity Products

Novell prides itself on providing product integration and connectivity. The network connectivity products support multiple LAN protocols, and the workstation connectivity products support OS/2, Macintosh, and UNIX environments. Novell's interconnectivity products open the NetWare LAN to non-NetWare systems such as SNA, asynchronous communications, and T-1.

Network Connectivity. Novell provides software solutions for connectivity to UNIX, VMS, and OSI FTAM networks. LAN WorkPlace is a multiplatform solution that connects DOS, OS/2, and Macintosh workstations to UNIX servers. LAN WorkPlace for DOS provides DOS and Windows users with direct access to a broad range of TCP/IP hosts, including UNIX, DEC's VAX, IBM mainframes, and reduced instruction-set computing (RISC).

NetWare for VMS is portable software that enables DEC VMS systems to function as NetWare servers. NetWare for VMS provides transparent integration of LAN workstations, VMS terminals, and stand-alone PCs. Features include virtual file storage, hardware independence, security, NetWare-compatible administration, and transparent file storage/print sharing.

NetWare FTAM is two products in one: FTAM server responder and OSI client initiator. The NetWare FTAM server responder enables NetWare DOS workstations to attach to OSI networks and communicate with a wide variety of FTAM hosts. The NetWare FTAM OSI client initiator permits OSI FTAM clients to access NetWare v4.0 and v3.11 file systems. NetWare FTAM supports GOSIP (Government OSI Protocols) systems and X.400 gateways.

Workstation Connectivity. Novell provides software solutions for OS/2, Macintosh, and UNIX connectivity. NetWare Requester for OS/2 provides NetWare printing and file services to OS/2 workstations. The OS/2 Requester is a shell that is installed on the user's local hard disk and supplies the network with connection protocols and IPC mechanisms for OS/2 distributed applications.

NetWare for Macintosh v3.01 is designed for the NetWare v4.0 and v3.11 operating systems. It operates as a server NLM and provides NetWare file, printing, routing, and administrative utilities to the Macintosh workstation. Features include AppleTalk Filing Protocol (AFP) support, AppleTalk internetwork routing, Chooser integration, and 32-bit NetWare processing.

NetWare for Macintosh v2.2 is designed for the NetWare v2.2 operating system. It operates as a server VAP and provides the same transparent Macintosh connectivity as v3.01. NetWare for Macintosh v2.2 uses a Service Protocol Gateway (SPG) to access the NetWare file system.

NetWare NFS transparently integrates UNIX workstations with NetWare v4.0 and v3.11. NetWare NFS uses Sun Microsystem's Network Filing System (NFS) to share files, UNIX printers, NetWare resources, and TCP/IP connectivity features.

Interconnectivity Products

Novell's interconnectivity products are designed to extend NetWare-based LANs into larger wide area networks. Novell currently offers 10 interconnectivity products that connect LANs, hosts, remote workstations, and multiprotocol systems.

LAN-to-IBM Host. Novell has always supported LAN connectivity to IBM host platforms. The myriad LAN-to-IBM products have increased substantially over the past few years—specifically with the introduction of newer IBM mainframes and the AS/400 product line.

NetWare for SAA is a server NLM that provides multiplatform workstations with 506 simultaneous display, printer, and APPC sessions to multiple IBM hosts.

NetWare 3270 LAN workstation products provide terminal and printer emulation services to DOS, Windows, and Macintosh workstations.

Dial-In/Dial-Out Connectivity. Telecommuting is gaining momentum as a NetWare LAN requirement. More users are demanding remote asynchronous connectivity. Novell has responded with three dial-in/dial-out connectivity products: NACS, Access Server, and the NetWare Asynchronous Remote Router. NetWare Asynchronous Communication Services (NACS) is a server NLM that provides dial-out capability to 32 simultaneous users.

NetWare Access Server is Novell's dial-in solution. It operates as a dedicated communications server with up to 16 simultaneous connections. The NetWare Access Server provides remote dial-in connectivity for DOS, Macintosh, and ASCII users.

NetWare Asynchronous Remote Router is Novell's software solution for asynchronous connectivity between remote NetWare LANs. It allows multiple asynchronous connections between remote networks at 19.2 Kb/s. The link is completely transparent to users on both LANs and provides network managers with an inexpensive solution to WAN connectivity problems.

Miscellaneous. In addition to the interconnectivity options just described, Novell provides products that support and administer local and wide area communications. The NetWare Communication Services Manager is a Windows-based network management application that monitors multiple NetWare communications products. Currently it supports simultaneous activity from NetWare for SAA and NACS.

NetWare Link products enable interconnectivity between geographically separated LANs. NetWare Link/64 supports wide area networking over 64 Kb/s data lines, whereas NetWare Link/T1 offers speeds up to 2.084 Mb/s. NetWare Link products operate as dedicated communications servers with routing, multiplexing, and processing capabilities.

Services Software

The core of Novell's network services matrix consists of printing, database, and messaging. The previous connectivity products focused on communications within and between NetWare LANs. These next three categories deal with LAN functionality and user effectiveness.

Print Services. The NetWare Print Server is at the heart of network printing. It offers centralized document handling, spooling, remote printing, and supports up to 16 shared printers per server. NetWare Print Server can be implemented in three different ways: a server NLM, a server VAP, or a dedicated print server. Regardless of the configuration, Print Server simplifies printing management by offering centralized administration of print users, queues, devices, forms, and job configurations.

Database Services. NetWare database services offer advanced client/server functionality to popular database applications. NetWare supports all database standards and provides 32-bit processing for record indexing, queries, and high performance data retrieval.

NetWare Btrieve is Novell's client/server key-indexed record management system. It offers high-performance, secure data management functions to business support applications such as accounting, sales management, development, and project management. NetWare Btrieve operates as a server NLM for NetWare v4.0 and v3.11 and a server VAP for NetWare v2.2.

NetWare SQL is Novell's relational data access system that works in concert with NetWare Btrieve. NetWare SQL (Sequential Query Language) operates as a server NLM and provides a stable database engine to popular front-end applications. Features include direct access to NetWare Btrieve, declarative referential integrity (DRI), high performance, and superior memory management.

Messaging Services. Novell provides excellent support to third-party electronic mail systems. Novell's E-mail solution is called NetWare MHS, or Message Handling Service. NetWare MHS provides distributed E-mail developers with a convenient, reliable, high-performance store-and-forward communications platform. MHS supports all applications that require data cooperation, centralized file storage, and interconnectivity.

NetWare Messaging CONNECT is a related messaging product that provides IBM SNA connectivity to NetWare MHS clients. It operates as a dual-platform solution running on both the NetWare server and the IBM host. Features include remote access, automatic data conversion, and PROFS support.

A world community can exist only with world communication, which means something more than extensive shortwave facilities scattered about the globe. It means common understanding, a common tradition, common ideas, and common ideals.

—Robert M. Hutchins

Network Management Products

The final network services category is network management. These products are vital to the continued operation and success of NetWare LANs, WANs, and MANs. Novell's network management products control the functionality of the following NetWare components: SFT, performance, configuration, security, and accounting.

NetWare System Management. *System management* refers to the control of system resources. NetWare Hub Services integrates the functionality of a centralized topology hub with the features of the NetWare file server. It operates as a hardware/software solution. The hardware consists of a centralized HMI-compatible hub card (hub management interface) in the server; the software consists of NetWare v4.0 or v3.11 and NetWare Hub Services. The combination provides a powerful system for centralized network management. The Hub Management Console (HUBCON) displays hub statistics and controls vital hub parameters.

NetWare Services Manager is a Windows-based solution that provides centralized management of multivendor systems. NetWare Services Manager is a very comprehensive system that monitors network traffic, identifies node problems, maps enterprise-sized WANs, and simplifies asset management. The system operates as a dedicated management server with client hooks to NetWare servers in the form of NetWare Management Agents software. Features include Windows navigation, centralized fault management and security, SNMP (Simple Network Management Protocol) support, and adjustable alarm thresholds and notification. NetWare Services Manager also supports OS/2.

Network Monitoring and Analysis. Network monitoring and analysis is becoming more important as NetWare systems increase in complexity. Novell currently offers two monitoring and analysis tools: LANtern and LANalyzer. LANtern Network Monitor is a hardware solution that collects vital communications information from Ethernet LANs. It plugs into the cabling trunk as would any other node and continuously monitors packet transmissions and critical network statistics. LANtern relays data to a centrally located console where it is interpreted by a secondary product, LANtern Services Manager. LANtern Services Manager is a Windows-based application that turns any LAN workstation into a powerful network management console. LANtern uses SNMP to reach beyond routers and bridges.

LANalyzer Network Analyzer is a precision analysis and diagnostic tool for quick and easy correction of network problems. It operates as a combination of hardware components and software applications. The advanced hardware plugs into any IBM-compatible machine and supports Ethernet or Token Ring topology standards. The software runs on the dedicated LANalyzer machine and includes a product called the Automated Troubleshooting System (ATS). ATS is a comprehensive set of tests that will analyze your network's components and provide clear troubleshooting solutions.

NetWare Administrative Utilities. Novell provides two NetWare administrative utilities beyond the inherent GUI NetWare Administrator and text-based SYSCON. NetWare Remote Management Facility (RMF) is a client/server application that provides remote access to NetWare console functionality. It operates as two workstation utilities and three server NLMs on NetWare v4.0 and v3.11 systems. The first utility, ACONSOLE, provides supervisory access to the server console over asynchronous lines. The complementary utility is called RCONSOLE; it provides the same console access over NetWare SPX LAN lines. Both of these utilities enable network supervisors to use a remote virtual console. Any command that could be entered at the file server console can be accessed remotely through RMF. RMF requires the following three server NLMs: REMOTE.NLM, RS232.NLM, and RSPX.NLM.

NetWare Name Service (NNS) is an enterprise WAN naming service that provides transparent connection across multiple NetWare LANs. NNS enables users to log into multiple LANs with a single login and password. This product has become somewhat obsolete in the wake of NetWare v4.0 and NetWare Directory Services.

Distributed Application Development Tools

Distributed application development tools provide network developers with a set of NetWare-compatible applications for designing, creating, and managing LAN programs. Novell's development tools cover database, communications, and Application Programming Interface (API) applications.

Database Developer Tools

Novell supports third-party database development on the NetWare server platform. Btrieve Developer's Kits enable developers to integrate NetWare's popular Btrieve record management system with their own custom applications. The kit includes a record manager engine, language interfaces, developer utilities, and a programmer's manual with API documentation and code examples.

The NetWare SQL Developer's Kit includes code and utilities for the development of client/server database applications on the NetWare SQL platform.

Xtrieve Plus is a front-end relational browser and report writer. It supports NetWare SQL and Btrieve-formatted data, enabling users to catalog, retrieve, analyze, and update their critical database files. A server-based version of Xtrieve Plus is included with NetWare SQL.

Communications and Protocol Tools

Novell provides three tools for the interface and development of advanced LAN platforms. NetWare RPC (Remote Procedure Call) is a real-time technology that provides process-to-process communications by extending program calls across the network. NetWare RPC is a set of sophisticated tools designed to assist developers in creating truly distributed applications. Applications that use RPC can take advantage of multiprocessing across a variety of RPC hosts throughout the LAN. Programming calls are distributed throughout the network to increase speed, efficiency, and processing power.

NetWare for SAA LU 6.2 Tools is a developer's toolkit that provides reference material and programming examples for the development of LU 6.2 applications on the NetWare SAA platform. Developers use this kit to create server-based LU 6.2 NLMs.

NetWare 3270 Tools is a set of reference manuals, sample programs, source code, and API drivers for the development of enhanced 3270 connectivity products.

Network API Tools

The NetWare APIs afford developers the opportunity to write applications for the NetWare server platform. With NetWare API tools developers can directly access NetWare methods of handling security, directory management, transactional tracking, printing, file management, communications, and accounting.

NetWare C Interface for DOS is a set of C libraries that allow developers to make NetWare system calls directly from C-based applications. This product supports the modularity of NetWare v4.0 and v3.11.

NetWare System Calls for DOS provides system access to NetWare 2.2 LANs.

Support and Education

Novell is dedicated to serving all LANkind. Support for the customer has become an important part of the Novell philosophy. At the onset, managers set goals to support NetWare on all major LAN platforms. Unfortunately, they didn't expect to be supporting 3 million LANs in 10 years! The challenge facing Novell today is how to distribute customer support while maintaining quality control and corporate image. The company has developed a series of satellite organizations that serve to distribute the workload and responsibility of supporting the millions of NetWare users worldwide. Some of the Novell organizations are centralized and some are distributed. Here is how it works.

Customer Support Programs and Services

Novell's customer support programs and services are primarily centralized. This setup includes the organizations and services that ensure customer satisfaction, technology integration, and product distribution. The Customer Satisfaction department was created to resolve immediate customer concerns and propagate goodwill throughout the Novell user base. That department's phone number is (800) 453-1267, extension 7695.

Novell's Technical Support Alliance (TSA) is a technology integration strategy for cooperation within and between hardware and software manufacturers. Product engineers from a variety of participating companies meet often to discuss support for multivendor applications and network platforms. Players include DEC, Intel, Lotus, Microsoft, IBM, Novell, NEC, Borland, UNISYS, SMC, and 3Com.

Novell Technical Support (NTS) is a centralized support organization that answers routine NetWare-based questions over the telephone. It is designed to support gold and platinum resellers, who in turn support users. The service is available directly to users at a staggering $150 per hour, in 15-minute increments. NTS is available 24 hours a day, 7 days a week at (800) NETWARE (638-9273).

NetWare Users International (NUI) is a worldwide network of NetWare user groups that provide open channels to Novell corporate and other NetWare installations. NUI members represent themselves and their companies at monthly user group meetings and discuss troubleshooting, new products, NetWare integration, and LAN strategies. To find out more about your local NetWare users group, call NUI's administrative staff at (800) 228-4NUI (228-4684).

The NetWare maintenance and upgrade program consists of three services: NetWare Software Maintenance, NetWare Express, and NetWare Upgrade. The NetWare Software Maintenance program is an annual, renewable contract that provides NetWare users with immediate fixes, press releases, product enhancements, site licensing, and a private information forum.

The maintenance program is delivered through the new NetWare on-line service called NetWare Express. NetWare Express uses GE Information Services to provide worldwide access to a NetWare-specific on-line information warehouse. NetWare Express includes the NetWare Buyer's Guide, press releases, trade show schedules, and the Network Support Encyclopedia. This service will soon replace NetWire and costs $20 per hour in the U.S. and $40 per hour internationally.

NetWare Upgrade provides an economical upgrade path for NetWare users who require the most current level of NetWare technology. This program offers upgrade discounts, free patches, and vital information about enhancements to the existing product.

Novell's sales and distribution strategy centers around the Reseller Authorization Program. Novell authorized resellers are distributed organizations that have proven to be professional, knowledgeable, and dedicated to the Novell philosophy. Resellers can qualify in one of three categories:

- *Normal* authorized resellers serve small to medium-sized accounts and must pass stringent Novell standards—including an on-site visit, business plan, reseller profile, application, and specific sales goals.
- *Gold* authorized resellers must demonstrate a significant commitment to Novell and meet specific sales quotas.
- *Platinum* authorized resellers serve large Fortune 1,000 corporations.

Other Novell programs and services include NetWire, Novell Research, Novell Press, and the Network Support Encyclopedia. NetWire is a set of Novell-supported information forums on CompuServe. NetWire is open to the public at CompuServe rates $12 to $24 per hour and provides press releases, file patches, question-and-answer forums, user forums, and NetWare product information. Novell is moving support away from NetWire and toward NetWare Express.

Novell Research provides technical information and publications concerning the design, installation, and management of NetWare LANs.

Novell Press is a new organization that supports in-house and independent NetWare publications. The press staff members have been an invaluable resource in the development of this book.

The Network Support Encyclopedia is an electronic information retrieval database that contains Novell Technical Notes, hardware and software test bulletins, product documentation, a library of NetWire files, and valuable troubleshooting decision trees from Novell Technical Support. The product is available in a Standard or Professional volume and is distributed regularly on CD-ROMs.

If a man empties his purse into his head, no man can take it away from him. An investment in knowledge always pays the best interest.

—Benjamin Franklin

Novell Education and Training

Novell is committed to providing professional and comprehensive NetWare training through Novell Authorized Education Centers and Novell Technical Institutes. Novell Authorized Education Centers (NAEC) are education partners that provide certified NetWare education to consultants, independent service organizations, technicians, support professionals, and general users. The NAEC program establishes very stringent education standards and accepts only the highest level resellers, distributors, OEMs, and private training organizations.

Novell Education Academic Partners (NEAPs) are authorized education centers within public colleges or universities. NEAPs affiliates must meet the same stringent education standards as private NAECs but offer certified NetWare courses in the traditional college format. Both of these Novell affiliated education centers provide quality NetWare training by certified NetWare instructors (CNI) and Novell-prepared materials. Lectures, educational facilities, and laboratory exercises are strictly controlled by Novell's centralized department of education.

The goal of Novell education is to provide high-quality NetWare education to potential NetWare support engineers. This way Novell can distribute the support of its 3 million LANs to qualified independent professionals. Qualified professionals who complete the rigorous seven-course engineering program from a Novell Authorized Education Center are certified as CNE, or certified NetWare engineers. Currently there are approximately 18,000 CNEs supporting all of NetWare's U.S. and international installations. That's roughly 167 LANs per CNE—plenty of work.

Novell currently supports three levels of CNE: the standard CNE, the enterprise CNE (ECNE), and the certified NetWare administrator (CNA).

- The standard CNE is the original certification. It consists of 19 credits (roughly 7 courses), 7 proficiency exams, and continuing certification requirements.
- The enterprise CNE is an advanced specialization degree. It consists of CNE certification, an additional 19 credits, 7 more proficiency exams, and continuing certification requirements.
- The new CNA program is designed to provide a limited network management education to current administration professionals. It consists of two courses (v4.0, v3.11, or v2.2), one comprehensive proficiency exam, and Continuing Certification requirements.

The NetWare proficiency exams cover materials taught in CNE, ECNE, and CNA courses. Candidates can attempt to pass the exams without taking the courses, but it's difficult to do so and definitely not recommended. The exams use an advanced form of computerized adaptive testing. They are accurate measurements of proficiency in a given discipline. Following is a progress chart for CNE, ECNE, and CNA certification.

CNE
CNE Core Requirements (10 credits)
DOS / Microcomputer Concepts
NetWare Service and Support
Networking Technologies
CNE Operating System Requirements (5 credits)
NetWare v2.2: System Manager
NetWare v2.2: Advanced System Manager
or
NetWare v3.11: System Manager
NetWare v3.11: Advanced System Manager

CNE Electives (4 credits)
NetWare v2.15 to v2.2 Update
NetWare v3.11: OS Features Review
Product Information Course
NetWare for Macintosh Connectivity
NetWare NFS
LAN WorkPlace for DOS
NetWare TCP/IP Transport
LANalyzer for Ethernet
LANtern Service Manager
NetWare Dial-in, Dial-out Connectivity
Any of the five NetWare v4.0 courses
NetWare v2.15: System Update
NetWare for SAA Installation and Troubleshooting

ECNE
ECNE Core Requirements
CNE Certification
ECNE Operating System Requirements (5 credits)
NetWare v3.11: System Manager
NetWare v3.11: Advanced System Manager
ECNE Electives (14 credits)
Same as CNE

CNA
CNA Core Requirements (5 credits)
NetWare v2.2: System Manager
NetWare v2.2: Advanced System Manager
or
NetWare v3.11: System Manager
NetWare v3.11: Advanced System Manager

The introduction of NetWare v4.0 has changed the face of Novell education. As NetWare topics become more complex, the courses are becoming more specialized. Modular NetWare courses enable prospective engineers to pick and choose skills from a variety of Novell topics. Courses are now available that specialize in design, installation, management, printing, and interconnectivity. Currently Novell offers five modularized NetWare v4.0 courses:

- *NetWare v4.0 Administration* (4 days): The new administration courses replace the previous system manager courses. NetWare v4.0 administration is designed for first-time network administrators with responsibility for day-to-day LAN operations.
- *NetWare v4.0 Advanced Administration* (3 days): The advanced administration course continues the NetWare v4.0 education process in the realm of advanced enterprise WAN fundamentals. This course is designed for experienced administrators with responsibility for the management of complex WANs.

- *NetWare v4.0 Design and Implementation* (3 days): The design and implementation course is designed for advanced NetWare v4.0 administrators. This course provides an effective model for the analysis and design of large enterprise WANs.
- *NetWare v3.11 to v4.0 Update* (3 days): The NetWare v4.0 update course is designed for advanced NetWare v3.11 administrators who plan to integrate NetWare v4.0 into an existing NetWare v3.11 environment. This course and a subsequent test are required for continuing Category I CNIs.
- *NetWare v4.0 Installation Workshop* (2 days): The NetWare v4.0 installation workshop provides NetWare v4.0 installation experience for advanced NetWare v3.11 administrators. This course is designed to follow the NetWare v4.0 update course.
- *Fundamentals of Internetworking Design and Management* (2 days): This introductory course is designed for NetWare v3.11 or NetWare v4.0 administrators who need experience with the fundamentals and concepts of internetworking. The lecture-only course will provide a broad conceptual base for NetWare v4.0 design and management. This course and a subsequent test are required for continuing Category II CNIs.

New and old CNEs can choose to specialize in any of the following NetWare v4.0 fundamentals: administration, design, interconnectivity, or installation. The CNE certificate is the same, but the candidate's skills are diversified. The CNA program offers a separate certification for CNE candidates who complete the NetWare v4.0 track, including the first two courses just listed. Look for future changes that make it easier to specialize in any given NetWare discipline.

The intelligence-testing business reminds me of the way they used to weigh hogs in Texas. They would get a long plank, put it over a cross-bar, and somehow tie the hog on one end of the plank. They'd search all around till they found a stone that would balance the weight of the hog and they'd put that on the other end of the plank. Then they'd guess the weight of the stone.

—John Dewey

This chapter completed our discussion of LAN fundamentals with a peek inside the features and benefits of NetWare and Novell. Now we are ready to begin the big show: building NetWare LANs. Strap yourself in tight, it's going to be a wild ride!

USER LAB SETUP

Following is a brief list of steps required to set up a NetWare LAN environment for the following five labs. You can perform these steps on either a NetWare v2.2 or v3.11 system. Unfortunately, NetWare v4.0 is too different and complex to warrant inclusion in these exercises. Keep in mind that each lab builds on the fundamentals of previous exercises. So in order to set up a particular lab, you must follow the setup steps for all prior labs as well.

User Lab I: Introduction to NetWare

Create a different user for each person who may want to participate in the lab exercises. Make sure they have access to the PUBLIC directory and various menu utilities—SYSCON, SESSION, FILER, PCONSOLE, and PRINTCON. Require a password for each user. In addition, create the following drive mappings in each user's login script:

```
MAP U:=SYS:USERS\%LOGIN_NAME
MAP F:=SYS:LOGIN
```

User Lab II: Network Directory Structure

Create a directory structure identical to the training directory structure as shown in Figure UL2.2. Put some sample files and directories in the GROUP\ADMIN directory.

User Lab III: Network Users and Groups

This lab has no special requirements.

User Lab IV: Network Security

This lab is sensitive to security rights. In creating the security structure, make sure that users don't inherit rights from other users or groups. Try to keep the LAN's users isolated if possible. The following rights apply to user trustee assignments and should be entered for each user in SYSCON. Note: These assignments can be created through a special Novell group.

```
SYS:APPS\GRAPHIC        [  WC   F ]
SYS:APPS\WP             [ RWCE  F ]
SYS:GROUP               [ RWCEMFA]
SYS:USERS               [ R   EMFA]
SYS:USERS\LARRY         [   C     ]
```

Also create a directory named HIDDEN under the GROUP/EVERYONE directory and flag it hidden—**FLAGDIR SYS:GROUP\EVERYONE\HIDDEN H**. Finally, use FILER to modify the inherited rights mask (IRM) for the following directory:

```
SYS:USERS\MOE -- IRM    [SRWCE F ]
```

User Lab V: Printing on a Network

Make sure there is a print queue the users can access. Have the queue assigned to an active printer. Create a file in the SYS:GROUP\EVERYONE directory named LIFE.DOC and ask a question similar to "What is the meaning of life for you?" Also create a default form on the user's server using the PRINTDEF utility:

1. Type **PRINTDEF** at the command line and press Enter. Highlight Forms from the PrintDef Options screen and press Enter.

2. Press Ins at the Forms menu and type in the following parameters to the right of the prompts:

```
Name:           default
Number:         0
Length:         67
Width:          80
```

3. Press Esc and Enter to save the new default print form. Press Esc twice to exit PrintDef and highlight Yes at the confirmation box. To complete the step, choose Save Data Base, then EXIT from the Exit Options screen.

Have fun!

USER LAB I

Introduction to NetWare

The five user labs have been designed for NetWare version 3.11. They assume that you have access to a NetWare LAN and can coax the supervisor into setting up the exercises for you. If you are working with NetWare version 2.2, the labs will appear almost identical. If you are working with NetWare version 4.0, many of the labs will differ. I will note the differences as we go along. If you do not have access to a NetWare LAN, refer to the Preface for a way to complete these labs remotely. Good luck and keep your mind open.

Welcome to NetWare

Working on a NetWare network means your personal computer is connected to other computers and peripherals in order to share files and resources. This increase in communications creates a situation of high connectivity. *Connectivity* is a popular computer buzzword that simply means that your computer is highly connected to other locally available systems, thus opening the lines of communication and allowing a more efficient flow of data and information from node to node.

You and your computer together are referred to as a *node*. Nodes communicate with each other through the central file server, or *hub*. Nodes can

- share network resources such as hard disks, data, applications, and printers
- communicate with each other through electronic mail systems
- use external network services such as mainframe gateways, LAN bridging, and communication servers

In order to fully understand how a NetWare LAN operates, we must first review the principal hardware components of the LAN (workstations and file server) and the software that runs on each (DOS and NetWare).

The Network Components

Figure ULI.1 shows a simple LAN configuration. The *workstations* are the personal computers on which network users, like you, perform work. Workstations are used much like ordinary, nonnetworked personal computers, until they are connected to the LAN. LAN connection opens up an exciting world of informational opportunities. Connection to the file server is achieved through the process of logging in. Each workstation processes its own files and uses its own disk operating system (DOS).

The *file server* is a personal computer that uses the NetWare operating system to control the network. The file server coordinates all of the workstations in the network and regulates the way they share network resources. All of the LAN's shared files are stored on a large hard disk in the file server, instead of on diskettes or hard disks in the individual workstations.

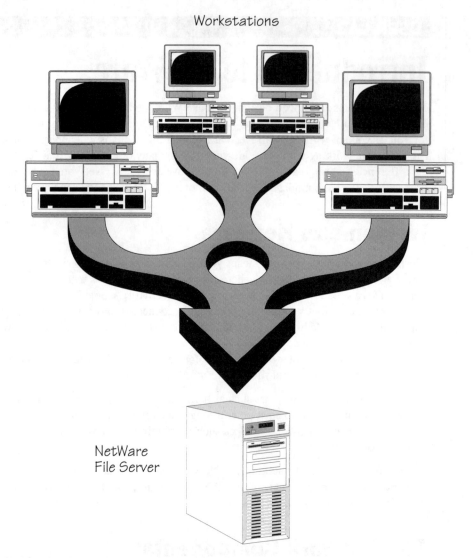

Workstations

NetWare
File Server

FIGURE ULI.1   A Simple LAN Configuration

The Network Shell

Workstations communicate with the file server through a special set of software called *network shells*. The shells must be loaded into each workstation before that particular workstation can function on the network—a LAN liaison of sorts. The NetWare shells work together in two parts: NETx and IPX.

Part 1: NETx

The first part, NETx, directs the workstation's primary requests to DOS or NetWare. If the workstation's primary request is something of a local nature (a workstation command such as DIR), the shell will direct it to the specific workstation's DOS. On the other hand, if the workstation's primary request is network oriented (such as a network command like NDIR), the shell will redirect the request to part 2 and let IPX direct it to the proper network location.

Part 2: IPX

IPX is the second half of the NetWare shell combination. This miniprogram is responsible for directing the workstation's secondary requests from NETx through the internal NIC over to the LAN file server. IPX follows the message as it traverses the LAN and makes sure it doesn't get into any trouble along the way.

The Network Directory Structure

All network information is stored on the file server's internal hard disk. The filing structure resembles an electronic file cabinet, as Figure ULI.2 illustrates. Network directory structures differ from local disks in three important ways: security, drive designation, and mapping.

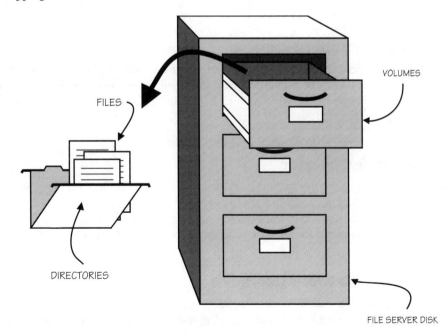

FIGURE ULI.2 Comparison of a Paper and an Electronic Filing System

Security

Network files are more complex than their local counterparts, mostly because they are shared. This complexity lends itself to a more sophisticated system of file attributes and security.

Drive Designation

Local drives use the letter designations A: through E:. A: and B: are floppy drives, whereas C:, D:, and E: are reserved for hard disks. Network drives use the remaining 21 designations, F: through Z:.

Mapping

Because network disks have so much space and so many drive designations to choose from, they require a built-in system for mapping directories and file locations. Mapping is NetWare's system for assigning directories to drive letter designations. This makes it much easier for users to find files and access network applications.

Network Users

Before people can begin working on a network, they must be registered as network users. During registration, they are given one of three classifications: network Supervisor, network operator, or regular network user.

Network Supervisor

Every network includes only one Supervisor, who is responsible for the smooth operation of the entire LAN. The network Supervisor establishes NetWare security, tracks NetWare users, troubleshoots NetWare problems, and updates the NetWare operating system as needed. This classification of network user has the highest level of NetWare security rights.

Network Operator

The network operator is the next level of classification and represents only a few users who are responsible for specific tasks in network operations or maintenance. The network operator helps the Supervisor when needed but carries limited security rights. Operators are normally designated for network printing, file server maintenance, and workgroup management.

Regular Network Users

The regular user classification of network user represents the other 99.99 percent of the people using the network. Regular network users only have security rights to their own or their workgroup's data, and must receive assistance from a network operator or the network Supervisor if anything goes wrong.

Network Security

All network files are stored on the central file server's hard disk. Without proper security, any registered user may access these shared files and modify them. Some files, however, are not meant to be shared; they are personal, confidential, or copyrighted. NetWare provides an extensive multilevel security system that controls access at the user, directory, and file levels. Figure ULI.3 illustrates NetWare security as an inverted pyramid.

NetWare security consists of a combination of passwords and rights (or privileges) that are assigned to specific users. Additional security characteristics are assigned to directories and files. This creates an environment whereby only specific users with correct passwords and privileges can access specific directories and files. NetWare security can also restrict when and how users can work on the network, and can charge them for the time and resources they use when working on the LAN. The network Supervisor is responsible for customizing, installing, and managing NetWare security.

Logging In

In order to use the network, you must connect your node to the file server and log yourself into the active user roster. To log into NetWare, follow these four steps:

1. Boot DOS in the workstation.
2. Load the NetWare shells.
3. Change the default drive to a network drive.
4. Enter a username and password.

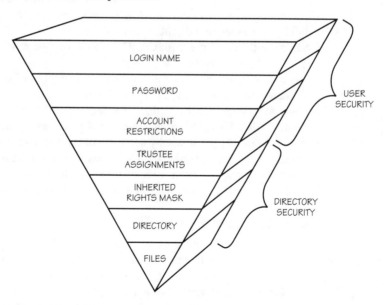

FIGURE ULI.3   The NetWare Security Pyramid

As mentioned earlier, each user is registered with NetWare security and given a unique username and password. The network Supervisor or a workgroup manager is the only person who can register a username and password. This process occurs very early in the life cycle of the network installation. Once your username and password have been established, you can log into the LAN and begin accessing network resources.

The following exercise is designed to give you some experience with the login process. This exercise also gives you an opportunity to explore the NetWare environment and become comfortable with network directories, mapping, and shared applications.

Exercise 1: Logging In

Somewhere on your local workstation disk (hard disk or floppy) is a network directory, which is usually called NET, NOVELL, NETWARE, or LAN. The local network directory contains your two workstation shells, IPX.COM and NETx.COM. In the case of a diskette, these files are usually located in the main root directory of the A: or B: diskette. Complete the following steps to log in:

1. Power on your workstation and boot DOS. Switch to the drive letter that contains the NetWare shells—A: or C:. Change directories to the network directory by entering **CD\NET**.

2. Load the IPX shell by typing **IPX** at the C:\NET> prompt and pressing Enter. Notice the messages on the screen. These are the parameters that IPX is using to initialize the internal workstation network interface card (NIC).

3. Load the NETx shell by typing **NETx** at the C:\NET> prompt and pressing Enter. Notice the messages on the screen. These are the workstation defaults that describe the workstation's specific networking environment. The message `Attached to Server NIRVANA` indicates that your workstation is successfully connected to the central LAN file server.

4. Change the default drive from C:\NET> to the first network drive, F:\LOGIN>. Type **F:** and press Enter.

   Some complex wide area networks include multiple file servers. In order to keep them straight, we name them. The file server name consists of 2 to 45 characters containing no spaces. In these user labs, we work with a fictitious file server named NIRVANA. Substitute the name of your server wherever appropriate.

5. Log into the proper file server by using the file server name and your own unique username. Type **LOGIN NIRVANA/*username*** and press Enter. (Remember our typestyle rules and substitute your own specific login name for ***username*** here.) The file server will ask for your password. Type it in and press Enter.

Exercise 2: Exploring the LAN

Once you have logged into the network, you can explore the many available drives and directories. Some directories will appear to have no files in them; this is not necessarily the case. If you don't have the proper security rights, files and directories will not appear in the list. Compare what you see to what your neighbor sees . . . is it the same? What about the Supervisor's list? Try exploring the F:\> drive with the following:

1. Change directories to the F:\PUBLIC and check out all of the files. What are they used for?
2. Explore the F:\MAIL directory. What's with all of the numbers?
3. Now check your own directory by entering **CD \USERS\\username**. What's there? This is your home directory. You should have all rights here. Type **RIGHTS** and press Enter.
4. What's at Z:? Are these the same files as F:\PUBLIC? This is an example of drive mapping.
5. Where does the U: drive take you? How does it do that?

As you can see, moving around the network isn't so intimidating. Your screen looks just like it does in DOS, except the directory structure is bigger. The directories and drives are all part of one single hard disk located in the central file server. Each command you type is sent to NetWare through the workstation NIC and over the LAN cabling. The file server processes your request and sends the response right back. This all happens very quickly: Most of the time you don't notice the delay. Let's experiment with a popular NetWare utility, SYSCON.

1. Switch to F:\USERS\\username by typing **CD \USERS\\username** and pressing Enter. To enter the SYStem CONfiguration utility, type **SYSCON** and press Enter. SYSCON is used to create NetWare users, groups, and system operators. Network managers configure security, account restrictions, and login scripts with this menu utility.
2. As a user, you can explore your own personal parameters in the User Information screen. Highlight the User Information option at the SYSCON main menu and press Enter. Highlight your username and press Enter. Can you see your password? Why not? Can you change it? Take a look at some other parameters. We will explore SYSCON in more depth later in Lab III. Exit SYSCON by pressing Alt+F10 and then Enter.
3. Now try another popular menu utility: FILER. FILER provides network users and Supervisors with file and directory management capabilities. To access FILER, type **FILER** at the F:\USERS\\username directory and press Enter. Highlight Directory Contents and press Enter. This screen enables you to add, view, copy, delete, and modify NetWare files. Users can also erase entire directory structures from this screen with one keystroke. Return to the main menu by pressing Esc.
4. Highlight Current Directory Information and press Enter. This screen provides valuable file, directory, and security information. When was the directory created? Who created it? What are your rights? Exit FILER by pressing Alt+F10 and highlighting YES at the exit confirmation screen.

LAB QUIZ I

Introduction to NetWare

1.   Where does NetWare reside? Where do the two shells reside?

2.   What does the NETx shell do? What does the IPX shell do?

3.   What is mapping?

4.   At what three levels does NetWare control security?

5.   List the four steps involved in logging in.

6.   What happens if you log in without specifying the file server's name (such as by entering LOGIN *username*)? Does the login still work? Why or why not?

7.   What do all of the numbers under the F:\MAIL subdirectory mean?

USER LAB II

Network Directory Structure

As described in Lab I, NetWare's directory structure is very similar to that in DOS. The hard disk is divided into volumes, which are divided into directories, which are further divided into subdirectories, which contain files. Remember there were three important differences between DOS and NetWare directory structures:

- *Security:* Network files are more complex than their local counterparts, mostly because they are shared. This complexity lends itself to a more sophisticated system of file attributes and protection. This feature enables network users to protect their secret data without burdening themselves with multiple passwords.
- *Drive Designation:* Local drives use the letter designations A: through E:, network drives use F: through Z:. You have already seen how different drive letter designations can help you move through complex network directory paths.
- *Mapping:* Because network disks have so many drive designations to choose from, NetWare enables the user to assign a specific directory path to a drive letter. Let's explore this feature in more detail.

Directory Paths

The *directory path* is the route through NetWare's directory structure that leads to a specific directory, subdirectory, or file. In concept, the directory path for a network is the same as for a local disk, but in practice the network directory name is more complex. Figure ULII.1 describes a common directory name and the conventions that are used to describe its specific path. Because these directory names can get quite long, NetWare has devised a method of representing them with single drive letters. This shortcut is known as *drive mapping.*

Drive Mapping

Drive mappings point to certain network locations and provide straightforward access to data or information found at that location. They simply assign drive letter designations to complex network or local paths. There are three types of drive mappings: network, search, and local.

Network Drive Mappings

Drive mappings provide users with a convenient way of moving through the network directory structure. To switch directories, users simply type a drive letter instead of the entire directory path. Drive mappings are temporary, though, and are removed when users log out. You can save drive mappings permanently by placing them in a login script. You will see more about that later.

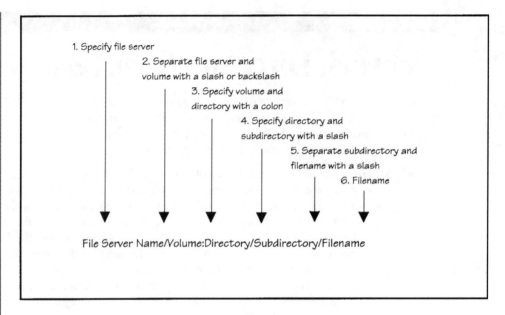

1. Specify file server

2. Separate file server and
volume with a slash or backslash

3. Specify volume and
directory with a colon

4. Specify directory and
subdirectory with a slash

5. Separate subdirectory and
filename with a slash

6. Filename

File Server Name/Volume:Directory/Subdirectory/Filename

FIGURE UL11.1   Syntax for a Typical Directory Path

Each network user has his or her own drive mappings. For example, one user may have the letter H mapped to NIRVANA/SYS:HOME/MARY, and another might have the same letter H mapped to NIRVANA/SYS:HOME/DAVID. On the other hand, some drive mappings may be shared. The Z: drive, for example, is assigned to NIRVANA/SYS:PUB-LIC for everyone. It is a good rule of thumb to always specify the drive letter and path when sharing files.

Search Drive Mappings

Search drive mappings affect the users' ability to access network applications. When a user wants to open an application or data file, the file server looks through the current directory for the file first. If the application or data file isn't there, the file server responds with the message `Bad Command or Filename`. Search drive mappings extend the users' ability to find applications and files. The search mappings build a list of directories to search in case the file isn't located in the current directory. This particular type of drive mapping is similar to the commonly used DOS PATH command.

Search drives are useful because they seemingly break down the walls between directories and provide users with a way of accessing application programs from anywhere on the file server disk. NetWare serves users best when search drive mappings have been optimized. This feature saves users from having to place duplicate copies of common files throughout the shared disk.

Local Drive Mappings

Local drive mappings point to disk drives installed in or attached to the local workstation. These disk drives may be floppy disk drives (high or low density), hard disk drives (C:), or logical drives (usually D: or E:). DOS always reserves a certain number of drive letters for local drives (A: through E:), but you can reserve more by using the DOS LASTDRIVE command in the CONFIG.SYS file.

The Training Directory Structure

Your Supervisor will need to create a special directory structure on the file server's hard disk that will be used for the remaining laboratories. Figure ULII.2 illustrates the training directory structure in detail. Have the Supervisor refer to the user lab setup information at the beginning of these labs.

Exercise 1: Working with Drive Mappings

This exercise is designed to help solidify the drive-mapping concepts by walking through some of its practical applications. First, you must log in:

1. Boot the workstation with the DOS diskette and load the NetWare shell by typing **IPX** and pressing Enter. Then type **NETx** and press Enter.
2. Make F: the default drive. Type **LOGIN NIRVANA/*username*** and press Enter. Input your secret password and press Enter.
3. Now that you are logged in, start by viewing a list of the current drive mappings. For all of the drive-mapping functions we will use the SESSION menu utility. Type **SESSION** and press Enter.
4. To see your current drive mappings, highlight DRIVE MAPPINGS in the Available Topics menu and press Enter.
5. On your current screen, you can see that some drive letters are reserved for local drives, and other drives are mapped to directories already set up on the network. Now we are going to map an additional drive to the directory NIRVANA/SYS:APPS/WP. At the Current Drive Mappings list, press Ins to display the next letter available for drive mapping; it should be G. At the drive letter box, press Enter. The Select Directory box will be displayed.

FIGURE ULII.2   Detailed Structure of the Training Directory

6. To see the list of file servers to choose from, press Ins. The File Servers/Local Drives list will be displayed. Highlight NIRVANA and press Enter. The Volumes list will be displayed, and NIRVANA will appear in the Select Directory box.

7. Highlight the volume SYS and press Enter. Volume SYS will be added to the Select Directory box, and the Network Directories list will be displayed.

8. Highlight the directory APPS and press Enter. The directory APPS will be added to the Select Directory box, and the three subdirectories for that directory will appear in the Network Directories list.

9. Highlight the subdirectory WP and press Enter. The subdirectory WP will be added to the Select Directory box. At this point the mapping path has been completed. Press Esc to confirm it and Enter to add G: to the Current Drive Mappings list. The system will ask whether you want to map root this drive. Highlight No and press Enter.

Drive mappings can also be created at the NetWare command line. The following steps walk you through the MAP command-line utility:

1. Exit SESSION by pressing Alt+F10 and Enter at the Exit SESSION confirmation box. At the NetWare prompt, type **MAP H:=NIRVANA/SYS:APPS/WP** and press Enter.

2. To use your new drive mapping, type **H:** at the prompt and press Enter. Notice which subdirectory the prompt jumps to!

Now that you are such a pro with drive mappings and the SESSION menu utility, try a few additional exercises on your own:

1. Get back into SESSION by typing **SESSION** and pressing Enter.

2. Change your current default drive to SYS:USERS/MOE.

3. Generate a list of the search drive mappings.

4. Add a search drive mapping to the directory NIRVANA/SYS:APPS/DBASE.

5. What is the significance of a search drive mapping versus a network drive mapping?

6. If you are feeling really clever, send a nice message to your neighbor.

Exercise 2: Working with Directories

NetWare's directory structure is very similar to DOS's local directory structure—so similar, in fact, that many of the fundamental concepts will carry over into this exercise. The major difference is that in Exercise 2 you use the FILER menu utility to work with directories instead of DOS commands at the local prompt.

1. First move to the SYS:GROUP/ADMIN directory by typing **G:** at the prompt and pressing Enter. Then type **CD\GROUP\ADMIN** and press Enter. To access the FILER menu utility, type **FILER**, then press Enter. Highlight Directory Contents in the Available Topics menu and press Enter. A list of subdirectories and files in the SYS:GROUP/ADMIN subdirectory should appear. It may be blank.

2. Now we would like to add an additional subdirectory, called MYOWN, beyond the ADMIN directory. Press Ins. Type **MYOWN** in the New Subdirectory Name box and press Enter. Notice that the new subdirectory is displayed in the Directory Contents list.

3. Nah, we decided we didn't like the name MYOWN and want to change it to MINE. The FILER menu utility enables you to rename subdirectories—something that DOS does not allow. Highlight MYOWN in the Directory Contents list and press the modify key (F3). The Edit Directory Name box appears.

4. To rename MYOWN to MINE, press the Backspace key until MYOWN is deleted from the box. Then type **MINE** and press Enter.

5. Well, now that we think about it, we don't need this subdirectory after all—let's just delete it. (Don't you feel fickle?) To delete the subdirectory MINE, highlight MINE and press Del. The Delete Subdirectory Options box appears.

6. Highlight Delete Entire Subdirectory Structure and press Enter. Confirm your choice by highlighting YES and pressing Enter. Notice that the MINE subdirectory no longer appears in the Subdirectories list.

If you are feeling up to the task, try some of the additional functions that can be found in the FILER menu utility:

1. Move from the SYS:GROUP/ADMIN subdirectory to the SYS:USERS/LARRY subdirectory without leaving FILER.

2. Move back.

3. Find out when the SYS:APPS/DBASE subdirectory was created.

4. See who owns the SYS:APPS/WP subdirectory.

5. View a list of the TRUSTEES of the SYS:APPS/WP subdirectory.

6. View the file attributes of the files in the SYS:USERS/CURLY subdirectory.

7. View the volume information for the volume SYS:.

LAB QUIZ II

Network Directory Structure

1. In what three ways does NetWare's directory structure differ from that in DOS?

2. Give an example of a full network directory name.

3. List the three types of network drive mappings and briefly explain each.

4. How many network drives do you have already mapped when you log in? What are they?

5. How many search drives do you have already mapped when you log in? What are they?

6. What happens when you type Z:?

7. When was the SYS:GROUP/ADMIN subdirectory created?

8. Who owns the SYS:GROUP/ADMIN subdirectory?

9. How many total bytes are there on the SYS volume?

USER LAB III

Network Users and Groups

Network Users

Before users can begin working on a network, they must be registered as network users. The network user is registered under a unique username—typically the person's first name or last name and first initial. The username is used for login procedures, security, and accounting identity. The network recognizes the user by his or her username and distributes security rights based on the user's classification: Supervisor, operator, or regular user. Figure ULIII.1 represents the level of user control by the type of key card.

Network Supervisor

There is only one *network Supervisor*. The Supervisor is responsible for the smooth operation of the LAN. He or she maintains the system, establishes directory security, assigns users and operators, creates network groups, and installs additional NetWare facilities. The network Supervisor has *all* rights and privileges to all aspects of the network—these rights are not removable. In addition, NetWare supports *assistant-Supervisors*. These specialized users are called *workgroup managers* or *user account managers*. Workgroup managers can create, delete, and manage users within their workgroup. User account managers are created by workgroup managers, and they can only manage users—not create or delete them.

Network Operator

This is the next level of classification and represents only a few specific users who are responsible for specific tasks in network operations or maintenance. The network operator

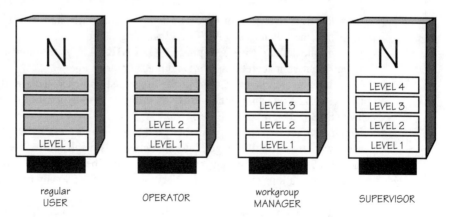

FIGURE ULIII.1   User Types and Their Levels of Control

helps the Supervisor when needed but carries limited security rights. Network operators are given additional privileges by the network Supervisor to run specific maintenance utilities such as FCONSOLE and PCONSOLE.

Regular Network User

This classification of network user represents the other 99.91 percent of the people using the network. Most network users are registered as regular users. This user classification limits security rights to only personal files. The security differences among these three classifications are completely transparent and do not interfere at all with the normal running of the NetWare LAN. The key is this: You wouldn't know you have limited security privileges if I hadn't told you.

Network Groups

Network users are organized into groups for convenience. NetWare creates groups according to security, tasks, and drive-mapping requirements. The network Supervisor creates groups during the user registration process. These groups can perform many centralized operations, including login scripts, messages, trustee assignments, and drive mappings. Network management is simplified by applying it to groups instead of individual users. The group EVERYONE is automatically created during NetWare's installation, and it contains all users. In Exercise 2, you will explore some of NetWare's group options.

Exercise 1: Understanding Network Users

Like each NetWare user, you are registered as a regular network user with a unique username. In addition, you have been assigned to a variety of network groups. This exercise is designed to demonstrate techniques used to gather information about network users. The next exercise explores network groups.

First, you must log in:

1. Boot the workstation from DOS and load the NetWare shell by typing in **IPX**, pressing Enter, then typing **NETx** and pressing Enter.
2. Make F: the default drive by typing **LOGIN NIRVANA/*username*** and pressing Enter. Input your secret password and press Enter again.
3. Now that you are logged in, start by viewing a list of the users currently active on the network. You can use the SESSION utility to display a list of network users. Type **SESSION** and press Enter.
4. Highlight User List in the Available Topics menu and press Enter. A list of the users who are currently logged into the network is displayed with a reference to the STATION # they are currently logged into. The STATION # refers to the actual workstations they are using. NetWare is designed so any network user can log in from any workstation.
5. Exit SESSION by pressing Alt+F10, highlighting YES to confirm, and pressing Enter.
6. You can also view a list of the current network users from the command line. At the NetWare prompt, type **USERLIST** and press Enter.

7. To view information about your own user account, type **WHOAMI /A** and press Enter. The /A parameter displays all available information.

Centralized user management is controlled from the SYSCON utility. We explored it earlier in Lab I. Now we will examine additional SYSCON options.

1. To access SYSCON, type **SYSCON** at the NetWare prompt and press Enter. Highlight Names User Information screen and press Enter. The User Names screen will appear. This screen differs from the SESSION list in that it displays all network users, not just those currently logged in.
2. Highlight the name of any user other than yourself and press Enter. Notice that only two options appear: Full Name and Groups Belonged To. These windows are informational only; you cannot change any of this information.

⇨ **INFORMATIONAL WINDOWS:** *Windows that have one solid border line; input windows, on the other hand, have a double-lined border.*

3. Now try viewing your own user information. Return to the User Names screen by pressing Esc. Then highlight your own username. Press Enter. Notice a much larger list of choices. Highlight Account Restrictions and press Enter. Notice that this window is also informational. The only people who can alter user information are Supervisors, workgroup managers, and user account managers.

Now that you are such a pro with SYSCON, try some more exciting user functions:

1. Change your password.
2. Identify your user ID number.
3. Find your minimum password length.
4. Describe your login script.

Exercise 2: Understanding Network Groups

Now that you have worked with network users, take a look at network groups.

1. We will use the SYSCON menu utility to perform the rest of the network functions in this lab. To access SYSCON, type **SYSCON** and press Enter.
2. Highlight Group Information and press Enter. A list of the network groups is displayed: group names. The group EVERYONE is automatically created on each network. Highlight EVERYONE and press Enter. The Group Information screen will appear.
3. The Group Information screen provides information about group lists, security, and workgroup managers. To view a list of the members of EVERYONE, highlight Member List and press Enter.
4. Experiment with the other Group options. Which network groups do you belong to? Try to find another way to view a list of your groups. Hint: Check Understanding Network Users.

LAB QUIZ III

Network Users and Groups

1. Name the three classifications of NetWare users.

2. Give two examples of the kind of maintenance utilities a network operator would use.

3. What station number are you logged into?

4. What network groups have been created on NIRVANA?

5. To which network groups do you belong?

6. What is your user ID number?

7. Examine your login script. What is its purpose?

USER LAB IV

Network Security

Security is crucial to any network environment. NetWare provides a multifaceted security system that relies on rights and attributes. Security *rights* are privileges that control user access to directories and files. NetWare v2.2 supports seven types of rights, and NetWare v3.11 and v4.0 support eight. Security *attributes* are more complex privileges that affect the availability of network directories and files. A user's *effective* rights are a combination of user and directory security. Sound confusing? It is.

Let's start from the beginning. NetWare security is managed in seven different layers. The levels are given in the following list. Those on the left affect users; the three on the right affect directories and files.

User Security	Directory/File Security
Login name	Directory rights (IRM)
Password security	Directory attributes
Account restrictions	File attributes
Trustee assignments	

Each layer of security builds on the level listed above it and creates a much more secure and complex system. Let's start with user security.

User Security

Login name is the first level of NetWare security. It controls initial access to the LAN. Only registered users can access a NetWare system. Once the login name has been entered, NetWare may ask for a password.

Password security is not required, but it is highly recommended. If a user enters the login name or password incorrectly three times in a row, the file server will lock the account and no longer allow that user to log in. This security feature is designed to stop intruders from continually attempting to access the network under a "borrowed" login name.

Additional restrictions can also be set up by the Supervisor to increase the strength of login or password security. These additional *account restrictions* represent the third layer of user security. Account restrictions include

- *Time restrictions:* The network Supervisor can limit a user's login to a specific time of day.
- *Station restrictions:* The network Supervisor can assign specific workstation addresses so a user will only be able to log in from assigned workstations.
- *Account disabling:* The network Supervisor can disable the login abilities of any user at any time.

Trustee security is used to control individual users' ability to work with files in a given directory. A *trustee* is a user who has been given rights to a particular directory. A trustee assignment is a set of specific rights within the directory. *Trustee assignments* represent the final level of user security.

Trustee rights must be granted to each user for each directory he or she needs to access. Once a user is given trustee rights in a directory, those rights extend down through all subdirectories, until they are redefined at some lower level, as Figure ULIV.1 shows.

The trustee rights consist of eight privileges:

S: Supervisory—all rights
R: Read from open files
W: Write to open files
C: Create new files and subdirectories
E: Erase existing files
A: Access control—the ability to alter a file or directory's rights
F: File scan directories and files
M: Modify the file or directory attributes

Trustee rights are normally granted directly to the particular user by the network Supervisor, but in some instances the network Supervisor prefers to grant the trustee assignments indirectly. This is done through security equivalence. A *security equivalence* enables one user or group to exercise rights equivalent to those of some other user. This is a quick way of indirectly updating the trustee assignments of a user or a group. Trustee assignments are established during the Network Management phase through SYSCON or the NetWare Administrator utility.

Directory/File Security

Directory/file security represents the bottom three layers of the NetWare security model. *Directory rights* are used to control the rights of all trustees in a given directory. The inher-

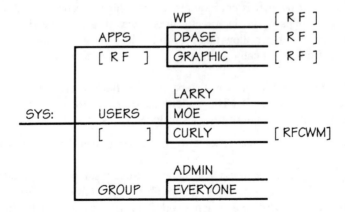

FIGURE ULIV.1   Filtering Trustee Assignments

ited rights mask (IRM) establishes the maximum number of rights available to any user in that specific directory. This level of security overrides trustee security in that only the rights that are in a directory's rights mask can be exercised by subsequent trustees.

The bottom line is this:

To exercise a right in a given directory, a user must have both directory and trustee rights in that directory.

This combination is called *effective rights*. Figure ULIV.2 illustrates the concept of effective rights. The final layers of NetWare security involve attributes. *Attributes* are aimed at protecting individual directories or files from being accidentally changed or deleted. Attributes are simple and straightforward, and only apply to specific directories and files. Attributes are not inherited like rights. Directory attributes include Normal, System, Hidden, Delete Inhibit, and Rename Inhibit. File attributes include Non-Sharable, Sharable, Read-Only, Read-Write, Normal, Execute Only, and Indexed.

The Training Directory Structure

Once again we will use our familiar training directory structure to illustrate the fundamentals of NetWare security. If you forgot what the Training Directory Structure looks like, Figure ULIV.3 should refresh your memory.

Exercise 1: How Security Works—Rights

Exercises 1 and 2 are designed to help you practice some of the network security concepts you learned earlier in this lab. In the first exercise, you explore two directories and learn what it is like to work with all levels of rights as opposed to limited rights. In Exercise 2, you compare the Trustee and Directory rights of the MOE directory, and combine the two to calculate the total effective rights.

Let's begin by logging in:

1. Boot the workstation with DOS, then load the NetWare shell by typing **IPX**, pressing Enter, typing **NETx**, and pressing Enter.
2. Make F: the default drive, type **LOGIN NIRVANA/*username***, and press Enter. Input your secret password and press Enter again.

Inherited	R	W		E	M	F	A
IRM	R		C		M	F	
Effective Rights	K				M	F	

FIGURE ULIV.2   Effective Rights

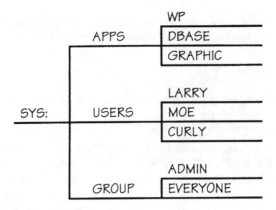

FIGURE ULIV.3   The Training Directory Structure

3. Now that you are logged in, we can start by moving to the SYS:APPS/WP directory. Changing directories in NetWare is very similar to changing directories in DOS. Type **CD \APPS\WP** and press Enter.

4. Now we will test our rights in this directory by trying to create a file. Type **COPY CON** *username* and press Enter. Now type **This is MY file, and nobody can have it** *username*. and press Ctrl+Z, then press Enter. Did it work? You must have Create rights in this directory.

5. We will now test our file scan rights by trying a DIR command. Type **DIR** and press Enter. Did you see a list of different files? You must have File Scan rights to this directory.

6. Try reading the file. Type **TYPE** *username* and press Enter. You should see This is MY file, and nobody can have it. displayed. This means that you also have Read rights in this directory.

Life sure can be easy in a directory with full rights. Now let's explore a directory in which we have limited rights.

1. Type **CD \APPS\GRAPHIC** and press Enter. Try your copying rights. Type **COPY \APPS\WP***username* and press Enter. Did it copy your file? You must have Write, Create, and File Scan rights.

2. Let's try looking for the file. Type **DIR** and press Enter. It's there. Let's try to read the file. Type **TYPE** *username* and press Enter. What? It says the file cannot be found? You must not have Read rights.

3. Now let's test your Erase rights. Type **ERASE** *username* and press Enter. Nope. Well, you must not have Erase rights, either.

Life can be tough in a directory with limited rights! Now for some additional fun:

1. Try to figure out the exact rights you have in the SYS:USERS\LARRY directory. (Hint: Create a file with COPYCON and try to read it. Type **DIR**.)

2. There is a hidden directory named HIDDEN somewhere hidden in the training directory structure . . . try to find it. (Hint: The only way to find a hidden directory is to go there. Use the **CD** command.)

Exercise 2: Effective Rights

In this exercise, you move to the MOE directory and compare its two primary security tools: trustee assignments and the inherited rights mask. You will use this information to calculate the effective rights of that directory. Begin by moving to the proper directory:

1. Type **CD \USERS\MOE** and press Enter. Now, we will use the FILER menu utility to determine this directory's IRM. Type **FILER** and press Enter.
2. Highlight Current Directory Information in the Available Topics menu and press Enter. Take note of the rights assigned to the IRM; write them down. Exit FILER by pressing Esc twice, then pressing Enter.
3. To view trustee assignments, we will use the SYSCON menu utility. Why? When you're done pondering this factoid, type **SYSCON** and press Enter.
4. Highlight User Information in the Available Topics menu and press Enter. The User Names list will appear. Highlight your username and press Enter.
5. To view your own specific trustee assignments, highlight Trustee Directory Assignments in the User Information screen and press Enter. The trustee rights you have for each directory will be listed. Find the rights for the SYS:USERS directory and write them down. Remember that rights flow down, so the right in SYS:USERS dictates the right in SYS:USERS\MOE.

Now that you have a list of your trustee assignments and IRM for SYS:USERS\MOE, you can calculate the effective rights . . . remember how?

All done? Good! Now let's show how to reach the correct answer:

1. To view the effective rights of the MOE directory, should we use SYSCON or FILER? We should use FILER. To exit SYSCON, press Alt+F10 four times and highlight YES at the confirmation box. Then press Enter.
2. To access FILER, type **FILER** and press Enter. Highlight Current Directory Information in the Available Topics menu and press Enter. The Current Directory Information box will appear.
3. The effective rights list appears on this screen. The list should look familiar. You did well.

Now for something completely different. . . .

1. Where would you find information about your own personal security equivalence? Do you have any security equivalences? If so, what are they?
2. Do you have any account restrictions? If so, what are they?

LAB QUIZ IV

Network Security

1. Briefly describe the four levels of NetWare user security.

2. What are the eight different privileges that make up trustee rights?

3. Which two types of rights combine to create effective rights?

4. What are the four file attributes? What are the four directory attributes?

5. Where is the HIDDEN subdirectory?

6. Why would you use FILER to view a directory's inherited rights mask and SYSCON to view trustee assignments?

7. What are your effective rights to the SYS:APPS\GRAPHIC subdirectory?

8. Do you have any station restrictions? If so, what are they?

9. Do you have any time restrictions? If so, what are they?

10. Does your account have an expiration date? If so, what is it?

Printing on a Network

Networks are designed to allow a number of people to share resources. One of the primary shared resources is the network printer. Network printers are typically attached to the file server rather than to individual workstations. When you print to a network printer, you do not send the print requests directly to the printer. Instead, you send your request to the file server, where the request waits in a print queue, along with other users' print job requests, until the printer is ready. Print job requests follow the path from workstation to queue to network printer, as shown in Figure ULV.1.

This level of printing complexity requires a great deal of organization, preparation, and maintenance. There are three areas in the network environment where you can access, configure, and maintain network printers: application printing, printing menu utilities, and printing command-line utilities.

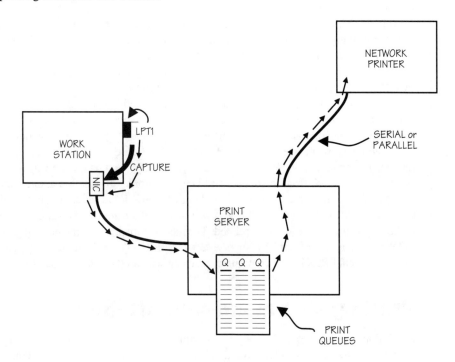

FIGURE ULV.1 Print Job Path from Workstation to Queue to Printer

Application Printing

Although the network handles printing requests much differently than a stand-alone personal computer does, you might not notice the difference when you're printing from a network application. WordPerfect, for example, is designed to operate on a network in exactly the same manner as it does on a stand-alone system. Although network printing requires additional commands, WordPerfect hides these commands from the network user. This type of simplicity is called *transparent network printing*. That is, the complexities of print queuing and network printing are "hidden" from the network user. Microsoft Windows and complementary products also support transparent network printing.

Printing Menu Utilities

If you cannot print on the network from within your application or if you want to take advantage of the printing flexibility NetWare offers, you must use the NetWare printing utilities. PCONSOLE, PRINTCON, and PRINTDEF are the NetWare menu utilities used for printing. CAPTURE, ENDCAP, and NPRINT are the NetWare command-line utilities used for printing. This section concentrates on the printing menu utilities. The next section delves more into the printing command-line utilities.

The PCONSOLE menu utility controls printing setup, management, and security. PCONSOLE enables network users to access a print queue and manage or insert jobs. Users designated as print queue operators can edit any other user's print queue entry information, delete any entry from the queue, and modify the queue status by changing the operator flags. Queue operators can also prioritize the order of print jobs in the queue.

Regular network users can use PCONSOLE to access and print files on local and remote file servers, view jobs that are waiting in the queue, change the way a job is printed, delete a print job from the queue, and view additional information about print queues.

All of the configuration options found in PCONSOLE are set up by individual network users in the PRINTCON menu utility. A *print job configuration* is a customized description of the way you want the job to be printed. The modes, forms, and parameters used in PRINTCON are set up by the network supervisor in the PRINTDEF menu utility. Figure ULV.2 shows a typical PRINTCON configuration screen with all the available parameters.

Printing Command-Line Utilities

If you don't feel comfortable using the printing menu utilities, you can still print to a network printer by using NetWare command-line utilities. Granted, these three command-line utilities do not give you the same flexibility and complexity of the menu utilities, but they are much easier to use.

The NPRINT utility transfers network files directly to the shared printer. With this utility, you can print files that exist in exactly the form you want them, including any necessary formatting. The files must either be in ASCII format or already be formatted by your specific application with the proper printer control characters. NPRINT is a primitive utility and should be reserved for printing simple files that have little or no formatting.

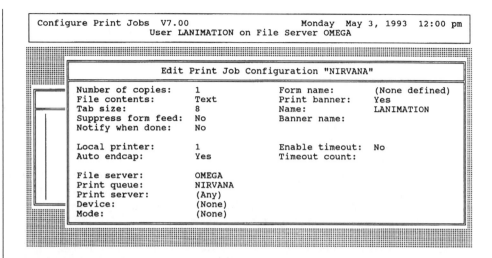

```
Configure Print Jobs  V7.00                Monday  May 3, 1993  12:00 pm
                     User LANIMATION on File Server OMEGA

              Edit Print Job Configuration "NIRVANA"

    Number of copies:    1          Form name:       (None defined)
    File contents:       Text       Print banner:    Yes
    Tab size:            8          Name:            LANIMATION
    Suppress form feed:  No          Banner name:
    Notify when done:    No

    Local printer:       1          Enable timeout:  No
    Auto endcap:         Yes        Timeout count:

    File server:         OMEGA
    Print queue:         NIRVANA
    Print server:        (Any)
    Device:              (None)
    Mode:                (None)
```

FIGURE ULV.2   Print Job Configuration Screen for the NIRVANA Print Queue

The CAPTURE and ENDCAP command-line utilities redirect local printing to a network device. They simply fool local applications into printing to NetWare queues. These utilities are useful when you cannot send a file directly to a printer using NPRINT, PCONSOLE, or a network application. Many applications, however, are not designed to run on a network. These applications are designed to send data to a local printer through one of the parallel LPT printer ports on the back of workstations. CAPTURE allows these applications to send data from your workstation to a network printer.

When you issue a CAPTURE command, you place a software sign in front of the LPT port that reads, "All data to be redirected to the network." Then, when you send a file to that LPT port, it is immediately redirected to a network printer. ENDCAP stops the capturing of the LPT port and returns printing to a local mode. This use of CAPTURE and ENDCAP is especially valuable for new networks.

Exercise 1: Printing with Menu Utilities

This exercise is designed to illustrate the fundamentals of NetWare's printing menu utilities—specifically, PCONSOLE and PRINTCON. These two utilities should make your network printing much easier and more flexible. Begin by logging in:

1. Boot the workstation with DOS, and load the NetWare shell by typing **IPX** and pressing Enter, then typing **NETx** and pressing Enter.
2. Make F: the default drive, type **LOGIN NIRVANA/***username*, and press Enter. Input your secret password and press Enter.
3. Once you are logged in, move over to the SYS:GROUP\EVERYONE subdirectory, type **PCONSOLE**, and press Enter.
4. Highlight Print Queue Information in the Available Options menu and press Enter. Highlight any available print queue from the Print Queues list and press Enter. To see the contents of the queue, highlight Current Print Job Entries in the

Print Queue Information menu and press Enter. You should see a list of the jobs waiting to be printed. If this list is blank, there are currently no jobs printing.

5. To add a print job entry, press Ins. The Select Directory to Print From box will appear. Make sure that NIRVANA/SYS:GROUP/EVERYONE is the selected directory. Highlight LIFE.DOC in the Available Files list and press Enter.

6. Now that you have specified the file you want to print, you must choose the printing configurations you would like to use. For this example we will use the PCONSOLE defaults. Later, we will use PRINTCON to change them and print this file again. Highlight Console Defaults and press Enter.

7. You will get the New Print Job to Be Submitted screen. Take a good look at your specific configurations, because later we will change some of these parameters. To send your print job to the queue, press Esc and then Enter. Your file, LIFE.DOC, has now been added to the queue with everybody else's work. How do you know which print job is yours?

You have just printed a file using the PCONSOLE default configurations. Let's create our own set of configurations, using PRINTCON, and print the file again.

1. To exit PCONSOLE, press Alt+F10 until the Exit Console confirmation box appears. Highlight YES and press Enter. To access PRINTCON, type **PRINTCON** and press Enter.

2. Highlight Edit Print Job Configurations in the Available Options menu and press Enter. To add a print job configuration, press Ins. At the Enter New Name box, type your username and press Enter.

3. You may now define your print job configuration in the Edit Print Job Configuration box. An example of this box can be seen in Figure ULV.2. Use the arrow keys to move to the Print Banner selection and make sure it is Yes. Now move down to the Banner Name selection and type in a string of characters only you would recognize (up to 12 characters); then press Enter. This is now the banner name that you will use to identify your print job as distinct from everybody else's.

4. Now move to the Notify when done choice and type **Y**, then press Enter. This option will activate a user console message when your print job has been completed. Finally, move to the Number of Copies choice and type **3**; press Enter.

5. Once you have set up your print job configurations, press Esc. Highlight YES and press Enter to confirm that you want to save the changes. To exit PRINTCON, press Alt+F10 until the Exit Printcon confirmation box appears. Highlight YES and press Enter. Press Enter again to confirm that your Print Job Configurations have been saved.

Now that you have created a custom print job configuration with your username, you can print LIFE.DOC again, with the new configurations.

Repeat steps 3 through 5 of the first list in this exercise—the one with PCONSOLE instructions. Now instead of specifying PCONSOLE defaults as your configuration, highlight your username configuration set and press Enter. Now you should receive a printer notification and be able to identify your three printouts by the banner name you designated in PRINTCON.

Exercise 2: Printing with Command-Line Utilities

Now that you are experienced at printing with the NetWare menu utilities, let's compare them to the ease and simplicity of command-line printing utilities.

1. Exit PCONSOLE if you have not already done so. All of the work with command-line utilities is performed at the NetWare prompt. Move to the EVERYONE directory by typing **CD \GROUP\EVERYONE** and pressing Enter.

2. To print the LIFE.DOC file, simply type **NPRINT LIFE.DOC** and press Enter. A message similar to the following should be displayed:

```
Queuing data to Server NIRVANA, Queue queuename
```

3. The file LIFE.DOC should print now. Does it print with your new banner? Why or why not?

   Even though this utility doesn't have the complexity of PCONSOLE, understand that it doesn't have its sophistication, either. In order to make any configuration changes, you really have to use a MENU utility. Now let's try our hand at CAPTURE and ENDCAP.

4. To experiment with the features of CAPTURE and ENDCAP, we will print a screen display of our drive mappings. Type **CAPTURE** and press Enter. A message similar to the following should appear:

```
Device LPT1: re-routed to queue queuename on server
NIRVANA
```

5. This message tells us that the LPT1: parallel port has been redirected to the network printer. Now type **MAP** and press Enter. A list of your drive mappings should appear. To send this map list to the printer, type **MAP > LPT1:**. This redirects the output to the parallel port.

6. A list of your drive mappings should print on the network printer. Does it contain your new banner name? Why or why not?

7. To end the CAPTURE session, type **ENDCAP** and press Enter. A message similar to the following should be displayed on your screen:

```
Device LPT1: set to local mode
```

LAB QUIZ V

Printing on a Network

1. What is transparent network printing?

2. Describe the three different printing menu utilities.

3. Describe the three different printing command-line utilities (CLU).

4. What is your answer to the question proposed in LIFE.DOC?

5. What is your default tab size?

6. In addition to the banner name, what other information is printed in your banner?

7. Explain capturing.

Building NetWare LANs: Analysis and Design

"LAN ho!"

Probably the most exciting experience for anyone is the realization of a dream or idea. For some, a dream can be as simple as more money, a better job, or pickles on ham and cheese. For others, dreaming is very serious business: president of the United States, a cure for cancer, peace on Earth. Reality should never get in the way of your dreams. For example, I want to score the winning run in the seventh game of the world series. Unfortunately, reality has a way of sneaking up on you. So to combat the sobering effects of reality, I suggest we aspire to attainable dreams: I want to build a castle. You want to build a network. Let's work on our dreams together.

All great projects are first conceived in the mind, then put to paper, and finally materialized as the consolidation of available resources. The real "magic" in all of this is the process of transforming a dream into a reality. My castle begins with an idea—20 rooms, a moat, and central heating. The idea is drafted into blueprints, and the land is bought. Next, the builders acquire the necessary materials—rocks, wood, kitchen appliances—and begin construction. In the final step, I hire the management staff that will materialize my dream—hang tapestries, bake pies, feed the alligators.

Building NetWare LANs is no different. The first step is the recognition of a need and the conceptualization of a solution. Second comes construction. And finally, the integration of available resources into a working system. Analysis and design is the first step in the building of a NetWare LAN. Once the needs have been determined and the solution conceived, it is necessary to acquire the appropriate resources and begin constructing the dream. Installation is the second step in the process of building the network. Once the generalized system has been developed, it is necessary to "mold" it to fit the specific needs as determined in the first step. Only after a system has undergone intense network management can it fully realize its potential. The final three parts of this text will provide you with some detailed insights into each of these steps, and act as a guide to the goal of successfully building NetWare LANs. You also might learn a thing or two about castles along the way.

Never put off until tomorrow what you can do the day after tomorrow.

—Mark Twain

Chapter 4

Systems Analysis

"After long, careful consideration of technical requirements, user demands, and costs, all I came up with was a headache."

This first chapter in Part II deals primarily with the process of determining a system's needs and developing a plan or design to meet those needs. The functions of system analysis and design are greatly misunderstood, and often overlooked. Many network administrators think this process is unnecessary, opting to build their NetWare LANs in the dark. Imagine for a moment, building a castle without blueprints. Where would the living room go? How many rocks should we buy? Is there enough room for the indoor pool? A complete network design is as important to your LAN as the blueprints are to my castle.

The first step in building your NetWare LAN involves the cooperation of three distinctly different functional areas of computer science: analysis, design, and integration.

Analysis: The network analyst is responsible for investigating the players, concepts, and equipment that make up the existing system and developing a theory about how the system can be improved or changed. Then the analyst must determine which factors are relevant and important to the materialization of his or her theory. Finally, the analyst must prioritize the factors and brief the network designer.

Design: The network designer is responsible for exploring available resources and determining which combinations of hardware and software best accommodate the priorities he or she received from the network analyst. It is imperative for the network designer to work in close cooperation with the network integrator to avoid developing a design that can never be implemented.

Integration: The network integrator is responsible for balancing the resources that he or she received from the network designer and integrating them into a workable plan. The integrator must be aware of the network analyst's original theory to avoid developing a plan that, although it might work, does not meet the system's initial needs. The network integrator is not responsible for the implementation of the plan but should work in close cooperation with the installation team to ensure the team members are fully aware of the ultimate goal.

Each of these responsibilities is a full-time job in and of itself and should not be considered three aspects of one employee's responsibility. Having said that, it is unfortunate that a high percentage of projects are developed by one person. In addition, no doubt a good majority of this book's readers are expected to perform all of these tasks in an unreasonably short period of time. It is so all of you remain sane and employed that I dedicate this book to the understanding of *all* aspects of building NetWare LANs! We begin with systems analysis.

Preliminary Investigation

As if understanding all of the many technological aspects of local area networking isn't enough, now you have to make it work. Your next task will be to build a sound, productive network that balances technical requirements, user demands, and cost. This is not an easy endeavor, albeit a very rewarding one. In this chapter, I will guide you down the proverbial path of enlightenment by showing you how to spend your LAN time, energy, and resources.

The first concern for the network analyst is whether he or she should be bothering with this network at all. There is nothing worse than finding out you are wasting your time after you've spent it. In some rare cases, building a NetWare LAN can prove to be costly and unwarranted. A preliminary investigation should always be your first step. Through this process, the network analyst can determine whether the LAN should be built. The product of this step is the feasibility report. Management uses this report to choose one of three different avenues of action: do nothing, build the LAN immediately, or continue with data gathering and analysis.

The preliminary investigation consists of four phases: problem definition, scope, objectives, and feasibility report. The problem definition phase is where the network analyst asks the question: "Why a LAN?" Most analysts start with, "I don't know" or "Why ask why?"

Once the question has been adequately answered, the scope of the project must be determined—how big will this system be? Are we talking LAN, WAN, MAN, or CAN (colossal area network)?

During the third phase, objectives, it is important for the network analyst to start thinking about possible solutions. Not complete, viable solutions; just ideas. To begin, the analyst can express the system as a list of objectives. Finally, with the definition, scope, and objectives in hand, the network analyst will prepare a brief feasibility report for management. This report summarizes the analyst's findings and recommendations. The central purpose of the report is to help management decide whether the LAN is worth pursuing. It is imperative that the analyst be as objective as possible in preparing the feasibility report.

Problem Definition

Somebody called the system analyst. Somebody had a reason. This is always a good place to start. Are the users frustrated with their existing system? Do they need a system to start with? Are they pursuing some sort of competitive advantage? Are they trying to save money? Your initial aim is to find out why the users called you and what they expect you to do. Further investigation might reveal that the stated problem is actually only a symptom of the real problem. Let's say a group of users call you because management is consistently unresponsive to their needs. After careful analysis, you find that what they really mean is that management doesn't read their memos. Further analysis shows that management doesn't ever receive their memos. The problem definition quickly changes:

Original: Management doesn't listen to its staff.
Actual: Management doesn't receive staff memos.

Scope

Establishing the scope of a project is critical in order to keep the LAN under control. Scope provides physical boundaries for the network as well as financial and personnel limitations. After defining the problem accurately, the network analyst must explore the system resources and determine how far they can stretch. In many cases, the scope acts as a restraint to keep unworkable solutions from expanding too far. If the scope is too broad, the LAN will never be finished. If the scope is too narrow, the LAN will surely not meet the users' needs.

As you can see, the scope is a very important aspect of the preliminary investigation. It is critical to establish a LAN's scope early in the analysis process, because it has a strong influence on cost, expectations, environment, and time. Management is looking for the bottom line: "How much will it cost and how long will it take?" In the earlier example, it is important to establish scope right away. How many memos are being lost—all of them or just a few? It turns out that the missing memos are originating from one floor of the building: the seventh floor. In this instance the system analyst visited the mailroom and found that the courier who handled mail for the seventh floor had a pet goat—a finicky goat who would only eat memos written on company stationery.

Objectives

Once you have determined what the system is and how big it should be, you will need to ascertain exactly what the users think the system should do. The LAN objectives are the cornerstone of the preliminary investigation. Objectives should clearly and concisely outline the capabilities of the new system. The objectives should also explain how the system will complete the problem definition, and more importantly, satisfy the user's needs. Again, the goal here is not comprehensive solutions, just simple ideas.

Objectives should be phrased along the following lines:

- a castle with 20 rooms, a moat, and central heating
- a mail system that delivers all staff memos to management
- a relational database that allows simultaneous multiuser access
- a baseball card with 3-D pictures, current statistics, and ERA rankings
- a reliable NetWare LAN for 20 users in two different buildings

The language used to list the objectives is very important. Management can easily misunderstand your emphasis if you are not clear and concise. Also, there is no guarantee that the same network analyst will perform both the preliminary investigation and the data gathering/analysis. In many cases these are two different people. It is imperative that all your work be documented precisely.

Feasibility Report

At the culmination of the preliminary investigation, you will present a feasibility report to the users' management. These presentations are typically short and informal, generally consisting of a two-page report and half an hour of questions and answers. Management uses this report to decide whether to pursue the project. In most cases, management opts for further study. It is rare for management to order a preliminary investigation for something the managers do not intend to ultimately carry through. Of course management, in general, has been known to surprise the world now and again.

The feasibility report should contain brief paragraphs on the following topics:

- problem definition
- scope
- a list of objectives
- preliminary solution ideas
- estimated costs and benefits

Careful consideration is critical at this juncture. The feasibility report stands as a model for the network analyst's thoughts and points of view with respect to the project. As the project moves forward, this model can become a guideline for network design, installation, and ultimately network management. Although informal, this report is the first blueprint for the process of building a NetWare LAN. Our sample feasibility report about the memo problem would read like this:

> *Problem Definition:* Staff memos are not being delivered to management.
> *Scope:* All staff memos from the seventh floor.
> *Objectives:* A mail system that delivers all staff memos to management.
> *Solution Ideas:* It was discovered that a finicky goat has been eating the memos. The goat belongs to the mail courier who delivers mail to the seventh floor. We suggest management find some more desirable, less destructive food for the malicious mammal.
> *Estimated Costs and Benefits:* A 50-pound bag of grain costs $25. Written communications between staff and management on the seventh floor would resume.

Data Gathering

Assuming the preliminary investigation is a success, the next step in systems analysis is data gathering. *Data gathering* is the process of determining who is doing what to whom and why. In other words, just the facts ma'am. Objectivity is crucial in data gathering. There are all sorts of distortion effects that have been found to alter data as it is gathered. The *Hawthorne Effect* states that individuals who know they are part of a study behave differently from those who are not part of a study or don't know they are part of a study. The *learning curve* shows that data gathered early in an experiment is not always as accurate as data gathered later.

Let's return to my castle for just a moment. After preliminary investigation, I was able to define the problem as "I want a castle, and I don't have one." The scope included 20 rooms, 30,000 square feet, and 25 surrounding acres. My objective is a castle with 20 rooms, a moat, and central heating. Careful analysis of the feasibility report leads me to conclude that I need more data. So I will continue with my systems analysis by gathering as much data as possible. I will find a suitable oceanside region, survey possible land plots, research real estate pricing, and try to learn something from people who have done this all before.

Data gathering for your LAN is just as important. You must survey the existing system, talk to users, research business operations, and observe the surrounding environments. Network analysts use a variety of methods for data gathering: observation, interviews, written documents, questionnaires, and sampling. I recommend that you use a combination of these methods in gathering your LAN data.

Observation

Observation is the most useful and powerful of the data-gathering methods. It is amazing how much you can see with your eyes wide open. Observation can be effective when it is performed independently or with the help of users. Be careful, though, when you ask the users for help in guiding you through existing systems and business operations. The first question they ask is "Why?" Be sensitive to the Hawthorne Effect from users who feel threatened by the possible introduction of a new LAN.

While observing, you should examine procedures, existing technology, and people. Watch the users at work. Explore their business procedures. Can the procedures be improved so employees are more efficient or productive? Identify the existing technology. How do the users interact with their current systems? How are they likely to interact with a new system? Observe the people. Examine their interpersonal relationships. Identify the users who will be most likely threatened by a new LAN. Find users who can calm the cyberphobia. Look for the following factors that affect LAN design:

- electronic data exchange—file transfers
- interoffice communications—memos or electronic mail
- ergonomics in workstation design—keyboards/monitors
- user interface—menu systems, applications, and operating systems
- training and documentation—categories of user skill levels
- business operations—what the business does
- organizational chart—feelings among staff, management, and others
- automated tasks—tasks that are and aren't currently automated (but should be)
- existing technology—catalog hardware, software, and other types
- security—identify data and resources that require specific security
- environments—office layout, building, power sources, interference

Another key element of observation is intuition. Each network analyst approaches data gathering with a different combination of personal skills. Some analysts are good listeners, some write well, and others have great intuition. While you're observing a system, pay attention to your feelings about the system. How does it make you feel? Would you like to work here? If not, what can be done to improve the atmosphere? Feelings are difficult to express on paper, but they can be very useful in choosing an approach for data analysis.

Interviews

Interviews are another powerful tool for data gathering. They can provide a great deal of insight for the network analyst that he or she may not have picked up during the observation phase. Some users will reveal more information during interviews than others. The key is to filter out the complaints and anxiety and gather as much useful, objective data as possible. Opinions will also surface. Be very careful when you are dealing with these little half-truths.

The more he talked of his honor, the faster we counted our spoons.

—Ralph Waldo Emerson

There are two different kinds of interviews: structured and unstructured. In structured interviews, the analyst prepares a list of common questions that are asked of all users. The questions and their answers are then analyzed across the population to determine trends and majority facts. Unstructured interviews, on the other hand, pursue a more flexible path.

The network analyst prepares a general guideline in advance but is free to stray from it as data-gathering opportunities present themselves. Unstructured interviews can be more productive than planned ones, because you can adapt your investigation based on preliminary findings and follow tangential paths of information based on previous answers.

Another important interview element is body language. Pay attention to inflections in the user's voice. Notice body movements and hand gestures. As the user becomes emotional about a certain topic, categorize the emotion—rage, anxiety, anticipation, or joy. Observation is a great tool in interviewing a system's key personnel.

Written Documents

Written documents can yield insight into how a system works. The network analyst should examine forms, manuals, letters, memos, charts, diagrams, and other paperwork in order to better understand how the business operates. It is important to determine early on which documents hold the most information. A midsized organization produces thousands of documents each day, and few analysts enjoy shuffling through a million pages in order to gather a little data. Some documents of interest include invoices, bills, interoffice communications, financial reports, and training manuals.

Questionnaires

Questionnaires are great tools for gathering large amounts of data quickly and easily. They let the users do all the work. Ideally, questionnaires consist of short-answer, well-written questions that elicit clear, concise responses. The trick in preparing a questionnaire is to ask the right type of questions without directing or influencing the responses. Also, the questionnaire should elicit quantitative responses whenever possible. This makes data analysis a little more meaningful. Following are three examples of how you should and should not ask for responses to various types of needs:

Directional issues
Should Not: "Do you think a LAN will solve your current problems?"
Should: "Are you satisfied with your current system? If not, how can it be improved?"

Quantitative issues
Should Not: "Do you like your current user interface?"
Should: "Rate your current user interface on a scale of 1 to 10."

Subjective issues
Should Not: "Please describe your job."
Should: "List your five most important tasks."

In general, users prefer a questionnaire that is quick and simple. A variety of question types is a good idea, because it elicits a variety of different responses. Some analysts ask the same question in two or three different ways to test the consistency of the respondent. Whatever approach you use, remember that questionnaires are only effective when used in combination with interviews and other data-gathering methods.

Sampling

Sampling is used to gather quantitative data. Network analysts use sampling as an efficient alternative to collecting all the data of a given system. With sampling, the analyst collects a representative subset of the total data and then extrapolates the results across the total population. For example, you are asked to analyze the need for a LAN at Santa's workshop. Part of your data-gathering process is to determine how many letters originate from little boys and girls in North America. Santa receives approximately 42 trillion letters each year, so an accurate count of all the letters would be impossible. Sampling is your friend. Through sampling you need only count 500 letters, and extrapolate the number of North American children across the population of 42 trillion—a considerable savings in time and energy.

Now that you have observed the system's daily operations, conducted endless interviews, photocopied documents, collected questionnaires, and sampled large amounts of data, you are ready for the real fun—analyzing it all!

Data Analysis

Data analysis is the meat and potatoes of systems analysis. The grueling legwork has been completed, and now it is time to make sense of it all. You will organize the questionnaires, documents, notes, and sampling data into 10 different categories. Each of these categories will ultimately serve the requirements report in the form of objectives, needs, requirements, and recommendations. Following is a list of the 10 data analysis categories:

- load factor
- distance
- environment
- security
- future expansion
- cost
- protection
- changing technology
- existing equipment
- intangibles

These categories help to differentiate the data you collected and organize it into a meaningful form. As the data analysis process continues and you organize your findings into categories, you should begin to notice a LAN taking form. Right before your eyes, the answers will begin to appear and the requirements report will take shape. Keep in mind that the following 10 categories are only the major arteries of your LAN. Many additional criteria will grow from each topic. It is your job to try to sanely differentiate between a "real" issue and a user's meaningless "brush fire."

Load Factor

The LAN load factor is determined through a combination of related principles. Answers to some of the following questions will help you narrow the possibilities to a specific LAN architecture:

- How many users will the LAN have?
- How many users will work at the same time?
- How complex are the independent applications?
- Are the applications "disk-intensive"?
- Will the network provide multiuser applications?
- Will many users and applications require high levels of performance?
- Is the experience level of your "average" user fairly high?

If the answer is many or yes to a few of these questions, you might be leaning toward a high-load network. High-load systems require special handling with respect to data protection, speed, and disk integrity. Load factor also dictates which topology you choose. A high load factor, for example, would require the power of a star configuration with coaxial cabling, while a lighter load factor would tend to favor a less-expensive bus topology with twisted-pair cabling.

Distance

The distance between network components is a critical factor is determining LAN architecture. The one aspect of the LAN architecture that hinges on distance criteria is cabling. The transmission medium you choose will stick with you for a long time. Prepared analysts choose a medium that allows for future growth. There are typically three different types of LAN cabling to choose from:

- twisted pair
- coaxial
- fiber optic

Twisted-pair cabling is ideal for short, light-load LANs. Coaxial cabling is a good fit for small to medium-sized LANs using heavy loads. Keep in mind, the Ethernet standard limits the distance of each coaxial trunk to 685 feet or 208.7 meters. Fiber optic cabling is ideal for large networks using very heavy loads. Fiber optic hardware is pricey, but the cost is dropping as technology advances.

Be careful as you determine cabling distances. Most of the time, the distance between workstations is not the distance traveled by the cabling. Some cabling runs are so convoluted that the actual distance traveled can exceed the distance between workstations by 200 percent.

Environment

The network analyst must also consider the type of building that houses the LAN. In addition, the structure and composition of the building's walls can have an adverse effect on the network cabling. As you consider the structural environment that houses your LAN, ask these simple questions:

- What kind of access will I have to hollow ceilings?
- Are there cable channels built into the floor?
- Do the walls have conduit available for use?
- If none of the above is true, will the building fire codes allow me to run cable loosely throughout the building?

If the answer to all of these questions is no, you'll be in for a lot of work. In addition, pay attention to the surrounding businesses and the equipment they are using. Does the nearby electrical machinery cause electromagnetic interference or electrical problems with your topology? Is the electrical power supplied to the building reliable? If not, you will need to explore Energy SFT, or devices to ensure the even flow of power to the network.

Another important consideration is ergonomics. *Ergonomics* is the concept of fitting the tool to the hand that uses it. Consider the plight of the network users. Are they staring at green screens all day? How many of them are exposed for long periods to harmful VDT radiation? What kind of lumbar support do they have? Some ergonomic factors to consider are the keyboard angle, layout of the keys, display screen (resolution and color), lighting, screen glare, desk organization, desk height, noise, air quality, temperature, work breaks, and employee morale.

Security

The importance of security depends primarily on the LAN's greatest functionality. Is the purpose of the LAN to organize monetary transactions for a banking firm with hordes of confidential information? Or is it a drug store that's trying to keep track of vitamin C? Security in the first scenario involves all levels of protection, from login names to file attributes, whereas the second example requires nothing more than simple password protection.

Beyond the seven-layered NetWare security model is LAN security that takes on not-so-obvious shapes. Intangible aspects of a network that normally go unnoticed can quickly become questions of primary security. Things such as leakage, tapping, user authentication, audit trails, and encryption are issues that the network analyst must address. Security exists in stages, from least to most secure. First, there is software security: NetWare. Next, there is hardware security: locking the keyboard. Finally, the analyst may want to install media security: line monitors. Typically, the seven-layered security model from NetWare is sufficient. Chapter 12 explores NetWare's security model in greater depth.

Future Expansion

Probably the single most overlooked aspect of data analysis is, "Where will this network be in three years?" Many great LAN strategists are guilty of becoming so wrapped up in current projects that they forget to look ahead. For all their planning, strategists can forget to plan ahead. Future expansion can be as simple as adding a few extra workstations or as elaborate as calculating load factors 10 years into the future. No matter what the precaution, future expansion cannot be ignored. One of the best ways of exploring future expansion is to look at internetworking. *Internetworking*, as discussed in Chapter 1, includes bridges, routers, and gateways.

Cost

The nemesis of network analysts is money. Money has shattered more dreams than has any hardware, software, or space limitation. Your involvement with systems analysis will not go far until you run into this age-old roadblock. When you are analyzing cost issues, it is imperative to be realistic and fair. Objectively evaluate LAN functionality within a reasonable cost arena. It is not your job to determine whether management can afford the LAN. It is your job to tell the managers how much the LAN will cost. Also, try not to get wrapped up in the cost of the solution, because there is no solution yet. At the same time, don't ignore the cost issues either. Technology isn't cheap, and very few organizations can afford the latest and greatest inventions.

Beware of hidden costs. Items such as training, new software, hardware upgrades, and maintenance/repair are not always factored into the original equation. It is very important to evaluate exactly what the system needs. Here are some helpful hints to try when you must cut costs:

- Never sacrifice tape backups or uninterruptible power supplies (UPSs).
- Use multiuser, site-licensed software applications whenever possible.
- Opt to upgrade the disk space in the file server instead of upgrading each workstation.
- Clone hardware is fine for workstations, but try to use name-brand topology components.

Protection

System fault tolerance (SFT) is a critical aspect of LAN design. Most unemployed network analysts have forgotten SFT somewhere along the line. Protection exists on many different levels in NetWare. Energy SFT consists of surge protectors, SPSs, and UPSs. Storage SFT includes read-after-write verification, hot fix, disk mirroring, disk duplexing, and file server duplexing. SFT costs a little more initially, but the peace of mind and protection are well worth it.

Changing Technology

Problems that seem insurmountable today could be solved in three months with the release of a new network technology or device. Keep on top of rapidly shifting computer trends. There are a multitude of advantages in being a leader rather than a lagger. As a network analyst, you should perform this type of research every week. Take a quick look at where the industry is going. Then take a look at where your network is going. Explore any new technology that could make your LAN more productive or efficient. There are endless periodicals and resources available that can help you with your weekly research: *LAN Times, LAN Technology, NetWare Application Notes, NetWare Buyer's Guide,* user groups, and this book, just to name a few.

One of the most comprehensive resources available is CompuServe. CompuServe is an on-line data bank that contains many networking forums, user groups, and file libraries. Two of the resources that I use extensively on CompuServe are NetWire and the Executive News Service. NetWire is a NetWare forum that contains information and press releases about all NetWare-related products. There is also an on-line library that contains thousands of support drivers, utilities, and program files. The Executive News Service is a CompuServe resource that enables you to selectively retrieve specific networking articles and press releases from most of the global news services. Refer to Chapter 3 for a discussion of these networking services. Keeping on top of changing technology will help you ride the crest of networking success instead of getting drowned in the white-wash.

Existing Equipment

Local area network installations are often an upgrade of existing systems. Typically, this means you are forced to integrate new NetWare LAN components with existing computer equipment. Fortunately the computer industry is becoming more homogeneous, and today's LAN systems will meld easily with any given flavor of computer system. This molding process can be as smooth as simply adding cabling, a few network interface cards (NICs), and a file server, or as complex as replacing dumb terminals with workstations and opening up a whole new world of LAN-to-host communications. Gateways permit internetworking between unlike systems—a LAN to a minicomputer or mainframe, for example.

Recently, great advances have been made in the areas of hardware connectivity and software integration. *Hardware connectivity* allows transparent communications between a variety of different hardware platforms. An Ethernet NetWare LAN, for example, can transparently integrate IBM-compatible, Macintosh, PS/2, and UNIX workstations. A few years ago, this level of hardware connectivity required an act of Congress. Software integration has come a long way as well. Today, these same machines can share files across many different proprietary operating systems: DOS, OS/2, System 7, Windows NT, and UNIX. Today's new integration technologies are making it much easier for everybody's computers to communicate in a seemingly standardless world.

Intangibles

Just when you thought it was safe . . . oops! You will never think of everything. If some data pops up that you cannot fit into any of the previous nine categories, there are always intangibles. Intangibles are those annoying little somethings that never quite conform. In every analysis, I always find one or two intangibles. The best advice is to take note of them and move on with the idea of heading them off at the pass.

Requirements Report

Now that data gathering and analysis are complete, it is time to put our findings on paper. The requirements report is the final product of all our systems analysis efforts. This report is not necessarily for management, because managers have already committed to the project. This report is directed toward the network designer and network integrator. The network designer will use the requirements report as a guideline for his or her design. The ultimate goal of the network design is to create a LAN plan (nice ring!) that satisfies the requirements set forth by the network analyst in the requirements report. The network integrator will then take the plan and consolidate the necessary resources for installation and ultimately network management.

The requirements report consists of four different sections—vital statistics, preliminary investigation, requirements, and initial recommendations—with the following functions:

1. The first section, vital statistics, deals primarily with introductory background information for the network designer.
2. Preliminary investigation is simply a recap of the feasibility report. The network designer normally doesn't receive the preliminary investigation, so you should include it in the requirements report in case there are some facts he or she can use.

3. The third section, requirements, is the core of the requirements report. Here the network analyst outlines the data-gathering and analysis phases. The requirements section consists of a list of the design requirements necessary to complete each of the 10 analysis categories.

4. The final section, initial recommendations, serves as a transition from systems analysis to network design. The network analyst should be very general in recording initial recommendations. The detailed plan will be worked out by the more experienced network designer.

Following Chapter 6 you will find five design case studies. These semifictional scenarios have been carefully developed to give you a taste of what is involved in systems analysis and network design. The first scenario, The Simpsons, is an example of how to create a useful, informative requirements report. Following is a copy of Case 1.

CASE 1

The Simpsons
Production Company

The production team for Fox television's hit cartoon series "The Simpsons" is housed in a small production studio on Sunset Boulevard in Hollywood. They write the scripts, develop preliminary sketches, and create the voice tracks for each episode. In addition to their production responsibilities, this office handles all of the administrative and financial paperwork for the show and sends nightly update reports to Fox television.

Currently, there are 4 writers, 3 cartoonists, 3 producers, and 5 administrative assistants working as part of this production team. They spend their time fiddling with Rolodexes, filing away Simpsons data, passing verbal and hand-written messages, enhancing poor quality output, manually scheduling meetings, and typing letters on 5 old Smith-Corona typewriters. In addition, they each take their turn fighting through rush-hour traffic to get the daily reports to Fox's headquarters before 5:00 PM.

One day, the producers visited Disney Studios and CBS and marveled at the sophistication of their office system designs. The Simpsons producers decided that they too should have the benefits of 20th century technology and decided to hire you to design their new electronic office. The only drawback was an experience they witnessed at CBS: the LAN crashed and took all of its valuable data with it. They vowed that their system would never go down or lose data.

The Studio is organized into a square with fifteen 50' x 50' offices lining the perimeter. In the center of the square is a large work space for the cartoonists, and a central wiring closet directly at the midpoint. The entire studio covers about 40,000 square feet of land. In addition, all of the offices have been wired with coaxial cable for television feeds—unfortunately, none of these lines are available for data. The producers were hoping you could build their magical office system for less than $65,000. Good Luck!

Assume that we have already completed the data-gathering and analysis phases. The first step in creating a requirements report is preparing vital statistics.

Vital Statistics

The vital statistics section covers mostly general background information. Subjects such as who, where, and when should be included in this section. Simple facts are as follows:

VITAL STATISTICS

Who:	"The Simpsons" Production Company
	Homer Simpson, Producer
	4 writers
	3 cartoonists
	3 producers
	5 administrative assistants
Where:	"The Simpsons" Production Studio
	700 Sunset Boulevard
	Hollywood, California
	phone: (213) 555-1234
	fax: (213) 555-0007
	15 offices - 50' x 50'
When:	Analysis: May 3, 1993
Report:	May 31, 1993
Design:	September 3, 1993
Installation:	October 3, 1993
Completion:	November 1, 1993

The vital statistics section should be kept short and to the point.

Preliminary Investigation

Include a summary of the feasibility report:

FEASIBILITY REPORT

Problem Definition:	Old, manual office technology is nonproductive and inefficient.
Scope:	15 workstations—8 administrative, 4 word processing, and 3 financial.
Objectives:	(1) An automated, electronic office system that handles word processing, interoffice communications, financial analysis, and Rolodexes; (2) a data communications system for file transfer to Fox's headquarters; (3) good quality output; (4) reliability.
Solution Ideas:	A LAN with word processing, spreadsheeting, and electronic mail capabilities. Also, include modem communications, system fault tolerance, electronic scheduling, and an on-line Rolodex.

Estimated Costs and Benefits:	Project should not exceed $65,000. The benefits of an electronic office were evident at Walt Disney Studios and CBS: better communications, increased productivity and administrative efficiency, improved quality of life, lower long-term administrative costs, and better quality output.

Requirements

The requirements section deals primarily with the results from data gathering and analysis. This is where the network analyst transforms the results into useful system requirements. Be careful not to make assumptions or recommendations in this section. The network designer needs clear, objective facts at this point. Your initial assumptions and recommendations will be expressed in the next section. Begin the requirements section with a brief review of the data-gathering methods:

DATA GATHERING	
Observation:	43 hours unattended; 23 hours attended.
Interviews:	12 unstructured; 15 structured.
Written Documents:	492 pages, including forms, invoices, financial reports.

Next, outline the results of your data analysis by structuring them into a series of system requirements. Organize these requirements according to the same 10 categories you used during the data analysis phase.

DATA ANALYSIS	
Load Factor:	15 inexperienced users grouped into 3 functional categories.
	8 administrative—word processing, electronic office functions.
	4 writers—word processing.
	3 financial—spreadsheets, electronic office functions.
	The cartoonists still sketch manually.
	Reliability is more of an issue than speed.
	This LAN will have a small to medium load factor.
Distances:	15 50' x 50' offices in a 40,000-square-foot area.
	Two-story building
	12 offices in the perimeter; 3 offices in a central open area.
	Central wiring closet located at the midpoint.
	All offices must be connected to the LAN.
Environment:	Coaxial television cabling runs to all offices.
	Existing coaxial cabling is run in shielded conduits.
	Electrical power is not reliable.

All desks and chairs are ergonomically designed.
The production team is very interested in physical
comfort.

Security: The LAN must be highly secure.

The producers are concerned about data confidentiality, especially with respect to the modem communications.

Users will store shared data as well as private documents.

Future: There is currently no interest in future expansion.

Cost: The producers are highly aware of cost.

The project cannot exceed $65,000.

Costs for systems analysis, network design, training,
and maintenance will be included in the $65,000
limit.

Protection: This LAN must never crash.

Technology: There is currently no new technology that can substantially increase this LAN's productivity or efficiency.

Existing: There is currently no existing computer equipment.
There are 5 Smith-Corona typewriters.

Intangibles: There is a slim chance the cartoonists will begin to
explore computer graphics in the next 3 to 5 years.
None of the employees has ever used a computer
before.

Initial Recommendations

The final step in preparing your requirements report is initial recommendations. This section is less objective than any of the previous sections. It gives the network analyst an opportunity to speak his or her mind and get the network designer off to a flying start. The initial recommendations should be general in scope and specific in context. They will follow the same format as the network design:

Hardware Design	**Software Design**
Topology Components	Network Operating System
Cabling	Workstation Operating Systems
File Server	Menu Systems
Workstations	Network Applications
SFT Components	Office Systems Design

Following is an example of what the initial recommendations would look like for "The Simpsons" Production Company:

HARDWARE DESIGN

Topology Components:	The small to medium-sized load factor points to a simple Ethernet BUS design. This is also a low cost alternative.
Cabling:	I recommend coaxial cabling for the long distances between offices and to satisfy the need for ultimate reliability.
File Server:	An IBM PC clone will do fine—possibly a 80486/33-MHz model.
Workstations:	All of the user's requirements can be satisfied within the IBM PC platform. Again, clones will work as good, low-cost workstations—possibly 80386/33-MHz machines. I also recommend no local workstation hard disks, because omitting them would increase security and decrease cost. Data communications to the Fox headquarters should be handled through a communications gateway.
SFT Components:	The overwhelming need for ultimate reliability points to a need for high levels of system fault tolerance. I recommend a UPS, surge protectors, and network tape backup. Although it is expensive, I would also explore the possibility of disk mirroring or duplexing.

SOFTWARE DESIGN

Network Operating System:	NetWare v3.11 will satisfy all of "The Simpsons" LAN requirements.
Workstation Operating Systems:	DOS will perform well on the IBM PC workstations. In addition, a graphical user interface (GUI)—Microsoft Windows, for example—could help to alleviate some of the users' initial computer shock.
Menu Systems:	The GUI could act as the menuing interface. Otherwise, I recommend a good, solid LAN interface such as Lazy Susan or WordPerfect Library.
Network Applications:	All of the users' application requirements can be satisfied with commercially available LAN software. I recommend WordPerfect

Office Systems Design: and Lotus 1-2-3 in the DOS environment and Microsoft Word and Excel in the GUI environment. The need for electronic scheduling, mail, and a shared Rolodex can be satisfied through WordPerfect Office in the DOS environment or Windows for Workgroups in the GUI environment. These products will provide a consistent interface and groupware functionality: electronic mail, menuing, scheduling, and an on-line Rolodex.

The requirements report has been completed. Typically, the network designer will ask for two to three days to absorb the report, and then he or she will want to meet with you to discuss any questions. Once the requirements report has been completed and you have met with the network designer, your involvement in this project is over. Don't be too worried, though—there are probably 33 more projects waiting for you. Also keep in mind that most network analysts work on a variety of different projects simultaneously. This helps to stimulate the gray matter.

"One cannot believe impossible things," he said. "I daresay you haven't had much practice," said the Queen. "When I was your age, I always did it for half-an-hour a day. Why, sometimes I've believed as many as seven impossible things before breakfast."

—Lewis Carroll

Before you begin investigating network design, let's get a quick update from my castle project. The feasibility report led me to believe that this was a viable project that deserved further study. I entered the data-gathering phase. In gathering my castle data, I used three of the five gathering methods: observation, interviews, and written documents. I observed 23 different castles in similar oceanside regions. I examined their construction, size, surrounding gardens, and need for central heating. Then, I interviewed the occupants. I asked questions regarding atmosphere, neighbors, and interior decorating. Most of the castle dwellers expressed a need for central heating, but stood firm in their cold, damp architectural traditions. I interviewed castle architects and gathered information regarding the cost of materials and timelines for construction. Finally, I inspected hundreds of castle documents to determine the most suitable location and size of garden.

The next step, data analysis, offered some interesting results. It turns out that I want a 25-room castle—not 20—with central heating *and* air-conditioning. Who would have thought it? In addition, the oceanside region would require entirely too much garden maintenance. The castle will encompass 30,000 square feet within 25 surrounding acres. I need a multifloor infrared motion-detecting alarm system and alligators in the moat. A remote-controlled drawbridge will offer safe passage to the castle's occupants and approved guests. It turns out that new technology in castle construction will enable me to build the structure entirely out of recycled L.A. freeway rock. The final cost is estimated to fall somewhere between $1 and $1 billion.

With my requirements report in hand, I am ready to find a castle designer who can transform my dream into a reality. The next step involves careful attention to detail and a vast knowledge of castle components. Network design works the same way—careful attention to detail and a vast knowledge of networking components. The remainder of this part explores the process of network design through an in-depth study of the required LAN hardware and software components. You will become the network designer who is sought by so many users to transform their LAN dreams into a reality.

Chapter 5

Hardware Design

"Sorry, Jack, but we had to cut back on something!"

The network analyst has investigated your LAN's objectives, prioritized them, and developed an initial solution. He or she comes to you as the network designer and says, "Make it so!"

Of course your response is, "Sure! No problem," and you proceed to drown yourself in the 342-page requirements report.

I have a better idea. . . .

Factors and Components

It has been my experience that all the factors, details, and lexicon in the world of networking can be narrowed down into two very important classifications: people and performance.

As the network designer, you only have to concern yourself with these two categories. Analyze the requirements report and prioritize the results with respect to their influence over the people in the office and the performance of the LAN. It's that simple. Then you can work together with the network integrator to develop a balance of hardware and software components that create a design synergy.

⇨ **SYNERGY (SIN'ER-JE):** *The whole is greater than the sum of its parts.*

Synergy in networking is the product of well-orchestrated software and hardware components. In the best scenario, these components complement each other to create a LAN that exceeds the productivity and performance of individual systems. As we saw in earlier chapters, each of the hardware and software components provides its own networking functionality: topology components connect workstations and file servers, operating systems control messages as they traverse the LAN cabling, and software applications give the system practical usefulness. As the network designer, it is your job to understand these components well enough to create a design synergy that meets the demands set forth in the requirements document. Following is a list of the hardware and software components that must be included in the network design:

Hardware
- *Topology components:* NICs, hubs, MSAUs, and connectors
- *Cabling:* unshielded twisted-pair, shielded twisted-pair, coaxial, fiber optic, microwave, satellite, infrared, T-1
- *File server:* CPU, RAM, disk drives, and so on
- *Workstations:* CPU, RAM, ergonomics, and so on
- *SFT Components:* SPS, UPS, backup systems, disk duplexing, and so on

Software
- *Network operating systems:* NetWare, Banyan VINES, NT LAN Manager, and so on
- *Workstation operating systems:* DOS, OS/2, UNIX, System 7
- *Menu systems:* Microsoft Windows, NetWare's menu system, and so on
- *Network applications:* word processing, spreadsheets, database, integrated applications, and so on
- *Office systems design:* electronic mail, scheduling, calendars, and so on

Design synergy is just as important for my dream design as it is for yours. The hardware and software components of my castle parallel your LAN:

Castle Hardware	Castle Software
Cement	Central heating, air conditioning
Electricity, phone, TV	Paint, interior decorating
Rocks	Furniture
Rooms, indoor pool	Appliances
Moat, drawbridge, alarm	Tapestries, pies

Castle hardware consists of construction materials—the physical components required to build the structure. The rocks are at the heart of my design. They create the foundation and support the walls. The cement binds the rocks together. Cabling is also very important in a castle. My domestic cabling consists of electricity, telephone, and TV. Without castle cabling, the software would be useless. The real focus on castle hardware is the rooms. A castle would be nothing without living rooms, bedrooms, dining rooms, a sports bar, and indoor pool. The rooms are supported by the rocks and cement. Finally, the castle needs protection, reliability, and security. My castle SFT consists of a moat with alligators, a drawbridge, and a multifloor infrared motion-detecting alarm system.

Castle software consists of productivity tools—the internal resources that are required to build a comfortable, home-like atmosphere. The central-heating and air-conditioning components are at the heart of my castle software. They will provide the occupants with happiness and peace-of-mind. At a more personal level, interior decorating produces a feeling of warmth and security. Resources such as paint, wall-paper, pictures, and candles are required to give the castle that "lived-in" feeling. The true productivity tools of my castle are the chairs, tables, sofas, and beds. Furniture complements paint and central heating by providing the occupants with somewhere to go. Appliances are required to keep the occupants happy. They provide user interface and software design. Without appliances, occupants would have to cook and clean the old-fashioned way, and we don't want that. Finally, the castle software design wouldn't be complete without tapestries and mincemeat pies.

A well-constructed design is critical to any project. Network projects rely on the hardware and software components for performance, reliability, productivity, and user interface. The network designer and integrator must do their homework in order to create the best possible design synergy. This chapter's discussion of network design begins with an in-depth study of the hardware components and their impact on the LAN's people and performance.

Topology Components

An average conversation about topology design can quickly digress into the electronic twilight zone of IEEE 802 standards and interconnectivity buzzwords. More often than not these specific elements are underlying ingredients of a larger pie. They are the foundations of the properties that concern us. So in the interest of clarity and sophistication, this discussion focuses on the network design characteristics of topology components, not the underlying electronic principles that create them.

The first hardware-oriented decision facing the network designer is how to physically configure the components of his or her plan. Many different factors must be weighed and balanced in constructing the best formula for efficiency, performance, and reliability. Fortunately, 95 percent of the networking world has settled on one of five standard topology designs:

- Thin Ethernet bus
- Thick Ethernet bus
- Ethernet 10Base-T
- ARCNet star
- Token Ring

The network designer works in concert with the network integrator to find the best match for topology design, people, and performance. It is imperative for both players to fully understand the boundaries of their responsibility:

- The network designer controls the balance of design synergy, and clearly understands the relationship between network resources and requirements.
- The network integrator is technologically aware of which hardware and software components can best fit the ultimate design.

Each of the topology designs has its own set of strengths and weaknesses that makes it uniquely suitable for a given balance of resources and requirements. Some are less expensive, some are more reliable, some handle communications faster, most are easy to use, and all of these designs are intelligent candidates for building a NetWare LAN. Table 5.1 gives a "cheat sheet" summary of these strengths and weaknesses.

Ethernet

Ethernet is clearly the global standard for computer networks. It is supported by all facets of computer science, from PCs to Macs to UNIX. The Ethernet standard was developed in 1973 at Xerox Corporation's PARC facility in Palo Alto, California, as part of Xerox's ALOHA network design experiments. In the PC marketplace, you can find a very wide range of Ethernet manufacturers: 3COM, Novell, Intel, Excelan, Western Digital, Tiara, Gateway, and SMC. There is also a market for Ethernet clone manufacturers. Not quite as reliable, these components are normally sold for less than $100.

Ethernet currently provides the widest support of any network topology with respect to multiple protocols, including NetWare's IPX/SPX, TCP/IP, Xerox's XNS, and Sun's NFS. This makes it relatively effortless to interconnect dissimilar LANs using Ethernet.

Thin Ethernet Bus
The standard Ethernet design uses a bus topology. In this configuration, the coaxial cable acts as a linear trunk and each of the Ethernet NICs is connected to it. The thin Ethernet standard uses a thinner coaxial cable and operates on less expensive hardware.

Components. Figure 5.1 illustrates the topology components required to install a thin Ethernet design. The network interface card contains the circuitry necessary to ensure reliable communications between the workstation and the rest of the LAN. It contains an inter-

TABLE 5.1 Comparing Features of Topology Designs

Topology Design	Low Cost	Low-Loads Speed	High-Loads Speed	High Reliability	Flexible Installation
Thin Ethernet	X	X			X
Thick Ethernet			X		
Ethernet 10Base-T		X			X
ARCNet	X			X	
ARCNet Plus			X	X	
Token Ring (4 Mb/s)				X	
Token Ring (16 Mb/s)			X	X	
LocalTalk	X				X

nal transceiver that provides the direct electronic interface between the card and the Ethernet cabling. The card itself attaches to the coaxial cabling through the use of a BNC T-connector that joins two lengths of the cabling trunk and the network interface card (NIC). The cabling scheme is terminated and grounded through the use of BNC terminators and grounded BNC terminators.

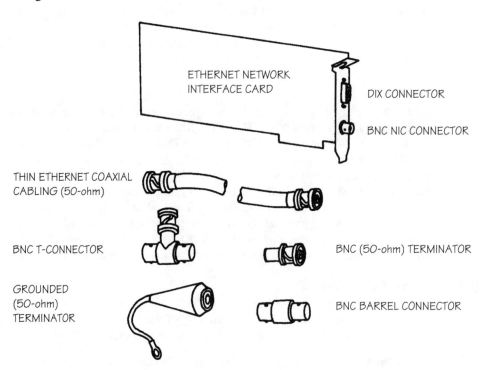

ETHERNET NETWORK INTERFACE CARD

DIX CONNECTOR

BNC NIC CONNECTOR

THIN ETHERNET COAXIAL CABLING (50-ohm)

BNC T-CONNECTOR

BNC (50-ohm) TERMINATOR

GROUNDED (50-ohm) TERMINATOR

BNC BARREL CONNECTOR

FIGURE 5.1 Topology Components for Thin Ethernet

By grounding terminators, you can strip harmful electromechanical interference (EMI) noise from the coaxial cabling shield.

Topology/Protocol. Figure 5.2 describes a typical thin Ethernet topology design. Notice how the coaxial cabling is organized into a bus trunk segment. The workstations are connected to the trunk through network interface cards and BNC T-connectors. A repeater is included to illustrate how two trunk segments can be attached without exceeding cable length limitations. Thin Ethernet is limited to only 5 trunk segments per LAN, and 30 workstations per trunk. The maximum cable length for one trunk is 607 feet or 185 meters. The entire network topology is limited to a total cable length of 3,035 feet or 925 meters.

Cabling. Thin Ethernet operates on 0.2 inch RG-58A/U 50-ohm coaxial cabling. This specific network cable can be purchased from NIC manufacturers in precut lengths with the BNC connectors already attached. But most network installations require a huge diversity of lengths, and these components should be purchased separately in bulk. The minimum distance between BNC T-connectors is 1.5 feet or 0.5 meter.

Cost. The primary advantage of using the thin Ethernet topology design is the cost of the network components. If your entire network system can operate within the 3,035-foot cable limitation and your traffic requirements are light, this layout is most likely for you. Many different manufacturers produce thin Ethernet NICs, each offering its own mix of cost and performance trade-offs. In my experience, most reliable cards fall into the $150 to $250 range. Intel

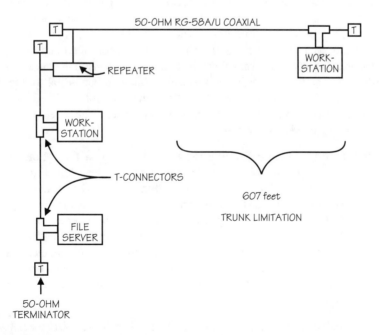

FIGURE 5.2 Topology Design for Thin Ethernet

Corporation manufactures an especially nice Ethernet NIC: EtherExpress. The EtherExpress NIC contains internal intelligence that allows it to easily conform to any unique workstation configuration.

Performance. All of the Ethernet designs run at 10 megabits per second (10 Mb/s). This throughput is relatively speedy when compared to the other designs, but it can also be somewhat misleading. The Ethernet protocol slows down dramatically when faced with heavy traffic. In some cases, the 10-Mb/s standard has been known to drop below 1 Mb/s. In addition, some have doubted the reliability of a CSMA/CD bus design over thin Ethernet cabling because of the lesser bandwidth in the coaxial trunk and the throughput sacrificed by having the transceiver on the NIC. All in all, though, thin Ethernet is a sound topology design for small, word-processing LANs. It is comparatively fast, easy to install, and doesn't cost an arm and a leg.

Thick Ethernet Bus

The thick Ethernet topology design differs from its thinner cousin in ways far beyond the diameter of the coaxial cabling trunk. The thick Ethernet standard represents a commitment to reliability and speed. Thick Ethernet also runs the CSMA/CD protocol on a BUS topology but requires the use of separate transceivers for the connection from NIC to trunk. In addition, the thick Ethernet design uses DIX (Digital/Intel/Xerox) connectors on the NIC instead of the clumsy BNC T-connectors. All these factors combine to create a fast, reliable Ethernet design with much better throughput in high load environments.

Components. Figure 5.3 describes the network topology components required for the installation of a thick Ethernet system. The NIC is exactly the same as the card used for thin Ethernet, but the internal transceiver is not used and the 15-pin DIX connector is used instead of the BNC T-connector. The 15-pin female DIX connector attaches to one end of a 10-, 50-, or 150-foot transceiver cable which in turn connects to the thick Ethernet external transceiver. The transceiver is an independent box that handles all of the trunk communications and fastens directly into the thick Ethernet cabling. The end of the trunk cabling run must be terminated with an N-series terminator. The other end of the cabling scheme must be grounded to the earth.

Topology/Protocol. Figure 5.4 illustrates the design of a thick Ethernet topology. Notice that the external transceivers are attached directly to the cabling trunk and interface with the workstation's NIC through a specialized transceiver cable. Also, the three trunk segments are connected through two Ethernet repeaters in exactly the same manner as with the thin Ethernet design. The cabling limitations of a thick Ethernet topology extend to 1,640 feet (500 meters) per segment with a total network cabling length of 8,200 feet or 2,500 meters. As with thin Ethernet, the maximum number of trunk segments is 5, but with the thicker design you can have up to 100 workstations per segment. The minimum distance between transceivers is 8 feet (2.5 meters), and the transceiver cable cannot exceed 164 feet or 50 meters.

Cabling. The thick Ethernet topology design uses 0.4-inch RG-8A/U specialized coaxial cabling. The transceiver cable is a distinctly different type of cabling and should be purchased precut with the DIX connectors already attached.

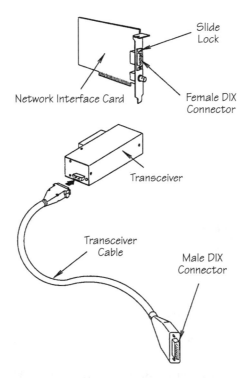

FIGURE 5.3   Topology Components for Thick Ethernet

Cost. Well, you didn't think you were going to get all of these great improvements for free, did you? The thick Ethernet topology design is not nearly as inexpensive as the thin Ethernet design, but it still offers the network designer a cost-effective solution. Additional costs include transceivers, N-type connectors, and DIX transceiver cables.

Performance. Thick Ethernet also runs at 10 megabits per second and has the same NIC throughput as the thin Ethernet design. But as I discussed earlier, the added functionality of an external transceiver and thicker cabling increases this topology's overall speed and reliability, especially in heavy traffic situations. In addition, the extended cabling distances and larger number of tolerated workstations allow the network designer to create a topology that can better handle interconnectivity and bridges to more complex systems. This added flexibility, along with Ethernet's place as a de facto standard within the networking industry, makes thick Ethernet the design choice of most large, interconnected wide area networks—Internet, for example.

Ethernet 10Base-T
With all of its successes as a network standard for speed, connectivity, and cost, Ethernet has fallen far short of the mark in one key category: existing cabling. A large number of network installations require the network designer to use existing cabling in an effort to avoid the many costs associated with pulling new wire. Nine-tenths of the time this existing cabling is not the type of coaxial cable required by both the thin and thick Ethernet

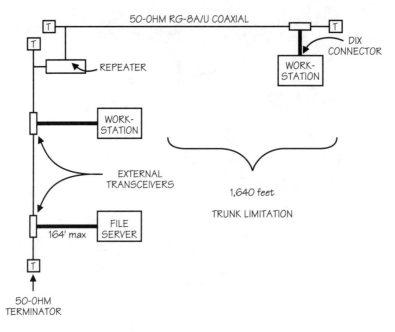

FIGURE 5.4   Topology Design for Thick Ethernet

topology designs. Nine-tenths of the time it's twisted-pair (UTP or STP). In these cases, the network designer is forced to look beyond Ethernet to a topology design that can operate on UTP or STP: ARCNet or Token Ring. A few years ago, the Ethernet community banded together and created a 10-Mb/s, CSMA/CD, star topology standard that runs very smoothly on UTP: Ethernet 10Base-T.

Recently, manufacturers have introduced Ethernet NICs that support all three topology standards. These versatile cards are equipped with three different ports: BNC, DIX, and RJ-45.

Components.   The Ethernet 10Base-T topology design is like a young child who has something of an image complex. The IEEE has only recently established it as a standard, and many of the early manufacturers differed in their approach to this unique design. The dust has settled now, though, and most 10Base-T manufacturers are standardizing on one way of doing things. The 10Base-T NIC contains an internal transceiver and RJ-45 twisted-pair connector. In some cases, the 10Base-T NIC does not have an RJ-45 connector and uses an AUI interface to an external 10Base-T transceiver. Either way, the 10Base-T RJ-45 plug connects into a twisted-pair hub that sits at the center of the star topology. The 10Base-T hub can connect up to 12 independent legs, each attaching to one workstation, for a maximum length of 328 feet or 100 meters.

Topology/Protocol.   The Ethernet 10Base-T topology uses the same CSMA/CD protocol as the other two Ethernet designs but differs in its fundamental cabling scheme.

10Base-T organizes its design into a star configuration, with each leg of twisted-pair cabling terminated at a workstation NIC or transceiver. Figure 5.5 demonstrates the 10Base-T star topology design. This blueprint requires approximately 300 percent more cabling than the other designs but greatly surpasses those designs in performance, versatility, and ease of maintenance. The Ethernet 10Base-T star configuration can be expanded by attaching two or more hubs together through internal AUI connectors. The maximum number of devices allowed on one network is 1,024.

Cabling. The beauty of Ethernet's 10Base-T design is that it can use a large variety of different twisted-pair cabling types and configurations. The problem with this concept is that most twisted-pair installations were made with telecommunications, not data communications, in mind. Refer to the cabling section of the chapter for more information about Ethernet 10Base-T installations that use existing UTP. If you have the luxury of installing your own twisted-pair cabling scheme from scratch, use 2 or 4 pairs of 24-AWG solid copper, low-capacitance unshielded or shielded wire. If you can afford it, use Teflon or plenum-coated cabling. These specialized cables are discussed later in the chapter.

Cost. Unfortunately, the high cost of 10Base-T hardware just about blows the money saved by using existing twisted-pair cabling. The standard 10Base-T NIC runs about the same as the earlier Ethernet designs: $100 to $200. The real cost in this design is the twisted-pair hub: It typically goes for between $800 and $1,200. The overhead costs associated with implementing a twisted-pair 10Base-T topology are a little higher than the standard Ethernet design, but the added cabling flexibility and increased performance are improvements that more than justify the additional expenditure.

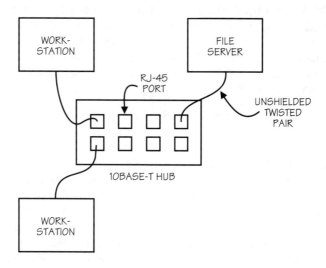

FIGURE 5.5   Topology Design for Ethernet 10Base-T

Performance. The Ethernet 10Base-T topology also operates at 10 megabits per second and has proven to handle heavy traffic situations much better than the standard Ethernet design. This increased level of network throughput can be attributed to the star topology and centralized twisted-pair hub. These topology elements combine to route Ethernet packets much more effectively and efficiently than the traditional bus design. In addition, the star layout allows the network manager to quickly isolate bad cabling legs and repair them without bringing down the entire network. This topology maintains the same connectivity advantages as the standard Ethernet, and network designers have recently found it to be a good, low-cost solution for medium to large-sized LANs.

ARCNet

The ARCNet topology design was created in 1977 at the Datapoint Corporation by a scientist named John Murphy. ARCNet stands for Attached Resource Computer Network. This topology scheme predates the token-passing standards as adopted by IBM and others, but uses very much the same technology. ARCNet does not offer the same overall connectivity as Ethernet, but its hardware components are sufficiently standardized so that any ARCNet device from any manufacturer can be used on any other ARCNet LAN. Over 100 manufacturers currently produce ARCNet components, among them notables such as Standard Microsystems Corporation, Novell, Thomas Conrad, Network Innovations, Black Box, Tiara, and Earth. ARCNet uses the token-passing protocol over a distributed star topology. Currently, it runs at 2.5 Mb/s, but ARCNet Plus NICs are in the works that are said to run at 20 Mb/s. ARCNet components are less expensive than Ethernet devices, and the topology design is more reliable. The two advantages Ethernet has over ARCNet are connectivity and speed, although the latter may be misleading.

ARCNet Star

The ARCNet standard uses a distributed star topology. This topology uses active and passive hubs for the routing and control of tokens as they move from one workstation to the next. The star topology can operate on either coaxial or twisted-pair cabling, but the most reliable design calls for 93-ohm coaxial cabling and low-impedance NICs. The ARCNet star is similar to 10Base-T in design, but offers additional functionality by distributing the hubs throughout the ARCNet layout.

Components. The ARCNet distributed star design uses three unique hardware components: low-impedance boards, active hubs, and passive hubs. Figure 5.6 details these components along with their supporting connectors. The low-impedance board performs a dual function with its internal NIC capability and an added low-impedance transceiver. The internal transceiver allows the board to generate a data "token" strong enough to travel 2,000 feet (609.6 meters) to an active hub over 93-ohm coaxial cabling. This distance limitation is significantly decreased when the accepting device is a passive hub at 100 feet or 30.5 meters. The passive hub is a signal splitter that allows the network designer to create distributed mini stars of three workstations at the end of each active leg. The file server must always be attached directly to an active hub, and the central anchoring device must also be an active hub.

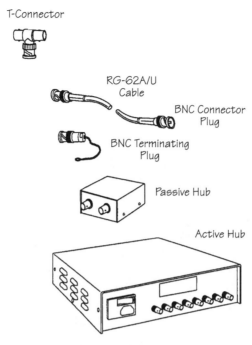

FIGURE 5.6   Topology Components for ARCNet

Topology/Protocol.   Figure 5.7 illustrates how the low-impedance boards, active hubs, and passive hubs all combine to create a distributed star topology. Notice how the active hub is used as the central star anchor, and the passive hub is distributed among the workstations. Active hubs can be linked together to create a more evenly distributed topology. This design has many advantages in speed, reliability, maintenance, and troubleshooting.

It's important, though, to keep within the distance limitations of 2,000 feet to active hubs and 100 feet to passive hubs. The entire network from one end to the other cannot exceed 20,000 feet or 6,096 meters. Other rules of thumb:

- Do not connect passive hubs together.
- Do not create a closed ring of hubs.
- Terminate all unused ports on passive hubs.
- Add file servers, bridges, and gateways to active hubs only.

The ARCNet token-passing protocol has many advantages in its capacity to handle heavy traffic situations. ARCNet is said to get faster as the network load increases. (Sounds a little far-fetched to me.) In any case, it is proven that ARCNet token-passing topologies do not slow down in heavy traffic environments; Ethernet definitely does. The token-passing protocol operates as a logical ring with the data token being passed from node to node in an organized manner. The ring itself contains many levels of system fault tolerance: ring maintenance and initialization at each node, lost token recovery, and effortless LAN reconfiguration once workstations are added or removed.

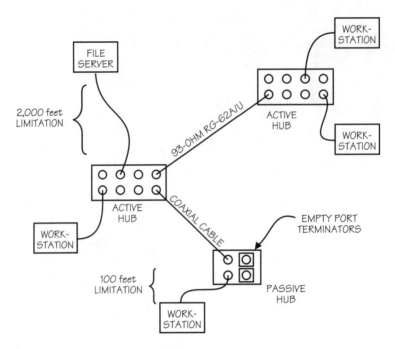

FIGURE 5.7   Topology Design for ARCNet

Cabling. The ARCNet star topology design can operate on coaxial or twisted-pair cabling. The preferred choice is RG-62A/U 93-ohm coaxial cable, because it allows much longer distances between devices and includes an inherently superior level of stability in heavy traffic environments. Twisted-pair cabling is supported and works quite well in small LANs. ARCNet over twisted-pair requires one pair of unshielded or shielded 24-AWG solid copper, low-capacitance wire. The distance between active twisted-pair hubs and workstations is limited to 400 feet or 121.9 meters. You cannot use passive hubs on a twisted-pair ARCNet topology. Be cautious when using existing UTP or STP cabling for ARCNet designs, because sometimes it's hard to tell how far the cable is actually running in the wall. It could appear to be well within the distance limitations, but with loopbacks and rerouting the actual distance may exceed 400 feet.

Cost. All things considered, the ARCNet star topology design is a cost-effective choice for medium-sized networks with medium to heavy load requirements. The ARCNet low-impedance NICs run about $245 each for coaxial cabling and $295 for twisted-pair. Faster and more advanced cards can be purchased for up to $700. Passive hubs are relatively inexpensive at $69 each. They come standard with 4 ports, 1 in and 3 out. Active hubs come in two flavors: 8 ports at $549 and 20 ports at $1,780. Twisted-pair hubs are active by design and contain 8 RJ-11 ports for $750.

Performance. The many advantages of the token-passing protocol give the ARCNet design a few distinct advantages compared with Ethernet. One principal advantage is the lack of packet collisions with the ARCNet star. The organized distribution of tokens over a logical ring furnishes ARCNet with the reliability and stability required in heavy traffic situations. The token-passing protocol is substantially slower than CSMA/CD, but ARCNet systems are in the works that will run at speeds twice as fast as does Ethernet. In addition, the ARCNet star topology has the advantages of maintenance, troubleshooting, and fault-tolerance that give it a further edge over the Ethernet bus design.

Note: There are a few new ARCNet devices that have been created to further enhance the performance and reliability of this topology design. A few of the most exciting are these:

- Intelligent hubs: active hubs with internal network management software.
- Hub cards: a 4-port active or twisted-pair hub on a card. It plugs into a workstation.
- Nodal priority cards: boards that plug into the file server and provide 25 percent more access to passing tokens.

Token Ring

The Token Ring topology standard uses token-passing protocol to transmit network messages over a ring topology. IBM developed the Token Ring design and continues to greatly influence the introduction of improvements to this standard. Even though a number of manufacturers currently produce Token Ring components, IBM pretty much owns this market and relies heavily on it for the introduction of IBM equipment into smaller offices. A few companies have developed proprietary variations on the Token Ring standard: Proteon, NCR, Thomas Conrad, Western Digital, and Black Box. Even though these manufacturers claim to have improved IBM's standard design, the majority of network designers prefer to go with IBM's Token Ring design because it has one thing these others will probably never have: IBM connectivity. Any IBM Token Ring network can easily attach to any of IBM's other computing products, including minicomputers and mainframes.

The Token Ring standard is very fast (4 or 16 Mb/s), very reliable (by using token-passing protocol), very durable (with its ring topology), and very proprietary. Once you choose to enter the Token Ring arena, you must stay with one particular manufacturer. Ethernet and ARCNet, on the other hand, are sufficiently standardized to allow for crossover from one manufacturer to another. The proprietary nature of Token Ring makes it more expensive.

The Token Ring topology design looks similar to the physical star of ARCNet and transfers data tokens in the same manner: a logical ring. The difference with Token Ring is that all of the central hubs are connected together in a physical ring by running patch cables to specialized ring-in and ring-out ports. This configuration creates a ring of hubs, thus the term *Token Ring*. All Token Ring components use a specialized cabling scheme that was standardized by IBM. The cables are typically shielded twisted-pair housed in a PVC-coated jacket with strange IBM-type connectors—hermaphroditic. It is nearly impossible to avoid IBM when an installation uses the Token Ring design.

Components. Figure 5.8 illustrates the standard Token Ring components as introduced by IBM. The 16/4 adapter is a specialized NIC that can run at either 16 or 4 Mb/s. All NICs

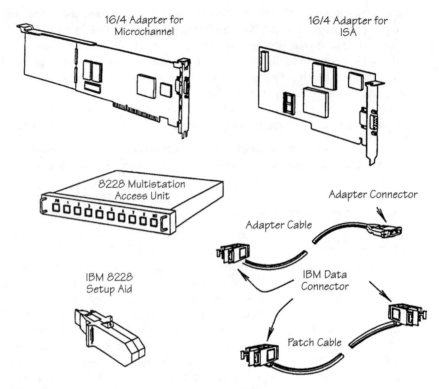

FIGURE 5.8   Topology Components for Token Ring

in the ring must run at the same speed. The 16/4 adapter/A is a specific NIC for use in IBM PS/2 Microchannel computers. At the core of the Token Ring topology is the MSAU (Multistation Access Unit). The MSAU is the centralized network hub that connects up to 8 workstations in a physical star configuration. Multiple MSAUs are attached in a ring of hubs through IBM patch cables and specialized ring-in and ring-out receptacles.

IBM has introduced a new internetworking protocol called *Source Routing*. This token direction protocol enhances Token Ring's interconnectivity to larger networks by monitoring token paths through bridges and gateways. The source node is responsible for communication integrity and token routing.

Topology/Protocol.   The Token Ring topology represents an integration of the best characteristics of all the other network designs. It has the most reliable protocol (token-passing), the most trouble-free configuration (physical star), and the fastest connectivity scheme (ring of hubs). Figure 5.9 illustrates how these three components merge to create a superior LAN topology design. The largest Token Ring network can have up to 96 workstations and 12 MSAUs. The MSAUs cannot extend more than 150 feet (45 meters) from

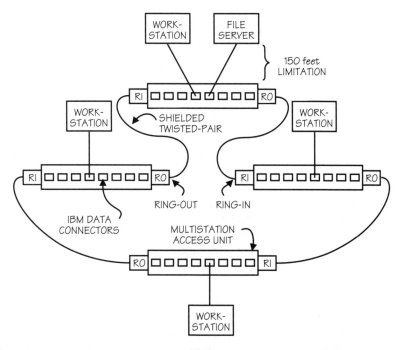

FIGURE 5.9   Topology Design for Token Ring

each other or from a workstation. The ring of hubs is limited to 400 feet (120 meters) in total cable length. In order to ensure a fast and stable design, it is imperative that you follow a few more Token Ring rules:

- Do not splice patch cables.
- IBM Type 6 cabling is very susceptible to electromagnetic noise, heat, office floors, and air-conditioning ducts. Avoid these hazards in a Token Ring environment.
- Adhere to legal restrictions regarding PVC- or plenum-coated cabling.
- The ring of hubs must be a closed loop.

Cabling.   The standard cabling scheme for Token Ring topologies was introduced by IBM and bears its name. This cabling scheme specifies five different types of Token Ring cabling. Refer to the cabling section of this chapter for details on IBM-type cabling.

Most Token Ring networks use IBM Type 1 patch cables for long distances and IBM Type 6 cabling for shorter distances and adapter cables. All of these cables are terminated with proprietary IBM data connectors. It is important to follow cable installation instructions closely when you design a Token Ring LAN. IBM-type cabling and data connectors can be finicky and fragile during installation. Be careful.

Cost.   You'd better sit down for this one. IBM has never been known for its introduction of cost-effective components. The company's pricing theory seems to be, "Great Technology— regardless of cost!" The Token Ring topology design is expensive no matter how you slice it—partially because of its proprietary nature and partially because it is such a dominant design. Token Ring NICs typically go for around $595—more if you want the 16/4 technology. The Token Ring MSAUs each house 8 workstation ports and 2 in/out receptacles. They usually go for about $795. The IBM-type data connectors are a whopping $16 each, with 8-foot adapter and patch cables going for around $47. Even the wall plates are expensive at $3.75 each. The Token Ring topology design is going to cost you, but if you compare it with the cost of network slowdowns and downtime, you may be getting a long-term bargain.

Performance. The Token Ring standard is without a doubt the strongest and most commanding of all the network topology designs. It integrates the best of all the other standards, and crosses network bridges and gateways smoothly. Token Ring is the de facto standard for large corporations that run heavy traffic on a variety of IBM machines. But it can also be the choice of a smaller company that cannot tolerate network downtime or sluggish data switching. Remember, though, that Token Ring is expensive. It is not for everybody. Although there are times when the costs can be justified, most of the time they cannot. Ethernet and ARCNet offer the network designer a great variety of alternatives at a fraction of the cost.

Other Networks

The Ethernet, ARCNet, and Token Ring topology designs represent about 95 percent of all installed NetWare LANs. These three standards cover all conceivable combinations of cabling architecture, hardware topology, and communications protocol. There are a few specialized applications, though, that cannot be satisfied by one of these three designs. At the forefront of these specialized applications are three popular network designs: IBM PC LAN, G/Net, and LocalTalk.

IBM PC LAN

This specialized topology design targets small, inexpensive networks that require high levels of IBM connectivity. The IBM PC LAN is a CSMA/CD design over bus topology and offers few of the advanced features of the standard Ethernet design. IBM PC LAN comes in two flavors: broadband and baseband. IBM's broadband design operates on broadband coaxial cabling organized into a tree topology. The transmission rate is around 2 Mb/s, and it can handle up to 72 workstations on one network. The baseband design operates on baseband twisted-pair cabling organized into a daisy-chain or star topology. The transmission rate is also 2 Mb/s, but baseband can only handle 8 workstations per network without an extender. With an extender, baseband can handle up to 80 workstations.

G/Net

The G/Net topology is a specialized networking design from Gateway Communications, Inc. It also targets small, inexpensive LANs but offers more cabling simplicity than the IBM PC LAN. G/Net is very similar to Ethernet in its use of trunk cabling and T-connectors. G/Net differs from Ethernet in that it operates via CSMA/Collision-Avoidance communications protocol, not CSMA/CD. G/Net runs at about 1.43 Mb/s, but starts to slow down considerably once the total number of workstations climb above 20. The G/Net cabling scheme is a bus topology over RG-58/U (50-ohm), RG-59/U (75-ohm), or RG-62A/U (93-ohm) coaxial cabling. G/Net NICs, or Network Interface Modules (NIMs), are very inexpensive and quite reliable under light loads.

LocalTalk

With the rising popularity of Apple's Macintosh line, an effort has been made in the networking community to accommodate the Mac's unique design. All Apple computers come equipped with an internal networking standard called LocalTalk. LocalTalk operates on a bus or tree topology at a transmission rate of about 230.4 kilobits per second, or 0.23 Mb/s. This standard uses a protocol similar to CSMA/CA called AppleTalk. AppleTalk is composed of four subprotocols: ALAP (AppleTalk Link Access Protocol), DDP (Datagram Delivery Protocol), ATP (AppleTalk Transaction Protocol), and ASP (AppleTalk Session Protocol). LocalTalk runs on unshielded twisted-pair cabling that connects to proprietary connectors on the back of each Macintosh. The specialized LocalTalk connector is part of an internal NIC that is produced at the factory and combined with the standard motherboard.

An additional Macintosh topology design is EtherTalk. EtherTalk is a new Ethernet application of the LocalTalk standard. EtherTalk NICs plug into high-end Macintosh workstations and offer 10Mb/s connectivity throughout traditional Ethernet LANs.

Cabling

Cabling is a critical LAN component. Decisions made here will make or break the most well-considered network design. Cabling directly affects the overall performance and reliability of the network. In fact, more network problems are caused by cabling than by any other single component. Cabling decisions play an important role in choosing a LAN topology. Investigate the cabling media: how will each potential solution meet operational needs?

- Ethernet and ARCNet both support UTP, STP, coaxial, and fiber optic cabling.
- Token Ring has become more versatile and now supports UTP, STP, and fiber optic cabling.

Each of these cabling choices has advantages and disadvantages. Each has a niche for which it is especially suited. It is your job as the network designer to match the correct medium to the mix of people and performance.

Currently there are four cabling media specially suited for local area networks: UTP, STP, coaxial, and fiber optic. In addition, there are seven expanded communications media that are specially suited for wide area networks: infrared, laser, microwave, satellite, radio, PSTN, and T-1. This section details the advantages and disadvantages of each of the LAN media, then discusses the feasibility of expansion through WAN communications.

Local Area Networking Media

The term *local area network* implies a communications scheme within a tight geographic zone. LAN media are produced with this idea in mind: The distance limitation of the medium is at best three miles (for fiber optic cabling). LANs use true cabling—that is, communications channels housed within a physical wire or fiber. This property has advantages in security, reliability, and speed. LAN media consist of UTP, STP, coaxial, and fiber optic.

Regardless of which LAN medium you select, you will have to consider installation costs. This is the largest single cost of cabling a LAN. Take some time to look at the actual costs associated with installing LAN media. The heavier cabling (thick Ethernet and IBM-type cabling) is less easily handled and therefore, more labor intensive. Fiber optic cabling, on the other hand, installs like lighter copper media. It is essentially the same size and weight as UTP and coaxial cabling. Lighter media are well-understood and very easy to install. Let's take a detailed look at each of the four LAN media.

UTP

Unshielded twisted-pair (UTP) cabling comes in two distinct flavors: *voice grade* (sometimes referred to as *D grade*) and *data grade*. Most LAN protocols require the use of data grade UTP. Data grade UTP comes in specific levels. Its level rating scheme refers to conductor size, electrical characteristics, and twists per foot. Nothing lower than level 3 should be considered for high-speed network installations. LAN grade UTP starts at level 3 and escalates through level 5. The higher the level, the greater the LAN characteristics of the medium—its speed, reliability, and expansion capabilities.

LAN grade UTP is made up of four or eight solid copper wires that are twisted together—hence the term *twisted-pair*. Twisting reduces susceptibility to crosstalk and electromagnetic interference (EMI). A UTP cable that contains four conductors is referred to as *2 pair wire*. All of the topology designs that support UTP require at least four conductors, or 2 pair. Spare pair nodes are inexpensive insurance for future growth. However, you should never use these spare pairs for anything other than network communications. Never mix data communications and telecommunications in the same UTP cable.

Fire and Building Codes. UTP conductors are contained within a jacket of either polyvinyl chloride (PVC) or plenum (Teflon and Halar). PVC is a dangerous cabling jacket; it releases lethal chlorine gas if burned. Plenum is a safe alternative to PVC; unfortunately, it is expensive. The physical location of the cabling dictates which jacket you should use. PVC cabling is limited to conduit piping or floor ducts only. Plenum, on the other hand, can be installed loosely throughout walls, ceilings, and floors. Either way, you should never install low-voltage network cable in conduits or floor ducts that contain electrical wiring. Some general rules of thumb:

- Don't assume that conduits or ducts are available; check out all cabling paths prior to installation.
- Don't assume that local fire and building codes allow PVC in conduits. Some communities outlaw PVC altogether.

Electrical Characteristics. The size of the individual conductors is measured according to the American Wire Gauge, or AWG. The standard AWG measurement for LAN cabling is 22 AWG to 24 AWG. The higher the number, the smaller the diameter of the conductor. Typically, higher data transmission rates require larger gauge (22 AWG) or a conductor with more efficient electrical characteristics.

The National Electronics Manufacturers Association (NEMA) has developed a series of cabling levels that describe varying degrees of electrical standardization. These measurements currently run from level 1 to level 5; the higher the number, the better the cable. Low-speed topology standards can operate over voice grade media (levels 1 or 2). These topologies include LocalTalk, ARCNet, and IBM PC LAN. If you must make use of existing telephone wire, these are the topology standards you should consider. Level 1 and 2 UTP can be purchased for $0.04 to $0.05 per foot (PVC) or $0.09 to $0.10 per foot (plenum). You can purchase level 3 UTP for $0.07 to $0.08 per foot (PVC) or $0.13 to $0.14 per foot (plenum). The difference in cost is greatly outweighed by the increase in performance.

The minimum UTP required for high-speed LAN applications is level 3. Level 3 media are classified as low loss but not extended frequency. Level 3 UTP has debatable capability to support advanced 16 Mb/s Token Ring loads. Level 4 has improved electrical characteristics, specifically in the higher frequency ranges. It also has more tightly twisted pairs for improved crosstalk protection. You should be able to find Level 4 cabling for $0.12 to $0.17 per foot (PVC) or $0.25 to $0.28 per foot (plenum). Level 5 is the top-rated UTP standard. This is the medium of choice for current and future high-speed standards (of 20 Mb/s to 100 Mb/s). Level 5 is low-loss extended frequency cabling, priced from $0.18 to $0.21 per foot (PVC) and $0.35 to $0.42 per foot (plenum).

In selecting UTP, you should concern yourself with three basic electrical characteristics: attenuation, capacitance, and crosstalk.

- *Attenuation.* Attenuation describes the reduction in amplitude of a communications signal as it is transmitted across UTP media. Attenuation directly affects the ability of the NIC to distinguish between a real signal and meaningless EMI noise. Typically this specification is presented as the db (decibel) loss at a specific frequency over 100 or 1,000 feet. Example: 3.0 db @ 1,000 feet @ 16 MHz.
- *Capacitance.* Capacitance is the measure of a cable's ability to store electrical charge and withstand changes in voltage. These changes in voltage produce the digital signals that are transmitted from NIC to NIC. Unacceptably high levels of capacitance can distort digital transmissions and prevent the NIC from understanding the signal. Capacitance is measured in pf' or pico farads per foot. A typical cable measurement would look like this—18 pf'—read as 18 pico farads per foot.
- *Crosstalk.* Crosstalk is the condition of signal reduction due to EMI from other conductors. Crosstalk is exactly what its name implies: the crossing of signal from one conductor or pair of conductors to another. It is always preferable to isolate data cabling from other cabling such as telephone, alarm, or power cables to minimize crosstalk.

STP

Shielded twisted-pair (STP) is identical in every facet to UTP, except for one: STP provides a protective shielding. The shield is usually aluminum/polyester located between the outer jacket and the central conductors. The addition of the protective shielding makes STP a more robust cable for extreme LAN environments. The shielding isolates the conductors from EMI. In order for the STP shielding to be effective, it must be grounded. Grounding should be performed at only one end of a cable run. The ground should be isolated to assure that it doesn't also introduce foreign signals to the media.

STP is available in 2, 3, or 4 pairs, both PVC and plenum-coated. STP cabling is also more expensive than UTP. You can expect to pay $0.20 to $0.23 per foot (PVC) or $0.52 per foot (plenum) for level 4 STP. You should use level 4 regardless of your protocol speed when you determine the installation requires shielded media. Level 5 cable in a shielded configuration is just now being introduced on the market.

IBM-type STP. Until recently, IBM has stipulated that IBM Token Ring products would only operate reliably on IBM-type cabling. Other Token Ring manufacturers suggest otherwise and have proven that Token Ring LANs can operate reliably over non-IBM-type STP. Nonetheless, it is important to differentiate IBM-type cabling from standard STP.

- Type 1, the most common STP, consists of 2 twisted pairs of 22-AWG solid copper, shielded with a T-screen foil and braided shield. PVC Type 1 costs $0.42 per foot, and the plenum medium costs $1.15.
- Type 2, a combination data and telephone cable, consists of 2 twisted pairs of 22-AWG solid conductors for LAN and an additional 4 pairs of 22 AWG for telephone. Type 2 costs $0.65 per foot (PVC) or $1.48 per foot (plenum).
- Type 3 is essentially level 3 unshielded twisted-pair cable.
- Type 5, a fiber optic cable, contains two 100/140 micron optical fibers.
- Type 6, a more supple version of Type 1, is used to cross connect patch panels between adjacent MSAUs. Type 6 uses 2 pairs of lighter 26-AWG stranded (not solid) conductors with a braided shield and a PVC jacket. Type 6 cables are usually purchased as prefabricated patch cables or in bulk at $0.41 per foot.
- Type 8, a special flat cable designed to be installed under carpets, has a maximum thickness of 0.090 inch. Type 8 cabling consists of four conductors of 26 AWG that run parallel to each other. This cable costs like gold at $4 per foot.
- Type 9, the smallest IBM-type medium, has an outer diameter of 0.210 inch nominal. Type 9 uses 2 pairs of 26-AWG solid conductors, individually shielded with aluminum foil and a braid of tinned copper. This cable is plenum-coated at $0.70 per foot.

Coaxial Cabling

Coaxial cabling, commonly known as "coax," gets its name from its two conductors that run down the same axis. The inner conductor is 20- to 21-AWG solid copper or sometimes stranded wire. Stranded wire can withstand tighter bends without breaking. The central conductor is encased in one of three kinds of insulating material: foam, PVC, or Teflon. This insulation helps to isolate the central conductor from the outer braided conductor. The central core wire, insulation, and foil shield is then further encased in a braided conductor or outer shield. The jacket can be either polyvinyl chloride (PVC) or plenum.

Coax is measured by the same electrical characteristics as UTP, and has comparatively more capability with respect to capacitance and attenuation. A level rating scheme is not used with coaxial cables; instead, the cable is rated for impedance. *Impedance* is an electrical measurement of the cable's opposition to signal flow. The workstation NIC and the coaxial cabling must have matching impedance values. Ethernet requires a 50-ohm cable, whereas ARCNet and broadband Ethernet run at 93-ohm impedance.

Coaxial cable can support much higher transmission rates than UTP or STP—up to 100 megabits per second. Coax costs more as well. Thin Ethernet coax is RG-58 50-ohm PVC at $0.27 to $0.37 per foot, and RG-58 50-ohm plenum at $0.46 to $0.78 per foot. ARCNet coax is RG-62 93-ohm PVC at $0.18 to $0.40 per foot, and RG-62 93-ohm plenum at $0.64 to $0.74 per foot. Thick Ethernet coax is RG-8 and RG-11 at $1.60 to $1.90 per foot (PVC) and $2.20 to $2.50 per foot (plenum).

RG-59 75-ohm coaxial cabling is used for cable TV and is not suitable for LAN communications.

Fiber Optic

Fiber optic technology is the future of network cabling. Ethernet star, ARCNet star, and Token Ring all support fiber optic media. Fiber optic cabling is comparable in cost to STP and Thick Ethernet coax, dispelling the myth that fiber optic is too expensive. Fiber optic is the most reliable of all LAN media, and interconnectivity between fiber devices is ensured by an American National Standards Institute (ANSI) committee. ANSI has developed a set of fiber optic standards that govern token-passing communications at 100 Mb/s: the Fiber Distributed Data Interface (FDDI). Ethernet has three fiber optic standards: FOIRL, 10Base-FA, and 10Base-FP. FOIRL stands for Fiber Optic Inter Repeater Link. FOIRL describes a point-to-point protocol to connect Ethernet LANs over great distances. 10Base-FA is similar to the Ethernet 10Base-T standard: 10Mb/s, CSMA protocol over a star topology. The FA represents the centralized fiber active hub. 10Base-FP is unique and takes advantage of the properties of light. The FP designates a fiber passive optical hub that consists of multiple glass tubes fused together to distribute a light signal to each node. The Token Ring optical standard is controlled by IEEE's 802.5J standard and supports both 4 Mb/s and 16 Mb/s. The ARCNet standard is supported without additional acronyms or sub committees.

Fiber optic cabling consists of very fine fibers of glass. In the not-too-distant future, we will most likely see plastic fiber optic cable. The "secret" of fiber optic technology is really quite simple. Each fiber cable consists of a light-conducting inner core of glass. This fiber conductor actually has two parts: an inner glass cylindrical core and an outer concentric glass cladding. The cladding is reflective and acts as a container for the light signal as it travels through the cable. Think of the cladding as a cylindrical mirror surrounding the inner core. The inner core is very pure and transparent. The purity level required for fiber optics is the current stumbling block for plastic media. The inner core glass is composed of pure silicon dioxide (SiO_2) and wrapped in Kevlar, a material used to construct bulletproof vests. Multiple cores are typically bundled in a PVC or plenum jacket.

Fiber optic cabling is measured by the diameter of the core fiber. Most LAN components use 62.5-micron fiber (one matching the diameter of a human hair). The transmission of light through these miniature fibers is accomplished in one of three types of cable: single mode, step-index multimode, or graded-index multimode. The single mode medium is the most expensive fiber cabling because of its incredibly small core of 7 to 9 microns (1/300 inch). Single mode is used for WAN communications that cover long distances and require high speeds. The step-index multimode medium was primarily used in early fiber installations. Currently, the graded-index multimode medium is the most popular fiber optic LAN cabling. The graded-index type uses an enhanced cladding that reduces reflectance in the fiber core. Fiber optic cabling is relatively inexpensive at roughly $0.50 per foot. The current cost factor in fiber optic technology is not the cabling but the networking components—NICs, hubs, and fiber optic modems (FOMs), which cost 1,000 percent more than electronic components.

Table 5.2 summarizes the trade-offs among cable types.

Advantages and Disadvantages of LAN Media

Twisted-pair media share the advantages of being low cost, well-understood technologies. Both offer flexible configurations and conventional telephone style terminations, except for IBM Type cabling. Disadvantages for both UTP and STP include distance limitations, insecurity, and eavesdropping. IBM-type cables are large and heavy, making for more costly and difficult installations. Coaxial media offer higher data rates, greater distances, and high EMI protection. The downside to coax is its more difficult installation procedure and noncompatibility among different impedance cables. Coax is more secure than twisted-pair media, but not impervious to eavesdropping. Fiber optic cabling offers speed, reliability, and EMI protection. The fiber optic medium provides the highest level of security and connectivity across multiple protocols. Fiber optic cable installation, however, requires precise quality control.

Wide Area Networking Media

The term *wide area network* implies a communications scheme beyond geographical boundaries. WAN communications media must be able to extend beyond buildings, cities, and even countries. Of the seven WAN media discussed here, only two are physical cabling: PSTN (Public Switched Telephone Network) and T-1. Incidentally, both are more accurately described as protocols, not media.

The majority of the WAN channels use the characteristics of unbound communications. Unbound WAN media include infrared, laser, terrestrial microwave, satellite, and radio. These media accomplish the task of communications without electrical or optical

TABLE 5.2   Comparing Features of LAN Media

Cable Medium	Low Cost	High Security	High Bandwidth	Flexible Installation	Greater Distance	High Reliability
UTP	X				X	
STP						X
Coax	X		X	X	X	X
Fiber Optic		X	X		X	X

conductors. The lack of physical restrictions provides larger bandwidths as well as wide area capabilities. These properties make it possible for geographically distributed LANs to communicate with one another on a "real-time" basis. WAN media are expensive and complex, but compared to the alternative—nothing—they are easily manageable. WAN media will continue to grow in popularity as LANs proliferate and interconnectivity becomes commonplace.

Table 5.3 lists the strengths and weaknesses of WAN media.

Infrared

Infrared (IR) is a child in WAN communications. IR uses LEDs, ILDs, and photodiodes to exchange digital signals. IR has similarities to bounded fiber optics without using cable. We use IR communications every day to operate TV remote controls. IR communications are best suited for attaching LANs that are less than a mile apart. IR transmissions are sent from a transmitter across a thin beam of infrared energy to a receiving station. IR signals travel in a straight line and are classified as *line of sight*. This means that no obstructions can break the plane between the sender and receiver. IR energy can be reflected off mirrors mounted on walls and ceilings to circumvent the straight-line properties of this medium.

IR doesn't require an FCC license to use, and it promises WAN transmission speeds around 10 Mb/s. Unfortunately, IR is susceptible to adverse weather conditions, including fog, rain, and snow, and birds. Even though these natural phenomena don't actually break the beam, they absorb (attenuate) the IR energy and affect the signal's strength and integrity.

Laser

A communications laser transmits data over a narrow beam of coherent light. This light beam is usually infrared energy that is modulated into digital pulses. The modulated beam is captured by photodiodes and translated into traditional electrical digital signals. Lasers are also line-of-sight devices and are extremely directional: Sending and receiving elements must be precisely aligned.

Major advantages of this medium are its use of high frequency light energy. Like bound fiber optics, lasers are capable of extended bandwidths and correspondingly high data transmission speeds. No FCC license is required to construct such a system, and, like the glass in fiber optic cabling, lasers are highly resistant to interference, jamming, and

Table 5.3 Comparing Features of WAN Media

WAN Medium	Low Cost	High Security	High Bandwidth	Flexible Installation	Greater Distance	High Reliability
Infrared	X				X	
Laser		X	X	X		
Microwave			X		X	
Satellite		X	X		X	X
Radio	X			X		
PSTN	X				X	X
T-1		X	X			X

eavesdropping. However, lasers *are* sensitive to attenuation from rain, fog, and other degraded atmospheric conditions.

Microwave

There are two forms of microwave transmission: terrestrial (earth-based) and space (satellite-based). We will describe terrestrial microwaves here and move on to satellite communications in the next section. Microwave communications extend the geographical boundaries of your WAN up to 50 miles. Microwave relay towers (MRT) extend WAN communications by regenerating the signal and sending it off to another MRT 50 miles away. Earth-based transmissions are commonly in the low-gigahertz frequency ranges and are line of sight. Microwaves are sent from a parabolic "sending" antenna as specific very high frequency radio waves to a similar parabolic "receiving" antenna. This arrangement is referred to as a microwave link. Microwave links are best suited for midrange connections where cabling installation is too difficult or expensive. Microwaves have large bandwidths and send data quite reliably. Higher-frequency microwaves travel shorter distances and experience signal reduction in rain and fog. This is a normal property of all radio frequency communications.

In discussing radio waves, we refer to propagation properties as the medium's ability to carry a signal forward. As frequency increases, the signal becomes more directional and range decreases proportionally. Like all radio frequencies, microwaves propagate farther across water. Note that higher frequency microwaves use smaller, less-expensive antennas. High frequency microwave is reserved for short-haul systems—hops between buildings or across campus facilities. The FCC requires licensing of microwave systems. This process can prove to be time consuming and expensive.

Satellite

The most spectacular advancement in data communications has been the development of satellite transmissions. This WAN medium virtually opens the entire globe to your network. Like terrestrial microwaves, satellite microwave links use low-gigahertz (4- to 30-GHz) microwaves. These transmissions use essentially the same properties as terrestrial microwave and are also line of sight. However, satellite signals travel much longer distances; they are beamed from earth stations known as *uplinks* to a geosynchronous satellite and back down to another earth station called a *downlink*. The satellite's geosynchronous orbit positions it 22,300 miles above the equator in a fixed location. Uplink and downlink stations use different frequencies so as not to interfere with each other's transmission. Earth stations are usually fixed structures, but they can be mobile on aircraft, marine vessels, or land vehicles.

Satellites offer very good throughput; however, uplink and downlink delays dramatically decrease performance. Currently, there are over 20 commercial communication satellites in orbit, providing hundreds of voice, data, and television channels. The implementation of NetWare-based satellite communications requires complex telecommunications equipment and one or more gateway machines.

Radio

Terrestrial and satellite microwave transmissions use very high frequency radio signals. Radio transmission, on the other hand, uses midrange frequencies of 3 MHz to 3,000 MHz.

Radio transmissions referred to as RF (radio frequency) use omnidirectional broadcasts to send signals in a 360-degree wave pattern. Radio equipment is mobile, flexible, and relatively inexpensive. These devices can be placed on a variety of different land, air, and water vehicles. Cellular radio offers the benefits of wireless portability with the range of traditional dial-up telephone lines. All radio systems, except cellular radio, require an FCC license and are susceptible to interference from EMI and atmospheric conditions.

PSTN

The Public Switched Telephone Network (PSTN), as do all telephone networks, represents perhaps some of the world's largest WANs and offer vast connectivity to any location serviced domestically or internationally by phone lines. The PSTN is configured as a hierarchical star topology using up to five levels. The focus here is not to make you an expert on this expansive WAN medium but to introduce the basic PSTN concepts and terminologies.

PSTN is a viable WAN alternative that is often overlooked. This is how it works. The NIC connection is typically made to an RJ-style wall jack that runs back to a telephone closet. Network managers are responsible for this segment. At the telephone closet, circuits are cross connected to a Demarc (demarcation point) provided by the phone company. The Demarc designates the point where the telephone company's lines intersect with your building. This is where the local loop begins. The local loop consists of multiple pairs of UTP that run from the Demarc to the central office (CO). The CO is a fortress that houses an organized mass of wire terminations from many different local loops. There are about 20,000 COs in the United States alone. The major purpose of the CO is to switch calls from incoming loops to outgoing trunks; hence the term Public Switched Telephone Network.

Trunk lines connect COs. They are multichannel broadband circuits that use frequency division multiplexing to carry thousands of simultaneous transmissions. Voice-grade trunks are filtered to limit bandwidth to 3,000 Hz. This filtering causes attenuation and distortion of digital signals and limits the practicality of high-speed transmissions. High-speed data communications max out at 14,400 bps. Digital lines are conditioned differently and provide much higher bandwidths and reliability. We will discuss digital lines in the next segment.

Think of PSTN as a hierarchical network. This system has built-in flexibility and can route calls in a very efficient manner. This medium offers a simple, cost-effective solution for remote site connectivity. For real-time connectivity to multiple remote sites, you may want to consider a digital line such as T-1.

T-1

T-1 is a WAN protocol. T-1 is a dedicated, not switched, digital circuit. Dedicated circuits connect a workstation NIC directly to the long distance carrier, bypassing the local CO. T-1 operates as a digital signal level 1 (DS-1) using standard phone lines and transmission equipment. T-1 transmits data at a rate of 1.544 megabits per second. The T-1 protocol breaks a DS-1 signal into 24 DS-0 64-Kb/s channels. These 24 channels can be shared by voice and data devices or monopolized by one large piece of data equipment. T-1 devices can be purchased or leased from the long distance carrier. The T-1 standard is cost effective for large corporations that require multiuser, full-time access to distributed NetWare WANs.

Companies and individuals who need digital connections are not out of luck if they cannot cost justify an expensive T-1 service. All of the major RBHC (Regional Bell Holding Company) carriers provide data grade private circuits. Private lines are also dedicated and offer data rates from 2.4 Kb/s to 64 Kb/s—a fractional T-1. These systems are ideal for the many network applications for which switched voice channels are too restrictive and T-1 is too expensive.

File Server

Now we come to the rocks—the heart of our hardware design. The cement has been chosen and the castle cabling has been designed. The cabling provides connectivity for the castle design. It creates an efficient path over which the software can travel. Without electricity, telephone, and TV, the occupants would be bored, out-of-luck, and useless. Cabling works with cement to bind the rocks together. A good cement design provides performance and reliability to the castle rocks.

Castle rocks come in many different shapes and sizes, so choose them carefully. Oversized rocks can produce cracks in our walls. Undersized rocks are inefficient and weak. Some characteristics to look for in rock design are size, weight, strength, composition, and age. Rocks are used to build castle rooms. The rooms are the true focus of our design: that's where castle people live and play. When choosing your rocks, think about the size of the rooms and their purpose.

Network design isn't much different. The cabling scheme you choose will physically connect the computers of your LAN together. The topology design you choose will dictate which networking language the computers use to interact. The overall hardware design of your NetWare LAN is a web of interconnected computers. Do you see a pattern here?

Everything we have discussed so far is the supporting cast for the real stars of our show: the network *computers*. The file server and workstations are at the heart of your NetWare LAN. As the network designer, it is your responsibility to integrate these intelligent components as efficiently as possible. There are myriad manufacturers, components, and features to choose among, so again, choose carefully. One of the most important criteria for making these choices is Novell certification. The Novell certification program is important for many reasons:

- Hardware certification allows Novell to curb the integration of bizarre equipment into the NetWare standard.
- NetWare LANs are software oriented. Hardware certification permits control of the hardware over which the software is run.
- Novell tests third-party hardware on a regular basis, and certifies equipment that peacefully co-exists with NetWare.
- Novell will not directly support any LAN that is not totally composed of Novell certified hardware.

The Novell Certification program also protects Novell from having to support an infinite number of hardware/NetWare combinations. If you are using equipment that Novell has tested, the customer support people can count out equipment malfunctions and concentrate on what they know best: troubleshooting NetWare. If you do not use hardware the Novell labs have certified, Novell will not even talk to you!

Having said that, I must report that less than half of NetWare LANs are constructed with Novell-certified hardware. "Money talks"; it is a grim fact of life. Novell-certified hardware products are consistently more expensive than their noncertified counterparts. In addition, Novell is not in the business of continually testing equipment. The company will lag in its certification of new technology, and many times misses products completely. Keep in mind what I have said about Novell certification, but don't be too shy about using noncertified hardware.

Before we begin our detailed exploration of NetWare file servers and workstations, here are five important hardware tips:

- When in doubt, choose a well-known manufacturer: IBM, Compaq, Wyse, DEC, HP, NEC, or Dell. Although these components may cost a little more, the peace of mind and customer support are definitely worth it. Remember, this is an important network running critical applications: the twist on the adage, "penny foolish, pound wise" applies here.

- Once you have chosen a manufacturer, pay attention to the bus type: Is it a standard IBM AT, EISA, Microchannel, or Macintosh architecture? Bus architecture is tied directly to topology/NIC compatibility. Be careful when you choose IBM PS/2 Microchannel machines, because some NICs don't support that bus architecture. Additionally, even fewer Macintosh-supported NICs are available.

- The number of expansion slots available is important. At least five additional expansion slots will be necessary for the file server, and three for each workstation. Expansion slots are necessary for additional disk coprocessor boards (DCB), UPS monitoring, internal NetWare bridging, additional RAM, use of up to four NICs per server, video boards, printer ports, and additional disk controllers.

- Additional disk bays are necessary in the file server and workstations. The file server should be a large box with at least three full-height disk bays. The additional bays are available for storage expansion once the network gets byte-tight. In addition, the workstations should support a variety of disk media: 5.25-inch double and high density, as well as 3.5-inch double and high density. Also, a few selected workstations should install internal tape backup units for nightly system fault tolerance. These SFT components typically require a full-height bay.

- Additionally, it is a good idea to have some level of physical security for the file server: remove the keyboard and monitor when the server is not in use, lock the keyboard, or physically enclose the file server in a locked cabinet.

With these additional tips in mind, let's jump into our investigation of what makes a great NetWare file server. The following three components detail the key factors in building a NetWare file server: CPU, RAM, and disk storage.

CPU

The core of what a computer does is found in its Central Processing Unit or CPU. The CPU of any computer has two primary responsibilities: control and arithmetic/logic functions. The microprocessor is designed to perform simple arithmetic operations at very high speeds. There is nothing amazing about what the CPU can do, it is how fast it does it that boggles the mind. After all, the computer can really only do math—the rest is just sophisticated software.

The only seven things a computer can really do are
    Arithmetic—add, subtract, multiply, and divide.
    Logic—less than, greater than, and equal to.

The file server's main function is to process requests from the network. These requests are stored in the file server's RAM and shuffled to the CPU over a specific bus line. The architecture of the bus is critical to the file server's performance. Currently, there are three standard bus architectures: Industry Standard Architecture (ISA), Extended Industry Standard Architecture (EISA), and the proprietary IBM Microchannel Architecture. The most important bus line is from the NIC to RAM to CPU. All high-performance machines (386 and 486 models) offer a 32-bit bus channel across this critical line.

In addition, the EISA and Microchannel architectures use a concept called *bus mastering*. Bus mastering allows the file server to pass network requests from the NIC to internal RAM without having to wait for a CPU clock cycle. This direct bus line from NIC to CPU to disk controller can increase the file server's performance as much as 400 percent. In order to take full advantage of EISA/Microchannel bus mastering, you must install specialized bus mastering components: 32-bit bus mastering NIC, 32-bit EISA disk controller, 32-bit EISA 80486 bus mastering motherboard. Keep in mind that these components are typically five times more expensive than standard ISA components.

The processor clock speed is also an important consideration when you choose a NetWare file server. The EISA/Microchannel bus mastering systems operate mostly independent of the internal clock but at times do rely on a fast count. The performance of the ISA relies completely on the processor clock speed. A 33-MHz or 40-MHz machine is adequate as a NetWare server. Recent tests of faster CPUs have shown that NetWare's timing routines max out by 50 MHz. The 80386DX2 and 80486DX2 clock doubler chips are not worth the extra money.

Finally, pay attention to future trends in NetWare when you choose a long-term file server. A year ago, designers felt the 80386 technology was sufficient for five years. They were wrong. The recent release of NetWare v4.0 has proven that software can indeed take advantage of the 80486 EISA technology. The existing 80386 ISA file servers will also run NetWare v4.0, but not with the superior performance of the current 80486 or the new Pentium machine.

An 80486/50-MHz EISA file server will ensure high performance today and compatibility with future releases of NetWare.

RAM

The file server's main memory, or RAM, works very closely with the CPU and NetWare operating system. The server's performance hinges a great deal on the RAM's ability to do its job. Many of the network's file server processes (FSPs) are loaded into file server RAM. Without enough RAM, the network can slow down or even come to a screeching halt.

NetWare's use of RAM can be differentiated into two functional areas: system and speed. The system requirements for RAM differ from version to version, ranging from 1.52MB (v2.15) to 5MB (v4.0). A file server containing this amount of memory would operate reliably but at very unacceptable speeds. Additional RAM is needed to enhance NetWare's speed. Memory affects network speed in three distinct ways:

■ Directory caching—the process of storing the network File Allocation Table (FAT) in RAM to speed up user indexes of file addresses. This feature increases the speed of file searches up to 100 times.

■ Directory hashing—the process of indexing FATs in RAM. This feature reduces the response time of I/O requests by 30 percent.

■ File caching—the process of storing heavily used files in RAM, for quicker retrieval. Subsequent requests for cached files are answered over 100 times faster.

The bottom line is: The more RAM in the file server, the more caching and hashing the network can do. This leads to incredible increases in overall performance.

A good rule of thumb to follow is to start with 4MB of RAM in the file server, then add 500K per user up to 64MB.

Disk Storage

Network disk drives are complex and temperamental animals. It is imperative that you put a great deal of thought into choosing the correct disk for your design. The disk drive is the principal resource on the LAN and contains all of the useful information that gives the system value. Disk drive "crashes" literally destroy companies, which in turn fire network designers. Think of your network design as a self-defense mechanism and adequate back-ups as job security.

The network designer needs to work in close cooperation with the network integrator when choosing the disk drive components. Four critical components make up the NetWare disk subsystem: the drive itself, the disk controller, disk coprocessor boards, and supporting NetWare disk drivers. Consult Novell's hardware certification guide for a complete list of Novell certified disk drives. The file server disk technology must be standardized and precise, because it houses the NetWare operating system.

Disk Drive

Before the server disk can be used as a NetWare host, it must undergo two processes: low-level formatting and computer surface analysis (COMPSURF). The low-level formatting procedure is manufacturer-specific and controlled by the appropriate disk controller. Use the manufacturer's software, not NetWare's COMPSURF format option. The second of the disk preparation procedures is a NetWare utility called COMPSURF. COMPSURF performs a simple disk surface analysis that marks bad blocks and records faulty addresses. Once a disk has been formatted and COMPSURFed, it is ready for NetWare installation.

NetWare v2.2 provides an additional COMPSURF utility called Z-TEST. Z-TEST runs a comprehensive surface analysis of the Zero boot track only. Z-TEST takes minutes instead of days to run, and offers nearly the same peace of mind.

Disk Controller

The disk controller acts as a mediator between the disk drive and the NetWare operating system. The disk controller must speak the same language as NetWare and still interface with the physical disk drive. This protocol is accomplished in one of four ways: standard AT hard disk controller, ESDI, SCSI, or disk co-processor boards.

Standard AT Hard Disk Controller. This option is available at installation with all levels of NetWare. The drivers to support this technology are inherent in the installation process. This option applies to most of the standard IBM ISA clone 386/486 internal disk drives and controllers—MFM, RLL, and IDE. Some of the newer IDE controllers require a unique IDE driver (available from NetWire or Novell). Note: Do not perform a low-level format on an IDE drive. The process will destroy the drive. I recommend IDE drives for network workstations.

ESDI. The Enhanced Small Device Interface (ESDI) is an established standard that supports disk transfer rates ranging from 10 to 24 Mb/s. The IBM PS/2 line has adopted this controller standard for use in most of its machines.

SCSI. The SCSI (pronounced "scuzzy"), or Small Computer Serial Interface, standard has a large following because of its logical rather than physical nature. Any SCSI device from a tape backup unit to a hard disk can be plugged into any other SCSI device and integrated almost effortlessly. The SCSI flexibility allows for intelligent on-line expansion as more hard disks are added to the file server. I recommend SCSI drives for all NetWare servers.

Disk Coprocessor Boards. A disk coprocessor board (DCB) is a disk controller card that contains a small CPU (80188) that manages all of the file server's disk requests. This added functionality relieves a great deal of the disk processing load from the resident CPU and frees it to perform more critical network processing. Although DCBs are relatively expensive, they can improve the LAN's overall performance by up to 34 percent! DCBs are also used for disk mirroring and disk duplexing levels of NetWare SFT.

Novell NetWare inherently supports disk drives and controllers that fall into the first two categories. Beyond that, it is the network designer's responsibility to provide NetWare with the appropriate disk drivers for the integration of specialized equipment. The disk drivers, called VADDs (value-added disk drivers), are provided by the component's manufacturer at the time of purchase. Make sure to get the appropriate VADD before you install NetWare.

A good rule of thumb for file server disk storage is 35MB per user. A minimum of 300MB is recommended.

Workstations

The workstation is the user's link to the network. The workstation is also the LAN workhorse for distributed network applications. No other network component epitomizes people and performance more than the LAN workstation. The network designer must try to balance user needs and network performance in configuring LAN workstations. People appreciate color monitors, ergonomics, mice, and well-designed keyboards. Performance requires 32-bit architecture, 8MB of RAM, and very fast CPU clock speeds. In an ideal world, both people and performance could be satisfied. Unfortunately, we don't live in a perfect world, and all of these technologies cost money.

The following three components are key factors for configuring NetWare workstations: CPU, RAM, and ergonomics.

CPU

The workstation CPU is where 95 percent of the network processing occurs. It is important to address processing requirements of individuals on the network and not to buy blanket workstations for completely different tasks. Think of the many different workstations as islands attached with long, narrow bridges. They can stand alone or in synchronicity. Here are some minimum configurations:

Application	CPU
word processing	80386SX/20 MHz ISA
database inquiry	80386/25 MHz ISA
spreadsheets	80386/33 MHz ISA
graphics	80486/33 MHz ISA
CAD	80486/50 MHz EISA

The speed and quality of Intel-based processor chips are measured in strange ways. The clock speed, for example, is not determined by the hardware; all 80386 chips are manufactured the same. The clock speed is determined at quality control. If an 80386 chip passes quality control at 33 MHz, it is sold as a 33-MHz chip. If not, it is tested at 25 MHz. If the chip passes quality control at 25 MHz, it is sold as a 25-MHz CPU. This procedure continues at 20 MHz and 16 MHz. This means that an 80386 33-MHz computer has the same CPU as an 80386 20-MHz machine, but the 20-MHz computer is *guaranteed* to run at 20 MHz (it may run faster). I have an 80386 20-MHz laptop computer I swear runs faster than my 80386 33-MHz desktop machine.

Another interesting scenario surrounds the Intel 80486SX microprocessor. This chip is marketed as a full 80486DX processor without the math coprocessor functionality—a glorified 80386, a half-truth. The 80486SX is the same microprocessor as the 80486DX, except that the SX chip comes with an additional read-only memory (ROM) component that turns off the math coprocessor. Intel will gladly upgrade your SX chip to a DX by selling you another DX chip and ROM, so that this time the math coprocessor is on and the main CPU has been turned off. So in the end, you have two full 80486DX chips, each with half the intended functionality. If you currently have an 80486SX machine, ask your dealer to remove the ROM and activate your existing math coprocessor. This is a good example of how marketing can destroy technology.

RAM

Workstation memory requirements are dictated by network applications. NetWare shells and the WOS eat up 25MB to 150MB of conventional RAM; the rest is available for downloading network applications. Figure 5.10 graphically illustrates a typical workstation RAM table. Additional memory can be added beyond conventional workstation RAM: expanded and extended memory. Both types of additional RAM exist beyond the 640K barrier and require memory management programs to make them work. Microsoft Windows, QEMM/386, DOS 5.0 and 6.0, and OS/2 are all equipped with advanced memory management subroutines. Novell also provides NetWare shells that load into additional RAM: EMSNETx.EXE loads into expanded memory and XMSNETx.EXE loads into extended RAM. Chapter 6 discusses memory management software in greater detail.

From a hardware standpoint, it is a good idea to install as much workstation RAM as possible. Most network designers agree 4MB is a good place to start. I recommend at least 8MB of workstation RAM. For advanced machines (80486, UNIX, and high-end Macintoshes) running advanced network applications (CAD/CAM, desktop publishing, or graphics), I recommend 16MB of memory. Another popular design strategy is diskless workstations, which are network nodes that do not contain an internal disk. In these cases, the internal RAM takes on even more responsibility. All LAN functions are performed in workstation RAM. The NetWare shells and WOS boot commands are loaded from firmware on the internal NIC.

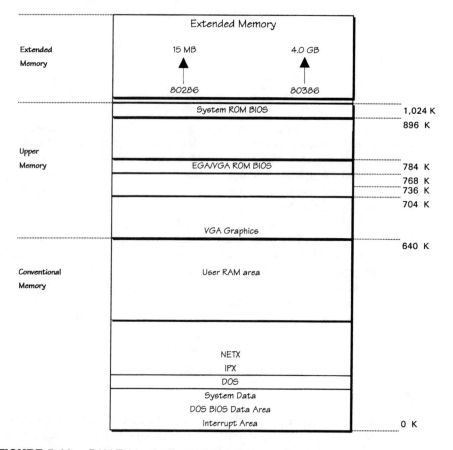

FIGURE 5.10   RAM Table of a Typical Workstation

From the "I told you so" category, stay away from terminate and stay-resident (TSR) programs. These memory hogs clutter workstation RAM to the point of confusion. Some TSRs wrap themselves around critical network shells and block network applications from functioning properly. Other TSRs simply gobble up so much workstation RAM that network applications cannot load. A few TSRs to look out for are NetWare's internal menu program, the # sign in login scripts, pop-up calendars and utilities, and most E-mail notify commands. Some memory management utilities that can be used as TSR alternatives include QEMM/386, LANSpace, and AboveDisk.

Ergonomics

Because the workstation is the user's link to the network, it is imperative for you to pay attention to "people design." *Ergonomics* is a fancy word for people design. Take a look at the workstation computer and ask yourself, "Is this machine friendly? Would I want to spend eight hours a day with it? Is it a people machine?" These questions might sound silly, but to the users who spend their life at the keyboard, these are emotional issues. In addition, ergonomics can serve to alleviate many of the health hazards facing today's network user, as outlined here.

Radiation and VDTs

Many recent studies have suggested that the radiation emitted from standard video display terminals (VDTs) is not trivial. As the display technology advances, the radiation concerns may deepen. One recent alternative is the low-emission color VGA monitor. Also, consider nonglare color instead of monochrome green; it will do wonders for productivity and morale.

Physical Discomfort

A poorly designed network workstation can produce a variety of different physical discomforts: eyestrain, neck pains, backaches, fatigue, and severe wrist injuries. A few minor design improvements can make a world of difference: screen hoods, antiglare filters, nonglare monitors, appropriate keyboard height, indirect lighting, adjustable chairs, adjustable desks, and upright copy holders.

Stress

Technology increases office productivity. Productivity increases user expectations. High expectations produce stress. Network users can now produce 300 percent more work than they could before. Increased levels of productivity and prolonged periods of exposure to network terminals have produced an epidemic of technology-related stress. To alleviate some of this anxiety, I recommend limiting the time users spend in direct contact with computers. Diversify their tasks so users spend at least one or two hours a day away from the source of their technostress.

Isolation

As local area networks grow into wide area networks, the distances between network users expand. The University of Southern California's Center for Future Research estimates that 10 million people will work from home by the year 2000. The further isolation of network workstations leads to user isolation. As appealing as it may sound to work from home, many people need the human interaction they receive at the office. There is a growing fear that as workstations extend into the home and society becomes increasingly linked by computers, people will hide away by themselves and tap away on electronic keyboards. Job diversity, weekly staff meetings, and task rotation are viable options for curbing user isolation.

Cyberphobia

Cyberphobia is the fear of computers. Many users are intimidated by new technology. Especially technology they do not understand. LANs have only recently arrived on the scene, and many traditional mainframe operators fear that their skills are useless. Education and computer literacy are the cures for cyberphobia. Spend time with the network users and show them that the workstation is there to serve them, not the other way around.

Microsoft Corporation has recently introduced a wonderful ergonomic device: a PC sound card that accepts simple verbal commands in Windows. The best news is the product costs less than $300. Keyboards are quickly becoming obsolete.

People design is a very important factor in designing network workstations. Ergonomics, the CPU, and RAM should be balanced evenly in order to create a synergy of people with performance. An overpowered computer that users fear is as useless as an underpowered computer that users welcome.

SFT Components

To guard against unscheduled network downtime, follow this wise and simple rule: Don't turn off the server. Unfortunately, it's not that easy to avoid disaster. Sometimes the natural forces of physics are too overwhelming for your hardware design, and the whole thing goes up in smoke. No problem; you thought ahead. And by thinking ahead, you get to keep your head—and your job.

Many unemployed network designers spend all of their time and resources on topology design, cabling, file servers, and workstations. In doing so, they miss the most important lesson of all: precaution. Precaution implies forethought, and forethought implies preparedness, and preparedness equates to system fault tolerance (SFT). The concept of the system fault means that no matter how good your system design is, the system will crash. Tolerance is a measure of how badly the crash affects you and your users. An intelligent mix of SFT components can delay network crashes and prevent the LAN from being destroyed beyond recovery. SFT is categorized into two functional areas: energy SFT and storage SFT.

Energy SFT Concepts

Energy SFT controls the quality and quantity of LAN electricity as it feeds file servers, workstations, and active topology components. Energy SFT protects against anomalies in the commercial power from wall outlets. Spikes, surges, harmonic distortion, gradual brownouts, and blackouts are all enemies of LAN file servers and workstations.

Spikes

Large voltage *spikes* can severely damage computer motherboards, disk drives, and active topology components. Spikes are high-magnitude, split-second power surges. The most dramatic cause of spikes is lightning striking on or near a power line. Electrical spikes can be quite eventful: I have seen high-voltage impulses actually blow holes in computer chips. Spikes can also corrupt data, cause printer errors, and wreak general havoc with network software.

Surges

A *surge* is an overvoltage that lasts longer than a split-second spike. A spike becomes a surge when it lasts for longer than 1 cycle (1/60 second). Standard commercial power is rated at 60 cycles per second. Surges occur when other equipment on the line has been drawing large amounts of power, then suddenly cuts off. Surges are far more dangerous than spikes because they last much longer.

Harmonic Distortion

Computer systems run best on sine-wave power. Sine waves are smooth electronic hills with peaks and valleys. *Harmonic distortion* deforms the normal sine wave. Harmonic noise can be sent back into the AC line by nonlinear components: computers, copiers, FAX machines, and variable speed motors. Harmonics cause communications errors and make transformers overheat, creating a potential fire hazard.

Brownouts

Gradual *brownouts* place undue strain on networking hardware. They are difficult to detect and, left unchecked, can cause a literal "meltdown." These events are long-term under-voltages, lasting minutes or even hours. Brownouts often are instituted by utility companies when peak demand exceeds the capacity of power generated. Motherboards and disk drives respond quite unfavorably to low power for even the shortest period of time.

Blackouts

Blackouts are complete power failures over an extended period of time. Blackouts are becoming more frequent as power distribution grids are pushed to the extreme. Blackouts are caused by ground faults, accidents, lightning, or any other act of nature. It goes without saying that blackouts are bad news. Disk drives and subsystems can be irreparably damaged when power fails suddenly.

Energy SFT Components

Energy SFT is accomplished through the use of four specific devices: surge protectors, power conditioners, SPSs (standby power supply), and UPSs (uninterruptible power supplies).

Surge Protectors

Surge protectors are the most inexpensive and widely used energy protection devices available. They are designed to monitor incoming voltage levels and redirect surges that exceed 250 volts to a neutral conductor. The neutral conductor is the third prong on conventional power plugs. Make sure each piece of your equipment has a three-pronged plug and is plugged into an appropriate receptacle. Better-quality surge protectors feature multistage designs. These designs place several suppression components between equipment and the line. The best surge protectors can withstand peak suppression levels of 310 volts (UL 1449, 330 V rating) and do this in less then 1 nanosecond. More often surge protectors will also offer electromagnetic interference (EMI) and radio frequency isolation (RFI) protection.

Surge protectors are plugged into the wall outlet and contain internal sockets for connection to networking hardware components. Most surge protectors contain multiple numbers of plugs and can handle an equivalent number of devices simultaneously.

Power Conditioners

Power conditioning devices are super surge suppressors. They also protect your equipment from voltage swings and harmonic distortion. Power conditioners are independent transformers that sit in-line between the wall outlet and network devices. They provide computer equipment with conditioned power—smooth sine waves. Good-quality power conditioners will meet ANSI/IEEE C62.41 Category A and UL 1449 standards for lightning and surge suppression, respectively. Power conditioners regulate the output power to ±5 percent of nominal voltage and put out sine-wave power typically with less than 5 percent THD (Total Harmonic Distortion).

SPS

The standby power supply sits in-line between the wall outlet and the network device. It contains a relatively strong battery that can keep a LAN file server or workstation alive for 5 to 60 minutes, depending on its size and the computer's load. The SPS monitors electrical voltage levels as power is fed to the computer from the wall. At this point, energy is flowing directly from the wall to the network device. If the voltage level falls below a given threshold (approximately 88 volts), the SPS almost immediately switches over from commercial power to its internal battery. Quality SPSs can make this transition in a maximum of 4 milliseconds (ms). A longer delay will crash the network device. In the event of a complete electrical outage, the SPS supplies the network device with electrical energy from its battery until the normal current is restored or it runs out of juice. There are two major problems with this scenario:

- If the SPS runs out of battery energy before the normal current is restored, the network device will crash.
- The short delay between the commercial power outage and SPS switching is not always short enough. In some cases, the delay is so long that it brings down the network device anyway. Pay close attention to the transfer time.

UPS

The uninterruptible power supply works in a slightly different way. The UPS also sits in-line between the wall outlet and network device, but the similarities end there. Early UPS technology continually fed conditioned power to the network device from its internal battery. Current UPS technology feeds raw wall power into a transformer. On the input side of the transformer is usually a control microprocessor that manages a charging system. The battery and this device together are called an *invertor*. The invertor is used to convert the DC current (as opposed to AC) from the internal battery into AC power, which is required by active network components. The UPS recharges the internal battery with a small charger system.

A good UPS will monitor the battery periodically and always keep it at full charge. In the event of a power outage, the UPS beeps loudly and usually has light indicators that will flash. The UPS then switches from highly conditioned wall power to inverted power supplied from the battery. It continues to serve the network device with the same internally conditioned battery power. Once the UPS battery drops below five minutes of reserve power, another advanced UPS function kicks in: UPS monitoring.

UPS monitoring is a watchdog software protocol that allows the file server to supervise the levels of energy available from the UPS. The system will close files and down the server when UPS battery levels fall below five minutes of power. The connection from the NetWare server to the UPS device can be made through a serial port or an additional UPS card. UPS monitoring requires additional server software—a value-added process (VAP) or a NetWare loadable module (NLM).

UPS monitoring is specifically important in situations where workstations continue to operate even though remote file servers have lost electricity. Without UPS monitoring, the system would continue to function normally until an abrupt crash occurred, at which time all open files would be corrupted.

How to Choose the Correct System

Unfortunately, the networking industry is a little confused about the difference between SPSs and UPSs. Intentionally or not, many of the energy SFT manufacturers advertise their SPS products as UPSs. UPS and SPS systems are rated for size in volt-amperes (VA). Computers and peripheral devices are often measured in watts or volts and amperes (amps). You will find this information usually on a plate attached to the power supply or in the computer manual. The following formulas show you how to convert either rating into VA:

Total Volts $\times$ Total Amps = VA
Watts $\div$ 0.7 (or $\times$ 1.43) = VA

Simply total all of the ratings for the equipment you wish to protect and allow a reasonable growth factor (approximately 25 percent). This gives you a margin of safety as well. Select a UPS that has a VA rating closest to your total load. Be careful in this regard. If you are shopping for a UPS, here are some additional pointers:

- Read the specifications sheet. If the UPS has a "switch delay" of greater then 2 ms (milliseconds), chances are it is not a UPS.
- Cost is another key factor. A UPS is more difficult to manufacture than an SPS. Most quality UPSs cost well over $500. A $400 UPS is most likely an SPS.
- Size is important. Most network file servers require 200 to 300 watts for the CPU alone. Typically a UPS should have a minimum capacity of 750 VA per server supported.
- Some suggested manufacturers are American Power Conversion, Best Power Technology, Elgar, and Network Security Systems.

Storage SFT

Earlier we touched on the value of network disk drives, and more specifically, the information stored on them. Routine backups and on-line redundancy are not just good ideas; they are job security. A network without some level of storage SFT is like a catcher without shin guards: ouch! There are two types of storage SFT: backup systems and on-line redundancy. Both of these SFT strategies require additional hardware and should be automatically written into the network design regardless of cost. I'm serious!

Backup Systems

The primary concern in choosing a backup system for your network is this: "Can I get my data back?" It is a fact that most people only realize the value of their information once it is gone. A good network designer realizes the value of the user's data now, and will make every effort to protect it. Most current backup systems use high-density magnetic tape media in a high-speed cartridge. These devices are usually installed into a full-height disk bay and operate via a specialized controller. Some internal backup systems can connect directly to the workstation's internal floppy/hard disk controller. Keep in mind that 95 percent of all network backups are conducted from a workstation. The NetWare file server disk is only accessible from LAN workstations. It is a myth that network backups are performed from the file server.

Following are additional features to consider when you are evaluating tape backup systems:

- Flexibility—file-by-file backup and restore features are helpful. Also consider the system's file and directory selection procedures.
- Security—how easily unauthorized users can gain access to the NetWare bindery for users, groups, security, and so on.
- Reliability—check the file validation and error correction features, as well as the reliability of restore procedures.
- Convenience—there should be automated time-specific backup procedures for those long 3 A.M. procedures.
- Speed—Speed is directly related to cost: Low-cost machines operate at about 500KB to 1MB per minute. The more expensive models can handle 5MB to 10MB in a minute.
- Size of tape—smaller QIC-40 formats store 120–240MB of data on a minicartridge, whereas the medium-sized models use large cartridges to store 250MB to 525MB. And the big guns use digital audio tape (DAT) or optical disks to store gigabytes worth of information.
- Cost—the most cost-effective backup solution is from Colorado Memory Systems. That company's Jumbo 120 and 250 models plug directly into workstation floppy controllers and use inexpensive minicartridges. These internal drives cost $250 and $350, respectively. Next is the midsized range. Emerald, Mountain, and Maynard dominate this category with backup solutions ranging from $495 (250MB) to $9,995 (5GB). The high-end products come from Palindrome Corporation. The Palindrome Autoloader System uses robotic arms and complex archive algorithms to handle up to 50GB of data storage. This system retails for about $20,000.

Once again, refer to Novell's hardware certification guide to make sure that the tape Backup System you choose is Novell certified. NetWare offers a software backup solution in the command utility NBACKUP. NBACKUP backs up and restores critical network files, including the bindery, to and from diskettes. Also, NBACKUP can be configured to work with hard disks or network drives.

Whichever backup solution you choose, make sure to create a backup schedule. This schedule should include five nightly backups, a weekly set, and one monthly set. The weekly and monthly tapes or diskettes should be stored in a cool, dry place offsite—a safe deposit box, for example. Many insurance companies issue policies for data recovery. In addition, there are disaster recovery centers popping up all over the world. In the event that all of your machines have been destroyed, these centers will emulate your work environment for as long as it takes to restore your original system—assuming, of course, that you have stored some backup tapes offsite.

On-line Redundancy

On-line redundancy protects network data as it is being used by the system. This level of storage SFT uses real time protection components to prevent file loss and data mismatching before it is too late. On-line redundancy is also known as NetWare SFT level II and is implemented through four different on-line strategies: hot fix, transactional tracking system (TTS), disk mirroring, and disk duplexing. Chapter 3 provided a detailed discussion of the four on-line SFT strategies.

The *grand slam*: It's when opportunity knocks and a big stick answers!

—Anonymous

Well, that just about does it for hardware design. Congratulations! You have completed another step in building a NetWare LAN. The most challenging phase of analysis and design is the transition from network analysis to hardware design. The next step, software design, should be a breeze. In software design, you will breathe life into your local area Frankenstein (LAF). Without the productivity and purpose of network applications, operating systems, and groupware, your hardware design *is* a LAF. It's time to step up to the plate and give your dream a whack. Speaking of dreams, I wonder how my castle is doing. . . .

Chapter 6

Software Design

"Another case of one too many software design changes"

T he software design of a NetWare LAN is dictated more by user needs than by performance requirements. On the one hand, software design must work in harmony with hardware components to provide an effective balance of people and performance. On the other hand, the purpose of software design is to offer the network users a productive work environment. In the development of the software design, the designer must not solely rely on his or her own expertise. In this process, the users will have as much to say about the acquisition of software components as the network designer—sometimes even more.

The value of user opinion is never more evident than in the process of buying furniture. The castle software design is dominated by the opinions and preferences of the castle people. The occupants choose paint color, wallpaper patterns, dishwashers, furniture style, and tapestries. They live, work, and play within the environment of the castle software, so they figure they should have a say in designing it. I guess you can't blame them.

The only software component left to the designer is the type and style of central heating. The castle people are not well versed in such things and really don't care as long as it works. The choice of central heater and air conditioner is a very important task. These components support the entire software design and establish an atmosphere for occupants, furniture, wallpaper, and tapestries. If it is too cold, the occupants would freeze and the furniture could begin to crack. If it is too hot, the wallpaper could decay and the tapestries would melt. It is a good thing that the most important decision is left to the most qualified castle person—the network designer.

This holds true for network design as well. The users have the upper hand in choosing workstation operating systems, menus, network applications, and groupware. Fortunately, the really important decision is left to you—the choice of a network operating system. The network operating system establishes an atmosphere for DOS, Windows, WordPerfect, and E-mail. If the NOS is too strong, it will overpower DOS and confuse the users. If the NOS is too weak, it won't be able to support document sharing for WordPerfect, communications for E-mail, and file caching for Windows. Once you have established the network operating system, the software design builds from there. It is important to note that the software design process never ends. The development of the software design is an ongoing process. The system is constantly being upgraded and improved. Try not to get all wrapped up in the development of the perfect software design—it will probably change 23 times before the system is complete.

The beginning of wisdom is to call things by their right names.

—Chinese Proverb

One of the most puzzling aspects of network software is *version numbering*. Version numbering is a necessary part of the software development process, but it is often misunderstood. The procedure calls for incremental numbering as software releases evolve technically. A full point increment indicates revolutionary enhancements or a complete rewrite of the software core. Fractional increments are used to indicate minor revisions or the addition of significant improvements. Currently there are *seven* new versions that span the globe of network software:

- Windows NT version 1.0
- OS/2 version 2.0

- Microsoft Windows 3.1
- NetWare version 4.0
- UNIX System V
- MS DOS version 6.0
- System 7

Some software develops faster than others. It all depends on the strategy of the software manufacturer. UNIX, for example, evolved for almost 23 years before reaching version V, whereas DOS jumped from version 2.1 to version 6.0 in only 9 years. The most significant of recent advancements is NetWare's move from version 3.11 to version 4.0. Novell's engineers returned to the proverbial drawing board and rebuilt NetWare's core operating system functions. The new product is not necessarily a 3.11 upgrade—it is a whole new GUI WAN NOS.

Version numbering is just one piece of the vast network software pie. This chapter explores the strengths and functionality of network operating systems, workstation operating systems, menu systems, network applications, and groupware. We will analyze each of these components in depth and develop an understanding of how they fit into the overall design of our NetWare LAN.

Remember to balance people and performance as you integrate software into the network design. In this case, your focus should be on *people*—user productivity, user interface, and application efficiency.

Network Operating Systems

The network operating system is the *heart* of the LAN. It resides on the central file server and controls most of the network operations, including file requests, packet routing, security, users and groups, shared printing, system management, and interconnectivity. In addition, the network operating system also integrates all of the other software design components.

As Chapter 2 discussed, there are two types of NOS designs: client/server and peer-to-peer. Client/server operating systems reside in a central file server and control all aspects of the network from a central site. Peer-to-peer operating systems reside in all the workstations and distribute the responsibilities of file sharing and resource allocation. Client/server systems—NetWare, for example—are more powerful than their peer-to-peer counterparts. This book focuses on client/server network operating systems.

Currently, there are five major client/server operating systems that control approximately 95 percent of the network market. They are, in descending order of popularity:

- NetWare v3.11
- NetWare v4.0
- NetWare v2.2
- Windows NT/LAN Manager
- Banyan VINES v5.5

Each of these operating systems has its own audience for varying reasons:

- NetWare v3.11 has the highest portion of new installations. Many first-time LANs buy NetWare v3.11 because of its power, versatility, and ease-of-use.
- NetWare v4.0 is the new kid on the block. This advanced 32-bit NOS was only recently released but has already made an impact. NetWare v4.0 is not a replacement for NetWare v3.11—it has a completely different focus. NetWare v3.11 serves medium to large-sized LANs, whereas NetWare v4.0 serves corporate, enterprise-sized WANs in addition to smaller systems.
- NetWare v2.2 is an ideal upgrade path for small to medium-sized LANs. A good portion of the NetWare v2.x user base upgraded to NetWare v2.2 instead of NetWare v3.11 because v2.2 costs less and runs on the same 80286 server platform as v2.1x.
- Windows NT/LAN Manager is also a very young NOS. NT was also recently released and includes many of the functions of LAN Manager. Windows NT can operate as a client/server or peer-to-peer NOS. NT's client/server functionality is provided by a built-in version of Microsoft's LAN Manager.
- Banyan VINES v5.5 serves the UNIX crowd. It is based on the UNIX workstation operating system and offers the same cryptic interface. Banyan VINES has typically served a specialty audience on the east coast of the United States. This new version with its improved features should reach a more diverse network audience.

If we devote our time to disparaging the products of our business rivals, we hurt business generally, reduce confidence, and increase discontent.

—Edward N. Hurley

Table 6.1 is a brief product stratification that compares the most important features of these five network operating systems.

As you can see, there are many features to consider in choosing the correct network operating system. The choice you make here will impact the rest of your software design, so choose carefully. In an effort to prepare you for this unenviable task, I will explain these important NOS components in more depth. To review, they are

- configuration
- security
- system fault tolerance
- speed
- connectivity
- user interface
- network management

Our discussion focuses on NetWare as the operating system of choice. I will spend a little time on Windows NT, though, because it is quickly becoming a new force in network computing. Let's begin with NetWare v2.2.

TABLE 6.1   Comparing Features of the Five Most Popular NOSs

	NetWare v2.2	NetWare v3.11	NetWare v4.0	Windows NT/LAN	Banyan VINES v5.5
Configuration					
Operation	Server	Server	Server	Peer	Server
32-bit NOS	No	Yes	Yes	Yes	Yes
80486 "aware"	No	Yes	Yes	No	Yes
Number of users	100	250	1,000	>1,000	Unlimited
Number of open files	1,000	100,000	100,000	8,000	Unlimited
Maximum storage	2GB	32TB	32TB	4GB	Unlimited
Shell	NETx	NETx	Requester	Requester	Built-in
WOS Window	No	No	No	Yes	No
MHS	Yes	Yes	Yes	Extra	No
Chatting	No	No	No	Yes	Yes
Accounting	Yes	Yes	Yes	Extra	Extra
Auditing	No	Extra	Yes	Yes	No
APIs	Yes	Yes	Yes	Yes	Yes
Indexed files	Yes	Yes	Yes	No	No
Peer disks	No	No	Yes	Yes	No
Peer printing	No	Yes	Yes	Yes	No
Security					
Access restriction	Yes	Yes	Yes	Yes	Yes
WOS flush	No	No	No	Yes	No
Supervisor restrict	No	Yes	Yes	No	Yes
Intruder detection	Yes	Yes	Yes	No	Yes
User rights	Yes	Yes	Yes	Yes	Yes
Directory rights	Yes	Yes	Yes	Yes	No
File attributes	Yes	Yes	Yes	Yes	No
IRM	No	Yes	Yes	No	Yes
Security sharing	No	No	No	Yes	No
System Fault Tolerance					
Write verification	Yes	Yes	Yes	No	Yes

	NetWare v2.2	NetWare v3.11	NetWare v4.0	Windows NT/LAN	Banyan VINES v5.5
System Fault Tolerance (cont.)					
Duplicate FATs	Yes	Yes	Yes	No	No
Hot Fix	Yes	Yes	Yes	Yes	Yes
Disk mirroring	Yes	Yes	Yes	Extra	Yes
Disk duplexing	Yes	Yes	Yes	Yes	No
TTS	Yes	Yes	Yes	No	No
UPS monitoring	Yes	Yes	Yes	Extra	Yes
Resource management	No	Yes	Yes	Limited	No
Salvage files	Yes	Yes	Yes	No	No
Speed					
Indexed FAT	Yes	Yes	Yes	No	No
Directory hashing	Yes	Yes	Yes	No	No
Directory caching	Yes	Yes	Yes	Yes	Yes
File caching	Yes	Yes	Yes	Yes	No
Elevator seeking	Yes	Yes	Yes	Yes	No
Multitasking	Yes	Yes	Yes	Yes	Yes
Optimization	No	Yes	Yes	Yes	Limited
Multiple LANs	4	16	32	2	4
Volumes/server	32	64	64	24	10
Optical media	No	No	Yes	Yes	Extra
Disk migration	No	No	Yes	Yes	No
Connectivity					
DOS	Yes	Yes	Yes	Yes	Yes
OS/2	Yes	Yes	Yes	Yes	No
UNIX	No	Extra	Yes	No	No
Macintosh	Yes	Yes	Yes	No	No
Windows	Yes	Yes	Yes	Yes	Yes
OSI	No	Yes	Yes	No	No
TCP/IP	Extra	Extra	Yes	Yes	Yes
VAX	No	Extra	Extra	No	No
AppleTalk	Yes	Yes	Yes	Extra	No
NetBEUI	Yes	Yes	Yes	Yes	Yes
Asynchronous	Yes	Yes	Yes	Yes	Extra
Routing	Yes	Yes	Yes	Yes	Extra
NetWare	Yes	Yes	Yes	Yes	No
Windows NT	No	Yes	Yes	Yes	No

	NetWare v2.2	NetWare v3.11	NetWare v4.0	Windows NT/LAN	Banyan VINES v5.5
Connectivity (cont.)					
VINES	No	Yes	Yes	No	Yes
Remote WS	Yes	Yes	Yes	Yes	Yes
LANs per server	4	8	8	2	4
X.25	Extra	Extra	Extra	Yes	Extra
User Interface					
Menu Utilities	Yes	Yes	Yes	Yes	Yes
GUI utilities	No	No	Yes	Yes	No
GUI install	No	Yes	Yes	Yes	No
On-line help	Yes	Yes	Yes	Yes	Yes
Modularity	No	Yes	Yes	Yes	No
Diskless WS	Yes	Yes	Yes	Yes	No
Virtual console	No	Yes	Yes	Yes	No
User menu system	Yes	Yes	Yes	No	No
Native interface	DOS	DOS	Windows	Windows	UNIX
Network Management					
GUI administrator	No	No	Yes	Yes	No
Security check	Yes	Yes	Yes	No	No
Centralized rights	Yes	Yes	Yes	Yes	Yes
Multiserver administration	Yes	Yes	Yes	Yes	Yes
Auto WS update	No	No	No	No	Yes
Intruder alert	No	No	No	Yes	No
Cache statistics	Yes	Yes	Yes	Yes	Extra
CPU usage	Yes	Yes	Yes	Yes	Extra
Disk usage	No	No	No	No	Extra
Packet analysis	No	Yes	Yes	No	Extra
Files open	Yes	Yes	Yes	Extra	Extra
CPU stats	No	Yes	Yes	Yes	Extra
Printer management	Yes	Yes	Yes	Yes	Extra

NetWare v2.2

NetWare v2.2 is a complete 16-bit network operating system designed for small to medium-sized LANs that require resource sharing, workgroup productivity, and average connectivity. NetWare v2.2 is actually more similar to NetWare v3.11 than it is to NetWare v2.15. NetWare v2.2 was designed as an intermediate upgrade path to v3.11 for existing NetWare v2.15 LANs. The features, utilities, security, and printing components of NetWare v2.2 are huge improvements over its 80286-based predecessor—NetWare v2.15. As a matter of fact, NetWare v2.2 was released within months of the release of NetWare v3.11. There are still some limitations to NetWare v2.2 that are attributed to the restrictive 80286-based server technology:

- *Nonmodularity*—NetWare v2.2 still relies entirely on a compiled OS core. The complete NetWare v2.2 functionality is combined into one operating system file—NET$OS.EXE. This system file is hidden in the SYS:SYSTEM directory. Any NOS modifications require a complete reconfiguration of this network operating system file. Figure 6.1 illustrates the rigid NetWare v2.2 OS core.
- *Lack of connectivity*—NetWare v2.2 supports a limited number of protocols and workstation platforms.
- *Storage limitations*—the 16-bit 80286 technology limits NetWare v2.2's ability to handle large disks and memory requirements.
- *Value-added processes (VAPs)*—NetWare v2.2 accepts server applications as value-added processes. VAPs are limited in scope and not easily loaded or unloaded.

Overall, NetWare v2.2 is a good investment. It is less expensive than NetWare v3.11 and much more powerful than NetWare v2.15. NetWare v2.2 supports 5, 10, 50, or 100 simultaneous users over DOS, Windows, OS/2, or Macintosh platforms.

Configuration

NetWare v2.2 is the only client/server NOS that supports two modes of operation: dedicated or nondedicated. In dedicated mode, NetWare v2.2 supports all facets of security, network management, printing, and system fault tolerance (SFT) level II. In nondedicated mode, NetWare v2.2 operates somewhat normally, except that it supports only SFT level I. Nondedicated NetWare v2.2 allows the server to function as a workstation for most DOS applications. One important note: If the workstation application freezes, so does the entire NetWare v2.2 server.

In dedicated mode, NetWare v2.2 supports a minimum of 2.5MB of server RAM and a maximum of 12MB. In nondedicated mode, the NetWare v2.2 server supports 2.5MB minimum RAM and 8MB maximum. NetWare v2.2 allows 1,000 concurrently open files and a maximum of 32,000 directory entries per volume. There can only be 32 disks or volumes per server with a maximum volume size of 255MB. NetWare v2.2 has a storage capacity of 2GB.

The key to the NetWare configuration is the *bindery*. The NetWare bindery is an object-oriented database that contains definitions for users, groups, security, and other objects on the LAN. The bindery consists of three components: objects, properties, and data sets. *Objects* are any physical or logical entity that interfaces with the NetWare OS.

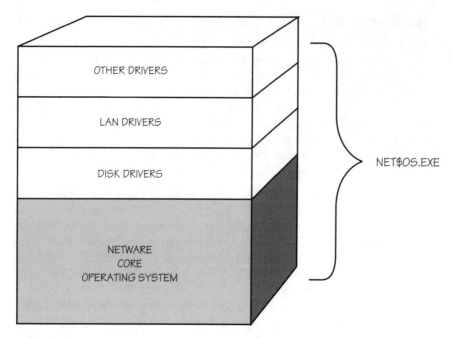

FIGURE 6.1   The Nonmodular NetWare v2.2 Operating System Core

NetWare objects include users, groups, workgroups, routers, gateways, file servers, and print servers. *Properties* are characteristics of bindery objects. Properties include passwords, account restrictions, account balances, addresses, user profiles, client authorization lists, and group members. *Data sets* are values assigned to object properties.

The NetWare v2.2 bindery consists of two hidden system files: NET$BIND.SYS for objects and properties, and NET$BVAL.SYS for data sets. In addition, NetWare v2.2 includes a disk management utility called DISKED that provides Supervisors with emergency access to the NetWare bindery.

Too many people are thinking of security instead of opportunity. They seem more afraid of life than death.

—James F. Byrnes

Security

NetWare provides a multifaceted security system. It is based on a seven-layer security model. Security becomes more complex as users work their way down the ladder. The first four layers of the NetWare v2.2 security model affect users and groups. The final three layers affect directories and files. Here is a brief look at the NetWare v2.2 security model.

Layer 1: Login Name. The login name (*or username*) identifies users on the LAN. It can be up to 47 characters in length—no spaces, no forward slash (/), and no backslash (\). The login name is supplied during the login process and must be preceded by a file server name, as in the format LOGIN NIRVANA/*David*.

Layer 2: Password. The password usually follows the login name during the login procedure. NetWare systems do not automatically require a password. This option must be set during the network management phase. Passwords can contain up to 20 characters and no spaces. To avoid short passwords, the default minimum password length is 5 characters. Sophisticated programs exist that can determine a password of 5 characters or less in 30 minutes, so insist that the network users select passwords of 6 or more characters. NetWare v2.2 passwords are encrypted at the workstation and sent along the topology in a form only the file server can understand. Previous versions of NetWare used text-based passwords that were easily siphoned with protocol analyzers.

Layer 3: Account Restrictions. Once a valid login name and password have been entered, the user is subject to a series of account restrictions. These security restrictions limit users' access to the entire system. Account restrictions include time restrictions, station restrictions, account balance restrictions, and account locking.

Layer 4: Trustee Assignments. The final layer of user security is trustee assignments. If a user has passed through the first three layers, he or she must be given *rights* to access certain areas of the network directory structure. Trustee assignments are user-specific rights within specific network directories. NetWare v2.2 rights include

> **R**ead—read an existing file
> **F**ile Scan—search the directory or subdirectory
> **W**rite—write to an existing file
> **C**reate—create and write to new files or subdirectories
> **E**rase—delete existing files or subdirectories
> **M**odify—modify file names and attributes
> **A**ccess Control—change the existing rights

NetWare v2.2 trustee assignments can be granted to either users or groups. As a user, you will receive rights individually or as part of a group. Trustee assignments cascade from the original directory to all subdirectories below it. The only way to change a trustee assignment in a subdirectory is to completely reassign the rights.

Layer 5: Directory Rights. Directory rights are the first layer of directory/file security. Directory rights are the same as trustee assignments, except directory rights are assigned to directories—not users. In order to exercise a given right, the user must have both the trustee assignment and the directory right—this is called *Effective* rights. If the network manager wants to eliminate a right for all users in a specific directory, he/she will revoke that directory right. This is called the *Maximum Rights Mask (MRM)*. The default MRM is all rights for all directories. This is a very complex level of security.

Layer 6: Directory Attributes. Directory attributes affect directories regardless of trustee assignments or directory rights. Attributes are security properties that affect a user's ability to use or modify directories and files. NetWare v2.2 supports the following directory attributes:

> **N**ormal—default directory attribute with no special security
> **Sy**stem—protects the directory from searches, deletion, and copying

Hidden—hides the directory from the DIR command—not NDIR
Private—protects the directory from searches and deletion.

Layer 7: File Attributes. File attributes are used to add security to specific files on the LAN. NetWare v2.2 supports a wide variety of file attributes, including

Non-Sharable—only one user may access the file at a time
Sharable—multiple users may access the file simultaneously
Read/Write—users may see the file and alter the content
Read Only—users may see the file, but not alter the content
Normal—default file attribute is NS/RW
System—identifies a file as being system-owned and operated
Execute Only—protects .EXE and .COM files—no copy, no delete
Archive Needed—files that have been modified since the last backup
TTS—transactional tracking system file
Indexed—provides an additional level of file indexing—like hashing

File attribute security is rarely used. It is common for complex database files, system directories, and shared applications. This is the most complex level of NetWare security.

NetWare v2.2 provides security features beyond the seven-layered model. On the top, NetWare v2.2 provides *user types.* On the bottom, NetWare v2.2 provides *cable-encrypted passwords.* NetWare v2.2 supports eight user types, each with a different level of security:

- Supervisor
- Workgroup Manager
- Console Operator
- Print Server Operator

- Supervisor Equivalent
- User Account Manager
- Print Queue Operator
- Regular Network User

Another interesting security feature is *ignorance.* Ignorance is not tied to the network operating system; unfortunately, it is a global trait. User ignorance can work in favor of the network Supervisor if users don't understand the system well enough to cause any damage. This is a double-edged sword, though, and I do not recommend ignorance as your only line of defense.

System Fault Tolerance

NetWare v2.2 supports system fault tolerance levels I and II. SFT is built into the NetWare operating system. Therefore, NetWare v2.2 can provide a high level of reliability without sacrificing performance. SFT level I includes duplicate DETs, duplicate FATs, and read-after-write verification. SFT level II includes hot fixing, disk mirroring/duplexing, UPS monitoring, and the NetWare transactional tracking system. Chapter 3 gives a detailed description of NetWare SFT.

Speed

Speed and performance are measured by *file server response time,* which is the response time for disk reads, disk writes, packet requests, and resource allocation. NetWare v2.2 incorporates all of the standard NetWare speed features: distributed processing, directory hashing, directory caching, file caching, and elevator seeking. In addition, NetWare v2.2 includes a few additional speed features: FSPs, DMPs, and statistics.

FSPs. *File server processes (FSPs)* are NetWare routines that handle workstation requests. Workstation requests, called *network core protocol (NCP)* requests, arrive at the server as file service packets. These packets are escorted directly to the OS core, where the FSPs reside. If an FSP is available, it will process the request. If not, the request must wait in a *packet receive buffer (PRB)*. If the FSPs are really busy, the PRBs will begin to fill up. Once full, they will discard subsequent packets, and users will receive the bad news, `Error sending on the network`.

Here is a good analogy. Think of the OS core as a bank. The FSPs are tellers that service requests from bank customers. If all the tellers are busy, customers wait in the lobby (PRB). NetWare v2.2 has refined its memory management procedures to the point that FSPs get better, faster service from the OS core. This means they are more efficient and that fewer requests are relegated to the NetWare lobby. In addition, NetWare v2.2 adds FSPs as needed.

Using NetWare v2.2 you can increase the number of file service processes. The minimum is 3 and the maximum is 20. The default is 10. You cannot modify the size of the packet receive buffer.

DMPs. *Dynamic memory pools (DMPs)* are used as temporary workspaces for most critical NetWare OS services. Each time an FSP begins processing a request, it uses between 2 and 1,024 bytes of DMP memory. There are 4 dynamic memory pools. DMP1 is used exclusively by FSP and workstation requests. DMP2 is used by LAN adapters and DMP3 is used by the disk channels. NetWare v2.2 has added DMP4 as an overflow area for DMP1. This addition adds a substantial amount of FSPs to the system and relieves potential request bottlenecks. Therefore, requests are processed faster and the system grants a higher level of performance.

Statistics. NetWare v2.2 provides a wonderful maintenance utility called FCONSOLE. FCONSOLE provides the network manager with a plethora of server statistics, one of which is *statistics summary*. The Statistics Summary screen may look like Greek to the untrained eye, but to the professional NetWare number-cruncher, it affords a wealth of performance knowledge. Some usage level results to look out for:

- *File service processes* should never fall below 3.
- *Current server utilization* above 80 percent means the server needs more RAM.
- *Disk requests serviced from cache* should not drop below 80 percent.

Other screens to examine are Cache Statistics and Disk Statistics:

- The number of *cache misses* should never exceed 20 percent of the total cache count.
- The *thrashing count* should be near zero.
- Dirty LRU blocks equal more server RAM.
- *I/O error count* on the rise means it's time to reformat your server disk.
- If the *hot fix remaining* parameter continually decreases, the disk is probably going bad.

NetWare v2.2 is a relatively fast network operating system as it is. But these techniques can help you give NetWare that extra boost your network might require. Don't be afraid to experiment with OS parameters. Just make sure you have a solid backup before you begin.

Connectivity

NetWare v2.2 is media independent. This enables your network's team to integrate incompatible types of network hardware. In addition, NetWare v2.2 supports server applications as VAPs. These VAPs can be used to incorporate multiple protocols and various workstation platforms.

Also, NetWare v2.2 supports internal and external routers. This enables the LAN to extend beyond the boundaries of a single topology to multiple LANs or a workgroup WAN. Let's examine these connectivity features in a little more depth.

Media Independence. NetWare v2.2 supports all popular topology designs, including Ethernet, ARCNet, Token Ring, and LocalTalk. The OS core relies on hardware drivers to provide protocol translations and connectivity support. The hardware drivers are integrated with the OS core during the installation procedure. NetWare v2.2 supports most popular LAN drivers and disk drivers.

VAPs. NetWare v2.2 Macintosh VAPs enable a PC-compatible network to integrate Macintosh workstations. The NetWare for Macintosh v2.2 VAP provides NetWare functionality to Macintosh workstations over Apple's own *AppleTalk Filing Protocol (AFP), Printer Access Protocol (PAP),* and AppleTalk protocol phases I and II. Additional name services are added to support Macintosh folders and extended naming structure. NetWare v2.2 also supports *Open Data-Link Interface (ODI)* drivers for TCP/IP connectivity. With ODI, a single workstation adapter can handle both IPX/SPX and TCP/IP packets. Other VAP functions include printing, UPS monitoring, and third-party processes.

Routing. NetWare v2.2 allows four independent NICs in the file server. Through internal routing functions, NetWare v2.2 will communicate between these NICs and allow connectivity within and among the four separate LANs. In addition, NetWare v2.2 supports external routers on dedicated or nondedicated workstations. The router installation procedure (ROUTEGEN) creates a router OS file called ROUTER.EXE. ROUTER.EXE is executed at the workstation and binds multiple LANs together.

Because of the limitations of the 80286-based file server architecture, NetWare v2.2 doesn't inherently support any other connectivity options. NetWare v3.11 provides a much higher level of connectivity to UNIX clients, mainframes, remote workstations, and diverse protocols.

Half the work that is done in this world is to make things appear what they are not.

—Elias Root Beadle

User Interface

NetWare v2.2 looks like DOS. Many users think that NetWare *is* DOS; it isn't. NetWare v2.2 is its own operating system, but it operates in the client's native environment—DOS, Windows, OS/2, or Macintosh. This client-based interface makes it easy for users to get comfortable with the NetWare environment. In addition, NetWare v2.2 introduces an entirely new on-line help system. The product is called *Infobase,* and it was developed by Folio.

The Infobase supports full text searches and context-sensitive help. NetWare v2.2 and v3.11 include their own Infobase. NetWare v4.0 includes a new information database called ElectroText. Also, NetWare v2.2 provides two different types of utilities: command-line utilities and menu utilities. Command-line utilities are designed for advanced users who require an immediate response from the command line. Command-line utilities can also be used in batch files and login scripts. Menu utilities are for users who don't enjoy the cryptic command-line language. Menu utilities also provide additional functionality for users.

Network Management

The most noticeable improvement from v2.15 in NetWare v2.2 is network management. Novell has completely rewritten some of the earlier management utilities, as well as introduced some entirely new ones. In addition, the installation process has been revamped and simplified—it now takes three hours instead of three days to install a NetWare v2.2 NOS. Also, Novell has added a centralized print server function and remote printing facilities.

Network management functions are distributed among various user types. The Supervisor (or Supervisor Equivalent) has access to all management functions and all security levels. Workgroup Managers can create, delete, and manage users within their workgroup—they are assistant Supervisors. Console Operators are given special privileges to manage the file server console—FCONSOLE. Print Server Operators are printing supervisors with all printing rights and privileges.

NetWare v2.2's network management capabilities are broken down into three areas: utility management, installation, and printing.

Utility Management. The NetWare v2.2 management utilities are categorized in four ways: command-line utilities (CLU), menu utilities, Supervisor utilities, and console commands. Command-line utilities are executed at the network command line. CLUs can be used to manage users, security, directories/files, and printing. Table 6.2 lists NetWare v2.2's utilities by category.

Menu utilities enable users and Supervisors to perform multiple management tasks by using a menu interface. Most of the CLUs have been incorporated into one of various menu utilities. In addition, NetWare v2.2's menu utilities include commands that cannot be performed at the command line.

Supervisor utilities are specialized management commands that are reserved for the Supervisor's use. These utilities are stored in the SYS:SYSTEM directory, and only the Supervisor is granted access rights to that directory. Supervisor utilities control the file server, user accounts, communication shells, and NetWare accounting. Refer to Table 6.2 for the list of NetWare v2.2's Supervisor utilities.

Console commands are part of the NetWare v2.2 file server operating system. These commands are executed at the file server console prompt. Console commands can also be executed at an external router prompt. These utilities are used to manage shared network resources.

Installation. The NetWare v2.2 installation procedures are a dramatic improvement from v2.15's. The installation process determines critical NetWare features, including performance, security, printing, and system fault tolerance. NetWare v2.2's installation procedure is flexible enough to accommodate an endless number of configuration options.

TABLE 6.2   Network Management Utilities in NetWare v2.2

Command-line Utilities

Users	Security	Dir/Files	Printing
ATTACH	FLAG	CHKDIR	CAPTURE
CASTOFF	FLAGDIR	CHKVOL	NPRINT
CASTON	GRANT	LISTDIR	PSC
LOGIN	REMOVE	MAP	PSTAT
LOGOUT	REVOKE	NCOPY	
SEND	RIGHTS	NDIR	
USERLIST	SETPASS	NVER	
VERSION	SLIST	PURGE	
WHOAMI	TLIST	RENDIR	

Menu Utilities

COLORPAL	PRINTCON	USERDEF
HELP	SYSCON	FILER
PCONSOLE	FCONSOLE	NBACKUP
SESSION	MENU	SALVAGE
DSPACE	PRINTDEF	VOLINFO
MAKEUSER		

Supervisor Utilities

ATOTAL	PAUDIT	DCONFIG
DOSGEN	BINDREST	WSGEN
BINDFIX	SECURITY	

Console Commands

BROADCAST	CLEAR MESSAGE	CLEAR STATION
CONFIG	CONSOLE	DISABLE LOGIN
DISABLE TTS	DISK	DISMOUNT
DISPLAY SERVERS	DISPLAYS NETWORKS	DOS
DOWN	ENABLE LOGIN	ENABLE TTS
MONITOR	MOUNT	NAME
OFF	PRINTER	PURGE
QUEUE	RESET ROUTER	REMIRROR
SEND	SET TIME	SPOOL
TIME	TRACK ON	TRACK OFF
UNMIRROR	UPS	VAP
VER	WATCHDOG	

Initial NetWare installation consists of one menu utility that is executed at the file server console. This utility, INSTALL, configures the installation options and generates NetWare's OS core—NET$OS.EXE. INSTALL also has options for disk testing, disk formatting, and copying of the NetWare system and public utility files.

Workstation installation is performed by the WSGEN menu utility. WSGEN generates the workstation-specific NetWare shell—IPX.COM. Additional installation options can be included in the form of *VAPs*. VAPs are file server application processes that run on top of the NetWare OS core. VAPs provide enhanced services, including system fault tolerance, security, database functions, and interconnectivity. NetWare v2.2 incorporates the following installation options:

OS Mode	Installation Style	NIC Drivers
NIC Configuration	Network Address	Printing Services
Disk Channel	Disk Drivers	Disk Configuration
SFT	File Server Name	Communication Buffers

Printing. NetWare v2.2's printing capabilities are extremely versatile. Network managers can configure network printing to satisfy a variety of communication requirements. NetWare v2.2 printing feature consists of four components: core printing, print servers, print queues, and print management. *Core printing* is used for printers attached directly to the NetWare v2.2 file server. Core printing is established during the NOS installation procedure. *Print servers* are extensions of core printing for printers attached to dedicated or nondedicated workstations. A print server is executed as a VAP on the file server or an EXE file on a dedicated workstation. Nondedicated workstations can provide remote printing services through the RPRINTER utility. It occupies only 4,928 bytes of workstation RAM.

Print queues are temporary holding cells on the server disk that store print jobs while the network printers are busy. Print queues exist as subdirectories within the SYS:SYSTEM directory structure. Regardless of where the printing services are installed, all print queues reside on the NetWare v2.2 file server.

Print management consists of a set of CLUs, menu utilities, and console commands. Network managers, print server operators, and print queue operators manage NetWare v2.2 printing through the use of the utilities listed in Table 6.3.

NetWare v2.2 is an ideal solution for small to medium-sized LANs with limited connectivity needs. It also provides excellent NOS functionality within the 80286-based server environment. But if you require more flexibility and better performance, you should probably explore the NetWare v3.11 solution.

Be aware of the limitations of the NetWare v2.2 environment. Unfortunately, those who live by the 80286 also die by the 80286.

TABLE 6.3 Print Management Utilities for v2.2

CLUs	**Menu Utilities**	**Console Commands**
CAPTURE	PCONSOLE	PSERVER (VAP or EXE)
NPRINT	PRINTCON	PRINTER
PSC	PRINTDEF	QUEUE
RPRINTER	RPRINTER	SPOOL

NetWare v3.11

NetWare v3.11 is a complete 32-bit network operating system designed for medium to large-sized LANs that require high performance, modularity, and flexible workstation connectivity. NetWare v3.11 is a substantial improvement over all previous versions of NetWare. The most notable improvements are in the areas of modularity, storage capacity, and connectivity.

- *Modularity*—NetWare v3.11 is the first truly modular network operating system. The core OS consists of three components: the NetWare File System, System Executive, and NLM Software Bus. These components are integrated into one file—SERVER.EXE. All other network services are NetWare loadable modules (NLMs). NetWare v3.11 NLMs are attached to the NLM bus without disrupting the LAN. A huge variety of server applications are written as NLMs, including connectivity drivers, disk drivers, security, SFT, routing, gateways, multiprotocol support, MHS, and printing. Figure 6.2 illustrates the modular NetWare v3.11 OS core and its NLMs.
- *Storage Capacity*—NetWare v3.11 takes full advantage of the 32-bit 80386 file server architecture. This NOS supports almost unlimited amounts of disk storage, memory, and concurrently open files. In addition, the High-Capacity File System (HCFS) supports as many as 2,097,152 directory entries per volume.
- *Connectivity*—NetWare v3.11's 32-bit processing and modular architecture create an open environment for a variety of multiple protocols and workstation platforms. NetWare v3.11 supports IPX/SPX, TCP/IP, AppleTalk, and OSI protocols. NetWare v3.11 also supports DOS, Windows, OS/2, Macintosh, and UNIX workstations. Connectivity is supported as NLMs.

Overall, NetWare v3.11 is an ideal solution for high-performance, interconnected LANs. NetWare v3.11 is available in 5-, 20-, 50-, 100-, and 250-user versions. The street price for a 5-user license is approximately $595. A 20-user package can be bought for around $1,100. NetWare v3.11 might be overkill for some small, workgroup installations. But most LANs with aspirations of connectivity and performance should invest in NetWare v3.11 and not settle for NetWare v2.2. Let's take a longer look at the features and functionality of NetWare v3.11.

Configuration

NetWare v3.11 supports only one mode of operation—dedicated. This fact is due to the high-performance NCP and multiprotocol support. NetWare v3.11 is the first of Novell's open architecture solutions. It is designed to provide file sharing, security, printing, SFT, and network management to a huge variety of platforms. NetWare v3.11 supports open architecture through NetWare Loadable Modules (NLMs). These programs are loaded and unloaded from the file server console without disrupting the integrity of the LAN. NLMs link disk drivers, LAN drivers, name space, enhancement utilities, and server management functions to the central OS core. NetWare v3.11 has four types of NLMs:

- Disk Drivers (*.DSK)—disk drivers control communications between NetWare and internal server disks. NetWare v3.11 supports five internal disk drivers: ADISK.DSK, DCB.DSK, PS2ESDI.DSK, PS2MFM.DSK, and PS2SCSI.DSK.

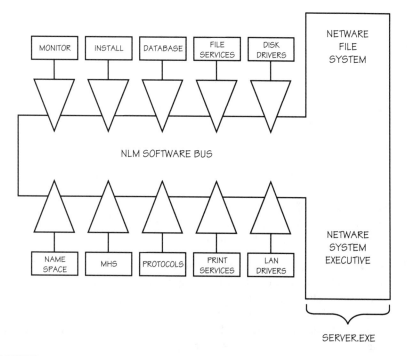

FIGURE 6.2 The Modular NetWare v3.11 Operating System Core and Its NLMs

- LAN Drivers (*.LAN)—LAN drivers control communications between NetWare and internal server NICs. NetWare v3.11 supports 11 internal LAN drivers: TRXNET.LAN, 3C503.LAN, 3C505.LAN, 3C523.LAN, NE2.LAN, NE232.LAN, NE1000.LAN, NE2000.LAN, NE3200.LAN, TOKEN.LAN, and PCN2.LAN.
- Name Space (*.NAM)—name space modules provide NetWare support to non-DOS naming conventions. Currently, NetWare provides file and directory support for OS/2, Macintosh, NFS, and OSI naming conventions: OS2.NAM, MAC.NAM, NFS.NAM, and FTAM.NAM.
- Management NLMs (*.NLM)—management modules provide configuration options to the NetWare OS core. Management modules support disk tests, volume repair, UPS monitoring, remote console, remote booting, multiple protocols, and many various third-party specifications. NetWare v3.11 currently supports several internal management NLMs:

INSTALL	CLIB	DISKSET	ETHERRPL
MATHLIB	NMAGENT	REMOTE	RSPX
STREAMS	TLI	TOKENRPL	UPS
MONITOR	IPXS	SPXS	VREPAIR

NetWare v3.11's high-capacity file system supports third-party drivers for WORM (write once, read many), CD-ROM, and removable media devices. The new system employs a mainframe-style filing system called *Universal File System (UFS)*. UFS allows 100,000 concurrently open files and a maximum of 2,097,152 directory entries per volume—a substantial improvement over version 2.2. There can be 64 volumes and 32 disks per volume, for a total of 2,048 server disks. NetWare v3.11's maximum storage capacity is well beyond current technology—4GB file size and 32TB of maximum addressable storage—that's 32 *trillion* bytes. NetWare v3.11 requires a minimum of 4MB of server RAM and a maximum of 4GB.

The NetWare v3.11 bindery consists of three files: NET$OBJ.SYS for objects, NET$PROP.SYS for properties, and NET$VAL.SYS for data sets. NetWare v3.11 does not support the DISKED utility for accessing locked binderies.

Security

Security for NetWare v3.11 is based on the same seven-layer model as NetWare v2.2. The newer version introduced a few security enhancements, but for the most part, the model remains the same. Following is a brief description of NetWare v3.11's enhancements to the seven-layer security model. Note that layers 1 through 3 and 5 are the same as in v2.2; covered here are the layers that changed in v3.11.

Layer 4: Trustee Assignments. The most substantial security improvement for NetWare v3.11 is in the area of trustee assignments. As mentioned earlier, trustee assignments cascade from directories to all subsequent subdirectories. Also, recall that Effective rights are a combination of trustee assignments and directory rights.

Note: The Maximum Rights Mask (MRM) has been renamed in NetWare v3.11 to more accurately reflect what it does—inherited rights mask (IRM). With NetWare v3.11, effective rights can be calculated in two ways:

1. You can calculate the combination of inherited trustee assignments *(from the parent directory)* and IRM, which is the same as in v2.2.
2. You can calculate a set of explicitly assigned trustee assignments in a given subdirectory that override the IRM, which is unique to v3.11. This means that trustee assignments cancel IRM in the directory where they have been granted, but only in that directory. NetWare v3.11 rights include
   Supervisory—all rights in this directory and all subdirectories
   Read—read an existing file
   File Scan—search the directory or subdirectory
   Write—write to an existing file
   Create—create and write to new files or subdirectories
   Erase—delete existing files or subdirectories
   Modify—modify filenames and attributes
   Access Control—change the existing rights

NetWare v3.11 rights are the same as v2.2, with one exception—Supervisory. The Supervisory right has been added to create *assistant Supervisors.* The Supervisory right overrides all other rights security. Also, in NetWare v3.11, trustee assignments can be granted to files as well as directories.

Layer 6: Directory Attributes. A few additional directory attributes have been added for NetWare v3.11. This level of security emulates the NetWare v2.2 strategy with the addition of the following:

- **D**elete Inhibit—ultimate protection against directory deletion
- **R**ename Inhibit—ultimate protection against renaming directories
- **P**urge—purges all files in a directory—they cannot be retrieved

Layer 7: File Attributes. File attributes have also been enhanced in NetWare v3.11. The improvements were in response to users' needs for ultimate protection against Delete, Rename, and Copy commands. These attributes can be given to any network file. They will overwrite the security granted at previous layers of the NetWare security model. The additional NetWare v3.11 file attributes are as follows:

- **C**opy Inhibit—limits the copy rights of only Macintosh users
- **D**elete Inhibit—limits the delete right of all users
- **R**ename Inhibit—limits the rename ability of all users

All other NetWare v3.11 security features are identical to NetWare v2.2.

System Fault Tolerance

NetWare v3.11 supports system fault tolerance levels I, II, and III. SFT Level III, server duplexing, is an additional product that requires two identical servers. In addition, the machines must be connected with a 100-Mb/s fiber optic line. This level of server SFT is highly protective and expensive. See Chapter 3 for a detailed description of NetWare SFT.

Speed

One of the most notable improvements to the NetWare v3.11 operating system is better performance. The 32-bit architecture has led to considerable improvements in the file server's throughput and response time. File server processes have been refined, and the four dynamic memory pools have been combined into one. File capacity has been improved, and a feature called *Turbo FATs* has been integrated. Turbo FATs provide faster access to large database tables, substantially improving the response time of file reads. In addition, NetWare v3.11 supports 32-bit server NICs and bus mastering. Bus mastering increases server response time over 400 percent.

In addition to these improvements, NetWare v3.11 has introduced two new performance optimization utilities: SET and MONITOR. SET is a console command that offers immediate NOS configuration. MONITOR is a server NLM that provides performance management and optimization functionality. Let's take a look.

SET. The SET console command provides the following nine parameters:

```
1  Communications
2  Locks
3  Memory
4  Transaction tracking
5  File caching
6  Disk
7  Directory caching
8  Miscellaneous
9  File system
```

The SET utility is the most versatile NetWare v3.11 tool. It provides fine-tuning capabilities at the OS core level. As you can see, it provides a huge variety of different configuration options. Some of the more notable parameters with respect to speed and performance are these:

- SET minimum packet receive buffers = 500
- SET maximum concurrent disk cache writes = 100 (favor writes)
- SET maximum concurrent disk cache writes = 10 (favor reads)
- SET dirty disk cache delay time = 1 (favors writes)
- SET maximum outstanding NCP searches = 100
- SET new service process wait time = .3 (for FSPs)
- SET maximum service processes = 35
- SET maximum alloc short-term memory = 3000000

MONITOR. The NetWare v3.11 MONITOR.NLM utility is the most widely used server configuration utility. It offers a variety of options similar to the SET command's, but in a menu environment. MONITOR is loaded at the server console and displays the following seven options:

```
1  Connection Information
2  Lock File Server Console
3  Disk Information
4  File Open/Lock Activity
5  LAN Information
6  Resource Utilization
7  System Module Information
```

In addition to these menu choices, MONITOR provides a server information screen at all times. The screen displays information about CPU usage, cache buffers, disk requests, PRBs, FSPs, and connections in use. This screen can be valuable in optimizing NetWare v3.11 performance. A well-trained network manager can analyze these screens and fine-tune NetWare for increased speed and performance. Following are a few red lights to look for in optimizing NetWare v3.11:

- Memory usage—check total server memory and compare it to memory available for file caching. If cache buffers fall below 25 percent, add memory immediately.
- Dirty cache buffers—these are disk buffers waiting to be written to disk. If this number exceeds 50 percent of total cache buffers, consider increasing the performance of your disk channel to favor writes.
- Service processes—FSPs process incoming user requests. If the number approaches 20, you need more. Consider increasing the maximum with a SET command.

Refer to Chapter 15 for a full discussion of server optimization and the MONITOR utility.

A man travels the world over in search of what he needs, and returns home to find it.

—George Moore

Connectivity

NetWare v3.11 has substantially more connectivity than earlier versions provided, due primarily to NetWare v3.11's open architecture. The NLM software bus supports a diverse variety of multiplatform tools. NetWare v3.11 supports DOS, OS/2, UNIX, Macintosh, and Windows clients, as well as OSI, UNIX, SNA, and DEC VAX hosts. Later, this chapter discusses NetWare connectivity from a variety of different client platforms. Chapter 3 outlined Novell's product strategy for support of multiple host platforms. Following is a brief list of NetWare v3.11 connectivity solutions for multiple clients and hosts:

Client Connectivity

DOS	The only built-in client support uses workstation shells IPX and NETx
OS/2	The NetWare Requester for OS/2, a set of OS/2 client and server tools
UNIX	NetWare NFS, a set of server NLMs for connectivity to UNIX clients
Macintosh	NetWare for Macintosh v3.01, a set of AppleTalk client and server tools
Windows	NetWare Tools and NWADMIN, utilities for optimizing NetWare LANs

Host Connectivity

OSI	NetWare FTAM, a set of client and host services for OSI-compatible systems
UNIX	LAN WorkPlace, a set of NetWare client tools for accessing UNIX hosts
UNIX	NetWare NFS, a version of NetWare to support UNIX hosts
SNA	NetWare for SAA, a set of NLMs for client access to SNA hosts
DEC VAX	NetWare VMS, a version of NetWare for DEC VAX hosts

User Interface

NetWare v3.11 is even easier to use than NetWare v2.2. It uses the same DOS-like interface and a greatly improved on-line help system. The plethora of connectivity products make for a simple integration of NetWare v3.11 and native client environments. NetWare for Macintosh makes NetWare look like a Macintosh, whereas NetWare NFS makes NetWare look like a UNIX machine. NetWare v3.11's open architecture makes this all possible, and that is probably the most friendly interface of all.

Network Management

As with security, NetWare v3.11 network management operates on the same foundations as NetWare v2.2. Utility management has changed little and the printing services are unchanged. The most notable difference is in the installation procedure. Following is a description of NetWare v3.11's network management capabilities, focusing on the improvements over NetWare v2.2.

Utility Management. The NetWare v3.11 management utilities have changed little. The only considerable enhancement is in the console commands. Table 6.4 lists the NetWare v3.11 management utilities—utilities new in v3.11 are identified by ***bold italic***.

Installation. The NetWare v3.11 installation process has been dramatically improved over NetWare v2.2. The modular nature of NetWare v3.11 makes it easy to install and uninstall LAN components. The NetWare v3.11 installation procedure consists of one

TABLE 6.4   Network Management Utilities for NetWare v3.11

Command-line Utilities

Users	Security	Dir/Files	Printing
ATTACH	*ALLOW*	CHKDIR	CAPTURE
CASTOFF	FLAG	CHKVOL	ENDCAP
CASTON	FLAGDIR	LISTDIR	NPRINT
LOGIN	GRANT	MAP	PSC
LOGOUT	REMOVEN	COPY	RPRINTER
SEND	REVOKE	NDIR	
SLIST	RIGHTS	NVER	
USERLIST	SETPASS	PURGE	
VERSION	SYSTIME	RENDIR	
WHOAMI	TLIST		

Menu Utilities

COLORPAL	MAKEUSER	PRINTDEF
JUMPERS	PRINTCON	USERDEF
PCONSOLE	SYSCON	NBACKUP
SESSION	FILERHELP	SALVAGE
DSPACE	MENU	VOLINFO

Supervisor Utilities

ACONSOLE	PAUDIT	BINDREST
COMCHECK	*UPGRADE*	ECONFIG
FCONSOLE	BINDFIX	SECURITY
SMODE	DOSGEN	WSUPDATE
ATOTAL	*RCONSOLE*	
DCONFIG	WSGEN	

Console Commands

ADD NAME SPACE	*BIND*	BROADCAST
CLS	CLEAR STATION	CONFIG
DISABLE LOGIN	DISABLE TTS	DISMOUNT
DISPLAY SERVERS	DISPLAYS NETWORKS	DOWN
ENABLE LOGIN	ENABLE TTS	*EXIT*
LOAD	*MODULES*	MOUNT
NAME	OFF	*PROTOCOL*
REGISTER MEMORY	*REMOVE DOS*	RESET ROUTER
SEARCH	*SECURE CONSOLE*	SET
SEND	SET TIME	*SPEED*
SPOOL	TRACK ON	TRACK OFF
UNBIND	*UNLOAD*	*UPS TIME*
UPS STATUS	*VERSION*	*VOLUMES*

step—load the SERVER.EXE file. It is that simple. Of course, you can't communicate with anything, but you *do* have a NetWare v3.11 server. The new installation procedure consists of four components: NetWare OS core, disk driver, LAN driver, and support NLMs. The *NetWare OS core* is a 1MB file called SERVER.EXE. This file contains the three components necessary for a NetWare v3.11 OS core—the NetWare File System, System Executive, and NLM software bus.

All other LAN components plug into the SERVER.EXE file. The disk driver is necessary to establish reliable communications between SERVER.EXE and the internal hard disk. The LAN driver handles communications with the internal network interface card. Finally, the NLMs plug into SERVER's NLM Software Bus and provide management, configuration, and connectivity functions.

The NetWare v3.11 installation process consists of seven steps: disk preparation, SERVER, disk driver, LAN driver, INSTALL, copy SYSTEM and PUBLIC files, and startup files. These steps are

Step 1: Disk Preparation

1. Boot DOS.
2. Create DOS partition.
3. Format DOS partition.
4. Copy SERVER to C:.
5. Create AUTOEXEC.BAT.

Step 2: Server Installation

1. Run SERVER.EXE.
2. Name file server.
3. Enter internal IPX number.

Step 3: Disk Driver

1. Load *.DSK.
2. Load DISKSET (optional).

Step 4: LAN Driver

1. Load NMAGENT (optional).
2. Load *.LAN.
3. Bind IPX to *.LAN.
4. Enter net number.

Step 5: INSTALL.NLM

1. Load INSTALL.
2. Create NetWare partition.
3. Create SYS: and other volumes.
4. Mount volumes.

Step 6: Copy Files

1. Copy SYSTEM files.
2. Copy PUBLIC files.

Step 7: Startup Files

1. Create AUTOEXEC.NCF.
2. Create STARTUP.NCF.

NetWare v3.11 is an ideal solution for medium to large-sized LANs. The open architecture and 32-bit server platform provide multifaceted network users with transparent connectivity to a variety of different host environments—including NetWare servers. The security structure is sophisticated, and server performance rates well above NetWare v2.2. NetWare v3.11 represents almost 90 percent of all new NetWare LANs, and its total installation base is quickly surpassing NetWare 2.2.

So, is NetWare v3.11 for everybody? No. NetWare v3.11 serves a diverse market, but it is not for everybody. Smaller LANs don't need all the power v3.11 affords, and larger WANs need more connectivity tools. NetWare v3.11 fits extremely well between the low-end NetWare v2.2 and high-end NetWare v4.0.

NetWare v4.0

NetWare v4.0 is not an upgrade from NetWare v3.11. It is a *migration*. NetWare v4.0 is a completely different way of approaching local area networking. It splits the realm of networking into two halves: logical and physical. The logical half defines organizations and workgroups; the physical half defines users and servers. NetWare v4.0 could be overkill for many small to medium-sized LANs with fewer than five servers. Network designers everywhere will have to decide whether their LAN warrants the sophistication, complexity, and high price tag of NetWare v4.0.

NetWare v4.0 is the big *Kahuna*. It represents Novell's ninth generation of the NetWare network operating system. The original architects of NetWare—Drew Major and Superset—returned to the proverbial drawing board and completely redesigned the interface, communications, and functionality of NetWare. The result is a GUI, flexible, fast WAN NOS. NetWare v4.0 epitomizes *transparent connectivity*. It unobtrusively provides the user with simultaneous access to multiple network resources from one login. Users no longer belong to servers, they belong to the NETWORK as a whole. All resources on the network are treated as objects in a hierarchical tree—much like files in a directory structure. Users, servers, printers, volumes, and groups are treated equally and given simultaneous access to each other's resources. This is all made possible through NetWare v4.0's newest wonder—*NetWare Directory Services (NDS)*.

NDS is an object-oriented database that organizes network resources into a hierarchical tree. The global NDS tree is fully replicated and distributed throughout the network, thus providing efficient connectivity and network fault tolerance. NDS also features a single login and hidden security system that makes access to any server, volume, or network resource completely transparent to the user. NDS takes care of the complexities of network topology, communications, protocol translation, and authentication in the background—far away from the general user. NDS is simplicity through sophistication.

In addition to NetWare Directory Services, NetWare v4.0 offers better RAM management, disk utilization, auditing services, GUI utilities, and on-line documentation. Following is a brief description of the new features offered in NetWare v4.0.

RAM Management

NetWare v4.0 manages file server RAM more efficiently than does NetWare v3.11. Earlier versions of NetWare allocated memory to multiple pools that served specific purposes. In NetWare v3.11 these pools expanded as needed but rarely returned unused memory. Occasionally a server application ran out of RAM even if there was plenty of memory available in the main pool. NetWare v4.0 has consolidated all server RAM into one main pool, and memory is reallocated as needed. The server operates much more efficiently and applications rarely run out of valuable file server RAM.

Disk Utilization

NetWare v4.0 incorporates three impressive disk usage strategies: block suballocation, data migration, and file compression. These three disk usage strategies were designed to solve some serious disk space management problems with NetWare v2.2 and v3.11. *Block suballocation* solves the problem of wasted space with medium to large block sizes. This feature divides any partially used disk block into 512-byte suballocation blocks, thus saving the remainder of the block for other files.

Here's an example of the serious effects of wasting disk space with block allocation. Imagine you have set your volume block allocation to 64KB blocks and you need to save a 65KB file. Without block suballocation, the 65KB file would require two disk blocks, or 128KB. That's 63KB of wasted space. A user could run out of space on an 80MB server disk before loading the SYSTEM and PUBLIC files if he or she set the block allocation size to 64KB. With block suballocation, the file would require a 64KB block and two 512-byte suballocation blocks, resulting in no wasted space.

Data migration solves the problem of disk cram by providing an efficient method for "near-line" storage. Near-line storage is somewhere between on-line (hard disks) and off-line (tape backup). Data migration provides near-line storage by automatically transferring inactive data to a tape drive or optical disk without actually removing the data's entries from the server's DET or FAT. The data still appears to be on the volume and users can transparently access the data without having to worry about the near-line device.

File compression eases the pain of purchasing expensive on-line disks. This feature allows NetWare v4.0 volumes to hold more on-line data by automatically compressing inactive files. Users can save up to 63 percent of the server's disk by activating file compression—that's 1GB of files in 370MB. File compression is activated in one of two ways: by flagging directories and files as IC (immediate compress) or by using the SET console commands to configure the inactivity delay for compression. By default, file compression is turned on and the inactivity delay is set to seven days. Users can avoid file compression by flagging specific files DC (don't compress). Files are automatically decompressed when users access them.

Drew Major is excited about the new algorithms that he and Superset used to develop NetWare v4.0 file compression. They are the most efficient and effective software-based file compression routines known to exist. Not only are the routines fast but they are also processed in the background to avoid any interference with critical OS operations. This makes for a fleet, unobtrusive file compression feature.

Auditing Services

NetWare v4.0 includes a sophisticated and secure group of auditing services that act independently from network administration. One of the biggest complaints about previous versions of NetWare was that the auditing features were both limited and integrated with network management. Novell answered these complaints with AUDITCON—a fully functional auditing console. The auditing administrator uses a different password than the network Administrator and has all rights needed to perform auditing functions only. Auditing administrators can monitor and track network activity at two different levels: throughout the NDS tree and within server volumes. A full list of auditing features is discussed later, under Security.

GUI Utilities

NetWare v4.0 has vastly improved the interface for both user and Administrator utilities. In addition, NetWare v4.0 offers a group of integrated utilities that perform the functions of numerous NetWare v2.2 and v3.11 programs. At the forefront of the new utility revolution is NWADMIN—a fully integrated, Windows-based graphical Administrator tool. The other GUI Administrator utility is PAR—a graphical partition manager for creating NDS partitions and replicas. NetWare v4.0 also offers text-based menu versions of these integrated utilities for Administrators who would rather steer clear of the GUI environment. They are NETADMIN and PARTMGR, respectively. In addition to the GUI utilities, NetWare v4.0 features enhanced console commands, server NLMs, workstation menu utilities, and command-line utilities. We will discuss these utilities in more depth later, under Network Management.

On-line Documentation

Novell has integrated the NetWare v4.0 documentation library into the operating system files. The CD-ROM installation enables you to load the on-line documentation ("ElectroText") onto the server disk and make it available to all network users. ElectroText uses the NetWare Communication Services browser to display documentation text and figures graphically. The ElectroText browser provides a straightforward interface for electronic documentation of any kind. It includes a library window, book display, and search engine. The library window offers the opportunity for Novell to integrate a variety of documents in multimedia form—in fact, *The Complete NetWare Construction Kit* may be available someday in browser form. The browser is currently available for Windows. Later versions will support Presentation Manager, X Windows, and Finder.

In addition to the five major features, NetWare v4.0 offers a few auxiliary improvements. These improvements are designed to provide subtle fine tuning of existing NetWare strengths. Following is a brief description of these subtle improvements:

- *High-Capacity Storage System (HCSS)*—NetWare v4.0 transparently supports optical disk changers (jukeboxes) as extensions of existing volumes.
- *International language support*—NetWare v4.0 provides utility and installation compatibility with multiple languages. Standard NetWare v4.0 supports English, French, German, Italian, Spanish, and Japanese. Language modules will be available for U.K., Canadian French, Russian, Chinese, Norwegian, Dutch, Portuguese, Danish, Finnish, Korean, and Swedish.
- *NLMs in protected mode*—NetWare v4.0 enables you to load misbehaved NLMs in a protected segment of server memory called the OS_PROTECTED domain. This way you can test third-party NLMs before you load them into the OS domain—ring 0.
- *Protocol optimization*—NetWare v4.0 provides the capacity for packet bursting and LIP (Large Internet Packets). Packet bursting transmits multipacket messages between workstations and servers in a bursting mode. This increases communications performance over large internetwork lines. In addition, Large Internet Packets are created to increase throughput over network bridges and routers.

To activate packet bursting and LIP, add the following two lines to the workstation's NET.CFG file:

```
PACKET BURST BUFFERS = 3

LARGE INTERNET PACKETS=ON
```

- *Enhanced print services*—NetWare v4.0 enables users to print directly to printers without worrying about their corresponding print servers and queues. Printers are treated as objects just the same as printer servers, volumes, users, and queues.
- *Time synchronization*—NetWare v4.0 supports global networks by providing time synchronization for critical NDS servers. Time synchronization is a method of ensuring that all NDS objects report the same timestamp. This is important for updating replicas and ensuring accurate auditing records. Time synchronization is controlled by four types of time servers: Single Reference, Primary, Reference, and Secondary Reference. Chapter 10 discusses time synchronization servers.
- *User authentication*—Novell is paranoid about packet theft and communications siphoning in NetWare v4.0. In order to avoid these security breaches, Novell has incorporated a sophisticated system of user authentication. User authentication establishes a session-specific, unique user code for each user at login. All subsequent network requests for that session are authenticated using this unique code. Furthermore, the code and critical user data (passwords) are never sent over the communications lines. They permanently reside on the server. User authentication has been incorporated to make NetWare v4.0's security system C2 compliant—a high level of security.
- *Yellow Pages*—NetWare v4.0 includes a simple NDS searching tool called *Yellow Pages*. It is a fully functional searching engine for NetWare Directory Services. Yellow Pages works in conjunction with NWADMIN and NETADMIN to provide searching capabilities to network managers. Yellow Pages includes a fuzzy-logic searching algorithm you can use to search for any object in the NDS

tree by using normal English sentences, for example, "Find all LaserJet printers on the third floor of building 7."

NetWare v4.0 is ideal for large, sophisticated internetworks with multiple locations, protocols, and client architectures. Figure 6.3 shows a typical NetWare internetwork structure that could best benefit from NetWare v4.0. Don't be fooled, though; v4.0 does offer myriad features for small to medium-sized LANs: file compression, GUI utilities, and on-line documentation. *You* will have to decide whether these features justify the product's additional cost and relatively high learning curve. NetWare v4.0 is not for everybody. The goal here is to arm you with the tools you need to make the right decision. Let's take a long, hard look at NetWare v4.0, starting with NetWare Directory Services.

NetWare Directory Services

NetWare v4.0 introduces a completely new way of approaching LANs, WANs, and MANs—NetWare Directory Services (NDS). NDS is a combination of features from OSI X.500, Banyan StreetTalk, and some stuff nobody has heard of before. The result is an object-oriented, hierarchical directory structure with complex access rights and distributed partitions. NDS classifies all network resources in 19 different object types. These objects are organized into a logical tree that resembles an organizational chart or directory filing

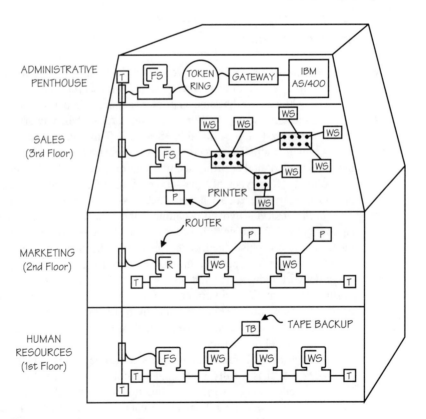

FIGURE 6.3   A Typical NetWare Internetwork

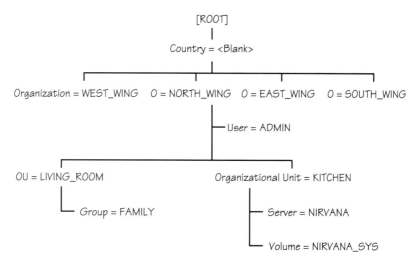

FIGURE 6.4 The Castle NDS Tree

structure, as shown in Figure 6.4. Objects can be organized by function, location, size, type, color—it doesn't matter. The point is that the NDS tree organizes objects independently from their physical location or proximity to users. When a user logs into the network, he or she can access any object in the tree regardless of its location—assuming of course that he or she has sufficient access rights.

The NDS tree is stored in a fully replicated, globally distributed, object-oriented database called the "Directory." The Directory consists of approximately four hidden/system files in a hidden directory attached to the root of the SYS: volume on each server. The directory is named _NETWARE and the files are

BLOCK.NDS   ENTRY.NDS   VALUE.NDS   PARTITION.NDS

The directory consists of objects, properties, and values. The objects define logical or physical entities that provide organizational or technical function to the network. Refer to Figure 11.3 in Chapter 11 for an illustration of the 19 objects and their associated icons. Each object has a list of properties that define its function. Values define the data that outlines the object properties. For example, the following chart would define me as a user object:

```
Object:    USER
Property:  LOGIN NAME
Value:     DAVID
```

NDS objects come in two flavors: container objects and leaf objects (as you can see, the tree analogy is alive and well). *Container objects* define the organizational boundaries of the NDS tree and house other container objects or leaf objects. *Leaf objects* are the physical network entities that provide technical services and functionality. Leaf objects define the lowest level of the NDS structure.

Figure 6.4 shows my castle NDS tree. The highest level is defined by the [Root] container object. This level cannot be redefined. The next level is the *COUNTRY (C)* container object. This level can be skipped. To use the COUNTRY object, you must be explicit about its place in the tree. NDS assumes the highest level is *ORGANIZATION (O)*. The third level is mandatory—the ORGANIZATION container object. The ORGANIZATION object is typically the beginning of a custom NDS tree. When I used the ORGANIZATION level to define the four corners of my castle, I established that this tree will be organized according to location and function. The ORGANIZATION level can only be one layer deep. Further stratification is provided by the last container object—the *ORGANIZATIONAL UNIT (OU)*. The ORGANIZATIONAL UNIT is the most versatile NDS object, because it can exist throughout the tree.

OUs house leaf objects or other OUs. Notice how I used the OU objects to define the rooms of my castle—again according to geographic location and functionality.

The remaining 16 object types are all leaf objects. Of the 16 object types, 4 are logical and 12 are physical. The 4 logical objects define aliases, groups, organizational roles, and profiles. This discussion focuses on the workhorses of our NDS tree—the physical leaf objects. Here is a brief description of each of them:

- *AFP Server*—represents an AppleTalk Filing Protocol server for native Apple Macintosh workstations.
- *Bindery*—represents an object that is placed in the Directory tree from a NetWare v2.2 or v3.11 migration and cannot be accurately represented by any one of the other leaf objects. This object is used for backward compatibility with older NetWare utilities.
- *Bindery Queue*—represents a bindery-based print queue from a NetWare v2.2 or v3.11 migration. This object also provides backward compatibility for older NetWare utilities.
- *Computer*—represents a specific computer in the network. The computer's properties include serial number, location, physical characteristics, network address, and the specific user to whom it is assigned.
- *Directory Map*—represents a global mapping to a specific directory within a specific volume anywhere in the network. The map's properties include a reference to the home server and the directory to be mapped. Also, properties of this object enable you to establish a variety of security rights.
- *NetWare Server*—represents a NetWare-based server in the network running any version of Novell NetWare. The server's properties include network address, operators, location, users, resources, and supported services. You can also define the version of NetWare and install NetWare accounting.
- *Print Server*—represents a NetWare-defined print server.
- *Printer*—represents any kind of physical printing device.
- *Print Queue*—represents a specific mapping to a printer or group of printers.
- *User*—represents the users who access network resources and add value to your network. The user's properties are complete. They include the real name, office location, postal address, E-mail address, description, title, function, home server, and even default language spoken. In addition, the user properties define valuable security information, including time restrictions, password configurations, intruder detection status, volume space restrictions, memberships, profiles, and security equivalences.

- *Volume*—represents logical volumes on physical disks within NetWare-based servers or HCSS devices. The volume's properties include name, host server, location, and volume restrictions. In addition, the properties display useful statistics and feature summaries for network management and disk optimization.
- *Unknown*—an NDS object that cannot be recognized by or classified as any of the other 18 object types.

An object's location in the Directory tree is defined by its context. *Context* is established as the object's complete path from point A to the top of the tree. Let's use my castle structure as an example. In Figure 6.3, the FAMILY object would have the following context:

```
CN=FAMILY.OU=LIVING_ROOM.O=NORTH_WING
```

Capital abbreviations define the object's type. In this case, CN stands for *common name*. Context is important, because it establishes where you are in the tree and provides a tool for navigating through the NDS utilties—NWADMIN and NETADMIN. Users can change their current context by using the CX (Change conteXt) command-line utility. Context is also important because it helps the system find your user object when you try to log in. Users must either provide their home context with the LOGIN command or change to the correct context first—the CX command.

Following are two examples of defining user context during login:

```
LOGIN CN=ADMIN.O=NORTH_WING
```

and

```
CX O=NORTH_WING
LOGIN ADMIN
```

Once a user has logged into the NDS tree, his or her ability to access other objects is determined by a complex NDS security structure. At the heart of NDS security is the *access control list (ACL)*. The ACL is a property of every NDS object. It defines who can access the object (trustees) and what each trustee can do (rights). The ACL is divided into two types of rights: object rights and property rights. *Object rights* define an object's trustees and control what the trustees can do with the object. *Property rights* limit the trustee's access to only specific properties of the object.

Working with NetWare Directory Services reminds me of a word my father used to use when I was growing up—*planning.* **The key to life and to a successful NDS tree is planning. A well-designed Directory can increase fault tolerance, decrease network traffic, increase global access to network information, and make it much easier to administer network resources. Plan carefully to ensure that you understand the ramifications of your NDS design before you install your first NetWare v4.0 server. I guess my dad was well ahead of his time.**

For example, let's say the group object FAMILY is a trustee of the user object DAVID. FAMILY has the *Browse* object right, which means any member of the group can see DAVID and view information about him. But David is shy. He only wants the family members to see his last name, telephone number, and postal address. So DAVID limits the group's rights by assigning the *Read* property right to only these three properties: last name, telephone number, and postal address.

NDS security is further complicated with trustee assignments, effective rights, and the inherited rights filter (IRF). We will explore NDS security later, under Security.

In summary, the NDS feature adds value and flexibility to NetWare v4.0. It is relatively simple at first glance but can get complicated quickly. This section gave you a general feeling of what NDS is about and how it applies to the average NetWare v4.0 LAN. The following sections will fine-tune your understanding of NDS and show how it combines with the other features of NetWare v4.0 to create operating system synergy.

Recall from earlier sections that our exploration of NetWare v4.0 will focus on seven different NOS components:

- configuration
- security
- system fault tolerance
- speed
- connectivity
- user interface
- network management

The discussion of NetWare v4.0 will build on our understanding of NetWare v3.11, which built on the understanding of NetWare v2.2. Compare these earlier sections across versions to grasp all the evolutionary improvements. Let's begin the exploration with NetWare v4.0 configuration.

Configuration

To a certain degree, NetWare v4.0 follows in the footsteps of NetWare v3.11. They share the same open architecture model and reliance on one central component for the operating system core—the SERVER.EXE file. Their installation processes are nearly identical, and security hasn't changed much within the NetWare server.

The biggest change is the migration from a bindery-based system to NetWare Directory Services. The bindery was a flat-file database that contained information about one server only. It didn't know anything about other servers or network resources. NetWare v4.0 replaces the bindery with the NDS Directory, which is a hierarchical database and contains information about every network resource on the LAN or WAN. The bindery files have been replaced by four database files in a hidden directory named _NETWARE. These files can grow to enormous sizes quickly. (Note: The Directory files start at about 100KB in total.)

In an effort to ease disk cram and provide NDS fault tolerance, the NDS Directory is distributed throughout the network in the form of partitions and replicas. *Partitions* are pieces of the NDS tree that define the objects within a server's current context. *Replicas* are copies of other server partitions. Each server in the NDS tree only contains information about its own partition. Typically, no one server will contain the entire Directory. If a specific server needs information about objects outside its own partition, it can request a replica from another NetWare server. Partitions and replicas are described in more depth later, under System Fault Tolerance.

The biggest concern with NetWare v4.0's radical new approach is compatibility with bindery-based servers. Fortunately, NetWare v4.0 contains a sophisticated bindery emulation system. *Bindery emulation* provides backward compatibility with bindery-based servers by making the NetWare v4.0 Directory look like a bindery to NetWare v2.2 and v3.11 servers in the same container object.

Because the bindery database is a flat-file structure, bindery emulation can only exist within one container object—an organization or organizational unit. This means that NDS servers outside the current container object will not exist for NetWare v2.2 or v3.11 servers. The current context of bindery emulation for a specific NetWare v4.0 server is called its *bindery context*. This value is set automatically at installation for all NetWare v4.0 servers and can be changed by using the SET BINDERY CONTEXT = command at the file server console. Bindery emulation makes NetWare v4.0 servers available to NetWare v2.2 and v3.11 users and enables NetWare v4.0 users to see NetWare v2.2 and v3.11 resources.

Regardless of all these strange new additions, NetWare v4.0 is still based on the Intel 80386 32-bit architecture. This means that most of the server specifications from NetWare v3.11 still hold true. The maximum number of users is still 1,000, with 4GB of maximum RAM and 32TB of addressable disk storage. The Universal File System allows 100,000 concurrently open files and a maximum of 2,097,152 directory entries per volume.

The minimum server requirements are a little more demanding than NetWare v3.11: An 80386DX is required (no 80386SX servers allowed), with 8MB of minimum server RAM and 70MB of disk storage for system/public files and on-line documentation. In addition, NetWare v4.0 shares the same approach to NetWare loadable modules as NetWare v3.11: disk drivers, LAN drives, name space, and management NLMs. NetWare v4.0 offers a few additional NLMs—DOMAIN, DSREPAIR, and RPL to name a few. The most amazing improvement is SERVMAN—a Server Management NLM. SERVMAN is covered later, under Network Management.

Security

NetWare v4.0 security is organized into two functional groups: above the server and within the server. Security *above the server* is controlled by NDS objects and their access control lists. Security *within the server* applies to directories, files, and volumes. This security is nearly identical to the seven-layered security model of NetWare v3.11. In addition, NetWare v4.0 provides an independent auditing feature called AUDITCON.

In order to understand the two functional groups of NetWare v4.0 security, use the server as a midpoint. In the first group (NDS security), the server is at the bottom of the tree. It is treated as an object just like users, volumes, printers, and groups. In the second group (directory/file security), the server is at the top of the tree. It houses the volumes, directories, and files. Understanding the server's point of view will help you to understand the concepts behind each security design.

Security above the server is analogous to directory/file security in concept, but the rights are different and they apply to NDS objects instead of specific directories or files. As you saw earlier, NDS rights are assigned to objects (object rights) and properties (property rights). Object rights can be acquired in three ways: by trustee assignment, inheritance, or ancestral inheritance. Global property rights can be inherited, but rights to specific properties must be assigned explicitly. Following is a breakdown of NDS security rights:

- *Trustee assignment*—an object can be given explicit access to any other object or its properties through the process of trustee assignments. A trustee assignment is granted by adding the object's name and associated rights to a host object's ACL property. This procedure can be performed in NWADMIN or NETADMIN.

- *Inheritance*—an object can also acquire object and property rights through inheritance. If rights are granted at the [Root], country, organization, or organizational unit level, the rights are inherited for all container and leaf objects underneath. This means that rights assigned to the [Root] object are inherited by every object in the NDS tree, so be careful. Inheritance can be blocked using the Inherited Rights Filter (IRF). The IRF will block inherited rights but not trustee assignments. The resulting rights after inheritance and the IRF are called *effective rights*. These are the actual rights an object can use within another object.

- *Ancestral inheritance*—objects can inherit rights by being associated with other objects. For example, if OU=LIVING_ROOM was granted object rights to the NIRVANA server, then every object in the organizational unit would ancestrally inherit the same rights. Furthermore, all members of the group FAMILY would also ancestrally inherit rights to NIRVANA, even though they are twice removed from the original trustee assignment. Wow, NDS security can really get weird!

Be careful with ancestral inheritance (AI). AI can quickly become a rights nightmare and create gaping holes in your NDS security structure. The best way to avoid AI is to avoid assigning container objects as trustees. If you want to make the same trustee assignment to a variety of different objects, create a group and assign the object rights there. Group assignments are not as dangerous as container object assignments.

Object and property rights are designed to provide efficient access to NDS objects. Following is a brief description of these important NDS rights:

Object Rights

Browse	See the object in a graphical view or search of the NDS tree.
Create	Create objects within the context of this container object.
Delete	Delete objects from the NDS tree.
Rename	Modify the common name property of the object.
Supervisor	All object and property rights; Supervisor can be inherited.

Property Rights

Compare	Compare any value to the value of the property and return True/False.
Read	Read values of the property, including compare.
Write	Modify, add, or delete any value of the property, including self.
Add or Delete Self	Add or delete self as a value of the property.
Supervisor	All property rights; Supervisor can be inherited.

Security within the server is nearly identical to NetWare v3.11. NetWare v4.0 follows the same seven-layered security model once we get inside the server. Volumes, directories, and files are subject to the same access restrictions, user rights, IRM (actually IRF), and attributes. Following is a brief description of directory/file security improvements in NetWare v4.0. Note: Layers 3 through 5 of the security system remain unchanged from v3.11. Refer to the earlier discussion of NetWare v3.11 security for a description of those three layers.

Layer 1: Login Name. When logging into a NetWare v4.0 system, users don't log into the server, they log into the network. Earlier you learned the process of establishing user context when users log in. This works well for NetWare v4.0 servers but not for bindery emulation. To log into bindery-based servers using the NetWare v4.0 LOGIN command, use the /B option.

Layer 2: Password. NetWare v4.0 accepts PC passwords of up to 127 characters, which is a substantial improvement over earlier versions of NetWare. This limit is significantly different—and much more limited at 11 characters—for Macintosh clients. In fact, one way of locking out Macintosh clients is to set the Minimum Password Length to 12.

Layer 6: Directory Attributes. Directory attributes have been enhanced in NetWare v4.0 to reflect the changes in file compression and data migration:

Immediate Compress—all files are immediately compressed.
Don't Compress—files in the directory can never be compressed.
Don't Migrate—files in the directory are never migrated to near-line.

Layer 7: File Attributes. File attributes have also been enhanced in NetWare v4.0. The improvements correspond to additional features only available in NetWare v4.0, namely file compression and data migration:

Can't Compress—set by NetWare. The file cannot be compressed.
Compressed—set by NetWare. The file is compressed.
Migrated—set by NetWare. The file has been migrated to near-line storage.
Immediate Compress—the file will be immediately compressed.
Don't Compress—the file will never be compressed.
Don't Migrate—the file will never be migrated to near-line.

An additional feature of NetWare v4.0 security is AUDITCON. This menu utility provides a sophisticated suite of auditing services that act independently of traditional network management. The key to AUDITCON is its password strategy. Unique passwords are required at multiple stages throughout the auditing process. These passwords are kept independently from ADMIN and other administrative users. Auditors can track network transactions according to a variety of different activities: logins, logouts, trustee modifications, file access, file modifications, NDS access, NDS modifications, queue management, and object alterations. The beauty of NetWare v4.0 auditing is that AUDITCON auditors can track network resources without actually having any other rights to the resources. Auditors can only audit.

As you can see, NetWare v4.0 provides a vast system of security levels, groups, and functionality. Here we've touched on the major points of NDS and directory/file security, but in order to fully understand their intricacies you will have to work with the system for a while. Be patient and try not to get bogged down in the millions of choices. Take the new security system one step at a time. This list starts you off with a brief description of the default security structure for NetWare v4.0. You can build from here:

- *NDS*—the default NDS tree is built from the server context you create during the NetWare v4.0 installation process. In Figure 6.4, the original NDS structure would be defined as CN=NIRVANA.OU=KITCHEN.O=NORTH_WING. The [Root] is automatically created with the first NetWare v4.0 server and cannot be modified.

- *Users*—the user ADMIN is created and placed in the same organization object as the NetWare v4.0 server. The ADMIN object's password is defined during server installation. ADMIN is granted the Supervisor object right to [Root] and NIRVANA (NetWare server object). This equates to all rights throughout the NDS tree and NIRVANA_SYS volume.

- *Volume*—the SYS: volume object is created for the default server. The container object that houses SYS: is granted read and file scan rights to SYS:PUBLIC. This means all users in the same container object inherit RF to the PUBLIC directory. In addition, new users are granted all rights to their specific home directory.

- *[Public]*—a special trustee called [Public] (brackets are required) is created during installation and granted *Browse* rights to the [Root] object. This trustee establishes a global assignment for all objects that have not otherwise been granted rights—it creates a minimum trustee assignment. Users can assign the [Public] trustee to objects they want to make available to everybody.

System Fault Tolerance

NetWare v4.0 SFT is identical to NetWare v2.2 and v3.11. It offers SFT levels I and II with read-after-write verification, duplicate DETs and FATs, hot fix, disk mirroring/duplexing, transactional tracking, and UPS monitoring. Also, NetWare v4.0 shares SFT level III (server duplexing) with NetWare v3.11 (although the product is not yet available for NetWare v4.0). The only unique SFT strategy that NetWare v4.0 brings to the table is NDS partitions and replicas. As mentioned before, the NDS Directory is fully distributed as partitions. NDS partitions contain a subset of the entire tree. The information in a specific server's partition encompasses the objects within the server's current context. The NIRVANA partition, for example, would contain information about the NIRVANA_SYS volume and ADMIN user. The first server in a container object houses the master partition, while subsequent servers receive replicas—read/write copies of the NIRVANA partition. In addition, the first server of the entire NDS tree gets the [Root] object as part of its partition.

If a user from another container (partition) wants to access a resource in the NIR-VANA partition, the user's host server will have to request a replica. Once the replica is copied to the user's host server, the user can access the resource through the NIRVANA replica. This strategy serves two purposes. First, partitioning breaks up the NDS database into more manageable pieces. The pieces are then distributed so that the most frequent requests are made to nearby NDS servers. This is fast and it reduces network traffic. Second, partitioning avoids a single point of failure for the entire NDS tree. If a server crashes or a partition becomes corrupt, the NDS tree can be rebuilt from nearby replicas. Partitioning is automatic in NetWare v4.0 and can be managed through the PAR GUI and PARTMGR menu utilities.

Speed

NetWare v4.0 is based on the same 80386 32-bit architecture as is NetWare v3.11. Although the NOS doesn't have the benefit of improved hardware, it has been fine-tuned to take better advantage of the Intel-based ISA structure. The most notable performance enhancement in NetWare v4.0 is server RAM consolidation. All memory management tasks are now served from one memory pool instead of five. This feature increases caching efficiency and decreases the chances of running into RAM bottlenecks. Another key improvement is NetWare v4.0's versatility in managing server optimization. SET and MONITOR are still the key server tools, as they were with NetWare v3.11, but the new versions have been substantially improved. In addition, the integration of SET parameters into the server startup files has been automated with the SERVMAN utility. Following are a few tips on fine-tuning the NetWare v4.0 server for maximum speed and memory efficiency using SET, MONITOR, and SERVMAN:

- *Cache Utilization*—view the percentage of Long Term Cache Hits from the Cache Utilization screen in MONITOR. If this number falls below 90 percent, add more memory to the server. You can return additional RAM to the server pool by removing DOS or unloading management NLMs—such as INSTALL, MONITOR, and SERVMAN—when you are done.
- *Packet Size*—most Ethernet and Token Ring NICs can handle large packet sizes (in excess of 1,024 bytes). Large packets can improve network communications performance tremendously. Choose Maximum Physical Receive Packet Size from the Communications menu within SERVMAN. Set the value to 4202.
- *Disk Access*—NetWare v4.0 offers a plethora of opportunities for optimizing server disk access. Each of these options is activated using SET parameters and can be integrated into the server startup files with SERVMAN. The following tips build on the suggestions I made earlier in the NetWare v3.11 section:
  Maximum Concurrent Disk Cache Writes = 100 (favors writes)
  Dirty Disk Cache Delay Time = 7
  Dirty Directory Cache Delay Time = 2
  Maximum Concurrent Directory Cache Writes = 25
  Maximum Concurrent Disk Cache Writes = 10 (favors reads)
  Directory Cache Buffer Nonreferenced Delay = 70

NetWare v4.0 performance is great as it stands. But you have a large variety of tools available to make it even better, so avail yourself of them. Study the subtleties of MONITOR, SET, and SERVMAN. Beware, though—you could spend a lifetime toying with performance optimization.

Connectivity

NetWare connectivity is split into two categories: physical and logical. *Physical connectivity* refers to the actual connections and protocol translations that occur between two like or unlike systems. *Logical connectivity* is the capacity of the host NetWare system to support transparent movement throughout the network. NetWare v3.11 is well advanced in physical connectivity but lacks any transparent logical connectivity. NetWare v4.0 includes few improvements in the area of physical connectivity, but its logical connectivity is excellent.

NetWare v4.0 combines the physical strength of v3.11 with the logical sophistication of NDS. The Directory structure makes it easy to integrate multiple unlike objects into one cohesive WAN. Communications within and between unlike clients is completely transparent to the user. Network Administrators will also benefit from the logical strengths of NetWare v4.0 through remote management facility, multiprotocol support, and additional language modules. Furthermore, NDS supports all client and host connectivity products from NetWare v3.11.

One of the most exciting connectivity advancements in NetWare v4.0 is Open Data-Link Interface (ODI) drivers and virtual loadable modules (VLM). These workstation connectivity tools will carry network computing into the next century by providing seamless integration of IPX/SPX, TCP/IP, and AppleTalk protocols on the same NIC at the same time!

User Interface

The most notable improvement in NetWare v4.0's user interface is the integration of native client environments. NetWare v4.0 is transparent to users in that it appears to them in a form they are comfortable with—command prompt for DOS users, GUI for Windows users, Presentation Manager for OS/2 users, X Windows for UNIX users, and Finder for Macintosh users. All of these facades are made possible through dramatic enhancements in the workstation software. The ODI specification and VLM versatility make client integration a snap. In addition, the multiple environments can use identical NICs and share server volumes through protocol translation and NetWare name space.

Another improvement is the separation of Administrator and user utilities. In earlier versions of NetWare, the users had to share the same utilities as Supervisors, and in many cases the users were lost and intimidated. Also, Administrators complained because users were muddling around with features they shouldn't access. NetWare v4.0 provides a series of user utilities aimed at simple user tasks. Furthermore, the user utilities are presented in native client environments:

DOS   NETUSER
Windows   NWUSER

OS/2	NetWare Tools for OS/2
Macintosh	The NetWare Desk Accessory

On the surface, NetWare v4.0 is integrated and friendly. Underneath, it provides a vast sea of administrative opportunities. The system can be as simple or complex as you would like. The important part is this: It's your choice!

Network Management

NetWare v4.0 has incorporated a wide variety of network management improvements. The most dramatic improvement has been the integration and consolidation of NetWare v3.11 utilities into a few *all-in-one* NetWare v4.0 management utilities. NWADMIN, NETADMIN, FILER, RIGHTS, and SERVMAN, for example, consolidate many of the features of NetWare v3.11 utilities into one central program. In addition to utility enhancements, NetWare v4.0 has an improved installation procedure, printing interface, and SET suite.

Utility Management. The NetWare v4.0 management utilities have improved dramatically. In addition to the new GUI utilities, many of the command line and menu utilities from NetWare v3.11 have been integrated and consolidated into new NetWare v4.0 utilities. The number of command line utilities dropped from 34 to 21, with the introduction of 4 completely new CLUs. Table 6.5 lists the NetWare v4.0 management utilities. New or significantly modified utilities are identified by ***bold italic.***

To avoid confusion with the new NetWare v4.0 command-line utilities, Novell has included a full complement of NetWare v3.11 utilities as batch files in the SYS:PUBLIC directory. These 24 batch files use the same names as the obsolete v3.11 utilities and display help messages that point the new user in the right direction. For example, the SYSCON.BAT batch file says

```
SYSCON is no longer supported with NetWare v4.0 USE NETADMIN
```

Following is a brief list of some NetWare v3.11 utility batch files (left column) and their v4.0 counterparts (right column):

FLAGDIR	**FLAG /DO**
ATTACH	**LOGIN /NS**
ALLOW	**RIGHTS/Filter**
SESSION	**NETUSER**
USERLIST	**NLIST user**
LISTDIR	**NDIR**
GRANT	**RIGHTS**
CASTOFF	**SEND /A**
REVOKE	**RIGHTS**
REMOVE	**RIGHTS /REM**

Installation. The NetWare v4.0 installation follows the same fundamentals as NetWare v3.11, but the user interface is dramatically improved. NetWare v4.0 automates the disk

TABLE 6.5   Network Management Utilities in NetWare v4.0

GUI Utilities

NWADMIN	The NetWare Administrator performs most of the functions of the other CLU and menu utilities in one graphical, Windows-based program.
PAR	The Partition Manager is used to manage Directory partitions and replicas.

Command line Utilities

Users	**Security**	**Dir/Files**	**Printing**
LOGIN	*AUDITCON*	*CX*	CAPTURE
LOGOUT	*FLAG*	MAP	ENDCAP
NLIST	*RIGHTS*	NCOPY	NPRINT
SEND	SETPASS	*NDIR*	*NPRINTER*
WHOAMI	SYSTIME	NVER	PSC
		RENDIR	

Menu Utilities

COLORPAL	*PARTMGR*	*PSETUP*
NETUSER	PRINTDEF	*NETADMIN*
PRINTCON	*HELP*	PCONSOLE
FILER	*MENU*	

Supervisor Utilities

DCONFIG	*UIMPORT*	WSUPDATE
RCONSOLE		

Console Commands

ABORT REMIRROR	ADD NAME SPACE	BIND
BROADCAST	CLEAR STATION	CLS
CONFIG	DISABLE LOGIN	DISABLE TTS
DISMOUNT	DISPLAY NETWORKS	DISPLAY SERVERS
DOWN	ENABLE LOGIN	ENABLE TTS
EXIT	*KEYB*	*LANGUAGE*
LIST DEVICES	LOAD	*MAGAZINE*
MEDIA	MEMORY	*MIRROR STATUS*
MODULES	MOUNT	NAME
OFF	PROTOCOL	REGISTER MEMORY
REMIRROR PARTITION	REMOVE DOS	RESET ROUTER
SCAN FOR NEW DEVICES	SEARCH	SECURE CONSOLE
SET	SEND	SET TIME
SET TIMEZONE	SPEED	SPOOL
TIME	TRACK OFF	TRACK ON
UNBIND	UNLOAD	UPS STATUS
UPS TIME	VERSION	VOLUMES

GUI Utilities (*continued*)

NetWare Loadable Modules

CDROM	CLIB	DISKSET
DOMAIN	*DSREPAIR*	EDIT
INSTALL	IPXS	MATHLIB
MATHLIBC	MONITOR	NMAGENT
NPRINTER	*NWSNUT*	PSERVER
REMOTE	ROUTE	RPL
RS232	RSPX	*RTDM*
SBACKUP	*SERVMAN*	SPXCONFIG
SPXS	STREAMS	*TIMESYNC*
TLI	UPS	VREPAIR

preparation stage with the INSTALL.EXE utility. In addition, NetWare v4.0 offers a CD-ROM installation for convenience and speed. Installation from a CD-ROM is almost 700 percent faster than from a floppy diskette. CD-ROM installation also offers the complete ElectroText on-line documentation library. Workstation installation is also improved. Now it offers an installation option for all native client environments—DOS, Windows, and OS/2. Refer to Chapter 10 for a complete look at NetWare v4.0 server and workstation installation.

Printing. NetWare v4.0 offers the same printing design as NetWare v2.2 and v3.11, but with a new twist. Users no longer print to queues, they print directly to printer objects. This feature makes printing management much easier and straightforward. In addition, a group of new printing Management utilities have been introduced: PSETUP, NPRINTER.EXE, and NPRINTER.NLM. PSETUP automates the process of installing network printing by creating printer, print server, and print queue objects. NPRINTER.EXE provides network printing services through workstation printers, and NPRINTER.NLM does the same thing for server printers. In addition, NetWare v4.0 printing services provide support for third-party print job configurations, Macintosh and NFS clients, and a new feature to optimize print queue polling time. For a complete description of NetWare printing, refer to Chapter 14.

SET. The NetWare v4.0 SET console command is substantially improved over NetWare v3.11. It provides 11 parameters with more than three times the number of configurations. Following is a brief look at the 11 SET parameters:

```
 1 Communications
 2 Locks
 3 Memory
 4 Transaction tracking
 5 File caching
 6 Disk
 7 Directory caching
 8 Time
 9 File system
10 NCP
11 Miscellaneous
```

The best way to ensure the integration of SET commands into your operating system is to use the NetWare v4.0 SERVMAN utility. SERVMAN provides a menu interface for using SET commands and automatically assigns new values to the appropriate startup files. The SET commands epitomize the power of change in NetWare v4.0.

I've never met a person, I don't care what his condition, in whom I could not see possibilities. I don't care how much a man may consider himself a failure, I believe in him, for he can change the thing that is wrong in his life any time he is ready and prepared to do it. Whenever he develops the desire, he can take away from his life the thing that is defeating it. The capacity for reformation and change lies within.

—Preston Bradley

NetWare v4.0 is ideal for large WANs or sophisticated LANs with multiple protocols and client environments. NetWare v4.0 is also ideal for medium- to large-sized LANs that require file compression, GUI utilities, on-line documentation, and the security of future technology. As I stated in the opening of the v4.0 discussion, NetWare v4.0 is not for everybody. It is not an automatic upgrade from NetWare v3.11. Now you are armed with enough information to make the right decision for your network. Remember to balance the needs and resources of your system in making a decision about NetWare v4.0.

To NetWare v4.0 or not to NetWare v4.0. This is the new question!

Windows NT/LAN Manager

Microsoft Windows NT is a complete 32-bit GUI workstation operating system. NT represents the latest evolution of NOS-to-WOS connectivity. It supports 32-bit and 16-bit applications in Windows, DOS, or OS/2 environments. Windows NT is a 32-bit WOS, a peer-to-peer NOS, and a client/server NOS all wrapped into one:

- Windows NT as a *workstation WOS* comes with built-in LAN drivers. Connectivity to peer-to-peer or client/server systems is controlled simply from within the Networks applet in the Control Panel. This setup is much like the Chooser function for the Apple Macintosh.
- *Peer-to-peer* functionality is achieved through resource sharing. Directories, files, and printers can be shared through the Server applet in the Control Panel. Once a *share* has been established, other Windows NT workstations will automatically recognize it and assign an appropriate drive letter mapping or print queue.
- As a *client/server* NOS, Windows NT incorporates many of the advanced features of LAN Manager. Windows NT comes with a built-in version of LAN Manager for Windows NT. This new 32-bit NOS expands the peer-to-peer sharing functions across multiple LANs by using domains. Also, LAN Manager for Windows NT provides additional network tools for managing users, groups, domains, security, and shared resources.

Windows NT can also interact with NetWare. While connected to a NetWare server, NT behaves as a normal 32-bit workstation operating system. NetWare Tools for NT are available to improve network administration from the NT workstation. In addition, NT supports multiple protocol sessions with NetWare, UNIX, and LAN Manager servers. NetWare messages are sent as TCP/IP packets to NetWare NFS, LAN Manager connections are established using NetBEUI, and UNIX messages use TCP/IP and various popular UNIX management utilities—FTP, RCP, TELNET, and RSH.

One of NT's most notable advancements is security. The security features of Windows NT satisfy the U.S. government's C2 classification: the highest rating for a commercially available operating system. This security scheme provides the ultimate protection against viruses, intruders, Trojan horses, and NT-impostors. UNIX and NetWare v4.0 are the only other operating systems to support the C2 security classification.

Windows NT is a viable NOS solution for critical application platforms and GUI development. NT's strengths are intrusion security, its user interface, and resource sharing. NT's weaknesses are lack of connectivity, platform dependence, relatively low performance, and unreliability. Windows NT is currently the most sophisticated WOS available, but it doesn't quite stack up as a full client/server network operating system. Following is a comprehensive examination of the three faces of NT: WOS, peer-to-peer NOS, and client/server NOS.

Windows NT WOS

Windows NT is the wonderful wizard of WOS. It's secure, 32-bit compatible, GUI, and network-ready. You can't ask for any more than that. Well, every silver lining has a cloud, and NT's is that it eats hardware for lunch. A stripped-down version of Windows NT requires a *minimum* of 8MB of RAM, an 80386-based CPU, and 55MB of hard disk space, including a 20MB paging file. In reality, NT requires 16MB of RAM, an 80486/50-MHz CPU, and 120MB of hard disk space.

If you can get beyond the hardware requirements, NT is a wonderful workstation operating system. NT looks just like Windows v3.1, but don't be fooled—NT offers substantial improvements. Specifically, NT has improved on security, registry, the file system, networking, and system applications. Refer to Figure 6.5 for an illustration of the Windows NT look-and-feel.

Security. Windows NT is a secure operating system—class C2. Users must log onto the system with a Ctrl+Alt+Del. This action performs a complete flush of all existing RAM and reboots the machine. NT bypasses the boot sector and jumps directly to a login dialog box. This security precaution protects NT workstations from intruding TSRs, password hounds, DOS applications, Trojan horses, and viruses. The only way to access an NT machine is to piggy-back the boot routine. Fortunately, nobody knows how to do it—not even Microsoft. The NT login dialog screen includes username, password, and domain. Once logged in, users can press Ctrl+Alt+Del once again to change their password, lock the computer, log off, or reboot.

Access to workstation resources is controlled in two steps: shares and permissions. *Shares* are granted for local printers and files. An NT user can grant other NT users sharing rights to local printers or specific directories/files. All NT shares are controlled by the

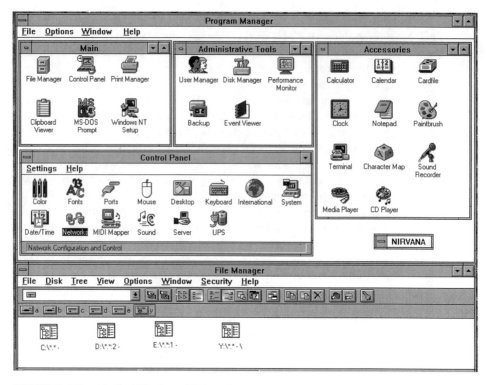

FIGURE 6.5 Typical Windows NT Interface: Program Manager and File Manager

Control Panel's server applet. *Permissions* are security rights for shared directories and files. NT permissions are similar to NetWare's directory/file attributes. Permissions include

read	edit	all access
no read	no edit	no access

Once a directory/file share has been established, users can configure permissions through the File Manager Security menu.

Registry. Windows NT stores its configuration information in a database system called the registry. The registry uses a treelike format to incorporate on-line system modifications. If allowed by the Administrator, users can use the registry editor to inspect or modify their workstation parameters. The registry editor resembles File Manager with key folders on the left and database properties on the right. The NT registry has four predefined configuration roots—current user, users, local machine, and classes:

- The *current users* root contains configuration information for the user who is currently logged in. He or she can view screen colors, program groups, and Control Panel settings.
- *Users* are profiles for all users who have share access to the current workstation.
- *Local machine* describes configuration information for the current workstation. Local machine parameters include system, security, software, and hardware.

- The *classes* root is used to define file associations for File Manager and Object Linking and Embedding. The NT registry replaces the standard Windows configuration files, including CONFIG.SYS, AUTOEXEC.BAT, and WIN.INI. This new system is much more organized and easier for users to follow.

NT File System. Windows NT incorporates its own high-performance file system called NT File System (NTFS). In addition, NT supports DOS's File Allocation Tables (FATs) and OS/2's High-Performance File System (HPFS). NTFS includes three main advantages: no limits, excellent recoverability, and security. NTFS supports 64-bit file addresses, giving NT files an almost unattainable size limit. In addition, NTFS provides primitive transactional tracking functions and auditing for better file recoverability. Finally, security permissions are applied to NTFS directories and files. Enhanced NT File Manager and Disk Manager utilities allow for better access to critical hard disk configurations.

Networking. Windows NT is network-ready. LAN drivers are built into the operating system, and NIC communications are easily initialized. Enhanced resource sharing functionality is provided by three new Control Panel applets: Server, Network, and UPS. Server controls workstation shares, user connections, and file locks. Network handles LAN drivers and NIC initialization. UPS provides internal UPS monitoring. In addition, NT provides network functionality through File Manager, Disk Manager, User Manager, Print Manager, and Backup.

System Applications. Windows NT uses the Windows v3.1 interface. The program groups, icons, windows, pulldown menus, applets, dialog boxes, and scroll bars are identical. That is where the similarities end. On a high-end 80486 machine, NT is much faster than Windows v3.1. On a low-end 80386 machine, NT is much slower than Windows v3.1. Beyond the speed issues, Windows NT provides a large number of improvements and additional GUI features:

- *Main Group:* The Windows NT Main Group contains the following five system applications: File Manager, Print Manager, Control Panel, MS-DOS Prompt, and Windows NT Setup.
  - ❑ *File Manager* provides the same Windows v3.1 functionality plus an enhanced toolbar, integrated peer-to-peer shares, security permissions, and auditing.
  - ❑ *Print Manager* has a completely new design for Windows NT. All local and shared printing functions are now centralized in the Print Manager. Enhancements include automatic file redirection, transparent connectivity to shared printers, a toolbar, and usability improvements.
  - ❑ The *Control Panel* is substantially improved in Windows NT.
  - ❑ Windows NT supports 16 and 32-bit DOS applications through an improved *MS-DOS Prompt.* In addition, the NT prompt supports OS/2 character-based applications, Windows v3.1, and Win32-based applications—Microsoft's new 32-bit application standard.
  - ❑ The *Windows NT Setup* application is used to reconfigure the NT operating system, delete information about remote users, or create a Repairman diskette. The Repairman diskette is used to stabilize an NT system that has become corrupted.

- *Control Panel:* The Windows NT Control Panel provides more networking functions than does Windows v3.1. Improvements include Server, UPS, System, and Networks applets.
  - ❑ The Server applet establishes shared peer-to-peer resources on the workstation machine.
  - ❑ The UPS applet provides centralized UPS uninterruptible power supply (UPS) monitoring.
  - ❑ The System applet enables users to set Cold Boot Loader options and user-specific configurations.
  - ❑ The Networks applet is greatly enhanced to include software and hardware driver support.
- *MS-DOS Prompt:* The Windows NT MS-DOS Prompt offers a more versatile command line for Windows v3.1 users. NT uses a *Single Command Shell (SCS)* window to provide DOSKEY support, multitasking applications, and icon-based configurations. The NT prompt automatically initiates DOSKEY so that previous commands can be recalled by using the up and down arrows. In addition, DOSKEY provides a popup window of your command history and loads a file of stored aliases. The Windows NT MS-DOS Prompt supports the following application types: MS-DOS, 16-bit Windows, 32-bit Windows, and OS/2 character-based. Multitasking is achieved by starting an application and returning to the MS-DOS prompt for additional commands. In addition, the NT prompt supports icon-based configurations for features relating to fonts, cut and paste, screen colors, windows sizing, and screen buffers.
- *Administrative Tools:* Windows NT has added an entire group of system applications that Windows v3.1 never had—administrative tools. These are five handy applications that provide rudimentary system management functions. Administrative tools consists of Performance Monitor, Event Viewer, Backup, Disk Manager, and User Manager.
  - ❑ *Performance Monitor (PM)* is a graphical representation of key system resources. PM monitors CPU utilization, committed pages, and context switches.
  - ❑ *Event Viewer* is used to view the NT events log. Event Viewer provides a story of what happened for system configurations and applications.
  - ❑ The NT *Backup* tool provides system backup and restore procedures.
  - ❑ *Disk Manager* is a graphical disk management system that provides a variety of useful tools: partition management, volume sets, stripe sets, and disk mirroring.
  - ❑ *User Manager* provides centralized management functionality for shared users, groups, and workstation security.

Windows NT Peer-to-Peer

Windows NT has built-in peer-to-peer NOS functionality. It requires a LAN adapter in each workstation and appropriate NT drivers. Currently, Windows NT supports 25 of the leading NIC manufacturers. In addition, Microsoft and third-party developers are actively working on providing driver support for older, less popular NICs. The LAN driver is configured in Control Panel through the Network applet.

Once configured, the NIC is initialized with the Bindings button. NT shares can be established for workstation printers, directories, and files. Shares are also configured in the

Control Panel—through the Server applet. Server is used to manage shares, user accounts, and file locks.

Directory/file permissions are controlled by the File Manager Security menu. Shared printers are controlled by the Print Manager Security menu. NT's peer-to-peer functionality is limited to workstations and peer-to-peer servers within the local LAN. Connectivity to other NT LANs requires Windows NT client/server functionality.

Windows NT Client/Server

Windows NT client/server NOS functions are provided by a built-in version of LAN Manager called LAN Manager for Windows NT. When Windows NT is configured as a client/server NOS, it still operates as an NT workstation or peer-to-peer system. The client/server functionality is simply integrated into the existing configuration. It operates with the same LAN drivers and uses the same peer-to-peer shares. LAN Manager for Windows NT adds domain controlling functionality and additional tools for network management. Domain controlling servers are interconnected LANs within a local geographic region. With this additional feature, users can log into client/server systems outside their local LAN. This function is not available with peer-to-peer systems.

Windows NT uses two protocols for interconnectivity: NetBEUI and TCP/IP. *NetBEUI (Network Basic End-User Interface)* is LAN Manager's protocol for connecting two NT servers or an NT server and an old LAN Manager server. *TCP/IP* is used for interconnecting all other LAN platforms. TCP/IP supports UNIX, NetWare, and VINES servers. NT's TCP/IP connectivity is established and controlled by the Control Panel's Network applet. Once the TCP/IP service has been successfully installed, NT provides a series of standard network utilities:

- ARP
- NETSTAT
- RCP
- ROUTE
- TELNET
- FTP
- PING
- REXEC
- RSH
- TFTP

The scientific theory I like best is that the rings of Saturn are composed entirely of lost airline luggage.

—Mark Russell

Windows NT supports additional user-level network security. Users are classified into four groups:

- *Administrators* can create and delete user accounts, share printers, control network management functionality, and access directory/file permissions.
- *Power Users* are workgroup managers who can control users within a specific local group. They also have access to printer shares and limited directory/file permissions.
- *Users* can create and manage their own local system.
- *Guests* can log onto a workstation, but have very limited network permissions.

The first step in configuring a client/server system is to change the Administrator's password. This is achieved through the User Manager applet within Administrative Tools. In addition, NT supports Administrator-equivalence for users who would like the security under their own username. To become Administrator-equivalent, simply add yourself to the Administrators group in User Manager.

Windows NT is a flexible, well-designed workgroup system. It operates well within the Windows environment and extends local resources to network users. Unfortunately, Windows NT is unfocused. It tries to achieve all levels of operation simultaneously. This is a classic example of an operating system that knows a little about a lot of things, but not much about client/server operability. Some of NT's weaknesses include

- shallow security
- limited connectivity
- weak performance on midrange machines
- restricted interconnectivity
- lack of server application support

Windows NT is a great WOS. It excels as a workgroup peer-to-peer NOS solution. However, Windows NT is too limited to be considered an enterprise solution for large, high-performance client/server LANs.

Workstation Operating Systems

One of the most critical functions of the workstation operating system is *compatibility*. The WOS must be compatible with workstation hardware, network applications, workstation shells, and (most importantly) the network operating system. In a distributed system, all processing occurs at the local workstation level. The workstation operating system must be able to handle the complex demands of locally processed network files—a difficult proposition.

Another critical function is *user interface*. As discussed earlier, the workstation is the user's link to the LAN. The workstation operating system is the user's interface to the LAN. A friendly, familiar interface is vital for LAN workstations, because it helps to alleviate initial feelings of LAN-phobia. Also, users are more productive in an environment they like and understand.

Finally, the workstation operating system must be able to support high levels of LAN *connectivity*. Not only does the WOS have to handle local processing, network resources, and user interface, but it must also remain forever connected to the LAN's topology components. The WOS is connected to the workstation NIC through a set of complex network programs called *shells*. The shells are specific to the network operating system, WOS, and internal workstation NIC. Whatever happens on the LAN is communicated to the WOS through the workstation shells.

Initially, WOSs were designed to operate with stand-alone machines—they fell apart in multiuser environments. Others were designed for connectivity. Today, most of the new WOSs have been tweaked to deal with connectivity and the stresses of network processing. Unfortunately, LAN functionality is still not in the fabric of their being. Sure, they excel in their own environments—UNIX with VINES and OS/2 with LAN Manager—but what about interoperability? What about connecting with other machines using other network operating systems? Not yet. Soon, when *all* computers are networked, WOSs and NOSs will connect on *all* levels. There will be little difference between the workstation operating system and the NOS—Windows NT is a great example. Until then, we will have to live with a dozen workstation shells and the marginal interoperability of DOS, OS/2, UNIX, and System 7.

DOS

The *disk operating system (DOS)* is the most popular NetWare WOS. There are many different types, manufacturers, and versions of DOS. Currently, the leaders are Microsoft DOS versions 3.3, 5.0, and 6.0; Digital Research DOS version 6.0; Compaq DOS; and IBM PC DOS.

DOS provides NetWare users with a simple, familiar command line. It relies on third-party products for GUI integration. The marriage of DOS and NetWare has withstood the tests of time and many assaults by Windows, OS/2, and UNIX. The bottom line is this—NetWare looks like DOS. NetWare v4.0 has altered the bottom line a little, so for that version read, "NetWare looks like DOS and Windows." Whichever environment you choose, NetWare and DOS get along well.

NetWare and DOS rely on a set of communication programs—shells—to translate application requests into IPX packets that are shuttled across the LAN topology through internal network interface cards. In some cases, the shells must support additional protocols like TCP/IP and AppleTalk. The two main NetWare shells are IPX and NETx. *IPX (Internetwork Packet Exchange)* handles low-level communications between workstation NICs and LAN cabling. The other shell, *NETx*, handles communications between DOS, NetWare, and IPX.

Here is how it works:

1. When a request is made by a local workstation application for some data, the message travels past DOS and directly to the workstation shell—NETx.
2. NETx analyzes the message and determines whether it is destined for NetWare or DOS. If the request is for local data, it is forwarded to the local workstation operating system—DOS. If the request is for network data, it is transformed into something the network can understand and given to another network shell, called IPX.
3. IPX communicates the request to the workstation's internal NIC, which quickly and directly transmits the message along the communication media to the file server.
4. Once at the file server, the request is handled by available file server processes and an answer is generated.
5. The answer is given back to the file server's IPX and returned to the originating workstation NIC.
6. The local IPX shuttles the answer to NETx and ultimately back to the workstation application.

NetWare supports additional shells for specialty applications: NetBIOS, ODI, and LSL. *NetBIOS (Network Basic Input/Output System)* is an IPX complement that provides

NetWare connectivity to NetBIOS applications. *Open Data-link Interface (ODI)* is Novell's new workstation strategy for supporting open systems. ODI shells handle a much more diverse selection of workstation platforms as well as simultaneous multiple protocols. *Link Support Layer (LSL)* is a low-level support shell for ODI communications. The NetWare shells are supported by a text configuration file called NET.CFG. NET.CFG provides specialized configuration parameters for the main four NetWare shells. NET.CFG supports all configuration options from the earlier SHELL.CFG, plus some new parameters of its own. In addition, NetWare v4.0 organizes these shells into an ODI-compliant system called the *NetWare Requester*.

Following is a detailed examination of IPX, NETx, NetBIOS, ODI, NET.CFG, and the NetWare Requester.

IPX

Internetwork Packet Exchange (IPX) is the most critical NetWare shell. It binds to the local workstation NIC and controls communications between topology components and operating systems. The IPX shell must be configured during the NetWare installation procedure (WSGEN) and contains specific hardware drivers that dictate the flow of data from WOS to media to NOS. Further shell customization can be achieved by linking an auxiliary data file to the IPX shell—NET.CFG.

NET.CFG contains specialized commands that enhance and support the primary functions of IPX. It is critical for users to load the correct IPX shell. Novell publishes a new revision of IPX.OBJ almost quarterly. The new revision can be found on NetWire and must be bound to the LAN driver through WSGEN to create IPX.COM. The network will "bog down" and sometimes even crash if users access the incorrect IPX revision. Windows is especially sensitive to old IPX.COM files. Use the *Windows Setup* application to accommodate the updated shell file. Revision information can be viewed by typing **IPX i** at the NetWare command line. IPX cannot be unloaded once it has been placed in workstation RAM.

NETx

NETx is the director of the network shells. It analyzes workstation requests and determines whether they should be forwarded to the local operating system (WOS) or the network operating system (NOS—NetWare). If the request is forwarded to NetWare, the NETx shell hands it over to IPX, which in turn sends the packet to the workstation NIC. The NIC then guides the message over the communications channel to the file server for processing. All NETx shells are identical, because all DOS operating systems are functionally similar. Prior to 1991, NETx was NET2, NET3, NET4, and NET5—according to the version of DOS. Also in 1991, Novell released a set of memory management NETx shells: EMSNETx and XMSNETx. These shells save conventional workstation memory below the 640KB barrier by moving into Expanded or Extended RAM. EMSNETx supports the LIM 4.0 standard. XMSNETx supports the XMS 2.0 memory standard. When loaded, IPX and NETx occupy a total of 67KB of workstation memory. NETx can be unloaded from RAM by typing **NETx u** at the NetWare command line.

NetBIOS

NetBIOS is an IBM network communications standard. Many software manufacturers develop applications that adhere to the NetBIOS standard because it provides them with a large umbrella of network compatibility. NetWare LANs support NetBIOS applications through the use of the NetBIOS shell. The NetBIOS emulator is a front and back end for IPX. NetBIOS is loaded similarly to IPX and NETx, and requires additional workstation RAM. NET.CFG supports additional NetBIOS configurations.

ODI

Open Data-link Interface (ODI) is Novell's new interface technology that allows multiple LAN protocols to share the same network interface card. IPX and TCP/IP, for example, could operate on the same workstation NIC at the same time. ODI drivers operate at the data-link layer of the OSI communications model. The drivers comprise two shells: *MLID (Multiple-Link Interface Driver)* and *LSL (Link Support Layer)*. Among other features, ODI drivers allow NetWare clients to use TCP/IP gateways, UNIX NFS hosts, and AppleTalk printing devices.

ODI offers many benefits:

- Multiple protocols can reside on one NIC.
- Connectivity is possible to a variety of platforms without rebooting the workstation.
- NET.CFG is supported for specialized configurations.
- ODI has modularity; it can be loaded and unloaded freely. Also, new revisions are provided as independent shells—no binding, installation, or extra fuss.
- Workstation RAM is optimized with enhanced shell drivers.

The ODI solution consists of three components: LSL, LAN drivers, and protocol stacks.

LSL. The ODI link support layer is a critical element in multiprotocol LAN operations. The LSL driver acts as a switchboard, routing network packets between MLID and multiple protocol stacks. LSLs support many frame types. LSL.COM is loaded first in the ODI solution.

LAN Drivers. The LAN drivers are the hardware support programs that communicate with NICs. In the IPX solution, LAN drivers are bound to IPX.OBJ to create IPX.COM. This is cumbersome, because it requires regenerating the workstation shell each time NICs are changed or configurations are modified. In the ODI solution, LAN drivers are independent files that execute in conjunction with LSL and protocol stacks. The LAN driver .COM file is loaded second.

Protocol Stacks. Protocol stack shells control communications within and between workstation NICs. The protocol stack is a third independent file that establishes TCP/IP, IPX, or AppleTalk protocols. IPXODI.COM and TCPIP.EXE are examples of NetWare protocol stacks.

Novell has recently hinted that ODI drivers will replace IPX and NETx, thus narrowing the scope of network shells.

NET.CFG

NET.CFG is the DOS workstation configuration file. It contains a plethora of communication options that you can use to customize the DOS/NetWare connection. NET.CFG replaces the older SHELL.CFG. It is fully compatible with the older parameters and introduces some new ones. The NET.CFG file must reside on the workstation disk in the same directory as the NetWare shells. In the case of diskless workstations, the NET.CFG file must be part of the centralized boot mirror. Table 6.6 lists the NET.CFG commands and the shells they work with.

NetWare Requester

NetWare v4.0 bundles all of these workstation shells into an ODI-compliant system, the NetWare Requester. The NetWare Requester distributes the communications and redirecting functions into separate workstation files. These Requester files are organized into two classes: ODI files and VLM files. The ODI files are identical to the ODI drivers discussed earlier. The VLM files replace NETX with a full complement of NetWare v4.0 Requester files called virtual loadable modules. Some of the required VLMs include CONN, NDS, IPXNCP, BIND, REDIR, NWP, and F10. NetWare v4.0 supports the NetWare Requester for DOS and the NetWare Requester for OS/2. Chapter 15 discusses the NetWare Requester in more detail.

DOS users can maintain their native commands through a special directory on the NetWare disk. A DOS system subdirectory should be created under SYS:PUBLIC. The DOS subdirectory contains support for internal transient commands (COMMAND.COM) and external DOS commands like EDIT, MEM, FORMAT, and CHKDSK. Most of the common DOS commands have NetWare counterparts, but it is a good idea to maintain centralized command support for users who enjoy the DOS-only utilities. In addition, the DOS system subdirectory is a good place to send COMSPEC. *COMSPEC (Command Specifier)* protects DOS users from losing their COMMAND.COM system file.

OS/2

OS/2 operates well as a workstation operating system. It is multitasking, DOS-compatible, and network ready. IBM's OS/2 version 2.0 has opened new doors for the second-genera-

TABLE 6.6   NET.CFG Commands for DOS Workstation Shells

IPX.COM	NETx.COM	NetBIOS.EXE	ODI
config option	all servers	abort timeout	bind
int64	cache buffers	broadcast count	buffers
int7A	file handles	broadcast delay	frame
ipatch	local printers	command	link driver
IPX packet size limit	long machine	type internet	link stations
IPX retry count	preferred server	listen timeout	mempool
IPX sockets	print header	receive buffers	node address
SPX abort timeout	set station time	retry count	protocol
SPX connections	share	retry delay	saps
SPX listen timeout	short machine type	send buffers	sessions
SPX verify timeout	show dots	verify timeout	slot

tion WOS. Improvements include greater application support, more reasonable hardware overhead, extended features, and increased LAN connectivity. NetWare provides a set of OS/2 connectivity tools called the *NetWare Requester for OS/2.*

NetWare Requester for OS/2 provides OS/2 users with transparent NetWare connectivity. The Requester is a set of client shells and NetWare utilities. The client shells interface between OS/2, NetWare, and the LAN topology design. The NetWare utilities consist of OS/2 versions of common NetWare commands—public, login, and security. In addition to the OS/2 shells and utilities, there are special considerations for OS/2 workstations—login scripts, mapping, HPFS, and capture.

OS/2 Client Shells

The NetWare Requester for OS/2 workstation configuration consists of an automated, GUI installation program. The workstation installation procedure accomplishes three things: It specifies the local destination directory, modifies the CONFIG.SYS file, and copies the appropriate Requester files to the appropriate workstation directory. The default directory for OS/2 Requester client files is C:\NETWARE. The OS/2 CONFIG.SYS file is the central point for all system configurations. Many critical NetWare changes need to be made to the workstation configuration file. These changes include

- LSL support
- IPX
- Named Pipes
- NetBIOS
- LAN drivers
- SPX support
- Requester driver

Copy the OS/2 versions of LOGIN and SLIST to the workstation disk. This way OS/2 users can log in to all NetWare servers—regardless of whether the servers support OS/2 utilities.

Once you've installed the Requester, reboot the workstation. The OS/2 workstation is now ready to attach to the NetWare server. But before a peaceful communication can occur, we must install the OS/2 utilities on the NetWare disk.

NetWare OS/2 Utilities

The NetWare OS/2 utilities consist of OS/2 versions of common NetWare utilities. These utilities fall into three categories: public, login, and security. Another GUI installation program is used to install the NetWare OS/2 utilities. The procedure creates three directories: SYS:PUBLIC\OS2, SYS:LOGIN\OS2, and SYS:SYSTEM\OS2. The Requester copies OS/2 versions of all the critical NetWare utilities into each of these new subdirectories. The PUBLIC\OS2 directory incorporates all of the OS/2 public utilities. The LOGIN\OS2 directory receives ATTACH, LOGIN, MAP, and SLIST. The SYSTEM\OS2 directory receives special security utilities, including ATOTAL, SECURITY, PAUDIT, BINDREST, and BINDFIX.

Special Considerations

You must take into account some special considerations when you connect OS/2 workstations to NetWare servers. These considerations cover login scripts, mapping, HPFS, and print job redirection:

- OS/2 workstations do not execute the system login script. All login script commands for OS/2 users must be executed from individual login scripts. This can be cumbersome.
- In order for OS/2 users to access NetWare OS/2 utilities, they must have the drive letter **L:** mapped to the following directory—SYS:PUBLIC\OS2.
- OS/2 doesn't support the NetWare MAP command. Instead, the WOS prefers PATH.
- OS/2 users enjoy a High Performance File System (HPFS). HPFS accepts 254-character-long filenames and supports both upper- and lowercase entries. NetWare supports the OS/2 HPFS as a name space module. In order to support HPFS, add the name space to the OS/2 volumes and load the OS2.NAM module.
- The CAPTURE command is kind of wacky in the OS/2 arena. CAPTURE is used to redirect print jobs from local ports to NetWare queues. OS/2 workstations support capture, but they don't process the following options—timeout, autoendcap, noautoendcap, and create.

OS/2 is a solid workstation operating system, but it's subject to too many cons and too few pros. It seems as though all the extra effort to accommodate OS/2's incompatibilities is not justified by its marginally better performance. Windows NT and MS DOS 6.0 will most likely replace what little OS/2 exists in the mainstream market.

And now for something completely different . . . UNIX.

UNIX

UNIX is inherently networkable. It is both a WOS and a peer-to-peer NOS. UNIX has unique network functionality that makes it an ideal solution for client/server workstations. Unfortunately, UNIX has only recently enjoyed widespread success. In the past, UNIX appealed to a small, specialty market—scientific workstations, government, and research institutions.

Originally, UNIX was monolithic, cryptic, cumbersome, and hardware-dependent. It was designed by a small group of engineers at AT&T in 1969. The product quickly evolved when it was handed off to a band of U.C. Berkeley students in 1974. They added network functionality, full text editing, and a very fast file system. The golden age of education and research quickly gave way to commercialization. By 1989, there were 25 independent versions of UNIX available, including SunOS, SCO Xenix, HP-U X, AT&T's System V release 4.0, and IBM's AIX.

The UNIX explosion fostered mind-boggling features and vendor-dependence. Two very important components were sacrificed—reliability and ease of use. The dominating PC market never gave UNIX a second thought.

The minority status of UNIX has only recently changed. Windows NT provided the 25 independent UNIX manufacturers with a common adversary. Suddenly, they were forced to work together toward a common goal—providing a reliable, GUI, multitasking connectivity WOS for PC LANs and larger open systems. Three major manufacturers have come to the forefront in providing a UNIX-based WOS for the PC platform: Univel, NeXT, and SunSoft. Univel is the result of a merger between UNIX System Laboratories (USL) and Novell. Univel has introduced a new PC-based UNIX WOS called UnixWare. USL offers the same product as System V release 4.2. In addition, we can expect greater UNIX/NetWare connectivity in light of Novell's aquisition of USL.

Another exciting move for UNIX is the release of NextStep—an Intel 80486-based version of NeXT's amazing workstation operating system. NextStep is full multitasking, GUI-based, and written with UNIX connectivity tools. SunSoft is a software-based spin-off from the immensely successful SUN Systems—a hardware vendor. SunSoft has introduced a PC-based UNIX WOS called Solaris 2.0. Solaris is a derivative of SVR4.2. SunSoft will enjoy huge distribution channels and the sales momentum of SUN Systems.

Although UNIX is beginning to gain momentum in the PC LAN arena, it has always excelled with high-end workstations and large Internetwork. NetWare v3.11 and v4.0 currently support many different levels of UNIX connectivity. There are three critical components that influence UNIX–NetWare communications: TCP/IP, UNIX Utilities, and NetWare/UNIX products.

TCP/IP

TCP/IP stands for *Transmission Control Protocol/Internet Protocol*. TCP/IP is a set of two protocols that govern LAN messages as they travel within and between UNIX systems. The TCP protocol is similar to NetWare's NetBIOS in that it handles point-to-point communications between network nodes. The IP protocol provides IPX-like communications through network devices (NICs).

At the heart of the TCP/IP system is a global naming scheme called *internet addressing*. Internet addresses are unique router assignments that describe where destination nodes reside. Internet addresses have four parts—111.222.333.444. The fields are separated by periods. The fields are organized into a *class, network,* and *host* ID. The first two fields describe the class ID. The length of the network ID is determined by the class. The host ID is the remainder of the address. Each Internet field consists of three decimal-based numbers. Because these numbers are hard to remember, TCP/IP provides a naming scheme called *domain naming*. In domain naming, the decimal field is represented by a word. Since Internet traverses the globe, each progressive field in domain naming must describe a larger, more comprehensive area. Following is my Internet address:

dciv@garnet.berkeley.edu

In my address, the first field represents my name—David Clarke IV. The next field represents the name of my native UNIX server. The third field broadens to include the place I work—U.C. Berkeley. And finally, the fourth field represents the type of organization it is—edu for educational, gov for government, or com for commercial. If you wanted to send me a message from Ireland, you would simply enter my Internet domain name and it would find its way to California. An amazingly simple and effective system. NetWare supports TCP/IP protocols and domain naming. UNIX users can access NetWare servers through unique Internet addresses. In addition, NetWare users can access UNIX servers in the same manner.

UNIX Utilities

Seven UNIX utilities influence its incorporation into NetWare LANs: NFS, FTP, RPC, SNMP, SMTP, RLOGIN, and TELNET. NFS stands for *Network File System*. NFS is the UNIX standard for sharing directories and files across TCP/IP channels. NFS is an application-layer protocol that sits on top of TCP/IP and *mounts* remote directories to local client workstations. NFS is very similar to the Windows NT share procedure. FTP stands for *File Transfer Protocol*. FTP is used to transfer files between UNIX clients and hosts. The FTP protocol provides dissimilar systems with file transfers, file translation, and automatic login/logoff procedures.

RPC stands for *Remote Procedure Call*. RPC is an amazing NFS concept that allows multiple UNIX hosts to act as one processor. Independent modules of one application can be processed by different computers at different locations. The results of the distributed processes are shared by all NFS machines. *Simple Network Management Protocol (SNMP)* is the network management standard for TCP/IP networks. SNMP shares client configurations across the network as *managed objects*. These objects exist in a large SNMP database called the Management Information Base (MIB). Each client retains the MIB and keeps track of everybody else's configurations. This level of distributed management makes it very easy to remotely modify existing client configurations. SMTP stands for *Simple Mail Transfer Protocol*. SMTP is used to send electronic mail over a TCP/IP network. The SMTP message consists of a domain name that is conveniently translated into a decimal-based Internet address. SMTP is a rudimentary standard for all nodes on the TCP/IP network. The *rlogin* command is used to log remote clients into UNIX hosts. Once logged in, users can use RCP to remote copy and RSH to remote execute. *TELNET* is a built-in TCP/IP terminal emulation system. It allows users to access remote applications on remote UNIX hosts as if they were running locally.

NetWare/UNIX Products

NetWare supports UNIX in three configurations: NetWare clients connected to UNIX hosts, UNIX clients connected to NetWare servers, and NetWare functionality on a UNIX server. In addition, Novell provides *NetWare v3.11 TCP/IP Transport*—a set of NetWare v3.11 NLMs designed to offer TCP/IP connectivity to UNIX applications. NetWare TCP/IP transport is required for most of the following configurations. Here is a description of how UNIX–NetWare connectivity works.

NetWare Clients Connected to UNIX Hosts. Novell's *LAN WorkPlace* solution provides workstation connectivity to NetWare servers or TCP/IP hosts. LAN WorkPlace supports DOS, OS/2, and System 7 operating systems as well as the Windows GUI environment. Currently there are three products:

- *LAN WorkPlace for DOS v4.0*—DOS and Windows v3.1
- *LAN WorkPlace for OS/2 v2.0*—OS/2
- *LAN WorkPlace for Macintosh v1.1*—System 7

LAN WorkPlace uses TCP/IP for communications to UNIX hosts, VAXs, IBM mainframes, and various other TCP/IP machines. It uses ODI drivers to allow IPX and TCP/IP packets within the same workstation NIC. LAN WorkPlace supports the following UNIX utilities: FTP, RCP, RSH, and TELNET. LAN WorkPlace uses NetWare v3.11 TCP/IP Transport for *IPX Tunneling* through TCP/IP channels. IPX tunneling is a packet routing procedure that transmits IPX packets over Internet lines.

UNIX Clients Connected to NetWare Servers. *NetWare NFS* offers the superior performance and disk storage capacity of NetWare to UNIX clients. NetWare NFS maintains all aspects of the UNIX environment, providing connectivity to NetWare security, file structure, mail, and application support. NetWare NFS uses the NetWare v3.11 TCP/IP Transport application for UNIX communications over IPX or TCP/IP lines. NetWare NFS provides all of the functionality of the UNIX NFS standard, including remote procedure calls.

In addition, NetWare NFS provides UNIX clients with native filing, shared printing, UNIX naming conventions, FTP functionality, and file/record locking. NetWare NFS runs on the NetWare v3.11 or v4.0 server, and workstation communications are handled through native NFS commands.

NetWare Functionality on a UNIX Server. *NetWare for UNIX* is a portable version of NetWare designed to run on general-purpose operating systems. NetWare for UNIX runs as a set of application programs in a multiuser, multitasking UNIX environment. The name is a little misleading, because NetWare for UNIX can also run on non-UNIX operating systems—hence it earned the name *portable* NetWare. NetWare for UNIX provides HOST/PC integration, transparent connectivity, NetWare security, host security, file sharing, print servers, and NetWare application development interfaces.

What is algebra exactly? Is it those three-cornered things?

—*J. M. Barrie*

System 7

NetWare connectivity to Macintosh clients is provided through a set of programs called *NetWare for Macintosh.* NetWare for Macintosh is a set of client and server programs that provide file, printing, security, SFT, and performance features for Macintosh workstations. The Macintosh operating system, System 7, interfaces with NetWare for Macintosh through the internal Chooser utility and an additional NetWare desk accessory.

NetWare for Macintosh uses the AppleTalk Filing Protocol (AFP) for distributed applications and AppleTalk Phase I and Phase II for connectivity. In addition, NetWare for Macintosh supports SNMP and AppleTalk MIB for UNIX-like management of network objects. NetWare for Macintosh operates as a NetWare loadable module on NetWare v3.11 and v4.0, and as a value-added process (VAP) on NetWare v2.2. NetWare for Macintosh supports the Macintosh's internal LocalTalk connection as well as industry-standard ODI LAN adapters. In addition, NetWare for Macintosh supports the internal Ethernet adapters that are integrated into the Macintosh Quadra line.

NetWare for Macintosh is implemented in two parts. First, the NetWare for Macintosh server files must be installed and configured at the NetWare server. Second, the NetWare for Macintosh client files must be installed and configured at the workstation. Once the configurations are complete, Macintosh workstations can attach to NetWare servers as if they were DOS clients; the same functionality is available to Macintosh users. Let's take a look at these two Macintosh connectivity steps.

NetWare for Macintosh Server Configuration

The NetWare configuration process for Macintosh workstations is relatively simple. NetWare for Macintosh is loaded as an NLM for NetWare v3.11 and v4.0, and as a VAP for

NetWare v2.2. The functionality is identical, except for some additional protocol translations that occur on NetWare v2.2 servers. NetWare for Macintosh consists of the following NLMs:

- *APPLETALK.NLM*—AppleTalk protocol stack and router. This is the main AppleTalk module that handles protocol stacks, Macintosh routing, and NIC communications.
- *AFP.NLM*—AppleTalk Filing Protocol. This module handles all AFP requests from Macintosh workstations. It is responsible for Macintosh application support, file structure, folders, and security.
- *ATPS.NLM*—AppleTalk print server. This module processes AppleTalk printing requests. Macintosh and DOS workstations can share AppleTalk printers.
- *ATCON.NLM*—AppleTalk console utility. This is a server application that provides AppleTalk management functions.
- *MAC.NAM*—Macintosh name space. This module formats NetWare volumes for Macintosh naming conventions. DOS and NetWare only support 11-character names; System 7 supports 31-character names. Macintosh name space adds considerable overhead to NetWare file server processes. In addition, volumes that share DOS and Macintosh data create duplicate data entry tables that substantially decrease network performance.

To alleviate NetWare overhead, follow this simple strategy concerning Macintosh name space. Create three separate volumes: DOS, MAC, and BOTH. The DOS volume will contain DOS-only files and applications, the MAC volume will contain MAC-only files and applications, and the BOTH volume will contain only the data that is shared by both DOS and MAC users. This strategy will minimize duplicate DETs. Add the MAC name space NLM to only MAC and BOTH.

NetWare for Macintosh is installed on NetWare v2.2 servers through the INSTALL program. In addition, it must be configured as a set of similar VAPs.

NetWare for Macintosh Workstation Configuration

System 7 clients have a head start over DOS users, because System 7 is inherently networkable. The workstation operating system already has many of the networking hooks required to attach to a NetWare LAN. The Chooser utility provides login, printing, routing, and management services. NetWare for Macintosh provides a second desk accessory (DA) for specialized NetWare commands. In addition, the workstation requires the Notify startup document, NetWare UAM, and the NetWare Control Center. In order to use NetWare for Macintosh, workstations must have the following system components installed:

- *System* version 6.0 or above
- *Finder* version 6.1 or above
- *Chooser* v3.3 or above
- *AppleShare Workstation* v2.0 or above
- *LaserWriter* v5.2 or above
- *ImageWriter* drivers v2.7 or above

The NetWare DA consists of four network programs:

- The About program provides a brief description of the NetWare DA functionality.
- The Message program provides short messaging capabilities across NetWare channels.
- The Print Queue program provides standard print queue management functionality (PCONSOLE).
- The Rights program provides security management and rights lists.

The Notify startup document is Notify INIT. Notify INIT is copied to the workstation's system folder to allow receipt of network messages.

NetWare UAM (User Authentication Method)

UAM is copied to the workstation's AppleShare folder and provides NetWare password encryption features. The NetWare Control Center (NCC) is an administrative feature for managing users, groups, and security. Macintosh clients can use NCC to access a subset of SYSCON's management facilities.

This ends our exploration of workstation operating systems. We have covered 95 percent of the software components that provide network *performance*. The NOS and WOS combine to provide connectivity, security, performance, SFT, and application platforms. This is the heart of NetWare performance. What about people? Earlier we stated that LAN synergy is achieved through a balance of people and performance. The next few sections explore people design through menu systems, network applications, and office systems design.

Menu Systems

The network menu system integrates all facets of software design. It penetrates the design, surrounds it, and binds the components together. The menu system usually represents the user's first point of contact with the network and can have a considerable psychological impact on a user's acceptance or denial of the LAN. Make your choice of a network menu system carefully. There are myriad components to consider: interface, look and feel, hardware requirements, software overhead, ease of use, management capabilities, and (of course) cost.

Recent advancements in menu design have split the industry into two halves—graphical user interface and text-based. GUI systems are easy to use and beautiful to look at but hardware-intensive. Most GUI menu systems effectively eliminate 80286-based workstations; the 286s simply run too slowly with a GUI. The GUI arena is led by Microsoft's Windows system. The alternative, *text-based* menus, uses sophisticated programming techniques and little hardware overhead to accommodate almost any LAN configuration.

For the most part, text-based systems are more powerful than GUI systems, but they lack the user-friendly look. There is a huge variety of text-based systems to choose from, including NetWare's own internal menu system. This section takes a brief look at the best available GUI and text-based network menu systems.

Microsoft Windows

Microsoft Windows has revolutionized software design. Its GUI system has refined the look and feel of many of today's applications. Major software developers are scrambling to release Windows 3.1 and NT versions of favorite software—WordPerfect, Lotus 1-2-3, dBASE, Harvard Graphics, and on and on. No longer is software judged solely on productivity. Today's applications must contain a second elusive quality: usability. Users demand intuitive applications, standardized menus, compatibility, and icons.

Microsoft Windows is now in its third generation—version 3.1. It has evolved as far as the 16-bit DOS architecture can take it. Windows NT is the next generation of 32-bit Windows operating systems. Unfortunately, people like DOS. And with the improvements in DOS 6.0, people are inclined to stick with DOS. So for the millions of DOS-heads, Microsoft is working on Windows 4.0. The evolution of Windows 4.0 focuses on interface, because the core of Windows' performance will remain forever attached to the 16-bit DOS architecture. The Windows 4.0 interface is more modern, consistent, and standardized. The design of Windows 4.0 is a collaboration of developers, software manufacturers, and users. It promises to excite all of the senses, including digital sound, animated icons, and full-motion video.

Unfortunately, Windows 4.0 isn't here yet. We must make the best of Windows 3.1 for now. Microsoft's current Windows interface has remained intact for almost four years. Networking Windows is not hard. *Optimizing* Windows in a NetWare environment is hard. Follow the 10 easy steps outlined next for optimizing NetWare and Windows.

Hardware

Windows is a very hardware-intensive application. The biggest problem with GUI is the large hardware investment it requires. The Windows graphic look puts a heavy load on workstation CPU, RAM, video, and disk.

To optimize the hardware:

- The workstation CPU must operate at a minimum of 80386, 32-bits, 25 MHz in order to take advantage of Windows' enhanced 386 features. Windows supports an 80286-based CPU, but only in standard mode—this is limiting.
- The workstation should support at least 4MB of RAM, although 8MB is recommended. Memory is so inexpensive at roughly $35 per megabyte at this writing, that the investment makes sense for Windows optimization. Extra memory provides disk caching, multitasking, and better compatibility for DOS applications under Windows.
- Workstation video is a very important component. The speed of the video controller has a substantial impact on the speed of the GUI. Various manufacturers provide Windows accelerator video controllers that are designed to optimize graphical output. The Paradise card increases video speeds up to 1,500 percent.
- Consider the workstation disk, which is presumably where Windows will reside. You can run Windows from a centralized server, but it is not recommended. Windows optimization relies on virtual memory, disk performance, and caching. These procedures are not available to users from central file server disks. The size, speed, and format of the workstation disk can have a considerable effect on the speed of Windows. The disk should be at least 100MB in size, no slower than 15 milliseconds, and formatted to 1:1 interleave. We will discuss these concepts in more detail later.

Software

In order to take full advantage of the Windows environment, all applications should be designed for it. Windows applications operate much faster and more reliably in a Windows environment than do non-Windows applications. Also, Windows optimization is not just a matter of speed. It is also a matter of productivity. And many studies have shown that users are more productive in an environment they like and understand. Also, a consistent interface can help eliminate confusion and frustration. Most Windows applications have been designed to take advantage of Windows' inherent networkability. Features such as file locking, print queues, and drive mapping are incorporated into Windows applications. This level of network compatibility is not a standard in the non-Windows software world.

Disk Format

As stated earlier, the workstation disk is very important in optimizing Windows. The disk component to consider is format type, which refers to how the disk reads and writes Windows data. The *interleave factor* describes a method of alternating sectors to read and write data. The older IBM-compatible machines have an interleave factor of 3:1. This means that numerically ordered sectors are organized three sectors apart. This also means it takes three times longer to read and write Windows data than if the sectors were organized sequentially. Many third-party utilities describe and manage disk formatting—Norton Utilities and Central Point PC Tools are examples.

In addition to interleave factor, the fragmentation of the disk impacts Windows' performance. *Fragmentation* describes a common condition of DOS disks whereby files are scattered throughout the disk in noncontiguous blocks. This scattering can considerably slow down disk access. Windows relies on many temporary files. If the disk is highly fragmented, the temporary files are difficult to retrieve and the system slows down tremendously. There are many third-party utilities available that can nondestructively defragment your workstation disk—Norton Utilities and OpTune, for example. I recommend defragmentation at least once a month.

Disk Performance

Windows is also impacted by the workstation disk's performance. The speed of the disk is important, but not of major concern—most manufacturers have standardized on 15 to 19 milliseconds. The configurable improvement to disk speed is the integration of a caching disk controller. Windows provides two disk performance procedures: 32-bit access and disk caching.

Windows' *32-bit disk access* is achieved through FastDisk. FastDisk is a Windows procedure that provides Windows users with twice the disk throughput of normal machines. In order to use FastDisk, the user must be operating in 386 Enhanced mode and be using a 100 percent Western Digital WD1003 compatible disk controller—which most disks do. To activate FastDisk, use the 386 Enhanced applet under Control Panel. Choose Virtual Memory and Change. If your system supports the WD1003 controller, a checkbox will appear in the lower left corner next to `Use 32-Bit Disk Access`.

Disk caching, another Windows disk optimization procedure, refers to Windows' ability to store frequently used files in workstation RAM. The system can access files from RAM 100 times faster than from disk. Windows' disk caching feature is called *SmartDrive*.

SmartDrive is activated in the AUTOEXEC.BAT file. There are additional third-party disk caching programs that provide more features and flexibility than does SmartDrive—Norton Cache and HyperDisk are examples.

Memory Management

The workstation RAM is a focal point for Windows optimization, especially in a NetWare environment. Windows relies on workstation RAM for application processing, multitasking, performance, disk caching, and system control. The more RAM, the merrier.

Workstation RAM is divided into three types: conventional, expanded, and extended. Conventional memory is important to non-Windows applications. As a matter of fact, they can't live without it. DOS applications can only access the first 640KB of workstation RAM. If this memory is cluttered with system components, drivers, and terminate-and-stay-resident (TSR) utilities, the workstation performance slows considerably—a condition known as *RAM cram.*

Fortunately, Windows alleviates this problem by leaving conventional RAM alone and concentrating on extended memory—RAM above 1MB. That leaves us with 384KB of wasted RAM—from 640 to 1024. This wasteland is known as the *upper memory area (UMA).* Windows provides a utility called EMM386 that enables users to convert their UMA into expanded memory. This expanded memory can then be used by DOS drivers, system components, and TSRs. This procedure alleviates RAM cram by moving DOS components from conventional to expanded RAM.

There are five memory management techniques you can use to free conventional workstation RAM:

DOS=HIGH,UMB   Add this to CONFIG.SYS to move DOS system components into the first 64KB block of extended RAM, called the *high memory area (HMA).*

DEVICE=C:\WINDOWS\EMM386.EXE noems /i=e000-efff   Add this to CONFIG.SYS to convert as much of the UMA as possible into usable expanded memory.

DEVICEHIGH=   Add this DOS command to CONFIG.SYS to replace DEVICE=. It moves DOS device drivers from conventional to expanded RAM.

LOADHIGH=   Add this DOS command to AUTOEXEC.BAT to enable users to load TSRs, drivers, and other memory programs in expanded rather than conventional RAM.

EMSNETx   Use this expanded memory version of NetWare's NETx workstation shell. Add it to AUTOEXEC.BAT.

Use the MEM /C command to monitor the migration of programs from conventional to expanded RAM. These simple techniques saved me almost 150KB of conventional workstation RAM. If you run out of physical RAM, Windows enables you to use hard disk space as virtual memory. *Virtual memory* looks and acts just like real memory, except it is slower. Virtual memory is available through 386 Enhanced mode only, and can be configured in the 386 Enhanced applet under the Control Panel.

Following are samples of CONFIG.SYS and AUTOEXEC.BAT files that optimize workstation memory under Windows:

CONFIG.SYS	AUTOEXEC.BAT

```
DEVICE=C:\WINDOWS\HIMEM.SYS        @ECHO OFF
DOS=HIGH,UMB                       CLS
STACKS=9,256                       PROMPT $P$G
DEVICE=C:\WINDOWS\EMM386.EXE noems /i=e000-efff
DEVICEHIGH=C:\DOS\SETVER.EXE       LOADHIGH C:\WINDOWS\SMARTDRV.EXE
                                   4096 1024
DEVICEHIGH=C:\WINDOWS\MOUSE.SYS    PATH C:\;C:\DOS;C:\WINDOWS;C:\NET
FILES=40                           LOADHIGH IPX
BUFFERS=40                         EMSNETX
SHELL=C:\DOS\COMMAND.COM C:\DOS\   /P/C:1024
```

Printing

Windows printing is network-aware. Printing from Windows to NetWare queues is simple. Most DOS applications must be fooled into printing to NetWare queues. NetWare uses the CAPTURE command to redirect print jobs from the local workstation LPT1: port to a NetWare queue—WordPerfect 5.1 is the lone exception. It can print directly to a NetWare queue without the CAPTURE command. Windows provides the functionality to print directly to NetWare queues as well. Windows printing is faster, simpler, and easier to manage than printing done from NetWare.

Windows provides two utilities to optimize NetWare printing: Printers applet and Print Manager. The Printers applet on the Control Panel enables users to redirect print jobs directly to NetWare queues. It lists the queues, jobs, and printers in a graphical format. Choose Connect and Network under Printers. The Windows Print Manager provides NetWare queue management from within Windows. Print Manager is a desktop application that features job prioritization, queue shuffling, queue connection, job deletion, and printing options. To activate Print Manager, choose the Use Print Manager checkbox under the Printers applet.

Network Installation

Windows provides two strategies for network installation: workstation and server. Installing Windows on a workstation has many advantages: availability of virtual memory, disk optimization, performance, and integrity. On the downside, the Windows files and virtual memory occupy approximately 40MB of workstation disk space.

Installing Windows on a workstation is simple. Run the SETUP utility and specify Novell NetWare on the System Information screen. Windows will copy the appropriate files to the workstation disk and make special network modifications automatically. The key to this strategy is using the correct NetWare shells; the next step discusses shells in more detail.

The other network strategy is installing Windows on the server. Windows server installation centralizes shared files, saves disk space, and increases workstation connectivity. On the down side, the server installation doesn't support disk optimization procedures.

Installing Windows on a server is a two-step process. First, the Windows SETUP utility copies the appropriate files to a shared server sub-directory—type **SETUP /a** and enter **F:\APPS\WINDOWS** at the directory prompt. Second, Windows configures user definition files for each NetWare user—log in as a specific user (such as David) and type **SETUP /n** from the U:\USERS\loginname directory (such as U:\USERS\DAVID). This is where the user definition files are stored. Repeat this procedure for each user.

NetWare Shells

NetWare shells are especially important in a Windows environment. The shells process communications between Windows and shared applications or data. The IPX shell handles Windows requests for network resources, and the NETx shell directs Windows requests between DOS and IPX. The most important aspect of Windows and NetWare shells is the shell version. Windows doesn't work well with shells that predate version 3.10. Ideally, NetWare shells should be as current as possible. This includes updating them every four to five months. Currently, Windows works best with the following versions:

- IPX versions 3.10 and later
- NETx versions 3.26 and later

To find the version of shells you are using, type **NVER** at any NetWare prompt. The best way to keep on top of shell revisions is by checking NetWire—Novell's CompuServe forum. You can download the latest shells at no charge. The IPX shell can be upgraded in one of two ways: WSGEN or ODI. Standard IPX shells are compiled from two components: LAN driver and IPX.OBJ. Windows interfaces with the IPX.OBJ component.

To upgrade IPX, simply copy the new IPX.OBJ file from NetWire to the WSGEN diskette and run the WSGEN shell generation utility. The new IPX.COM file will reflect the updated IPX.OBJ.

An easier solution is ODI. Because ODI supports modular shells, no compiling is necessary. Simply copy the new IPXODI.COM from NetWire to the workstation disk. The NETx shell upgrade is much easier. NETx is a noncompiled shell, so simply copy the new NETx.COM from NetWire to the workstation disk. This procedure has been automated with the WSUPDATE NetWare utility. Currently, Windows supports four NETx shell revisions at installation: below 3.01, below 3.21, 3.21 and above, and 3.26 and above.

To support the symbol .. as a representation of previous directory in Windows, add the line SHOW DOTS=ON to the NET.CFG workstation file.

Network Utilities

Windows provides a number of built-in network utilities: Network applet, Network Assistant, Print Manager, File Manager, and WinLogin.

- The *Network Applet* choice on the Control Panel supports the NetWare Device Driver Set for Windows. The Network applet provides checkboxes to control network drives, messages, printing, share handles, and warnings. NWPOPUP is a Windows application that loads at startup and provides a graphical interface for NetWare SEND messages.
- The *Network Assistant* is a Windows application of three components: Network Connections for drive mapping, login, and server attachments; Previous Connections List to provide information about where you have been; and Network Utilities, another interface to the NetWare Device Driver Set for Windows.
- The *Print Manager* is network-ready for NetWare printers and queues. It provides a feature for attaching to known servers.

- The *File Manager,* also NetWare-ready, displays volumes of data concerning network drives, directories, and files. The Disk-Network Connections menu supports drive mapping, server attachments, and directory browsing over multiple servers.
- *WinLogin* is a Windows add-in that Microsoft developed after the fact. WinLogin was released in response to numerous complaints that Windows didn't directly support NetWare login procedures. WinLogin is free, and provides an icon for NetWare login procedures from within Windows.

NetWare Tools for Windows

NetWare Tools for Windows is a set of nine Windows utilities from Novell. These utilities were designed to provide Windows optimization in the NetWare environment. Novell provides the utilities for free on NetWire. NetWare Tools for Windows provides the same fundamental network features that Windows does, but in clearer, more precise manner. NetWare Tools for Windows also contains some features Windows doesn't: Windows versions of favorite NetWare utilities, including USERLIST, VOLINFO, SETPASS, and SEND. The tools include Map, Printers, Attachments, UserList, VolInfo, SetPass, Send, Messages, and Scripts.

Other GUI Menu Systems

GeoWorks Ensemble

GeoWorks Ensemble is a multitasking GUI menu environment. It provides application support, file management, and printing services. Ensemble supports its own application development platform—PC/GEOS. It is compliant with Motif, Windows, and Presentation Manager interfaces. Features include GeoWrite, GeoDraw, GeoManager, GeoDex, GeoPlanner, GeoComm, and GeoWorks Pro spreadsheet application.

Ensemble is actually more than a GUI menu system. It exists somewhere in between menu systems and groupware. GeoWorks Ensemble is available as a site license and offers EMS functionality. The product requires 3MB of local disk space. Its retail price is $200, available from GeoWorks, Inc., (800) 772-0001.

SuperGUI

SuperGUI is a graphical-based menu system with enhanced network support. Features include point-and-click, file and directory management, autodialer, time-tracking system, report generator, macro language, and on-line help. The retail price is $100 to $130, available from Media Management Systems, Inc., (404) 564-5610.

NCDware

NCDware is a GUI menu system for UNIX compatible systems. It works with DEC VAX/VMS, ULTRIX, Sun/SunOS, and IBM AIX workstation operating systems. NCDware supports Ethernet LANs and was written in the C programming language. Its retail price is $50, available from Network Computing Devices, Inc., (800) 235-7889.

WISh2

WISh2 is also a UNIX-based GUI menu system. This product has much wider support than does NCDware. WISh2 is compatible with SCO UNIX, SPARCstation/SunOS, IBM AIX,

HP, DECstation, and Silicon Graphics. WISh2 demands large hardware overhead, including 7MB of local disk storage and 8MB minimum RAM. The product is an icon-based desktop shell for UNIX machines running under X Windows. Its retail price is $695, available from Non Standard Logics, Inc., (617) 482-6393.

PM Assistant

PM Assistant is an automation and customization tool for OS/2's Presentation Manager. PM Assistant is more than simply a menu system; it is a task automation utility. Its retail price is $125, available from Utilis, (800) 745-7757.

Text-Based Menu Systems

+Menu

+Menu is a simple, text-based menu building program. It is available in a single-user or LAN package. +Menu requires no script files or programming. The LAN version supports diskless workstations and password protection. Its retail price is $29 for the single user version and $195 for the LAN version, available from Abelson Communications, Inc., (516) 546-2286.

EASY-DOS-IT

EASY-DOS-IT is a simple, old text-based menu system. It provides one-stroke access to programs, DOS commands, and tutors. Its retail price is $29, available from BMS Computer, Inc., (800) 283-4267.

LANMenu

LANMenu is a true multiuser, text-based menu system. It uses the NetBIOS protocol standard for LAN communications and supports access rights and restrictions. Its retail price is $250, available from Circle Development, Inc., (800) 676-0333.

Turbo Menu

Turbo Menu is a successful NetWare-compatible LAN menu system. It is text-based and offers complete user transparency. Features include automatic installation, scrolling menu bars, hot keys, clock, unlimited submenus, colors, password protection, hard disk management, hypertext documentation, and file management. Its retail price is $40, available from Decisis, Inc., (309) 655-0177.

Direct Access Network

Direct Access Network is a LAN implementation of the popular Direct Access menu system. It offers the same text-based interface and automated menu generation to a variety of different LAN platforms—NetWare, VINES, and LANtastic. Its retail price is $995, available from Fifth Generation Systems, Inc., (800) 873-4384.

Lazy Susan

Lazy Susan is a popular no-frills network menu system. It requires only 77KB of local disk storage and less than 25MB of workstation RAM. Features include single-keystroke selections, 100 options per menu, multilevel passwords, and auditing. Site licensing and free technical support are available. Its retail price is $80, available from GETC Software, Inc., (800) 663-8066.

Automenu

Automenu has been around for a long time. The company probably enjoys the largest installed base of text-oriented DOS menu systems. Automenu currently supports NetWare, VINES, and Alloy LANs. Its retail price is $70, available from Magee Enterprises, Inc., (800) 662-4330.

Q*Menu

Q*Menu is an interesting DEC solution for VAX/VMS menuing. It requires 760KB of local disk and 204KB of workstation RAM. It provides simple menu management features, including management of menu structures, point-and-shoot operations, and shared menu linking. Check its price tag: $595 to $8,495! (I'll take a dozen.) Q*Menu is available from W. Quinn Associates, Inc., (800) VAX-FILE.

NetWare's Menu

NetWare's application menu system is based on the Menu Utilities structure. It provides a header across the top of the screen that describes the menu title and provides the user with date and time information. The main window appears in the middle of the screen, with one to nine numbered choices. In addition, NetWare offers a moving selection bar that highlights available options. Double lines around the perimeter indicate *input* windows, whereas single lines identify *information-only* windows. The main drawback with NetWare's Menu System is its mode of operation—it works by creating cryptic text files with titles, menu options, and commands. Simple, but cumbersome. The good news is that NetWare v4.0's version of the menu system incorporates many of the advancements of Saber Menu. I'm not complaining—it's free!

WordPerfect Library

The WordPerfect Library is a menu *shell* that sits above NetWare or DOS and controls the execution of network applications. It sports a simple design—a full screen with letters designating available choices. WordPerfect Library is also sophisticated—it doesn't take much memory and offers a consistent interface for users who are comfortable with the WordPerfect environment. In addition, WordPerfect Library gets along very well with NetWare. Available from WordPerfect Corporation, Inc., (800) 321-5906.

Network Applications

Earlier this book described network applications as the *swords that users wield to carve out company profits.* They are in fact double-edged swords. On the one hand, network applications enhance users' effectiveness and productivity—these applications crunch numbers, organize words, and paint pictures. On the other hand, network applications are complex programs that must balance the demands of network resources and local workstation processing—they are stored at the central file server and processed at the local workstation. If anything, network applications are schizophrenic.

There are two kinds of network applications: stand-alone and network-aware. *Stand-alone* network applications are programs that were never designed to run on a LAN. NetWare supports multiple access to stand-alone applications. But it can get you in trouble.

This is how it works. When a user requests a network application, NetWare downloads a copy to the local workstation RAM—the user works locally. If another user requests the same application, NetWare checks whether the Sharable attribute has been assigned to the application files. It has. So NetWare downloads a second copy of the application to a different user's workstation RAM—everybody is happy—for a while. The problem with stand-alone applications is that they contain no concurrency-control mechanisms. *Concurrency-control mechanisms* protect against two users inadvertently deleting each other's changes. User A could open a file and begin making changes. User B opens the same file, because NetWare allows her to, and she also begins making changes. Whose changes are saved—A's or B's? The user who finishes last. This can be a very dangerous scenario. There are two solutions for this horrifying scenario: install a well-designed network directory structure (Chapter 12) or purchase a network-aware application.

Network-aware applications are software programs that were designed to run on a LAN. There are many advantages to network-aware software, but the most notable is concurrency-control mechanisms. Network-aware applications support one of three different concurrency-control mechanisms: file locking, record locking, or field locking.

- *File locking* is the process of restricting application and data files to only one user at a time. Some sophisticated file locking allows users to open a file, but not make any changes. File locking is common with network-aware word processing and spreadsheet applications.
- *Record locking* allows multiple access to network files, but restricts users from accessing the same record within the file. A record is a range of bytes that designates a person, place, or thing.
- *Field locking* is a further refinement of record locking. It enables users to share records but restricts their access to simultaneous fields. A *field* is one of many characteristics that describe a record. A record, for example, would be a database of information about a person—say, John Doe. The record contains multiple fields that describe John's address, phone number, age, and so forth.

Record locking would restrict all of John Doe's information, whereas field locking would allow multiuser access to the record, but not the same field—the address, for example. Record locking and field locking are complex and difficult to master. They are common features among high-end spreadsheets and database programs for multiple users.

Some of the other advantages of network-aware software include

- *cost effectiveness*—many manufacturers provide discounts on multiuser packages of 5, 10, and 20 users. They will sell you one set of disks and multiple licenses. In addition, network designers can save money by eliminating large workstation disks.
- *software maintenance*—network managers can focus on one copy of the software, not 50 individual versions.
- *centralized enhancements*—updates, macros, and fonts can be centralized. Users can share macros and can take advantage of others' expertise with a given software package.

- *shared data files*—users can share data files and integrate projects. NetWare security supports shared and private directories.
- *increased storage*—one network-aware application can save googols of local disk space. Also, users have access to a larger network disk than they would have had locally.

The world of network applications is organized into four categories: word processing, spreadsheets, database, and integrated software. Following is a brief description of the best applications in each category.

Word Processing

Word processing is the most common application of network software. Network-aware applications offer many advantages over word processing stand-alone:

- shared style sheets
- editing documents
- spooled printing
- user configurations
- forms processing
- shared printing
- mail merging

Microsoft Word

Word is Microsoft's best-selling word processor application. It has enjoyed a great deal of success across three major platforms: DOS, Macintosh, and Windows. Microsoft Word for DOS is intended for purists who don't like the Windows interface or don't have enough workstation horsepower. Word for DOS is a well-behaved program with most of the features of the other versions, but it is not very easy to use. Microsoft Word was originally designed to run in DOS, but the product really shines when it is combined with Windows or System 7. Microsoft is concentrating on GUI word processing. Word for Windows is a revolutionary improvement over the DOS version. It offers toolbars, grammar-checking, consistent menu structures, charting, a thesaurus, envelopes, a ruler, desktop publishing, and help—*all with one button.*

The current version of Word for Windows, version 3.0, features enhanced customization and intelligence. The interface remains consistent, but the task automation functionality has been dramatically improved.

Word for Macintosh has been around longer than Word for Windows and shares many of the same GUI features. Microsoft Word is network-aware. It offers networking hooks for file locking, master documents, and shared applications. The bottom line is that Microsoft excels with GUI. Word is fast, flexible, and easy to use. By the way, Microsoft also offers a version of Word for OS/2's Presentation Manager.

WordPerfect

WordPerfect dominates the DOS world. The world-famous word processor prides itself on the ability to support almost any computing platform. There isn't any other application available for so many platforms—DOS; Windows; Macintosh; OS/2; Data General; NeXT; VMS; IBM mainframes; and more than 30 different UNIX, Xenix, and RISC systems.

WordPerfect is a classic example of function over form. It is cryptic to use and difficult to learn, but once you have mastered WordPerfect, there is nothing like it.

WordPerfect for Macintosh features a DA with mail, a calendar, Rolodex, file manager, and forms maker.

WordPerfect for OS/2 supports extended edition, multitasking, enhanced memory, and integrated text and graphics.

WordPerfect for UNIX supports the IBM RS/6000, DECstation, SCO Xenix, Silicon Graphics, UNIX V, Sun's SPARCstation, and others.

WordPerfect Corporation is located two miles from Novell, Inc., in Utah, and it is rumored that the engineers from both companies do lunch. Needless to say, WordPerfect is very well behaved on NetWare LANs. Available from WordPerfect Corporation, Inc., (800) 321-5906.

Borland Multimate

Multimate has been adopted by many word processing professionals. It's a unique, high-powered word processor, not in the formatting and font sense, but in the connectivity and application interaction sense. Multimate is not a terrific word processor, but for power users it offers more.

Borland Fullwrite Professional for Macintosh

Fullwrite Professional is Borland's offering to the Macintosh community. It is a full-featured word processing application with the power of Multimate and the look of a Macintosh. Fullwrite Professional offers built-in outlining, a 100,000-word spell checker, a 220,000-word thesaurus, automatic hyphenation, autosave, and on-line help.

Lotus Manuscript

Believe it or not, one of the first Lotus products to exploit networking was Lotus Manuscript. Manuscript is a flexible word processor with excellent networking features—including master documents, *include files* for multiuser sharing, a comments section for colleague reactions, and excellent connectivity with other Lotus products. Manuscript is available in three editions: standard, server, and node. Retail prices are $495 standard, $595 server, and $295 node, available from Lotus Development Corporation, (800) 872-3387.

Spreadsheets

Led by the popularity of Excel, Quattro Pro, and Lotus, use of spreadsheets is on the rise. The simplicity of a spreadsheet lends itself to a huge variety of business applications—from financial reporting to employee records to taxes. Networking features include

- linking
- shared file access
- master spreadsheets
- advanced printing
- macros, templates, and programming
- goal seeking
- financial models

Microsoft Excel

Microsoft Excel is an excellent addition to the Windows family of network applications. As with all the other Microsoft products, Excel is network-ready right out of the box; no special software is needed.

Microsoft Excel supports three platforms: DOS, Windows, and Macintosh. Excel for DOS uses a run-time version of Windows for the familiar GUI interface. Excel on an 80286 machine will work, but excruciatingly slowly. Excel truly shines on a Windows-supported 80386 or 80486 workstation or a fully functional high-end Macintosh. Features include a programmable toolbar, automatic graphing, spreadsheet linking, drag and drop, autoformat, autofill, Crosstab Wizard, Scenario Manager, Analysis Toolpak, Report Manager, and an enhanced spell checker.

Microsoft Excel looks great and it is easy to use, especially if you are familiar with the other Microsoft products. Microsoft Excel has many *gee-whiz* features the other spreadsheet applications lack.

Borland Quattro Pro

Quattro Pro is a relative newcomer to the spreadsheet scene. Borland studied the other products carefully before designing Quattro Pro. The wait was well worth it—Borland successfully integrated all of the best features of the other spreadsheet applications into one powerful business tool, including Excel and 1-2-3 emulation modes.

Recent versions of Quattro Pro offer more power and ease of use. Release 3.0 includes advanced analytical tools and intelligent graphs that help business professionals decipher the meaning of the spreadsheets. Quattro Pro earns its ease of use through its *SpeedBar,* a row of clearly labeled, context-sensitive buttons that provide instant access to frequently used features and macros. Other features include WYSIWYG (what you see is what you get) displays, scalable fonts, zoom and pan, line drawing, the Annotator, slide shows, Paradox database compatibility, and the Optimizer to help solve complex multivariable equations.

Quattro Pro is also network-aware. It fully supports NetWare file locking, print queues, logins, and drive mappings. Quattro Pro comes network-ready right out of the box. Borland's Quattro Pro isn't as pretty as Excel, but for serious spreadsheeters, no other package compares. Available from Borland International, (800) 331-0877.

Lotus 1-2-3

Lotus 1-2-3 is the grandfather of spreadsheet packages. It is a world-famous application that has mellowed with age. Like a good cheese, Lotus 1-2-3 has matured over time, but no revelations. Lotus 1-2-3 was a role model for Quattro Pro and Excel, and unfortunately they learned too well. 1-2-3 offers a huge installed base, solid spreadsheet functionality, great analysis tools—but nothing extraordinary. The saving grace for 1-2-3 is an enormous number of third-party add-ins.

Lotus offers two different LAN strategies: stand-alone and network-aware. The stand-alone 1-2-3 applications are network-ready and can be installed on a workstation or the server. The major drawback is lack of file locking in the stand-alone version. The network-aware applications consist of server and node packages. The server package is loaded on the server and includes a license count utility and file locking.

Lotus 1-2-3 is available for DOS, Windows, OS/2, and Macintosh platforms from Lotus Development Corporation, (800) 872-3387.

PlanPerfect

PlanPerfect is WordPerfect's integrated spreadsheet application. The product is comprehensive, but it falls well short of the big three. PlanPerfect is a good spreadsheet solution for WordPerfect integration in small to medium-sized offices. It is a complete package with all of the standard spreadsheet features, but nothing else. The true test of a great application is that it gives you what you need before you know you need it. PlanPerfect has no surprises. Available from WordPerfect Corporation, Inc., (800) 321-5906.

Borland Full Impact for Macintosh

Borland's Full Impact is an integrated spreadsheet/graphics application. It offers the power of desktop spreadsheeting with the superior graphics capabilities of the Macintosh environment. Data analysis is enhanced through 3-D bar charts, 3-D surface charts, 3-D perspective pies, line charts, and scatter plots. Graphic analysis has advantages over staring at a screen full of numbers, and Full Impact makes it very easy. Available from Borland International, (800) 331-0877.

Databases

Probably the first application to take advantage of a LAN's shared resources was a *database*. Network databases must support multiple users accessing shared files simultaneously—file locking, record locking, and field locking. In order to achieve this level of connectivity, database applications rely on complex network protocols, security schemes, and TTS backout.

NetWare-compatible systems use IPX/SPX and NetWare Core Protocol (NCP). Most common database applications rely on the file server for processing, communications, and resource allocation. Some advanced systems are too taxing, so they run on their own server: a database server. The most common NetWare-compatible database servers are NetWare SQL and Microsoft SQL Server. SQL (Structured Query Language) is an IBM standard for database management and connectivity. It is supported by most large database management systems (DBMS). Some advantages of network databases are these:

- record and field-level locking
- large data storage
- file sharing
- centralized management
- concurrent data entry
- concurrent data queries
- system fault tolerance

Borland Paradox

Borland has become a leader in advanced software design. Probably the company's greatest achievement is Paradox. Paradox is a full-featured, easy-to-use, power-packed DBMS. Borland paid a great deal of attention to Paradox's user interface. Many of the database systems have been accused of ignoring user's needs, so Borland made an effort to provide intuitive menus, on-line help, and readable documentation—and succeeded. The clear, straight-forward interface makes database development easy for beginners and professionals.

Features include the SpeedBar, BLObs (binary large objects), VROOM (virtual run-time object-oriented memory manager), diverse file import/export, an automated graphing tool, QBE (query by example), and a separate SQL module for IBM connectivity. The Paradox Applications Language (PAL) is easy to learn. It includes a scripting feature that enables programmers to transform keystrokes into database scripts.

Paradox supports 256MB of data per field, 255 fields per record, and 2 billion records per database—that's a whopping 130,560,000,000,000,000,000 bytes. Paradox's network-ability is extraordinary. Multiuser locking is performed automatically and changes made by users instantaneously appear on all user screens. Available from Borland International, (800) 331-0877.

dBASE IV

Ashton-Tate introduced dBASE IV a few years ago to mixed reviews. The company had been the leader in network database applications for many years, but its grip was slipping fast. In an effort to bolster market share and save the dying product, Borland International purchased Ashton-Tate in 1991. Borland quickly revitalized dBASE and offered it as a low-end alternative to Paradox. The new dBASE IV provides first-time database users with a place to start. It is ideal for maintaining small address lists or medium-sized inventory systems. The development environment is clear and the report generator is easy to use.

Some of dBASE IV's new features include QBE, Label Designer, Design Tools, and IQ!. dBASE is well designed for networks and supports NetWare, VINES, LAN Manager, and IBM PC LAN. The longevity of dBASE has served it well in one key area—platform diversity. dBASE IV currently supports DOS, Windows, Macintosh, VMS, SQL, SAA, and UNIX platforms. Available from Borland International, (800) 331-0877.

Fox Pro

Microsoft responded to Borland's dominance in database applications by purchasing Fox Software in early 1992. Microsoft has put a great deal of effort into developing its own Windows-based DBMS to complement Word and Excel—it failed. When Microsoft purchased Fox Software, it acquired the fastest available database application—Fox Pro. Microsoft is now committed to improving the product and integrating it into the Windows desktop solution—Word, Excel, and Fox Pro.

Fox Pro is a very well-designed system. It is powerful, efficient, versatile, and hard to use. The new Fox Pro offers a graphical user interface, smaller memory footprint, network traffic reduction, and platform diversity. Features include a virtual memory manager to eliminate cumbersome overlays, an integrated SQL module for IBM connectivity, Rushmore query optimization to reduce network traffic, and compound indexes for efficient file locking. Fox Pro supports DOS, UNIX, Windows, and Macintosh clients. Fox Pro serves the advanced DBMS professional who demands speed, flexibility, and cryptic tools.

R:Base

R:Base has also been around for a while. The product started as an alternative to dBASE but never quite materialized. It offers similar functions to dBASE, including menu-driven

QBE, multiple tables, an application-code generator, and a sophisticated report writer. Some additional improvements include R:Base Procedural Language and an unlimited number of records per database. Available from Microrim, (800) 628-6990.

DataPerfect

DataPerfect is WordPerfect's integrated database application. As with PlanPerfect, it is a good-quality product—nothing more. DataPerfect is ideal for WordPerfect users' offices that require connectivity and application consistency among word processing, spreadsheets, and database management. Available from WordPerfect Corporation, Inc., (800) 321-5906.

Integrated Software

Integrated software consists of network applications that have been designed to *do it all*. Integrated network applications are a great idea, but unfortunately nobody seems to be able to get it right. Each manufacturer excels in one or two areas but never in all. It makes more sense to purchase separate packages from manufacturers who specialize in a given area: WordPerfect for word processing, Lotus for spreadsheets, and Borland for database management. Microsoft is probably the closest to achieving the triple crown with Word and Excel. Also, the Windows environment lends itself to application integrity and interface consistency.

All four of the leading software manufacturers offer integrated applications. Usually these applications consist of five functional components:

- word processing
- database
- communications
- spreadsheet
- graphics

Microsoft Works—Multimedia

As mentioned earlier, Microsoft has the best chance of achieving successful software integration. Microsoft Works is currently the top-selling integrated application, with more than 3 million copies sold worldwide. It offers complete Windows compatibility and a version for the Apple Macintosh. Works is ideal for small businesses that require task integration and limited functionality. It is a cost-effective solution and offers fundamental word processing, spreadsheeting, database management, charting, and graphics.

Works has two extraordinary features that set it apart from the other packages—WorksWizards and OLE. WorksWizards are interactive templates that walk users through customized documents, address books, form letters, and charting. Object Linking and Embedding (OLE) is a Windows standard that enables users to exchange charts, files, drawings, documents, and spreadsheets within and among all the different Works modules. The word processing module features document linking, a spell checker, thesaurus, and network compatibility. The spreadsheet module features Autosum, performance analysis, toolbar, and multiple file formatting. The database module includes an efficient filing system for small businesses, built-in reporting, handling of up to 32,000 records, and dBASE IV compatibility. The charting module features spreadsheet importing, 31 different chart formats, and a standard toolbar. The graphics module is Microsoft Draw for Windows.

The most exciting aspect of Microsoft Works is Multimedia support. Microsoft Works—Multimedia is a full CD-ROM application that supports digitized sound, full-motion animation, and multimedia OLE. The multimedia version of Works also supports animated help and a comprehensive on-line reference. The on-line reference walks users through a graphical representation of commonly used Works features.

WordPerfect Works

WordPerfect also offers an integrated software application named Works. This version of Works integrates the familiar WordPerfect interface with integrated application programs. WordPerfect Works includes word processing, spreadsheets, database, communications, and graphics. Works borrows fundamental features from WordPerfect, PlanPerfect, DataPerfect, and DrawPerfect. WordPerfect Works integrates well with NetWare LANs.

Lotus Symphony

Lotus Symphony is one of the oldest integrated applications. It was founded on the immense success of 1-2-3. Symphony has evolved over the past seven years into a solid integrated package with adequate functionality in word processing, spreadsheets, database, communications, and graphics. It borrows fundamental features from 1-2-3 and Manuscript.

Symphony is at its best when connected to another Lotus product called Notes. Lotus Notes is a groupware package that provides network users with object storage and retrieval. A Notes object can be text, numbers, files, graphics, and images. Another Lotus offering is Lotus SmartSuite for Windows. SmartSuite is a GUI-based integrated application that supports 1-2-3, Ami Pro, Freelance Graphics, and cc:Mail. Available from Lotus Development Corporation, (800) 872-3387, extension 6860.

Borland Framework IV

Framework IV is an integrated business application that combines seven software components: word processing, spreadsheet, database, communications, graphics, outlining, and electronic mail. Borland has a reputation of providing powerful business productivity tools, and the company hasn't disappointed anybody with Framework IV. It is the most versatile and complete of the integrated network applications. The only downside is that it doesn't have a recognizable, consistent user interface. Microsoft Works uses Windows, Symphony uses the look of 1-2-3, and WordPerfect Works relies on the popular WordPerfect interface. Framework IV is ideal for advanced network users who don't require a comfortable user interface.

The word processing component features boilerplate hot keys, multiple fonts, and dBASE merging. The spreadsheet component is the most powerful in its class with support for 32,000 concurrent spreadsheets. The database function follows dBASE logic with simple flat-file features. The communications component features 11 terminal emulations, on-line support, and sending/receiving in the background. The graphics component converts spreadsheet and database information into 3-D graphs. Outlining provides users with a simple organizational tool, and the electronic mail component helps them communicate over the LAN. Framework IV also includes a built-in programming language called FRED (seriously!). Available from Borland International, (800) 331-0877.

Office Systems Design

Office systems design software is a critical component for today's *electronic office*. Office systems design uses a set of network applications called *groupware*. Groupware consists of electronic task integration tools that automate simple and mundane business functions.

Groupware functions include

- electronic mail
- automated group scheduling
- individual user calendars
- network-wide calendars
- network applications integration
- network management
- task automation

The need for groupware in today's electronic office is growing as managers realize the flexibility and productivity of these tools. In five years, an office without groupware will be at a competitive disadvantage.

Groupware fits in well with our NetWare design, because it is inherently networkable. Groupware applications are designed for network environments and integrate with them well. Features such as file locking, security, shared printing, and user configurations are built into the groupware tools. One of the most important groupware functions is electronic mail.

NetWare integrates E-mail in the Message Handling Service (MHS). Since early 1988, Novell has been bundling MHS with all versions of NetWare. MHS represents messages as envelopes that contain key X.400 control information. X.400 is a routing protocol that offers many advantages to existing electronic mail systems.

Currently, the most popular groupware applications are Microsoft Windows for Workgroups, WordPerfect Office, and Higgins.

Microsoft Windows for Workgroups

Windows for Workgroups is basically a DOS version of Windows NT. It is an excellent GUI application that provides all of the traditions groupware features: electronic mail, scheduling, shared calendars, a Rolodex, and chat—a realtime conferencing capability. Windows for Workgroups goes beyond the traditional boundaries of groupware applications by offering some built-in networking functions: It can operate as its own peer-to-peer operating system for file sharing, printer sharing, and network Dynamic Data Exchange. If your network needs extend beyond the limitations of a peer-to-peer LAN, Windows for Workgroups also supports many of the existing client/server architectures—including NetWare and LAN Manager.

The implementation of Windows for Workgroups is simple and convenient. There are four options: Starter Kit, User Kit, Add-On, and Upgrade. The Windows for Workgroups Starter Kit includes a two-user license, two network interface cards, some coaxial cabling, a screwdriver, and a "getting started" video. This kit is enough to start a small peer-to-peer

LAN for two workstations. The Windows for Workgroups User Kit enables you to add additional users to an existing peer-to-peer LAN. It also includes a NIC and some cabling. The Windows for Workgroups Add-On provides the functionality of Workgroups for users who are already attached to a LAN and using Windows v3.1. The Windows for Workgroups Upgrade provides the same functionality for users of Windows v3.0.

Whichever implementation you choose, Windows for Workgroups is an excellent groupware solution for Windows users. It provides excellent functionality and a consistent/familiar user interface. For more information, call (800) 642-7676, extension QF2.

WordPerfect Office

WordPerfect Office is an excellent office design tool for network users who are familiar with the WordPerfect interface. WordPerfect Office integrates automated scheduling, individual calendars, and electronic mail. Office consists of seven components: Shell, Mail, Scheduler, Calendar, File Manager, Notebook, and Calculator. The Office Shell is a text-based, front-end menu system that provides some fundamental memory management functions. It emulates the familiar WordPerfect screen, and provides a clear, efficient interface for WordPerfect users.

Office Mail is one of the most sophisticated enterprise mail systems available. It supports a wide variety of mail formats, including TCP/IP, SMTP, multiple servers, X.400, X.25, DEC VAX, and IBM's PROFS. Office mail is integrated into the groupware system to provide store-and-forward access to memos, phone messages, letters, and files. WordPerfect Office Scheduler ties into the mail system and provides connectivity between individual user calendars. Users can request meetings directly from other user's calendars by entering the information into Office Scheduler. The Calendar function in Office works independently or in concert with network scheduling. It is a simple date/time format with appointments, an alarm, and memo fields. Office File Manager is a network version of WordPerfect's file manager. Office Notebook is a flat-file database with straightforward screen programming. It provides an excellent interface for shared Rolodexes over the LAN. Finally, the WordPerfect Office Calculator provides graphical arithmetic operations. WordPerfect Office supports DOS, Windows, Macintosh, UNIX, and Data General platforms.

He who chooses the beginning of a road chooses the place it leads to. It is the means that determine the end.

—Harry Emerson Fosdick

Just as the quote says, the last two chapters have been all about *choice*. The decisions you make now will shape the strength and functionality of your LAN forever. Be patient, spend some time, and take great care in fitting your LAN design to the system's needs and requirements. Use the information you have learned in these last two chapters to mold your road toward success. Use the information you will learn in the next two parts to pave the road with gold.

SUPERVISOR LAB I

NetWare Design Cases

The first step in building a NetWare LAN is systems analysis and design. Chapters 4 through 6 discussed the key responsibilities of the network analyst, designer, and integrator. There you explored the requirements report, data gathering, analysis, hardware design, and software integration. Analysis and design procedures have the most substantial impact on the success of a NetWare LAN, so grant them substantial attention.

In this project, you will be asked to use your newfound analysis and design skills to develop a solid network design for each of four fictional companies. The following ingredients provided in the case descriptions will add reality to your assignments in these cases:

- a brief description of the company and the type of work it does
- a list of the system needs as revealed through a series of management and staff interviews
- a brief discussion of existing equipment
- a detailed layout of the physical office space and cabling measurements
- a price list and cost umbrella to ensure a strong dose of reality

The network analyst in you will use the company description and list of system needs to develop a preliminary Requirements Report. Then, the network designer in you can integrate existing equipment and new technology with the report to create a detailed Network Design. The network integrator in you will finally take the design and suggest actual components to purchase from the price list, at the same time remaining within the cost umbrella. This is as real as it gets—at least until you're actually making these decisions and purchases on the job!

CASE 1

"The Simpsons" Production Company

The production team for Fox Television's hit cartoon series "The Simpsons" is housed in a small production studio on Sunset Boulevard in Hollywood. Here team members write the scripts, develop preliminary sketches, and create the voice tracks for each episode. In addition to their production responsibilities, team members handle all of the administrative and financial paperwork for the show and send nightly update reports to Fox Television.

Currently, there are four writers, three cartoonists, three producers, and five administrative assistants working as part of this production team. They spend their time fiddling with Rolodexes, filing away Simpsons data, passing verbal and hand-written messages, enhancing poor-quality output, manually scheduling meetings, and typing letters on five old Smith-Corona typewriters. In addition, they each take their turn fighting through rush-hour traffic to get the daily reports to Fox Television's headquarters before 5:00 P.M.

One day, the producers visited Disney Studios and CBS and marveled at the sophistication of their office system designs. "The Simpsons" producers decided that they, too, should have the benefits of up-to-the-minute technology and decided to hire you to design their new electronic office. The only drawback was an experience they witnessed at CBS: the LAN crashed and took all of the production people's valuable data with it. "The Simpsons" producers vowed that their system would never go down or lose data.

The studio is organized into a two-story square with fifteen 50-by-50-foot offices lining the perimeter. In the center of the square is a large work space for the cartoonists and a central wiring closet directly at the midpoint. The entire studio covers about 40,000 square feet. In addition, all of the offices have been wired with coaxial cable for television feeds. Unfortunately, none of these lines are available for data. The producers were hoping you could build their magical office system for less than $65,000. Good Luck!

CASE 2

Smith, Jones, Xenon, and Associates

John Smith, Bill Jones, and Quorest Xenon grew frustrated with the world of Big Eight accounting, so they decided to branch off and start a Small Eight accounting firm of their own. By a stroke of good fortune, they attracted a *huge* base of clients from their previous organization. Push came to shove, and soon there were 150 partners from all races, cultures, and linguistic backgrounds. It came time to expand their business physically and technologically, and they hired you to make their dreams come true.

Smith, Jones, Xenon, and Associates is primarily a client-oriented firm; the partners serve the average Joe. They work extensively with Quattro Professional as a spreadsheet package, WordPerfect 5.1 for word processing, and PC Anywhere remote communications. They have expressed an interest in retaining these packages in the new LAN environment, although they currently have no hardware or software. In addition, this firm would like to investigate electronic mail and computer fax technologies. The partners want all of this with a simple user interface, because they don't want to be bothered with prompts, Windows, or bizarre DOS commands. Speed is more of an issue than reliability; these accountants simply do *not* have time to wait.

They have already chosen their new international headquarters: two four-story buildings with internal unshielded twisted-pair cabling (phone and data). The two buildings act as bookends to a huge PG&E transformer, as well as being located beside a local airport and KJIV Rap Radio. There are 20 full offices on each floor, each sized about 20-by-25 feet. The partners settled on 5 printers per floor. Each floor contains approximately 15,000 square feet of total floor space.

Smith, Jones, Xenon, and Associates have asked you to design the layout of their offices in coordination with the networking project so as to create a sense of office synergy. They would like to have everybody electronically connected to ensure equal access to all data, applications, and resources. The price tag for the project should come in under $500,000. Good Luck!

CASE 3

Manhole Conglomerate, Inc.

Manhole Conglomerate, Inc., is the largest designer, manufacturer, and distributor of—you guessed it—manhole covers. Its company motto is "Covering all of your international needs." Every time you drive over a manhole cover, chances are it's a Manhole beauty. Sales have skyrocketed in the last decade because of the boom in car sales and the spread of suburbia, and the future seems very bright for Manhole.

Recently, the powers-that-be at Manhole decided to integrate their international offices using existing equipment and the latest networking technology. The following seven international offices will be connected into local NetWare LANs, and then interconnected into one huge global WAN:

- San Francisco: Administration, 4 Floors
- Chicago: Sales, 1 Floor
- New York: Marketing, 2 Floors
- Los Angeles: Sales, 1 Floor
- London: Financial, 3 Floors
- Paris: Design, 2 Floors
- Tokyo: Sales, 1 Floor

There are exactly 25 offices on each floor, each with an IBM PS/2 computer. There are 5 LaserJet printers on each floor, and they all need to be shared easily. San Francisco and London each have an additional IBM AS/400 minicomputer that is attached to only 1 stand-alone PS/2 terminal. Manhole would like to see a more global use of this technology. In addition, the cities of Tokyo, London, and New York have installed satellite dishes for international communications—and those hard-to-get cable shows. All of the local offices have been wired with IBM Type 2 cabling for telephone, and connected to a central communications closet on each floor.

Manhole has hired you to orchestrate this incredible integration using all of the company's existing workstations, minicomputers, and printers. The system must be fast, reliable, and capable of "connecting everybody to everybody"! You have $1 million to spend. Good Luck!

CASE 4

University of California, Pleasant Hill, Computer Science Lab

The University of California regents have hired you to design a new state-of-the-art technology hub for the University of California at Pleasant Hill. The board of regents has asked you to make a design proposal and include an "acceptable" budget figure—an open figure. The design should accommodate the university's unique student body and financial constraints while at the same time remaining consistent with its highly acclaimed reputation as the foremost technology center of the Pacific Rim.

Your proposal should address the integration of the following hardware and software components into a transparent design that allows students the freedom of local or remote access. In addition, the students should be able to communicate with each other using a consistent user interface.

UCPH Computer Hardware	UCPH Computer Software
25 IBM PS/2 computers	WordPerfect
50 IBM personal computers	Microsoft Word for Windows
10 Apple Macintosh computers	Microsoft Excel for Windows
1 DEC VAX minicomputer	PageMaker
1 IBM AS/400 minicomputer	Quattro Professional
10 generic dot-matrix printers	Paradox
5 HP LaserJet printers	Harvard Graphics
1 Apple LaserWriter printer	

The lab is housed in one expansive room with open ceilings and floor ducts for cabling. Remember to address the user interface concerns of the various students while at the same time integrating the diversity of technologies. It is also very important to remember that schools do not like to spend money! Good Luck!

Pricing for All NetWare Design Cases

Price List for Hardware Components

Topology Design

Ethernet

Ethernet NIC—8 bit	249
Ethernet NIC—16 bit	295
Ethernet NIC—Mac	395
Ethernet 10Base-T NIC—8 bit	325
Ethernet 10Base-T NIC—16 bit	395
Thick Ethernet Transceiver	399
Transceiver Cable	109
Twisted-Pair Transceiver	299
Twisted-Pair Concentrator	795
Ethernet Repeater	495
BNC Connectors	1.20 each
BNC T-Connectors	2.00 each

BNC Terminators	1.00 each
Ethernet Coaxial Cabling, PVC	0.75/foot
Ethernet Coaxial Cabling, Plenum	4.00/foot
Ethernet UTP Cabling (includes labor)	0.35/foot

ARCNet

Thomas Conrad ARCNet Star NIC—Coax/UTP	195
Thomas Conrad ARCNet Star NIC—Coax/UTP	379
Thomas Conrad ARCNet Bus NIC—Coax/UTP	249
Thomas Conrad ARCNet Bus NIC—Coax/UTP	395
Active Hub—8 port	495
Passive Hub—4 port	95
Twisted-Pair Hub—8 port	495
ARCNet Intelligent Hub	699
Nodal Priority Card	695
ARCNet Coaxial Cabling, PVC	0.75/foot
ARCNet Coaxial Cabling, Plenum	4.00/foot
ARCNet UTP Cabling (includes labor)	0.35/foot

Token Ring

Token Ring 4-Mb/s NIC	595
Token Ring 16/4 NIC	695
Token Ring 16/4A NIC	695
Token Ring MSAU	795
Adapter Cable—8 foot	47
Patch Cable—8 foot	47
IBM Data Connectors	16 each
IBM Type 1 Cabling	1.00/foot
IBM Type 2 Cabling	1.50/foot
IBM Type 3 Cabling	0.50/foot
IBM Type 6 Cabling	1.50/foot
Token Ring Fiber NIC	2,795
Fiber Optic Cabling	4.00/foot

Computers

File Server

386/33-MHz Box 8MB RAM	3,295
486/50-MHz EISA Box 16MB RAM	5,995
Pentium 586 Box 16MB RAM	7,995
Internal 155MB Hard Disk with Controller	795
Internal 335MB Hard Disk with Controller	1,395
2 External 320MB Hard Disks with Controllers and Power Supply	3,995
Disk Coprocessor Board	1,295

Workstations

286/12-MHz Box 1MB RAM	995
386sx/16-MHz Box 1MB RAM	1,995
386/33-MHz Box 2MB RAM	2,995
Internal 40MB Hard Disk with Controller	325

Additional Hardware Components

SFT Components

External 300MB Tape Backup Unit	2,899
SEVEN 300MB Tapes	395
Surge Protectors	35 each
SPS	475
Intelligent 800-VA UPS	895
UPS Monitoring Kit	89

Peripherals

HP LaserJet III	1,739
High-speed Printer	4,995
Color Plotter	1,295
Serial/Parallel Printer Cable	25 each
High Speed Modem	649
Internal FAX Board	279

Price List for Software Components

Network Operating System (20 users)

NetWare ELS I	495
NetWare ELS II	1,795
NetWare v2.2	3,295
NetWare v3.11	4,995
NetWare v4.0	7,995
Banyan VINES v5.5	5,995
LAN Manager for OS/2	3,795
Windows NT	3,495

Management

Microsoft Windows v3.1	95/Node
Automenu	25/Node
Direct Access LAN	259
MenuWorks	25/Node
WordPerfect Office—5 nodes	495
WordPerfect Office—20 nodes	1,495
Windows for Workgroups—20 nodes	1,295

The Coordinator	795
cc:Mail LAN Package—25 nodes	695
cc:Mail LAN Package—Gateway	1,295
cc:Mail LAN Package—FAX	1,995
DaVinci eMail	1,200
PC Anywhere	350/Node

Applications

WordPerfect v6.0 LAN—5 nodes	279
WordPerfect v6.0 LAN—20 nodes	1,139
Quattro Pro LAN—5 nodes	349
Quattro Pro LAN—20 nodes	1,239
Lotus 1-2-3 3.1 LAN—5 nodes	599
Lotus 1-2-3 3.1 LAN—20 nodes	1,349
Paradox LAN	699
Harvard Graphics LAN	649
Microsoft Excel for Windows LAN—5 nodes	925
Microsoft Word for Windows LAN—5 nodes	749
dBASE IV LAN	649

Price List for Interconnectivity

NetWare Gateway Software—Runs on an Independent 386 Server

NetWare AS/400 Gateway	2,995
NetWare VAX Gateway	2,995

Complete Interconnectivity Systems

TCP Gateway for NetWare	3,995
NetWare T-1 Server	4,895
Complete Infrared System	11,995
NetWare Microwave Server	7,995
NetWare Satellite Server	7,995

Part III

Building NetWare LANs: Installation

"This is Mr. Spock. He's here to help with installation."

The network analyst has investigated the system's players, functions, and equipment. He or she has molded these results into a theory of how the components can be optimized into LAN synergy. The network designer has used the analyst's requirements report to develop a network blueprint: a LAN plan that outlines the effective integration of people, performance, and available resources. The network design consists of 10 components:

LAN Hardware	LAN Software
Thin Ethernet	NetWare v4.0
50-ohm coaxial cabling	DOS v6.0
80486/50 EISA server	MS Windows v3.1
Ten 80386 workstations	Word, Excel, Paradox
UPS and tape backup	Windows for Workgroups

Now it's your turn. As a member of the installation team, it is your responsibility to acquire the hardware and software components and construct the LAN foundation. The remainder of the LAN functionality will be installed by the network manager as part of the third phase of building a NetWare LAN—network management.

It's time to get busy. We've done all of our thinking, now it's time to construct our dream. Installation is the second step in the process of building a NetWare LAN. During installation, we will review the network design, acquire the appropriate materials, and construct my castle—oops, I mean our LAN. LAN construction consists of two phases: hardware installation and NetWare installation. This process is known as NetWare framing.

The first move in NetWare framing is hardware installation. This step involves the consolidation, installation, and configuration of hardware resources. These resources include topology components, cabling, file servers, workstations, and SFT. Hardware installation requires a unique understanding of microcomputer operations and component configuration. The second move in NetWare framing is NetWare installation. This step involves the construction and customization of the NetWare network operating system. NetWare installation requires a completely different set of construction skills. In order to successfully install a NetWare server, the installation team must have a complete understanding of NetWare's functionality and the intricacies of each version. Construction of a NetWare v2.2

server differs dramatically from the construction of a NetWare v4.0 system, just as the construction of a castle differs dramatically from the construction of a shopping mall.

Veni, Vidi, Visa.
(We came, we saw, we went shopping.)

—Jan Barrett

Chapter 7

Hardware Installation

"You guys got references?"

Hardware installation is the first move in NetWare framing. This step is especially critical because LAN hardware represents the foundation of the NetWare LAN, just as the mortar and rocks are the foundation of my castle. All components and functionality of my castle, and your LAN, will be built on the strong foundation of hardware installation. The LAN hardware determines speed, performance, reliability, and ergonomics. A solid hardware installation can set the stage for a strong, productive LAN, whereas a weak installation will introduce many potential network hazards: cabling faults, NIC conflicts, RAM cram, token loss, and unreliable SFT. The chance of isolating hardware-specific problems decreases tremendously as the installation process proceeds and the LAN becomes more complex. Pay attention to these issues: documentation, component standardization, configuration standardization, and testing.

Hardware Installation Guidelines

Documentation

The prospect of installing hardware components into a stand-alone PC is complex enough; imagine how confusing it can get when you're installing 20 integrated systems simultaneously. It is easy to forget what went where, who did it, and how the systems were configured. The guardian of the network installation team is documentation. NetWare documentation provides network installers and managers with a centralized collection of critical hardware settings and configurations. Follow these 10 simple worksheets for a clean, well-documented hardware installation:

DOS Workstation Worksheet	Hard Disk Worksheet
File Server Definition Worksheet	Printing Worksheet
OS Generation Worksheet	Directories Worksheet
Trustee Security Worksheet	Login Scripts Worksheet
Users Worksheet	System Configurations Worksheet

The network installation team will work in conjunction with the network manager in completing these worksheets. This process is outlined in detail in Chapter 15.

Component Standardization

The integration of network hardware is infinitely easier when the network uses only standardized components. Whenever possible, lobby the network designer for hardware standardization. Systems work better when they are used to being together. Talk to the network designer before he or she specifies 20 heterogeneous workstations. Component standardization is especially important for topology, cabling, and workstation components.

Configuration Standardization

Even though you don't have much influence on the standardization of hardware components, you do control the standardization of hardware configurations. The installation team is responsible for hardware settings, addresses, memory configurations, SFT, and interrupts. It is a good idea to standardize these configurations whenever possible. Some areas to standardize include NIC interrupts, cabling connectors, workstation RAM, peripherals, addressing schemes, and distributed SFT (surge protectors, for example).

Testing

A good hardware installation becomes a *great* hardware installation once it has been tested. Before, during, and after the hardware installation, you should thoroughly test component settings and configurations. Here are a few ideas:

1. Pretest the file server and workstations with hardware diagnostics (Norton Utilities, PC Tools, or Microsoft Diagnostics, for example).
2. Make connections to the LAN one machine at a time.
3. Send test signals down the cabling scheme to ensure media continuity.
4. Unplug an active UPS from the wall to test power reliability.
5. Always troubleshoot network problems one at a time.

Patience is definitely a virtue, as well as a prerequisite, in hardware installation.

Idealism increases in direct proportion to one's distance from the problem.

—John Galsworthy

If you follow these simple guidelines and don't lose your head, you should have no problems with hardware installation. This chapter discusses the procedures for installing each of the five LAN hardware components: topology, cabling, file server, workstations, and SFT.

Topology Components

The topology components control communications within and between NetWare LANs. These components are closely tied to the network cabling; one cannot exist without the other. The network designer has chosen a specific topology design and determined the optimum LAN cabling. Now it is your job to integrate these components into a functional LAN. You must install the topology and cabling at the same time, because they rely on each other. Once these components are in place, the network computers can plug right in.

The focus of topology/cabling installation is the network interface card (NIC). The NIC establishes the LAN topology, initializes communication protocols, and determines cabling type. The NIC is also the only topology component that directly interfaces with the network computers. Pay careful attention to optimizing NIC configurations.

The NIC Niche

The NIC communicates with three different devices: LAN cabling, network computers, and topology design. LAN cabling interfaces with the NIC through a specific network connector. Each topology design specifies a different type of connector. Network computers interface directly with the NIC through bus connections. LAN file servers and workstations require a complex set of configuration parameters to control internal NIC communications. The topology design configurations are specific to Ethernet, ARCNet, and Token

Ring. These components are covered later in the chapter. These three devices control the NIC environment and make it necessary for the NIC to seek out a specific NIC niche.

LAN Cabling

The network cabling is closely tied with the topology design and protocol. It is the medium over which network messages travel. The workstation/server NIC interfaces with LAN cabling through a specific type of connector. Here is a brief list:

Thin Ethernet	50-ohm BNC T-connector
Thick Ethernet	15-pin DIX connector
Ethernet 10Base-T	RJ-45 UTP connector
ARCNet	93-ohm BNC connector
Token Ring	15-pin AUI connector, IBM-type data connector
IBM PC LAN	75-ohm BNC connector, RJ-45 UTP connector
LocalTalk	Apple-type 9-pin DIN connector

Network Computers

The most critical NIC connection is to the network computer. Workstations and file servers are a complex maze of bus channels, RAM addresses, and interrupt requests. The NIC must carve out its own niche in this forest of internal communications: the NIC niche. In order to control these overwhelming channels of information, network computers employ a sophisticated set of internal configurations. Communications within and between critical workstation/server components are policed by four different parameters:

- Interrupt request line (IRQ)
- Input/output (I/O) port
- Base memory address
- Direct memory access (DMA) channel

RAM and DMA values are typically given as one hexadecimal address. This address defines the starting location of the memory range. Be careful not to assign incremental RAM and DMA addresses; their ranges could overlap. Also, most systems reserve specific IRQ and I/O addresses. Never assign the following values:

IRQ: 0, 1, 2, and 9

I/O: 220-249, 2F0-2F7, and 3E0-3E7

The *interrupt request line* defines a direct hardware channel to the central processing unit (CPU). Each peripheral device in the computer must have a unique IRQ, including the NIC, serial port, parallel port, modem, internal mouse, disk controller, video card, floppy drive controller, and tape controller. The IRQ provides the hardware device with a way of interrupting the CPU when the device needs some processing time.

This is how network requests are transferred from cabling to NIC to internal NetWare shells. The input/output port defines a pathway for incoming and outgoing CPU messages. The CPU will send and receive network data through a specific NIC I/O port. Each peripheral must communicate on a unique I/O port. The base memory address defines a system

RAM location for incoming network requests. The base memory address is assigned as a range of RAM locations, because most network packets are quite large. Included in the RAM address are LAN drivers, disk drivers, packets, and NetWare instruction sets. Direct memory access refers to an internal controller that buffers incoming network requests. The NIC packets can be temporarily stored in the DMA buffer instead of system RAM. This procedure bypasses the busy CPU and increases NIC performance substantially. Unfortunately, 90 percent of the current workstation/server NICs do not take advantage of DMA channels.

In a simple configuration with few peripherals, it is easy to avoid configuration conflicts, because the default NIC settings usually work. However, in a fully loaded workstation or server with multiple serial and parallel ports, NIC configuration can get very tricky. Table 7.1 lists some common peripherals and their corresponding parameters.

Notice that the IRQ and DMA addresses are given in decimal notation, whereas the RAM and I/O addresses are given in hexadecimal ranges. The hexadecimal notation uses a base 16 system of 0 through 9 and A through F (that is, 01, 02, 03, 04, 05, 06, 07, 08, 09, 0A, 0B, 0C, 0D, 0E, 0F, 10 . . .). Hex numbers may look weird, but they behave the same as decimal numbers.

NIC configurations are assigned through three methods: hardware jumpers, hardware switches, and software EPROM. Hardware jumpers consist of metal pins that protrude from the NIC. A butterfly attachment makes an electronic connection between two of the pins, which sends a specific configuration message to the workstation/server bus. Hardware jumpers come in various shapes and sizes. Most NIC jumpers fall into two categories: 3-pin or multipin. The 3-pin jumpers consist of one bank with 3 pins. This convention allows for one of two configurations: pins 1 and 2 covered or pins 2 and 3 covered. Multipin jumpers consist of multiple banks of 2-pin assignments. Each assignment represents a value for IRQ, I/O, or RAM address. Jumpers are used to assign IRQ, I/O, RAM

TABLE 7.1   Hardware Parameters for Common LAN Peripherals

Peripheral	IRQ	I/O	RAM Address	DMA
Serial 1	4	3F8-3FF		
Serial 2	3	2F8-2FF		
Parallel 1	7	378-37F		
Parallel 2	5	278-27F		
XT Controller	5	320-32F	C8000-3FFF	3
AT Controller	14	1F0-1F8	C8000-CBFFF	
		170-177		
Floppy Controller	6	1F0-1F8		2
		3F0-3F7		
Tape Controller	5	280-28F		
Monochrome		3B0-3BF	B0000-B3FFF	
EGA Video	2	3C0-3CF	A0000-AFFFF	
VGA Video		102, 46E8	C0000-C7FFF	
Internal Mouse	5			

address, DMA, remote reset, connector-type, and network timeouts. A jumper typically consists of 3 pins and a connector block. The jumper can have 1 of 3 possible configurations: 1 and 2 connected; 2 and 3 connected; or none connected.

Hardware switches offer a great deal more flexibility than jumpers. Switches consist of one bank of 8 tiny on/off levers that can be set in any of 256 possible binary combinations; the switches are similar to an external byte. The decimal equivalent of the binary switch represents a number between 1 and 255. These numbers are typically used to designate node addresses in the ARCNet topology design.

Software EPROMs are the latest advancement in NIC configuration. EPROM stands for Erasable Programmable Read-Only Memory. EPROMs are programmable chips on the NIC that store valuable configuration parameters. These boards allow for software-controlled configuration assignments—no jumper, no switches. IRQ, I/O, RAM address, and DMA are assigned through a software program called SOFTSET. Most of the NIC manufacturers are providing new boards with software EPROM—Intel, SMC, and others.

Topology Designs

Ethernet, ARCNet, and Token Ring control network communications in different ways. Each standard relies on specific cabling, a unique NIC, connectors, and additional LAN components—hubs, repeaters, and MSAUs. Let's take a moment now to outline the hardware installation differences among these three fundamental topology designs.

Ethernet

As you know, Ethernet is available in three flavors: thin, thick, and 10Base-T. Although these three designs use different connection strategies, they all share the same Ethernet protocol standard: IEEE 802.3. In addition, they all share the same Ethernet NIC. The connectors differ, but the internal components remain the same. In fact, manufacturers are beginning to introduce Ethernet NICs that simultaneously support all three flavors.

Figure 7.1 illustrates the typical Ethernet NIC. This NIC has four configuration components: base I/O and interrupt jumpers, cable-type jumpers, remote reset jumpers, and remote reset PROM socket. The base I/O and interrupt jumpers are used to set IRQ, I/O, and RAM addressing. The cable-type jumpers define the connector type: BNC or DIX. If DIX is chosen, the NIC bypasses its internal circuitry and transfers control to an external transceiver. Remote reset describes the process of booting a workstation from the file server instead of an internal disk. This option is available for workstations without an internal hard disk or floppy. The remote reset jumpers establish this procedure, and the remote reset PROM socket houses the directional remote PROM chip. Remote booting is covered later in the chapter under Workstation Installation.

Installation of the Ethernet bus topology components is relatively simple. Some rules of thumb follow:

- Use the correct terminator impedance.
- Attach T-connectors directly to the NIC BNC port.
- Allow at least eight feet between transceivers.
- Do not exceed 25 workstations (thin) or 50 workstations (thick).
- Use two NICs in the server for heavier loads.

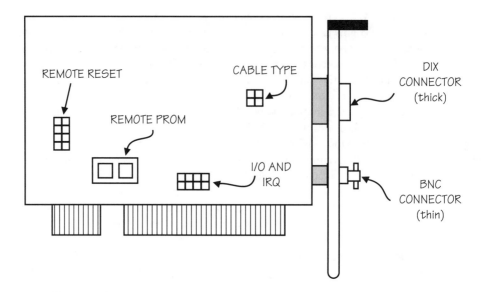

FIGURE 7.1   Components of a Typical Ethernet Network Interface Card

Installation of the Ethernet 10Base-T topology components is a little bit harder. Ethernet 10Base-T is a star topology over UTP cabling. The 10Base-T star relies on a central controlling hub called a *concentrator*. The concentrator consists of 12 RJ-45 ports that connect 12 legs of the Ethernet star. Multiple concentrators can be connected through special in/out receptacles. Traditional Ethernet NICs can be integrated into the 10Base-T design through a DIX-to-RJ-45 external transceiver. This is usually not cost-effective though, because the external transceiver costs almost as much as a new 10Base-T NIC. Another interesting Ethernet oddity allows for a BNC connection to an RJ-45 port; it is called a *balun*.

ARCNet

The ARCNet design uses a star topology over 93-ohm coaxial cabling. ARCNet NICs support a direct BNC connection; they have built-in terminators. Figure 7.2 illustrates the typical ARCNet NIC. This NIC is heavily standardized. I guess it would be safe to say "If you've seen one ARCNet NIC, you've seen them all." These NICs use three configuration components: IRQ and base I/O address jumpers, remote reset PROM socket, and node address switch. The IRQ and base I/O jumpers establish values for the NIC's IRQ and I/O addresses. ARCNet cards rarely take advantage of DMA buffering. The remote reset PROM socket houses the directional remote PROM chip.

The node address switch is unique to ARCNet. It defines the hexadecimal equivalent of a NIC address, between 1 and 255. The ARCNet LAN uses the node address to determine the token path. If two NICs share the same address, the token will get confused and crash. Refer to the ARCNet documentation for a complete listing of switch settings and corresponding node addresses. Other than the NIC, the key component in an ARCNet LAN

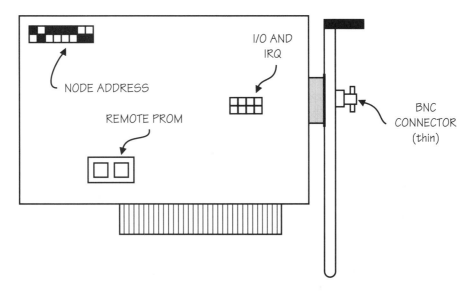

FIGURE 7.2   Components of a Typical ARCNet Network Interface Card

is the distributed hub. ARCNet hubs come in two flavors: active and passive. *Active hubs* regenerate network messages as they travel from node to node; they require electricity. *Passive hubs* are simple signal splitters requiring no electricity. Multiple ARCNet hubs are connected through normal hub ports. This strategy allows for a true distributed ARCNet star.

Token Ring

Token Ring and its components are controlled by IBM. Token Ring installation is supposedly reserved for certified IBM engineers, but you can do it. The Token Ring NIC is a simple design, including interrupt and base memory jumpers, a base I/O switch, and a remote reset PROM socket. The configuration components act exactly the same as for Ethernet and ARCNet. The only oddity with Token Ring NICs is the speed factor. These NICs can operate at 4 Mb/s or 16 Mb/s, whichever is fastest. Speed settings are changed automatically. The only problem is that these NICs follow the least common denominator rule: The entire LAN will operate at the speed of the slowest NIC.

The Token Ring design relies on a central hub called an MSAU (Multistation Access Unit). The MSAU contains eight passive ports that accept hermaphroditic IBM data connectors. In addition, the MSAUs provide two additional ports, ring-in (RI) and ring-out (RO), for MSAU-to-MSAU connections. Make sure to complete a full ring by connecting the last MSAU's RO with the first MSAU's RI. The complete ring cannot exceed 400 feet. This design creates a physical star, logical ring. Before connecting cables to any of the MSAU ports, initialize the connection with IBM's Setup Aid. The Setup Aid is a small active device that opens and closes active MSAU relays. You simply insert the aid and wait for a click.

Whichever design you choose, make sure to test the topology components thoroughly before you continue. In addition, check the NIC configurations against system parameters with a hardware diagnostics program such as Norton Utilities, PC Tools, or Microsoft Diagnostics. Check IRQ, I/O, RAM address, and DMA. Document your findings in the appropriate worksheet.

≋ Cabling

LAN cabling is the next critical hardware component. It provides the topology design with a pathway for network packets, so that cabling and topology are inseparable. Pay attention to the smallest details when you're installing network cabling. Seventy percent of hardware faults are the result of oversight during the installation of cabling or topology design components. Here is my top 10 list of things to look out for as you install LAN cabling, listed here in "countdown order":

10. Hire a qualified cable installation contractor as part of your installation team. Small distractions such as local building codes, fire restrictions, and licensing can become large issues if they are not handled correctly. Also, there are future costs associated with improper technical installation or complete rewiring, so do it right the first time.

9. Use the correct cable. This may sound silly, but the small technical discrepancies between different types of cabling can loom large over your high-speed LAN. Pay attention to such details as cable size, impedance, twists per foot, shielding, fiber diameter, distance limitations, and crosstalk.

8. Use the correct connectors. The use of incorrect connectors can result in poor connections, bottlenecks, and data loss.

7. Adopt component standardization. Whenever possible, use the same cabling manufacturer and model throughout the LAN. Component standardization reduces second guessing during cable testing and troubleshooting.

6. Follow accepted color codes. Twisted-pair cabling uses a standard color code scheme for matching specific wires. It is important to consult the cabling documentation for the correct color code standard when you install UTP or STP.

5. Label everything—the cabling, the NIC, the outlet, the adapter cable, your shoe, the wall, and the kitchen sink. Each cable run should be labeled with the workstation's physical and node address. You should be able to find which cable attaches to each machine without having to turn the LAN upside-down.

4. Be neat. Cables can be crossed, detached, or destroyed if they are left out in the open. Cables should be used and not seen. For safety and aesthetic reasons, run cabling through conduit, ceilings, or floor ducts. In open environments, use 3Com's stick-on conduit, which is available in many nice colors.

3. Use the proper tools. Each cable type requires a unique set of installation skills and industry tools. Cabling tools are specifically designed for crimping, connecting, shredding, cutting, and fusing. Don't use a coaxial crimping tool for fiber optic cabling; the result could get messy. Also, practice on dead cable before you start attaching live connectors. Practice makes almost perfect.

2. Be patient. "Rome wasn't built in a day." I don't think anybody expects you to install 3 miles of UTP over 52 workstations in 3 hours. Take the time to review the cabling layout and walk the entire run before you start.

1. Document what you plan to do. Plan the entire cabling scheme before you do anything. Go over the plan with your installation team. Also, create a detailed cabling diagram when you are finished. Include physical workstation addresses, floor numbers, office numbers, and node addresses.

Cabling installation is part common sense and part practice. Each medium requires a specific set of procedures and skills. It is a good idea to leave cabling installation to the professionals—or at least the semiprofessionals. But if you really want to go at it yourself, here are a few fundamentals with respect to UTP, STP, and coaxial cabling.

UTP

UTP describes a diverse category of physical cabling. The different types of UTP are too numerous to name here. Fortunately, the networking industry has standardized on one specific type of UTP: DIW, or D-inside wire. The most common type of DIW is telephone wire. DIW is easy to identify, because it's housed in a gray or beige vinyl jacket with multicolored internal wires. The colored wires correspond to a standard color code. The color code defines specific wires as a combination of wire color and stripe color. Consult your cabling manual for specific color code standards. Three types of connectors are commonly used for UTP: RJ-11 (telephone), RJ-45 (LAN), and 50-pin (data). Workstation connections are typically wired as home runs to a central wiring closet. The connection in the wiring closet is made to a punch-down block. The punch-down block connects to a central UTP concentrator.

STP

STP cabling is most commonly used in Token Ring LANs. IBM has developed an entire classification system that specifies different types and levels of shielded twisted-pair cabling. The primary cable used in Token Ring LANs is IBM Type 1: two twisted pairs of 22-AWG wire inside a copper braided shield. IBM Type 2 is identical to Type 1, except that Type 2 has four additional twisted pairs outside the shield. IBM Type 3 is UTP.

The strange component of IBM STP cabling is the proprietary IBM data connector. This hermaphroditic connector is difficult to make, and homemade connections typically don't work. In this arena, you are almost forced to purchase ready-made cables. The IBM data connector provides a locking component that prevents the connection from coming loose, so use it. Minus the IBM connectors, STP is also a good choice for Ethernet 10Base-T LANs.

Coaxial Cabling

Unlike twisted-pair, coaxial cabling has not yet been standardized. Different LANs use different types of cabling—different in size and impedance. Thin Ethernet uses RG-58A/U 50-ohm, thick Ethernet uses RG-8/U 50-ohm, and ARCNet uses RG-62/U 93-ohm cabling. The most common connector for LAN coax is the BNC connector. BNC is designed for quick connections and comes in three flavors: crimp, screw, and bolt. Crimp connectors are soldered to the coax conductor and crimped to the protective jacket with a special crimping tool. Screw connectors are screwed onto the jacket, whereas bolt connectors are bolted on. Make sure to finish with a solid connection. If a weak connection is made, the workstation will experience intermittent cabling faults that are difficult to isolate and potentially embarrassing.

The specific cabling issues with respect to Ethernet, ARCNet, and Token Ring are detailed in Chapter 5's coverage of topology design. The specific properties of LAN cabling and their advantages and disadvantages are discussed in Chapter 5's discussion of cabling.

File Server

The file server houses all of the LAN's shared resources for both software and hardware. Installation of the file server software—that is, NetWare—is covered in the next three chapters. Installation of the file server hardware is covered here. The installation of a NetWare file server involves five critical hardware components: CPU, RAM, disk, printers, and interconnectivity. The server CPU determines NetWare's functionality and the capacity of the internal NIC. The server RAM shuffles network requests to and from LAN resources. The server disk houses applications and network data. The network printer is typically attached to the server. Interconnectivity defines pathways to other systems, both local and wide. Let's take a longer look at the installation of a NetWare file server.

CPU

The primary purpose of the NetWare file server is to process network requests. The server CPU is a key player in LAN performance and functionality. For example, an 80286-based CPU can only run NetWare v2.2 or below. Pay attention to the CPU capabilities and NetWare version. The main CPU factor with respect to hardware installation is bus type. The server bus type determines the server's capacity for processing multiple LAN requests. If the server CPU supports a 32-bit bus mastering EISA NIC, install one. ISA machines autoconfigure internal NICs; EISA machines don't. Before you install a 32-bit bus mastering EISA NIC, you must run the specific EISA configuration utility so the server will recognize the card.

RAM

The file server's RAM is a key ingredient in the performance of NetWare LANs. Beyond the implicit minimum RAM of 2MB to 8MB, there are advantages to increasing the file server's memory capacity, including caching, hashing, and applications support.

Server RAM exists in two forms: system RAM and peripheral RAM. *System RAM* refers to memory chips on the system's motherboard. Most 80386 machines support two banks of single in-line memory modules (SIMMs). Each bank supports four SIMMs modules, which are commonly available in 1MB and 4MB configurations. SIMMs modules plug directly into the RAM banks that support multiple configurations, but not within the same bank. Most 80386 servers can address 32MB of system RAM. *Peripheral RAM* is memory on an expansion card. The memory card plugs into a 32-bit slot on the server's expansion bus and communicates with system RAM and the CPU through a 32-bit bus line. This memory is a little slower than system RAM but supports memory above 32MB. NetWare addresses both system and peripheral RAM as extended memory.

Disk

Network disk systems are very complex and temperamental animals. They consist of two hardware components: the disk controller and disk drive. The *disk controller* is the interpreter between NetWare and the server disk drive. Pay attention to the installation of server disk controllers: Beware of bad cables, make sure to connect the drive cables correctly (notch pointing up), make a firm bus connection, and check the controller jumpers for configuration settings (IRQ, I/O, and RAM address). The disk drive is the medium for NetWare and shared LAN files. Handle the drive with kid gloves: Ground the drive, install sliders, plug in the power correctly, and screw the drive in tight. Don't worry about partitioning, testing, or formatting the server disk. These processes are covered during the NetWare installation phase.

Printers

NetWare supports two types of network printers: direct and remote. *Direct printers* attach directly to the file or print server through a parallel (LPT) or serial (COM) port. Up to five printers can be connected to each server, but the connections require additional parallel/serial cards. If you are going to insert additional printing cards into the server, be sure to adjust the hardware configurations and document them in the appropriate worksheet. *Remote printers* are attached to distributed workstations. These devices are shared through a workstation printing utility called RPRINTER. To use remote printers, the workstation must be attached and RPRINTER activated. Remote printing allows 5 printers per workstation and 16 per LAN.

Interconnectivity

The best installation team looks to the future. Plan ahead for interconnectivity by leaving one or two server expansion slots open. If you're installing an internal router, make sure the NICs are using different hardware configurations and unique network addresses. External routers are configured on distributed workstations through the ROUTEGEN utility. NetWare supports dedicated and nondedicated external routers.

Workstations

The network requirements for workstations are much less dramatic than those for file server. From a strict connectivity sense, the workstation is only attaching the LAN. By contrast, the server is running the LAN. Workstation installation in a NetWare environment is not much different from a normal stand-alone installation.

Installation Steps

Following is a list of workstation installation steps required for all machines:

1. Install the internal hard disk.
2. Install the diskette drive(s).
3. Install the video board.
4. Connect the keyboard.

5. Attach the monitor to the video port.
6. Plug in the computer. Turn it on.
7. Format the internal hard disk for DOS.

Following is a list of additional installation steps required for NetWare workstation:

8. Install the workstation NIC—configure the IRQ, I/O, RAM address, and DMA.
9. Attach the cabling to the NIC.
10. Install workstation boot files—IPX.COM and NETx.COM.

Note: The next three chapters outline the steps required for installing workstation software.

Workstation Strategies

Two strategies are integral to workstation connectivity: LAN independent and LAN dependent. *LAN-independent workstations* can exist with or without the LAN. These machines are self-sufficient workstations with internal hard disks and local applications. LAN-independent workstations use NetWare connectivity for printing, shared data files, and electronic mail. *LAN-dependent workstations* rely on the NetWare server for all computer operations. These machines contain no internal disk or diskette drives and boot DOS from the central server through a process known as *remote booting*.

Remote booting is accomplished through the DOSGEN utility, as follows:

1. DOSGEN creates a NetWare boot image of DOS's critical boot files, including COMMAND.COM, CONFIG.SYS, and AUTOEXEC.BAT. The boot image is stored in the F:\LOGIN directory as NET$DOS.SYS.

Copy the LAN-dependent workstation's AUTOEXEC.BAT file to the F:\LOGIN directory to avoid the `Batch file missing` **error.**

2. When a user activates a LAN-dependent workstation, the boot sequence bypasses the missing disk and relinquishes control to the NIC's remote reset PROM. The PROM activates an internal version of IPX.COM and NETx.COM and attaches to the NetWare server.
3. The NetWare server downloads the NET$DOS.SYS file to workstation RAM where it is expanded and run.
4. In the event of having multiple LAN-dependent workstations in one network, the network manager can build a text table named NET$DOS.SYS. The table will establish a direct correlation between node address and boot file. Remote booting offers security, virus protection, and cost savings.

∰ SFT

System fault tolerance is LAN insurance against inevitable hardware failures. The installation of NetWare SFT provides two strategies: internal and external. Internal SFT refers to software and hardware processes that operate inside the file server. Internal SFT consists of software processes such as TTS, hot fix, and UPS monitoring as well as hardware components such as disk mirroring and duplexing. External SFT refers to hardware components that protect the NetWare LAN from outside the file server. External SFT consists of tape backup, surge protectors, UPS, and server duplexing. Let's take a closer look at SFT installation.

Internal SFT

Internal SFT processes rely on file server processing and hard disk channels. NetWare controls all aspects of internal SFT. The first two software components of internal SFT are automatic: TTS and hot fix. TTS is turned on during the NetWare installation phase, and critical files are flagged TTS by the network manager. Hot fix is also activated during NetWare installation, and the redirection area is configured by the installation team.

UPS monitoring is activated as a file server process: NLM or VAP. Most UPS manufacturers provide specific UPS monitoring kits with their hardware.

The hardware components of internal SFT focus on disk protection. Disk mirroring is redundancy at the most fundamental level. With mirroring, the server houses two identical disk drives that "mirror" each other's movements. In this scenario, the two disks are installed on the same channel. Disk duplexing is more advanced storage SFT. With duplexing, the server houses two disks, two controllers, and two cables. In this scenario, the two disks are installed on two separate channels, with different IRQs, I/Os, and RAM addresses.

NetWare unwillingly supports mirroring among different size disks. The key matching parameter is partition size. You can fool NetWare into thinking two drives are identical by altering the partition size of one of the disks. Simply increase the larger disk's hot fix area until the active partition matches the smaller disk. It works!

External SFT

External SFT supports NetWare but doesn't rely on it. With the exception of server duplexing, external SFT components exist independently of the file server. There are four external SFT processes: tape backup, surge protectors, UPS, and server duplexing. Tape backup is one of the most misunderstood SFT components. Many users think the tape backup system should be attached to the file server because it is backing up server files, but that's wrong. The cardinal rule in NetWare LANs is that only a workstation can access server files. The network backup system must be installed in a workstation and operate over traditional LAN channels. Pay close attention to security risks before, during, and after automatic tape backup procedures. Surge protectors should be installed on all active network components, such as workstations, file servers, print servers, printers, routers, gateways, and active hubs.

Although I state that network tape backup systems must be attached to workstations, this is not entirely true. Some manufacturers are developing tape backup units that plug directly into the server. This is a more efficient process but not without difficulties. Server backup systems are tricky to install, less secure, and more rigid in their configuration. Stick to the old way.

UPS is the highest level of energy SFT. UPS connectivity can only be justified for critical LAN components, including the file server, routers, and gateways. Make sure the UPS device is sufficiently charged and has enough battery capacity to handle the server load for at least ten minutes. Test the UPS by pulling the cord from the wall while the UPS is attached to the file server.

Server duplexing is the ultimate level of NetWare SFT, and it is only available in v3.11 and v4.0 through a feature known as *SFT Level III.* This SFT strategy provides complete server redundancy through two identical servers and a fiber optic connection. Each server handles network requests and stores identical NetWare parameters—data, security, users, groups, printing, SFT, and system files. Installation of server duplexing is complex and expensive.

Regardless of which SFT components you choose and where they operate, it is imperative for them to work! Imagine how much fun it would be to discover that your tape backup system didn't work the day after your server disk crashed. This is called "adding salt to the wound." Test all of your SFT components *before* you need them. Then test again.

I shot an arrow into the air, and it stuck.

—Graffito

That completes our discussion of hardware installation. Now you're ready to move on to the second step of NetWare framing—NetWare installation. The next three chapters provide a detailed discussion of NetWare installation through the eyes of NetWare v2.2, v3.11, and v4.0. Enjoy the show.

Chapter 8

NetWare Installation, Version 2.2

"Then the brave installation team installed the Cold Boot Loader . . ."

NetWare installation is the second phase of NetWare framing. This procedure breathes life into an otherwise cold, dead hardware design. Currently, our NetWare LAN consists of NICs, cabling, computers, and a tape backup unit—a useless heap of junk. Through the process of NetWare installation, we will bring life, connectivity, and usefulness to the hardware design.

Beyond this NetWare installation phase is the third and final step in building a NetWare LAN: network management. The network manager will build on the NetWare foundation and complete our dream construction. He or she will add users, groups, security, functionality, software, NetWare SFT, and printing.

Think of the network manager as your LAN's interior designer. I would hire this person to inspect my empty, framed-out castle and suggest quality improvements, such as furniture, tapestries, staff, crocodiles, and a washer/dryer. But before the interior designer could work with my dream home, I would have to finish the construction and build walls and floors over the castle frame. Similarly, you must fill in the NetWare frame with an operating system and default configurations.

NetWare currently supports three versions—v2.2, v3.11, and v4.0. This and the next two chapters outline the installation procedure for each of these network operating systems. Each installation improves on the fundamentals of the previous version: Version 3.11 improves on version 2.2 and NetWare v4.0 is the best yet. Even though these procedures differ in content, they share fundamental similarities—network drivers, addressing, file server naming, volumes, and the NetWare console. We will begin with the most archaic of the three: NetWare version 2.2.

Requirements

The NetWare installation procedure has specific hardware and software requirements. These values are firm limits, there are no compromises. Once we have established the minimum NetWare v2.2 server configuration, we can begin the five stages of NetWare installation.

Hardware

File Server

Your network file server should be at least an 80286-compatible CPU with 2.5MB of memory. Larger internal disks require greater amounts of RAM for hot fix, disk caching, and administrative utilities, a 10MB internal hard disk, and at least one Novell-certified network interface card.

Workstation

The minimum workstation is an 8086-compatible CPU with 640KB of memory. The minimum RAM is needed for WSGEN, the NetWare workstation shell generation program. Network applications and graphical user environments require additional workstation RAM. A Novell-certified network interface card must be installed in the workstation.

Topology Components

Cabling and the topology components should be NetWare compatible and certified by Novell. They may use the Ethernet, ARCNet, or Token Ring topology design.

Software

DOS

NetWare's installation utilities are DOS-based programs. DOS is initially required to boot the file server and must always run under the NetWare shells on the workstation.

NOS Install

The INSTALL utility is used to generate the NetWare network operating system. The NetWare v2.2 operating system consists of one executable file: NET$OS.EXE.

DOS Install

The WSGEN utility is used to generate the NIC-specific workstation shell, IPX.COM. The NETx.COM shell is DOS-specific and therefore common to all workstations and distributed with the NetWare v2.2 disks.

NetWare v2.2 Disks

The complete set of NetWare v2.2 SYSTEM and PUBLIC diskettes contain files that must be copied to special system directories on the internal file server disk. Those directories are SYSTEM, PUBLIC, LOGIN, and MAIL. Following is a list of all the required NetWare v2.2 diskettes:

```
SYSTEM-1          DOSUTL-1          HELP-1
SYSTEM-2          DOSUTL-2          HELP-2
LAN_DRV_001       DOSUTL-3          WSGEN
OSEXE             DOSUTL-4          PRINT-1
OSOBJ             PRINT-2
```

Installation

NetWare v2.2 installation consists of five stages:

1. Define the operating system.
2. Link and configure the operating system and utilities.
3. Test the hard disk using ZTEST.
4. Define the file server and install the operating system and utilities.
5. Use WSGEN.

The purpose of the NetWare v2.2 installation is to create the operating system file NET$OS.EXE. This file controls all NOS functions and resides hidden in the SYSTEM directory. The stages break out like this:

1. Stage 1 defines the operational parameters for creating NET$OS.EXE.
2. Stage 2 links and configures the OS file as well as some system-specific utilities—ZTEST, INSTOVL, COMPSURF, and VREPAIR.
3. Stage 3 tests the server disk and marks bad blocks.
4. Stage 4 defines the file server and copies the SYSTEM and PUBLIC files to the new server disk. During stage 4, the OS file is copied to the appropriate location and the server disk is initialized for NetWare booting using the Cold Boot Loader.
5. Stage 5 defines, links, and configures the workstation-specific NetWare shell, IPX.COM.

NetWare v2.2 supports three installation methods: floppy-drive, hard-drive, and network-drive. The floppy-drive method is the most popular and standard installation mode. This operation requires a high-density floppy drive on the file server and DISKCOPY backups of four NetWare v2.2 installation diskettes: SYSTEM-1, SYSTEM-2, OSEXE, and OSOBJ. The floppy-drive method performs all four NOS stages at the file server computer in one complete cycle.

The hard-drive method breaks the installation stages into two parts. In part 1, the installation team uploads the NetWare v2.2 installation diskettes to a workstation hard-drive and performs stages I and II. In part 2, the installation team downloads the configured files to floppy-disks and performs stages 3 and 4 at the file server. This method is used for multiple v2.2 installations on independent file servers.

The network-drive method emulates the hard-drive method, except it performs the configuration on a network-drive. In part 2 of the network-drive method, the configured files are downloaded directly to the new file server, bypassing the floppy-disk step. This method is used for multiple v2.2 installation on connected file servers.

This chapter concentrates on the floppy-drive method. This is the most common, straightforward, and flexible installation method. Before you move to the first major stage in the installation process, follow these steps:

1. Boot the server in DOS.
2. Insert the SYSTEM-1 diskette and make A:> the default drive. Type **INSTALL** and press Enter.

Stage 1: Define Operating System

The install screen appears, displaying four options: Basic Installation, Advanced Installation, Maintain Existing System, and Upgrade from NetWare v2.x. The Basic Installation option is for first-time installers and makes numerous assumptions along the way that are not always appropriate. The Advanced Installation follows the same format as the basic method, but it enables you to make configuration input. The Maintain Existing System option provides NET$OS.EXE modification and reconfiguration after the initial installation. Later in the chapter, we will explore the maintenance options with command-line parameters.

You might notice that Novell uses a curious naming scheme for all important system files: a $ symbol is part of the filename. I guess you can say Novell knows on which side its bread is buttered!

To begin the definition process, follow these steps:

1. Highlight Advanced Installation and press Enter.
2. Press Enter again to continue past the welcome screen.

The first stage of the NetWare v2.2 installation focuses on defining the OS parameters, as shown in Figure 8.1—operating system mode, communication buffers, server status, core printing, network drivers, and disk drivers.

Money often costs too much.

—Ralph Waldo Emerson

Operating System Mode

The OS mode may be dedicated or nondedicated. If nondedicated, you must supply a Nondedicated Network Address. Most NetWare client/server environments require a dedicated file server. Highlight Dedicated and press Enter.

Number of Communication Buffers

Communication buffers store network requests until the server CPU is ready. Estimate the number of buffers as 2 per user and 10 per server NIC, for a total of no fewer than 150. The maximum number of buffers is 1,000. Type **150** and press Enter.

Defining the Server

NetWare asks, `Will this machine be the server: yes or no?` If yes, INSTALL creates a NetWare drive that is stored on the local hard disk. If no, INSTALL will prompt you for diskettes on which it will load the configured operating system files. You can reuse these working master diskettes for a later installation. Highlight Yes and press Enter.

```
         <ESC> = Cancel   <F1> = Help   <Alt><F10> = Quit

      ┌──────────────────────────────────────────────────────┐
      │               Operating System Generation             │
      ├──────────────────────────────────────────────────────┤
      │ Operating system mode:          Dedicated             │
      │    Nondedicated network address:                      │
      │ Number of communication buffers:  150                 │
      │ Will this machine be the server?  Yes                 │
      │ Include core printing services?   Yes                 │
      │                                                       │
      │                                                       │
      │ Network board A                                       │
      │  Driver: (Press <Enter> to see list)                  │
      │  Configuration Option:                                │
      │  Network address:                                     │
      │ Network board B                                       │
      └──────────────────────────────────────────────────────┘

          ┌──────────────────────────────────────────────┐
          │ To scroll the screen, use the arrow keys. Modify │
          │ highlighted field with <Enter> or <Delete>. When all the │
          │ information is correct, save and continue with <F10>. │
          └──────────────────────────────────────────────┘
```

FIGURE 8.1   NetWare v2.2 Operating System Generation Screen

Printing Services

NetWare asks, `Include core printing services?` *Core printing* describes print services from the internal file server ports. Core printing can only be installed at this point in the installation. If you have printers attached to the server, highlight Yes and press Enter.

Network Drivers

LAN drivers for software/hardware interface to the internal file server NIC. Three options are used in the configuration of network drivers: driver, configuration option, and network address. Highlight the appropriate network driver and press Enter.

The following three options will appear:

- *Driver.* Highlight yours from an internal list of nine drivers or provide a manufacturer-specific diskette. The custom LAN driver must be provided on a diskette labeled LAN_DRV_*???*, where *???* represents a three-digit manufacturer code.
- *Configuration Option.* This describes the configuration parameters for the internal NIC. Parameters include IRQ (interrupt), I/O Base Address, and DMA (Direct Memory Access) Channel.
- *Network Address.* This is the hexadecimal eight-digit address that identifies the specific LAN cabling topology.

Disk Drivers

Disk drivers provide the hardware/software interface to the internal file server disk. Two options are available for configuring disk drivers: Driver and Configuration Option. Highlight the appropriate disk driver and press Enter.

The following two options appear:

- *Driver.* Highlight yours from an internal list of five drivers or provide a manufacturer-specific diskette. The custom disk driver must be provided as a file named *.DSK, where * represents the manufacturer's driver name.
- *Configuration Option.* This option describes the configuration parameters for the internal drive. Parameters include Disk Type (ISADISK), Primary/Secondary Drive, Verification (on/off), I/O Base Address, and IRQ (usually 14).

Stage 2: Link and Configure OS/Utilities

The linking and configuring stage of NetWare's installation requires no user input. The system uses the configuration parameters that were defined in the previous stage and creates critical NetWare OS files and utilities.

Utilities

The system will now automatically link and configure the NetWare v2.2 utilities. It will install the following utilities on the appropriate diskettes:

ZTEST	SYSTEM-2	INSTOVL	SYSTEM-1
COMPSURF	SYSTEM-2	VREPAIR	SYSTEM-2

Operating System

Once the utilities have been configured, INSTALL will link and configure the NetWare v2.2 operating system. The entire operating system is compiled into one system file—NET$OS.EXE—that is loaded onto the OSEXE diskette.

Stage 3: Test Hard Disk (ZTEST)

ZTEST stands for track zero hard disk test. This utility is an extremely grueling and comprehensive *destructive disk test*—that is, it comprehensively destroys the data on your disk. Be extra careful when you use this utility. ZTEST checks all facets of the file server disk and ensures drive/controller integrity. If a disk fails the ZTEST procedure, that disk must be replaced before you continue with the NetWare v2.2 installation.

ZTEST will display critical drive information for you to verify: Channel #, Controller #, Drive #, and Disk Type. The typical internal ISA (Industry Standard Architecture) disk will use channel 0, controller 0, drive 0, and ISADISK type 2 or 47 (user definable). Two ISA disks would show channel 0, controller 0, and drives 0 and 1. ISA disks support up to 4 internal drives—2 controllers with 2 drives each. Small Computer Serial Interface (SCSI) drives follow the same scenario, but their inherent daisy-chaining design provides file servers with a great deal more flexibility. SCSI configurations support 4 channels with 8 daisy-chained controllers per channel and 2 drives per controller. That is 64 drives! Unfortunately, NetWare v2.2 only supports 32 file server drives. In order to take full advantage of the SCSI potential, NetWare enables you to mirror 32 drives, therefore using the 64-drive SCSI capacity.

To activate the NetWare v2.2 ZTEST, press Enter at the ZTEST information screen. Choose Yes at the confirmation box, then press Enter. To avoid the testing procedure, press Esc at the same screen.

Stage 4: Define File Server and Install OS/Utilities

The final steps in installing the NetWare v2.2 operating system are server definition and software installation. Now that the utilities, NICs, NOS, and drives have been linked and configured, it is time to define the server and install the system onto the internal disk. The File Server Definition screen shown in Figure 8.2 consists of the following four components: file server information, hard disk information, partition information, and volume information.

File Server Information

File Server Name. The name must be a unique server designation of between 2 and 47 alphanumeric characters that contains no spaces, periods, slashes, or backslashes. Type **NIRVANA** and press Enter.

Maximum Number of Open Files. This is the maximum number of files that can be opened on the server simultaneously. To calculate the maximum open files, multiply the number of users by 20, then multiply the product by the number of network applications. Type **240** and press Enter.

```
┌────────────────────────────────────────────────────────────────┐
│        <ESC> = Cancel   <F1> = Help   <Alt><F10> = Quit         │
│  ┌──────────────────────────────────────────────────────────┐  │
│  │             File Server Definition                        │  │
│  ├──────────────────────────────────────────────────────────┤  │
│    Server name:                    NIRVANA                      │
│    Maximum open files:             750                          │
│    Maximum open index files:       50                           │
│    TTS backout volume:             SYS                          │
│    TTS maximum transactions:       100                          │
│    Limit disk space:               Yes                          │
│    Maximum bindery objects:        1500                         │
│    Install NetWare for Macintosh:  No                           │
│                                                                 │
│  Hard disk information                                          │
│                                                                 │
│  Disk #0  Type 43:  ISA Disk type 43          Ch:0 Con:0 Dr:0   │
│  Physical size: 10452   Logical size: 10242   Hot Fix size: 210    2.0%  │
│  └──────────────────────────────────────────────────────────┘  │
│    ┌──────────────────────────────────────────────────────┐    │
│    │ To review or modify the information, use the arrow keys. Modify │
│    │ a highlighted field with <Enter>. Save and continue with <F10>. │
│    └──────────────────────────────────────────────────────┘    │
└────────────────────────────────────────────────────────────────┘
```

FIGURE 8.2   NetWare v2.2 File Server Definition Screen

Maximum Number of Open Indexed Files. This is the maximum number of index-flagged database files that can be opened simultaneously. The default is 0.

TTS Backout Volume. The default TTS backout volume is SYS:.

Maximum Number of TTS Transactions. The maximum number of TTS transactions should be twice the number of applications using TTS. Type **100** and press Enter.

Limit Disk Space: No or Yes. NetWare v2.2 enables you to limit the amount of disk space users can access. To activate this feature, highlight Yes and press Enter.

Maximum Bindery Objects. This parameter works in coordination with disk space limitations. The bindery objects are tracked in limiting disk space. Type **1500** and press Enter.

Hard Disk Information

Disk #. The first NetWare v2.2 disk is 0.

Disk Type. The disk type defines the disk controller type. IBM-compatible servers use ISA Disk Type 02, Channel 0, Controller 0, Drive 0. Other types include MFM, ESDI, and SCSI.

Physical Size. The physical size parameter defines the physical size of the internal disk.

Logical Size. The logical size determines how much of the server disk is used for data storage. The remainder is assigned to hot fix.

Hot Fix Size. The hot fix size establishes the size of the hot fix redirection area. The default is 2 percent of physical disk size.

Mirror Status. Choose between Not Mirrored or Primary/Secondary. Highlight Not Mirrored and press Enter.

Partition Information

OS Type. NetWare v2.2 supports multiple OS partitions on the same server disk. The table that is displayed lists the unique partitions and their corresponding OS type. The default is NetWare.

Status. The status parameter defines whether the OS partition is bootable. Only one internal partition can be bootable; the rest are nonbootable. Set the NetWare partition to Bootable and press Enter.

Start. The starting disk cylinder for the current partition. The default is 0 for the bootable NetWare partition.

End. The ending disk cylinder for the current partition. The default is the last physical cylinder for the solitary bootable NetWare partition.

Megabytes. The physical size of the current OS partition. The default is the entire disk for bootable NetWare partitions.

Volume Information

Volume Name. The volume name distinguishes this logical partition from other volumes on the same physical NetWare partition. The name must be between 2 and 15 alphanumeric characters and may contain no spaces. The first default system volume is SYS:.

Disk Number. The disk number refers to the physical parameter from Hard Disk Information. The default is 0.

Megabytes. The megabytes setting defines the size of the current volume. If SYS: is the only volume, Megabytes should correspond to the total capacity of the server disk.

Cache: No or Yes. Volumes should always be cached. Highlight Yes and press Enter.

Dir Entries. The directory entries setting defines the number of files, directories, and subdirectories a volume can support. Be careful not to assign a low number. The default is tied to the volume size with the following formula: 4 blocks plus 1 block for every 2MB. Then take the result and multiply it by 128 entries per block. A 40MB disk, for example, defaults to 3,072 directory entries. I recommend tripling the default, up to 32,000 entries.

When the File Definition screen is completed, press F10 to continue. The system will generate the NET$OS.EXE file and copy it to the SYS:SYSTEM directory. Next, NetWare v2.2 will establish the Cold Boot Loader of the server disk. Finally, the system will prompt you to insert 10 different diskettes sequentially. It will use these diskettes to copy the SYSTEM and PUBLIC files to the appropriate NetWare directories.

Congratulations! You now have a NetWare console prompt. The heart and soul of a NetWare server is the : -. Get used to it.

Stage 5: WSGEN

The final stage in building a NetWare v2.2 server is workstation installation. WSGEN stands for workstation shell generation. WSGEN is a NetWare menu utility that has one purpose: to create IPX.COM. IPX.COM is the NIC-specific workstation shell that communicates with internal NICs and NETx. IPX generation requires NIC-specific LAN drivers. Make sure you have the manufacturer's driver diskettes before you start WSGEN.

WSGEN is a relatively simple utility that requires an IBM PC with 640KB of RAM and an internal floppy drive. Boot the workstation under DOS v3.1 or higher and insert the NetWare v2.2 WSGEN diskette in the floppy drive. Move to the A: drive by typing **A:** and pressing Enter. To activate the shell generation utility, type **WSGEN** and press Enter. A welcome screen will appear. Press Enter to continue. WSGEN operation consists of three simple steps: NIC selection, NIC configuration, and IPX creation.

NIC Selection

The next screen is the NIC selection menu. NetWare v2.2 lists 10 default NICs. If you are using one of these cards, highlight the NIC and press Enter. Otherwise, press Ins to specify a manufacturer-specific driver diskette in the format LAN_DRV_*???*.

Insert the diskette in any drive and press Enter. The system will copy the driver to the NIC selection menu. Highlight the NIC and press Enter.

NIC Configuration

The next screen is the NIC configuration menu. A list of possible configurations will be displayed. Refer to the DOS Workstation Worksheet from Chapter 15 for the correct parameters. Highlight the appropriate option and press Enter.

IPX Creation

To begin creating the IPX.COM shell, highlight Yes, generate workstation software, and press Enter. The system will start linking, binding, and generating the IPX.COM shell. At one point, the system will probably ask you for the LAN_DRV_*???* diskette. Insert the diskette and press the Spacebar to continue.

When you are finished, the following message appears:

```
Generation of workstation software with the
requested driver and configuration is complete.
Press Enter to exit.
```

You have successfully completed the NetWare v2.2 installation. Next we will explore the advantages of installing a NetWare v3.11 system. It is much more flexible than what you have seen for v2.2.

Aim at perfection in everything, though in most things it is unattainable. However, they who aim at it, and persevere, will come much nearer to it than those whose laziness and despondency make them give it up as unattainable.

—*Lord Chesterfield*

Chapter 9

NetWare Installation, Version 3.11

"We always have a bit of fanfare before loading the NetWare Operating System disks."

The installation of a NetWare version 3.11 LAN is dramatically improved compared with version 2.2. The 80386 32-bit server platform and modular design make NetWare version 3.11 more powerful, reliable, and versatile. The installation process reflects these improvements. The most notable difference is in the NOS architecture. Refer to Figures 6.1 and 6.2 for a comparison of v2.2 and v3.11 NOS architectures. The NetWare v2.2 architecture relies on one generated operating system file: NET$OS.EXE. This file is a union of LAN drivers, disk drivers, and the core operating system (OS). Any changes to a NetWare v2.2 LAN require the complete regeneration of NET$OS.EXE. This is both cumbersome and inefficient.

The NetWare v3.11 architecture, on the other hand, is completely modular. Each installation component exists independently of the others and is fused to the overall NOS through a common NLM software bus. The OS core is one file (SERVER.EXE) that consists of three NOS components: NetWare File System, System Executive, and NLM software bus. All other installation components exist as NetWare loadable modules (NLMs). They include LAN drivers, disk drivers, print servers, communication devices, SFT, network management utilities, OS patches, Message Handling Service, and protocol engines. The greatest asset of NetWare v3.11 is that multiple installation components can be loaded and unloaded without affecting the performance and integrity of the LAN.

A simple analogy can help to clarify the differences between NetWare v2.2 and v3.11 installation procedures. Think of building a castle. What material would you use? In a NetWare v2.2 environment, you would use rocks and cement. The essence of the castle is literally set in stone, and the only way to change the design is to rebuild the castle. NetWare v3.11 is much more flexible. This castle is built out of Legos. The essence of the castle is modular, and it can be altered easily. Ironically, in this analogy, plastic is stronger than stone.

The only drawback to this system is autonomy. NetWare v3.11 installation autonomy means there are no prompts, no screens—nothing to tell you how to proceed (except this book, of course). You must make a conscious effort to complete each step. Let's take a closer look at the NetWare v3.11 installation procedure.

Requirements

The NetWare v3.11 server requirements are more demanding than those in v2.2. The most notable difference is the 80386 32-bit server platform. This hardware requirement is necessary for the complex operations involved in NLM management. Also, NetWare v3.11 is a true 32-bit multitasking network operating system. Other additional requirements include server RAM, workstation RAM, disk space, and a set of enhanced NetWare v3.11 diskettes.

Hardware

File Server

Your network file server should be at least an 80386-compatible CPU with 4MB of minimum memory. Larger internal disks require greater amounts of RAM for hot fix, disk caching, and administrative utilities. A 20MB internal hard disk and at least one Novell-certified network interface card are other server requirements.

Workstation

The minimum workstation is an 8086-compatible CPU with 384KB of memory. The minimum RAM is needed for IPX.COM and NETx.COM, the NetWare workstation shells. Network applications and graphical user environments require additional workstation RAM. A Novell-certified network interface card must be installed in the workstation.

Topology Components

Cabling and the topology components should be NetWare compatible and certified by Novell. They may use the Ethernet, ARCNet, Token Ring, or LocalTalk topology.

Software

DOS

NetWare's installation utilities are DOS-based programs. DOS is initially required to boot the file server and must run under the NetWare shells on the workstation.

SERVER.EXE

The NetWare v3.11 operating system core consists of one file: SERVER.EXE. Once loaded, this file defines the foundation of NetWare v3.11 and offers expandability to NetWare loadable modules. SERVER.EXE is the console prompt.

DOS Install

The WSGEN utility is used to generate the NIC-specific workstation shell, IPX.COM. The NETx.COM shell is DOS-specific and therefore common to all workstations and distributed with the NetWare v3.11 disks.

NetWare v3.11 Disks

The complete set of NetWare v3.11 system and public diskettes contain files that must be copied to special system directories on the internal file server disk. Those directories are SYSTEM, PUBLIC, LOGIN, and MAIL. Following is a list of all the required NetWare v3.11 diskettes:

SYSTEM-1	DOSUTL-1	HELP-1
SYSTEM-2	DOSUTL-2	HELP-2
SYSTEM-3	DOSUTL-3	WSGEN
LAN_DRV-001	DOSUTL-4	PRINT-1
		PRINT-2

Installation

You will find the NetWare v3.11 installation to be a substantial improvement over that of NetWare v2.2. There is only one installation method, the installation components can be loaded and unloaded on the fly, and any of the following steps can be repeated or changed at any time without adversely affecting the rest of the LAN. Let's walk through the simple stages of building a NetWare v3.11 NOS.

NetWare v3.11 installation consists of seven stages:

1. Prepare the NetWare hard disk.
2. Run SERVER.EXE.
3. Load and bind the NetWare drivers.
4. Load INSTALL.NLM.
5. Define startup files.
6. Load additional NLMs.
7. Use WSGEN.

The actual process of creating a NetWare server consists of Stages 1 and 2. The remaining five stages add incremental functionality to the existing NOS. The stages break out like this:

1. Stage 1 prepares the server disk through local partitioning and DOS formatting.
2. Stage 2 creates the raw NetWare v3.11 server with the SERVER.EXE file.
3. Stage 3 adds connectivity to the NOS by adding the NetWare drivers.
4. Stage 4 creates further functionality by defining a NetWare partition and initializing the system volume.
5. In Stage 5, we define the two critical startup files, STARTUP.NCF and AUTOEXEC.NCF.
6. Stage 6 provides additional NOS functionality through the introduction of various NetWare loadable modules—MONITOR, patches, PSERVER, and RMF.
7. Stage 7 is the final installation stage. Stage 7 defines, links, and configures the Workstation-specific NetWare shell IPX.COM.

Stage 1: Prepare the NetWare Hard Disk

The NetWare v3.11 operating system consists of one file—SERVER.EXE—and various auxiliary NetWare loadable modules (NLMs). SERVER.EXE runs on DOS. In order to generate the NetWare v3.11 system, you must first boot the server under DOS v3.3 or v5.0. The process of preparing a NetWare DOS disk consists of disk partitioning (FDISK) and disk formatting (FORMAT).

FDISK

Disk partitioning will organize the server disk into two parts: a DOS partition for booting and a non-DOS partition for NetWare. Novell recommends at least a 5MB DOS partition, but I recommend 3MB; the smaller the DOS partition, the larger the NetWare partition. The purpose of the DOS partition is twofold: to boot the file server in DOS and then load

SERVER.EXE, and to house the critical server drivers—disk drivers, LAN drivers, and NLMs. FDISK is a DOS utility that enables you to create specific-sized DOS partitions.

To activate FDISK, boot the file server with a DOS boot diskette and type **FDISK** at the A> prompt. At the FDISK Options screen, choose 4, Display Partition Information. If a partition already exists, you must delete it. Press Esc to return to the FDISK Options and choose 3, Delete Partition or Logical DOS Drive. Delete all partitions and return to the FDISK Options screen.

To create a DOS partition, choose 1, Create DOS Partition or Logical DOS Drive. At the Create DOS Partition screen, choose 1, Create Primary DOS Partition. A screen will appear indicating that the current fixed disk drive is 1. The system will ask you whether you would like to use the maximum available size for the primary DOS partition. Answer No. Next, enter the partition size as a percentage of the total disk space. If your disk is 300MB, for example, you will enter 1 percent, or 3MB. Press Esc to return to the FDISK Options screen.

The final step is to activate the new DOS partition. Enter 2 to select Set Active Partition. The system will prompt you for the number of the partition; input **1** and press Enter. The primary DOS partition has been made active. Press Esc twice to exit FDISK.

FORMAT

Now that we have a primary DOS partition, we must format it. The server disk will not boot DOS unless we format the active partition as a system disk. To format the DOS partition, boot from the A: drive and input **FORMAT C: /s /v** at the A> prompt, then press Enter. The system will respond with a warning that all data on drive C: will be lost. This is fine, because we have no data on drive C:. Type **Y** and press Enter. The actual format will only take a few seconds. Once this process is completed, the system will ask for a volume label. Input the name of your server and press Enter. Reboot the file server after you remove the A: drive diskette.

Your server disk is now ready to accept the NetWare operating system. Before we progress to the next stage, we must copy the NetWare SYSTEM diskettes and create two DOS boot files. Find the three NetWare SYSTEM diskettes and copy the contents to the C> root directory. Type **COPY A:*.* C:** with the SYSTEM-1 diskette in drive A:. Press Enter. Repeat this procedure for SYSTEM-2 and SYSTEM-3. Next, create two DOS boot files, AUTOEXEC.BAT and CONFIG.SYS. Type **COPY CON AUTOEXEC.BAT** at C> and press Enter. Type **SERVER** and press Enter. To exit and save the file, press Ctrl+Z and press Enter. Next, type **COPY CON CONFIG.SYS**. Input **FILES=40** and press Enter. Input **BUFFERS=40** and press Enter. To exit and save the file, press Ctrl+Z and press Enter. The disk is ready. Reboot from C: and move on to the next stage.

Stage 2: Run SERVER.EXE

Once the server disk has booted under DOS 3.3 or 5.0, it is time to run the NetWare v3.11 operating system file, SERVER.EXE. The AUTOEXEC.BAT file should activate the SERVER file and begin the NetWare installation process. You might notice that the SERVER file reboots the file server machine; the lights on the keyboard will flash. This is done to flush out DOS and activate NetWare v3.11. At this point, the core of the NetWare operating system will load into memory and the following message will appear:

```
Novell NetWare v3.11 (# user) 2/20/91
Processor speed: 322
(Type SPEED at the command prompt for an explanation of the
speed rating)
```

The NetWare SPEED rating is a measurement of the server's processing capabilities. The rating is calculated as a percentage of the number of CPU cycles that pass in three clock ticks. It is tied to processing power and clock speed:

80386/16MHz   121

80386/25MHz   242

80386/33MHz   342

80486/33MHz   914

The system will then prompt you for the items described next.

File Server Name

The name must be a unique server designation of between 2 and 47 alphanumeric characters that contains no spaces and does not begin with a period. I recommend the name **NIRVANA** to remind you of your pursuit of NetWare Nirvana.

IPX Internal Network Number

The IPX internal network number is the first of three NetWare addresses: IPX internal network number, network address, and node address. The IPX internal network number is a hexadecimal eight-digit address that distinguishes this file server bus from any other on the LAN.

The network address is used to distinguish the physical cabling trunk. All distinct segments of cabling that include a file server NIC must have a unique network address. The network address is also an eight-digit hexadecimal number. It is established during the LAN binding phase, stage 3. The node address distinguishes the physical server and workstation NICs from all other NICs in the world. Each NIC on the LAN has a unique 12-digit hexadecimal address that allows it to communicate with all other NICs. Ethernet, Token Ring, and LocalTalk node addresses are programmed onto the NICs at the factory. ARCNet addresses are programmed by the network manager during the hardware installation phase. The IPX internal network number must differ from all other IPX numbers and network addresses.

Each independent server NIC must have a unique network address. NICs that share cabling trunks must use the same network address.

Keep in mind that hexadecimal numbers are base 16, not base 10. This means that network numbers consist of digits 0 through 9 and letters A through F. You can make meaningful addresses by using the alphabet. Some interesting combinations include DAD, ADA, BA5EBA11, and CAFE. You can also combine the words, as in BADCAFE. Have some fun with it!

Once the file server name and IPX internal network number have been established, the following message will appear:

```
File server name: NIRVANA
IPX internal network number: DAD
Total server memory: 7.7 Megabytes
Novell NetWare v3.11 (# user) 2/20/91
(C) Copyright 1983-1991 Novell Inc.
All Rights Reserved.
NetWare release for The Complete NetWare Construction Kit
Monday May 3, 1993 11:11:07 PM
:
```

The : prompt indicates the existence of a NetWare v3.11 server in the raw. We cannot print, save files, or communicate at this point, but we do have a living, breathing server. Congratulations! The next step is to add functionality to the system, one component at a time. We will begin by loading and binding the NetWare drivers.

Stage 3: Load and Bind the NetWare Drivers

The primary NetWare drivers control two very important LAN functions: storage and communications. The disk driver interfaces with the server disk controller and processes network requests for shared data. The LAN driver interfaces with the internal server NIC and shuffles network requests from LAN cabling to server RAM. There are three steps in this stage: load disk driver, load LAN driver, and bind LAN driver.

Load Disk Driver

In order to set NetWare partitions, generate NetWare volumes, and save network files, we must load the proper NetWare disk driver. NetWare v3.11 inherently supports 5 disk drivers:

ISADISK	standard AT-style disks (MFM, RLL)	PS2MFM
DCB	disk coprocessor board	PS2SCSI
		PS2ESDI

You can exit the installation process at any point by typing DOWN at the console prompt. This will close the NetWare v3.11 server. Then type EXIT to leave the NetWare shell and return to DOS. To return to NetWare, type SERVER at the c:\> prompt. If you haven't established startup files, you will need to follow the instructions from the top.

In addition, Novell provides the IDE disk driver through NetWire and authorized resellers. Other specialized disk drivers are normally supplied with the disk at the time of purchase. To load the ISADISK driver, type **Load C:\ISADISK** at the console (:) prompt and press Enter. The system will ask for the input of two parameters:

I/O port	1F0, 170
Interrupt number	E, B, F, C

The I/O port defines the I/O address for the disk controller. The interrupt numbers define the controller's IRQ. The default values are I/O port = 1F0 and IRQ = E. If you are using an IDE server disk, copy the IDE.DSK driver to the C: drive and type **Load C:\IDE** at the console prompt and press Enter. The system will ask for the same parameters, but with more choices: I/O ports = 1F0, 170, 1E8, and 168, and IRQ = E, B, F, C, and A. The defaults are the same. Once the disk driver has been loaded, the system returns you to the console prompt.

Load LAN Driver

The LAN driver initializes the server NIC and controls communications between the NIC, RAM, and LAN cabling. NetWare v3.11 supports multiple server NICs, creating an internal router. This configuration bridges dissimilar topologies or distributes traffic among similar topologies. NetWare v3.11 inherently supports 9 LAN drivers:

NE1000	NE2000	NE3200	NE2-32 } Novell Ethernet
3C503	3C505	3C523 } 3Com Ethernet	
TRXNET generic ARCNet			
TOKEN generic Token Ring			

To load the NE2000 driver, type **Load C:\NE2000** at the console prompt and press Enter. The system will prompt you for some additional information:

```
I/O Port:            300, 320, 340, 360
Interrupt number:    2, 3, 4, 5
```

The default configuration is I/O = 300 and IRQ = 3. To load a manufacturer-specific LAN driver, copy the *.LAN driver to the C: drive, type **Load *driver name*** at the console prompt, and press Enter. NetWare v3.11 supports a variety of additional LAN driver parameters: DMA, INT, MEM, PORT, NODE, RETRIES, SLOT, NAME, and FRAME. Each of these parameters specifies a particular configuration for the server NIC. DMA, INT, MEM, and PORT are NIC configuration parameters. NODE specifies a unique NIC address, whereas NAME specifies a unique NIC name. SLOT defines a specific bus location for EISA and Microchannel architectures. FRAME and RETRIES are communication parameters.

Bind LAN Driver

Once the LAN driver has been loaded, it must be attached to the communications protocol stack. This process is known as *binding*. Protocol binding allows the NIC to send and receive packets in a specific language, such as IPX, TCP/IP, or AppleTalk. Most NetWare LANs use the IPX protocol stack. To bind the IPX protocol to our NE2000 LAN driver, type **BIND IPX TO NE2000** and press Enter. The system returns with a very important prompt:

```
Network Number:
```

The network number defines this server's unique cabling trunk. All servers on this trunk must share the same network number. Input an eight-digit, hexadecimal number and press Enter. The system will return with `IPX LAN protocol bound to NE2000`. We're in business.

Stage 4: Load INSTALL.NLM

Once the NetWare drivers have been loaded and bound, we are well on our way to NetWare Nirvana. The next step is to add functionality to the LAN. The INSTALL procedure establishes partitions, volumes, system utilities, product options, SFT, disk integrity, and startup files. INSTALL.NLM consists of four parts: disk options, volume options, system options, and product options. Figure 9.1 graphically illustrates the INSTALL.NLM options. To access the INSTALL.NLM utility, type **Load C:\INSTALL** at the console prompt and press Enter.

Disk Options

The disk options section provides utilities for working with NetWare disks. Disk options include four choices: Format, Partition Tables, Mirroring, and Surface Test. The only required component of the section is Partition Tables; the other three are optional. To access NetWare v3.11 disk partitioning, highlight Partition Tables and press Enter. The Available Disk Drives list will appear. Highlight the first server disk (Device #0) and press Enter.

The Disk Partition screen appears. This screen is composed of two boxes: the informational Partition Type box and Partition Options menu. The Partition Type box displays the bootable DOS partition and the amount of free space outside the DOS partition. Our goal is to convert the free space into an active NetWare partition. Choose Create NetWare Partition from the Partition Options menu and press Enter. The system will create a NetWare partition with all available free space. The new partition will appear in the Partition Type screen.

NetWare hot fix size is a critical factor in disk performance and SFT. The default is 2 percent, and this works well in most systems. But in LANs with large database files, small hot fix sizes can create a disk bottleneck. Increase the hot fix size to 5 percent for disk-intensive LANs.

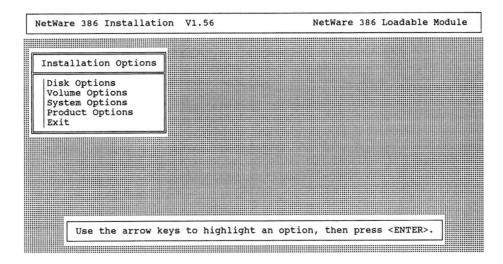

FIGURE 9.1   The NetWare v3.11 INSTALL.NLM Options

Volume Options

Return to the Installation Options menu by pressing Esc at the Partition Options screen. Highlight Volume Options and press Enter. The Volumes list will appear; it is empty. To add the default SYS: volume, press Ins. Highlight Yes at the confirmation box and press Enter. The Volume Information screen appears. The default SYS: volume has a block size of 4KB and occupies the entire NetWare partition. In addition, notice that the status is not mounted. We have to create the volume before we can mount it. To complete the volume creation, press Esc and highlight Yes at the confirmation box. Then press Enter. The system will create the volume and return to the Volumes list. To mount the volume, highlight SYS: and press Enter. Move to the Status option and press Enter. Highlight Mounted and press Enter. The volume is now mounted.

Mounting **is a term left over from the mainframe world when computer operators were required to physically mount tape reels in order to access the data. In NetWare,** *mounting* **refers to making a disk volume active.** *Dismounting* **a volume is an effective way of avoiding data theft or software piracy.**

System Options

With the partition set and the SYS: volume mounted, we can copy the SYSTEM and PUBLIC files to the appropriate NetWare directories. Highlight System Options from the Installation Options screen and press Enter. The Available System Options screen consists of two main components: Copy Files and Startup Files. The Copy Files option moves all NetWare SYSTEM and PUBLIC files from the installation diskettes to the SYS: volume. The Startup Files option provides a way of creating and editing STARTUP.NCF and AUTOEXEC.NCF. Refer to Stage 5. Highlight Copy System and Public Files and press Enter. The copying process takes approximately 27 minutes for a 386 33-MHz server, so have a cup of tea or help me plan the color of curtains for my castle's west wing.

Product Options

The Product Options menu provides an installation utility for additional NetWare support products, including NetWare for Macintosh, SAA, NetWare for NFS, and additional Novell NLMs.

The NetWare v3.11 installation procedure has been completed. Let's review the steps:

1. Partition the server disk using FDISK.
2. Format the server disk for DOS using FORMAT.
3. Run SERVER.EXE.
4. Load the disk driver.
5. Load the LAN driver.
6. Bind IPX to the LAN driver.
7. Load INSTALL.NLM.
8. Create the NetWare partition.
9. Create the SYS: volume.
10. Copy SYSTEM and PUBLIC directories' files.

Users can now log in and access shared NetWare data and utilities. The next phase of building a NetWare LAN focuses on network management procedures such as printing, maintenance, and troubleshooting. But before we move on to greener pastures, we must add a few levels of customization and reliability to our new NetWare server.

Stage 5: Define Startup Files

Once the NetWare v3.11 installation has been completed, we must secure all of our work in the NetWare v3.11 server startup files. The startup files activate critical server parameters during the NetWare booting procedure. They consist of two files: STARTUP.NCF and AUTOEXEC.NCF.

STARTUP.NCF

The STARTUP.NCF file automatically loads NLMs prior to the INSTALL step. It loads from the server's DOS partition and typically activates the NetWare v3.11 disk driver. The STARTUP.NCF file also loads advanced SET parameters, including warning options, cache buffer size, physical receive packet size, packet receive buffers, and maximum subdirectory tree depth. To create a STARTUP.NCF file from this session's installation, highlight Create STARTUP.NCF file from the Available System Options screen and press Enter. The system will prompt you for the path; accept the default of C:\ and press Enter. Notice that this session's changes have already been incorporated. The following line should be displayed:

```
load C:\ISADISK port=1F0 int=E
```

To exit and save the new STARTUP.NCF file, press F10 and highlight Yes at the confirmation box, then press Enter. From this point forward, if you want to modify the STARTUP.NCF file, choose Edit STARTUP.NCF file from the Available System Options menu.

AUTOEXEC.NCF

The AUTOEXEC.NCF follows the STARTUP file. The AUTOEXEC.NCF automatically loads all remaining system NLM modules. Any command that is entered at the console prompt can be loaded automatically by AUTOEXEC.NCF. To activate this session's AUTOEXEC.NCF file, highlight Create AUTOEXEC.NCF file on the Available System Options menu and press Enter. Notice again that today's changes have already been incorporated:

```
file server name NIRVANA
IPX internal net DAD
load C:\NE2000 INT=3 PORT=300
bind IPX to NE2000 net=1234567
```

These commands follow the path of this session's installation. Here are some additional startup file commands that can be used to optimize the AUTOEXEC.NCF file:

- `mount all`, which mounts all volumes automatically.
- `load PSERVER NIRVANA_PS`, which establishes the NetWare print server. (Note: Make sure to configure the print server first using the PCONSOLE utility. Refer to Chapter 14.)

- `load REMOTE`, which defines NetWare Remote Management Facility (RMF).
- `load RSPX`, which establishes RMF.
- `load MONITOR`, which is the NetWare console management utility.
- `SET Allow Unencrypted Passwords = ON`, which accommodates earlier NetWare servers.
- `load VREPAIR`, which monitors and repairs server volumes automatically.
- `load INSTALL`, which edits installation options.

In addition, refer to Optimizing NetWare with SET Commands in Chapter 6. To complete the AUTOEXEC.NCF file, press F10 and highlight Yes at the confirmation box, then press Enter. To modify the AUTOEXEC.NCF file, choose Edit AUTOEXEC.NCF file from the Available System Options menu.

Stage 6: Additional NLMs

At this point, you can polish off the NetWare v3.11 installation by activating additional NetWare NLMs. These NLMs can be activated independently at the console prompt or automated in the AUTOEXEC.NCF boot file. Either way, here are a few NetWare v3.11 NLMs from Novell or third-party manufacturers, any of which can be run by preceding it with the command load.

PATCHMAN

PATCHMAN is a patch manager for minor NetWare upgrades. This utility must be loaded before all NetWare v3.11 patches. It tracks and manages dynamic patch modules. Some current NetWare v3.11 patch NLMs to explore are

DOTFIX	EVENTFIX	SYNCTIME	TRSTFIX
GETQFIX	BIGRFIX	REQFIX	RPLNFX
NCPSPFIX	GETSEFIX	EAINFIX	DIAGRFSX

Contact NetWire or LANimation for a detailed description of these patches and information about current availability.

EDIT

EDIT is a server editor utility.

CLIB

The CLIB utility is required to load NLMs that make NetWare system calls.

NMAGENT

NMAGENT is required to load Network Management Agents, NLMs.

STREAMS

STREAMS is required to load interface protocol NLMs.

Stage 7: Use WSGEN

The final stage in building a NetWare v3.11 server is workstation installation. WSGEN stands for workstation shell generation. WSGEN is a NetWare menu utility that has one purpose: to create IPX.COM. IPX.COM is the NIC-specific workstation shell that communicates with internal NICs and NETx. IPX generation requires NIC-specific LAN drivers. Make sure you have the manufacturer's driver diskettes before you start WSGEN.

WSGEN is a relatively simple utility that requires an IBM PC with 640KB of RAM and an internal floppy drive. Boot the workstation under DOS v3.1 or higher and insert the NetWare v3.11 WSGEN diskette in the floppy drive. Move to the A: drive by typing **A:** and pressing Enter. To activate the shell generation utility, type **WSGEN** and press Enter. A welcome screen will appear. Press Enter to continue. WSGEN operation consists of three simple steps: NIC selection, NIC configuration, and IPX creation.

NetWare v3.11 WSGEN is exactly the same as NetWare v2.2 WSGEN. Refer to the WSGEN stage in the previous chapter for a detailed discussion of the WSGEN procedure.

Men trifle with their business and their politics; but never trifle with their games. It brings truth home to them. They cannot pretend that they made a magnificent drive when they foozled it. The Englishman is at his best on the links, and at his worst in the Cabinet.

—George Bernard Shaw

Chapter 10

NetWare Installation, Version 4.0

NetWare v4.0 is the big *kahuna*. Novell's new network operating system introduces a huge variety of improvements and functionality. Here's a quick recap of the latest version's features:

- NetWare Directory Services
- RAM management
- data compression and migration
- GUI utilities
- auditing services
- on-line documentation
- WAN connectivity

The installation of NetWare version 4.0 follows the same fundamentals as NetWare v3.11, but the user interface is dramatically improved. The most apparent enhancement is INSTALL.EXE. This utility automates the NetWare disk preparation stage—FDISK and FORMAT. Other improvements include choices of three installation media, including CD-ROM; multiple INSTALL.NLM options; on-screen help; an IDE disk driver; and more information at the console prompt. In addition, the NetWare v4.0 installation procedure is fully prompted, unlike that in NetWare v3.11. NetWare v4.0 guides the installation team through the first five of seven stages, from disk preparation to definition of startup files. This feature makes the installation process easier, faster, and more reliable. Let's take a closer look at the NetWare v4.0 installation procedure.

Requirements

The NetWare v4.0 requirements are more demanding than v3.11. The most notable difference is the workstation GUI environment. A good portion of the NetWare v4.0 enhancements are graphically oriented; these features at minimum require an 80286 workstation, 1MB of memory, and Microsoft Windows. NetWare v4.0 is also a true 32-bit multitasking network operating system and requires an 80386 server with a minimum of 8MB RAM.

Hardware

File Server

An 80386-compatible CPU with 8.0 MB of minimum memory is required. Additional server RAM is required for advanced NetWare v4.0 features, including NetWare Services Directory, NLMs, multiple volumes, NetWare Name Space, block suballocation, data migration, and large internal disks. A 30MB internal hard disk is required—5MB DOS partition and 25MB for NetWare v4.0 system files. Additional options are available that require large amounts of incremental file server disk space—on-line documentation (40MB), OS/2 utilities (90MB), and other NetWare products. A Novell-certified network interface card is also required.

Note: NetWare v4.0 currently ships as a CD-ROM. In order to install the operating system from this medium, the file server must support a CD-ROM drive as a DOS device.

Some early 80386-based computers (such as those manufactured in 1987) may not correctly process full 32-bit instructions. These machines will not support a NetWare v4.0 server; NetWare will display a warning message. Contact your local reseller for information on possible ROM corrections.

Workstation

An 8086-compatible CPU with a minimum of 384KB of memory is required. The minimum RAM is needed for NetWare Requester for DOS—the NetWare workstation shells. Additional NetWare v4.0 GUI user tools require an 80286-based workstation with 1MB of RAM and Windows 3.x. Keep in mind that these processor types and memory levels are the *absolute minimum* workstation configuration. I recommend an 80386DX/33-MHz machine with at least 4MB of RAM to run efficiently as a workstation. Network applications and graphical user environments require additional workstation RAM. A Novell-certified network interface card is required.

Topology Components

Cabling and the topology components that are compatible and certified by Novell are required—Ethernet, ARCNet, Token Ring, and LocalTalk are supported.

Software

DOS

NetWare's installation utilities are DOS-based programs. DOS is initially required in booting the file server and must always run under the NetWare shells on the workstation.

GUI Windows

NetWare v4.0 provides additional GUI-based Windows utilities. These workstation utilities offer enhanced network management features for network managers, Administrators, and users. NetWare GUI tools require Microsoft Windows version 3.x or OS/2 v1.x or later.

SERVER.EXE

The NetWare v4.0 operating system core consists of one executable file—*SERVER.EXE*. Once executed, this file loads the NetWare Executive, File System, and NLM Software Bus. SERVER.EXE can be upgraded as NetWare v4.0 improvements are introduced.

Workstation Software

The workstation software consists of DOS, Windows, or OS/2 utilities. The installation process is primarily DOS-based and works from four workstation diskettes. Due to the complex nature of the workstation software, it is recommended that each workstation be equipped with an internal hard disk.

NetWare 4.0 Media

The NetWare v4.0 operating system is currently available on two different media—a complete set of NetWare v4.0 *system* and *public* diskettes or one CD-ROM disk. Both media contain identical files that must be copied to special system directories on the internal file server disk. Those directories are SYSTEM, PUBLIC, LOGIN, and MAIL. Following is a list of all the required NetWare v4.0 diskettes:

```
NETWARE-1          NETWARE-8          ENGLISH-1 (language)
NETWARE-2          NETWARE-9          LICENSE
NETWARE-3          NETWARE-10         REGISTER
NETWARE-4          NETWARE-11         WSDOS_1
NETWARE-5          NETWARE-12         WSWIN_1
NETWARE-6          NETWARE-13         WSDRV_1
NETWARE-7          INSTALL            WSDRV_2
```

In addition, the CD-ROM disk contains a complete set of NetWare v4.0 documentation in electronic form. The electronic documentation can only be accessed from a Windows workstation.

Installation

NetWare v4.0 installation follows the fundamentals of NetWare v3.11. In addition, NetWare v4.0 has added four features: CD-ROM media, INSTALL.EXE, NetWare Directory Services, and workstation installation. The CD-ROM medium provides a solution to the installation disk-swapping tango. The INSTALL.EXE utility provides a menu-driven interface for partitioning and formatting the server boot disk. The installation of NetWare Directory Services is a complex set of procedures that establish root servers, directory trees, time synchronization, name context, and the ADMIN password. Workstation installation specifies various client environments—DOS, Windows, or OS/2.

This chapter supplements the NetWare v3.11 fundamentals covered in Chapter 9 by introducing NetWare v4.0 advancements. If you have any questions concerning a specific installation concept, refer to Chapter 9.

NetWare v4.0 can be installed from one of three locations: CD-ROM, diskette, or NetWare directory. The CD-ROM method requires a CD-ROM drive attached to the server as a DOS device. The diskette method requires an appropriate 3.5-inch or 5.25-inch diskette drive in the server. The NetWare directory installation method requires an existing NetWare v2.2, v3.11, or v4.0 server with enough available disk space for the entire set of NetWare v4.0 files (roughly 30MB to 170MB). Regardless of the method you choose, the fundamental installation steps are identical. NetWare v4.0 installation consists of seven stages:

1. Prepare NetWare hard disk.
2. Run SERVER.EXE.
3. Load INSTALL.NLM.
4. Install NetWare Directory Services.
5. Define startup files.
6. Install additional NLMs.
7. Perform workstation installation.

When copying the NetWare v4.0 files to an existing NetWare directory, use one of the following NCOPY commands:

CD-ROM: NCOPY E:*.* F:\SERVER.40 /s /e

DISKETTES: NCOPY A:*.* F:\SERVER.40 /s /e

Stage 1: Prepare the NetWare Hard Disk

The NetWare v4.0 operating system consists of one file—SERVER.EXE—and various auxiliary NetWare loadable modules (NLM). SERVER.EXE runs from DOS. In order to generate the NetWare v4.0 system, you must first boot the server under DOS v3.3, v5.0, or v6.0. The process of preparing a NetWare DOS disk consists of disk partitioning and formatting—just as with NetWare v3.11. This process has been simplified in NetWare v4.0 with the introduction of INSTALL.EXE. INSTALL.EXE automates the task of partitioning and formatting the server boot disk. This installation utility consists of five steps: disk partitioning, disk formatting, naming the server, assigning the IPX network number, and copying the server boot files.

NetWare v4.0 supports many language modules. If you are using the French installation option, during the instructions given here you'll replace the Install-English diskette with Install-Français. For German, substitute the Install-Deutsch diskette.

Disk Partition

To begin the NetWare v4.0 installation, insert the Install-English diskette in drive A: and turn on or reboot the file server. The Install-English diskette is programmed to boot the server under DR DOS and begin the INSTALL.EXE utility. If you are using the CD-ROM, boot the server from a floppy diskette and switch to the CD-ROM drive (in this case, D:). Switch to the D: root directory and type **INSTALL**. In both cases, the system will display the Select an Installation Option menu. Highlight Install new NetWare v4.0 and press Enter. If you are upgrading an existing v3.1x system, refer to the instructions under Upgrade later in this chapter.

If you are using the CD-ROM or NetWare directory methods and you booted the server from a diskette containing any DOS other than DR DOS, complete the FDISK and FORMAT steps manually using your DOS utilities. When this process is finished, return to INSTALL.EXE and choose Retain Current Disk Partitions from the Disk Partitions Options menu. You can now continue with the NetWare v4.0 installation from the NAME SERVER stage.

Next, the system displays two disk partition components: the Existing disk partition box (informative) and the Disk Partition Options menu. You can retain the current partitions or create new ones. Most installations require the creation of a new DOS partition. Highlight Create a new DOS partition and press Enter. The system will display a warning message indicating that all data and all partitions on your disk will be destroyed. If this is not what you intended to do, back up your data now! To exit, press Esc three times. To proceed, highlight Create a DOS partition and press Enter.

You are asked to input the partition size in megabytes (MB). The system defaults to 5MB—this is the minimum partition size for a NetWare v4.0 server. Press Enter to continue. Highlight Yes at the confirmation box and press Enter. The partitioning process takes less than a second. At this point, the system will display an informative message. Press the Spacebar to continue. The system will reboot to recognize the new partition.

Disk Format

Once the new DOS partition has been created, we must format it. After rebooting, the system will return to the Format the DOS partition screen. The Source path defaults to A:—FORMAT.COM is on the Install-English diskette. If you would like to change the default Source path, press F2 and input a new path. Press Enter to continue with the format. Another warning is displayed—press Y and Enter to continue. Once the format is completed, the system will prompt you for a volume label—up to 11 characters. Type the file server name and press Enter. The DOS partition information is displayed—press Spacebar to continue to the next step.

Name Server

INSTALL.EXE will now prompt you for the file server's name. The server name distinguishes this NetWare machine from any other on the LAN, WAN, or MAN. Choose an alphanumeric name with 2 to 47 characters—no spaces. Type **NIRVANA** and press Enter. This is to honor our quest for NetWare Nirvana.

Assign IPX Number

The next step is to identify the server's unique IPX Internal Network Number. This number must differ from all other IPX network numbers and network addresses. For more information on network addressing, refer to Chapter 9—NetWare Installation version 3.11. Backspace over the default number and type **DAD**—press Enter.

Copy Server Boot Files

The final step in disk preparation is to copy the server boot files to the DOS partition. The system will display two installation paths—Source path (`A:\` or `D:\NETWARE.40\FILES` or `F:\SERVER.40\NETWARE`) and Destination path (`C:\SERVER.40`). To accept these defaults, press Enter. To change the installation paths press F2 (Source) or F4 (Destination). If you are using the diskette method, the system will ask for five NetWare diskettes—NetWare-1, NetWare-2, NetWare-4, NetWare-5, and Install. Once the files have been copied, the disk preparation procedure is completed. Note: the CD-ROM and NetWare directory methods copy files 700 percent faster than the diskette method.

Stage 2: Run SERVER.EXE

Once you have used the INSTALL.EXE procedure and have partitioned the server disk, created a 5MB DOS boot section, established initial server configurations, and copied the

NetWare server files, it is time to load the NetWare v4.0 system file—SERVER.EXE. The system will prompt you

```
Do you want AUTOEXEC.BAT to load SERVER.EXE?
```

Highlight Yes and press Enter. The system will create an AUTOEXEC.BAT file on the server boot disk with one line—SERVER.EXE.

Once the AUTOEXEC.BAT file has been created, the system will reboot and load SERVER.EXE—you will notice the keyboard lights flash. The server name and IPX network number will automatically load. INSTALL.NLM will be automatically activated. You now have a valid NetWare v4.0 server. As with NetWare v3.11, you can't do anything—no file or printing services will be available yet. The next stages add incremental functionality to our raw NetWare v4.0 server.

If you ever get lost during the installation procedure, you can exit to the console prompt by pressing Esc and restart by typing LOAD INSTALL at the : prompt. At this point, highlight Install a new v4.00 server and press Enter.

Stage 3: Load INSTALL.NLM

The NetWare v4.0 INSTALL.NLM covers the same installation parameters as NetWare v3.11, but in a substantially different way. Refer to Figure 10.1 for an illustration of the INSTALL.NLM Main menu. The Main menu consists of three choices:

- *Install a new v4.00 server* activates the installation procedure at step 1 to load the disk driver. This option is automatically started when SERVER.EXE is loaded from INSTALL.EXE. To return to the main menu from this point, you have to unload INSTALL.NLM and initialize it from the console prompt.
- *Upgrade a v3.1x server* is a set of NetWare v4.0 utilities that automates the upgrade process. This procedure manages the NetWare v4.0 installation without destroying existing NetWare v3.1x configuration parameters and data. The NetWare v4.0 upgrade process is covered later in this chapter.

```
NetWare Server Installation   V4.00                    NetWare Loadable Module

        ┌─────────────────────────────────────────────────────────────┐
        │                    Installation Options                      │
        ├─────────────────────────────────────────────────────────────┤
        │ Disk Driver Options  (Configure/Load/Unload Disk Drivers)    │
        │ LAN Driver Options   (Configure/Load/Unload LAN Drivers)     │
        │ Disk Options         (Configure/Mirror/Test Disk Partitions) │
        │ Volume Options       (Configure/Mount/Dismount Volumes)      │
        │ License Option       (Install the Server License)            │
        │ Copy Files Option    (Install NetWare System Files)          │
        │ Directory Options    (Install NetWare Directory Services)    │
        │ NCF Files Options    (Create/Edit Server Startup Files)      │
        │ Product Options      (Install/Reconfigure Products)          │
        │ Other Options        (Other Optional Installation Items)     │
        └─────────────────────────────────────────────────────────────┘
```

FIGURE 10.1 The NetWare v4.0 INSTALL.NLM Main Menu

■ The *Maintenance/Selective Install* option enables experienced network managers to alter the sequence of installation events. This option also provides functionality for future enhancements to the installation configuration—adding new disks, mirroring, internal routers, new directory trees, updating LAN drivers, editing startup files, configuring NetWare volumes, and installing the server license.

Each of these three installation options provides a different pathway through the nine fundamental steps of installing a NetWare v4.0 file server:

1. Load the disk driver.
2. Create the NetWare partition.
3. Create and Mount NetWare volumes.
4. Install NetWare v4.0 server license.
5. Copy SYSTEM and PUBLIC files.
6. Load the LAN driver.
7. Install NetWare Directory Services.
8. Create startup files.
9. Install additional product options.

This stage discusses the first six steps and then moves on to NetWare Directory Services and startup files.

Load Disk Driver

The disk driver initializes communication between NetWare and the internal server disk. NetWare v4.0 automatically lists 32 disk drivers. Some of the most common are

■ *ISADISK:* Most standard AT-style disks (MFM, ESDI, IDE)
■ *IDE:* Some new 80386/80486 IDE disks attached directly to the system board
■ *DCB:* Disk coprocessor board or Novell SCSI

Notice the installation Black Box. This NetWare v4.0 feature provides network managers with on-line help and parameter explanations. The Black Box is apparent in every installation screen and provides brief explanations of highlighted options. Also, NetWare v4.0 supports two other installation boxes: informative and input menus. Informative boxes contain single yellow borders (single-line borders on monochrome monitors); input menus support double-lined borders.

To activate one of these choices, highlight the driver and press Enter. To activate a driver not listed, press Ins. The system will prompt you to insert one of two driver diskettes—NetWare-2 or vendor-specific driver diskette. Remember, CD-ROM and NetWare directory methods require no disk swapping. Disk drivers not listed require a vendor-specific driver diskette. Highlight Your Driver and press Enter. The Driver Parameters menu will appear. This screen is used to input critical disk parameters, including the interrupt number, I/O port, and in some cases scatter gather. Scatter gather batches disk requests—this is faster in high loads and slower in low loads.

Choose the default parameters and press F10 to load the driver. A message indicating that the driver was successfully loaded will appear—press Enter to continue. INSTALL.NLM now provides three choices: Load driver again, Load another driver, or Continue with installation. Few installations require additional disk drivers. Highlight Continue with installation and press Enter.

Create the NetWare Partition

The next step begins with the Create NetWare disk partitions screen. This menu contains two choices: Automatically and Manually. The automatic option creates one nonmirrored NetWare partition with all available disk space. In addition, the hot fix redirection area will be set at around 2 percent. The manual option provides customization for NetWare disk partition space, disk mirroring/duplexing, and hot fix redirection size. Most installations consist of one nonmirrored disk partition. Choose Automatically and press Enter. The Manage NetWare Volumes screen appears to inform you that the NetWare partition has been created and assigned to the SYS: volume. Press Enter to continue.

Create and Mount NetWare Volumes

The Manage NetWare Volumes menu will appear. This screen displays all the server's volumes and their corresponding sizes. If you performed an automatic installation, the menu will display one volume (SYS:) and its corresponding size. The volume size should roughly match the size of the entire NetWare disk partition. SYS: is the default NetWare volume and home of all SYSTEM and PUBLIC files.

To alter the SYS: defaults, highlight SYS: and press Enter. The Volume Information screen will appear. Volume information consists of six options:

- *Volume Name* distinguishes this NetWare volume from all others—do not change the name of the SYS: volume.
- *Volume Block Size* defines a specific configuration for disk caching. Small blocks (4KB) are more efficient for normal disk traffic, whereas large blocks (64KB) process large database requests more quickly. The default is 8KB.
- *Status* defines Mounted or Not Mounted volumes.
- *File Compression* is file-specific—an attribute set by the network manager. In order for files to be compressed, the volume must have file compression turned on. If you enable file compression at this point, it will increase storage capacity by 63 percent, but decrease disk performance. By default, file compression is turned on and the delay is set to 7 days.
- *Block Suballocation* saves server RAM by storing files in 512-byte blocks, thus avoiding wasted block space. Block suballocation should be turned on for all server disks—except very small ones (less than 80MB).
- *Data Migration* is a NetWare v4.0 feature that enables you to move volume data to alternative storage devices (tape, CD-ROM, removable disks). The advantage of data migration is that the data appears as if it were still residing on the default server disk. On the downside, migrated data is accessed much slower. Unless you have the capacity for data migration, turn it off.

To save the Volume Information parameters, press F10 at the Volume Information screen. To continue with creating and mounting the SYS: volume, press F10 at the Manage

NetWare Volumes screen. Highlight Yes at the confirmation box. The volume has now been defined, created, and mounted.

Install NetWare v4.0 Server License
Next, the licensing box appears. It states that the license files will be installed from drive A:. To change the source drive, press F3. The system will look for the server MLS license file on the LICENSE diskette. This file will authenticate the server for a variety of user connections—from 5 to 1,000, depending on what you bought. Insert the diskette in the appropriate drive and press Enter. It will only take a few seconds for the system to load the Main Server License.

Copy SYSTEM and PUBLIC Files
For the next step in the installation procedure, you copy the SYSTEM and PUBLIC files to the new SYS: volume. The Copy NetWare Files screen will appear. NetWare v4.0 automatically copies all critical system files to the SYSTEM, PUBLIC, MAIL, and LOGIN directories—6.7MB. Beyond that, NetWare v4.0 enables you to choose which file groups you would like to copy. Here is a complete list:

NetWare v4.00 CBT	3.40MB *(CD-ROM)*
NetWare v4.00 Online Documentation	30.61MB *(CD-ROM)*
NetWare v4.00 Utilities	20.70MB

All of these file groups are marked by default. It is a good idea to copy all NetWare files at this point, just in case you need them later. If you are strapped for disk space, choose NetWare v4.00 Utilities only. Use the Enter key to mark or unmark a file group. When finished, press F10 to copy the specified file groups to the new NetWare v4.0 server. The NetWare v4.0 files are compressed for all media, so the copying process is slow—approximately 90 minutes for the NetWare v4.00 Utilities from diskette and 15 minutes for all NetWare v4.0 files from CD-ROM or the NetWare directory. When the file copying is complete, you will receive an appropriate message—press Enter to continue.

An interesting quirk arises when you copy the NetWare v4.0 server files. The LOGIN.EXE file—probably the most critical NetWare file next to SERVER.EXE—is considered a NetWare v4.0 utility. Therefore, if you choose to skip the NetWare utilities and load only the critical system files, you won't be able to log in! You don't have much of a choice.

Load LAN Driver
The LAN driver provides communication services to the NetWare server. It is responsible for mediating communications between SERVER.EXE and the internal NIC. LAN drivers are loaded at the Load LAN Driver screen. Once the system has finished copying the appropriate files and utilities, it asks you to insert the NetWare-3 diskette. Insert the diskette and press Enter. The system will load 52 different LAN drivers into server memory. Be patient; this process takes a few minutes from diskette.

If the server NIC supports one of the listed NICs, the system will default to the correct driver. Otherwise, you will have to press Ins and provide the system with the NetWare-2 diskette or an additional vendor-specific configuration. To load the LAN driver, highlight your driver and press Enter. The system will copy a few files and respond with the Driver Parameters menu. This screen is used to input critical LAN parameters, including Interrupt number, I/O port, Node Address, and Frame Type. (Chapter 7 discusses NIC configurations.)

Input the correct parameters from the File Server Definition Worksheet and press F10 to load the driver. The Network Address to bind IPX to menu will appear with a strange default value. Backspace over the default address and type your network address—**1234567**—and press Enter. The system will bind IPX to the loaded driver and assign 1234567 as the network address. Note: If this server is part of an existing LAN, the installation program will automatically bind your driver to the existing network address.

You now have a functional NetWare v4.0 server with a NetWare partition, SYS: volume, SYSTEM and PUBLIC files, and LAN communications to the server NIC. Don't get too excited yet. Before anyone can log in, we must define the NetWare Directory tree and complete the Workstation Installation.

Stand firm in your refusal to remain conscious during algebra. In real life, I assure you, there is no such thing as algebra.

—Fran Lebowitz

Stage 4: Install NetWare Directory Services

The most exciting NetWare v4.0 enhancement is NetWare Directory Services (NDS). NDS is a global strategy for organizing NetWare resources in a natural, efficient manner—it replaces the previous NetWare bindery. NetWare resources include servers, volumes, users, organizations, and countries. NetWare resources are treated as objects in a hierarchical tree structure called the Directory. The Directory is maintained by an independent database called the NetWare Infobase (NIB). The NIB is distributed among all servers in the WAN to ensure connectivity and system fault tolerance. The Directory extends from [Root] at the top to server volumes at the bottom. NDS does not encompass NetWare directories or files—these objects are controlled by NetWare's DOS-like Network Directory Structure. Chapter 6 provides more information about NetWare Directory Services, and Chapter 11 gives more information about Network Directory Structures.

The main reason for using NetWare Directory Services is to organize NetWare resources so that users can find them easily. This level of organization requires a plan. Never try to install NDS before you plan the Directory tree. A Directory plan can be as simple as preparing for 1 master server and 10 users, or as complex as encompassing 1,000 servers in 12 countries for 1 million users. Whichever scenario fits your LAN, include these five NDS planning considerations:

- *Directory parameters*—the first decision is how big to make the Directory tree. At the top level is the [Root], then container objects, and finally leaf objects. You must also name the Directory tree—to distinguish it from other NDS structures. Also, large Directory trees should consider incorporating local replicas for traffic efficiency and system fault tolerance.

- *Container objects*—container objects form the top level of the tree. The top level is the most critical of the directory. Container objects include COUNTRY (C), ORGANIZATION (O), and ORGANIZATIONAL UNIT (OU). Based on the size of your tree, determine how many container objects you need—only the ORGANIZATION object is required. Use O for companies and OU for departments within companies. Draw a vertical tree illustrating the [Root], O, and OU designations.

- *Leaf objects*—leaf objects are the real workhorses of the Directory tree. These NDS structures are placed within container objects and represent the user's interface to the LAN. Leaf objects include users, volumes, servers, computers, profiles, group lists, and aliases. NetWare v4.0 installation creates the following default leaf objects: server, SYS: volume, and ADMIN Supervisor. Create a list of your LAN's leaf objects and place them under appropriate Os and OUs.

- *Access control*—NDS security emulates NetWare trustee assignments. Leaf objects are given access rights at various levels of the Directory tree. In addition, NDS rights can be removed through an inherited rights filter. NDS security affects the organizational structure of the Directory tree, but it is not established at installation; this level of NetWare security is controlled by the Network Manager through the NWADMIN utility. Refer to Chapters 12 and 13.

- *Time servers*—because the NetWare Directory tree is designed to span multiple organizations, countries, and time zones, NDS has a built-in time synchronization feature. This NetWare v4.0 feature relies on a combination of four time servers: Single Reference, Primary, Secondary, and Reference. A Single Reference server is the only time source for small LANs. These servers use their own internal clock to provide a timestamp to all other secondary time servers. Reference servers are for larger WANs and they rely on outside time sources (such as atomic clocks) for time synchronization. Primary servers negotiate with each other to provide one common timestamp to secondary servers. Primary servers replace reference and single reference time servers. Secondary servers provide time synchronization to NetWare v4.0 clients. Before NDS installation, determine which NetWare servers will perform which time server functions.

Once you have completed the NDS plan, continue with the initial NetWare v4.0 installation or access NetWare Directory Services from the Maintenance/Selective Install option under the INSTALL.NLM Main menu. During the first step of the NDS installation stage, the system searches for existing NDS objects. The search will return the Install Directory Services screen. It all begins with a question:

```
Is this the first v4.00 server on this internetwork?
```

The system provides you with three possible answers: Yes, No (Recheck), and No (Check a specific place). Highlight Yes and press Enter.

Directory Name

An input box will appear asking for a name for the Directory tree. Use any alphanumeric name that will distinguish this directory tree from others in the WAN. Remember: The NDS tree expands beyond single servers—avoid using server names. Type **CASTLE** and press Enter.

Time Zone

The Choose Time Zone screen will appear. It lists 27 different time zones from Australian, Central Time, to United States of America, Pacific Time. These options provide default values for the Time Configuration window. Highlight the appropriate time zone and press Enter.

Time Configuration

The Time Configuration Information screen will appear. The Time server type defines this server's synchronization status with respect to the other servers in the LAN. If this is the first NetWare v4.0 server, type **Single Reference** and press Enter. The Standard and Daylight time zone abbreviations establish time definitions for this NetWare server. If you are in San Francisco, type **PST** and **PDT**, respectively. For New Yorkers, type **EST** and **EDT**, respectively. If you are a Utahan, type **MST** and **MDT**, respectively. Standard time offset from UTC describes this server's synchronization delay from the Universal Time Coordinate (UTC). The offset is 8 hours behind for San Francisco, 5 hours behind for New York, 0 for England, and 1 hour ahead for Germany. Type **8:00:00 BEHIND** and press Enter. Current daylight time status is ON until the last weekend in October. Type **ON** and press Enter. Press F10 to save the configurations and highlight Yes at the confirmation box, then press Enter.

Object Context

The next NDS screen is Specify a Context for This Server and Its Objects. Server context is an NDS path for this server only. The highest NDS level for our NetWare v4.0 server tree is ORGANIZATION. Type a name for the ORGANIZATION object and press Enter. Type **NORTH_WING** and press Enter. The next three levels are defined as ORGANIZATIONAL UNITS. These levels are the structures under which this server object exists. They are usually departments or workgroups within the organization. Most NetWare v4.0 servers exist within a specific OU. Type **KITCHEN** for Level 1 and press Enter. The Server Context parameter defines the full NDS path that points to this specific server. Notice how the system automatically creates the path when you define the NDS organization levels above. In addition, the system automatically creates an Administrator object with the name ADMIN and puts it in the ORGANIZATION container. Type the ADMIN password here and press Enter. Retype the password and press Enter. Don't forget the password, or you will have to reconstruct the NDS tree. Press F10 to save the Object options and continue.

The Server Context window does not specify an option for COUNTRY. In order to add a COUNTRY container to your NDS tree, manually type the line .C=*COUNTRY* at the end of the Server Context parameter.

During the final NDS step the system will install the NetWare Directory Services and add the SYS: volume as a leaf object; press Enter to continue. The system will then display an information box with the Directory tree name, Directory context, and Administrator name. Write this information down! Press Enter to continue.

Stage 5: Define Startup Files

Once the NetWare v4.0 installation has been completed, we must secure all of our work in the NetWare v4.0 server startup files. The startup files activate critical server parameters during the NetWare booting procedure. They consist of two files: STARTUP.NCF and AUTOEXEC.NCF.

STARTUP.NCF

The system will jump into STARTUP.NCF. This startup file automatically loads NLMs during the server bootup. It loads from the server's DOS partition and typically activates the NetWare v4.0 disk driver. The STARTUP.NCF file also loads advanced SET parameters, including warning options, Cache Buffer Size, Physical Receive Packet Size, Packet Receive Buffers, Number of Watchdog Packets, Auto TTS Backout Flag, and Maximum Subdirectory Tree Depth. To create a STARTUP.NCF file from today's installation, highlight Create STARTUP.NCF file from the Available NCF Files Options screen and press Enter. The system will prompt you for the path. Accept the default of C:\SERVER.40 and press Enter. Notice that today's changes have already been incorporated. The following line should be displayed:

```
load ISADISK port=1F0 int=E
```

To exit and save the new STARTUP.NCF file, press F10 and highlight Yes at the confirmation box—press Enter. From this point forward, if you want to modify the STARTUP.NCF file, choose Edit STARTUP.NCF file from the Available NCF Files Options menu in INSTALL.NLM.

AUTOEXEC.NCF

The AUTOEXEC.NCF follows the STARTUP.NCF file. The AUTOEXEC.NCF automatically loads all remaining system NLM modules. Any command that is entered at the console prompt can be loaded automatically by AUTOEXEC.NCF. The system jumps into today's AUTOEXEC.NCF file. If you aren't following the new NetWare server option and you want to create today's boot file, highlight Create AUTOEXEC.NCF file at the Available NCF Files Options menu and press Enter. Notice again that today's changes have already been incorporated:

```
set Time Zone = PST8PDT
set Daylight Savings Time Status = ON
set Daylight Savings Time Offset = 1:00:00
set Default Time Server Type = SINGLE REFERENCE
set Bindery Context = OU=KITCHEN.O=NORTH_WING
file server name NIRVANA
ipx internal net DAD
load NE2000 INT=2 PORT=320 FRAME=Ethernet_802.3 NAME=NE2000
bind IPX to NE2000 net=1234567
```

These commands follow the path of today's installation. Here are some additional startup file commands that you can use to optimize the AUTOEXEC.NCF file:

- `mount all`, which mounts all volumes automatically.
- `load PSERVER NIRVANA_PS`, which establishes the NetWare Print Server. (Note: Make sure to configure the print server first using the PCONSOLE utility. Refer to Chapter 14.)
- `load REMOTE`, which defines NetWare Remote Management Facility (RMF).
- `load RSPX`, which establishes RMF communications.
- `load MONITOR`, which is the NetWare console management utility.

To complete the AUTOEXEC.NCF file, press F10 and highlight Yes in the confirmation box—press Enter. To modify the AUTOEXEC.NCF file, choose Edit AUTOEXEC.NCF file from the Available NCF Files Options menu in INSTALL.NLM.

The final step in NetWare v4.0 core installation is covered by the Install Additional Products screen. You are prompted to install the following four additional NetWare v4.0 components: Create a registration diskette, upgrade v3.1x Print Services, Install an additional Server Language, and Configure Communications Protocols. Press F10 to end the installation. You are greeted with a Completion screen. Congratulations!

Stage 6: Install Additional NLMs

At this point, you can polish off the NetWare v4.0 installation by activating additional NetWare NLMs. These NLMs can be activated independently at the console prompt, or automated in the AUTOEXEC.NCF boot file. Either way, here are a few NetWare v4.0 additions to the previous NetWare v3.11 list.

NWSNUT

NWSNUT is the NLM Utility User Interface. This utility is required for advanced management routines like SERVMAN and MONITOR.

SERVMAN

The SERVer MANagement utility provides options for viewing and changing critical server parameters, including IPX/SPX configurations, SET commands, NetWare drivers, volume information, and network information.

DOMAIN

DOMAIN is a server utility used to run NLMs in protected mode. DOMAIN creates a protected OS domain (OSP) to isolate nontested NLMs from the OS core domain—domain 0.

DSREPAIR

The DSREPAIR utility repairs problems with the NetWare Directory Services Database.

Stage 7: Perform Workstation Installation

The final step in NetWare v4.0 installation is the workstation installation. Before users can access your new version 4.0 server, you must establish a NetWare workstation environment. The workstation environment defines the native WOS, user utilities, interface standard, and communication shells. NetWare concurrently supports three workstation environments: DOS, Windows, and OS/2. In addition, UNIX and System 7 environments are supported with auxiliary workstation kits.

The NetWare v4.0 workstation software is quite different from what you might be used to in earlier versions—it is now called the *NetWare Requester.* It operates within the ODI specification and requires myriad different VLMs (virtual loadable modules). The older shells, IPX.COM and NETx.COM, have been replaced with IPXODI.COM and NETx.VLM. Now everything relies on the complex configuration of the NET.CFG file. Fortunately, the workstation installation procedure has been automated and handles these configurations for you.

DOS

To begin the DOS installation, insert the Workstation for DOS (WSDOS_1) diskette at the workstation and type **INSTALL**—press Enter. The DOS workstation installation is a simple, text-based list of five steps:

Step 1. Target directory for CLIENT software:
> This option defines the default directory for the workstation software. The standard choice is C:\NWCLIENT.

Step 2. Allow changes to DOS system files (Y/N):
> You can specify whether the system modifies your local AUTOEXEC.BAT and CONFIG.SYS files. If you choose the default, NO, the system will create two backup copies of the intended changes—AUTOEXEC.BNW and CONFIG.BNW. If you choose YES, the system will make the following two changes:
> AUTOEXEC.BAT: @CALL C:\NWCLIENT\STARTNET
> CONFIG.SYS: LASTDRIVE = Z

Step 3. Windows? (Y/N):
> At this point you must specify a DOS or WINDOWS installation. The Windows installation is discussed in more depth below. Choose No for DOS and Yes for Windows.

Step 4. Network interface card:
> Next, you must specify the NIC driver and configurations to match your workstation hardware. Press Enter to see a list of 27 different drivers. You will be prompted for either of the DRIVERS diskettes. Insert the WSDRV_1 diskette and press Enter to continue. Highlight the appropriate NIC driver and press Enter. You will be prompted for the correct configurations in the Jumper Settings for the Card menu. Input the correct settings and be sure to match the Frame Type of the server—Ethernet_802.3, for example.

Step 5. Press <ENTER> here to install.
> Once the appropriate configurations have been established, the system will copy the customized workstation software to the correct directory—C:\NWCLIENT, for example. The windows software will also be copied and the appropriate configuration files will be modified.

Windows

The Windows installation is performed as a subset of the previous DOS installation. Step 3 of the DOS installation procedure provides an option for choosing the DOS or Windows installation. If you choose the Windows installation, the system will ask for the Windows home directory—typically C:\WINDOWS—and prompt you for the WSWIN_1 Windows diskette. During the file-copying procedure, the Windows install procedure makes a few modifications to your existing Windows system. These modifications are

- copying the appropriate .DRV, .INI, and .DLL files to your Windows directory
- modifying WIN.INI and SYSTEM.INI to reflect the NetWare changes
- adding the ElectroText group to your Windows desktop
- replacing your existing wallpaper with a Novell bitmap

OS/2

The OS/2 installation is the only true Windows-based installation procedure. It displays a graphical interface for the definition of workstation NIC drivers and configurations. The OS/2 shells are packaged into one big interface called the NetWare Requester for OS/2. For the OS/2 workstation installation, follow these steps:

1. Open an OS/2 full screen and type *drive*:**INSTALL** (replace *drive* with the drive letter that contains the NetWare Workstation for OS/2 diskette). The NetWare Workstation for OS/2 Installation Utility window will appear.
2. Click Requester on Workstation from the Installation menu. The OS/2 workstation installation performs the following modifications to your system:
   - creates a NETWARE directory in the root of your boot disk
   - copies all Requester files to the NETWARE directory—drivers, utilities, and DLLs
   - creates a Novell group on the OS/2 desktop with a variety of NetWare-related programs
   - modifies the CONFIG.SYS file dramatically

Once you have completed the workstation installation, you are ready to log in. The login procedure is covered in more detail in Chapter 11.

Upgrading to NetWare v4.0

NetWare v4.0 supports migration from NetWare v2.x and NetWare v3.1x servers. You can accomplish the upgrade process in a variety of ways—each with its own advantages and disadvantages. *NetWare v2.x* upgrade supports two methods: NetWare Migration Utility and In-Place Upgrade. *NetWare v3.1x* upgrade supports one simple upgrade process.

Regardless of the method, each NetWare v4.0 upgrade shares one common goal—bindery/data retention. The all-important NetWare v2.x or v3.1x bindery objects are converted into NetWare v4.0 Directory objects. This saves a great deal of time and effort in assigning users, groups, security, and system configurations. NetWare v2.x and v3.1x data is retained in a variety of ways—from backup to direct migration. Let's take a closer look at NetWare v4.0 upgrade.

NetWare v2.x to v4.0

The most serious NetWare upgrade is from NetWare v2.x to v4.0. Novell has never before allowed an upgrade path to traverse more than one NetWare generation—this migration covers two full NetWare generations. Thus, this multigenerational upgrade poses some interesting problems, such as incompatible file attributes, outdated binderies, and incongruent drivers.

The NetWare v2.x to v4.0 upgrade is accomplished in two ways: through the NetWare migration utility and through an in-place upgrade.

NetWare Migration Utility

The NetWare migration utility performs a NetWare v4.0 upgrade from a NetWare v2.x system across the LAN or on a single server. The *across-the-wire* method requires a LAN with two available servers and a DOS workstation with at least 640KB of RAM. The NetWare migration utility is installed on the hard disk of the DOS workstation and moves files across the LAN from the source NetWare v2.x server to the destination NetWare v4.0 server. This method retains all network data and converts old NetWare bindery information into a NetWare v4.0 Directory tree. Follow these simple steps:

1. Install the NetWare migration utility on the DOS workstation from the migration diskette. Type **MIGRATE** from the C: drive and press Enter.
2. Select a working directory.
3. Define the source and destination servers.
4. Press F10 to begin the migration.
5. When the migration is complete, view the migration reports.

The *same-server* method requires a LAN with one 80386-compatible server and a DOS workstation with a backup device. This method relies on tape backup and bindery translation for data migration from v2.x to v4.0 on the same machine. Follow these simple steps:

1. Back up the old NetWare data from the DOS workstation.
2. Run the migration utility at the workstation to translate the bindery information.
3. Install the new NetWare v4.0 server.
4. Restore the data files to the new NetWare v4.0 server.
5. Run the migration utility to migrate the NDS tree to the NetWare v4.0 server.

In-Place Upgrade

The *In-Place Upgrade* method is a two-step process. First, the NetWare v2.x server is upgraded to NetWare v3.11. Second, the NetWare v3.11 server is upgraded to NetWare v4.00. The first step is accomplished in three phases:

1. During the *Analysis* upgrade phase, the NetWare v2.x server disk is analyzed for critical system parameters—hot fix addresses, FAT, Directory entry tables (DET), and data block addresses. The system also translates FAT and DET information to accommodate v3.11 file structures. Directory and file attributes are upgraded.

2. The *Modification* phase moves v2.x data blocks to a new location with the v3.11 parameters. The system tables are written to disk and the v3.11 partition table is created.

3. In the final phase, *Creation*, all of the v2.x bindery information is upgraded to v3.11—including users, groups, printing, security, and file structures.

The In-Place Upgrade requires an 80386-compatible server with at least 10 percent available disk space, a 5MB DOS partition, bootable DOS diskette, backup device, and the NetWare v4.0 Upgrade diskette.

The NetWare v2.x to v3.11 upgrade consists of 15 steps:

1. Back up the v2.x server twice.
2. Document the v2.x server information.
3. Run BINDFIX from a v2.x workstation to copy the old v2.x bindery.
4. Boot the server from a DOS diskette.
5. Insert the Upgrade diskette and type **SERVER**. Press Enter.
6. Test the NetWare v3.11 disk driver by loading it.
7. Test the NetWare v3.11 LAN driver by loading it.
8. Unload the LAN driver.
9. Type **LOAD A:2XTO311** at the console (:) prompt and press Enter.
10. Enter the DOS partition size (5MB).
11. Type **Y** to confirm creation.
12. Assign random passwords.
13. Down the new v3.11 server and type **EXIT**. Press Enter.
14. Format the DOS partition.
15. Create the STARTUP.NCF file on the C : \> disk.

Now that we have a viable NetWare v3.11 server, we can upgrade it to NetWare v4.0. Follow the steps outlined under NetWare v3.1x to NetWare v4.0.

NetWare v3.1x to v4.0

The upgrade process from a NetWare v3.1x server to NetWare v4.0 follows the same fundamentals as a new installation. The difference is that the upgrade process retains the old NetWare bindery and creates a default Directory tree. The NetWare v3.1x data is not transferred—it must be backed up and restored. The NetWare v4.0 upgrade requires a full NetWare v3.1x server backup, updated LAN and DISK drivers, 8MB of server RAM, a 5MB DOS partition, and working copies of the NetWare v4.0 installation diskettes or CD-ROM. The NetWare v3.1x to v4.0 upgrade focuses on four main components: NetWare v4.0 server boot files, NetWare v4.0 SYSTEM and PUBLIC files, NDS and bindery update, and startup files. Review the new installation procedures earlier in this chapter before you start a NetWare v4.0 upgrade—an understanding of key v4.0 fundamentals is essential.

NetWare v4.0 Server Boot Files

Before we begin the upgrade procedure, we must prepare the NetWare v3.1x server—perform two full backups, SALVAGE any deleted files, DOWN the server and EXIT, and copy old NetWare v3.1x bindery files to a backup diskette.

Then follow these steps:

1. Insert the INSTALL diskette into drive A: and type **INSTALL** at the A:\ prompt. Press Enter.
2. Highlight Upgrade NetWare v3.1x to v4.0 and press Enter. The system will copy the NetWare v4.0 server boot files to the C:\SERVER.40 directory.
3. In addition, you will be prompted for the path of the existing STARTUP.NCF file. Type **C:** and press Enter. The system will copy the old file to the C:\SERV-ER.40 directory.

Once the boot files have been established, the system loads SERVER.EXE, executes STARTUP.NCF, mounts SYS:, and loads the INSTALL.NLM utility.

NetWare v4.0 SYSTEM and PUBLIC Files
The INSTALL utility will take you directly to the Copy NetWare Files screen. The system automatically copies default SYSTEM and PUBLIC files. In addition, you have the choice of copying NetWare v4.0 files from three different file groups—refer to installation Stage 3. Press F10 to continue and be prepared to wait—it takes 90 minutes to copy all NetWare v4.0 files from diskette or 15 minutes from CD-ROM. Press Enter to confirm your copy completion.

NDS and Bindery Update
Once the file copying is complete, the NetWare v4.0 install routine will display the following message:

```
Examining network for a Directory Services server.
```

After careful analysis, the system will respond with the Install Directory Services screen. If this server is part of an existing Directory tree, highlight the tree name and press Enter. If this server is the first NetWare v4.0 server, it will act as the NDS master server. Highlight Yes (this is the first Directory server) and press Enter. The NDS installation consists of three steps: directory name, time configuration, and object context. Refer to installation Stage 4 for a complete explanation of NDS installation. Press F10 to save the Directory information.

The system now checks for NetWare v3.1x bindery conflicts and upgrades existing volumes. All bindery object IDs will be upgraded to appropriate NDS leaf objects. If there are any naming conflicts during this procedure, the system will prompt you to Rename the bindery object. Press Enter to continue.

Startup Files
The final step in the NetWare v3.1x to v4.0 upgrade is modification of the AUTO-EXEC.NCF startup file. The system will display the following message:

```
The AUTOEXEC.NCF file will be scanned to verify that the
Ethernet 802.2 frame support is loaded for Ethernet LAN
drivers.
```

NetWare v4.0 default FRAME type for Ethernet drivers is 802.2—as opposed to Ethernet 802.3 in all previous versions. This is unfortunate. Ethernet 802.2 drivers cannot communicate with NetWare v3.x or v2.x servers. If you have a mix of NetWare servers in your LAN, add the **FRAME=Ethernet_802.3** parameter to the LAN driver load command. If your LAN consists of only NetWare v4.0 servers, allow the system to change the FRAME type to 802.2. Press Enter to continue. The two AUTOEXEC.NCF files appear side by side. Other system changes include time synchronization parameters, NDS context, and IPX binding. Press F10 to save the new file and continue. The following message appears:

```
The NetWare server installation is complete.
```

Congratulations! You have successfully installed a NetWare v4.0 file server. Now it is time to hand the reins over to the Network Manager. You have done a wonderful job.

Last night I dreamed I ate a ten-pound marshmallow, and when I woke up the pillow was gone.

—Tommy Cooper

Be prepared to be *amazed!* The next part of this book will open a whole new world of network directory structures, system configurations, users, groups, security, GUI management, and NetWare flexibility features. The analysis, design, and installation are behind us; this is where the fun starts.

Part IV

Building NetWare LANs: Network Management

A network manager is open, sensitive, and understanding, regardless of his true feelings.

Now we're cooking! The first two stages of building a NetWare LAN were packed with questions, answers, knowledge, intrigue, mystery, decisions, and shopping. Here is where the fun begins. Network management is the adventure of building NetWare LANs. The lucky network manager gets to create users, establish security, define utilities, corral printing, and shoot troubles. Fasten your seat belt; it's going to be a wild ride.

The network analyst has developed a combination of system needs and prioritized them into a requirements report. The network designer and integrator have explored the available resources and integrated the system requirements into a synergy LAN plan. The network installation team has spent lots of money and fused the network components into a functional skeleton. . . . Now it's your turn!

Adventure is the champagne of life.

—G. K. Chesterton

As the network manager, it is your responsibility to take this unsophisticated network foundation and develop a thriving, dynamic NetWare LAN. It is your system to configure, manage, maintain, and troubleshoot. In addition, it is your responsibility to work in conjunction with other network managers to expand this LAN into the realm of interconnectivity—*if you build it, they will come.*

The network manager's role is probably the most excruciating and the most rewarding! The other players will move on to other systems, other designs, new frontiers, but you will stay and finish the castle. The network manager is the ruler of his or her own home: mapping out the boundaries of the building, filling it with furniture, hiring a staff, and laying down the laws. This is a huge responsibility, and the network manager must be willing and prepared to accept the scepter. The success or failure of network management hinges on three characteristics: network knowledge, management skills, and fire containment. The network manager must fully understand the intricacies of his or her LAN and be in touch with networking upgrades, enhancements, and technical improvements. In addition, the network manager must be sensitive to user issues and concerns, open to alternative configurations, and continually in touch with the evolving relationships among users, groups, applications, and security. Finally, the network manager must develop precautionary guidelines for network crashes and create an effective procedure for calmly and rationally dealing with everyday system brush fires.

If you dedicate a small amount of your daily time to developing these network management skills, your reign as King or Queen will be a long and fulfilling one.

Chapter 11

Network Directory Structure

**"No wonder we're lost, you're holding the
Drive Map upside down!"**

The next five chapters explore the roles and responsibilities of the network manager. Our goal is to complete your foundation of NetWare expertise, building on what you have already learned: LAN fundamentals, NetWare support products, systems analysis, design, and installation. Once your reading of these chapters is completed, this knowledge base will serve you well in designing, installing, and managing NetWare LANs. If you learn one thing from this book, learn that work can be fun and that the key to success is imagination, intuition, and a big heart.

You can't depend on your judgment when your imagination is out of focus.

—John F. Kennedy

All right now. You have inherited a LAN from the network analyst, designer, integrator, and installation team. Conceivably, you have been left with a working file server, interconnected workstations, NetWare OS, and a variety of off-the-shelf network applications. The second assumption is that it all works: The file server boots and the workstations connect. If so, the other players have completed their assignments; the rest is up to you.

As the king or queen of your new inherited castle, the first thing you want to do is define its functional boundaries: directory structure. The concept of directory structure exists on two different levels—above the server and within the server. *Above the server* is NetWare Directory Services (NDS) and NetWare v4.0. The purpose of NDS is to organize the logical objects of your network—the responsibilities, departments, locations, and job functions. The physical objects, like servers and printers, are at the lowest layer of the NDS tree.

The second level of directory structure exists *within the server.* The server is the highest layer of organization for data—volumes, directories, subdirectories, and files. NetWare v4.0, v3.11, and v2.2 are nearly identical once we get inside the file server. NetWare's internal disk is an empty frontier, waiting for organization and structure.

When the NetWare server is first created, there are standard configurations that exist by default. In NetWare v4.0, the NDS tree contains only the objects that were defined during the installation process. In our case that is the NORTH_WING organization and the KITCHEN organizational unit. Also, within the KITCHEN container are three physical objects: NIRVANA server, NIRVANA_SYS volume, and Admin user. Within the server, NetWare v4.0 creates four system directories: SYSTEM, PUBLIC, LOGIN, and MAIL. NetWare v3.11 and v2.2 also create these default directories. In addition, they also define two users—Supervisor and Guest—and one group—Everyone. Both Admin in NetWare v4.0 and Supervisor in NetWare v3.11 and v2.2 are granted all rights to the directory structure. The only difference is that you can delete Admin and not the Supervisor.

This chapter explores our new NetWare frontier from the top (NDS) to bottom (files). We will establish a clear, efficient directory structure and install drive mappings, network applications, and preliminary security. Let's start by logging in.

In NetWare v4.0, the default Supervisor user is replaced with Admin, and the password is defined in the NDS installation procedure. Also, there is no Guest or Everyone group. The directories remain the same.

Logging In

Before we can get too excited about creating the network directory structure, we must first log into the LAN. To log in to a NetWare server we must first attach to it. Assuming the workstation software has been loaded correctly, this can be a relatively simple step: Load the shells and switch to the first network drive. In most non-ODI LANs (NetWare v3.11 and v2.2) these steps consist of the following lines at the DOS prompt:

```
CD\NET
IPX          : the IPX.COM file for NIC communications
NETx         : the DOS redirector for LAN requests
F:           : the first network drive
```

Attaching to ODI LANs (NetWare v4.0) can be a little more complicated. The NetWare v4.0 Requester consists of two primary parts: ODI and VLM (virtual loadable module). The ODI components establish the network connection and initialize the workstation NIC. The VLM components direct LAN traffic between NetWare and the local environment: DOS, Windows, or OS/2. ODI connections are usually made with the following steps:

```
CD\NWCLIENT
LSL          : the Link Support Layer driver
NE2000       : the ODI NIC driver
IPXODI       : the ODI IPX for NIC communications
VLM          : the redirector for LAN requests, it
               consists of many different files including
               NETx.VLM, BIND.VLM, IPXNCP.VLM, NDS.VLM, and
               REDIR.VLM
D: or F:     : the first network drive
```

The NetWare v4.0 Requester is driven by virtual loadable modules. The following VLMs load automatically when the VLM.EXE file is invoked:

Required	*Optional*
CONN	**PRINT**
IPX NCP	**NETX**
TRAN	**RSA**
SECURITY	**AUTO**
NDS	**NMR**
BIND	
NWP	
FIO	
GENERAL	
REDIR	

NetWare v2.2 and v3.11

The process of logging in is simple in NetWare v3.11 and v2.2: Users log in to one server. The user's security, applications, and utilities are all controlled from that one server. Users may attach to up to seven other servers, but they can only log in to one. The command to log in to these servers is

```
LOGIN servername/username
```

For example, in our case the command is

```
LOGIN NIRVANA/Supervisor
```

Initially the Supervisor has no password, so you can log in without any difficulty. Once you are logged in, immediately create a Supervisor password using the SYSCON menu utility. Be careful in your choice of a Supervisor password; unwanted Supervisors can literally destroy NetWare LANs. On the other hand, if you forget the Supervisor password, you will be in even more trouble.

NetWare v4.0

Logging into a NetWare v4.0 LAN is a little more challenging. In these systems we don't log in to the server, we log in to the NETWORK. There is one login for all servers in the NDS tree. Security, applications, and utilities are controlled at all levels throughout the structure, not just the server. This has many advantages. The only requirement is that you know the organization that contains your user object. In our example, the Admin user is contained within the NORTH_WING organization. To log in to the CASTLE NDS, we would type the following at the first network drive:

```
LOGIN.CN=ADMIN.O=NORTH_WING
```

The Admin password was defined during the NDS section of the server installation. Input the password and press Enter. If the NDS tree can't find your user object in the defined context, you can move to the organization level with the CX (Change conteXt) command:

```
CX.O=NORTH_WING
LOGIN ADMIN
```

NetWare v4.0 supports two methods of object naming: typeful and typeless. Typeful naming requires specification of the object type, for example:

```
.CN=NIRVANA. OU=KITCHEN .O=NORTH_WING
```

Typeless naming is a shortcut method that assumes the leftmost object is the CN, the rightmost object is the ORGANIZATION, and everything in between is an OU, for example:

```
.NIRVANA.KITCHEN.NORTH_WING
```

In both cases, the leading period tells the system to start at the root. If you drop the leading period, the system will assume your naming scheme is starting from your current context. In addition, trailing periods instruct the system to start one, two, or three levels up.

Once you have successfully logged in to the network as Admin, you will find a relatively empty NDS tree. The following section describes how to use NetWare v4.0 utilities to complete the NDS structure.

The NDS Structure

Your new NDS tree contains only the objects you defined during the NetWare v4.0 server installation. Figure 11.1 shows a graphic example of the current CASTLE NDS tree. The first step in creating the structure is to complete our initial NDS design by adding container and leaf objects to the empty tree. The container objects define organizational structure, whereas the leaf objects do all of the work. In our CASTLE tree we will add a few more ORGANIZATIONs—three more wings—and fill them with ORGANIZATIONAL UNITS—rooms. The leaf objects will bring life to the rooms as people, furniture, appliances, and volumes. To complete the NDS structure, we will use the NWADMIN (GUI) or NETADMIN (text) utilities. In this example, we will focus on the Windows-based NWADMIN utility.

Figure 11.1 shows an example of the default objects in our CASTLE tree—NORTH_WING, KITCHEN, NIRVANA, NIRVANA_SYS, and Admin. In NWADMIN the different object classes are distinguished as unique icons. To begin creating this structure, follow these steps:

1. Move to the [Root] context and insert our three new ORGANIZATIONS. Click on Set Context from the View menu. Type **[Root]** exactly as shown in the figure, including the brackets. Then click OK. The [Root] is the highest level of the NDS tree and it is represented by an icon of the earth (cute!?!).

FIGURE 11.1 Beginning the CASTLE Tree Structure

2. To add a new organization, choose Create from the Object menu. The New Object menu will appear with three object classes: Alias, Country, and Organization. Choose Organization and click OK.

3. The Create Organization screen will appear with an Organization Name box. Type **WEST_WING** and click Create. The WEST_WING organization is alphabetically inserted in the list below [Root].

4. Repeat the previous steps to insert SOUTH_WING and EAST_WING.

The next step is to create ORGANIZATIONAL UNITS (OU) below the appropriate organizations. Unfortunately, OU wasn't a choice in the Object-Create menu. That is because our current context is [Root]. To create an OU we must move to a specific ORGANIZATION. Move to O=NORTH_WING. Hint: Try View-Set Context.

Notice that the NDS tree changes and KITCHEN and Admin appear again. This graphical screen is called the *Browser.* Now try Object-Create. The object list is much larger. As a matter of fact, this list of 14 objects represents the remainder of the 17 different NDS objects. See Figure 11.2 for an illustration of these 14 remaining NDS objects. Create an OU called **LIVING_ROOM**.

Now we would like to add a group called **Family** to the LIVING_ROOM; sounds appropriate, right? Simply highlight the LIVING_ROOM OU and use Object-Create to insert a family. Pretty easy!

Now to practice your newfound skills, try to create an NDS tree identical to the one shown in Figure 11.2. Be careful to ensure you're at the correct level when you create objects.

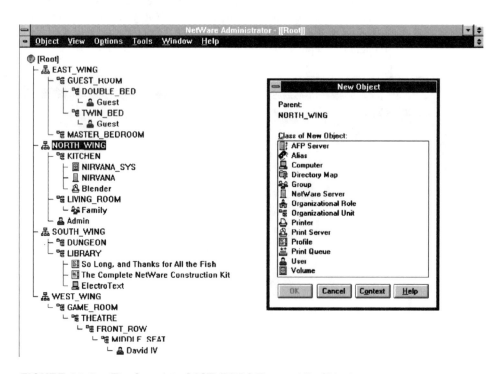

FIGURE 11.2   The Complete CASTLE NDS Tree and Its Objects

One very interesting thing to notice about the CASTLE tree is the use of identical object names. Notice that GUEST_ROOM OU has two different BEDS each with a user named Guest in it. This is possible in NetWare v4.0 because the NDS tree treats each object as an extension of its context. So the first Guest is actually CN=GUEST.OU=DOUBLE_BED.OU=GUEST_ROOM.O=EAST_WING. This is not possible in previous versions of NetWare.

Network Directory Structures Within the Server

Now that we have organized our NDS tree, we can concentrate on how data is organized within a server. NetWare v4.0 behaves much more like NetWare v3.11 and v2.2 once we get inside the server. I will point out the differences as we go along.

Once you have successfully logged into the network as Supervisor or Admin, you will notice a relatively empty disk; it contains only fundamental NetWare OS files and utilities. The NetWare disk is organized into a DOS-like *directory structure*. Figure 11.3 illustrates a typical NetWare directory structure, with volumes organized into directories, directories into subdirectories, and subdirectories into files.

The NetWare *directory path* is the route through the directory structure that points to a specific file. In order to identify a specific directory or disk location, NetWare has adopted a specialized directory naming scheme called *directory name*. Following is an example of the directory name convention:

FILE SERVER/VOLUME:DIRECTORY\SUBDIRECTORY\FILENAME

As the network manager, you will create a directory structure using a combination of three components:

- *System directories* are created during the NetWare installation procedure and include NetWare OS files, Supervisor utilities, login parameters, and user-specific ID configurations.
- *User directories* define a private area for user files and shared workgroup data. The user directory gives users a place to feel comfortable and secure.
- *Application/data directories* are a complex organization of private, shared, and workgroup files. There are a million different strategies for organizing application/data directories; I will share the most successful ones with you.

Keep in mind that the work you complete in this chapter is subject to personal imagination. There is no one right answer; feel free to add your own unique signature whenever appropriate. Let's begin with system directories.

System Directories

System directories contain and control operating system files. NetWare supports two types of system directories: NetWare and workstation operating system (WOS). NetWare system directories are created by NetWare and should not be changed. They are required for the smooth operation of the LAN. WOS system directories support the peaceful coexistence between NetWare and the many different workstation operating systems.

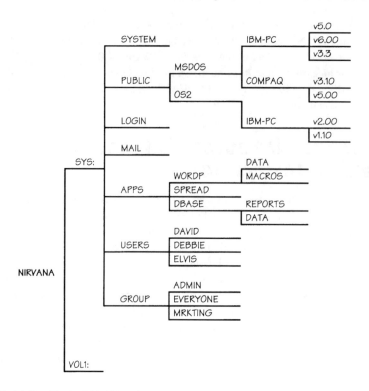

FIGURE 11.3   Typical NetWare Directory Structure

NetWare System Directories

When you log in to the NetWare server as Supervisor, you will notice four default directories:

- SYSTEM. This directory contains the NetWare Operating System and its associated databases, including the BINDERY in NetWare v3.11 and v2.2. Also included are LAN drivers, disk drivers, NLMs, and Supervisor utilities.

- PUBLIC. This directory contains the NetWare public utilities. These utilities provide user management for printing, files, user information, group information, and directory options.

- LOGIN. This directory is the front porch of our NetWare LAN—the place where users hang out before they are allowed in the door. The LOGIN directory contains critical login programs and utilities. Users in limbo (not logged in) can only access programs from the LOGIN directory; the rest of the structure is invisible. Login programs include LOGIN, SLIST, and NLIST (NetWare v4.0).

- MAIL. This directory contains each user's mail box. The subdirectories under MAIL correspond to each user's ID number and contain login scripts, mail, and print job configuration files. The Supervisor has the unique distinction of SYS:MAIL\1. To view other users' ID numbers, choose Other Information from the SYSCON User Information screen.

In addition, NetWare v3.11 includes ETC as a system-created directory for internetworking protocol services support. NetWare v4.0 adds ETC, DOC, WINDOWS, and CBT.

NetWare automatically creates these system-generated directories during the installation phase. (See coverage of how to copy SYSTEM and PUBLIC files in Chapters 8, 9, and 10.) They provide specific system functions to the LAN; don't delete them. In addition to the default NetWare structure, I recommend a functional WOS structure.

WOS System Directories

NetWare peacefully coexists with another type of operating system: WOS. The workstation operating system controls local workstation processing and connections to NetWare utilities. NetWare supports a huge variety of different WOS types and versions—DOS, OS/2, UNIX, System 7, and Windows NT. All of these diverse OSs share one common thread—the command processor. The WOS command processor controls all facets of local and network processing. For DOS the command processor file is COMMAND.COM. This critical WOS file resides in workstation RAM and communicates with NetWare shells or the NetWare Requester. NetWare needs to know where to find the WOS command processor in case it gets kicked out of workstation RAM.

If many assorted workstations are using different types and versions of WOS, we must have a way of showing NetWare where to find each specific command processor. Fortunately, the many WOSs share three distinct characteristics:

- OS describes the particular operating system—DOS, for example.
- MACHINE defines its default machine type—COMPAQ, for example.
- OS_VERSION establishes the current version of OS each workstation is using—v5.00, for example.

These three properties correspond to Login Script Identifiers in NetWare's management facility. For more details about the identifiers, refer to the System Login Script in Chapter 12.

The best way to handle this problem is to create subdirectories under PUBLIC that correspond to each of these Login Script Identifiers. That way the system can determine which WOS the user needs and where to find it. Figure 11.3 shows a sample directory structure under PUBLIC where MSDOS and OS2 are OS, IBM-PC and COMPAQ are MACHINE, and v3.3, v5.0, v3.10, v5.00, v6.00, v2.00, and v1.10 represent the OS_VERSION. The next step is to copy the appropriate command processor to each of the seven version subdirectories—COMMAND.COM, for example. Then we must set up a system-wide search drive mapping so NetWare can find the appropriate COMMAND.COM. This concept is covered later in the chapter. In the final step, we will insert a COMSPEC command in the System Login Script to point NetWare in the right direction. This trick will be illustrated in Chapter 12.

Pay attention to how NetWare configurations are assigned. User-specific configurations migrate across multiple workstation platforms. Machine-specific configurations apply to multiple users. A good rule of thumb is to set up application/environment configurations (color, macros, defaults, and so on) to be user-specific and to set up hardware/OS configurations to be machine-specific. WOS system directories should be machine-specific.

User Directories

The next goal for our castle is to create a place where each of the guests can feel comfortable and at home. You should outline each user's property, then build a private place where he or she can store valuable files. USER directories are a critical aspect of NetWare storage and security. The storage aspect of user directories refers to NetWare's ability to limit user disk space. The network manager can create subdirectories for each user and then monitor disk usage. Also, this branch provides users with an independent directory structure in which they can copy, delete, configure, and modify personal files. Windows, for example, uses the user directory for user-specific configurations.

The security aspect of user directories refers to NetWare's ability to limit user access to particular directories. User directories can be limited to appropriate users and workgroup managers. User directories provide a level of LAN customization without increasing the system's overall complexity. Users are responsible for their own subdirectories. The user directory structure should reside under the USERS umbrella.

In addition, it is a good idea to create subdirectories for each network group. Groups are fundamentally important, because they add a level of LAN connectivity and togetherness. Users who share functionally similar tasks are organized into groups, and these groups can share specific areas of the server disk. NetWare groups can have specific subdirectories with unique security under the umbrella directory of GROUPS. Group directories abide by the same guidelines as user directories and should also be continually monitored by the network manager.

Application/Data Directories

The final organizational structure for our NetWare disk is application/data directory structure. The directories in this structure represent organizational locations for network applications and shared network data. The guidelines for creating application/data directories are a little more complex than other boundaries, because they involve the specialized requirements of many different systems.

Network applications are generally well behaved, but sometimes you can run an application that is NetWare-unaware—these applications should be avoided at all costs. Chapter 6 gives a detailed discussion of the most well-behaved network applications. A good rule of thumb for generating application directories is to build them as specific subdirectories under the directory umbrella APPS. Each application's unique directory requirements can be satisfied through independent subdirectory structures without cluttering up the overall directory design. Here are a few guidelines for installing network applications:

- Specify the appropriate application directory name when you run the program's installation procedure.
- Install network versions of application software. Nonnetwork applications respond unfavorably to NetWare drives, attributes, shared access, and security.
- Provide additional user setup directories where unique user configurations can be stored. A good place for this is as an APPSETUP subdirectory under each user directory. This is a good example of user-specific configurations.
- Pay close attention to subdirectory security—trustee assignments, directory rights, file attributes, and so on. Most network applications are extremely sensitive to illogical subdirectory security.

■ Be thorough in configuring the network menu system—make sure to specify the correct application's directory. Some programs have to run in their specific subdirectory, whereas others require search mappings and user defaults.

Another important key to successful network applications is data directories. *Data directories* define storage parameters for documents, templates, macros, indexes, and reporting structures. There are basically three different types of data files: global, group, and private.

Global Files

Global files are files shared by all network users. Access to these files is either one-at-a-time or shared simultaneously; it is controlled by the specific network application. These globally shared files should be stored in a DATA subdirectory under each application directory. Trustee security should specify RF at the application level and RFCW at the data level. (See User Lab IV and Chapter 12 for more about security levels.)

Group Files

Group files are shared by functionally specific groups. Group files are accessed as needed from the specific GROUP subdirectory. All data files, regardless of application, should be stored in specific group directories to ensure trustee compatibility.

Private Files

Private files contain information that users want to keep to themselves. This type of data is typically personal (love letters) or confidential (James Bond stuff). It is a good idea to place these files in an APPDATA subdirectory under USERS/*username*. Trustee assignments keep everybody away from private directories; in fact, users don't even see other users' private directories. Encourage users to share information through global or group directories; private directories should be reserved for individual users only.

Once you have created the application directory structure, installed network applications, and assigned data directories, you should take a long, hard look at system security. Who gets access to what is a complex issue that requires a great deal of thought, time, and organization. This topic is covered in detail in the next chapter. Before we can establish system security, though, we must redefine the network boundaries with drive mappings.

∭ Drive Mappings

As you create the various system, user, application, and data boundaries, you are also creating isolated islands of technology. Each functional directory you create is physically isolated from the others, as if you were building large walls around each home—walls so high that nobody could climb over them.

Fortunately, NetWare has a vehicle for breaking down these walls and establishing communications among all the different homes and all the various towns. This magical link comes in two flavors: roads and telephone lines. The roads facilitate movement from house to house, but they aren't very fast and you can only travel one road at a time. Telephone lines, on the other hand, enable you to instantaneously attach to any room in the castle, with considerably less effort.

NetWare uses drive mappings to create transparent links among system, user, application, and data directories. NetWare provides two methods for drive mapping: network and search. *Network drive mappings* are the roads that facilitate movement from subdirectory to subdirectory across the LAN. *Search drive mappings* are the telephone lines that provide instantaneous access to a wide range of subdirectories all at once.

Network Drive Mappings

Network drive mappings represent specific NetWare directories as logical drives. Each logical drive is assigned a drive letter starting with F: up to Z:. Drive mappings are not physical. They simply provide the flexibility to represent long, complex directory names as single drive letters. For example, logical drive letter U: can be mapped to Mary's home directory:

```
MAP U: = NIRVANA/SYS:USERS\MARY
```

From now on, whenever you type **U:** and press Enter, the system will jump to Mary's home directory. Keep in mind that network drive mappings serve one function—directory movement. They do not provide any other feature; simply stated, they are a convenience.

Search Drive Mappings

It is important to reiterate that all you can do with a network drive mapping is move around. You can't search for application program files. Search drive mappings take the logical drive concept one step further: they enable you to create network drive mappings that search for program files—executable files (WP.EXE), system configuration files (COMMAND.COM), or application setup files (WP{DJC}.SET). The search drive mappings are telephone lines that connect multiple NetWare directories, except that these lines don't have voice mail.

Search drive mappings are handled a little differently than are network mappings. Search drives create an exploration list that NetWare follows to access application files. The assignment of search drives is a two-part process. In the first part, you prioritize directories and create an exploration list. In the second part, NetWare takes your list and assigns drive letters in reverse order starting from Z:. This is done to differentiate the search drives from network assignments, and to make sure they don't overlap. NetWare supports up to 16 simultaneous search drives out of the 26 total drive mappings.

For example, I would like to assign three directories to an exploration list: PUBLIC, APPS/WP, and APPS/DBASE. I distinguish the search mappings by using the letter S, and prioritize the directories by assigning them incremental numbers, 1, 2, and 3:

```
MAP S1: = NIRVANA/SYS:PUBLIC          Z:
MAP S2: = NIRVANA/SYS:APPS\WP         Y:
MAP S3: = NIRVANA/SYS:APPS\DBASE      X:
```

In the second part, the system will assign the letters Z:, Y:, and X: to my exploration list. The advantage of this setup is that no matter where I am, I can access any application file in any of these directories. For example, I would like to access the NETADMIN utility from PUBLIC. Unfortunately, my current directory is USERS\DAVID. If I type **NETAD-MIN** and press Enter, the system will first search the current directory, USERS/DAVID. Next, the system will look to the exploration list for a path of directory names. Once it finds the directory that contains NETADMIN, it will execute the application.

One important point arises in using NetWare drive mapping: Do not use the CD command to change directories once they've been mapped. Changing mapped directories with the CD command reassigns the mapping. This is especially serious for search drive mappings. If you must use the CD command to navigate the LAN, create a JUNK network mapping that can be reassigned without causing too much harm.

NetWare also provides some specialized mapping commands. Three of these commands are particularly useful: INSERT, NEXT, and ROOT.

MAP INSERT
The Insert option retains the internal DOS path. MAP INSERT S1: assigns all new search drive mappings to the first priority: S1. Also, the command MAP S16 will place the search drive at the end of the exploration list. This method is especially useful when you cannot remember the last priority number.

MAP NEXT
The Next option assigns a new network drive mapping to the next available letter.

MAP ROOT
The Root option creates a false root at the specified directory. Users can move forward in the directory structure but not back past the root. This is particularly useful when security is vital or applications require root installation.

Network and search drive mappings are stored in workstation RAM. This means they are machine-specific and temporary. Drive mappings are lost when the workstation is logged out or power fails and RAM is erased. Login scripts provide a simple method to ensure that you won't have to re-create your mappings every day.

Assigning Drive Mappings in Login Scripts
The *login script* is a list of commands that automatically loads every time you log in. NetWare uses the login script to load temporary system configurations, including drive mappings, informational messages, logic, WOS commands, and menu parameters. There are two main NetWare login scripts: SYSTEM and USER.

SYSTEM Login Script
The SYSTEM login script is automatically loaded for every user when he or she logs in. This script loads before the USER login script and contains special system configuration information. It is a good idea to include system-wide drive mappings in the SYSTEM login script:

```
Network Drives
MAP F:= NIRVANA/SYS:LOGIN
```

```
MAP G:= NIRVANA/SYS:GROUP
MAP U:= NIRVANA/SYS:USERS\%LOGIN_NAME

Search Drives
MAP S1:= NIRVANA/SYS:PUBLIC
MAP S2:= NIRVANA/SYS:PUBLIC\%OS\%MACHINE\%OS_VERSION
MAP S3:= NIRVANA/SYS:APPS\WINDOWS
MAP S4:= NIRVANA/SYS:APPS\WP
```

USER Login Scripts

The USER login script is loaded for individual users after the SYSTEM login script. This script contains user-specific configurations. Be careful not to cancel out the drive mappings that were established in the SYSTEM login script. With this in mind, we will use the MAP S16 command. It is a good idea to include user-specific drive mappings in the USER login script:

```
Network Drives
MAP NEXT = NIRVANA/SYS:USERS\DAVID\STUFF
MAP NEXT = NIRVANA/SYS:GROUP\ADMIN

Search Drives
MAP S16:= NIRVANA/SYS:USERS\DAVID\WPSETUP
MAP S16:= NIRVANA/SYS:UTILS\ADMIN
```

My advice is to steer clear of USER login scripts; they are too difficult to maintain. Accomplish as many mappings as you can in the SYSTEM login script. We will discuss login scripts in detail in the next chapter.

Let me add one last caveat concerning network directory structures: Document them! Everything you do as a network manager should be written in the *NetWare Log*. Every change, no matter how small, is important enough to be detailed in the log. Probably one of the most important items in the log is a detailed diagram of the network directory structure; all the directories, subdirectories, and drive mappings should be outlined and illustrated. These documents will probably save you about two trillion hours of pain and suffering in the future, believe me. Refer to Chapter 15 for a detailed discussion of network documentation.

For people who like peace and quiet: a phoneless cord.

—Anonymous

That completes our network directory structure design. We have filled in the NDS tree, established additional network objects, created WOS, user, and application/data directories, and provided access to these directories through network and search drive mappings. The next step in the realm of network management is SYSTEM CONFIGURATIONS. In the next chapter, we will establish global configurations both for the NDS tree and within the NetWare server. These configurations include access control lists, account restrictions, and the system login script. In Chapter 13, we will expand these configurations to include user and group-specific parameters. Ready, set, go!

Chapter 12

System Configuration

**"For configuring the tightest system security, the
David James Clarke IV award goes to . . ."**

N ow that you have established a network directory structure and installed an internal mapping system, you are well on your way to creating a vital, energetic LAN. The next step is to evaluate the LAN's system configurations and optimize the balance of user transparency and network performance. At this point, you should probably schedule one last meeting with the network designer to make sure you fully understand the balance of people and performance—essential components of system synergy.

So far, the LAN has been relatively quiet—this will change. The daily bustle of humming workstations and crazed users can quickly take its toll on an unorganized NetWare LAN. That's why it's preferable to establish preliminary system configurations while the LAN is still quiet. Initial system parameters such as account restrictions, login scripts, and system security can make or break your Kingdom. It is imperative for you to optimize these parameters *before* the network goes into hyperactivity—configuring an active system is like tuning a moving car.

Note: Many of the configuration activities in this chapter require the use of a mouse. These tasks are described with mouse actions such as the *click* and *double-click*.

The first step is to prioritize system configurations into some optimal combination. The best way to get a handle on the optimal balance is to ask a lot of questions:

1. How secure must the network be?
2. Should users be forced to change their passwords?
3. Should I set a minimum password length?
4. Are there specific times of the day at which I don't want specific users to log in?
5. Do I want to grant additional privilege to "advanced" users?
6. Do I need help?
7. Should I activate intruder detection lockout?
8. How many concurrent logins should my users be allowed?
9. Which directories should I hide?
10. Which files should I hide?
11. Do I want to install NetWare accounting?
12. How much should I charge?
13. Do I trust my users?
14. Should I restrict users to specific workstations?
15. How complex do I want the system drive mappings to be?
16. How many search drive mappings do we really need?
17. Do I trust the network applications to execute relatively buglessly?
18. Should I limit certain users' disk space?
19. How much disk space should I allow users?
20. Should I fire phasers?

So, balancing system configurations raises the ultimate 20 questions. Once you have answered all of them, you can retire. Believe me, it will never happen. NetWare LANs are constantly evolving. Don't strive for all the answers—compromise. This chapter discusses the three main components of system configuration: access control, login scripts, and system security. Our discussion focuses on the configuration concepts as they pertain to NetWare v2.2, v3.11, and v4.0. Fortunately, the conceptual differences among these three operating systems are minor. We will explore NetWare v2.2, v3.11, and v4.0 system configurations through the NetWare configuration tools SYSCON, NWADMIN, and NETADMIN. Although the concepts are quite similar, these tools differ dramatically in how they implement system configurations.

It is imperative for you to give this chapter your primary attention. NetWare's system configuration options can do wonders in decreasing a system manager's stress level. The configurations we will explore in this chapter are global parameters that affect the entire network. Understand that well-designed system configurations can dramatically reduce the need for user-specific parameters, thereby saving hours of user-specific setup and centralizing configuration maintenance.

Access Control

Access control refers to the critical and dangerous configurations that reside at the heart of the NetWare LAN. Typically, these components are absolutely off limits to everybody except the Supervisor. Access control is important because it sets the default restrictions for user-specific network access. Modifications made here will affect all the user records that are created from this point on. It is a good idea to concentrate on system configuration defaults before you create any users. Access control falls into four categories: NDS restrictions, default account balance/restrictions, default time restrictions, and intruder detection/lockout. Let's take a closer look.

NDS Restrictions

Default access to the NDS tree is limited to the ADMIN object. No other user objects exist. Once user objects are created, they will assume default restrictions from their closest home container. *Container configurations* are implemented during the creation of ORGANIZATIONs or ORGANIZATIONAL UNITS. At the point of creation, system managers can define a user template for each container object. Once this default container configuration has been created, all users created within that container will assume the configurations of the container user template. If the user template is undefined in a user's direct home container, he or she will assume the default restrictions of the home container's parent. The system continues to search up the NDS tree until it finds a user template that has been defined. Default NDS restrictions are defined through the NWADMIN and NETADMIN configuration tools.

Beyond the default restrictions, all new objects assume the NDS configurations of the [Public] object. [Public] is granted browse rights to the [Root] of the NDS tree and no access restrictions. This means that any new user can see the whole tree but not necessarily access any resources. Figure 12.1 shows [Public] and ADMIN as trustees of the [Root] object. NetWare v4.0's NDS restrictions are implemented differently from those in NetWare v3.11 and v2.2, but the default configurations themselves are identical: account balance/restrictions, time restrictions, and intruder detection/lockout. We will examine these three critical access control configurations in this section.

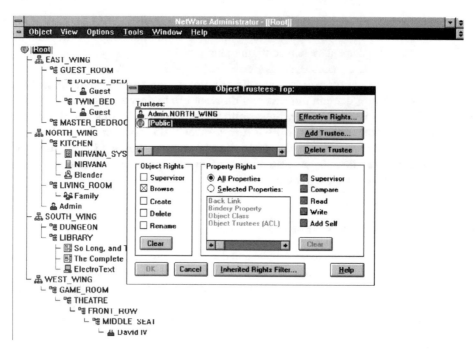

FIGURE 12.1   Trustees of the [Root] Object

Rights granted to [Public] can be inherited by users even if they are not logged in! A network connection is all that is required. This fact raises some very interesting security paradoxes.

Default Account Balance/Restrictions

The standard default account balance/restrictions provide default parameters for critical access control configurations. Default account balance/restrictions options perform three functions: password restrictions, setting the default accounting balance and credit limit for NetWare accounting, and setting up general default account restrictions for each of the NetWare users. We will illustrate default restrictions using SYSCON (NetWare v2.2 and v3.11) and NWADMIN (NetWare v4.0). Figure 12.2 illustrates the general restrictions in SYSCON, and Figure 12.3 shows password restrictions in NWADMIN. When a user's account is created, he or she adopts these default restrictions. A little early planning makes global user management a lot easier. Most of the options are self-explanatory, but a few justify some additional coverage here.

Limit Concurrent Connections

The Limit Concurrent Connections option tells the system to restrict the number of work-stations from which a user can simultaneously log in. This option is used to protect against user migration and workstation monopoly. It is a good idea to "limit" the concurrent connections made by most users—about three concurrent connections are enough.

```
SYSCON  7.02                          Monday  May 3, 1993  7:57 pm
                     User SUPERVISOR On File Server OMEGA
```

```
                  Default Account Balance/Restrictions
 Account Has Expiration Date:              No
    Date Account Expires:
 Limit Concurrent Connections:            Yes
    Maximum Connections:                  3
 Create Home Directory for User:          Yes
 Require Password:                        Yes
    Minimum Password Length:              5
 Force Periodic Password Changes:         Yes
    Days Between Forced Changes:          40
    Limit Grace Logins:                   Yes
       Grace Logins Allowed:              7
 Require Unique Passwords:                Yes
 Account Balance:                         10000
 Allow Unlimited Credit:                  No
    Low Balance Limit:                    100
```

FIGURE 12.2   General Restrictions in SYSCON

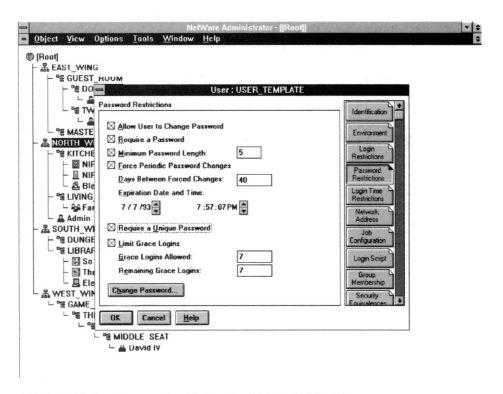

FIGURE 12.3   Password Restrictions Available in NWADMIN

Force Periodic Password Changes

The idea behind forcing users to revise their passwords is to create an additional level of access security. If users are forced to change their passwords every 40 days or so, the chances of unauthorized users getting into the system decrease tremendously. Usually it's a good idea to allow three to seven grace logins to give users time to come up with good replacements. In addition, it is a good idea to force users to come up with unique passwords each time.

Limit Disk Space

The Limit Disk Space option enables network managers to limit the amount of file server disk space specific users may use. This option should only be used as punishment in cases of network abuse. It goes against all of the concepts of network synergy to give people shared resources and then take them back.

 These default configuration options are integrated into one choice for NetWare v2.2 and v3.11 LANs: Account Balance/Restrictions. In NetWare v4.0, they are broken down into three choices: password restrictions, account balance, and login restrictions.

Additionally, here are a few more hints for default account balances/restrictions:

■ Leave Account Has Expiration Date set to "no."
■ Change Require Password to Yes and make the minimum password length around five characters.
■ Leave all the account balance options blank, unless you plan to use that feature. If you do use it, change Allow Unlimited Credit to No and put 100 as the Low Balance Limit. Be careful; users can easily spend their allotment and get locked out of the system.

Default Time Restrictions

This option is a good idea for sensitive networks and companies that employ late-night janitors. Many network managers have complained about "vulnerable" networks going down or being accessed after hours. Time restrictions add a level of sophistication and security to your network by limiting logins to only working hours. Any other time, the LAN is completely unaccessible, except to the Supervisor. Figure 12.4 illustrates the Default Time Restrictions menu in SYSCON. The * character indicates times when the system is accessible. If you are working and it approaches the cutoff time, the system will send you a warning message. Once the time period expires, NetWare will clear your workstation connection. Be careful when you create time restrictions; they can come back to haunt you.

Intruder Detection/Lockout

This system parameter allows for additional levels of access security. The concept is this: If an unauthorized user attempts to access the LAN with a stolen user login name, he or she should be limited in the number of times he or she can guess at that user's password. It makes sense, right? Detect intruders should always be set to Yes. Figure 12.5 illustrates the

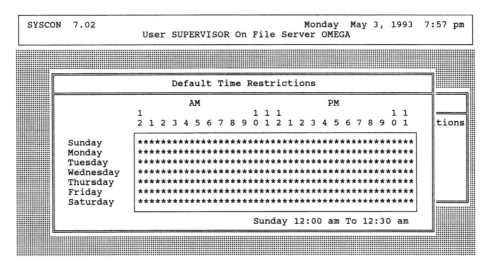

FIGURE 12.4   SYSCON's Default Time Restrictions Menu

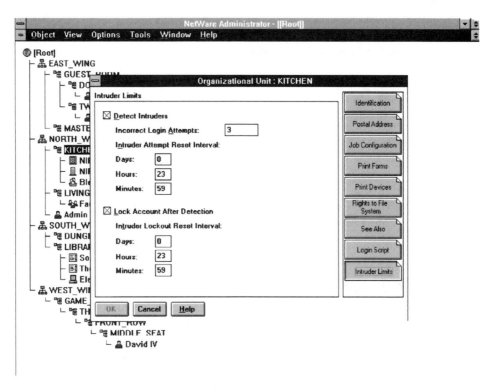

FIGURE 12.5   NWADMIN's Intruder Detection Screen

Intruder Detection screen in NWADMIN. The figure reveals two important configurations that work together to increase system security: Intruder Attempt Reset Interval and Lock Account After Detection.

Intruder Attempt Reset Interval

The number of times an intruder should be allowed to guess any given password should not exceed three. Intruder Attempt Reset Interval simply addresses the issue, "How long am I going to wait until I reset the bad login attempts counter?" Anything less frequent than 24 hours is begging the intruder to guess, then wait, then guess some more. Within a day, the network manager should get word that an intruder has been attempting to access the system.

Lock Account After Detection

The whole purpose of detecting an intruder is to lock him or her out after three incorrect login attempts. In addition, the account lockout should remain in effect for at least 24 hours—for the same reasons outlined earlier. Note: Once an account has been locked out, the system notifies the Supervisor through the file server console and error log.

In NetWare v2.2 and v3.11, intruder detection applies to individual servers. This means that intruders can rotate through alternative servers and try new passwords during the previous servers time out. Intruder detection and lock-out takes on a new importance with NetWare v4.0. In NDS security, the intruder detection applies to one login for the entire network. Detection applies at the container level. This locks the intruder out of the entire LAN for the entire account lockout period.

Login Scripts

The login script is the first file server process executed after a user's "authenticity" is verified. It is a set of instructions that informs all users, workstations, and NDS objects of specific system configurations. It is a powerful tool. Login script messages are written to the screen or sent electronically in the form of drive mappings and environmental parameters. There are four login scripts: system, user, default, and profile (NetWare v4.0 only).

Login scripts are primarily made up of commands and identifiers. The commands tell the login script what to do, and the identifiers tell the script how to do the job. This section discusses the purpose of each of the four login scripts, then delves into login script commands and identifiers.

Login Script Execution

As mentioned earlier, there are four login scripts, each of which is executed in a different order and each of which serves a specific purpose. Let's start with the system login script because it is always executed first.

System Login Script

The system login script contains global system configurations and environmental parameters. In NetWare v2.2 and v3.11 there is only one system login script, and it is executed by all users. In NetWare v4.0, each container object has its own system login script and it is only executed by the objects within the specific container. The system login script is the mother of all scripts. It is the focal point for all script configurations and should be treated with a great deal of respect. Many clever network managers can consolidate all of their script configurations into one system login script. This strategy has many advantages, but the most obvious is the existence of one script and one central point of script maintenance.

Login scripts are simple text files that follow a specific command syntax. The system login script is the file NET$LOG.DAT in the SYS:PUBLIC subdirectory. The user login script is the file LOGIN in each specific user's SYS:MAIL\USER_ID directory, and the default login script is built into the LOGIN.EXE program file.

User Login Script

Next is the user login script. Once the system login script is executed, NetWare looks for a specific user login script. The user script contains user-specific configurations that couldn't be integrated into the system login script. It is a good idea to avoid user login scripts at all costs; they create a maintenance nightmare.

Default Login Script

If a user login script doesn't exist, the system will execute the default login script. The default script is built into the LOGIN.EXE file and therefore cannot be changed. The default login script contains the minimum configurations and drive mappings for users who don't have their own system or user script. A problem arises when the default login script commands overwrite the system script. This occurs when a system login script exists without any user scripts—ironically, this is the ideal circumstance.

Two strategies can help you to avoid using the default script when no user login script exists. The first is to fool the system into thinking a user script really exists. This can be accomplished by placing the REM command at the top of each user login script. On the downside, this strategy requires maintenance of individual user scripts. The second strategy is to skip the default script altogether. To accomplish this, use the EXIT command at the end of the system login script. On the downside, this strategy will skip the default, user, and profile scripts. This is fine if no other scripts exist—ironically, that is the ideal circumstance.

Profile Login Script

The profile login script offers further configuration customization in NetWare v4.0. It contains group-specific configurations for NDS objects that are associated with the profile. A profile object defines a group of users who share similar configurations—including login scripts. The profile script will execute after the system login script and before the user or default login script.

All of these different login scripts share the same set of commands and identifiers. Now that we understand their purpose and order of execution, let's take a look at how to build NetWare login scripts.

Login Script Commands and Identifiers

Table 12.1 lists NetWare's login script commands. These commands work in conjunction with special login script identifiers. Tables 12.2 and 12.3 list NetWare's login script identifiers.

We will discuss each of these commands and identifiers in their order of importance and appearance in most login scripts. Few login scripts use *all* of these commands, but I have seen each of them used at least once or twice. Let's start with a brief discussion of login script identifiers.

Login Script Identifiers

Login script commands rely on special NetWare variables called *identifiers*. Login script identifiers return valuable network information, including time, date, workstation machine, node address, and login name. Table 12.2 lists all of NetWare's login script identifiers. Note: Identifiers are used by all versions of NetWare unless otherwise noted.

Refer to page 318 of the NetWare v3.11 Installation Manual for a further discussion of login script identifier variables.

All of the previous login script identifiers are valid for NetWare v2.2, v3.11, and v4.0 networks. Table 12.3 lists the few identifiers that work only in v3.11 or v4.0 scripts.

TABLE 12.1   Login Script Commands

NetWare v2.2 Only	NetWare v4.0 Only
PASSWORD_EXPIRES	CLS
MACHINE_NAME	CX
	LASTLOGINTIME
	NO_DEFAULT
	SET, SET_TIME, and TEMP_SET

NetWare v2.2, v3.11, and v4.0	
ATTACH	GOTO
BREAK	IF...THEN...ELSE
COMSPEC	INCLUDE
DISPLAY and FDISPLAY	MACHINE
DOS BREAK	MAP
DOS SET	PAUSE
DOS VERIFY	PCCOMPATIBLE
DRIVE	REMARK
EXIT	SHIFT
# (DOS Executable)	WRITE
FIRE PHASERS	

TABLE 12.2 NetWare Login Script Identifiers

Date	Time
DAY—Day Number, 01-31	AM_PM—Day or Night
DAY_OF_WEEK—Sunday, and so on	GREETING_TIME—Morning, and so on
MONTH—Month Number, 01-12	HOUR—12-hour scale
MONTH_NAME—May, and so on	HOUR24—24-hour scale
NDAY_OF_WEEK—1 through 7	MINUTE—00 through 59
SHORT_YEAR—93, and so on	SECOND—00 through 59
YEAR—1993, and so on	

User	Workstation
FULL_NAME—complete name	MACHINE—type of computer
LOGIN_NAME—unique login name	OS—type of WOS, DOS
MEMBER OF "group"—conditional	OS_VERSION—version of WOS
USER_ID—unique user id number	P_STATION—NIC 12-digit node address
	SMACHINE—short machine name
	STATION—connection number

Miscellaneous	
FILE_SERVER—server name	ERROR_LEVEL—0=no error
NETWORK_ADDRESS—cabling	*% variable*—DOS variable

Let's take a closer look at how to implement NetWare login scripts by exploring some common and not-so-common system login script conventions.

Commonly Used Commands

Let's focus for the moment on the system login script. In an ideal world, this script should be your central point for system configurations. If you feel compelled to create other scripts, you can use the system login script as a guide.

The following login script commands should be used in all system login scripts. I call this my top 10 list of login script commands.

TABLE 12.3 Identifiers Specific to NetWare v3.11 or v4.0

NetWare v3.11 and v4.0	NetWare v4.0 Only
SHELL_TYPE—version of NETx	NOT MEMBER OF "group"
ACCESS_SERVER—conditional	DOS_REQUESTER—version of VLM
	NETWARE_REQUESTER—OS/2 only
	%n—item entered at LOGIN command line

1. WRITE	6. IF...THEN...ELSE
2. MAP	7. DRIVE H:
3. COMPSEC	8. EXIT
4. DOS	9. REM
5. NO_DEFAULT	10. LASTLOGINTIME

WRITE. The WRITE login script command is used to display system messages to users during the login procedure. WRITE is used in conjunction with almost any of the login script Identifiers and can become quite sophisticated and complex. The syntax for the WRITE command is as follows:

```
WRITE "text string";...identifiers...
```

For example, let's create a WRITE statement that greets the user with the GREET-ING_TIME and his or her specific FULL_NAME:

```
WRITE "Good ";GREETING_TIME;", ";FULL_NAME
```

The output for user "John Smith" would look like this:

```
Good Morning, John Smith
```

or

```
Good Afternoon, John Smith
```

WRITE statements can also be informational:

```
WRITE "Your Workstation Number is ";STATION
WRITE "Your Physical Station ID is ";P_STATION
WRITE "The Time is ";HOUR;" ";MINUTE;" ";SECOND;AM_PM
```

Unfortunately, the syntax of the WRITE command can drive you crazy very quickly. So Novell introduced a dramatic improvement—the % sign. By preceding the identifier with a % sign, it can be included *within* the quotes:

```
WRITE "Today is %DAY_OF_WEEK, %MONTH_NAME %DAY"
WRITE "You are using a(n) %MACHINE Computer"
WRITE "Your workstation is running %OS Version
%OS_VERSION."
```

Write   `"You better go catch it! \7"`—in this case the \7 will sound a bell

Drive Mappings. To review, network drive mappings represent specific NetWare subdi-rectories as *logical drives*. Each of these logical drives is designated as a letter from F: to Z:. Drive mappings are not physical; there is typically only one physical disk in each file server. Mappings simply give us the flexibility of representing long, complex network directory names as single drive LETTERS.

For example, you could map logical drive letter U: to Susan's home subdirectory with the following:

```
U: = NIRVANA/SYS:USERS\SUSAN
```

It is important to understand that all you can do with a network drive mapping is *move around*. You can't "search" anywhere for a program or setup file. Search drive mappings take the logical drive concept one step farther, and allow you to create network drive mappings that also search for program execution files (WP.EXE), system configuration files (COMMAND.COM), or application setup files (WP{DJC}.SET). The search drive mappings are like telephone lines that connect various network subdirectories and instantaneously tell you if somebody is home.

Search drive mappings are handled a little differently than are network drive mappings. With search drive mappings you "prioritize" the subdirectories and NetWare assigns the logical drive for you—starting from Z: and moving backward. This is done to differentiate the search drives from the network drives and to make sure they don't overlap. At any given time you can install up to 16 search drives.

For example, if the first search drive (S1) is mapped to the PUBLIC subdirectory, then

```
S1: = NIRVANA/SYS:PUBLIC
```

So, no matter where I am, I can access a file from the PUBLIC subdirectory. This search drive is given the logical drive letter Z:. The next search drive will be given the logical drive letter Y:, unless it has been assigned already as a network drive. In that case, the second search drive will be mapped to X:.

Network and search drive mappings are temporary situations. You can change them at any time and they go away when you log out or turn off your machine. A simple way to ensure that you will always have the drive mappings you want is to put them into a login script. Furthermore, you should be able to fit all the system's drive mappings into the SYSTEM login script. Here's how:

******* Network Drive Mappings *******
MAP *1:=NIRVANA/SYS:LOGIN—assigns the first available network drive
MAP G:=NIRVANA/SYS:GROUPS*groupname*—see the IF...THEN statement
MAP U:=NIRVANA/SYS:USERS\\%LOGIN_NAME
MAP J:=FILE_SERVER/SYS:\\—used as a JUNK mapping for the CD command

******* Search Drive Mappings *******
MAP INSERT S1:=NIRVANA/SYS:PUBLIC
MAP INS S2:=NIRVANA/SYS:PUBLIC\\%OS\\%MACHINE\\%OS_VERSION—
    this particular mapping sets up a search drive to the specific workstation's DOS subdirectory so the system can find the correct COMMAND.COM with the COMSPEC command
MAP INSERT S3:=NIRVANA/SYS:APPS/UTILS
MAP INSERT S4:=NIRVANA/SYS:APPS/WINDOWS
MAP INSERT S5:=U:—assigns a search mapping to the user's home directory

NetWare search drive mappings occupy the same environment space as does the DOS path. Therefore, search mappings destroy local paths. In order to avoid this conflict, use the MAP INSERT command to add the search mappings to the front of the DOS path.

In addition to the standard network/search drive mappings, there are five auxiliary MAP commands that you should include in most system login scripts.

MAP DISPLAY OFF	This command stops the drive mappings from being displayed to the user during login script execution. This avoids screen clutter.
MAP DISPLAY ON	This command toggles the display of drive mappings back on.
MAP ERRORS OFF	This command stops the mapping errors from being displayed when the system login script maps users to directories where they have no rights. These errors can easily "panic" novice NetWare users.
MAP ERRORS ON	This command toggles the display of mapping errors back on.
MAP CHANGE U	The ability to change NetWare mapping types is an interesting phenomenon in NetWare v4.0, because it allows immediate mapping reversal. This is useful as users' needs change. This command changes a network drive mapping to a search drive mapping and vice versa.

COMSPEC. The COMSPEC login script command is used to tell the system where to find each user's specific DOS COMMAND.COM file. The correct COMMAND.COM file is critical to the smooth continuity of network applications. Many applications search for COMMAND.COM once they terminate. Earlier we set up different DOS subdirectories in the network directory structure and then created a search drive mapping to those directories. Now we will specify where the COMMAND.COM can be found by using the COMSPEC command. Note: The COMSPEC command must follow the system search drive mappings.

If the DOS subdirectory was mapped to search drive S2:, the following COMSPEC statement in the system login script is ideal:

```
COMSPEC = S2:COMMAND.COM
```

DOS. Three login script commands enable you to give important instructions to DOS, the disk operating system on your personal workstation. These three commands should all be used in this order:

DOS BREAK OFF	This command disables the Ctrl+Break keys from interrupting any DOS programs. This state prevents users from exiting to NetWare by "breaking" out of network-loaded DOS programs.
DOS VERIFY ON	This command establishes a level of "file verification" when users copy data from or to workstation disk drives. Typically, DOS does not verify when it copies files. On a network, data is too important to copy without verification.
DOS SET PROMPT = "PG"	This command gives NetWare the same "directory-specific" prompt that DOS enjoys. This feature greatly enhances user movement from directory to directory on the network.

NO_DEFAULT. This command is new to NetWare v4.0 and it provides a clever alternative for skipping the default login script. This becomes important for users with no user script and critical mappings in the system login script. The default mappings can sometimes cancel out the system configurations. Using NO_DEFAULT in the system login script gives you the flexibility to create a user login script for only specific users without having to worry about the default mappings. NO_DEFAULT completely skips the default script.

Its syntax is

```
NO_DEFAULT
```

IF...THEN. The IF...THEN command adds a level of logic to programming the system login script. It enables you to limit the execution of specific commands to special circumstances. This level of conditional execution adds sophistication and complexity to configuring system parameters with the system login script. Most importantly, the IF...THEN statement gives the supervisor enough versatility so he or she can get away with creating only one login script. The syntax of the IF...THEN statement is

```
IF identifier = "value" THEN command
```

Following is a list of some functional areas where the IF...THEN command can be useful:

```
IF NDAY_OF_WEEK = "7" OR NDAY_OF_WEEK = "1" THEN BEGIN
     WRITE "It's the weekend! Go Home!"
     EXIT "Logout"
END
IF NDAY_OF_WEEK = "2" AND MEMBER OF "Admin" THEN BEGIN
     WRITE "Welcome Back from Your Weekend!"
     WRITE "I hope you got plenty of rest %LOGIN_NAME"
     WRITE "Meeting in my office at 10:00 AM"
END
IF MEMBER OF "ACCT" THEN MAP G:=NIRVANA/SYS:GROUPS\ACCT
IF MEMBER OF "DP" THEN MAP G:=NIRVANA/SYS:GROUPS\DP
IF MEMBER OF "EXEC" THEN MAP G:=NIRVANA/SYS:GROUPS\EXEC
IF MEMBER OF "FUN" THEN MAP G:=NIRVANA/SYS:GROUPS\FUN
```

The last set of statements show how easy it is to establish group-specific network drive mappings without having to create separate mappings in each of the members' user login scripts.

DRIVE. The DRIVE command instructs the system where to leave the users once they exit the system login script. It is a good idea to direct users to their own specific home directories. This way they can run a configuration batch file for capturing, system variables, and a default menu system. The syntax for this command for drive U: (the home directory) is

```
DRIVE U:
```

EXIT. The EXIT command enables you to terminate the system login script and "jump" to the execution of another network application or program. The destination program can be a .COM, .EXE, or .BAT file. It is a good idea to create an exit batch file that includes any "command-line" instructions: CAPTURE, SET, and WIN or MENU. This way you can avoid using the "#" feature to execute these commands. The # locks the entire system login script into workstation memory—and rarely lets go!

```
EXIT "batch file"
```

Be careful when you use the EXIT command. It bypasses the execution of all other login scripts. This can be especially dangerous when the command is used in the system login script. Also, the EXIT command will not work with OS/2 workstations.

REMARK. Any line in the login script that starts with the REMARK command is ignored. This statement is intended for the creation of login script documentation. Documentation is very important for large scripts or systems that are maintained by multiple system managers. The REM command can be replaced by an * or ; as shown in this example:

```
REM ******* Welcome Messages *******
* ******* Network Drive Mappings *******
; ******* Exit to a Batch File *******
```

LASTLOGINTIME. This command helps you to track NetWare users. It displays the last time a user logged into the network when he or she ran the system login script. Users and system managers can informally track network usage by monitoring the LASTLOGIN-TIME command. It can also be useful in LAN troubleshooting.

Rarely Used Commands

The following login script commands are used only rarely in system login scripts:

1. ATTACH
2. DISPLAY and FDISPLAY
3. FIRE PHASERS
4. INCLUDE
5. MACHINE
6. PAUSE
7. PCCOMPATIBLE

ATTACH. This command automatically attaches your system to a second or third file server. To use ATTACH, your network must be physically connected to another server and you must have a valid account on the second system.

ATTACH is no longer valid in NetWare v4.0. To attach to a bindery-based server without running the second server's login script, use the /NS and /B parameters with LOGIN:

```
LOGIN OMEGA/DAVID /NS/B
```

DISPLAY and FDISPLAY. DISPLAY and FDISPLAY enable you to display a "text file" as a message at login time. FDISPLAY filters out control codes and printing configuration characters from nontext files.

FIRE PHASERS. This command causes the workstation to emit a piercing PHASER sound similar to the one used in the phenomenal television/movie series *Star Trek*. FIRE PHASERS can be used to draw attention to important messages on the screen. It can also be a lot of fun if it isn't overused. The maximum number of phasers allowed in one line is nine.

Beam me up, Scotty.

—James Tiberius Kirk

INCLUDE. The INCLUDE command branches to files created outside the login script and reads them as continuations of the login script itself. It is a method of login script branching. Keep in mind that the destination file must be written using valid login script commands.

Make it so.

—Jean Luc Picard

MACHINE. This command is necessary to set the NetBIOS machine name for some programs that require the use of the NetBIOS protocol. Also, it sets the long machine name for use with the DOS drive mapping and COMSPEC scenario. This command is not supported for OS/2 workstations.

Dammit, Jim, I'm a doctor, not an auto mechanic!

—Bones

PAUSE. The PAUSE command temporarily halts login script execution and displays the message `Strike a key when ready...` As soon as the user complies, the login script continues again. This command is most commonly used in conjunction with long WRITE messages.

You might have noticed that the message `Strike any key when ready...` has been modified to read `Strike any key when ready....` This was in response to the overwhelming frustration of many users who couldn't find the "any" key on the keyboard. Now they press the A key.

PCCOMPATIBLE. If your MACHINE is not the standard IBM_PC, your workstation will "lock up" during the execution of the EXIT command. In order to avoid this problem, simply tell the system you are using an IBM PC Compatible by issuing the PCCOMPATIBLE statement in the system login script.

The previous 22 login script commands compose 99 percent of the functionality of NetWare system login scripts. That leaves us with 9 unused commands. Of these 9 commands, there are a few that can prove to be useful in isolated instances. Following is a brief list:

- *# (DOS Executable).* This command is widely used by system managers, who quickly regret it. The # command enables you to execute external commands from within the system login script. Although this strategy has obvious appeal, it is greatly flawed. When the # command is issued, the system locks the login script into workstation memory and runs the specified external program. When the program is finished, the login script execution is continued. In many cases, the login script is never fully released from workstation RAM and approximately 70KB of valuable memory is lost. Avoid using this command.

A variation of the # command enables you to execute internal DOS commands. This is even more dangerous than the # command alone, because it calls a secondary COMMAND.COM. Following is the syntax for internal DOS commands:

#COMMAND /C DOS command

- *CLS.* This command can be useful in cleaning up the screen during complex login script execution. CLS is only available in NetWare v4.0.
- *SET TIME.* This command is useful in NetWare v4.0 systems, because it synchronizes the workstation with each primary reference time server.

With all of these many login script commands your system configuration can get complex quickly. It is a good idea to start with what you need and slowly add to the script as you go. Figure 12.6 provides you with a great place to start.

System Security

We have customized the core of our LAN's system configurations—NDS restrictions, default account balance/restrictions, intruder detection, and the system login script. Now it's time to complete the configuration process by establishing a tight security system. The safety and integrity of your Kingdom is directly related to how secure it is. If just anybody is allowed to waltz in and out of your main gates, harassing and plundering your citizens, the word will get out that "Clarkedom" is not a very nice place to live. It is imperative that you establish a firm, conservative, and organized security system throughout the castle Kingdom.

System security exists on three different planes:

- *NDS security:* This level of security focuses on the interrelationships of objects in the NDS tree. Each object has an access control list (ACL) that determines who or what can have access to it. The ACL defines object rights and property rights. NDS security on NetWare volume objects expands to include two more security planes: user security and directory/file security.

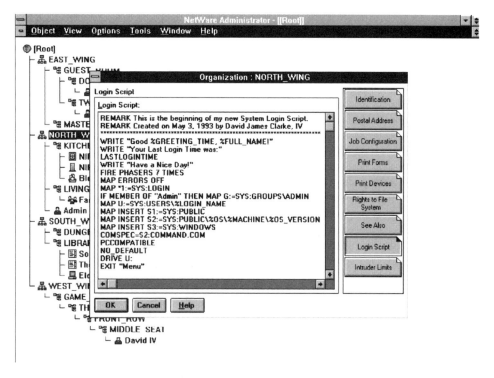

FIGURE 12.6   Beginning to Create a NetWare System Login Script

- *User security:* User security focuses on the restrictions and rights of individual users. Each user carries with him or her a unique combination of user restrictions and rights that dictate how he or she may move around the network. Earlier we defined the first three layers of user security—login, password, and account restrictions.

- *Directory/file security:* The final plane of system security focuses on the NetWare-specific data. Directories and files have their own level of security that is user-independent. Directory/file security is designed to protect specific directories and files from all users on the network.

The last two planes combine to create the seven-layer security model. This model is enforced from within each NetWare server. It applies to NetWare v2.2 and v3.11 servers and NetWare v4.0 volume objects. Refer to User Lab III and Chapter 6 for an in-depth discussion of the seven-layer security model. In review, it looks like this:

User	1.	Login Security
	2.	Password Security
	3.	User Restrictions
	4.	Trustee Assignments
Directory/File	5.	Directory/File Rights
	6.	Directory Attributes
	7.	File Attributes

System security is developed by logically combining the functional strengths of NDS, user, and directory/file security. The resulting combination of these three forces is called *effective rights*. Effective rights are the user's "real" privileges in a given area of the network and ultimately dictate which files he or she can access. As the network manager, it is your responsibility to create an efficient environment of system security that unites the transparency of NDS restrictions, flexibility of user rights, and the protection of directory/file attributes.

NDS Security

As discussed earlier in Chapter 6, NDS security is composed of two types of rights: object rights and property rights. *Object rights* define an object's trustees and control what the trustees can do with the object. *Property rights* limit the trustee's access to only specific properties of that object. Object and property rights are defined by an object's access control list (ACL). They can be assigned or inherited. If they are inherited, the rights may be blocked by the inherited rights filter (IRF).

NDS security can be implemented in a variety of ways. The most common implementation is to assign object and property rights to container objects—COUNTRY (C), ORGANIZATION (O), or ORGANIZATIONAL UNIT (OU). This strategy makes sense for global trustee assignments, because each object within the container will inherit the container's assignment. One of the problems with container assignments is that they rely on *ancestral inheritance*—a dangerous side-effect that can cause unwanted trustee inheritance. (See Chapter 6.) Another security strategy involves the assignment of rights to leaf objects. Leaf assignments are much safer because they limit the scope of inheritance.

Container trustee assignments are intended for limited system configurations. All other NDS security should be implemented through leaf assignments. This section explores some strategies for implementing container trustee assignments. Chapter 13 discusses the strengths of leaf security. Container assignments are organized into object rights and property rights.

Object Rights

The five object rights are listed in Chapter 6. Here is a summary list of them:

Browse   Create   Delete   Rename   Supervisor

Object rights control global object privileges. For example, if user object DAVID assigns the Supervisor object right to the organization NORTH_WING, all objects in the NORTH_WING organization will inherit all rights to DAVID. In addition, any objects associated with groups in the NORTH_WING organization will also inherit all rights to DAVID even though they are not part of the NORTH_WING organization. This can be dangerous. The best advice is to use container assignments sparingly and to focus most of your energy on leaf assignments. Following are a few tips for implementing system configurations through container trustee assignments:

- By default, the ADMIN object is assigned the Supervisor right to the [Root] object. Also, the [Public] trustee is assigned browse privileges to the [Root] object. These default assignments are illustrated in Figure 12.1.

FIGURE 12.7   NORTH_WING as a Trustee of Itself

- By default, each user object is assigned the Browse right to itself and Read rights to all properties. In addition, the user is granted Read/Write privileges to login script and Print Job Configuration properties.
- I would rename the ADMIN object for protection against hackers and experienced intruders. You should remove [Public] as a trustee of the [Root] object, because you don't want guests browsing the entire NDS tree.
- To provide browsing rights for leaf objects within their own ORGANIZATION, assign the browse privilege for each ORGANIZATION to itself. Figure 12.7 illustrates this point by assigning the NORTH_WING object as a trustee of the NORTH_WING organization. The browse object right allows objects within the NORTH_WING organization to see their own section of the NDS tree. This strategy limits user browsing to specific portions of the tree. If you would like these users to browse other partitions of the tree, simply assign the NORTH_WING object as a trustee of another organization.
- By default, the ADMIN user is assigned Supervisor rights to all volumes in its home partition. This provides the ADMIN user with all rights to the directory/file system.
- By default, the container of the SYS: volume is granted trustee rights to the SYS:PUBLIC directory. This means that all objects in the SYS: container can access the PUBLIC subdirectory.

Property Rights
The five property rights are listed in Chapter 6. Here is a quick review:

Compare   Read   Write   Supervisor   Add or Delete Self

Property rights supplement object security. Property rights enable you to customize the depth of object privileges. As discussed earlier, objects contain a variety of different properties: name, telephone number, account balance, and so on. Some object properties are more sensitive than others. For example, most users typically don't mind if you have access to their name or telephone number. But they might feel differently if you try to access their salary information or home address. Property rights enable users to limit access to sensitive properties. Here are some simple rules to keep in mind when you work with property rights:

■ By default, most trustees with browse object rights are granted read property rights to all properties within the host object. Keep in mind, read property rights also include Compare.

■ Most container object properties are harmless—that is, informational. To increase container security, restrict the following container properties: intruder detection, intruder login count, object trustees (ACL), and printer control.

■ Most leaf object properties are also harmless and informational. To increase leaf security, restrict the following leaf properties: account locked, higher privileges, incorrect login attempts, intruder address, minimum password length, object trustees (ACL), printer control, public key, security equivalences, and UID (User ID Number).

Once the NDS security configurations have been established, users must be able to access the NetWare server and directory/file system. The next two planes of NetWare security apply to NetWare v2.2 servers, NetWare v3.11 servers, and NetWare v4.0 volume objects. Next we will discuss the NetWare seven-layer security model.

User Security

The system configuration responsibilities with respect to user security are to establish default user restrictions. The heart of user security, which is trustee assignments, is developed at the time of user creation. This process is discussed in Chapter 13. Until then, the network manager can only establish a strategy for dealing with user access restrictions. There are many levels of user restrictions—we explored most of them earlier in this chapter.

Login Security
Login security, the first level of system security, involves primary access to the LAN. This level of user security hinges on whether the individual user has a valid account on the system. It's like knocking on the front door—if the network recognizes you, it might let you in.

Password Security
Sometimes a friend will ask you for the "secret password" before letting you in the door. Usually this tactic is reserved for highly secure systems—your NetWare LAN should be one! Users can be forced to use passwords and persuaded to change them periodically.

User Restrictions
User restrictions, the third level of NetWare security, involves access to network resources. Account restrictions limit user access through time, date, disk space, concurrent

connections, intruder detection, and station. We configured these restrictions earlier in the chapter.

Trustee Assignments

The final layer of user security pertains to the rights each user has to specific NetWare directories and files. If a user has rights to a directory, he or she is said to be a trustee of that directory. The trustee assignment rights are the same seven or eight rights we defined in Chapter 6. Trustee assignments are not system configurations—they are user/group configurations. We will explore these configurations in Chapter 13. In this section, we are concerned with security parameters that affect the entire LAN—directory/file security.

Directory/File Security

The directory/file level of system security is completely controlled by the Supervisor/ Administrator. It affects directories and files at a lower level than user security, therefore overriding any rights or privileges users are granted at a higher level. Directory/file security is controlled through the use of two different types of privileges: rights and attributes.

Directory/File Rights

Directory/file rights are used to mask or filter inherited rights. The directory/file shield establishes which rights any trustee may have in a given directory and guards against unwanted rights for misbehaving trustees. Directory/file rights are the same seven or eight rights used by user security trustee assignments. NetWare v2.2 allows seven rights and NetWare v3.11/v4.0 allows eight. The only difference is the Supervisory right that exists in both NetWare v3.11 and v4.0. The directory/file rights are defined in Chapter 6.

Each of the different versions of NetWare differs a little bit in its approach to directory/file rights. Here is a brief synopsis:

- **NetWare v2.2**—the earliest version of NetWare uses the term *maximum rights mask (MRM)* to define the directory/file rights. The MRM overrides all trustee assignments—whether the assignments are inherited or explicitly granted.
- **NetWare v3.11**—the middle NetWare kid uses the term *inherited rights mask (IRM)*. The IRM only overrides inherited trustee assignments. Explicit assignments are immune to the IRM in NetWare v3.11.
- **NetWare v4.0**—the new version of NetWare uses the term *inherited rights filter (IRF)* to define directory/file rights. The NetWare v4.0 IRF performs the same as the IRM in NetWare v3.11.

Of the three different acronyms used to describe directory/file rights, I think inherited rights filter is the most descriptive and accurate. I will use IRF to represent all three acronyms—MRM, IRM, and IRF.

Regardless of which version of NetWare you are using or what the directory/file rights are called, this level of system security can be very effective in restricting user access to critical NetWare directories. Here are a few tips on configuring directory/file rights:

- In NetWare v2.2 and v3.11, the FILER menu utility is used to define MRMs and IRMs. In NetWare v4.0, the network manager has many more choices: FILER, NETADMIN, NWADMIN, or the RIGHTS /F command.

- The default IRF for all directories is [SRWCEMFA]—all eight privileges. Any changes you make to a directory's filter will be to remove some of its rights. Figure 12.8 illustrates the inheritance filter for SYS:PUBLIC in NetWare v4.0's NWADMIN.

- Changes made to a directory or subdirectory's filter are specific to that directory only. IRFs do not extend downward through related subdirectories; trustee assignments do.

- Leave the IRF unchanged for user directories. This security will be handled through user-specific trustee assignments.

- Remove the create, erase, access control, and modify rights from all APP subdirectories that contain network applications.

- Remove the access control and modify rights from user APPSETUP subdirectories.

- Remove the access control, modify, and erase rights from the SYSTEM, LOGIN, and MAIL directories.

- Remove the access control and erase rights from the MS-DOS subdirectories under PUBLIC.

- Leave the PUBLIC directory unchanged.

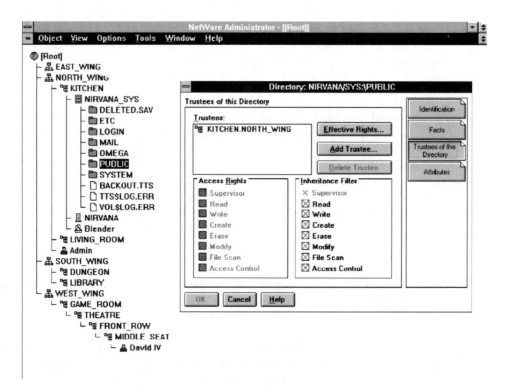

FIGURE 12.8   The IRF of SYS:PUBLIC in NWADMIN

IRF security is tricky; treat it with some caution. Once a right has been filtered, it cannot be regained by anyone except the Supervisor or a user with the access control right. It is a good idea to handle most user-specific security with trustee assignments.

Directory/File Attributes

This final level of system security is the tightest and most sophisticated of them all. Directory/file attributes affect system security at the most fundamental level and override all previous NetWare rights. Attributes are programmable features that attach themselves to specific directories and files. Attributes control access to subdirectories, visibility of files, multiuser access to files, and the functionality of the transactional tracking system. Directory and file attributes can be altered by any user who has the modify privilege, so it's a good idea to use discretion when you hand out this trustee assignment.

Chapter 6 defined the variety of different directory/file attributes that operate in NetWare v2.2, v3.11, and v4.0. This description offers a few tips for optimizing system security through the use of directory/file attributes.

- In NetWare v2.2 and v3.11, the FLAG command is used to define file attributes and FLAGDIR for directory attributes. In NetWare v4.0, the network manager can choose from NETADMIN, NWADMIN, or the RIGHTS command (/DO for directories).
- The default file attributes for all files on the network are Non-Sharable/Read-Write. It is a good idea to only make changes to files that need specialized attention.
- The default for directory attributes is nothing. This level of system security is only used in special cases, such as for hidden or system directories.
- All of the files in the system directories—SYSTEM, PUBLIC, MS_DOS, MAIL, and LOGIN—should be flagged Sharable/Read Only/Delete Inhibit/Rename Inhibit. Important SYSTEM files—all .COMs and .EXEs—should be further marked Sharable/Read Only/System.
- All application program files should also be flagged Sharable/Read Only. In addition, you should flag application executable files Sharable/Execute Only.

An interesting story recently surfaced involving a well-known software manufacturer (Brand X) and one of its clients. It seems that a company had installed a network version of Brand X software on a network, and many users were accessing it at the same time—this is legal. It also seems that many of the users were copying the program files and taking the Brand X software home—this is illegal. Brand X sued the company. The prosecuting argument was based on network management negligence. Brand X claimed that the company's network manager was begging for people to steal the Brand X software because he or she didn't flag the program files Execute Only. Brand X won the case.

- All shared files in DATA subdirectories should be flagged Sharable/Read-Write. All private files in DATA subdirectories should be flagged Non-Sharable/Read-Write.

- If you are worried about users navigating the system for reasons of curiosity, it is a good idea to FLAGDIR the system directories *hidden.*
- Flag all large database or critical system files as transactional. This activates NetWare's internal Transactional Tracking System and will protect these files from corruption should the network experience a sudden crash.
- In NetWare v4.0, it is a good idea to flag all application files Don't Compress. This is especially critical for shared Microsoft Windows files.

That completes our exploration of system configurations. By now, you should have a complete understanding of what you need to do to establish an organized, secure set of NetWare system configurations. Now the only mystery remains how to do it. The next section examines the three major system configuration tools—NWADMIN, NETADMIN, and SYSCON. Think of these utilities as the bulldozers of your LAN.

⁓ System Configuration Tools

Throughout this chapter, we have implemented various system configuration strategies with the use of three different tools: NWADMIN, NETADMIN, and SYSCON. *NWAD-MIN* is the most popular system configuration tool, because it provides hundreds of different functions and a clean, graphical interface.

NETADMIN is also very useful because it offers the same functionality as NWAD-MIN without the fuss of Microsoft Windows or Presentation Manager.

SYSCON is the NetWare v2.2 and v3.11 alternative to NWADMIN and NETADMIN, but it doesn't offer the same comprehensive utility coverage. Although we have been using these tools throughout the book, you haven't really been officially introduced to them. This section takes a few minutes to introduce the contrasting look-and-feel of NWADMIN, NETADMIN, and SYSCON.

NWADMIN

NWADMIN is the new kid on the block. It is a fully functional, integrated administration utility with the popular Windows look-and-feel. NWADMIN is more than just a pretty face. It consolidates almost all administrative utilities, including NETADMIN, PCON-SOLE, PARTMGR, and FILER. To view a list of tasks that can be performed in NWAD-MIN, choose Contents from the Help menu. Figure 12.9 illustrates the NWADMIN tasks window. NWADMIN has five functional menu choices in addition to Help: Object, View, Options, Tools, and Window. These menu choices control the functional window area— known as the NetWare Browser. In Browser you can view logical NDS objects as graphical icons. Each icon represents a physical or logical object. Beyond objects, the Browser enables you to view a volume's directory structure as well. Figure 12.10 illustrates the NetWare Browser and our own CASTLE NDS tree. Notice the breakdown of the NIR-VANA_SYS volume into directories and files.

To expand a container object, simply double-click on it. To view details about a container, choose Details from the Object menu. To view details about a leaf object, simply double-click on it. To view an object's trustees, choose Trustees of this object from the Object menu. To change the context, choose Set Context from the View menu. To perform

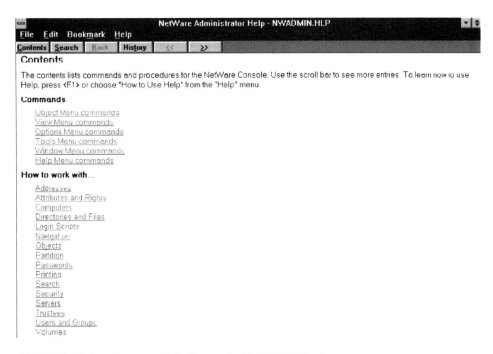

FIGURE 12.9   Contents Help Screen for NWADMIN Tasks

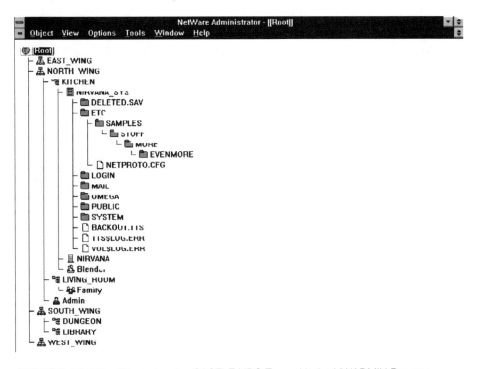

FIGURE 12.10   Displaying the CASTLE NDS Tree with the NWADMIN Browser

a Yellow Pages search of a partition of the NDS tree, highlight a container object and choose Search from the Object menu. We will explore more of NWADMIN in the next chapter.

NETADMIN

NETADMIN is also a new kid on the block, but he is not *the* new kid on the block. NETADMIN provides the same integrated functionality as NWADMIN, but it is a little harder to visualize the NDS tree. For example, compare Figure 12.10 with the same NDS tree in Figure 12.11—NETADMIN. The main menu in NETADMIN has three choices: Manage Objects, Manage according to search pattern, and Change Context. You use the Manage Objects option to perform housekeeping on objects, properties, object rights, and the directory/file system. Manage according to search pattern enables you to perform a Yellow Pages search of the NDS tree. Using Change Context, you can move to another container object in the NDS tree.

As with NWADMIN, it's simple to move around the NETADMIN screen. Any object with a + sign next to it is a container object. To move within a container, highlight the name and press Enter. To view details about a container, highlight the name and press F10. To view details about a leaf object, highlight the name and press Enter. NETADMIN is a fine utility for DOS-oriented NetWare v4.0 users. But to tell you the truth, it isn't nearly as powerful and easy to use as NWADMIN.

SYSCON

SYSCON is a solid, well-adjusted utility. Considering it is the only choice for NetWare v2.2 and v3.11 Administrators, it does a great job. I always liked SYSCON and was happy with what it could do. Of course that was before I used NWADMIN. SYSCON is a simpler utility, because NetWare v2.2 and v3.11 are simpler, kinder operating systems. SYSCON's

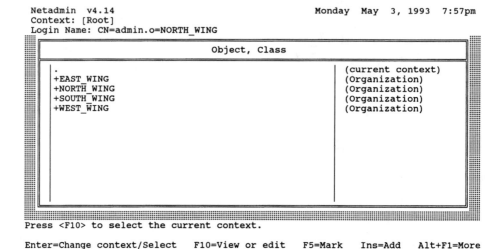

FIGURE 12.11   Displaying the CASTLE NDS Tree with NETADMIN

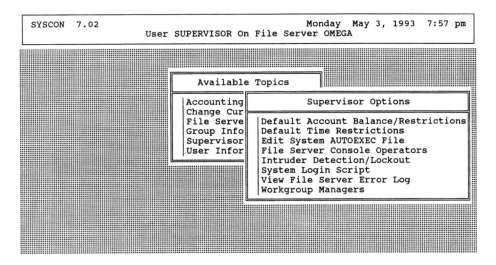

```
SYSCON  7.02                                   Monday  May 3, 1993  7:57 pm
                        User SUPERVISOR On File Server OMEGA
```

```
                              Available Topics

                      Accounting        Supervisor Options
                      Change Cur
                      File Serve   Default Account Balance/Restrictions
                      Group Info   Default Time Restrictions
                      Supervisor   Edit System AUTOEXEC File
                      User Infor   File Server Console Operators
                                   Intruder Detection/Lockout
                                   System Login Script
                                   View File Server Error Log
                                   Workgroup Managers
```

FIGURE 12.12   Options for Changing System Configurations in SYSCON

main menu is organized into four functional groups: Accounting, Supervisor Options, Group Information, and User Information. In addition, two informational groups provide File Server Information and the ability to Change the Current Server.

SYSCON's functionality is distinctly divided into two areas: system configurations and user/group configurations. System configurations are accessed through the Supervisor Options screen as shown in Figure 12.12. These options were discussed earlier in this chapter. User/group configurations are performed in the User Information and Group Information menus. Chapter 13 discusses these configurations.

Chapter 13

Users and Groups

"He gave the wrong password."

Your Kingdom is complete. You have developed houses for your people *(subdirectories)* and boundaries for their towns *(directories)*. You have created a functional government *(system configurations)* and laid down the laws *(system security)*. Now it's time to assemble the citizens!

Adding network users and groups is the final step in building a NetWare LAN. It involves the design, creation, and optimization of the network user environment. This step must be handled carefully, because it defines your LAN's productivity and autonomy. If approached correctly, this process can make your users happy and comfortable. If approached haphazardly, this process can completely ruin your NetWare LAN.

Following are a few points to consider before you add network users and groups:

- Be aware of the users' login names, full names, passwords, functional job responsibilities, security needs, and birth dates.
- Have a firm handle on how these people *interact* on a daily basis. Follow their "paper paths," review the "office cliques," and document internal department hierarchies.
- Understand their many different levels of education and technical competence. How do they "feel" around computers? Do they need a "challenge"? Where does training fit in? Some users will need a more friendly interface to the LAN; others would appreciate a more open system.

Once you have a detailed comprehension of these factors, you are ready to create a productive user environment. Remember in the back of your mind, that whatever configuration you create today must operate effectively and efficiently for the life of the LAN. Once you have established a user environment, it quickly *intertwines* itself with the system configuration spider web—this is common in a castle environment. The LAN and the users quickly become joined at the hip.

Marriage resembles a pair of shears, so joined that they cannot be separated; often moving in opposite directions, yet always punishing any one who comes between them.

—Sydney Smith

Adding Network Users

The process of adding network users is accomplished through the system configuration tools SYSCON, NWADMIN, and NETADMIN. This procedure can be completed by a variety of network managers:

- *Supervisor:* As the all-knowing, all-wise leader of your NetWare LAN, the Supervisor manages NetWare v2.2 and v3.11 LANs and his or her account cannot be deleted. The Supervisor has full rights to all management tasks in NetWare and these rights cannot be revoked. In addition, the Supervisor is the only user who can access the Supervisor Options screen in SYSCON.
- *ADMIN:* Serving as the administrator of NetWare v4.0 LANs, the ADMIN user object doesn't have the same special significance as the Supervisor. ADMIN is

simply the first user object created during NetWare v4.0 installation. ADMIN can be deleted. By default, the ADMIN user is given the Supervisory right to the [Root] object. This means that the ADMIN user has full rights to all NDS objects, including all servers and NetWare volumes.

- *Supervisor-equivalent:* The almost all-knowing, all-wise leader of your NetWare LAN, the Supervisor-equivalent user aids the Supervisor in managing and maintaining the LAN. The Supervisor-equivalent has all the same privileges and rights as the Supervisor. As a matter of fact, the Supervisor-equivalent is identical to the Supervisor except for two small details: the Supervisor-equivalent is created by the Supervisor, not by the system, and the Supervisor-equivalent account can be deleted.

- *Workgroup manager:* A distributed classification of user who is designed to delegate Supervisor management tasks, the workgroup manager is a Supervisor of a specific user group. Workgroup managers have the authority to manage specific users and create new ones if the need arises. The workgroup manager can further delegate network management tasks by creating user account managers. Workgroup managers and user account managers are assigned by the Supervisor, Supervisor-equivalent, or ADMIN.

Nothing is really work unless you would rather be doing something else.

—James Matthew Barrie

The concept of adding network users is approached in two ways: as object creation in NetWare v4.0 and as user addition in NetWare v2.2 and v3.11. This section explores the two approaches to adding network users and illustrates the management steps involved through NWADMIN and SYSCON.

Creating User Objects in NetWare v4.0

Users in NetWare v4.0 are leaf objects just like servers, volumes, groups, and printers. Just like these objects, users exist within containers of the NDS tree. To define a user's home context, you must highlight the appropriate container object—C, O, or OU—before you begin the creation process. Creating user objects is the same as creating any other object:

1. Select Create from the Object menu in NWADMIN.
2. Choose User from the New Object dialog box—as seen in Figure 11.2 of Chapter 11. User objects are special, because they define the productive workers of your NetWare LAN.
3. The Create User screen appears.

Creating accounts for NetWare v4.0 users can be as simple or complex as you want. The Create User option in NWADMIN has a variety of configurations, as seen in Figure 13.1. Following is a brief description of the Create User options in NWADMIN.

Login Name

The Login Name property is the most important field of the Create User dialog box. It defines the name used for logging in, the bindery emulation ID, and the subdirectory name

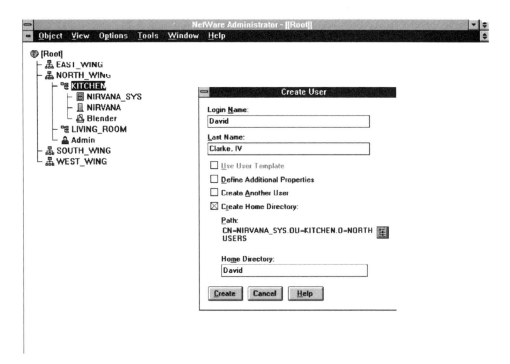

FIGURE 13.1 Creating User Objects in NWADMIN

for user HOME directories. In NetWare v4.0, a login name can contain spaces, symbols, and upper- and lowercase characters. However, if a login name is available to non-v4.0 servers through bindery emulation, it must match bindery naming rules—a maximum of 47 characters, no spaces, and no special characters (/ \ ; , * ?). Also, a login name must be unique in its home container branch of the NDS tree. Typically, first names or first initial and last names are used as login names.

Last Name
The Last Name property is also required in NetWare v4.0. The Last Name property is used for Yellow Pages searching or additional user identification. Once you enter a name in the Last Name box, the Create button becomes active. At this point, you may create the user account with no other configurations or continue with the following customization options.

Use User Template
The Use User Template option provides you with the opportunity to apply the default user template we created in Chapter 12. The user template is container-specific (OU=KITCHEN) and applies to all users within the specific OU.

Define Additional Properties
Select the option to Define Additional Properties when you want to customize user properties immediately. If you select this box and click the Create button, the system will jump

directly to the User Object dialog box. Otherwise, you can leave this box empty and manage the user objects later. We will discuss user management in the next section.

Create Another User

Use the option to Create Another User when you want to simultaneously create a batch of users within the same container object. If you mark this box and click Create, the system will open another new Create User dialog box.

Create Home Directory

Select the Create Home Directory option if you want to identify a HOME directory for this user. If you select this box, the Path option appears. The HOME directory path defaults to the nearest volume object within the same container. To browse the volume, choose the NDS browse icon. It is a good idea to specify a USER subdirectory within the NIRVANA_SYS volume.

Home Directory

In the Home Directory box you identify the user's HOME directory name. It should match the login name.

Home interprets heaven. Home is heaven for beginners.

—Charles H. Parkhurst

Once you complete the user's properties with the Create User dialog box, click the Create button. The user object will now appear as a cute people icon in its home context—the appropriate place of the NDS tree. The network manager can create other NDS objects that enhance the productivity of NetWare v4.0 users—including an alias, profile, and organizational role. An *alias* is an object that exists in the current user context but points to an object defined elsewhere. This feature is helpful for users who move between NDS partitions but don't want their accounts to be defined in multiple locations.

Profiles are used to define group-wide configurations for users who share common tasks. The profile properties include login script, rights, and identification. *Organizational roles* are primarily informational. They define job functions, positions in the organizational chart, or career titles. This object is particularly useful for users who migrate through diverse job functions—such as temporary workers, auditors, or management assistants. Figure 13.2 illustrates a typical user environment within the KITCHEN OU.

Now that we have created our NetWare v4.0 user objects, it is time to consider user management. But before we jump ahead, let's take a look at the procedures for creating NetWare user accounts in NetWare v2.2 and v3.11.

Adding NetWare User Accounts in NetWare v2.2 and v3.11

To add NetWare user accounts in NetWare v2.2 and v3.11, you use the SYSCON menu utility. Choose User Information from the Available Options screen. The User Names window lists each of the network users in alphabetical order. By default, the system creates two users: Supervisor and Guest. If you highlight a specific user and press Enter, a more

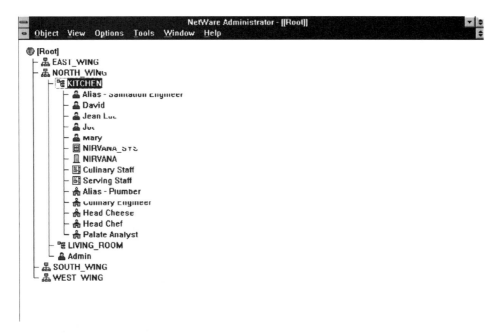

FIGURE 13.2   Sample User Definitions for OU=KITCHEN

detailed user window pops up—the User Information window. User Information provides 16 management options that enable network managers to configure and customize user accounts. This is where most of the user management occurs. The User Information window in SYSCON is shown in Figure 13.3. To view all 16 choices, you must be a Supervisor, Supervisor-equivalent, or an appropriate workgroup manager or user account manager. Regular network users can only view their menu or two choices from other user menus: Full Name and Groups Belonged To.

To add a new user, press Esc to back up to the User Names window. Press Insert. An additional window will pop up prompting you to enter the new User Name. The User Name is the login name, not the full name. It must be 47 characters or less and can contain no spaces or special characters (/ \ ; , * ?). Type the user name and press Enter. The Path to Create User's Home Directory screen will appear. The user's HOME directory path should default to

`NIRVANA/SYS:USERS\`*login name*

If this is the first network user, the path will default to:

`NIRVANA/SYS:`*login name*

To avoid creating user directories from the SYS: root, change the first HOME directory path to include the USERS directory. The system will then use this as the default for all subsequent users. Press Enter when the path is correct. The user's login name will appear alphabetically in the User Names window. You are now ready to manage your new NetWare users.

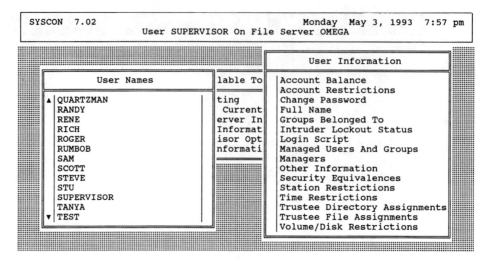

```
SYSCON  7.02                           Monday  May 3, 1993   7:57 pm
                    User SUPERVISOR On File Server OMEGA
```

User Names	lable To	User Information
▲ QUARTZMAN	ting	Account Balance
RANDY	Current	Account Restrictions
RENE	erver In	Change Password
RICH	Informat	Full Name
ROGER	isor Opt	Groups Belonged To
RUMBOB	nformati	Intruder Lockout Status
SAM		Login Script
SCOTT		Managed Users And Groups
STEVE		Managers
STU		Other Information
SUPERVISOR		Security Equivalences
TANYA		Station Restrictions
▼ TEST		Time Restrictions
		Trustee Directory Assignments
		Trustee File Assignments
		Volume/Disk Restrictions

FIGURE 13.3   Choices of the User Information Window in SYSCON

The Path to Create User's Home Directory screen will only appear if you set this parameter to Yes during the system configurations—Default Account Balance/Restrictions. This path works in conjunction with user's home mapping in the system login script. In order for the mapping to work, the user's HOME directory must match the login name exactly. For this reason, it is a good idea to limit user names to eight characters—the maximum length of a NetWare directory.

Managing Network Users

Once the NetWare user accounts have been created, you must configure their specific network environments. The process of managing new network users is accomplished in four distinct and sequential steps:

1. Install general user options.
2. Establish user restrictions.
3. Write user login scripts.
4. Configure user security.

We start with installation of general user options. These choices define typical user configurations for personal network environments. Next, we will establish user restrictions to augment the default account restrictions we set in Chapter 12. Writing user login scripts can offer additional user customization, but it is only recommended in special circumstances. Finally, we will configure user security. User security is the fourth level of the seven-layer security model. It is defined in two ways: user trustee assignments and a group trustee assignment. This chapter discusses both ways. We start with installing general user options.

Installing General User Options

The place to start with your new NetWare users is to install general user options. This procedure involves mostly administrative functions and can be outlined by the six areas described here. In NetWare v2.2 and v3.11, general user options are found in SYSCON. NetWare v4.0 introduces greater functionality in NWADMIN and NETADMIN.

User Type

The first general user option is User Type. There is no specific option for this configuration, but it is a critical user definition. As we discussed earlier, users can be classified in a variety of ways:

Supervisor	workgroup manager	print operator
ADMIN	user account manager	regular user
Supervisor-equivalent	console operator	

These classifications are defined in the User Information window of SYSCON or NETADMIN.

Full Name

The Full Name box is where you enter the user's full name. The full name should consist of first, middle, and last names; spaces are allowed. This function is primarily administrative in nature but can also prove to be a valuable network management tool for searching large wide area networks. In addition, NetWare v4.0's utilities include Last Name, Other Names, Description, and See Also.

Change Password

The Change Password option is important to network users and represents the second level of system security. Initially, passwords are assigned by the Supervisor/ADMIN, but soon the responsibility of password management falls onto the shoulders of the users themselves. Passwords are encrypted at the server and workstation, which means nobody can see them—not even the Supervisor/ADMIN. Network managers can change user passwords but not view them. This added security advantage exists to protect users from "Supervisors gone MAD!"

Groups Belonged To

When the LAN is initially installed, NetWare automatically creates the group Everyone and assigns all users to it. The network manager should create additional groups corresponding to common areas of functionality. Groups such as Administration, Accounting, Data_Processing, and Marketing are established to help develop security, electronic mail, and document sharing.

At this point, no additional groups have been created. Later in the chapter you'll see how to establish groups as areas of common functionality. Once groups have been established, the network manager can add a user through the Groups Belonged To (SYSCON) or Group Membership (NWADMIN) screens.

In NetWare v2.2 and v3.11, the network manager can use the group Everyone as a catch-all for global trustee assignments and generic configurations. In NetWare v4.0, the group Everyone doesn't exist. Instead, Novell has created a more sophisticated tool for global configurations—the [Public] trustee. The network manager can assign global trustee assignments to any NDS object by assigning [Public] as a trustee. Objects with no trustee assignments inherit [Public]'s rights by default.

Account Balance

The Account Balance option is available to systems that have installed NetWare's internal accounting system. The NetWare accounting system is a sophisticated monitoring utility that tracks user activity and charges them for resource utilization. The account balance function is used by network managers to establish user accounting balances and credit limits. Once a user reaches his or her credit limit, the system locks that user's login status. The network manager can use this option to reestablish user account balances.

Informational

There are a few remaining general user options that are primarily informational. These options provide specific user information and are used for network monitoring and routine maintenance. In NetWare v2.2 and v3.11 there are two informational options: Intruder Lockout Status and Other Information. In NetWare v4.0, there are significantly more informational windows: Identification, Intruder Lockout, Network Address, and Postal Address. Following is a brief description of Intruder Lockout Status, Other Information, and Identification.

- *Intruder Lockout Status:* If an intruder reaches the incorrect login count within the specified period, the account locked option will switch to Yes. This is valid for all versions of NetWare. In addition, this window will reveal the node address of the last Intruder to attempt access. This provides the network manager with an invaluable clue about the intruder's identity. The account locked option can be reset to No by the Supervisor/ADMIN or workgroup manager.
- *Other Information:* This window provides the network manager with valuable information on user disk usage, last login time, user ID, and console operator status. Refer to Figure 13.4 for an illustration of the SYSCON Other Information option. The Disk Space in Use field can be very helpful in tracking user disk use. This number reflects the total size of the files that are "owned" by this user. If the user approaches his or her disk space limit, the network manager can extend the Volume/Disk Restrictions parameter.
- *Identification:* This option is available in NetWare v4.0 only. The Identification window provides a plethora of valuable user data that you can use to build a personal user database. Sample user identification information is displayed in Figure 13.5. The entries in the dialog box can also be used for NDS searches. Users can view identification information about other users if they have the Browse object right.

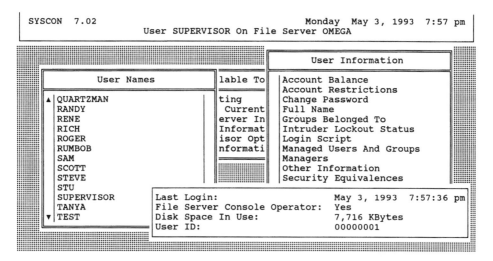

FIGURE 13.4   Information Displayed by SYSCON's Other Information Option

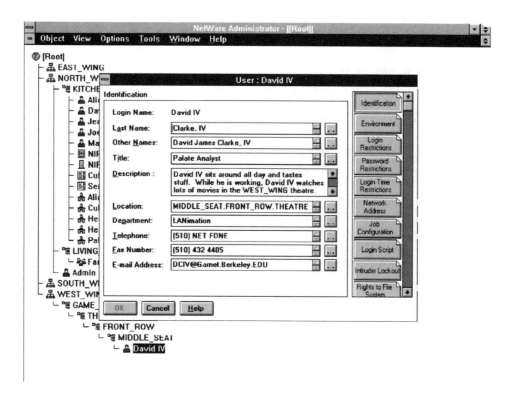

FIGURE 13.5   NetWare v4.0's Identification Window in NWADMIN

Establishing User Restrictions

Once the general user options have been installed, you should customize the user's account restrictions. During the system configuration phase, we established an elaborate web of default account restrictions. In this section, we will augment global restrictions with some user-specific restrictions. This step represents the third level of the NetWare seven layer security model. Beyond login and password security, user restrictions limit access to LAN resources through time restrictions, date restrictions, disk space restrictions, concurrent connections, and station restrictions.

You can't run a government solely on a business basis. . . . Government should be human. It should have a heart.

—Herbert Henry Lehman

Time Restrictions

Time restrictions are established in Netware v2.2 and v3.11 by using the Time Restrictions option under User Information in SYSCON. These restrictions are available in NetWare v4.0 through Login Time Restrictions in the User Object dialog box of NWADMIN. The default time restriction schedule is established during the system configuration phase and should be adequate for most NetWare users. Only in rare circumstances do you need to alter a specific user's restrictions—troublemakers, late workers, swing shift staff, and so on.

Date Restrictions

User accounts can be made to expire on any given date by using the Account Restrictions option in SYSCON or Login Restrictions option in NWADMIN. Date restrictions are primarily used to establish temporary accounts for guest users.

Disk Space Restrictions

File server disk space can be controlled by limiting a user's maximum disk space use. This total refers to the sum of all files that are "owned" by this specific user—measured in kilobytes. Disk space can be restricted through the Account Restrictions option in both SYSCON and NETADMIN. Figure 13.6 shows a user's Account Restrictions screen in NETADMIN. Disk space restrictions are not recommended because they typically interfere with user productivity. Disk space monitoring can be more cleverly audited with NetWare v4.0's AUDITCON feature. Disk space restrictions should only be used as a penalty for users who abuse their network privileges.

Concurrent Connections

Network managers can also restrict users from simultaneously logging into a number of different workstations with the Concurrent Connections option. Concurrent connections are managed from the Account Restrictions menu in SYSCON and the Login Restrictions menu in NWADMIN and NETADMIN. This function is primarily designed to prevent users from monopolizing network resources and to discourage user migration. Concurrent connection restrictions are a good idea, but you should give users more than one connec-

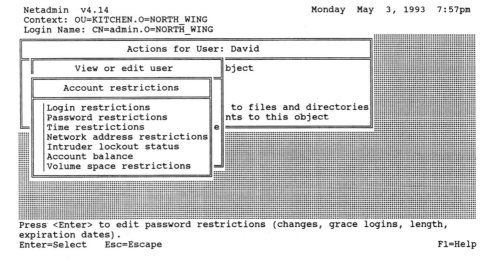

```
Netadmin  v4.14                              Monday  May  3, 1993  7:57pm
Context: OU=KITCHEN.O=NORTH_WING
Login Name: CN=admin.O=NORTH_WING
```

```
┌─────────────────────────────────────────────────┐
│              Actions for User: David              │
│  ┌──────────────────────────────┬──────────────┐ │
│  │       View or edit user       │bject         │ │
│  │ ┌────────────────────────────┐│              │ │
│  │ │    Account restrictions    ││              │ │
│  │ │┌──────────────────────────┐││              │ │
│  │ ││Login restrictions        ││ to files and directories
│  │ ││Password restrictions     ││nts to this object
│  │ ││Time restrictions         ││e             │ │
│  │ ││Network address restrictions│
│  │ ││Intruder lockout status   ││              │ │
│  │ ││Account balance           ││              │ │
│  │ ││Volume space restrictions ││              │ │
│  │ │└──────────────────────────┘│              │ │
│  │ └────────────────────────────┘              │ │
│  └──────────────────────────────┴──────────────┘ │
└─────────────────────────────────────────────────┘
```

```
Press <Enter> to edit password restrictions (changes, grace logins, length,
expiration dates).
Enter=Select    Esc=Escape                                    F1=Help
```

FIGURE 13.6   Accounts Restrictions Screen of NETADMIN

tion in case they need to employ another user's machine in an emergency situation. Typically, three concurrent connections are ideal—a limit that can be set for all users during the system configurations phase.

Station Restrictions

Access to the LAN can be further limited by restricting the physical workstations that users are allowed to use. Each NetWare workstation has a unique node address that the LAN topology uses to identify it. The Station Restrictions option enables the network manager to limit users to specific physical workstation addresses. This feature is important in wide area networking schemes because you typically have many different users attaching to your LAN from a variety of locations. If you notice one particular user who is getting a little "frisky," you can restrict that user to a physical location in the office and keep an eye on him or her. Station restrictions are established with the Station Restrictions option in SYSCON and the Network Address restrictions option in NWADMIN and NETADMIN.

User restrictions can be assigned to groups of users by using the F5 key. F5 marks multiple users in the User Names screen of SYSCON. If you mark multiple users and press Enter, the Set User Information window appears. This window enables you to define four different restrictions for all marked users: account balance, account restrictions, station restrictions, and time restrictions. This undocumented feature is not available in NWADMIN or NETADMIN.

Writing User Login Scripts

With the general user options and access restrictions in place, it's time to establish a more detailed user configuration. The user login script affords us the flexibility to generate a list of specific commands that, on execution, will customize each user's unique environment. The commands and identifiers used to construct the user login script were detailed in Chapter 12.

In the system login script, we organized these commands into a program that bred a generalized configuration for all users. In the user login script, we are interested in augmenting the system script with some user-specific customization. Remember: The user login script is executed by only one user and it follows the system script.

The following plan is a five-step approach to writing an effective user login script. It covers all of the important areas that must be addressed in each user's script. Note, however, that as unexpected situations arise, you may want to add additional functionality to this standard user script.

As stated in Chapter 12, the goal for network managers is to consolidate all configuration parameters into one system login script. Therefore, the user login script is obsolete. Well, the world is not a perfect place, and there are instances when the user login script can be necessary and effective. Following are guidelines for those instances—however rare. Keep in mind that if the system login script ends with the EXIT command, the user login script will not be executed.

Messages

Most of the important greetings and messages were taken care of by the system login script. The messages area of the user script is reserved for additional messages that are directed to one specific user. Typical messages will have some longlasting, global significance to the user in order to be placed in the user login script. Anything else should be communicated through regular channels—voice, electronic mail, fax, and so on.

```
WRITE "BOB, CONGRATULATIONS ON YOUR NEW BABY GIRL!"
WRITE "WE ARE ALL VERY HAPPY FOR YOU!"
```

Drive Mappings

The user login script is the perfect place for user-specific drive mappings. Network drive mappings should use logical drives that were not assigned by the system script, and search mappings should use the MAP S16 command to avoid canceling out previously created search drives. Following is a good example of some user-specific drive mappings that should be included in each user's login script:

```
MAP G:=NIRVANA/SYS:GROUPS\ACCT
MAP H:=NIRVANA/SYS:GROUPS\ADMIN
MAP I:=NIRVANA/SYS:GROUPS\UNITWAY

MAP S16:=NIRVANA/SYS:USERS\KAREN\WPDATA
MAP S16:=NIRVANA/SYS:GROUPS\ADMIN\DATA
```

IF...THEN

The IF...THEN login script command enables you to add a level of logic and sophistication to user configurations. It can be used to alert users of important meetings, greet them on birthdays, or provide reminders for Friday's backup:

```
IF DAY = "9" THEN BEGIN
    FIRE 7
    WRITE "DON'T FORGET!!!!"
    WRITE ""
    WRITE "TOMORROW IS THE MONTHLY BOARD MEETING!!!"
    WRITE ""
    WRITE "ARE THE REPORTS FINISHED?!!!"
END
IF MONTH_NAME = "August" AND DAY = "7" THEN BEGIN
    FIRE 2
    WRITE "HAPPY BIRTHDAY BOB!"
    WRITE "PUSHING 30, HUH?"
    FIRE 7
    END
IF NDAY_OF_WEEK = "6" THEN BEGIN
    WRITE "It's Friday!"
    WRITE "Time to BACK UP your local disk drive!"
    PAUSE
END
```

Default Drive

The DRIVE command establishes a default drive once the user script has ended. The system login script drops users into their own specific HOME directory, but some users need to be left somewhere else—configuration directories, local drive, and so on. In order to effectively configure each user's environment, find out which directory he or she would like to use as the default and use the DRIVE command to leave him or her there.

The syntax for establishing a default drive is

```
DRIVE G:
```

Exiting the Login Script

The last function of the user login script is to steer users in a specific network direction. Once the user exits the login script, he or she is on his or her own—no more handholding. This configuration represents the last point of control for the network manager; use it wisely. The last thing you can do as the network manager is to guide users in the right direction. The EXIT command enables you to terminate the user login script and "jump" to the execution of another network application. The best place to send most users is a menu system—NetWare's menu or Microsoft Windows, for example. Some users, on the other hand, may want to jump directly into a specific application. It's entirely up to them and you.

```
EXIT "Menu"...—jumps to a menu system
EXIT "WP"...—jumps to a specific network application
```

In NetWare v3.11, users can be locked out of their own login scripts by changing the following account restriction parameter:

```
Allow user to change password = No
```

In NetWare v4.0, the same effect can be accomplished by removing users' Read/Write access to their own login script property.

That concludes our discussion of user login scripts. I hope you never have to create one.

Configuring User Security

The final step in managing network users is configuring user security. As we discussed earlier, NetWare's security model exists in two planes: *User* security and *Directory/File* security. These two planes are organized into seven progressive levels—each more secure than the prior:

1. Login Security
2. Password Security   **User Security**
3. User Restrictions
4. Trustee Assignments

5. Directory's Maximum Rights Mask
6. Directory Attributes   **Directory/File Security**
7. File Attributes

The first four levels of NetWare's security model are user-specific. The final three are directory/file-specific. Earlier, in Chapter 12, we established the LAN's directory/file security through inherited rights filters and directory/file attributes. Now we will build on this existing security system with a more user-specific structure.

Login Security

By establishing an account for network users and giving them unique login names, you have completed the first step of user security. Only users with valid login names can access a NetWare LAN.

Once the system verifies a user's login name it will either ask for a password or continue to the system login script. If the login name is invalid, it will ask for a password anyway. This feature is designed to hide the fact that the login name doesn't exist. Furthermore, in NetWare v4.0, the system will authenticate the user with a session-specific authentication code. The code will be attached to all correspondence between the user and the NetWare v4.0 server.

Password Security

Once a user has been given a unique login name, he or she should be granted a secret password. Passwords should be more than five characters long and can extend up to 128 characters in total length. Here are a few ways to increase your LAN's password security:

- Set the *Minimum Password Length* parameter to 5 or 7.
- Require periodic password changes at 30- to 45- day intervals. In addition, require unique passwords each time. The system will keep track of the last 10 unique passwords.
- Users should type their passwords in upper- and lowercase. Although passwords are not case sensitive, this strategy confuses people when they look over your shoulder.
- A user password should not contain any of the following: any portion of anybody's real name, any user's pet name (or pet's name), or any known hobbies or interests. Passwords should be cryptic and boring.

User Restrictions

The third level of NetWare security focuses on user access restrictions. User restrictions use many criteria to limit network access: time, date, disk space, concurrent connections, and station. Earlier, this chapter established these user restrictions through SYSCON, NWADMIN, and NETADMIN. When combined intelligently, these restrictions can offer an effective method of user security. On the other hand, if used foolishly, user restrictions can completely destroy a LAN's productivity.

Trustee Assignments

The final level of user security involves trustee assignments to the NetWare directory/file system. As we mentioned earlier in the book, a *trustee* is a user who has been given specific rights or privileges to work in a particular directory. Trustee assignments must be granted to all users for all directories they intend to use. Once a user has been granted rights in a given directory, those rights extend down through subsequent subdirectories. Here are some points to keep in mind when configuring user trustee assignments:

- Pay attention to the difference between explicit and inherited rights. Explicit rights override a directory's IRM or IRF in NetWare v3.11 and v4.0. Inherited rights are subject to filtering in all versions of NetWare.
- Calculate effective rights. This is the combination of a user's inherited trustee rights and a directory's inherited rights filter. Granting inherited trustee assignments means nothing if the directory's IRF filters them out.
- Whenever possible, establish trustee assignments for users as GROUP assignments. Group trustee assignments save eons of time in design, installation, and security maintenance. We will delve into group security issues in the next section. User security is reserved for special circumstances.
- Grant each user full trustee rights in his or her HOME directory. The good news is that NetWare v2.2 and v3.11 will do this for you if you choose to create a HOME directory during user installation. NetWare v4.0 requires additional security maintenance.

User security can quickly become a huge spider's web of rights, masks, and restrictions. It is impossible to catch all of the holes that can develop in such a complex system. If you feel your handle on user security sliding away, there is a NetWare command-line utility that will identify holes in NetWare security. Type **SECURITY** from the SYS:SYSTEM directory and press Enter. Watch and learn.

> **Object rights in NetWare v4.0 have a profound effect on user security. By default each user object is assigned as a Browse trustee of himself. In addition, users inherit the rights of their home container object and the [Public] trustee. Refer to Chapter 12 for a discussion of object right security.**

Network Groups

One of the most productive and functional entities of a NetWare LAN is the *group*. The process of organizing users into functional work groups saves time, adds flexibility, and increases synergy throughout the whole system. Creating network groups is very simple— what they do is exciting:

- Groups can act as focal points for important electronic mail.
- Groups can be given trustee assignments as a whole.
- Groups can access specific network applications.
- Groups can create bonding and synergy between users.

Groups are good!

Groups are the towns of your Kingdom. They are the consolidation of similar people's interests. They promote global communications within and between citizens.

The process of organizing users into network groups is outlined in three simple steps:

1. Create groups.
2. Add users to the groups.
3. Configure group security.

Creating Groups

The process of creating NetWare groups resembles the process of creating NetWare users. To manage the process, in NetWare v4.0 we use NWADMIN or NETADMIN and in NetWare v2.2 or v3.11 we use SYSCON. Following is a brief look at creating groups using NWADMIN and SYSCON.

Creating Groups in NWADMIN

NetWare groups are leaf objects just as are users, volumes, printers, and servers. The first step in creating a group object is to move to the group's home container. Highlight the appropriate OU or choose Set Context from the View menu. Enter the group's home context. Next, choose Create from the Object menu. Highlight Group from the New Object box and click OK. The Create Group dialog box will appear. Within this box, you can name the group, define additional properties, or create another group. If you choose to define additional properties, the system will immediately jump to the group information box. The NWADMIN group information box prompts you for four entries: Identification, Members, Rights to File System, and See Also. Once you choose Create from the Create Group dialog box, the group icon will appear in its proper place in the NDS tree.

Creating Groups in SYSCON

SYSCON has a separate choice for groups from within the Available Options menu—it is called Group Information. Initially, the Group Names window contains one name—the group Everyone. This group is automatically created by the system and all users are assigned to it. To create a new group, press Ins. The New Group Name box will appear. Type a unique group name and press Enter.

Adding Users to Groups

To add network users to new groups, you create a member list. The member list identifies all the login names of the group users. To access the member list in NWADMIN, double-click the group icon. Choose Members from the group information window. Choose Add to insert user objects or Delete to remove them. To access the member list in SYSCON, highlight the group name from the Group Names list and press Enter. Figure 13.7 illustrates SYSCON's Group Information window. Choose Member List from Group Information and press Enter. Press Ins to add users. Mark multiple users in the Not Group Members window with F5. Press Enter to add the users to the member list.

Once the member list has been created, you can define custom user configurations through group assignments. (See Figure 13.7.) The most useful group management parameter is group trustee assignments.

Configuring Group Security

Groups can be granted trustee assignments. Group assignments are useful because they provide a vehicle for granting similar rights to a large number of users. Also, group assignments are maintained from one central location; member lists and group trustee assignments can be easily changed.

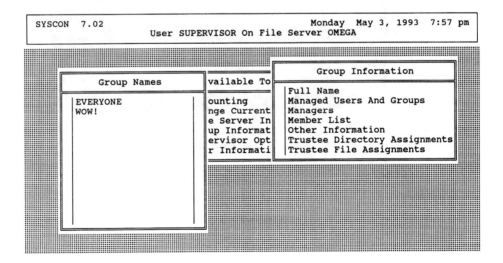

FIGURE 13.7   The Group Information Window in SYSCON

The most intriguing group in NetWare v2.2 and v3.11 is Everyone. This group includes all users and is automatically updated as users are created. Global trustee assignments should be granted to the group Everyone. In NetWare v4.0, the [Public] trustee serves the same purpose. Also in NetWare v4.0, network managers can assign trustee assignments to large groups of objects by assigning the container object as a directory/file trustee. This strategy is dangerous, though, because it incorporates ancestral inheritance—see Chapter 6.

Following are a few recommendations for configuring group security:

- Be careful when you assign container objects as trustees in NetWare v4.0. It is difficult to control organizational migration and ancestral inheritance. It is much safer to define NetWare groups and assign group trustee assignments.
- In NetWare v4.0, create a group for each container object and assign all local users to the group. Then assign the new group as a trustee of each local volume. Use the Include button in NWADMIN—see Figure 13.8. Next, assign the following trustee rights to each volume:

```
NIRVANA_SYS:APPS          [ R      F ]
NIRVANA_SYS:DATA          [ RWCEMF ]
NIRVANA_SYS:PUBLIC        [ RWC   F ]
```

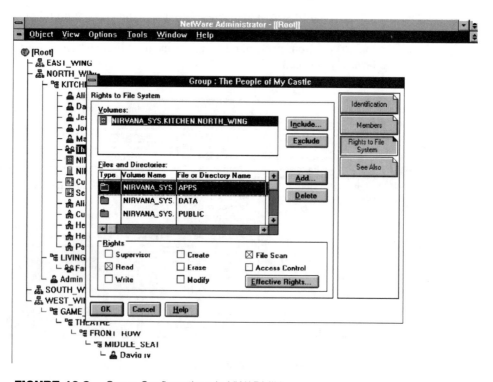

FIGURE 13.8   Group Configurations in NWADMIN

- In NetWare v2.2 and v3.11, grant the same global assignments to the group Everyone. Beyond that, group assignments can be granted as needed. User HOME directories should be defined using user trustee assignments.
- NetWare groups can be assigned according to function, job responsibility, application sharing, or data. Some sample groups include Admin, Network, Accounting, and Typing.

NetWare Tools for Users

NetWare provides various tools for network users. These tools give advanced NetWare users the functions they need to interact with their network environment. The user functions include mapping, userlists, security, volume information, server lists, messages, and so on. NetWare tools for users are text-based, menu-driven, or GUI. Following is a brief description of the four most popular user tools: NWUSER, NETUSER, NetWare Tools for Windows, and SYSCON.

NWUSER

NWUSER is a GUI-based user tool for NetWare v4.0. It is loaded in the WINDOWS directory of the workstation disk as part of the NetWare Requester installation. The NWUSER look-and-feel is illustrated in Figure 13.9. You can access this GUI user tool in two ways: by choosing File, Run from the Program Manager screen and typing **C:\WINDOWS\NWUSER** or by pressing F6 (the default NetWare hotkey) from within Windows. NWUSER provides five functional screens, on-line help, and two user-defined buttons.

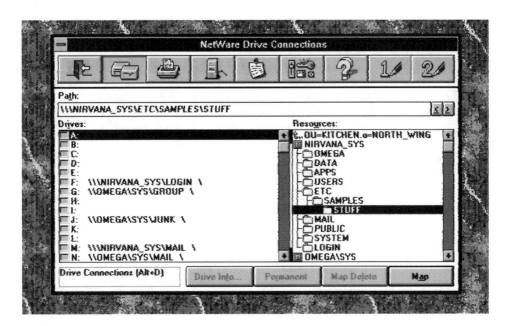

FIGURE 13.9　The NWUSER Tool in NetWare v4.0

The user-defined buttons enable experienced users to define NetWare command-line utilities from within the NWUSER interface. The NWUSER window consists of

- the upper button bar
- the lower button bar
- the left window
- the right window

Figure 13.9 illustrates these components. The upper button bar illustrates the nine user tools—five functional, help, two user-defined buttons, and exit. The lower button bar displays context-sensitive buttons and an information window. The left and right windows represent the work area for user configurations.

The core of NWUSER is in its five main user tools: Drive Connections, Printer Connections, Server Connections, Send Messages, and NetWare Settings. Let's take a moment to explore these five tools.

Drive Connections
The Drive Connections tool enables users to graphically define user drive mappings. The left window displays the drives; right window displays the volumes and directories. To map a drive, the user simply chooses the drive, highlights the directory, and clicks the Map button on the lower button bar.

Printer Connections
Printer connections are defined the same way as drive connections. The left window displays the ports; the right window displays the printers. The Printer Connections choice enables users to capture local ports to printers without having to use the CAPTURE command-line utility.

Server Connections
The Server Connections tool provides users with a graphical login utility. In previous versions of NetWare it was difficult to log in from within Windows. This tool makes it easy. Simply highlight the server from the right window and click on the Login button from the lower button bar. The left window lists the servers that are currently attached. The server connections tool also provides server information, a SETPASS utility, and logout functions.

Send Messages
The Send Messages button provides a graphical tool for sending one-line messages to NetWare users and groups. Simply highlight the user from the right window and click on the Send button from the lower button bar.

NetWare Settings
The final NWUSER tool is NetWare Settings. This button provides a detailed configuration screen for the NWUSER utility. Users can configure options such as Resource Display, NetWare Hotkey, Print Manager Display, and Message Reception.

NETUSER

NETUSER is the text-based menu version of NWUSER. It provides the same user functionality in a limited text-based format. Figure 13.10 illustrates the look-and-feel of the NETUSER menu utility. The Available Options screen displays five choices: Printing, Messages, Drives, Attachments, and Change Context. These five choices correspond with the five main functions of NWADMIN but don't provide user-defined buttons. On-line help is available through F1 and Exit is equivalent to Esc. In addition, with NETUSER users can change their user login script—a feature NWUSER doesn't provide.

NetWare Tools for Windows

NetWare Tools for Windows was introduced in Chapter 6. The utility tools in this package provide Windows optimization in the NetWare environment. They include GUI versions of USERLIST, VOLINFO, SETPASS, ATTACH, MAP, CAPTURE, and SEND. NetWare Tools for Windows is an earlier version of NWUSER for NetWare v2.2 and v3.11. It provides almost all of the same functionality, except for the GUI login. That procedure is reserved for another Windows/NetWare utility called WINLOGIN. NetWare Tools for Windows is available at no cost from Netwire or LANimation.

NetWare Tools for Windows can be configured as a hotkey dialog box by adding the following lines to NETWARE.INI in the C:\WINDOWS subdirectory:

NETWARE.INI

[options]
NetWare Hot Key = 123

Then you simply press F12 from anywhere within Windows and the NetWare Tools window will appear.

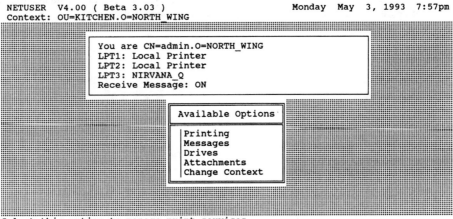

```
NETUSER  V4.00 ( Beta 3.03 )                Monday  May  3, 1993  7:57pm
Context: OU=KITCHEN.O=NORTH_WING

            ┌──────────────────────────────────────┐
            │ You are CN=admin.O=NORTH_WING         │
            │ LPT1: Local Printer                   │
            │ LPT2: Local Printer                   │
            │ LPT3: NIRVANA_Q                       │
            │ Receive Message: ON                   │
            └──────────────────────────────────────┘

                        ┌─────────────────────┐
                        │   Available Options  │
                        ├─────────────────────┤
                        │ Printing            │
                        │ Messages            │
                        │ Drives              │
                        │ Attachments         │
                        │ Change Context      │
                        └─────────────────────┘


Select this option to manage print services.

Enter=Select    Esc=Escape                              F1=Help
```

FIGURE 13.10   The NETUSER Tool in NetWare v4.0

SYSCON

SYSCON is primarily oriented toward the network manager, but it also offers some productive user tools. SYSCON is only available in NetWare v2.2 and v3.11. The User Information window provides 16 user options that users, as well as network managers, can configure. Using SYSCON, users can write login scripts, change passwords, and access full name information. The balance of the user information options are locked to users.

Congratulations! Your NetWare LAN is *alive.* You have

- an efficient topology design
- a functional NetWare operating system
- plenty of users and groups
- an organized network management system

All of the analysis, design, installation, and network management finally paid off. You will feel a rush of accomplishment when the first network user finally logs in. From now on, nothing will be the same. You have created an incredibly productive computing environment; now it is time to put it to use. The NetWare acid test is yet to come—daily use! Keep in mind, most LANs that fail, do so in the first seven months. Stay alert and keep your fingers crossed.

Our real problem, then, is not our strength today; it is rather the vital necessity of action today to ensure our strength tomorrow.

—Dwight D. Eisenhower

To ensure that your great new system doesn't crumble under the pressure of user demands, you will be asked to cut your vacation short and begin an intense campaign of network maintenance. Yes—that *M* word! Your role as network manager has really just begun. Although you performed admirably in *building* the LAN, your "real" challenge is going to be keeping it *alive.* The final two chapters of the book are dedicated to helping you prepare for all of the frolic and joy that await you in network printing, maintenance, and troubleshooting.

Chapter 14

NetWare Printing

Before the publication of *The Complete NetWare Construction Kit*, many managers complained of a 97.85 percent hair loss caused by network printing problems.

After reading *The Complete NetWare Construction Kit*, most managers reported network printing problems solved and offered to do hair-care product commercials.

Networks were originally created as a way to share resources. Before NetWare existed, computer users searched high and low for a way to share computer data. They wanted to share files, printers, fax machines, modems, plotters, and many other pieces of equipment. Early files were shared by putting files on disks and taking the disks to other workstations *(sneaker-net)*. Printers were shared in much the same way. Either users copied files and took them to the computer in the office that had a printer attached or they bought some kind of switching device. Early on, it was a manual device: an A, B box. Next to file sharing, network printing is one of the major reasons for choosing a NetWare LAN. NetWare provides a variety of different resources for sharing network printers.

In this chapter, we will explore the features and functions of NetWare printing—network printer installation and management. You will learn about PCONSOLE and queues. You'll study the four steps of printing installation and the difference between core printing and using print servers. We will even explore the features and advantages of third-party printing products. We will do what everybody else has done—talk about *how* to print on a NetWare LAN.

As knowledge increases, wonder deepens.

—Charles Morgan

Is that enough? Have you ever wondered why people print on a NetWare LAN? Or what they expect? Before we begin our brief journey into the hows of NetWare printing, I would like to offer a few viewpoints from the *why* perspective. I believe that you must understand the essence of printing, before you can optimize it on a NetWare LAN. If it sounds a little zenlike, bear with me. There is more to printing than meets the eye.

The Essence of Printing

On the surface, network printing may appear easy, but it is probably the most troubled and mysterious management issue in NetWare LANs. More hair has been lost over this matter than any other management responsibility. This frustration occurs because of the immense network complexities and the variety of users on the LAN. In our quest for the essence of printing, we need to concentrate on the people involved. Network users fall into three major categories: the user, the network Administrator, and the MIS director or the chief information officer (CIO). Some of the factors each group must consider are the application, the computer ports, the NetWare queue, and the printer (with its varied abilities and limitations). Network printing is a permutation of all these factors. The most complicated factor, however, is the individual needs and desires of the people. Let's take a look at the user segments and how they view NetWare printing.

There are as many opinions as there are experts.

—Franklin Delano Roosevelt

It seems like all of us have minds of our own. In fact, each person's personal needs greatly affect how well (or how poorly) printing will work on the LAN. But printing on a network is not the same as stand-alone printing. If users treat the printer as their own personal property and make changes to the printers at will, it creates chaos. To understand the components we will look at the three groups:

- the user
- the network Administrator
- the MIS director or the CIO

Each group has different expectations. These different needs can put a network Administrator onto the firing line every day. Once you see what's causing these fires, maybe they can be prevented. Let's take a look inside.

Adversity is the first path to truth.

—Lord Byron

The User

First, let's take a look at the essence of printing from the user's perspective. If we can see what the user is looking for and the intricacies involved, we can begin to realize just how difficult printing on a network can be for users. During the day each user needs to interact with printers and get some characters to appear on a piece of paper. Printing, to the user, is a necessary evil. If printing goes well, the day goes well and the user is productive. If not, the anguish caused can ruin the whole day. What the user wants to do is simple:

- Print correctly every time.
- Print as soon as possible.
- Find the print job.

It sounds simple, doesn't it? Well, let's look at what the user has to consider to accomplish this. Are there any road blocks in the way?

Print Correctly Every Time

Here is what often occurs:

1. Users set up the printing requirements in a particular application. They set it up in the way that they think a printer (the one they want to print to) will be set up when the print job gets there.
2. They send their jobs to a specific computer port that users hope is connected to the right Novell queue. They expect the printer they want is attached to that queue. They hope that no one has changed anything.
3. Then, they wait. If their print jobs don't come out right, users send the files again. If the print jobs don't come out of the printer the users think they sent the files to, users look around the office in hopes of finding the output.
4. If users don't find the output, they send the files again and maybe again and again and again!

What could users do to make their print jobs print using the right printer at the right location? What do they need to look for? What is involved in making print jobs process flawlessly? Users must consider many factors to print successfully on a network. Many factors besides the printer need to be looked at. The application used to output the print jobs, the computer ports used to send and receive the files, and the NetWare queue are three major factors. Let's take a look at each.

The Application. Applications don't talk directly to printers; the programs talk to either printer ports (a discussion coming up next) or the network queues (following a little later). First, users must take a close look at the application itself. Applications treat printing in different ways. The application may (or may not) be capable of producing the desired results.

The printer driver is a key factor: The application must have the correct printer drivers. A *printer driver* enables the application to send all the right commands to the printer so that it will print correctly. In the "olden days" (way back in 1985 or so) there were only a couple of drivers available. Applications could only print to Epson-emulating printers or to the now-all-but-extinct Diablo 630-emulating (daisy wheel) printer. Today, some applications provide more than 100 driver choices. Dot matrix printers generally have their own drivers, or they will emulate Epson or IBM printers. Whenever a user wants to change printers the printer driver must be changed. A unique driver exists within each application for nearly every type of printer. Some proprietary applications, though, give the users hardly any choice at all. In fact some of these applications still won't let the user print to laser printers because the programs lack the necessary printer drivers.

Once users have lined up the correct printer drivers for their application and printer, they must get their print jobs to the port.

The Printer Port. Within their applications, users must select the printer port, by type and by number. They may select either parallel or serial ports. Say users have five choices (a total of five parallel and serial ports on the back of their systems' CPUs):

- LPT1, LPT2, LPT3 (parallel ports)
- COM1, COM2 (serial ports)

Printing through a parallel port is faster than through a serial port, although serial communications support longer distances. The choice is yours. Now we have to get to the NetWare queue.

The NetWare Queue. These printer ports are then captured (associated with) certain Novell *queues* (sequences of print files "in line" to be printed). These queues have names that are not easy for users to relate to, for example: PrintQ_0, PrintQ_1, and PrintQ_2. Isn't that simple? The queue is associated with a particular printer. Will it be the right one? Let's take a closer look at the printer. Selecting the right printer is quite complex. The outcome of users' print jobs depends on it. We need to look at the printer itself, its native language, the paper and the paper trays, the fonts, and printer memory.

The Printer Itself. Last but not least, the user must consider the printer's capabilities. Each printer has a unique set of strengths and weaknesses. To what type of printer are users sending their print jobs—dot matrix, daisy wheel, laser, ink jet, or plotter? Laser printers fall into two main groups. These groups are separated by the Page Description Language (PDL) they speak. PDLs include Adobe's PostScript and Hewlett Packard's PCL. Hewlett Packard PCL language currently dominates the laser printer market. The user must also consider paper size and type; printer memory; fonts (internal, cartridge, and soft); simplex and duplex printing. You can see that the variables are myriad.

Print as Soon as Possible

To print as quickly as possible, users must find a printer that is nearby and available. Finding a printer physically located close by should be fairly easy. However, for users to determine and remember that printer's queue number is another story. As Administrators add, move, and change the location of printers, the queue numbers assigned to printers can be hard for users to keep track of. Users may send a job to a queue that is in another part of the building. They may *never* find their print jobs.

Another part of the puzzle users must contend with is how many people are in front of them in the queue. What are their jobs' positions in the queue and how long will the files take to print? This is not obvious! If a printer is currently printing out a job, the number of jobs that must be printed before the users' jobs will start can be 0 to 250 or so. How long it will take depends on the number of jobs ahead in the queue and the length of each one (in pages). A more complex job will also take longer to print. Graphics and soft fonts also add to the total print time.

Users could find out the number of jobs in the queue by using a Novell utility (PCON-SOLE). With all the other variables involved, though, this information is nearly useless. The network Administrator can also be quite burdened by trying to help users understand PCONSOLE.

Another contributing factor to delays is depletion of the printer's supplies. In a high-use area, this can be a constant dilemma, and each user must be made aware of the responsibility to replace supplies and the problems that can be avoided by not letting the printer run out in the first place.

Do not anticipate trouble, or worry about what may never happen. Keep in the sunlight.

—Benjamin Franklin

Find the Print Job

Because of confusion that queue numbers and far-flung network printers can create, users may not know where their print jobs will turn up. Sometimes users go all over the office in search of their long-lost print jobs. In fact, sometimes print jobs just disappear. Non-PostScript jobs sent to PostScript printers can disappear. Cabling problems can cause jobs to disappear.

How can we stop all the running around? One way is to turn on messaging by using Novell's CASTON feature. If messaging is activated, users can be notified which queue their print jobs actually went to and that their jobs have finished printing. This rectifies the "disappearing print job" that is repeatedly sent to be printed.

Sometimes, a print job is accidentally picked up by other staff. The Novell banner page (even though it may waste some paper) helps people learn who owns each print job. If jobs go somewhere that the user did not expect, other staff in the office can help the users track the printouts down.

> If a Novell banner page is enabled for a PostScript job, the job can also disappear. Most PostScript printers don't understand this command.

The Network Administrator

Now we'll explore the essence of printing from the network Administrator's perspective. The network Administrator looks at things slightly differently than do users. In many instances, users are the Administrator's clients. Instead of being on the firing line, constantly reacting to things as they happen, the network Administrator needs to plan ahead. The Administrator must make tactical decisions related to the users' needs in the following ways:

Users' Perspective	Administrator's Issues
Print correctly every time.	What print resources do we need?
Print as soon as possible.	Where do the printers need to be? How many do we need?
Find the print job.	What happened to the print job? Who needs information?

Many LAN environments still function this way: The network Administrator provides print queues and some basic printer information to the user. The rest is up to the user. If an additional printer is needed, it is up to the user's department to fund the purchase and choose the printer model. To completely manage the printer resources, the network Administrator must consider the factors of providing all the resources that the users need to get the job printed right. Most of the factors involve choosing the printer in the first place. Let's take a look at all of these factors, starting at the beginning.

What Print Resources Do We Need?

It isn't easy choosing the right printer for all of the possible jobs users may casually send to the queue. To choose the right printer, the network Administrator must consider all the factors that the users consider plus a few more. Here are many of the factors: the application, the paper types and sizes, the PDL, the printer memory, and the many fonts. The applications that are in use on the network will help determine the printer PDL needed. Some applications support mainly Hewlett Packard's PCL; others support mainly Adobe's PostScript Language. For many applications, users want to have the ability to print using both languages.

Memory. Applications that are highly graphic in nature or those with a large number of soft fonts require more memory than do applications that provide only plain-text printing. If you can standardize the applications used throughout the network, support is of course easier.

Paper. The paper types needed will help determine how many bins will be needed on the printer. If envelopes are printed out, an envelope feeder will be needed. If paper larger than $8^1/2$ by 14 is needed, you will have to look at a specialty printer capable of printing the size you need. The printer might also need to perform duplex printing.

Fonts. If the users want to print more than nonproportional text, fonts will become an issue. You will need to determine whether you can use internal fonts, cartridge fonts, or soft fonts. If users have trouble printing, the Administrator should set up training schedules for the users. The Administrator may need the help of printer operators to help keep the printers well supplied and to help users resolve difficulties. The less you add and move printers around the office, the easier it will be to manage the print resources.

Where Do the Printers Need to Be? How Many Do We Need?

To enable users to print their jobs as quickly as possible, the network Administrator needs to provide a printer that is nearby and available. The Administrator needs to establish a network architecture containing enough printers so that printers are close enough and easy to see. Users need to see the nearest printer to know

- whether the printer is busy and they should direct their jobs to another printer
- whether the printer is out for maintenance, off-line, or out of supplies

Printers should have plenty of supplies at hand. As the Administrator sets up all the queues for every printer, he or she should tell users what resources are available and what the queue number is. If the network Administrator could find out what volume each user usually printed, the printers could be placed close to the users that print the most. This would minimize the steps people spend walking back and forth to printers.

What Happened to the Print Job? Who Needs Information?

To let users know when their jobs have finished processing, the network Administrator will need to turn on job notification (messaging). We will take a look at how this is done a little later. In order for users to know whose job is in the printer tray, the Administrator should activate the banner page feature.

Without messaging and banners in place, the Administrator will spend a lot of time helping users find lost jobs. Users should be trained, as time allows, to send print jobs to print queues, and the Administrator should let users know which printers are attached to them.

Proactive Administrators set yearly preventative maintenance schedules. The network Administrator should aim never to run out of supplies for every printer. Try to manage network bandwidth for downloading soft fonts.

The MIS Director or CIO

The MIS director or the CIO makes strategic network decisions. These managers depend on the Administrator for the best information that they can get. Information traditionally is the "best guess" made by the network Administrator. Printing is an expensive company resource, but one that is difficult to get details about. There are few tools available that track network printing resources. The strategic decisions MIS directors and CIOs make may occur years before users and even Administrators witness the results of these decisions.

Let's see how MIS directors and CIOs may look at the issues raised earlier for users and Administrators:

Users' Perspective	MIS Director/CIO's Issues
Print correctly every time.	Information to cost justify the purchase of the asset.
Print as soon as possible.	How will this strategy make the users more productive?
Find the print job.	Do I have the information to manage ongoing costs?
	What about additional resources?

Giving the Boss Ammunition for Purchasing

The MIS director or the CIO looks at factors such as cost justification of hardware. If someone wants to spend money on equipment for the company, the managers want to know whether the company will benefit from purchasing the equipment in terms of time or money saved. The MIS director or CIO relies on the Administrator for this information. Often only some of the information is immediately available. The network Administrator may be forced to rely on other sources or projections of future growth for the information.

This is what typically happens. The network Administrator reports that the users are complaining. They are either complaining that it takes too long to print or that they have to go too far to the printer. The network Administrator takes their word for it. He gives this information to the MIS Director or CIO. The CIO then looks for the budget money or puts a new printer in the budget without knowing many details. CIO approves or disapproves without concrete basis either for or against. One way to get the information is to create a log of usage by printer or use accounting software available through a third party.

Explaining How This Strategy Makes Users More Productive

With this the MIS Director needs to decide what effect printers have on productivity of the office. Will more printers make users more productive or less? Should printers be centralized so we can get faster network printers? Should every user have his or her own printer? Productivity is the key here. Much more information is needed to determine the answers here. Each network is different and it is this complexity that makes gathering the information difficult. This burden usually falls on the network Administrator to get the information. This is what occurs on many networks: Users complain. The network Administrator complains. CIO must add systems and strategies as needed to stop complaining. Good luck to the network Administrator.

Obtaining the Information to Manage Ongoing Costs

The MIS director or the CIO wants the network Administrator to provide information needed to manage the ongoing costs properly. If the information is complete, the task is a huge one. Third-party software can help an Administrator to gather this information. Paper types and costs, toner usage, preventative maintenance schedules, and printer life cycles play a part in this big picture.

Perplexity is the beginning of knowledge.

—Kahlil Gibran

Now that you understand the many subtle complexities of NetWare printing, it is time to explore the how's and the what's. Are you in tune with the essence of NetWare printing?

NetWare Printing System Installation

NetWare printers are printers that are directly attached to the network. These printers can be accessed by all users on the LAN and shared "transparently." In a transparent NetWare printing environment, users print directly from their network applications and the output "magically" appears in the printer down the hall. This type of sophisticated resource sharing is the goal when Administrators install, configure, and manage network printers. Refer to Figure 14.1 for an illustration of NetWare's printing system.

The physical limitation for the number of printers that can be attached to a typical microcomputer is a maximum of five—three parallel and two serial. This is also the maximum number of printers that can be attached to a NetWare file server. The most popular method of NetWare printer installation is to attach the printers directly to the file server. This is accomplished through core printing or a nondedicated print server (NLM or VAP). Although this configuration has its advantages, it tends to bog down the server in high-load environments. Other problems include connectivity and convenience for users sharing printers from different rooms or floors of a building. Security also becomes an issue. To satisfy the printing needs of larger networks, NetWare provides dedicated print servers (.EXE) and remote printing. We will discuss these three different strategies for installing network printers: core printing, print servers (files with .VAP, .NLM, or .EXE extensions), and RPRINTER/NPRINTER.

Core Printing

During NetWare v2.2's standard configuration and installation procedure, you will be asked to specify whether you want to assign various parallel (LPT1, LPT2, LPT3) or serial (COM1, COM2) ports on the file server to network printers. Parallel printers do not

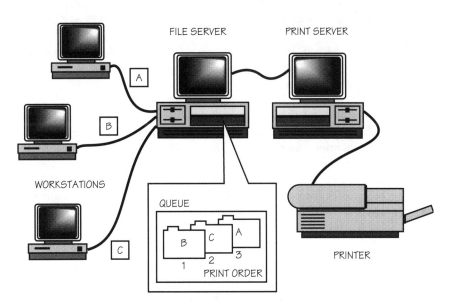

FIGURE 14.1 The Structure of NetWare's Printing System

require any additional hardware communications settings because they are speaking a language familiar to the file server.

Serial printers, on the other hand, use the data-transfer protocol, which must be custom configured. Serial printers tend to be slower because of their 9600-bps limitation. To configure a serial network printer you must inform the system which settings you are using for your data-transfer protocol.

Installing network printers through core printing is the simplest way to go, but it doesn't offer much flexibility. NetWare v3.11 and v4.0 no longer support core printing; they use print servers. Remember: Don't make the situation more confusing or complex if you don't have to. Core printing works just fine for most small NetWare v2.2 LANs.

Print Servers

Print servers provide additional functionality and location flexibility. Also, print server services are required when the number of printers exceeds the file server's limit of five. They will also be needed if the physical layout of the LAN is large or the system's printers require customized control hardware or software. NetWare v2.2 and v3.11 print servers support 16 printers over 8 file servers. NetWare v4.0 print servers support 256 printers over 32 file servers. NetWare print servers fall into two categories:

- dedicated, external—PSERVER.EXE
- nondedicated, internal—PSERVER.VAP (v2.2) and PSERVER.NLM (v3.11 and v4.0)

There are also third-party products such as Bitstream's MOSAIC that do many more tasks, including print job accounting.

In NetWare v4.0, each printer object occupies 20KB of file server RAM. Therefore, a LAN with 256 printers will require 5MB of file server RAM.

In addition, there are hardware connectivity products that are often called print servers. Many companies manufacture hardware/software products designed to integrate into a NetWare LAN and assume print server responsibilities. Products include the Intel Netport or HP's JetDirect internal card for the HP LaserJets.

Another set of products may be classified as *print directors*—utilities to help users get to the right printer or queue for the job. Windows' Print Manager may help get the user to the right printer for the job. Brightwork Development Inc. offers PS-Print, which supports both dedicated and nondedicated print server configurations. Fresh Technology Group offers a similar print directing product called Printer Assist Plus. One aspect of Bitstream's MOSAIC software is to analyze the print job and get it to the right print resource. We will take a closer look at some of these third-party solutions a little later in the chapter.

To install a print server, you must first define the server configurations in PCONSOLE (using steps given later in the chapter). Next, you must type the following commands:

Nondedicated NetWare v3.11 or v4.0—:**LOAD PSERVER** *print server name*
Nondedicated NetWare v2.2—**copy PSERVER.VAP to SYS:SYSTEM** and reboot
Dedicated—**copy PSERVER.EXE** to dedicated workstation disk and execute it

It is a good idea to add the line SPX CONNECTIONS = 60 **to the NET.CFG file of the dedicated print server machine. It will increase performance and prevent unexpected problems.**

RPRINTER/NPRINTER for Remote Printing

Another possible strategy for increasing a network's printing capacity is remote printing. *Remote printing* is the concept of using printers attached to workstations as network devices. This flexibility can alleviate the need for dedicated print servers and add as many as 16 printers to the LAN. Remote printing can also be handled in two ways: third-party or NetWare. There are many companies that offer "remote printing" products, but beware of the RAM stress they will put on the workstation. The other alternative is to use one of Novell's two remote printing utilities—RPRINTER.EXE and NPRINTER.EXE. Both remote printing utilities provide NetWare printing services to NetWare users from local workstation printers.

RPRINTER is supported by NetWare v2.2 and v3.11 and uses only 9KB of workstation RAM. To install RPRINTER, you must first define the remote printer in PCONSOLE (as described later in the chapter). Next, you move to the workstation with the remote printer attached and type the following command: **RPRINTER PS=***print server* **P=***printer number*.

NPRINTER is new to NetWare v4.0 and uses an efficient 3KB of workstation RAM. NPRINTER.EXE provides the same remote printing services as RPRINTER and loads with the same PS and P parameters. In addition, NPRINTER.NLM is required for printers attached to NetWare v4.0 file servers.

To provide remote printing services for two printers on the same workstation, load RPRINTER/NPRINTER twice with two different printer numbers.

RPRINTER/NPRINTER requires that the workstation attach itself to the LAN—you do not have to be logged in. To use RPRINTER without logging in, simply copy the RPRINTER.EXE or NPRINTER.EXE file from SYS:PUBLIC to the local workstation drive. Then type **IPX**, **NETX**, and the RPRINTER/NPRINTER command. In NetWare v4.0, users would not execute IPX or NETX. Instead they would type STARTNET.BAT from the C:\NWCLIENT directory.

RPRINTER/NPRINTER will not work if the workstation's NET.CFG file has the Local Printers = 0 **line. Also, add the following lines to the NET.CFG file:**

SPX Abort Timeout = 1500

IPX Retry Count = 50

Printing Configurations

Now that the network printers have been installed, we must define the printing configurations to use for each printer and the system as a whole. *Printing configurations* establish the system rules and restrictions for users with respect to sharing the network printers. These configurations determine *who* gets to use the system, *how* users attach to the shared devices, and *what* their output ultimately looks like. Printing configurations are established according to seven criteria:

- Print queues
- Print spools
- Queue users
- Queue operators

- Print jobs
- Printing parameters
- Printing forms

Print Queues

A *print queue* is a "holding cell" where print jobs are routed and customized before they are actually sent to the printer. The print queue is serviced by the print server. This means that the print server acts like a traffic cop directing the print jobs to the right queue. This happens whether the print server is internal or external from the file server. Print queues allow many different users to send print jobs to the same printer simultaneously; this is where they are all sorted out. Each printer must have at least one print queue. Print queues are defined as subdirectories of the SYS: SYSTEM subdirectory on the host NetWare file server. Queue subdirectories have the .QDR extension.

Print Spools

A *print spool* is a "gathering area" for large print jobs. Print spools will accept large jobs very quickly and free up the user's workstation for other tasks. The spool then organizes the print job and sends it to its own specific print queue. Each print queue must have at least one print spool "mapped" to it. In addition, print spools can act as compatibility devices for print jobs coming from networks running on different versions of NetWare. Print spooling is transparently integrated into NetWare v3.11 and v4.0 print queues.

Queue Users

Queue users are users who are authorized to use a specific print queue. Each print queue must have one or more queue users, or the queue is totally useless. By default, all NetWare print queues include the group Everyone as a queue user.

Queue Operators

A *queue operator* is a queue user who has been given additional print queue privileges. Queue operators can reorganize print job priorities, put print jobs on hold, or delete print jobs altogether. Queue operators are a good idea for delegating simple network maintenance duties. By default, the Supervisor is queue operator on all NetWare print queues.

Print Jobs

A *print job* is the actual data being sent to the network printer. The print job itself is bound by many different configuration options: number of copies, type of banner, destination print queue, and file server name. In addition, print jobs are assigned a specific set of printing parameters (mode) and a printing form name.

Printing Parameters

Print jobs are bound by a list of specific *printing parameters* that tell it exactly how to print. Parameters such as 10 cpi (characters per inch), near-letter quality, and 6 lines per inch are combined to create a print job's mode. The print mode describes exactly how the print job is to be printed, whereas the printer itself adds functions such as orientation, spacing, pitch, character set, and font.

Printing Forms

Printing forms define the type of paper the print job will use once it gets to the network printer. Each of the form options must be made available to the printer whether fed through manually or handled by a sophisticated paper tray setup. Some common print forms are continuous feed, letterhead, green-bar, address labels, checks, and envelopes. Most network printers prompt you for the insertion of specific paper types if the print form is anything other than the default $8^1/2$-by-11-inch paper.

Following is a brief description of NetWare's default printing configurations.

Default Printing Configuration

The printing configuration parameters are established by NetWare once the network printers are installed. Whether the installation was accomplished through NetWare or as a dedicated print server, the network operating system treats the printing configurations exactly the same. The default settings for our printing criteria are as follows:

Print queue	One print queue is created for each network printer that was assigned during the installation process. The queue for PRINTER_0 is named PRINTQ_0, and similarly PRINTER_1 is assigned the Queue PRINTQ_1. Additional network printers are assigned similarly named print queues.
Print spools	One print spooler is "mapped" to each assigned print queue.
Queue users	The group Everyone is assigned to each print queue as the queue user. This means everybody on the network can attach to every network printer.
Queue operators	The Supervisor is assigned as the queue operator to each print queue. Any other queue operators must be assigned by the Supervisor.
Print jobs	The default print job configuration prints one copy of the file with a banner using the user's login name. This setup will print to the first default print queue it can find and use the default print mode. The form name it recognizes is "default."
Printing parameters	The default print mode is set by the individual printer. These parameters do not change unless the Supervisor customizes them personally.
Printing forms	The default printing form is form 0 (standard). It defines a page that is $8^1/2$ inches wide and 11 inches long.

This default printing configuration satisfies 75 percent of the network Administrators and can be specialized with just a few small changes: customizing print queue names, adding queue users and operators, and maybe even modifying a few print job configuration parameters. These minor alterations won't take very much effort and shouldn't considerably increase the system's overall complexity. It's the big changes that can get "hairy."

If you make any changes at all (and you will) to the default printing configurations, you will instantly enter a new frontier—netware printing management.

NetWare Printing Management

Printing management is the network Administrator's responsibility. It includes configuring, maintaining, and troubleshooting the network's printing system. This is that "transitional" area between network management and network maintenance. Printer management does not only involve initially customizing the printer configurations but also "continually" customizing the printer configurations. As new printers are attached to the network, different forms are developed. As interconnectivity is established, it is the network Administrator's responsibility to ensure that everybody can peacefully coexist and print within the realm of the existing topology design. Now you can see where the loss of "hair" comes in.

All of these mind-boggling obligations can be accomplished through the use of three menu utilities: PCONSOLE, PRINTCON, and PRINTDEF. Get to know these utilities like the back of your hand!

PCONSOLE

PCONSOLE enables the Supervisor to add, delete, or modify print queues, print servers, and printers. In addition, PCONSOLE enables users to send print jobs to a specific queue and modify its job configurations. Figure 14.2 illustrates the PCONSOLE Main menu.

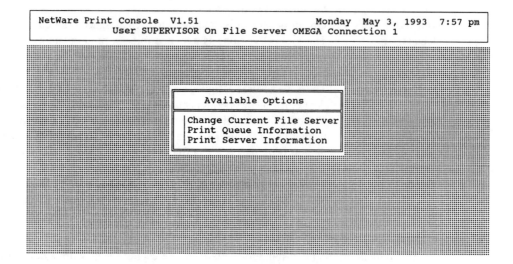

```
NetWare Print Console  V1.51                Monday  May 3, 1993  7:57 pm
                 User SUPERVISOR On File Server OMEGA Connection 1


                           ┌─────────────────────────┐
                           │     Available Options    │
                           ├─────────────────────────┤
                           │ Change Current File Server│
                           │ Print Queue Information   │
                           │ Print Server Information  │
                           └─────────────────────────┘
```

FIGURE 14.2   Available Options in PCONSOLE

Print Queues

To add a print queue to the system, press Ins at the Print Queues screen in PCONSOLE. To alter the configurations of a specific queue, highlight it and press Enter. The Print Queue Information window will pop up. The Print Queue Information screen provides customization of print queue parameters.

Queue Users. The Print Queue Information window has an option for Queue Users. Within this option we can add or delete specific users or groups as authorized users of this particular print queue.

Queue Operators. The Print Queue Information window also has an option for Queue Operators. This option enables the Administrator to add or delete users or groups as print queue operators. Queue operators have additional privileges in PCONSOLE that queue users don't, such as queue creation, configuration, and print job management.

In addition, PCONSOLE enables the Supervisor, operators, and queue users to display the "current print job entries" and view detailed information about each print job through the subsequent Print Queue Entry Information screen.

Print Servers

To create a NetWare print server, highlight Print Servers from the PCONSOLE menu and press Enter. Press Ins at the Print Servers list and specify a unique print server name—such as NIRVANA_PS. Once the print server has been created, you must define additional print server configurations, namely printers, attached queues, and print server operators.

Printer definition is discussed later. The final and most important step in a NetWare printing setup is to attach the printer to an existing queue. Highlight Attach Printer To Queue and press Enter. Press Ins to add the queue.

Printers

To define a network printer in NetWare v2.2 and v3.11, choose Configure Printers from the Print Server Information screen. Enter the name of the printer and define the local printing port. If the printer is attached to a remote workstation, choose Remote-LPT1: (or equivalent) and press Enter. To define a network printer in NetWare v4.0, follow the same instructions just given or use NWADMIN to create a printer object. To attach the printer to an existing queue in NWADMIN, highlight Assignments from the Printer window. Define the host print server and print queue, and click OK.

Printing Setup

Printing setup can be summed up in four simple steps:

1. Create the print queue: Print Queues in PCONSOLE.
2. Create the print server: Print Servers in PCONSOLE.
3. Create and configure the network printer: Configure Printers from Print Server Information in PCONSOLE.
4. Assign the network printer to the print queue: Attach Printer To Queue from Print Server Information in PCONSOLE.

All of these printing setup tasks are performed in PCONSOLE and covered in the previous discussion. NetWare v4.0 offers two administrative tools that automate this process: PSETUP and Quick setup from PCONSOLE.

The NetWare v4.0 version of PCONSOLE offers two display modes: Bindery and NDS. Bindery mode emulates the v2.2/v3.11 utility. Use F4 to switch between PCONSOLE modes.

Remember: Once NetWare printing has been installed, you must use PSERVER and RPRINTER/NPRINTER to activate it.

PRINTCON

PRINTCON enables the Supervisor to add, modify, or delete specific parameters about a print job's configuration. The network Administrator can establish a variety of print job configurations, name them, and then each time a user sends a print job to the network printer, a different configuration may be used. The system will automatically use the print job configuration that has been assigned as the "default." Users can select which configuration they want to be the default.

Print Jobs

To create a new print job configuration, choose Edit Print Job Configurations in the Available Options window of PRINTCON. Press Ins to display the Enter New Name window. A print job configuration name can be up to 31 characters long, but it must not contain spaces. Enter a new name and the expanded Edit Print Job Configurations screen shown in Figure 14.3 will appear. Most of the Print Job Configuration options are self-explanatory, but two look a little bit more interesting: MODE and DEVICE. We will explore these in the next discussion.

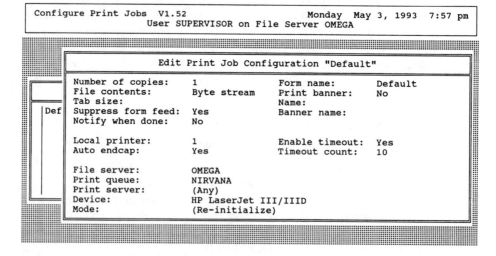

FIGURE 14.3 Print Job Configurations in PCONSOLE

To change the default print job configuration, choose the Select Default Print Job Configuration option and move to the name you would like. The next time you print to a network printer, this print job configuration will control your output.

Print job configurations are user-specific. Each user has a PRINTCON.DAT data file stored in his or her user-specific MAIL subdirectory, which contains all of the customized printing options. If the users don't have write privileges in the MAIL directory, then they cannot edit their own print job configurations.

PRINTDEF

The PRINTDEF utility enables the Supervisor, and only the Supervisor, to create a database of printing parameters for use by all of the network users. Once a parameter database has been created, it shows up as a choice in the Edit Print Job Configurations window. There are primarily two types of printing parameter databases: print devices and forms.

Print Device Parameters

Print devices are NetWare printer drivers that contain default print modes. A *mode* is a list of printing parameters and commands that are to be executed by the printer once the print job gets there. The print device is attached to the print mode. The modes are so complex and technical that they must be defined for specific printing devices. To define these parameters, choose Print Devices at the PRINTDEF Options Main menu. Using the Print Device Options window, you can edit, import, or export print devices.

NetWare provides a list of the print device *definition files* that are standard on most systems. If your printer is not on this list, you should have been supplied with a definition file from the printer's manufacturer. To add a new device to the system choose Import and specify the SYS:PUBLIC directory. To delete an existing device from the system choose Export. To edit an existing device, choose Edit. The Edit Device Option screen has two options: Device Modes and Device Functions. This is where you modify the device's mode. Each device can have multiple modes and functions, but for simplicity's sake, try to keep the number manageably low.

Printing Forms

The other option under PRINTDEF Options is Forms. Printing forms are much simpler than devices and modes. They simply define the length and width of the page. To define a print form, press Ins at the Forms screen, and the Form Definition window appears.

Once the devices, modes, and forms have been established, the users can choose from among them in the Edit Print Job Configurations window of PRINTCON. This window adds an additional level of flexibility and sophistication to the network printing system. Just make sure you don't bury your users in "sOPhiStIcAtioN." Simpler is better.

Well, now that we have established our "customized" network printing system, can you appreciate how quickly it gets out of hand? Remember the simple network printing picture at the beginning of this chapter? What happened to the good old days?

Printing is like castle cooking. Have you ever eaten castle food? It's very good. Culinary engineers spend decades learning the subtleties of red potatoes and mushy peas. Details such as the size of the vegetable, the amount of water in the pot, length of boiling, and additional ingredients quickly become overwhelming. It's not that difficult. Keep it simple. I recommend the cookbook method.

Network printing doesn't have to be a bowl of oatmeal. With enough common sense and a little compromise, we can develop a Network printing system that satisfies everyone's needs and doesn't require a troop of technicians to maintain.

Printing on a Network

Network printing can be accomplished in one of two ways: printing utilities or application printing.

Printing Utilities

Two NetWare utilities were primarily designed for sending files directly to a specific print queue. One is a menu utility (PCONSOLE) and the other is a command-line utility (NPRINT), yet both of them work exactly the same: they insert files directly into a specific print queue.

PCONSOLE. A user can insert a job into a specific print queue directly from the Current Print Job Entries window within PCONSOLE by pressing Ins. A prompt will ask you to enter a directory name to print from and then will list the files in the directory you choose. If you choose a specific file to print, another screen will prompt you for the print job configurations definition. Once you choose the appropriate "definition," the print job will be inserted into the queue, and sent off to the printer.

NPRINT. To print to a specific print queue from the command line, simply follow the correct "NPRINT" sentence structure:

```
NPRINT filename Q=print queue/option
```

where *option* can be any of the following:

```
S  = File server
PS = Print server
J  = Print job configuration name
F  = Form name or number
C  = Copies
B  = Banner name
NB = Send no banner at all
```

Applications Printing

We saw earlier that applications can cause trouble for printers. As you remember, applications don't "talk" directly to printers. The programs talk to ports or to queues. All applications are aware of ports. Some of the more sophisticated network applications are even aware of NetWare queues. On a network, users can be printing from applications that are Network-*aware* or Network-*unaware*. As the network Administrator, it is your responsibility to distinguish between the two, and take the appropriate strategy for configuring each user's specific printing needs.

Printing with network-aware applications is the simplest of the two scenarios, because we are talking about some sufficiently advanced software here. Not many applications are sophisticated enough to recognize a NetWare print queue; WordPerfect and Microsoft Windows are two exceptions. All of WordPerfect's network applications, from word processing to WordPerfect Office, are so Network-aware that they can recognize a NetWare print queue directly. You simply define the name of the queue in the program's Select Printer/Edit/Port option, and the rest is smooth sailing. In addition, Windows' Print Manager enables users to assign queues to local printing ports. This level of NetWare printing integration is unusual. Most network applications are network-unaware when it comes to printing.

Printing with network-unaware applications is another matter. Even if an application knows it's on a network, chances are it doesn't know how to find the network printer. These programs do, however, know how to find the workstation's local LPT port. With these applications, we have to fool them by "redirecting" their output from the local LPT port to the network queue. This concept is achieved through the use of the CAPTURE command-line utility. To "turn on" a workstation's capturing capabilities and send all application output to a specific network print queue, simply follow the correct "capture" sentence structure:

CAPTURE Q=*print queue* /*option*

where *option* can be any of the following:

S = File server
J = Print job configuration name
F = Form name or number
L = Local LPT port number
C = Copies
B = Banner name
NB = Send no banner at all

Figure 14.4 shows a complete table of the printing CAPTURE options. Once CAPTURE has been activated, the workstation's local printer cannot be used unless the user deactivates CAPTURE. This is accomplished by using the secondary command-line utility ENDCAP. Capturing is usually activated by batch files from NetWare login scripts: Use the SYSTEM login script for default capturing and the individual's USER login script if the user needs to capture to a specific print queue. Also, NetWare user tools enable users to configure specific capturing statements as needed. Refer to Chapter 13 for a discussion of NetWare user tools.

For network-unaware applications that "hold" onto print jobs until users exit the application, I have an answer. Simply use the /TI=10 (Timeout) parameter in CAPTURE and the queue will release the hostage job after a brief wait.

Is there any help in sight for us? Sure there is. Novell admits that the company can't solve every network need for every network user. Novell's emphasis is on the abilities of third parties to fill the gaps. Let's take a look at a few.

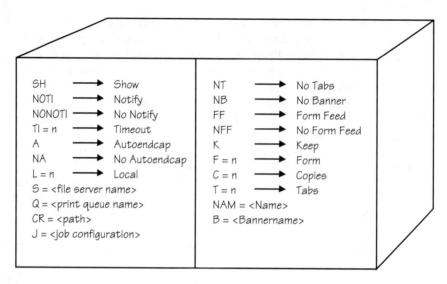

FIGURE 14.4   Using CAPTURE Options

Third-Party Products

The most sophisticated network printing product on the market is one by Bitstream: the MOSAIC print server. MOSAIC provides intelligence that analyzes the requests made by a user's software application (for example, paper type, font, and page description language) and matches the print job with a printer near the user that has the requested resources available. By doing so, MOSAIC can ensure that the print job is completed correctly on the first attempt. If for some reason the requested print resources are not available to that user, the network Administrator and/or the printer operator can be notified. That network decision maker can then make the appropriate resources available.

MOSAIC uses the instructions given to it by the network Administrator to determine where to send a print job. This is how the correct printer is chosen: By offering users a choice of several printers near their desks, MOSAIC can reduce the time most networks require to process print jobs. MOSAIC actually tracks which correctly configured printer will become available first, then directs the job to that printer. This means the job will be printed quickly and look the way the user expects it to.

The Bitstream MOSAIC print server tracks the print jobs to completion and then notifies the user when the job is complete and which printer processed it. A special banner page will help users to identify their print jobs among everyone else's if it is activated.

Using Novell's print server requires the Administrator to create a different print queue for each printer. By implementing MOSAIC, the Administrator can reduce the number of print queues needed, and MOSAIC will direct the print jobs to the proper printer. This product provides flexibility that enables the user to access a pool of printing resources. Department managers can offer their users different print resource types and let this intelligent print server deliver the print jobs to a printer. If the user only wants to print to one printer, this choice is also available. This means that printers can be physically attached wherever the Administrator wants them.

MOSAIC has complete accounting capabilities. This reporting gives information about the entire printing environment. The Administrator can track printing activity by user, printer, department, and project. This information can be used to help budget for purchases of toner and paper, scheduling printer maintenance, and cost justifying the next printer purchase. This accounting feature helps to provide tools to analyze printer usage and load-balance print traffic.

MOSAIC makes available the tools to make printing easier for both users and network Administrators while ensuring that the ongoing costs of network printing are managed carefully.

Chapter 15

Maintenance and Troubleshooting

"Tuesday—we back up data and water plants."

Now that you have read all the glamorous stuff about networking, let's turn to the least glamorous but very critical subject of maintenance and troubleshooting. These areas are vital to the ongoing smooth operation of any system. The many aspects of the Maintenance portion are outlined under Maintenance options in this chapter. Each will be covered in more detail.

Documentation

Documentation consists of gathering together different sets of data and assembling them into notebooks so the network manager has a hard copy of the system configuration and the node or user configurations. If you're a network manager a good premise to go on is disaster recovery. If your system was destroyed and you had to duplicate the whole software setup on new hardware, what would you need to do the job fast and accurately? The information you need for disaster recovery is what your documentation should consist of.

There are three documentation components to consider:

- hardware
- software
- network design

The hardware documentation is all the paperwork that's needed for verification (such as type of workstation, cards installed, and cables, plus serial numbers of hardware) on the file servers, workstations, and topology components. The software documentation is all the software installed on the servers and workstations with the licensing information included.

The configuration information is how the security levels are set up and who's in which group(s), user information, and printer configuration. Don't be surprised if this documentation grows into several notebooks!

Only those things are beautiful which are inspired by madness and written by reason.

—André Gide

Hardware Documentation

There are two philosophies of hardware documentation: Document as you go or document at the end of the installation. I prefer doing it at the end of the installation. The question is not *whether* it should be done but *when*.

If you assemble the hardware and software data as you install each workstation, you have all the paperwork and serial numbers in one place (such as a manila envelope or a plastic sheet protector). If you're installing a network in an existing location with people working around, under, and over you, it's hard to record all the information as you go because you can't leave the envelope with the information at the workstation site.

If you perform all your documentation tasks at the end of the installation, you can keep all your paperwork in one spot (or office) and go from node to node to collect your data. The down side is that when you're done with an installation, it's hard to sit down and document everything; it's easy to rationalize that the person taking over from you really doesn't need all this silly paperwork.

Hardware documentation consists of recording what hardware and software are installed. The easiest approach is to create a worksheet(s) with information that's needed. Don't forget to include the room number or the identification used for the cabling on one of the sheets.

One simple way to assemble all this information is to have a plastic sheet protector (top opening) for each node. Keep your worksheet in it so you can add paperwork as you go. If you send someone out to install a piece of hardware, make it a rule for the person to bring back the serial number or information that's needed for that node's configuration. If your recorded facts and figures are on a piece of paper, you can throw the paper in the plastic and transfer the information later. Let your installation team know up front what you're doing, what you're assembling, and what you expect from them.

File Servers and Workstations

A vital piece of information to include is the serial number of the workstation, the cards installed (and serial numbers, if necessary), the software installed with the licensing information, the printer (if any) with the serial number, any modems or external hardware, and anything else peculiar to that file server or workstation.

Topology Components

Topology documentation should include any hardware not included in file servers, workstations, and printers. Your records should be all-encompassing. Equipment to include encompasses hubs, NICs, and MAUs, and lists should record the addresses, routers, and external hard drives.

Printers

Printer documentation should include the type of printer, serial number, special fonts loaded, whether the printer is serial or parallel, its port address, and how it's configured on the network. In addition, the documentation should list the printer's host file server/workstation and its physical location.

All hardware, serial numbers, types, manufacturers, configurations, and other pertinent data should be on paper in an easily retrievable notebook. Another godsend during a crisis is a cleaned-up blueprint (full size or reduced) of the electrical/cable layout of the facility (or facilities). Overlaying placement of equipment on top of this gives you a complete picture of cable terminations, electrical and telephone outlets, and equipment placement.

Software Documentation

Software documentation should always include serial numbers and/or licensing numbers of all software. Start with the network operating system, then all the software on each file server, then the software on each workstation. Network software documentation should include at least the full name of the software, release number (and date, if applicable), licensing authorization number, and user limit (if applicable).

Network Design

Regardless of whether the installation team or the network manager assembles the book that records the network design, it's necessary. Even if you ignore my advice, you'll only ignore this documentation once. That's because you'll sweat bullets when you need the information and it's not at your fingertips. You'll document from then on.

System configuration documentation consists of

- the directory structure, which consists of system directories, user directories, and application/data directories
- volume configuration

An easy way to start your documentation on the system is with your installation layout notes. Before you began installing the system, you probably had paperwork showing how the operating system was going to be configured during installation (refer to the Novell worksheets in your NetWare documentation) and which user (or group) would get which security rights. That's a good beginning for this part of the documentation.

FILER

Go into FILER to document all your volume, directory, and subdirectory information. Once you've loaded FILER, display the Current Directory Information screen. The contents of whatever directory you're in will be displayed. You can go into the root directory, screen print those contents, then go into each directory as deeply as you want. I highly recommend you do this *before* you let users log onto the network so the structure recorded will be the most basic system directory configuration and if you ever have to duplicate it, you've got a starting point.

While you're in a directory (or while you're creating a directory), make note of the rights and attributes each directory has. This may seem basic when you have a new system, but once users start to create new directories, this clean, logical system configuration can evolve into specialized subdirectory pockets. Don't try to keep all the security information in your head—get it down on paper so it's easily accessible. By doing this, you're also making it easier on yourself to compare and keep track of growth on each volume to make sure it's still secure.

Once you're recorded one volume, do the same for each of the others. This venture is time consuming, but it's well worth the time and effort. Sensitive directories can be tagged Private so users can see a listing of files within the directory but not what's in the files. Make sure you have a hard copy of the filenames in all private-tagged directories.

If you have files within a directory that you need to secure in a special way (such as Read-Only), make note of those files. Generally those files would reside in only one or two directories (such as an accounting directory or a master forms directory) but make note of them anyway.

SYSCON

Enter the SYSCON utility and document the following information:

- Once you've loaded SYSCON, go into Group Names. Every group on the volume will be shown. Enter the first group and record the group's full name. If you haven't made note of this, do it now or screen print. Escape and go into Member List. This will list everyone in that group. If it's a general group, it's going to be long.

- Escape and go into Trustee Directory Assignments. This is a vital listing to have in hard copy. This lists the attributes of each directory. If you have to reinstall or duplicate your network, having this information on paper will make your job much easier.
- Once you're done documenting the groups, escape the last group and switch to Supervisor Options. This area lists your system defaults—such as the system login script.
- Switch to Default Account Balance and screen print this balance. This is important if you need to reconstruct the account configuration for billing.
- Next is Default Time Restrictions. If you start with 24 hours a day as your default, you probably need to make note of that but not screen print it.
- Next is the File Server Console Operator. Make a list of everyone on this list or screen print.
- Screen print the Intruder Detection Lockout so you know what you started with. If you ever change it, reprint it for your documentation.
- Screen print the System Login Script. If you change it, reprint it!
- The final data group is Workgroup managers. Print this one out—don't think that just because you only have one or two managers you can remember them. In an emergency, little things get by you.

User Information

There are two types of user documentation: records per file server and ones per user. If you've created a paperwork structure for individual users in the installation, these records may serve as a good basis for this part of the documentation. I recommend a User Information Sheet or a notebook with information for each user. This becomes huge if you have a large network, and it's time consuming to keep up. However, the records could help you if there's ever a security breach, data corruption by a disgruntled employee, or hacker damage.

If you have your user groups and user information on paper for the installation, all you may need to do is separate it into individual users. If you've listed groups of individuals with the same security rights, just copy your paperwork for each user. Although a nicely set out, handwritten or typed sheet for each user is great, let's be realistic. As long as you can put your hands on information for each user, that's what you start with. As you get comfortable with the network and as you have time, make your notebooks more detailed and "prettier." Just make sure you can produce the information that's needed when it's needed.

If you don't have paperwork to start with, load SYSCON, switch to the User Information area, and construct your documentation from the information there. If this is the way you have to do it, there are several approaches you can take. You can go into each User Information listing and screen print. That method is fine, but it may take a while to complete for many users.

The other way of capturing this material is to create a worksheet listing all the groups, the security equivalences, station restrictions, and so on, and then mark, cross out, or circle which ones apply for each individual user. That way you have a complete listing of what's on each volume and who has access privileges to what.

This technique is great in the beginning, but what happens when you add directories that users need? There's no answer to this great question but be creative. If you've started your documentation this way, you're going to be reluctant to redo everything just because someone needed something you hadn't thought of. Use tabs, stickers, labels—anything will do.

One thing to remember: If you're using a worksheet, allow for growth and additions. You've always got the back side of the paper to work with!

Don't make excuses for documentation—it's easy to put it off. Just accept it as part of the installer's or network manager's job description. It's also the network manager's job to maintain and *update* the documentation. Just imagine yourself after an earthquake as your bosses demand that you duplicate the system so work can keep flowing. If you have good documentation, the re-creation of your system will be fast and easy. Backups are great for data, but if you're restoring onto a new file server, you need to know what information to start with.

There's no one great way to document your network. Start with what other people have done and fashion your own set of documentation—whether it be notebooks, cards, or whatever. The best documentation is what you feel comfortable working with. There's no wrong way (except not doing it!). Just make sure you include all the information you'll ever need to reconstruct your system.

And think how impressed your bosses will be if you can hand them serial numbers of destroyed hardware while they're working on your reconstructed network in a temporary location. It's a nasty scenario, but it can happen. That's what documentation is all about.

Backup Systems

A sound backup system is a key player in maintaining your system. Be sure that the system you and your cohorts select is certified NetWare compatible. Then review your needs and develop a plan to use the backup product to its fullest capabilities.

In skating over thin ice our safety is in our speed.

—Ralph Waldo Emerson

Backup Systems and Features

Various types of backup systems are out there today: optical storage, tape (both $1/4$-inch and DAT formats, internal and external drives). Whichever type is chosen must be capable of backing up and restoring to the server all the files—including the bindery and any associated rights and attributes.

Bindery Files

So what is the bindery? Well, it's the critical part of NetWare. In fact, the *bindery* is where NetWare stores the security information pertaining to users, groups, directories, and files. In v3.11 it comprises three hidden files located in the SYS:SYSTEM directory:

- NET$OBJ.SYS file containing object information
- NET$PROP.SYS file containing property information
- NET$VAL.SYS file containing property values

Without these files little can be done to restore data. More will be said about the bindery later in this chapter.

NetWare Compatibility

Let me stress this one again: Be sure the backup system chosen is compatible with NetWare. DOS backup systems cannot be used to back up the NetWare File Server. Check whether the system can handle high capacities. With files reaching into the multimegabyte range, it is important to ensure the capability of the system to handle these file sizes. Also be sure that the backup program can handle the name space requirements of NetWare for Macintosh, OS/2, and so on. Remember: Additional name spaces require special backup treatment.

Backing Up Open Files/Backup Rate/Error Handling

If possible, when you back up the server wait till everyone is logged off. In many instances, the server is used around the clock. Consequently, there will always be files open on the network. It is important that the backup system chosen include a method that is acceptable. For example, some programs back up open files as long as they are flagged Sharable; others will stop and report there are open files, allowing the option to abort, retry, or skip the file. A list of skipped files then is maintained, thus giving you the opportunity to back them up later.

Another factor is the backup rate of the program. If you have a large amount of data—say 300MB—and the rate is 0.25MB per minute, it would take all day to complete the process. The longer the backup period, the greater the chance of something going wrong. In unattended backups, the chance of unauthorized network and file access is increased, because the system requires the individual performing the backup to be logged in as a Supervisor. This type of procedure should be done in a secure location such as a locked office.

Error handling is another important aspect of the backup system. Backups may not be completely error free, so the system should be able to detect both hard errors and soft errors and to correct them to prevent loss of data. *Hard errors* are ones caused by a physical defect on the medium; *soft errors* are created by foreign matter, such as dust, on the back-up medium. Backup programs provide a read-after-write verification option. This should be used, because the system will compare the data written to the backup with what is on the source disk and, if a discrepancy is found, rewrite the data to another location on the back-up media.

Backup Media

Magnetic tape is the main medium used in backup systems. DAT is becoming popular because of the large amount of data that can be stored on this type of tape. The problem with either tape medium is its "linearity." Because you have to sequentially access all the directories and files on a tape, it takes quite some time to locate a directory or file that you would like to restore. Depending on the amount of data stored there, it could take 20 to 30 minutes to locate the file before you can start the restoration.

Optical disks now include the ability to write over previously stored data, so this medium is an increasingly popular means of backup. As the write speed increases for optical disks, they'll become a more attractive option. The WORM (write once, read many times) disk is excellent for archival of data that should not be changed.

The remaining discussion in this section provides additional information about tape backup systems that were mentioned in an earlier chapter. They are discussed in order of cost, beginning with the less expensive option.

Implementing a Backup Plan

Regardless of which system is used for backup, a procedure to ensure regularly scheduled backups is absolutely critical. When and where a catastrophe will occur cannot be predicted. So a haphazard approach to backup will result in untold grief. Believe me, you *will* need to restore your data. It does not always happen to the other guy!

Most systems suggest a schedule. Daily backup of changed data is prudent, with a weekly backup of the entire server. Rotate the tapes/disks so that you have two sets of backup media. Be sure to identify the tapes/disks so you'll know to which group they belong. On a monthly basis, another complete set of backups should be made and kept offsite.

The set of weekly media should be stored offsite with the monthly set. This will provide security and safety in case of a major disaster at the worksite.

Be sure to have enough blank media on hand for use as they fill up and wear out. Tape systems will give a suggested schedule of replacing the backup tapes.

Maintenance Options

Maintaining the physical reliability of the hardware and software is essential to a smoothly operating network. By keeping these aspects in top shape, the need to use the systems described in the previous section will be minimized. So after the initial warranty period on your system ends, you must now decide on how to handle ongoing maintenance.

Let's explore the components of a maintenance program.

As machines get to be more and more like men, men will come to be more like machines.

—Joseph Wood Krutch

Maintenance Contracts

The two types of contracts available are "time and materials" and "annual." Time-and-material contracts may appear at first glance to be the cheapest way to go; look again. The charges for travel time, the computerless employees' hourly salary rate, plus parts would generally surpass the cost of an annual maintenance agreement in as little as one or two calls.

The annual contract has a higher initial cost. It is generally based on the quantity and type of equipment you have. This is the best type of contract to secure. It gives peace of mind knowing that all the equipment is covered. Also this type of contract usually provides for periodic maintenance on the equipment.

Comparison shop to find the best contract for you. The firm that provided you with your network will actively seek your business—after all, its staff installed it and know it best. That is a valid point, but the contract you select should provide a lot more than that. It should have a reasonable response time—ideally no more than four hours after reported problem—replacement equipment if yours cannot be repaired in a timely manner, periodic maintenance visits, and reasonable cost.

If the same company wishes to maintain the network software be sure that it has qualified personnel possessing a CNE certificate and how many. If it is a large firm and has only one or two with CNE certificates then they may have difficulty responding in a timely manner. In this case it may be wise to obtain software support from another source.

A potential problem arises when you use one company to provide hardware support and another to oversee software support. If the problem could be caused by *either* hardware or software, the multiple vendors may resort to finger pointing: "It's not *our* hardware's problem; call the software person!"

Internal Maintenance

Internal maintenance is just as important as having a maintenance contract. This task usually falls to the network Administrator. It is absolutely vital for this individual to be well trained. Also it is critical for the maintenance to be this individual's only job. A lot of organizations believe that the Administrator's job can be handled on a part-time basis. How wrong they are! This individual will be the key to the entire network's success. In addition, the network staff should include another equally trained individual as a backup Administrator. After all, the Administrator may someday want a vacation! Besides, if something drastic should happen, the backup person will be able to keep your network in operation.

Hot Spares Inventory

Having spare parts on hand will greatly enhance your capability to keep the show on the road. If possible, maintain a supply of the following spare items:

- NIC cards
- parallel cables
- SIMM strips
- patch cables with RJ-45 jacks
- T-connectors/terminators
- monitors
- workstation(s)

With items like these on hand, the Administrator can replace a defective item immediately. Then the service technician need only replace or repair the defective item.

Obviously, in order to perform this type of maintenance someone onsite must have experience in installing the devices just listed. Usually the Administrator is this individual.

On-Line Redundancy

As mentioned earlier in this book, disk mirroring and disk duplexing is a form of on-line redundancy. By placing data on two different disks, access reliability is increased. Remember that disk duplexing would provide better reliability, because each disk has its own channel to communicate with the server.

Another redundant procedure to provide access to the server is by loading both RSPX and RS232 modules onto the server. With these you can communicate directly or asynchronously with the server, thereby providing a backup system in case either one fails. The RS232 option requires that both the workstation and the server contain modems.

Troubleshooting Hardware

Troubleshooting is like being a detective. The system has a problem and it is up to the Administrator to determine what it is and fix it. This activity can be a lot of fun and at the same time very frustrating. One time I had a workstation that had worked just fine the previous day but was deader than a doornail when I got to work in the morning. I considered every cause imaginable—the plugs on the back of the unit, into the floor, on/off switch, fuses, and on and on. Then we called the service company to come to check it. A few minutes later, another user said her machine wasn't working. So I looked a little further. I went to the main circuit panel, and guess what? The problem turned out to be caused by a tripped circuit breaker! Needless to say I called the service company quickly to cancel the trouble call or our organization would have been out the $200 service charge for an unnecessary call.

This section outlines some troubleshooting suggestions for the file server and workstation—commonly encountered problems and troubleshooting utilities available. But first, let's list some troubleshooting techniques you can use to make your task easier.

Never trouble trouble till trouble troubles you.

—Anonymous

Troubleshooting Process

Begin by identifying the major components of your network, such as the power source, file server, NetWare, shared peripherals, workstations, interface boards, application software, and—last but not least—the topology (cabling).

Next, complete the following steps:

1. Do presite planning.
2. Check the error log.
3. Fetch your copy of the physical layout.
4. Isolate the problem.
5. Separate network components into assemblies.
6. Test each assembly.
7. Take corrective action.

Now we'll cover each of these steps a little more thoroughly. You can, for example, do the first four even before you visit the worksite.

Presite Planning

Preparation to investigate a problem is an essential part of network troubleshooting. It is possible with good presite planning to do a significant part of the problem isolation before you set foot on the site. This preparation gives you a better chance of arriving with the right tools, parts, and equipment to correct the problem. You may even solve the problem without going to the site. In any case, the planning process should include the following:

- a presite checklist
- an appointment to gain access to the site/system
- determination of which tools and parts to take

By completing the presite checklist, you have questions to ask the user on the phone before you travel to the site. It helps you gather useful information about the network and provides questions to help isolate/narrow the range of potential causes.

Also, this checklist should help you to decide which tools, spare parts, and materials to take to the site.

Error Log Records

Check the network's error log in an effort to identify the problem and ask the customer/user to replicate the problem, if possible.

Physical Layout

Obtain a copy of the physical layout of the network. Get information on cabling, location of components, number and type of workstations, each file server's operating system revision, and other such pertinent facts.

Problem Isolation

Isolate the problem by analyzing the symptoms down to the component level. Using a flow chart may help, because it shows the logical flow of a process involving the choices or decisions users or programs make.

Component Breakdown

Break down the component into assemblies to narrow the possible causes.

Assembly Testing

Test each assembly of the component replacing those that are faulty and that you have spare parts for.

Correction

Take the corrective action necessary to resolve the problem. Be sure to document the solution and the action taken. This will make it easier to identify if the problem should occur again.

File Server

The file server is the heart of the network. If you have problems here then everything else you have done is for naught. So in this portion we will take a look at some of the more common problems you may encounter. We begin with hard disk and volume problems.

Problem: The users complain that in the middle of projects the machine seems to hang. This problem has just started; previously the network has been operating well.

Possible Cause: Check the file server using MONITOR. Check whether the buffers are full, especially the Packets Received Buffer. If this buffer has reached its upper limit, the machine will lock.

Solution: After you reboot the server, have the users log on one at a time and remain idle. Monitor the Packets Received Buffer using MONITOR. If it continually goes up, do not have any other users log on. Ask the last user to log off. If the buffer contents stop increasing, replace the NIC card in the just-tested user's machine, because it has gone bad.

Problem: The file server hangs after mounting the last volume.

Possible Cause: The file server network board may not be initializing when the file server is booted because the board is not installed or seated correctly.

Possible Solution: Ensure that all file server and workstation network boards are seated properly and that the cabling and connections are secure. Also, run CONFIG at the file server console to see what settings appear. Check the network board configurations to ensure that the settings match.

Possible Solution: Check the network boards in all workstations for the correct station addresses.

Problem: None of the volumes, including the SYS: volume, mounted. The SYS: volume is the volume that contains the bindery files and NLMs. If this volume does not mount when the file server is booted, the AUTOEXEC.NCF file will not execute, LAN drivers will not load, the bindery won't open, and TTS will not be enabled.

Possible Cause: The SYS: volume is corrupted.

Solution: Run VREPAIR on the SYS: volume.

Possible Cause: The hard disk containing the SYS: volume has failed.

Solution: Replace the hard disk and follow these simple steps:

1. Load INSTALL to create the partitions and the SYS: volume.
2. Restore the data from a backup copy. (You *do* have a backup copy, right?)

Problem: The operating system reports memory errors when a volume is being mounted.

Possible Cause: Volumes require more memory during the mounting process because of the internal consistency checks.

Solution: Load MONITOR and check the status of available cache buffers. If the cache buffers are at levels less than 20 percent, add more memory.

Problem: Workstations can log in but periodically lose their connection to the file server.

Possible Cause: A network board in either the file server or a workstation is faulty.

Solution: Check the cabling for improper termination, loose connections, and faulty components. Use COMCHECK to check communication between the file server and workstations. If COMCHECK does not isolate the problem, use a LAN analyzer product to check whether the network boards, cables, and packets all operate properly. Replace faulty boards and cables.

Possible Cause: A user on the network is using an old shell file.

Solution: Check all boot files. Make sure everyone is using the latest version of the shell files.

Possible Cause: Two workstations have the same node (station) address.

Solution: Run USERLIST /A. Make sure all node addresses are unique. Make changes as necessary.

Problem: The server does not keep time correctly.

Possible Cause: The server will get the date and time from the internal clock on boot up. Then the operating system keeps track of time by counting the computer's clock ticks. If the oscillator on the system board is fast or slow, the time will be fast or slow, too.

Solution: If the server loses time when the server is off, the battery may be low or dead. Replace the battery. If replacing the battery does not correct the problem, replace the main system board.

Problem: The server does not boot after a network board was installed.

Possible Cause(s): The network board is not attached properly to the cable; the hardware conflicts with other boards, the monitor, or ports in the server; or the network board is faulty.

Solution(s): Attach the cable of the network board to at least one workstation and check the termination. Make a list of all I/O ports, interrupts, and memory addresses used by the equipment. Be sure no two pieces of hardware are using the same I/O port, interrupt, or memory address. Reconfigure the equipment so that no conflicts exist.

Problem: The servers do not recognize each other on the network.

Possible Cause(s): The hardware settings in the server are incorrect, the network or internetwork addresses conflict, or the directory database is corrupted.

Solution(s): Run CONFIG at the server console to see what settings appear. Then check network board configurations in the server to see that the board configurations match the settings shown when you run CONFIG.

Check the IPX internal network number for the server and the network address for the cabling. Multiple servers that share the same cabling system must have the same network address, but each server must also have a unique IPX internal network number and unique station address.

Reset the router with the RESET ROUTER console command.

Check the cabling system for faulty termination.

Down all servers except one. Reset its router with RESET ROUTER. Bring up each server, one at a time, establishing communications with it before bringing up the next. Run DISPLAY NETWORKS to check for duplicate network addresses as each is booted.

Problem: The server gets a General Protection Interrupt (GPI).

Possible Cause(s): NetWare switches between real and protected mode to access memory above 1MB. If a fatal error occurs at this switch, the processor will issue a General Protection Interrupt (GPI). Some of the more common causes are these:

- Memory chips—either system or extended memory—fail.
- Network boards fail, especially those that use shared memory.
- Other devices that use shared memory fail.
- Power spikes have occurred.
- Device drivers don't handle the device correctly during this switch.

Solution(s): Most of the time replacement of the defective hardware solves the problem. If power spikes cause the damage, check the power supply and install equipment to minimize these spikes. In cases of driver problems contact the manufacturer to see if it has had reports of failure and if a newer version of the driver fixed these problems.

Problem: The keyboard response on a nondedicated server workstation is slow.

Possible Cause: Check with the manufacturer to see if it has BIOS and keyboard controller chip updates. The computer could have a timing problem. Novell has certified some computers with the limitation that the keyboard response will be slow on nondedicated server workstations.

Workstation

Hardware can cause you a lot of heartache. So as with the software documentation, the hardware configuration should be well documented. Record the version of DOS on the machine, RAM installed, floppy drives, hard drive, NIC type, monitor, and CPU. This information will be very useful in troubleshooting hardware problems.

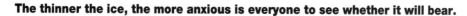

The thinner the ice, the more anxious is everyone to see whether it will bear.

—Josh Billings

Now on to the physical aspect of the LAN: hardware problems and solutions.

Problem: The user experiences frequent failure of the workstation and hard disk problems.

Possible Cause: Check whether the power supply works properly.

Solution: Have the power supply checked to see if AC current is constant. The line should be a dedicated line for the user(s) if possible. If a dedicated line is not possible, investment in a line/surge protector is highly recommended.

Problem: All the users on the network are having transmission problems with the server.

Possible Cause: The power supply to the server is not "clean"—that is, a dedicated line.

Solution: Check whether the server is on a dedicated line. No other office equipment (such as photocopiers) should share the same circuit. Have a dedicated circuit installed and be sure the server is on a UPS.

Problem: The user receives message saying `Parity error`, causing the machine to hang.

Possible Cause: The memory chips or SIMMs may not be properly seated or else a mix of speeds was created when additional memory chips were added to the system.

Solution: Check whether the memory chips or SIMMs are seated properly. Be sure to ground yourself first by touching the chassis to discharge any static electricity in your body; then it's safe to touch the chips. Push down on the individual chips or remove the SIMM strips and reinstall them. Also check to ensure that they all share the same speed rating.

Problem: The user has trouble reading a diskette in the floppy drive.
Possible Cause: The floppy drive may be defective.
Solution: Try the diskette in another workstation to see whether it can be read. If it can, replace the faulty drive on the workstation.
Possible Cause: The diskette is formatted at the wrong density or is using a different operating system.
Solution: Try another machine.

Problem: The user's monitor gets blurry or displays strange characters.
Possible Cause: The monitor needs adjusting or the video board may be going bad.
Solution: If the monitor allows for adjustment without removing the cover, try the brightness and contrast adjustments. If they are under warranty or a maintenance contract, call the service agency to replace the monitor or board.

Problem: The user receives a message similar to `Cannot initialize card` or the system hangs.
Possible Cause: The NIC card IRQ and I/O address may be in conflict with other devices in the workstation.
Solution: When you install NIC cards, the IRQ and I/O addresses of other devices should be checked first. Programs like Checkit provide this capability. Then check your NIC and make any changes necessary to eliminate the conflict. Also, the newer smart cards like Intel EtherExpress 16 LAN adapters check the system configuration and use the IRQ and I/O available. These cards are extremely easy to install.

Problem: The user receives a message that says `Cannot initialize the LAN card` or something similar. The configuration of the card setting is correct.
Possible Cause: The NIC has failed.
Solution: Replace the NIC board with one you have in inventory, then reboot the machine. These cards are relatively inexpensive and would be a good item to have in stock.

Problem: The user experiences communications problems between workstations on a network.
Possible Cause(s): These LAN communications problems can be caused by the following:

- cabling problems
- a faulty network board in any of the workstations
- a machine giving off noise that affects the network board
- driver problems with a network board

Solution(s): Run COMCHECK or some other network diagnostic program. This process may pinpoint the problem. As you run COMCHECK, each workstation should display all other workstations that are running COMCHECK along with itself. The elapsed time for each workstation should change. If one of these events does not occur, you could have isolated the problem workstation.

To check for cabling problems, use an ohm meter at various points in the cable to determine whether the ohm rating is within the specification for the cable you are using.

To check for a faulty network board, run each workstation separately to determine which one isn't functioning properly. Bring up one workstation, then add other workstations in succession. Check as each workstation is added to see whether it causes communications problems with the network.

Once you have determined a possible problem workstation, replace the network board and retest the workstation.

Cable

Roughly 60 to 80 percent of LAN downtime can be traced to cable-related factors. Network cabling is sensitive to materials used and termination techniques. Cable problems include breaks in continuity or opens, reversals, split pairs and crosstalk, excessive run lengths and attenuation, impedance mismatches, wrong materials, and worn connections or improper installation. The direct approach to troubleshooting your network's suspected cable problems starts with simple elimination. No special tools are required, just a good eye and basic logic. Always look first for the obvious and avoid making conclusions initially. It is truly amazing how many problems evaporate during this first step. This discussion outlines an approach to cable troubleshooting, presents symptoms and causes, and introduces troubleshooting tools.

Some obvious things to look for first are these:

- Have any connections come loose or been disconnected? If so, find out how and why.
- Are the connections mechanically sound or worn? Worn connectors often make an intermittent connection.
- In twisted-pair installations don't mix RJ connectors. If the ports on your hub or MSAU are RJ-45s, use RJ-45-terminated cables. RJ-11 plugs fit loosely in RJ-45 ports and cause an intermittent connection. This also goes for NICs.
- For Ethernet or ARCNet buses, are all connectors the proper impedance? Do both segment ends have the correct value terminators (50-ohm Ethernet, 93-ohm ARCNet)?
- All bus topologies must *always* be terminated at segment ends. Test terminators separately. Measure DC resistance with a digital volt meter (DVM) to confirm the value. Most terminators are marked either with their value or a manufacturer's part number. You can verify your terminators in this fashion. The full proof test is using the DVM.
- In Ethernet 10Base-T or Token Ring systems, never use flat patch cables (sometimes called *silver satin*) at the hub, MSAU, or anywhere. Flat cords aren't twisted and are susceptible to crosstalk and EMI. Flat cords are not always pin for pin or straight through. It is quite common—particularly with a cord you borrowed from the phone system—to have pair reversals. One golden rule in LAN cabling is that the data materials should be separated from the voice materials.

- In twisted-pair installations (10Base-T, Token Ring, and ARCNet) check for opens (breaks). A good installer will check all cables for continuity to avoid opens in any pairs. Continuity tests can be performed with continuity testers or tone generators and an amplifier. Tone generators and amplifiers work, but they are more cumbersome and time consuming tools.

- Pair reversals that are common in twisted-pair sites are exactly what the name implies. All network twisted-pair topologies use four conductors: TX+ (Transmit +), TX− (Transmit −), RX+ (Receive +), and RX− (Receive −). Reversing causes reversed polarity or incorrect configuration (node failure). Check any cable adapters you use for this same condition. If you use adapters and patch cords, remove them all. Test the cable to verify it is good (no opens, shorts, or reversals). Then begin adding back the adapters and patch cords one at a time to find your culprit. Always verify a cable from end to end with all of the connectors, adapters, and patch cords before you certify a node as good. A pair tester is the best method to check for reversals. Good units can identify reversals, opens, and some even show if you have AC voltages on the line. These units cost less than $150 at most cable suppliers.

- IBM Type cables and their proprietary connectors have their own testing device (cost is less than $400) called a *loopback tester* to find pair reversals. The tester will not detect reverse polarity caused by split pairs. Visual inspection is needed to correct split pairs. IBM Type cables can be verified for continuity and reversals using a good pair tester with adapters for the proprietary IBM style connectors.

- Shorts occur during cable installation if the cable's outer jacket and shielding are damaged. Use your meter to find which pairs are shorted and work backward to find the source. In any type of cable all conductors or shields must remain isolated. An exception is IBM Type cable installations. The proprietary connectors create shorted conditions when they are not plugged into anything. Cables terminated with IBM Type connectors need to be tested to verify isolation of all connectors with a connector plugged into both ends to open the shunt bar.

- If your cabling has no opens, reversals, split pairs, or shorts, check that it connects to the corresponding pin at either end. You can find this out the hard way as your NIC or hub goes up in smoke. Know the proper cable configuration and test all cables including any patch cords in the circuit before connecting to any equipment.

Long Cables

A frequently encountered cable problem is run lengths that exceed specifications. The effects of overly long cables vary:

- Stations may not always come up or come up but crash frequently. This symptom can also indicate use of a protocol that is faster than the speed your cable can support.

- Ethernet networks normally experience a large number of retransmissions or collisions.

- Token Rings may get "ring insertion errors" during parts of the day when stations on long cables are trying to reconnect to the MSAU.

- ARCNet networks can experience both of these types of problems.

There are several ways to measure cable runs. Installation is the best time to verify the accuracy of the cable design. Many cable manufacturers mark their cable in feet so installers can judge distances. If you are uncertain of a run and your cable is unmarked, you can run a measurement tape along with the cable as it is pulled in. Keep in mind that cables rarely follow straight paths to their destinations. Existing cables can be measured with handheld testers or more expensive, complex time domain reflectometers (TDRs). My perfect tool for the job, a wish list, might include Microtest's NEXTSCANNER ($3,320) in handhelds. This handheld will test all of the topology protocols in one unit. Microtest and other manufacturers like Startek make handheld testers for individual or combinations of topology protocols. These units cover most of the critical testing procedures, and some (like the NEXTSCANNER) offer TDR-like capabilities.

For longer cables and more challenging problems, the Tektronix 1503C TDR is one of the best ($4,950). Wish lists aside, a DVM can calculate cable lengths. The better DVMs are also helpful tools when you are troubleshooting opens and short problems. The best units available are made by Fluke. A high-sensitivity unit with tone signaling for continuity testing runs a little less than $600. You need high sensitivity because the resistance and voltages you will be measuring are minute.

Measuring Cable Runs with a DVM

The first step is to disconnect the bus or cable run at both ends. Second, you will short circuit a pair at one end of the cable being tested (coax, shield to center conductor). The third step is to set your meter to register ohms and take your measurement at the opposite end. By knowing the resistance per 1,000 feet (some manufacturers list it per 100 feet) of the cable you can calculate the length.

Terminations and Impedance Problems

What if you find your cable is within the specifications of the topology protocol for the access method? And further, say you have eliminated all of the simple problems. This is where a more precise analysis of the problem begins. At this stage it becomes important to have the proper tools along with your logic and keen eye. In high-speed networks the precision of the installation always comes shining (or glaring) through. Symptoms of termination problems (bad connections) or impedance mismatches often include frequent retransmissions, network hanging occurrences, stations that don't come up, and general inconsistent performance. The best handheld testers (like NEXTSCANNER) can't always indicate the precise problem. TDRs are costly but sensitive enough to find even the most obscure problems.

Some causes of termination and impedance problems are these:

- Most network media conductors are solid copper wire. During installation care needs to be taken in avoiding cable kinks. A severe enough kink causes damage that is irreversible. Cable kinks create points of reflectance that distort network communications.
- Another source of reflectance is mismatched impedance among cabling, connectors, and adapters.
- Twisted-pair terminations, including punch-down blocks and modular connecting blocks, should be new. Punch-down blocks that have been used over and over

may support voice and slower protocols but often fail in high-speed networks. Network terminations are best done with 110-style punch blocks as opposed to older style 66m types. The benefits of 110-style blocks are that they make a positive, gas-tight termination. They take up less space than do 66ms in wiring closets. At the workstation ends of twisted-pair installations you should use 110-style modular connecting blocks as well.

Why 110 Hardware Is Better

To install a conductor on a conventional screwdown terminal involves the following steps and their associated problems:

1. The PVC/Teflon shield is stripped off the copper. Even when you use a good wire stripper with skill, it is possible to nick the copper conductor minutely.
2. The bare wire is bent around under the screw lug. Any scarring of the conductor in the stripping process can be accentuated in this step. The conductor can break altogether or worse, wind up just short of actually breaking. This again will create a point of reflectance. Simple tests won't uncover this kind of problem.

    Think of it this way. When you take a garden hose and turn on the water, the flow fills the entire inner diameter of the hose. If you were to take your fingers and pinch the hose at any point, you would reduce the inner diameter and back up pressure behind the pinch. If you took the hose and bent it over abruptly the flow would be further reduced. Back pressure would push the opposite direction to the flow. In a network conductor the flow is packets of data. Damage or reduction of the overall diameter of the conductor creates reflectance and distorts the incoming packets.
3. You run the screwdown onto the bare copper wire. It is critical not to allow any of the insulation to wind up under the screw terminal. If this happens, an impedance mismatch occurs and creates another distortion factor.

You can solve all of these problems by using 110-style connections, which make tight, positive terminations that install more quickly and easily. Installation of a conductor on this type of termination is a one-step process. The conductor is not stripped of the PVC/Teflon shielding. It is placed into the proper groove and pushed down into the groove stripping just enough shield to create contact. The excess is cut off with the impact blade of the tool.

High-Speed Termination Hardware

Until recently network designers directed all concern to network media and less attention to the terminations themselves. With the evolution of very fast copper solutions, it has become imperative to apply the same kind of rating standards to terminations. Once the IEEE establishes a standard for 100-Mb/s speeds on copper look for manufacturers to introduce rated termination hardware. Some manufacturers like AMP and Krone are already producing high-speed termination hardware.

Noise

Noise is a large network problem detectable only with proper tools and methods. Retransmissions are problems commonly associated with noise. An example is a node that won't stay on line, one that crashes and exhibits general intermittent performance. These problems behave a lot like out-of-spec cable runs (that is, excessively long runs). Noise symptoms behave like those for excessive-length cables, provided the noise levels (voltages) aren't very high. The network signals need to be well above the level of noise for NICs to hear them. It isn't possible to eliminate noise completely, but a reasonable signal-to-noise ratio must be obtained. You need your meter or handheld tester to measure suspected noise problems.

Some topologies stand up better to noise then others. ARCNet on UTP is particularly noise tolerant, able to operate with noise levels up to 500 mV (microvolts). Token Ring 802.5 specifications call for noise levels to be as low as 24 mV or less (16 decibels below the received signal) to receive signal level at the NIC of 150 mV. A rule of thumb is that any noise level above 50 mV needs to be investigated. Handheld testers not only can give you a voltage reading of the noise but the frequency of the registering noise. Here are some noise sources and their frequencies:

Fluorescent Lights	10 KHz to 150 KHz
Video Signals	10 KHz to 150 KHz
RFI Signals	10 MHz and Up (TV, radio, and police transmitters)

Copiers, paper shredders, heating, ventilation, air conditioners, large rotating machines, or any equipment that cycles rapidly on and off or cycles faster, then slower, produces impulse noise. All of these signals can be measured with an oscilloscope attached to a properly terminated cable. The 60-Hz patterns are AC power noise.

The recommended approach for controlling noise problems is as follows:

■ Move cables away from noise sources. AC noise can be eliminated as a problem with a move as short as 12 inches.

■ Keep UPSs, SPSs, and power-conditioning equipment away from your equipment and cables. Make sure your noise is not self-induced.

■ Don't mix signals on a network cable; that is, avoid combinations of analog or digital phone pairs. Your installation may require shielded cable.

■ Don't, however, mix shielded and unshielded cable on the same MSAU or concentrator. If you need to mix cable types, isolate them by using a repeater or install separate cards in a concentrator for each cable type.

Crosstalk and Attenuation

Crosstalk between pairs is often caused by split pairs. Other causes are wire not to specification of the network (too few twists per foot), incorrect size, poor quality, and careless installation. Handheld testers shine for detecting *near-end crosstalk (NEXT).*

Attenuation is best measured with a unit that has built-in attenuation tests. A signal generator is attached to one end of the cable and the signal is measured at the opposite end. This type of test often requires the LAN to be taken down. Symptoms of excessive attenuation are intermittent symptoms. These will be more prevalent on longer cables. Du Pont has demonstrated correlations between attenuation and temperatures of cables with different insulation materials. Consider this factor if network performance changes with the seasons. Be prepared to test the cable at several different times of the day. The only fix for a bad cable is replacement with better quality and/or type of cable.

Cable Summary

All of the best and most sophisticated test equipment in the world won't take the place of good detective work. Most LAN problems stem from cabling. However, not every problem is cable related. Bear in mind that physical cabling is passive when properly installed. It only changes as a result of outside influences caused by the installation, environment, or people. You need to know when to open your magic bag of tools and when to suspect other hardware or software problems. In addressing cabling problems you cannot help but disrupt the working environment of the users on the system, so perform your magic only when required.

User Questions

The following questions answered for your installation by the people most intimate with the problems will go a long way to narrowing down and solving them.

- What time of day does the problem begin?
- What are the events and time sequences that lead to the problem?
- Have the user's system components or applications changed recently?
- Can the user make the problem stop? How?
- How long does the workstation operate properly once it has been fixed?

Installation Inspection

Following are some questions to ask of yourself during the installation inspection. The network standard appears in parentheses.

- Who are the upstream and downstream users (bus installations)?
- Do these users experience the same problems (bus)?
- What is the physical condition of the connections and the installation in general?
- Are RJ-11 plugs connecting to RJ-45 ports anywhere?
- Do symptoms change when you wiggle plugs or connectors?
- Are any flat silver satin patches being used (10Base-T, Token Ring)?
- Did you perform all standard troubleshooting tests?
- Are all the NICs working properly? (If not, run NIC Diagnostics.)
- Have you reviewed the network design?

Worry gives a small thing a big shadow.

—Swedish Proverb

Troubleshooting Software

File Server Software

Problem: The operating system reports disk errors when a volume is being mounted.
Possible Cause: The file server does not have enough memory to mount the volume.
Solution: Load MONITOR and check the status of the available cache buffers. If the cache buffers are less than 20 percent available, add more memory to your file server.

Possible Cause: The operating system is experiencing directory sector mismatching. This can occur if the media are defective or if the file server is turned off without the DOWN command.

Solution: Minor errors will correct themselves through normal network use. Example, if the FAT entry is wrong, it will be updated and corrected the next time it is written to. If errors do not correct themselves, run VREPAIR.

Problem: A volume can't be mounted because of corrupted directory tables or FATs.

Possible Cause: A power failure occurs and the server is not downed with the DOWN command.

Solution: Run VREPAIR and add a UPS system so that the file server is automatically downed when a commercial power failure occurs.

Possible Cause: A hard disk fails.

Solution: Replace faulty disks or controller.

Problem: The file server could not be found by the workstations.

Possible Cause: The network board may not be initializing when the file server is brought up because it is not configured properly or it has failed.

Solution: Run CONFIG at the server console to see what settings appear. Then check the network board configurations in the file server. Be sure the network board configurations match the settings revealed when you ran CONFIG.

Possible Cause: Address or interrupt conflicts may exist between two boards in the file server or between a board and the computer's hardware.

Solution: Make sure no two boards in the file server are using the same I/O port, memory address, or interrupt.

Possible Cause: The SYS: volume may not be mounted.

Solution: Run VOLUMES at the file server console to see that the SYS: volume is mounted. The SYS: volume must be mounted before the file server can advertise its name to the network. Mount the SYS: volume.

Problem: A file server running NetWare v2.x is out of directory entries but a lot of room remains on the hard drive.

Possible Cause: The users have exceeded the number of default directory entries.

Solution: Increase the number of directory entries by using INSTALL (NetWare v3.x and v2.2). The maximum number of directory entries for NetWare v2.x is 32,000 per volume. The default number of entries is 4 blocks plus 1 block for every 2MB of volume size. A directory entry is 32 bytes long and a block defaults to 4096 bytes. Therefore each block has 128 directory entries ($4096 \div 32 = 128$).

Problem: How can trustee assignments and binderies be duplicated from one server to another?

Solution: There are two ways provided by Novell utilities to back up just the binderies and the trustee assignments:

- LARCHIVE: Select the options to back up all directories and ignore all files.
- NBACKUP: Select Backup File Server and input **Yes** for Backup Bindery and Backup Trustees. Enter ***.*** for the Files to Exclude.

Problem: To boot the file server, the network uses the AUTOEXEC.NCF file to load and bind a LAN driver for NetWare v3.11. However, NetWare prompts for the driver parameters to bind the driver to the second board.

Possible Cause: The brackets are missing in the BIND statement.

Solution: Edit the AUTOEXEC.NCF and be sure the brackets are included in the BIND statement. See also the *NetWare System Administration* manual for more information on this command.

Workstation Software

Most workstations connected to NetWare are running DOS in a version by Microsoft, IBM, Novell, or Digital Research. The DOS system files must load first; then the network shell files will load. DOS 5.0 enables you to install it in high memory between 640KB and 1MB, leaving more of the 640KB for application use. IPX.COM and NETX.COM are the two programs that connect your workstation to the network.

Software documentation of each workstation is essential and will aid you as you troubleshoot workstation problems. It is recommended that you make printouts of AUTOEXEC.BAT, CONFIG.SYS, the NIC configuration, and (if the workstation is running Windows) the WIN.INI and SYS.INI files at the time the workstation is connected to the network.

So let's take a look at software problems and solutions.

Problem: The user turns on the machine and receives a message `Non-system disk or disk error`. The workstation stops and cannot load any programs.

Possible Cause: The system files are missing or corrupted.

Solution: Get another system disk, insert it in drive A, and reboot the machine. At the `A:\` prompt, type **SYS C:**. You should see a message `System transferred`. You should now be able to reboot your machine.

Problem: The user receives a message, `Bad or missing command interpreter`, and the machine locks up.

Possible Cause: The COMMAND.COM file has been corrupted or deleted.

Solution: Copy the same version of COMMAND.COM onto the hard drive. The workstation should then reboot.

Problem: The message `Insufficient File Handles` displays when the user loads an application.

Possible Cause: In the CONFIG.SYS file the value of `File=`n is not large enough.

Solution: Using a DOS edit program edit the CONFIG.SYS file and increase the `File=` statement to 40. If the workstation is running Windows v3.x, instead increase the statement to 60. While you are at it, you should increase the `Buffer=` statement to 25 to avoid sluggishness in execution speed of applications.

Problem: The user receives a message similar to either `Out of environment Space` or `Insufficient space in DOS environment`.

Possible Cause: DOS 5.0 allocates 256 bytes for the program and system environment. The workstation is using more bytes than are available.

Solution: Edit the CONFIG.SYS file to include the following statement:

```
SHELL=C:\COMMAND.COM /P /E:512
```

Monitor your system operation. You may have to increase the environment space again. Jump to 1024 and increase in 1024 increments..

Problem: When using NetWare 3.11 some users trying to log in receive the error message, `The following drive mapping operation could not be completed` *XXXX*.

Possible Cause: There is insufficient environment space, as described for the previous problem.

Solution: Add the `SHELL=C:\COMMAND.COM /P /E:`*XXXX* to the CONFIG.SYS file or edit the file to increase the environment.

Problem: The user receives a message `Bad command or file name` during bootup of the workstation.

Possible Cause: The AUTOEXEC.BAT file may have one or more statements pointing to an incorrect location for the file being called.

Solution: Edit the AUTOEXEC.BAT file and correct the appropriate statement(s). For example, if the NETX.COM file is in the NetWare subdirectory, the AUTOEXEC.BAT file should show `C:\netware\netx` and not just `C:\netx`.

Problem: The user receives a message saying `Could not load vipx.386 as the proper version of the IPX was not installed`.

Possible Cause: The AUTOEXEC.BAT file may be pointing to an old version of the IPX.COM.

Solution: Type **IPX-i** to see which version of the IPX the machine is using. Check the AUTOEXEC.BAT file to see where it is pointing to find the IPX.COM file. Edit the AUTOEXEC.BAT file to point to the correct location. Delete or rename all other IPX files. They can be easily located by using a utility program such as XTreeNet from XTREE company. Refer to NetWire for the latest release of IPX.OBJ.

Problem: The user who is trying to load Windows cannot get Windows to load in Enhanced Mode.

Possible Cause: The CONFIG.SYS file may be pointing to the incorrect version of HIMEM.SYS. Use the HIMEM.SYS in the DOS 5.0 directory.

Solution: Edit the CONFIG.SYS file to point to the DOS directory for the HIMEM.SYS file. Delete or rename all other HIMEM.SYS files.

Problem: The user gets a message that the `IPX has not been loaded. Load the IPX then run the shell`.

Possible Cause: The AUTOEXEC.BAT file is loading NETX before IPX.

Solution: Edit the AUTOEXEC.BAT file to load the IPX before NETX.

Problem: The user boots up properly and connects to the LAN but during operation receives a message `Network Error on Server` *XXXXXX*: `Connection no longer valid`.

Possible Cause: The machine may have a screen saver or other terminate-and-stay-resident (TSR) running that is causing a memory conflict.

Solution: Check the date of the screen saver or other program to see whether it is earlier than the version of NetWare you are running. Edit the AUTOEXEC.BAT file and "REM" out the screen saver or other TSR statement.

Problem: The escape code sequences set up in PRINTDEF are not sent with the print jobs.

Solution: If the sequences are correctly set up and this problem occurs, use the PRINTDEF.EXE (PRNTDF.ZIP) file available on NetWire. In addition, the NetWare shells v3.01a, v3.01b, and v3.01c will not send a correct print header. This was corrected in NetWare shell v3.01d and is available on NetWire as DSWIND.ZIP.

Problem: You are trying to set up a fake root using the syntax given in the manuals for MAP ROOT, but the process doesn't work.

Possible Cause: You are using an improper version of the NetWare shell.

Solution: Use the NetWare v3.x shell to create a fake root. Earlier versions do not allow fake roots.

Problem: The DOS BACKUP command will not back up files flagged as Sharable.

Cause: The BACKUP command in DOS 3.1 and above is not compatible with the Sharable flag in NetWare.

Solution: Use NetWare's NBACKUP utility to back up data.

Problem: When PATH is used, all the search drives are lost.

Cause: The DOS PATH command deletes and overwrites NetWare search drives.

Solution: Use the NetWare MAP command instead of PATH. Reboot the workstation or use MAP to set up the search drives again.

Problem: RENAME will not work on NetWare directories, but it will work on files.

Cause: The RENAME command is a DOS command and not a NetWare command.

Solution: Use the NetWare RENDIR utility to rename NetWare directories.

Problem: CHKDSK does not function to check a network disk.

Cause: CHKDSK is a DOS command, not a NetWare command.

Solution: Use NetWare VOLINFO or CHKVOL to check the status of a NetWare volume.

Miscellaneous Questions and Answers

The following are some more common questions/problems that occur that do not fall into any of the above formats.

Question: Can I automatically enter the name of the print server I am running on a NetWare file server running the PSERVER.VAP?

Answer: No. You can, however, automatically load the VAP by including the VAP name in the AUTOEXEC.SYS, but you will still have to type the name of the print server to be loaded.

Question: The user's print jobs are being sent to the printer and are getting intermixed. Why?

Answer: This often occurs with applications that take a long time to print. Increase the timeout or use **TI=0**.

What is happening is that the application is sending multiple print jobs through the queue because the timeout is too short. Because these jobs are sent intermittently, it is possible for other users' print jobs to be queued between them.

Question: Where can I find information on the physical layout of other topologies that are compatible with NetWare?

Answer: NetWare will accept any physical layout that adheres to IBM specifications.

Note: Application Notes are available on NetWire. If you do not have a CompuServe account, contact your local NetWare user group.

Question: Are IBM SCSI drivers available for IBM PS/2 Models 90 and 95?

Answer: NetWare v3.1 ships with PS2SCSI.DSK that supports Models 90 and 95. The drivers for NetWare v2.15c are available from NetWire as the PS2286.ZIP.

Question: In running NetWare v2.1x, why do we see excessively high utilization in FCONSOLE and MONITOR in 386 and 486 machines?

Answer: This requires a new operating system release. There are no plans for an operating system change to NetWare v2.x in the near future. However, any new products that are released will incorporate this fix.

Question: I am running NetWare v2.15c on an IBM PS/2 using the internal Enhanced Small Disk Interface (ESDI). I need additional disk space on the server, so is it possible to use the IBM SCSI controller and drivers in addition to existing ESDI drive?

Answer: No, NetWare v2.15c does not support ESDI drives with SCSI drives in a PS/2 server.

Question: Do current versions of NetWare support Integrated Drive Electronics (IDE) drives?

Answer: The IDE.DSK driver is available on NetWire.

Question: I am running NetWare v2.15c and linked the Token Ring drivers contained in the TRN050.ZIP file. I now have zero file service processes. What happened?

Answer: The new Token Ring drivers' default packet size is 4KB, so a larger portion of D group memory is used by the driver, leaving less room for file service process. Run the TRCONFIG.COM file against the Token Ring object file to reduce the packet size to 1KB or 2KB. Relink the operating system using this adjusted driver and additional file service processes will be available.

Question: After upgrading to NetWare v3.1a, we started receiving the errors Access denied and File not found when applications attempted to open files. They functioned correctly under the previous version. What happened?

Answer: In NetWare v3.0 and below, a file flagged Read-Only could be opened by applications using a Read-Write open DOS call. This was corrected in NetWare v3.1a security enhancements. However, many applications are written using file open calls that require Read and Write rights. The FIXOPEN.NLM available on NetWire as the FXOPEN.ZIP file is a dynamic patch that overrides the Read-Only security of NetWare v3.1a, providing pre-v3.1a access for these applications.

Question: I upgraded my workstation to NetWare v3.1a, then I was unable to see my drive channel. I am using the Novell disk coprocessor board and made no hardware changes. What happened?

Answer: Users who upgrade to NetWare v3.1 may need to upgrade their Novell DCB. NetWare v3.1 was written to support the latest in hardware, including DCBs with revision E or higher DCB firmware. DCBs with earlier firmware revisions will not work. This concern generally affects 50-pin DCBs that are a few years old.

It ain't no use putting up your umbrella till it rains.

—Alice Caldwell Rice

Troubleshooting Tools

NetWare has many tools (utility programs) you can use to help troubleshoot your network. This section lists some of these tools and indicates whether they are console commands— that is, whether they are entered at the console command prompt (:) or workstation command-line utilities.

Console Command/Command Line Utilities

ACONSOLE

ACONSOLE is a workstation utility you can use to control a modem. I mentioned using ACONSOLE as a redundancy option earlier in this chapter. It can be used to manage the transfer of screen and keystroke information to and from a remote file server.

Format: ACONSOLE

NetWare v4.0 incorporates the asynchronous console command, ACONSOLE, into the remote management feature, RCONSOLE.

BROADCAST

BROADCAST is a console command used to broadcast (Send) a message to all users logged in or attached to the file server.

Format: BROADCAST *"message"*

Replace *"message"* with the information you want to send (up to 55 characters).

CHKDIR

CHKDIR is a workstation command-line utility. Use it to view information about a directory and a volume.

Format: CHKDIR [*path*]

Information such as space limitations for the file server, volume, and directory you are checking will be given. Also, you'll get data about maximum storage capacity of the volume in kilobytes (KB) and the maximum storage capacity of the directory, if a restriction has been placed on it.

CHKVOL

CHKVOL is a workstation command-line utility. Use it to view information about a volume. This utility will give the file server name, volume name, total volume space, space used by files, space used by deleted files, remaining space on the volume, and space available to the user. It also supports wildcard characters.

Format: CHKVOL [*path*]

CLEAR STATION

CLEAR STATION is a console command to use when a workstation has "crashed" and left files open on the file server. The file server closes the workstation's files and erases all the server's internal tables for the workstation.

Format: CLEAR STATION *n*

The *n* represents the number of the workstation you want to clear from the file server. To ascertain the connection number, use MONITOR at the file server console to view connection information.

DISABLE LOGIN

DISABLE LOGIN is a console command to use to prevent users from logging into the file server because you are making repairs, backing up files, or loading software.

Format: DISABLE LOGIN

DISMOUNT

DISMOUNT is a console command used to make a volume unavailable to users. This utility enables you to maintain or repair a volume and to upgrade disk drivers while the file server is up.

Format: DISMOUNT *volume_name*

Be sure to notify all users that the volume is to be dismounted. Use BROADCAST to inform the users.

DISPLAY NETWORKS

DISPLAY NETWORKS is a console command that lists all networks and assigned network numbers that the file server router recognizes. All network numbers (internal and cabling system) are listed.

Use DISPLAY SERVERS to see a list of servers on the network.

Format: DISPLAY NETWORKS/SERVERS

DOWN

DOWN is a console command used to ensure data integrity before you turn off the power to the server. It ensures data integrity by writing all cache buffers to disk, closing all files, and updating the appropriate Directory and File Allocation Tables (FATs).

Format: DOWN

ENABLE LOGIN

ENABLE LOGIN is a console command used to reenable the login function. This command is also used to enable the Supervisor's account when the account has been locked by the intruder detection function.

If you are going to reboot the server after using DISABLE LOGIN, this command is not needed, because the login function is automatically enabled during the bootup procedure.

Format: ENABLE LOGIN

EXIT

EXIT is a console command to use to return to DOS after you have downed the file server. You are then able to access DOS files or rerun the SERVER.EXE file.

Format: EXIT

LOAD

LOAD is a console command used to link modules (NLMs) to the operating system.

Format: LOAD [*path*] *loadable_module*

LOAD Disk Driver. LOAD Disk Driver is used to establish communication between the hard disk controllers and the operating system during system installation. LOAD disk driver links a driver with your hard disk controller. Afterward it is used to link an updated driver or to link a driver to an additional hard disk controller.

Format: LOAD [*path*]disk_driver[*driver_parameter*]

LOAD LAN Driver. Use the LOAD LAN Driver command to link the appropriate drivers with the network boards installed in your file server.

Format: LOAD [*path*]LAN_driver[*driver_parameter*]

LOAD Name Space. Use LOAD Name Space if you have computers that need to store non-DOS files on your file server.

Format: LOAD [*path*]name_space

LOAD NLM Utility. Use LOAD NLM Utility to link management and enhancement programs with the operation system. These programs provide such services as installation, monitor, volume repair, backup, and diagnostics.

Format: LOAD [*path*]NLM-utility [*parameter*]

MONITOR

MONITOR is a NetWare loadable module. Use MONITOR to lock the file server console and to see how efficiently your network is operating. Figure 15.1 illustrates NetWare's MONITOR server utility. You can use MONITOR to view information about the following:

- utilization and activity
- cache memory status
- connection status
- disk drives
- mounted volumes
- LAN drivers
- loaded modules
- file lock status
- memory usage

```
┌─────────────────────────────────────────────────────────────────────┐
│ NetWare v3.11 (250 user) - 2/20/91          NetWare 386 Loadable Module │
└─────────────────────────────────────────────────────────────────────┘

┌─────────────────────────────────────────────────────────────────────┐
│                    Information For Server OMEGA                       │
├─────────────────────────────────────────────────────────────────────┤
│    File Server Up Time:    9 Days  8 Hours 29 Minutes 27 Seconds      │
│    Utilization:                5  │ Packet Receive Buffers:      10   │
│    Original Cache Buffers:  1,651 │ Directory Cache Buffers:     71   │
│    Total Cache Buffers:     1,350 │ Service Processes:            2   │
│    Dirty Cache Buffers:         0 │ Connections In Use:           2   │
│    Current Disk Requests:       0 │ Open Files:                   7   │
└─────────────────────────────────────────────────────────────────────┘

              ┌───────────────────────────────┐
              │        Available Options       │
              ├───────────────────────────────┤
              │ Connection Information         │
              │ Disk Information               │
              │ LAN Information                │
              │ System Module Information      │
              │ Lock File Server Console       │
              │ File Open / Lock Activity      │
              │ Resource Utilization           │
              │ Exit                           │
              └───────────────────────────────┘
```

FIGURE 15.1 NetWare's MONITOR File Server Utility

Cache usage and memory usage were covered earlier in the chapter.
Well, this is the utility you want to use in your troubleshooting.
Format: LOAD [*path*]MONITOR [*parameter*]

NMAGENT

NMAGENT is a NetWare loadable module. Use it to allow LAN drivers to register and pass network management parameters. NMAGENT must be loaded before LAN drivers can be loaded.
Format: LOAD [*path*]NMAGENT

PSERVER

PSERVER is a NetWare loadable module or VAP. Use this module to load the print server on the file server and establish print services for the network. However, before you load the print server, you must use PCONSOLE to set up a print server and configuration files. This utility will be listed shortly.
Format: LOAD PSERVER *print_server*

REMOTE

REMOTE is a NetWare loadable module. Use this module to access the file server console from a workstation. After REMOTE is loaded, you must load RSPS, or REMOTE will not function properly.
Format: LOAD [*path*]REMOTE[*password*]

RIGHTS

RIGHTS is a workstation command-line utility. Use it to view your effective rights in a directory or file. These are the rights that you can actually exercise in a given directory, subdirectory, or file. They are determined by a user's trustee rights if assigned, or, if not assigned, by the inherited rights mask and the previous directory level's effective rights.

Format: RIGHTS [*path*]

RSPX

RSPX is a NetWare loadable module. Use RSPX to allow the RCONSOLE utility to access a file server. Load REMOTE before you load RSPX. RSPX loads the SPX driver for REMOTE.

Format: LOAD [*path*]RSPX

SECURE CONSOLE

SECURE CONSOLE is a console command. Use it to implement the following security: preventing loadable modules from being loaded from any directory other than SYS:SYS-TEM, preventing keyboard entry into the OS debugger, and preventing anyone other than a console operator from changing the date and time.

SECURE CONSOLE also removes DOS from the file server. This prohibits intruders from accessing the server's DOS partition.

Format: SECURE CONSOLE

SECURITY

SECURITY is a workstation command-line utility. Use it to check for possible file server security violations. You must have Supervisor rights or equivalent to run SECURITY. SECURITY checks for possible violations by examining the bindery files maintained by each file server. It also identifies potential problems on your network but does not correct them—you must take this action. The output from SECURITY can fill more than one screen. You can redirect the output to a file and then print it.

Format: SECURITY

Happiness has many roots, but none more important than security.

—E. R. Stettinius, Jr.

SET

SET is a console command used to view the current operating system parameters and to configure the operating system to fit your requirements. Most of the parameters do not need to be changed, because they have been set to give maximum performance to most users.

Format: SET [*parameter*]

NetWare's SET parameters enable you to configure the core OS. In NetWare v3.11, the SET parameters are numerous and complex. NetWare v4.0 has incorporated a new server management utility, SERVMAN.NLM, which automates the process of configuring NetWare with SET commands.

SET TIME

SET TIME is a console command that sets the date and time kept by the file server.

Format: SET TIME [*month/day/year*] [*hour:minute:second*]

You can enter the time in either standard or military (24-hour) format.

TIME

TIME is a console command to display the date and time kept by the file server's clock.

Format: TIME

To reset the file server's date and/or time, use SET TIME.

TRACK OFF

TRACK OFF is a console command used to prevent the file server from displaying network advertising packets that are received or sent on the Router Tracking screen.

Format: TRACK OFF

TRACK ON

TRACK ON is a console command that performs the opposite action of the TRACK OFF command. Use this command to display the Router Tracking screen. TRACK ON signals the router to display all server and network advertising packets that are received or sent.

Format: TRACK ON

UPS

UPS is a NetWare loadable module. The hardware was described in the section on backup power supplies. Use this module to attach an uninterruptible power supply to your file server. UPS is the software link between the file server and the UPS hardware connected to the server.

Format: LOAD [*path*]UPS [*type port discharge recharge*]

UPS STATUS

UPS STATUS is a console command. The UPS module must be loaded for this command to execute. It checks the uninterruptible power supply attached to the server.

Format: UPS STATUS

UPS TIME

UPS TIME is a console command. The UPS module must be loaded for this command to function. This command enables you to change the amount of time you want the network to function on battery power or the time you estimate the battery will need to recharge.

Format: UPS TIME [*discharge recharge*]

USERLIST

USERLIST is a workstation command-line utility. Use this utility to view the following information:

- list of current users for a file server
- user's connection number
- login time
- network address and node address
- type of object that is attached to the server

Format: USERLIST [*fileserver/*][*name*] [/A] [/O] [/C]

VREPAIR

VREPAIR is a NetWare loadable module. Use this command to correct volume problems or to remove name space entries from File Allocation Tables and directory tables. This is a valuable utility, and I recommend that you review your *Novell System Administration* manual for more detail.

Format: LOAD [*path*]VREPAIR

WHOAMI

WHOAMI is a workstation command-line utility. Use this command to view the following about the file server(s) to which your system is attached:

- username on each server
- names of file servers you are attached to
- software version each server is running
- login date and time for each server
- groups you belong to on each server
- rights on each server
- security equivalences on each server

Format: WHOAMI [*fileserver*] [*option...*]

Replace *option* with one or more of the following:

```
/Security
/Groups
/Rights
/Object
/Workgroup
/System
/All
```

Menu Utilities

Along with the previously described utilities, NetWare has menu utility programs that are very useful in the maintenance of your system. These are command-line utilities. This discussion lists some of these menu utilities and their functions.

DSPACE

The DSPACE command performs the following tasks: lists and changes current file server attachments, limits user disk space on a volume, and limits disk space in a directory.

These tasks are organized according to the Available Options menu.

Format: DSPACE

FCONSOLE

Use FCONSOLE to accomplish the following tasks: Supervisors or console operators broadcast messages, view detailed current user connection information, see/alter the status of the file server, and allow system Supervisors to shut down the file server.

Format: FCONSOLE

MAKEUSER

MAKEUSER is used by a Supervisor or Workgroup manager to create and delete user accounts on a regular basis or to create many user accounts.

Format: MAKEUSER

The tasks you can perform with MAKEUSER are organized according to the topics in the Available Options menu:

- create new USR file
- edit USR file
- process USR file

MAKEUSER is a useful tool. Again select the option from the menu and supply or make changes to the information as necessary. Consult your *NetWare Utilities Reference* book on the details for using MAKEUSER to create or delete user accounts. You can edit a USR file with MAKEUSER before you process it or after you have processed it.

NBACKUP

Use the NBACKUP command to back up and restore data files in DOS or Macintosh formats on local drives and file servers. Use NBACKUP to back up and restore DOS and Mac files only!

Regular network users can use NBACKUP to back up information in directories where they have File Scan and Read rights. To restore information, they must have Create, Erase, File Scan, Modify, and Write rights. Only a Supervisor or Supervisor-equivalent user may back up a file server.

PCONSOLE

Use PCONSOLE to set up the print server, network printing, and view information about network printing. After you have set the configuration for the files you would run PSERVER. Refer to your Novell *Print Server* manual for more information.

RCONSOLE

RCONSOLE is a workstation command-line utility used to access the file server console from a workstation. This command turns the workstation into a virtual file server console. You can load and unload modules, execute all console commands, and copy files to the file server's NetWare directories or DOS partition.

Format: RCONSOLE

Certain keys on the number pad have specialized functions with RCONSOLE:

Key	Function
Number Pad ($-$)	Scrolls backward through the active console screens.
Number Pad ($+$)	Scrolls forward through the active console screens.
Number Pad (*)	Displays the Available Options menu.
Shift+Esc	Returns to the list of servers that have REMOTE and RPX loaded. Enables you to exit and use workstation as a workstation.

SALVAGE

SALVAGE can be a useful tool to restore files deleted by accident. With SALVAGE you can do the following: view all deleted files, recover files that have been erased from your workstation or other files to which you have rights, and restore files to their original directories or to the DELETED.SAV directory.

SYSCON

SYSCON is a versatile menu utility that you will use most frequently to troubleshoot problems with users, groups, rights, and so on. With this command you can control the file server, accounting features, and group and user information. The SYSCON menu is organized as indicated:

Accounting: This selection enables you to install the accounting feature, remove the accounting feature, set up and delete accounting servers, and set and modify charge rates for network use. For more detail on accounting, see your Novell documentation, *NetWare Concepts.*

Change Current Server: This selection enables you to attach to or log out of other file servers, choose an attached file server as the current server, and change to a different username on the current server.

File Server Information: This selection enables you to view information about the server such as file server name, NetWare version, system fault tolerance, transaction tracking, connections supported, connections in use, volumes supported, Network address and node address.

Group Information: Using this selection you list the groups on the file server; create, rename, or delete a group(s); assign or modify a group's full name; view, add, or delete managed users or groups; view, add, or delete managers; assign or delete users in a group(s); view a group's ID number; assign or modify a group as trustee of a directory; and assign or modify group trustee rights in a file.

This is one of the first places you would check if a user is having a problem accessing a directory or file.

Supervisor Options: You must have supervisory or equivalent rights to access this option. With it you can set up and change default account balances and restrictions, assign time restrictions to all users, create or modify the system's AUTOEXEC.BAT file, assign or delete a group or user as a file server console operator, activate the intruder detection feature, create or modify the system login script, view and erase the error log, and assign and modify system Workgroup managers.

User Information: With this selection you can create, rename, or delete users; set a user's account balance; set a user's account restrictions; assign or change a user's password; assign or change a user's full name; add or delete a user in a group; create or modify a user's login script; copy one user's login script to another user(s); view and modify managed users and groups, modify list of managers and view user's login information, including user ID; assign or delete a user's security equivalence; assign station restrictions and time restrictions to individual users; assign or modify a user as trustee of a directory, or modify user trustee rights in a file; and limit disk space for individual users.

As you can see, the SYSCON utility is a powerful tool. You will be using this feature daily in maintaining and troubleshooting your network. As I indicated under MAKEUSER, this program is much more versatile and easier to use when changes are necessary to make in a user's file. Review all of these functions thoroughly in your Novell documentation.

USERDEF

The USERDEF utility is similar to MAKEUSER, except that with it you can create multiple users' accounts by using a template. A Supervisor or Workgroup manager can do the following: create multiple users, provide simple login scripts, set up home directories, set up minimal login-password security, assign account and disk space restrictions, and establish print job configurations.

VOLINFO

Use VOLINFO to view information about each volume on the file server.
Format: VOLINFO

Third-Party Troubleshooting Utilities

Numerous troubleshooting utilities are available to help you to monitor your network. The size of your network will play an important part in which package you choose. Some utilities require certain hardware to be installed on the network server and workstations or require that you have intelligent hubs.

LANSight Express

From Intel, the LANSight Express utility requires that you have EtherExpress 16 or 32 LAN Adapters in all your workstations and on the server. By running this utility's TSR named USER, you can check the hardware configuration and software loaded on any workstation. The TSR requires 5KB of memory and will allow access to the workstation even if you are not logged on to the network. The components of this utility are SITEADMN.EXE, which is the administration program for LANSight Express; SIGHT.EXE, which allows access to the workstations; and USER.COM, which is the TSR placed in the AUTOEXEC.BAT file to be loaded on booting up the station.

XTree_Net

The XTREE Company provides another useful tool in managing the network. It provides features specifically designed for Novell NetWare. XTree_Net enables the Administrator to manage NetWare directory rights, file attributes, trustee assignments, and ownership within one environment. This is an excellent utility to determine user problems with regard to access rights to volumes, directories, and files.

LANalyzer and LANtern Network Monitor

These products combine software and hardware available from Novell. These products help you conduct tests of Ethernet and Token Ring networks. They enable you to determine network activity and to monitor performance of the file server(s), gateways, bridges, and so on. Together they can provide a detailed picture of what is going on in the network. It is a fairly expensive set, so check with your Novell reseller for pricing.

EtherStat

An Ethernet LAN monitor software program that monitors, captures, and displays statistical information for use by the manager for use in analyzing LAN performance and troubleshooting, EtherStat (by Gateway Communications Inc.) requires a dedicated network station installed with a G/Ethernet 16 or G/EtherTwist 16 LAN adapter with a minimum of 256KB RAM. EtherStat is operating system independent. It can be configured to capture, save to disk, and/or display any type of Ethernet LAN activity plus set event triggers and alarms. For price information call (800) 274-2733.

NetMenu

NetMenu is a packet of utilities from Network Enhancement Tools Inc. that can remove local drives while a user is logged in, and mask LAN drives while they use local drives. It can control access to DOS from within applications; totally secure job schedules to launch virus scans, periodic maintenance, mainframe downloads, and so on; ensure that login scripts are executed; change user/group security equivalence; plus much more.

NetMenu will create and maintain NetWare users accounts, groups, Workgroup managers and print queues from the command line, and modify security attributes of users. Combine with NetMenu user interface to create customized local versions of configuration utilities like NETCON, SYSCON, and MAKEUSER. For both products call (713) 240-4614.

NetWare Management System

Novell's NetWare Management System is the foundation for a series of cohesive, modular network management products that give the system administrator(s) centralized control of resources throughout the network computing environment from a single PC. It combines industry standards with NetWare's established open architecture. The NetWare Management System is the integration platform for the products from Novell, as well as for third-party management products.

Products from Novell include NetWare Services Manager (Windows or OS/2 versions that control the NetWare environment), which retails for $4,995; NetWare Management Enhanced Map (featuring IP discovery, SNMP management, location network mapping, and Hub Services Manager), available for $1,995; NetWare Management Agents (which send network information to the NetWare Services Manager console), at a price of $495 per server, 20 for $7,995, and so on; and Software Development Kits (APIs and specifications for third-party developers), for $4,995. For complete pricing call (800) 243-8526.

LattisNet Manager for DOS/Model 635

From SynOptics Communications Inc., LattisNet Manager for DOS is an open, SNMP-based system for physical and MAC-layer management of widespread Token Ring and Ethernet networks using SynOptics' intelligent hubs. Features include automatic mapping to provide real-time view of the network hierarchy, SynOptics' Expanded View of any hub in the hierarchy, geographic mapping based on HP's OpenView, the ability to set multiple user-defined thresholds, out-of-band signaling and logging. To order, call (800) PRO-NTWK.

Checkit

A utility that enables you to check what devices are using which IRQ and I/O addresses. It is a relatively inexpensive product that proves useful.

Never invest in anything that eats or needs repairing!

—Billy Rose

Appendix

Acronyms and Abbreviations

Abbreviations in This Book

ACL	access control list
AEM	Apple Events Messaging
AFP	AppleTalk Filing Protocol
ALAP	AppleTalk Link Access Protocol
ANSI	American National Standards Institute
APIs	Application Programming Interfaces
APPC	Advanced Program-to-Program Communication
ARCNet	Attached Resource Computer network
ASCII	American Standard Code for Information Interchange
ASP	AppleTalk Session Protocol
AT	advanced technology
ATA	ARCNet Trader's Association
ATP	Appletalk Transaction Protocol
ATS	Automated Troubleshooting System
AUI	auxiliary unit interface
AWG	American Wire Gauge; 22-AWG
BEB	binary exponential backoff
bit	binary digital
BNC	Bayonet Naval Connector
bps	bits per second
C	COUNTRY container object
CAD	computer-aided design
CAU	controller access unit
CCITT	International Consultive Committee for Telegraphy and Telephony
CD-ROM	compact disk read-only memory
CGA	color graphics adapter
CIO	chief information officer
CLU	command-line utilities
CNA	certified NetWare administrator
CNE	certified NetWare engineers
CNI	certified NetWare instructors
CO	central office
CPS	characters per second
CPU	central processing unit
CRT	cathode ray tube
CSMA	Carrier Sense Multiple Access
CSMA/CA	CSMA Collision Avoidance

CSMA/CD	CSMA Collision Detection
CX	change context
DA	desk accessory
DAT	Digital Audio Tape
dB	decibel
DBMS	database management systems
DCB	Disk Coprocessor Board
DET	directory entry table
DDE	Dynamic Data Exchange
DDP	Datagram Delivery Protocol
DEC	Digital Equipment Corporation
DIB	Directory Information Database
DIX	Digital/Intel/Xerox
DMA	direct memory access
DMPs	dynamic memory pools
DNA	Digital Network Architecture
DOS	disk operating system
DSK	Disk Driver
DVM	digital volt meter
E-mail	electronic mail
ECNE	enterprise CNE
EGA	enhanced graphics adapter
EIA	Electronic Industries Association
EISA	Extended Industry Standard Architecture
ELS	entry-level system
EMI	electromagnetic interference
EMS	Expanded Memory Specification
EPROM	Erasble Programmable Read-only Memory
ESDI	enhanced small device interface
ET	ElectroText
ETLA	Extended Three Letter Acronym
FAT	File Allocation Table
FCC	Federal Communications Commission
FDDI	Fiber Distributed Data Interface
FDM	frequency division multiplexing
FEP	front-end processor
FOIRL	Fiber Optic Inter Repeater Link
FSPs	File Service Processes
FTP	File Transfer Protocol
GHz	gigahertz
GOSIP	Government Open Systems Interconnection Profile
GUI	graphical user interface
HCFS	High-Capacity File System
HCSS	High Capacity Storage System
HMA	High Memory Area
HMI	hub management interface

HOS	host operating system
HPFS	High-Performance File System
IAC	interapplication communications
IBM	International Business Machines
IDE	intelligent drive interface
IEEE	Institute of Electrical and Electronic Engineers
I/O	Input/output
IPX	Internetwork Packet Exchange
IR	Infra Red
IRF	inherited rights filter
IRM	inherited rights mask
IRQ	interrupt request line
ISA	Industry Standard Architecture
ISDN	Integrated Services Digital Network
ISO	International Standards Organization
ITT	invitation to transmit
Kb	kilobits
KB	kilobytes
LAN	local area network
LIM	Lotus/Intel/Microsoft
LINC	LAN Innovators for Networking Communities
LIP	Large Internet Packets
LLC	Logical Link Control
LSL	Link Support Layer
LU 6.2	IBM's Logical Unit 6.2
MAC	Media Access Control
MAN	metropolitan area network
MAU	Media Attached Unit
Mb	megabits
MB	megabytes
Mb/s	megabits per second
MCA	Music Corporation of America
MCS	Macintosh Communications Standard
MFM	modified frequency modulation
MHS	Message Handling Service
MIPS	million instructions per second
MLID	Multiple-Link Interface Driver
MRM	maximum rights mask
MRT	microwave relay towers
MSAU	Multistation Access Unit
mV	microvolt
MUX	multiplexer
NAEC	Novell Authorized Education Center
NAM	Name-space Module
NCC	NetWare Control Center
NCP	NetWare Core Protocol

NDS	NetWare Directory Services
NEAP	Novell Education Academic Partner
NetBEUI	network basic end user interface
NetBIOS	Network Basic Input/Output System
NEXT	near-end crosstalk
NFS	Network File System
NIC	Network Interface Card
NLMs	NetWare loadable modules
NNS	NetWare Name Service
NOS	network operating system
NSE	Network Support Encyclopedia
NT	new technology
NTFS	Windows NT File System
NTIs	Novell Technical Institutes
NTS	Novell Technical Support
NUI	NetWare Users International
O	ORGANIZATION container object
ODI	Open Data-Link Interface
OLE	Object Linking and Embedding
OS/2	Operating System number 2
OSI	Open Systems Interconnection
OU	ORGANIZATIONAL UNIT container object
PAL	Paradox Applications Language
PC	personal computer
PM	Performance Monitor
PRB	packet receive buffer
PS/2	Personal System number 2
PSTN	Public Switched Telephone Network
PVC	polyvinyl chloride
QBE	query by example
RAM	random-access memory
RI	ring-in receptacle
RISC	reduced instruction-set computing
RLL	run length limited
RMF	remote management facility
RO	ring-out receptacle
RPC	remote procedure call
SAA	Systems Application Architecture
SCSI	Small Computer System Interface
SFT	system fault tolerance
SIMM	single in-line memory module
SMC	Standard Microsystems Corporation
SMTP	Simple Mail Transfer Protocol
SNA	Systems Network Architecture
SNMP	simple network management protocol
SPG	Service Protocol Gateway

SPX	Sequenced Packet Exchange
SQL	Structured Query Language
STP	shielded twisted-pair cabling
TCP/IP	Transmission Control Protocol/Internet Protocol
TDM	time division multiplexing
TDRs	time domain reflectometers
TLA	Three-Letter Acronym
TLI	transport layer interface
TSA	Technical Support Alliance
TTS	Transactional Tracking System
UAM	user authentication method
UFS	Universal File System
UMA	upper memory area
UNA	Universal NetWare Architecture
UPS	uninterruptible power supply
UTC	Universal Time Coordinate
USL	UNIX System Laboratories
UTP	unshielded twisted-pair cabling
VADDs	value-added disk drivers
VAP	value-added process
VAX	Virtual Access Extended
VDT	video display terminal
VGA	video graphics array
VLMs	virtual loadable modules
VM	virtual machine
VM	virtual memory
VMS	Virtual Memory System
WAN	wide area network
WORM	write once, read many
WOS	workstation operating system
XMS	Extended Memory Specification
XNS	Xerox Network System
ZIP	Zone Information Protocol
ZTEST	Zero-track test

Other Abbreviations in the Network Industry

ACK	acknowledgment
AMD	Advanced Micro Devices
ARPNET	Advanced Research Projects Agency Network
ATM	automated teller machine
CATV	Community Access Television
CMOS	complementary metal-oxide semiconductor
CONS	connection-oriented network services
CRC	cyclic redundancy check
DDN	Defense Department Network

DRI	declarative referential integrity
IC	integrated circuit
LED	light-emitting diode
MAP	manufacturing automation protocol
MVS	multiple virtual storage
PROM	programmable read-only memory
ROM	read-only memory
RPL	remote procedure load
SAP	service advertising protocol
SDLC	Synchronous Data Link Control
SIP	Service Identification Packet
SNAP	subnetwork access protocol
SONET	Synchronous Optical Network
TV	television
UHF	ultrahigh frequency
VAX	virtual access extended
VHF	very high frequency
VTAM	Virtual Terminal Access Method
XO	exactly one

Be very careful when you study these abbreviations—the mind is a terrible thing to waste. Current research suggests that the brain has a finite capacity. Experiments on propeller-head students have shown that excessive memorization of meaningless facts can eliminate childhood memories. One student in particular lost all recognition of his life prior to the age of 10. He did, however, demonstrate an amazing ability to recite data communication acronyms in rhyming couplets. If you are not careful, this could happen to you!

Index

Special Characters

M